SEARCHLIGHTS
ON
DELINQUENCY

SEARCHLIGHTS
ON
DELINQUENCY

New Psychoanalytic Studies

Dedicated to Professor August Aichborn, on the Occasion
of his Seventieth Birthday
July 27, 1948

Managing Editor: K. R. Eissler, M. D., Ph. D.

Chairman of the Editorial Board: Paul Federn, M. D.

INTERNATIONAL UNIVERSITIES PRESS, Inc.
New York   New York

PREFACE

By ERNEST JONES, M.D.*

(*London*)

I take this opportunity with pleasure to write a short envoi to this Commemoration Volume. I have known Professor Aichhorn for nearly forty years and have always admired the pertinacity and selflessness with which he devoted himself to the investigation of what was certainly a most difficult, and to many people rather unattractive field of study. To all who know him personally it is clear that he was greatly helped in his arduous labors by a profound love of humanity and a personal sympathy with those unfortunates whose inability to achieve harmony in their complicated environment had driven them into anti-social ways. To Professor Aichhorn's success in his work, the various contributions to this volume will doubtless bear witness. But I am sure that what he finds more gratifying is the extent to which his pioneering work has been taken up in other countries and coordinated into established institutions for the study and treatment of juvenile delinquency. Even the remedial work which has found such wide-spread application in prisons is only an extension of the work among juveniles inaugurated by Professor Aichhorn.

I should further like in my official capacity to congratulate Professor Aichhorn on the courage with which he held the fort in Vienna during the painful years of Nazi occupation. It was only fitting that he should be the one to revive the famous Vienna Society in its ancient habitation and that he should become its first President.

This volume is intended to mark not only Professor Aichhorn's scientific achievement but also the personal esteem in which his wide circle of friends hold him.

---

* President of the International Psycho-Analytical Association.

V

DEDICATION

By Paul Federn, M.D.

(*New York*)

The international tribute herein presented to August Aichhorn, had to be limited in scope by the editing staff who were forced to follow the reality-principle emphasized by our publishers. Following the pleasure-principle, a score of authors wanted to dedicate more papers to the venerated *Vorstand* in Vienna. The title, "Governor," characterized him and his method of working together with a team of devoted co-workers, constantly demonstrating his own ways yet constantly respecting the individuality of others. He himself was demanded as consultant for problem cases in the whole city. Aichhorn is diagnostician, therapist, and hygienist all in one. Yet he clearly distinguishes every measure and step which he takes in regard to all the three categories. He derived his own theories from his own methods of practice and from his theories he advanced new devices of action.

When his educational team was rebuilt after World War II, Aichhorn emerged not only as *Vorstand* but also as President of the re-established Psychoanalytic Society in Vienna. During the decade in which his own action was submerged and interrupted, his work continued everywhere on a world-wide scale. His book, *Wayward Youth* has become a kind of gospel and his papers the epistles to everyone whose work with juvenile delinquency was oriented to the psychological theories and methods Aichhorn had developed. Yet his popularity remained restricted to the circles of psychoanalysts and of social workers.

Therefore the volume presented here has a twofold aim: first, to give Aichhorn the satisfaction that his work has ripened in science and practice everywhere, secondly, to expand and enhance ever further the popularity of his work.

Psychoanalysis has become — whether accepted or debated — one of the main theoretical and practical bases of all professions dealing with human personality. Many of its applications developed into independent branches; they contributed new problems and new solutions to the central endeavor of psychoanalysis which we may define as genetic psychology and pathopsychology of the conscious and unconscious mind. The branch inaugurated by Aichhorn was fruitful in itself and also for the progress of the fundamental theories of psychoanalysis as a whole. He has clarified many problems of relations between neurosis, character formation, and delinquency. The empty term "psychopathy" needed to be replaced by meaningful concepts.

Aichhorn has been appointed a professor. He plans to create in Vienna an institute for research in delinquency which is backed by the Austrian Government. We hope that teachers and pupils and, of course, also scholarships will again find their way to the birthplace of psychoanalysis. We hope that what happened when Freud was the first President of the Viennese Society will happen again.

There is a symbolic as well as a practical significance to the fact that Aichhorn is the second President of the Viennese group. He is no physician. His profession was originally that of a teacher in the elementary schools. He founded the Viennese Knaben-Hort; he gathered more or less wayward children from the streets and rehabilitated them to peaceful and normal activities. Later he became the superintendent of a reformatory of the city of Vienna. His experiences induced him to join the psychoanalytic group. At that time he underwent his own training analysis with the writer of these lines. Had there then been those professional restrictions which have now been established in most countries, and which would have forced us to refuse to accept him as pupil and later as a member of the psychoanalytic society, we all, including Freud himself, would have been deprived of him as our teacher. The wayward youth and the adult delinquent — this world of its own — would have missed Aichhorn's contributions which have proved their value by daily use and daily experiment.

Therefore, this volume will also serve to remind whomever it may concern of Freud's statement that he would always oppose the pretension of medicine to monopolize psychoanalysis.

Freud's work was a contribution to the common task of all scientific professions which deal with the human mind and the human personality; it is dedicated to the whole of mankind. This is exemplified by the work of Aichhorn, a man admired and loved by us all.

A BIOGRAPHICAL OUTLINE

It would be a challenging but difficult task to write August Aichhorn's biography, a story sometimes amusing, sometimes tragic, but always stirring. For evident reasons barely an outline can be given here, but the highlights of such a fancied biography may be briefly presented.

It is proper to introduce the principal character of a novel, be he hero or villain, with a presentation of his ancestors' history. And so the author would take the reader back into the twelfth century when Austrian robber barons kidnapped Bavarian peasants to settle them on their estates. One of the kidnapped was an Aichhorn. Subsequent generations continued as peasants, tilling the same piece of soil for centuries until one of the Aichhorn clan moved to Vienna at the end of the eighteenth century. By an odd coincidence, his famous great-grandson's office was to be in a building adjoining the house old Jacob had bought, one hundred and fifty years before. The Aichhorns lived a colorful life after they moved from the country to the city. We find one the mayor of a suburb, another a member of the City Council. They were tradesmen and craftsmen, and one was a banker. Their days were happy and prosperous and then again beset with the sudden loss of wealth and hard work. They never seemed to feel discouraged, but fought rather than accepted their vicissitudes.

August Aichhorn was born the 27th of July, 1878. At the age of twenty, the year his twin brother died, he became a teacher in one of the grade schools of the City of Vienna. The course of his career seemed to be set from the start. He was a member of a conservative, well-established family; he lived in a feudal city and chose a profession which, like all professions in those days, was guild-like in character. At that time, once a teacher one remained a teacher and waited for two or three decades until he could retire on a government pension. But it was not Aichhorn's style to follow a routine and to wait for retirement. When in 1907 military settlements for boys were introduced in Vienna, he led a successful fight against that institution. In the following year he became the chairman of a new board which was officially assigned the duty of organizing boys' settlements. Thus he had prevented the penetration of the military spirit into the educational system. Aichhorn had devoted ten years to that task when he was given an unique opportunity. With a group of idealistic followers, he organized the institution for delinquent boys in Oberhollabrunn, Austria.

Out of the shambles of a refugee camp arose one of the most touching experiments in humanity. At a time when the Austrian monarchy fell apart and the fruits of a cultural tradition were ground to pieces between revolution and inflation, Aichhorn submerged himself in constructive work and created an entirely new method of curing an age-old scourge for whose cure many a device had been tried in vain. Crime and delinquency had taken their course without hindrance. Punishment, segregation, flogging, and execution were recommended by some; love, humaneness, understanding, mercy and charity by others. Neither approach satisfied Aichhorn. In Oberhollabrunn he had occasion to study a vast clinical material and to test his methods of treatment. Part of the exciting experience of these days was laid down in his book, *Wayward Youth*, the full impact of which only future generations will know.

Aichhorn became interested in delinquents when he started his work as a teacher. He groped around for a science which could help him in the understanding of his observations. Following the fashion of the day he studied neuropathology. But its contribution to the explanation of delinquency was inadequate and could not quench his thirst for knowledge. Next he tried experimental psychology and steeped himself into Wundt and Meumann, but again he felt frustrated. However, as soon as he came into contact with psychoanalysis he knew that he had found a key to the maze of his puzzling observations.

In Aichhorn's hands, Freud's technique, devised for the treatment of neurotics, seemingly became a new instrument so much did it differ from the original. Although still authentically analytic in its method, it yet was adapted to the requirements of the delinquent's personality structure which is so different from that of the neurotic. It was fortunate that a psychologist and clinician of Aichhorn's stature came upon psychoanalysis and made it his tool. Following the remarkable experiment in Oberhollabrunn which was mentioned with praise in the English Parliament he organized and conducted for the City Administration child guidance clinics throughout Vienna. After his retirement from the municipal service he was made chairman of the child guidance clinic of the Viennese Psychoanalytic Society. He soon became one of the foremost teachers of the Viennese Society and when Germany occupied Austria he remained at his post. He, his wife and their two sons miraculously survived, although one of the sons was sent to a concentration camp. Again surrounded by a holocaust he remained undaunted, and tried to preserve the little of Freud's work that could be rescued during those dreadful years. After the liberation he was elected president of the society, a position which he has held to this day.

It would be futile to attempt to compress the scope of Aichhorn's personality into a few sentences but a few words must be devoted to the teacher, the clinician and the man.

He possesses certain features that make him an unique teacher. It is his attitude of being "ignorant" about the subject-matter to which he has devoted his life work, his belief in always beginning anew, in being eternally a student and pupil, not a teacher, which make him a truly great one. He always acted as the "servant" of his pupils and met their queries for guidance not in the customary teacher-student fashion but sensed in every problem raised the underlying individual conflict which reality had imposed upon the questioner.

His lectures were not the dissertations of an instructor, but rather the talks of a man speaking about life as though reporting on a country he had visited. Even when presenting his theories, they seemed accurate descriptions of reality.

His intuition is uncanny. As the archeologist can visualize the entire temple from a half-broken column, so can Aichhorn reconstruct the whole of a human personality from a few meager details which seem only trifling superficialities to the unintuitive. This amazing gift he had acquired by hard work. He is a true psychologist, who could spend hours in the trolley car watching people and making guesses from what he saw. From the way a man held his newspaper, he guessed at the way he would leave his seat and walk to the exit. Until the passenger reached his destination Aichhorn would wait patiently to test his prediction, oblivious of the fact that by so doing he got farther and farther away from where he wanted to go.

He has a supreme faculty of identifying with the patient and of knowing his needs. It was a touching experience to hear him argue with a schizophrenic adolescent about the interpretation of some obscure passage in the Bible and to witness from week to week the patient's gradual recovery at a time when official psychiatry still maintained the dogma of the incurability of schizophrenia. Or who else would be able to spend six months of daily interviews with a patient who believed that Aichhorn would like to be instructed in the patient's vocation? But in this half-year, the foundation was laid for a transference which permitted him to achieve one of his brilliant therapeutic successes. His clinical stature is indicated in his statement that he who feels that he is being "patient" with the delinquent whom he is treating will by that feeling alone be deprived of the fruits of his good intentions.

Aichhorn may be called an impassioned psychologist. Wherever he went or in whatever he did he found problems of human nature to stimulate his quest for knowledge. The world became a huge stage crowded with innumerable dramas so that there was no difference to him between his office, the movie or the trolley car. Everywhere he detected problems of the human mind and puzzling questions demanding an answer. He succeeded in totally disengaging the problem of crime and delinquency from any religious, ethical or moral implications, thus approaching it as a question of nature exclusively. The result was his conception of delinquency not only as a problem of deviate behavior but more profoundly as a manifestation of deficient internal growth.

As a great artist has supreme command over his instrument, be it a flute or a harp, so can Aichhorn play his instrument, the human personality. In the shortest time he can turn a squanderer into a miser, a thief into a scrupulously honest fellow, a blackmailer into a defender of law and order. But such metamorphoses of a deviation into its opposite are meaningless to him and he never considers such stupendous changes of behavior a success. He is the enraged enemy of bigotry and conformity and knows that the new miser, the scrupulous fellow, the protagonist of law and order, are merely acting under the impact of a new compulsion. To him such changes only signalize the opportunity of starting his real work, namely to lead the patient to internal freedom and the integration of values. His amazing command over the human personality results in a technique enviable and uniquely effective. It is a rare pleasure to witness one of his interviews. It usually proceeds with a casualness which makes it seem uneventful and apparently merely flowing easily, yet at every moment it is expertly related to the dynamism of the total situation as subsequent checking would ascertain. He rarely makes a frontal attack, and is skillful in avoiding the precipitation of resistances, but he can implant a message in the unconscious of his subject with unfailing certainty and by means of indirections and innuendo. It would be difficult to find his peer in the great art of asking the well-timed questions which gives reassurance and the feeling of being understood. There are no routine questions in his repertoire interviewing, but a single question becomes a meaningful part of the comprehensive plan of his interview.

His questions are directed to provoke and create certain preconscious associations in his subject's mind as part of his strategy. By so doing he has forged an exquisite therapeutic tool out of a procedure which is usually merely a matter of routine and of gaining information.

A follow-up among the families who had sought his advice revealed that in a surprisingly high percentage of instances, a single interview had had a significant effect on the family equilibrium, an effect which persisted years after the interview had taken place.

Yet in spite of his command of the art of asking questions, Aichhorn can also level a magnificent frontal attack. Then narcissistic defenses crumble under his assault, the arrogantly smiling delinquent will leave the room in tears, a vengeful father becomes subdued and a nagging mother turns meek.

Yet to those who had the privilege of working with him, the most fascinating experience remains the personality of Aichhorn himself. He has achieved an enviable degree of mastery and harmony without losing the capacity for immersing himself in constructive conflict. The man who often spent sixteen or seventeen hours a day with patients, could say that he never has the feeling of working. To him work and play coincide. Despite his dedication to the treatment of delinquents he has never lost his capacity to enjoy the adventure of crime nor his understanding of how sweet to the criminal is the violating of a rule to which the community bows. His faculty for enjoyment is unlimited. A therapeutic success, a well-written mystery story, a ride in a car, a game of cards — for him everything can be an enticing adventure. Thus he is truly young, but spared the hardship of youth, and truly happy because oblivious of his own genius.

K.R.E.

EDITORIAL NOTE

The reader will not find throughout the papers of this book a uniform approach or uniform conclusions, but frequently mutually contradictory statements. The selection of papers was not determined by the viewpoint of any particular psychoanalytic school. It was the aim of the Editors to offer a representative cross-section of psychoanalytic theory and treatment of delinquency.

CONTENTS

GENERAL PROBLEMS

SOME PROBLEMS OF DELINQUENCY[1]

By K. R. Eissler, M.D., Ph.D.

(*New York*)

According to the Old Testament, man became as he is supposed to be today because of committing a crime. Before Adam and Eve tasted the fruit of the Tree of Knowledge of Good and Evil, they had only one obligation: to obey the Lord's command. Man's role before the Fall was that of an automaton, who could indulge in pleasure unharassed by conflicts or the necessity of making choices. Only after the Fall did human beings become that complex structure which modern psychiatry has tried to make intelligible. It was this first crime which thereafter forced man to serve simultaneously a triad of functions, his body, his conscience and external reality. Only after the Fall did man possess an insatiable curiosity, capable of striving for goals, of observing himself and of anticipating the future and making choices among infinite alternatives. In transgressing God's inscrutable command, Adam and Eve had no foreboding of the fratricide which was to follow, nor of man's future destiny of slaughter, injustice, and exploitation of his fellow man. Driven by an inexplicable urge to create ethical and moral values, an urge of equal intensity drives man to destroy and falsify these same values. However lofty his goals and ardent his strivings, the full record of each man's life is disfigured with the strain of acts and desires irreconcilable with his convictions of what is good and just.

We have assigned the generic term of delinquency to all these thoughts, actions, desires and strivings which deviate from moral and ethical principles. Delinquency is one of the most conspicuous configurations which come to the attention of the student of man and his history. The variety of ways in which man expresses this urge to cause pain to his fellow man, looms large. Love, which is its counterpart and which also exists in everyone and has made its

---

[1] This paper does not contain any original ideas but is based mainly on August Aichhorn's theory and therapeutic technique of delinquency. Since the author did not follow Aichhorn slavishly, it is possible that some points have suffered misrepresentation. In dealing with the structural aspect of neurosis and psychosis, the author has drawn heavily on Freud's papers, "Neurosis and Psychosis" and "The Loss of Reality in Neurosis and Psychosis" (*Collected Papers*, Vol. II, London, Hogarth Press, 1924).

3

imprint on history, does not seem strong enough to ward off or control man's desire to injure the members of his species by violence, either actual, symbolic or in thought. If we reflect on the importance which occidental imagination has assigned to sin and crime in the story of man's creation and development, it is astounding to realize that delinquency has remained psychiatry's stepchild. It has been far less investigated than the major psychoses and neuroses. Indeed, it is more attractive to devote one's attention to the latter. By his stubbornness and disrespect the delinquent makes the psychiatrist feel helpless and impatient, to say nothing of the effects on professional reputation and on income which follow a persistent preoccupation with the dregs of society.

We must analyze and clarify the concept of delinquency before we approach its clinical and therapeutic aspects since we believe that two misconceptions have blocked our understanding of its manifestations. It has been persistently asserted that delinquency is a behavior configuration which fits only an evaluative frame of reference and that it is therefore not comparable to neurotic or psychotic behavior. Neuroses and psychoses are considered diseases and are therefore not measured by that arbitrary yardstick which ethical judgments necessarily imply. Furthermore, neuroses and psychoses can be defined in descriptive terms which refer to objective personality factors, whereas delinquency can only be defined in terms of behavior deviating from a psychologically arbitrary norm of "goodness." But in the last analysis such a definition reveals that the use of the term refers to the reactions which the "delinquent" elicits from his environment. Consequently, these psychiatrists have claimed, those actions that have been called delinquent have varied with tradition, historical periods, and local customs.

The general conclusion follows that delinquency is a legal, moral, or ethical concept, as the case may be, but that it has no rightful place in medical, psychiatric terminology. Therefore, the concepts of modern psychiatry which were applied to neurotic and psychotic behavior as phenomena appropriate for the same scientific experimentation and deliberation as the other phenomena of nature, were not applied to delinquency. By reason of this conceptual classification, the study of this area of behavior would call for the methods of historical or esthetic research or any of the other methods in the field of humanities which serve the evaluation of human behavior.[2]

---

[2] Most of these objections to the scientific validity of the view that delinquency is a psychological conception can be raised likewise against concepts such as neurosis and psychosis. The contents of psycho-pathology are fluctuating. Behavior patterns which were abnormal yesterday, may be considered normal today and become abnormal in the public view tomorrow. Furthermore, the symptomatology of neuroses and psychoses changes in the course of history. These historical changes are perhaps slower and less conspicuous than their analogues in delinquent behavior. We shall enlarge on this subject later.

By the same token delinquency has also been considered a configuration which developed with the ego's conscious cooperation, except in those cases where it was found to be the direct result of a severe neurosis or psychosis. This view implies the offender's full responsibility for such behavior whereas the individual's responsibility for a neurotic or psychotic symptom has been repudiated by most modern psychiatrists. Indeed, such arguments must be conceded to be correct as long as delinquency is defined from the viewpoint of the jurist or society. The jurist relies on a set of codified rules; therefore he will call delinquent those behavior patterns that deviate from that code. Since the code appears to be quite arbitrary from the viewpoint of psychology, delinquency is then understandable only by the study of history, tradition, folklore, or religion. Such classification, however, prevents any psychological definition of delinquency. Our present attempt is to revise this definition. We believe that it is the restriction of the concept of delinquency to behavior deviating from an arbitrary standard that has doomed to failure most attempts to eliminate delinquency.

Whether certain behavior is delinquent or not, is entirely dependent on the motivation which lies behind that particular behavior. No external feature of behavior can ever be used as a reliable index of delinquency. No classification of behavior patterns can be undertaken without examining motivations although it must be conceded that the repetition of particular incidents in a life history or some conspicuous clinical features will prove exceptions to this rule. The essential validity of this rule can be demonstrated by the following deliberation. No doubt a man who enters a church and drives out any of those who are present with the permission of the Church Elders, would be considered guilty of disorderly conduct by any student of the law, especially after the culprit's sanity has been established. Nevertheless anyone who has read the gospels will agree that this behavior once occurred without signifying disorderly conduct. Since there are those who can conceive of the return of Jesus to this world, it is likewise conceivable that a man found guilty of having driven a person from his lawful place of worship might still not be guilty of disorderly conduct even though he was in the full possession of his senses. The true state of affairs can be established only after that man's motivation and the identity of his personality have been established. Crime, delinquency, and a variety of other terms are meaningful only if viewed as actions performed by individuals with a specific background and history, living in a specific social climate, and laboring under specific conflicts. On the other hand, behavior patterns which may not fall into the arbitrary delineations of juristic definitions might show all the earmarks of delinquent behavior in respect to their origin, motivation, clinical appearance, and also very frequently their social effect. Hence, a psychological definition of delinquency will greatly enlarge the number of cases which fall into this category and will remove from it only a few, as compared with the group which the law or society call delinquent.

The assumption underlying the psychological approach concerns the meaning of values and their role in the development of the child. It is necessary to recognize that the world of values is based on tasks that are psychologically similar to the tasks imposed on us by the physical and biological world. These tasks are facts which challenge the growing child but to which later the adult often responds with automatic behavior. To the child the bright light of a fire has the same attractiveness as his playmate's toy. He wants to touch both of them and desires to possess them both. The adult, later, will automatically avoid touching the one or appropriating the other. The child, however, has to learn to abstain from both these impulses — in short, this essential relationship to both physical and value stimuli is initially identical. They attract or repel a child; they invite manipulation; they elicit actions; they give pleasure or displeasure. Only later will the child learn that the structures underlying physico-biological stimuli and values are essentially different. Yet even the adult is often inclined to manipulate many of the value patterns as if they were physical structures. There is, however, one great difference between infringements upon the physico-biological world and upon the world of values. Punishment for violations of the former follows swiftly and almost automatically whereas perpetration of an act against the laws of values may or may not result in the pain of punishment depending on detection by authority and the shrewdness of the perpetrator. Moreover, the pain involved in touching fire coincides with the performance of the desired act. This makes it impossible to enjoy any aspect of the forbidden action whereas the stealing of the playmate's toy yields great pleasure before ending in the displeasure elicited by punishment. Yet in spite of the initial identity of physical and value stimuli in the child's life, society and psychiatrists take qualitatively different attitudes towards disturbances related to the one or the other. If a child lacks the ability to integrate the behavior pattern necessary for his protection from physical dangers, e.g., if a child persists in reaching toward fire or in cutting himself with knives, we assume a basic impairment of his intelligence. It is diagnostically labelled with a term running the gamut from moron to idiot. And mental deficiency is considered a medical problem. A person so afflicted might continue to act that way throughout his adulthood due to a defect in the structure of the brain and he will never lose the status of a patient deserving medical attention. If, however, a person as a child is deficient in his capacity or ability to integrate the behavior patterns necessary for his dealing with values and therefore persists in that deficiency throughout adulthood, he is not granted the status of a patient but the police and the courts are expected to deal with him. Yet, there is no theoretical justification for this marked difference in approach towards the two categories of disturbances. Integration of the behavior patterns necessary to physical preservation and those based on the acceptance and integration of social values, are both fundamental prerequisites for survival in the larger sense of the word. If he is to escape physical injury, a child in a modern occidental community with its traffic, mechanical utensils and electric outlets must learn things very different from those a child in a native African community must learn. Correlated to this difference in physical environment is a difference in the values and axioms accepted by each type of communities which impose indefeasible duties on the conduct of their respective group members. Children of both communities will likewise have to adjust to these sets of rules. Although mental deficiency in a primitive community leads to failure in tasks which are entirely different from those in which the mental defective fails who lives in a twentieth century metropolitan area, it will not be disputed that it constitutes a clinically and psychologically valid disease entity. The same train of thought is applicable to delinquent behavior. To be sure, the two categories of failure, that of the mental defective and of the delinquent, are qualitatively different. But this qualitative difference hardly explains why one kind of behavior disturbance should be called a disease requiring medical care and the other a punishable violation requiring incarceration. Both disturbances refer to human behavior and hence should be the exclusive concern of those who are experts in that field. Both are pathological reactions, disturbances in the relations of the individual to essential spheres of human existence and, therefore, are to be classified as diseases threatening the survival of those suffering from them. Delinquency — and this is the first point of our definition — refers to behavior, thoughts, and feelings that tend to infringe upon values. In human personalities these values find representation to a varying degree of intensity, consciousness, and awareness. The mental defective lacks such representation due to an organic defect. The ideal criminal has not structured his personality in accordance with any value system: he has merely retained the gain of pleasure and satisfaction as the exclusive goal of his behavior. He is asocial. Instinctual forces drive him on without any opposition from a restraining conscience. The adolescent, however, who seemed to have integrated social demands and devoted himself assiduously to his studies, but then abruptly throws to the winds his accustomed way of life and starts to drink or commits a theft, has become dissocial. He had accepted a representation of a value system but it was temporarily thrown out of working order by the impact of a strong instinctual demand. The instinctual demand, in this instance, had to work its way through strongly opposing forces; he became delinquent not because of the absence of represented values, but in spite of them. Hence values may not be represented at all or, they may be represented weakly or strongly as the case may be. Value representations must be classified under other aspects as well. They may be represented forcefully, even so forcefully that they become a burden to their bearers. Then the displeasure caused by them may become intolerable and lead to attempts at escape. Thus, in addition to considering the strength of value representation, we must also consider their effect on the person's ego. Furthermore, the degree of their integration will have its influence on manifest behavior. Value representations may be worked into the ego, integrated, and accepted by it or they may remain outside it. In the latter case, the ego will follow their demands as it does those of external coercing forces. Then instead of spontaneity there will be automatic and compulsive-mechanical behavior in the realization of values. And finally, value representation may be endowed with consciousness and awareness or they may be unconscious or its bearer may be unaware of their presence. When value representation is unconscious, the subject will automatically respond with value adequate behavior.

A clinical review of the phenomena of delinquency shows that it is the exception rather than the rule for such disorders to be based on only one of these constellations. The average clinical example is a composite of all factors: some values having not found any representation, others being endowed with too much or too little strength, some integrated, others extraneous while their representation in the subject varies all the way from full awareness to dim consciousness or complete unconsciousness.

The second set of defining factors in the phenomenon of delinquency concerns aggression. Although aggression has increasingly occupied the attention of psychiatrists, psychologists, and historians, little is really known about it. The terms aggression, hostility, and destructiveness are still used interchangeably although they surely designate psychologically different contents. A satisfactory phenomenology of aggression has not yet been established and, hence, its various developmental stages are not too well known, consequently our clinical understanding of such disorders in which aggression predominates is greatly impaired. Doubtless there are two different modes in which aggression may unfold its effects. Aggression may be turned against the subject who is the source of it, i.e., subject and object of aggression may coincide, or aggression may be channelized against the reality outside the subject. In its drive against reality it usually does not appear in a short-circuited form but undergoes manifold breaks and transitions until released in various behavior patterns. It may express itself through any function. Aggression can be carried out in thoughts, in looks, in gait, in actions. However there seems to be some closer affinity to the musculo-skeletal system one of whose functions is physical appropriation. Aggression can be best identified by a scrutiny of the purposes and origins of behavior patterns. Aggression is usually allied to and even fused with its counterpart: love. Often both are gratified in one and the same action or are directed towards the same object simultaneously either with or without undergoing a real fusion.

In the delinquencies, aggression is always directed towards the outside. For a tentative clinical approach it may suffice to say that instances of aggression directed against the subject's self fall into the neurotic or psychotic group. Psychiatric disorders may be classified on this basis into two groups: the autoplastic and the alloplastic. The hysterical symptom of conversion, e.g., is a representative example of the autoplastic. A conflict is temporarily solved or rather a state of tension is temporarily abated by a change within the system in which the conflict or tension arose. To give a simplified example: a person would like to attack an enemy, but for whatever reason refrains from doing so. The force aiming at the attack did not find discharge; shortly after a headache may develop which is a derivative of the undischarged energy originally directed towards an external object. The headache is a symptom of an autoplastic disorder; the aggressive impulse did not lead to any action resulting in a change of external reality.[3] Whereas the conversion symptom is the classic example of an autoplastic disorder, there are others which are also classified as autoplastic, but which involve some primary manipulation of reality. Examples are the numerous symptoms of the obsessional-compulsive neuroses. A compulsion, a compulsive ritual or a ceremony consists of actions. These actions are insignificant and trivial and so remote from the goal of the original impulse that the measure of reality change involved appears negligble. It is different in the symptomatology of some psychotics. The delusion of persecution is an autoplastic symptom, but it may lead the patient to murdering the assumed persecutor. Here the secondary effect on reality is very great, but it is important to keep in mind that this effect is the consequence of an autoplastic symptom.

Delinquencies, on the other hand, are genuinely and primarily alloplastic. The adolescent who steals, the gangster who kills, the clerk who embezzles, they all in their actions primarily impinge on external reality. To be sure, autoplastic symptoms, such as anxiety or guilt-feelings may occur, but the core of the disorder is alloplastic. It is, however, the alloplasticity of the delinquent action which has made it so difficult to recognize it as a symptom. For it shares this alloplasticity with normal action which always leads to a manipulation of reality. This alloplasticity of the delinquencies likewise explains their rapid changes in symptomatology in the course of history and the stupendous differences in symptomatology between one society and another. Since they can manifest themselves socially only

---

[3] Space does not permit to discuss here the ways in which the autoplastic symptom may lead secondarily to a change of reality inasmuch as the patient may become grouchy or irritable as a consequence of the headache and stop working, thus causing a real change in external reality. Most autoplastic disorders lead to such secondary manipulation of reality.

in that sphere where human actions reach reality they are dependent on the structure of that reality. Therefore the contents of the delinquencies are correlated to the variety of the social realities in which they occur. This dependency of the delinquencies on social realities does not militate against a psychological theory of delinquency since the mechanisms underlying alloplastic disorders are parts of the personality inventory. The result of a dysidentification (*Fehlidentifizierung*) will manifest itself in different action contents dependent on the kind of person with whom the subject has identified or tried to identify himself and hence depends on the delinquent's social environment but the pathology of the identification remains a psychiatric problem.

The definition of delinquency as an alloplastic infringement of values needs further qualifications. Man is often forced, for the sake of self-preservation, to act in a way offensive to his value system. A typical example is the act of killing in the course of self-defense. For theoretical reasons such aggressions cannot be rightly classified as symptoms of delinquency. But it is interesting to investigate the aggressive deeds which allegedly were forced on a person for the sake of self-defense. Almost invariably — according to my limited experience — such actions are found to cover up the release of forces aimed at goals remote from those of self-preservation, and they furnish pleasure which is extraneous to the aim of self-preservation. Though we do not deny that theoretically there are or can be actions motivated solely by the purpose of self-preservation, we must doubt that such acts are either typical or of frequent occurrence. The relationship between delinquency and self-preservation seems to be similar to that existing between physiological desire and unconscious wish in the production of dreams as described by Freud. A strong physiological desire, such as thirst or hunger, will prepare the way for a dream; but unconscious desires and, strangely enough, the very deepest and more repressed, will attach themselves to these biological urges and enter the dream. Likewise, situations of threat to self-preservation will mobilize the ever-ready delinquent tendencies. Since here there is an opportunity to discharge aggression under the cloak of a necessity imposed by the threat of external reality without the burden of responsibility, the most severely prohibited desires can find an undetected discharge. It is probably not possible for a human being to be aggressive without being delinquent. This differentiates him from the animal which is aggressive without ever becoming delinquent.

The symptoms of alloplastic disorders provide pleasure in contrast to autoplastic ones which yield displeasure. We know that autoplastic symptoms provide unconscious pleasure. Clinical experience shows that alloplastic symptoms may cause a corresponding unconscious displeasure. This contrast between conscious pleasure vs. unconscious pain is not encountered with that regularity in the alloplastic disorders with which the opposite contrast is found in the autoplastic. This conscious pleasure is an additional factor underlying the frequent objections to the classification of delinquency as a disease. Yet pain is certainly no necessary quality of disease. Were not the idea of injury or death associated with it or would sickness not interfere with other, pleasurable purposes, many physical symptoms would be conceded to provide bodily pleasure — a fact which becomes conspicuous in some disorders, such as tuberculosis. It is remarkable, however, how easily in delinquencies the pleasure derived from the gratification of aggression may turn into severe displeasure, sometimes without conspicuous external change. Furthermore, on closer study, the delinquent shows manifold deformities in his ego structure, such as feelings of isolation or depersonalization. Indeed, a large number of delinquents can be said to be very unhappy in spite of their frequent pleasurable discharges of aggression. In alloplastic disorders a desperate struggle can be observed against exposure to the conscious experience of displeasure. It is the delinquents' excessive sensitivity to displeasure, their persistent and often successful effort to repress all manifestations of displeasure rather than their actual gain of pleasure which often gives them the clinical appearance of persistent seekers of enjoyment. Nevertheless, it would be a great mistake to underestimate the direct role which pleasure plays in the delinquent. His primary disturbance, after all, concerns his unwillingness or incapacity to give preference to value enforcement over the immediate attainment of a pleasurable goal.

What are those pleasurable goals of the delinquent? We would expect to find a great variety of goals depending on the social group, the social community, the age and the individual history of the delinquent. There may be a few criteria, however, which these goals usually have in common. The gratification of a need, which, after all, is common to all goal-directed behavior, is too general a trait as to be of any help in defining delinquencies. One of the characteristics, possibly significant, is the fact that what makes a goal valuable to a delinquent is often only a superficially distinctive quality. The superficiality of his goals becomes evident as soon as we view the sector of reality toward which he strives, in relation to a wider reality and all its potentialities. It seems that in delinquent actions a subordinated part-structure receives overemphasis in a manner which is prejudicial to the whole. The delinquent in his relationship to the world becomes arrested at a preliminary step on the way towards comprehending and taking hold of it. The superficiality of the goal is sometimes overlooked in view of the delinquent's intensive interest in the world. In his attachment to the world he is superior to his neurotic counterpart. There is a strong tie that binds the delinquent to the world. This tie makes his clinical pathology and therefore the necessary therapy quite different from those of other psychiatric disorders. The psychotic may eventually waste his whole energy in hallucinations; he may live on a spiritual island; the neurotic, driven by phobias, may withdraw permanently to his room or into his bed, or he may discharge the object-directed energy in repetitive compulsions; not the delinquent. He does not live on an island; he is interested in the world; he needs the world; he is even too much interested in some aspects of the world. The isolation of the neurotic and of the psychotic may find its counterpart in the removal of the delinquent from the community and his physical isolation brought about by society's reaction to his misdeeds. The sexual life of patients suffering from alloplastic disorders, frequently shows the simultaneous existence of intensive interest in and superficiality of goals as manifested by fixation to a part-structure. The majority of delinquents are driven by strong interests in either heterosexual or homosexual pursuits. They are ready to make great sacrifices in the service of those objects to whom they feel attached. It seems sometimes as if the delinquent had preserved here an island of true devotion to a human being untainted by aggression or self-centered hostility. Closer scrutiny, however, invariably reveals that it is a matter of a perversion or, in the absence of any manifest disturbance of the physical performance, that the mental and emotional attitude accompanying the physical act is one of disregard for the happiness of the apparent love-object. This becomes evident in the delinquent's relationship to women. The object of his drive becomes a mere receptacle. The woman is degraded to a physiological tool and is never perceived in her totality as a human being with her own personality. This is not only significant of the delinquent's relationship within the sexual sphere. His partner becomes important only as a tool by which he can gratify his own ego needs, as for example, a subject on whom to show off jewelry; or a dummy to be dressed in beautiful clothes. In other words, what is only a part of a normal person's goal, constitutes the total and exclusive goal for the delinquent. To be sure, to find oneself in the object is an integral part in a wholesome relationship to the other sex. A finding of oneself in the partner is even one of the many prerequisites indispensable for a steady, mutually satisfactory and workable relationship. In the delinquent, however, the trait of finding oneself becomes the exclusive basis of interpersonal interest. Paul Schilder describes a correlation between the child's aggression and the level of unity it has achieved in regard to the body image of its objects.[4] I wish to enlarge on that idea and to suggest that the delinquent's disability to advance towards the representation of the whole may go back to a disturbance in his relationship to his own body, because he has been prevented from developing and integrating a unified total body image. It may be the distortion, the inharmonious and unbalanced state of

---

[4] Paul Schilder, *Goals and Desires of Man*, New York, Columbia University Press, 1942, xii—305 pp.

his own body-image that prevents him from enlarging the stunted representations of the world.

For clinical purposes I wish to mention an incident of delinquency in the history of a patient who otherwise showed no undue traits of alloplastic disorders. While doing some research work, he suddenly began to worry about the correctness of a theoretical conclusion he had drawn from some clinical material. At the same time he was dominated by a feeling of vanity and pride over what he considered the brilliance of his conclusions. Yet he was preoccupied by the idea that his point was not completely proven although it was clear that the evidence he presented was sufficient. He finally decided to send the paper to a professional journal in spite of his qualms. But doubts about the validity of his theory continued to occupy his mind for the next few weeks, although with lessened intensity. A new flare-up of doubts occurred when he corrected the galley proofs. The day subsequent to his returning the proofs to the editor, he felt an impulse to reread a paper which had no direct connection with his immediate work. This impulse appeared inexplicable until on reading the paper he found to his amazement that the author had drawn the identical conclusion about which he had previously worried with such intensity. It turned out that not only had he been present when the author read the paper, but that he also had read it several times thereafter. In view of those facts it became evident that his exaggerated worry about the alleged insufficiency of proof was the result of an unconscious conflict between his desire to appear as the originator of a new theory and a feeling of guilt about the aggression perpetrated by omitting an author's name and thus depriving a colleague of deserved recognition. As soon as the damage was done and could not be repaired, the repressive forces relaxed to the extent of permitting him to discover his error. The aggression in the form of mental stealing had been successfully carried out and the ego could dispense with further camouflage. Some of the earmarks of delinquency are demonstrated in this example. The infringement of a value and the impact on reality, in this instance by an omission, are present. Since the patient was not predominantly delinquent, the clinical appearance of the symptom was partly constructed like those encountered in autoplastic disorders. He did not plan the aggression but let it go by dint of simple forgetfulness. The readiness with which the truth was established indicated how ego-close the aggression was. The defense in the form of repression was particularly weak and no more than a superficial concession to customary restraint.[5] Had another person called his attention to the true source of his theory it would have become impossible for him to carry out the plagiarism. Furthermore, his fixation to a part-value configuration is quite evident. Scientists should be motivated by interest in values of

---

[5] The problem of the content against which the delinquent symptom is a defense will not be discussed here although the problem is of greatest clinical importance. It turns out that delinquent symptoms may keep a neurosis or psychosis in abeyance. The variety of structures held in abeyance by delinquency gives alloplastic disorders their specific clinical appearance. There is, however, a group of delinquents whose symptomatology is no longer a defense against an autoplastic disorder; they are a special group and show delinquencies untainted by another clinical entity. It must be stressed that in the majority of autoplastic disorders an alloplastic disorder is kept in abeyance. If the patient were able to carry out those impulses which he wards off by the neurotic or psychotic symptom he would be classified psychologically as well as juristically a delinquent or criminal.

the true-false order. Fame and honor are granted them by society as reward for their painful labor; yet they are consequences and not primary goals of their effort. In general terms it may be stated that the quest for fame, although it may be a potent factor in a scientist's endeavors, never ought to outweigh his love of truth. If the ratio of these two sets of motivations gets disturbed in favor of the rewards of fame a scientist may become delinquent not only by direct invidious aggression against a competitor, but he may consciously or unconsciously falsify results or limit his inquiries solely to contents befitting the society in which he lives and thus impair his primary goal of enlarging mankind's knowledge.

The clinical example presented also deserves attention from another aspect. The patient was never prosecuted for his violation, not only because it did not come to public attention; he could even have informed any number of persons, including the person he had damaged indirectly without incurring the danger of prosecution. In our present society it is customary to bring to justice those who infringe rights of physical property. Plagiarism is only rarely brought to court. This is all the more astounding since the bulk of scientific literature, as anyone who is familiar with it will agree, is brought about by plagiarism. Mental theft is condoned. Here society grants a large field in which delinquency may be carried out profusely without punishment. It is important to consider the sectors of condoned delinquency because only then will it be possible to ascertain and to outline the full scope of delinquency in our society. Oddly enough, it is the condoned delinquency which seems far more apt to destroy and disintegrate our civilization than the delinquency which society deems necessary to prosecute. Obviously, considerations neither of utility nor of damage to the group determine the condonation or prosecution of delinquency. The condoned and prosecuted categories appear to refer to society's reaction to the phenomena of delinquency while undetected delinquency to be mentioned here parenthetically only, involves a psychological problem, namely that of the delinquent's efficiency.[6]

Another almost invariable feature of the delinquent's attitude towards goals is the strong prevalence of magic. Magic attitudes are found in every kind of disorder and they are occasionally prevalent in individuals who are otherwise unaffected by psychopathology. In the personality makeup of the delinquent, however, magic plays a specific role which distinguishes it from the autoplastic group of disorders. It is surprising to note that the delinquent's efficient mastery of reality which is easily mistaken for a partial adjustment to a sector of reality actually often covers up a mass of magic beliefs. In the compulsive-obsessional neuroses the superstitions are separated

---

[6] Whether a person chooses a field of prosecuted or condoned delinquency in the process of discharging his hostilities is of significance and must not be viewed from a sociological viewpoint alone. The probability of embarking on one or the other course certainly depends at least partly on the *locus* of society in which the individual spends his formative years.

from the rational pursuits and recognizable as such because they are distinct symptoms to which a part of the ego usually objects. In the delinquencies on the other hand, superstition and reality manipulation coincide. In the same act in which the delinquent masters reality by imposing his will against the will of his environment or of society at large, he manages simultaneously to satisfy his magic beliefs. This must not be confused with the delinquent's conscious superstitions which he shares with the rest of the population, such as his belief in the propitiousness of certain days and numbers. The magic to which we here refer is that of the unconscious meaning which is attached to nearly all delinquent and criminal acts. They serve to enhance or to restore an inflated feeling of omnipotence which is essentially different from the feeling of mastery which normally is associated with efforts leading to success. The delinquent's destructive act becomes a necessity for him because of this psychological meaning. Were he prevented from acting the way he does or were he deprived of the prospect of indulging in delinquent acts, he would become depressed or stuporous or would develop panic. For such restraint may weaken his seemingly firm tie to reality. Sporadic or periodic destructiveness is an indispensable requirement for his maintaining a balanced feeling of well-being and of being in contact with reality.

There is an historical example of the delinquent's manifestation of magic beliefs when his destructive impulses are thwarted in their success. It is well known that Hitler, up to the last few days of his struggle, expressed the conviction that Providence was only testing him by this reversal of his good luck and that a sudden turn of the battle would restore his former glory if he only sustained his courage and his endurance. This was by no means a cheap propaganda trick nor a superficial self-deceptive illusion based on wishful thinking. From our clinical experience with delinquents we must assume that this was a true and deeply rooted conviction of a personality whose stability relied on the gratification of his destructive impulses. The religious person hopes and prays for the fulfilment of his wishes, the delinquent is confident of his ability to master the universe.

One feature in the history of delinquents must be mentioned because it occurs with such a surprising frequency that it may possibly be one of the prerequisites for the development of delinquency. It concerns a childhood situation in which the delinquent was exposed to an injustice on a reality level. We are not referring to those complaints familiar and prevalent in the histories of neurotics that their parents discriminated against them by loving them less than their siblings. These complaints of injustice may be justifiably called irrational.[7] The injustice of which the delinquent complains is concrete.

_____

[7] See Freud, S. (1915) Some Character Types met with in Psychoanalytic Work, *Collected Papers*, 4, where he shows the psychology of those who consider themselves "exceptions." He exemplifies his thesis in one of the greatest delinquents, Richard the Third, and considers the psychopathology of the latter as a reaction to discrimination by nature. I think some of the psychology of the "exception" can be discovered in each instance of clinical delinquency.

It often concerns a frank dishonesty which was perpetrated on him by his parents. The events reported by the delinquent and confirmed by others usually fall into the latency period. It is conceivable that the delinquent was exposed to a kind of trauma or traumata which is distinctive in its reality aspect[8] from that met by individuals who would later suffer from a neurosis, but my material did not show clearly whether the delinquent's complaints derived their great dynamic and structural effect from still earlier traumatic experiences during the preoedipal and oedipal phases. The awareness of having suffered a reality injustice at the hands of those with whom the child ought to identify and who should serve as prototypes of his later ideal and be the *fons and origo* of his conscience must interfere with appropriate identificatory processes and may well cause a disposition toward an unhampered release of aggression.

A certain mode of delinquency must be briefly mentioned here. It concerns latent delinquency. Clinical observation shows in a surprisingly large number of instances that alloplastic disorders may develop for long periods of time without causing any symptomatic manifestations. The patient's environment and the patient himself were unaware of the quiescent existence of a severe alloplastic disorder prior to the moment when an often seemingly trivial event may cause a sudden explosion and the abrupt appearance of the disorder with all the vigor accumulated in the course of years.[9]

It is necessary to emphasize that most psychopathology is composed of a mixture of alloplastic and autoplastic symptoms. Certainly, there are extreme cases in which one portion may become insignificantly small as compared with the other. In general, however, both are appreciably present albeit in varying proportions. The clinical classification will therefore depend on what kind of disorder predominates. But the ordinary therapeutic techniques which have been effective in the therapy of a large number of autoplastic disorders are not applicable to the alloplastic. The psychotherapy of a neurosis, after all, presupposes a person who experiences displeasure, is aware of suffering from a disease, and is desirous of being helped. The technique of treating autoplastic disorders presupposes the ability of self-observation and the desire and capacity to communicate to others the result of this self-perception. Since the attention of the neurotic is drawn towards himself because of the unpleasantness he feels in himself he usually does not lack these prerequisites. In alloplastic disorders none of these factors is present. The true delinquent certainly does not suffer unless he is caught and

---

[8] It is noteworthy that psychoanalysis may offer an indirect confirmation of a theory which is favored by sociologists, but must be rejected if taken literally, namely, that the root of delinquency is the unequal distribution of wealth and the economic discrimination against the majority of citizens.

[9] The important question arises here whether all members of society are suffering from latent, alloplastic disorders.

fears punishment; he denies that his behavior may be an illness: on the contrary he will claim that others who do not behave as he does are stupid and ignorant of the pleasures of life. He laughs at the idea of possibly needing that sort of help which the psychiatrist customarily gives. Last, but certainly not least, the delinquent is markedly lacking in ability to observe himself, and he is disinclined to communicate to any other person even the little which he may know about his subjective experiences. His conversation and the interest which he professes, are exclusively directed toward those contents of external reality from which he derives pleasure by infringing on values.

The psychoanalytic treatment of the delinquent falls into two parts of which the first only is of interest in this context. The average delinquent's personality contains autoplastic and alloplastic elements, but the latter in a larger proportion than the former. Only the autoplastic elements can be treated successfully with the usual techniques of psychoanalysis. The therapeutic problem therefore is to try to change the proportion of the two sets of elements in favor of the autoplastic. If this can be achieved and the prevailing ratio of the alloplastic elements can be changed to a predominance of the autoplastic then the way is open to proceed along the accustomed lines. The technique for achieving this reversal is founded on the principle of establishing a tight, fool-proof attachment between the psychoanalyst and the delinquent in the shortest possible time. Why this is necessary becomes clear. If the delinquent were not attached to the therapist he would discontinue his treatment but continue in his pleasure seeking behavior which in turn would eventually bring him into conflict with society. His subsequent imprisonment would make impossible any further therapeutic attempt. As is well known delinquents usually come or are brought for therapy at a late date when the prospect of arrest is imminent. Hence, very quick action is necessary, and an adequate, strong attachment must be established in the shortest possible time often within an hour if a final catastrophe is to be averted. Frequently the situation has reached such a critical point that the repetition of one simple delinquent act would be followed by arrest and a long term sentence. It is a task almost impossible to achieve, since it concerns a person who for years has developed a technique of living that amounted to free indulgence in selfish goals, disregarding the norms and demands of society. Within an incredibly short span of time this person is to be brought into a condition in which he will forego the gratification of his selfish desires and will behave as the community demands. This seems all the more impossible to accomplish because if the delinquent were able to forego his selfish interests he would be cured and would not need therapeutic help. Society, however, does not care so much what a person really is as how he behaves. If the psychoanalyst could make himself so important to the delinquent as to become for him a source of greater satisfaction than his delinquent pursuits or if he could make his patient temporarily substitute a field of condoned delinquency for that which is prosecuted, then the worst would be averted at least for the present emergency. The delinquent would still be far from cured. In either eventuality he would revert to his previous behavior pattern when separated from his therapist. Nevertheless time would have been won and the analyst could institute further measures without having to fear that the patient would get entangled with law-enforcing agencies.

The therapist of delinquents must become the delinquents' ideal if he wants to stand a chance of getting any hold on him. What are the delinquent's ideals? Does he have an ideal at all in view of his permanent impulse to infringe on values? It is that infringement on values which constitutes part of his ideals. We usually do not realize how difficult it is to infringe successfully on group values. An adolescent who specializes in the theft of cars needs an extensive technical knowledge. He must be an expert on cars; he must possess an elaborate knowledge of the locale and he must be aware of a score of techniques used by law-enforcing agencies. Actually it is a sign of considerable skill and ingenuity if a youth is able to steal a large number of cars without being caught. Or, let us consider how much intuitive psychological knowledge is required to carry out a successful hold-up. The proficient delinquent has a keen, alert mind. Owing to his great interest in surface values he has amassed a treasure of observations and experiences concerning the details of various sectors of reality unknown or scarcely noticed by the majority of citizens and, certainly, by the average psychiatrist. Since society tries to interfere with his preferred and cherished activities, he is forced to study people. Since he wants them to do things contrary to their advantage and wants to harm them and yet escape punishment, he has had to learn how to play on their prejudices, how to use their foibles and vanities and to predict the limit to which he could go in his exploitation. Moreover, he was compelled to learn in hard lessons the ways in which a victim would defend himself against his attack. All this made him a shrewd amateur-psychologist, an expert of the surface of the human mind, and an excellent manipulator of people. The development of these faculties was the outcome of necessity partly in order to escape punishment which was his great danger and the focus of his greatest fears, and partly to achieve his aggressive goals. Therefore, a person who reveals himself as being his superior in all these areas will become an object of admiration and interest. He will know that he can obtain valuable knowledge from him and there is no limit to the knowledge the delinquent needs in order to carry out his sinister plans and nevertheless escape punishment. If the analyst can convince the delinquent

of the shortcomings of the technique he had applied[10] and impress on him
that he, the analyst, knows more efficient and less dangerous techniques, then
the delinquent is bound to look up to him and to establish a relationship of
benevolent interest as all of us do when meeting persons who represent one
of our ideals. "But," one may object, "admitting that this will lead to an
attachment of the delinquent to his therapist, will this not merely make him
a more proficient delinquent without improving his capacity for socialization?" True, this would happen, if the therapist did no more than just this.
We must not forget that the preliminary goal was to create in the delinquent
some semblance of interest in the therapeutic situation. Afer all, the delinquent suspects that the therapist's goal is to make him a law-abiding citizen,
an idea which he profoundly hates. If he unexpectedly faces a person who
is more proficient in delinquency than he himself, he is taken off guard and
perceives a situation which is entirely different from what he had expected.
To place him in such a situation is an important therapeutic procedure.
When things take a course the delinquent has foreseen he feels himself master, which means that he feels contemptuous of his partner. Therefore it is a
general rule in the therapy of the delinquent never to act the way he
expects, but unceasingly to introduce new and unforeseen elements in order
to keep alive his interest in the therapeutic situation. Furthermore, two other
elements of importance are involved. The delinquent knows that his therapist is not engaged in criminal activities, but is in good standing in the
community. This must have a great effect on him. Why should a person
who possesses all the prerequisites of successfully tricking the world voluntarily
abstain from so doing? The analyst may hope that in the process of partial
identification the delinquent may also include this other part of the analyst's
personality. Moreover the delinquent notices that his analyst does not use
his knowledge to the delinquent's disadvantage. Hitherto his experience was
that people who knew how to cheat did it enthusiastically and whenever
there was an opportunity. The analyst, however, did not make him an object
of aggression, but of friendly protective action. This may lead to a devalua-
tion of the great value he had given to delinquent behavior. Another behavior
pattern the analyst must apply consistently in that initial phase of therapy is
an unfailingly helpful attitude. The delinquent must be taught by practical

---

[10] In order to institute this technique, expert knowledge of the delinquent's everyday life is necessary. The latter has little to do with the anatomy and physiology of the
central nervous system or with the usual subjects of psychiatric teaching. Since the
successful treatment of delinquents presupposes full command of the customs, habits,
traditions, idiosyncrasies, biases, preferences, folklore, superstitions of all walks of life
it is understandable that only rarely can a psychiatrist be found who is capable of dealing therapeutically with the difficult task of establishing the delinquent's transference.
Such knowledge is far less important in the therapy of the neurotic and psychotic. The
therapist's ignorance of the neurotic patient's daily life will quickly improve since the
neurotic patient will gladly tell the therapist all he needs to know of the secrets of
his life.

experience that there are no limits to which his partner will not go in helping him out of difficulties. This makes the therapy of delinquents an unremunerative occupation in view of the paramount importance which money plays in the delinquent's life. Money for him actually takes the place of love. Receiving money from a person is one of the signs which may convince him of being loved. Therefore usually no successful therapy of a delinquent is possible without his obtaining money from his analyst during that introductory phase of treatment when all possibilities must be mobilized to make the analyst a valuable person in the delinquent's eyes. The situation in which money is given to the delinquent for therapeutic reasons is wrought with danger and therefore requires special skill and tact. If the delinquent would be led to think that he tricked the analyst into giving money, this would make him feel contemptuous of his victim. Or if the analyst's money contribution became a matter of routine like the dole of the unemployed, then it would militate against any therapeutic benefit, and result in a therapeutic debacle. Money ought to be given only when the delinquent does not expect it. Again the delinquent must be taken aback by that therapeutic move. Never must the situation arise where the analyst could be considered a sucker or the victim of a sob-sister story. In spite of all the friendliness and love the delinquent obtains from his analyst, he must know that the analyst can act in an entirely different way if he wants to and that he has enough aggressiveness, vigor, and even combativeness to subdue the delinquent at any time. This double approach is one of the most difficult dynamic skills to achieve since the one aspect must almost always remain unverbalized, latent, potential, but active enough to reach the delinquent's unconscious, while the other is consistently and continuously acted out; yet both are necessary, presuppose each other, and either alone is ineffectual.

It should not be necessary to emphasize that all provocation of the delinquent must be avoided; he must never be made the object of even the slightest aggression, except for the one situation when his feelings of guilt are at the breaking point. Then some punishment or something that may be the equivalent of punishment will be necessary in order to reduce an acute tension based on feelings of guilt which otherwise may force him into active delinquency. Not to let oneself be provoked often subjects the analyst to a trying situation. The delinquent's distrust of the therapeutic situation is great, and he will be ingenious in testing out the therapist. The delinquent wants to make sure beyond doubt that his new and unexpected friend is a really reliable fellow. The friendliness he has encountered does not fit into his previous experience nor into his concept of the world. He feels that he might have to change if things continued on that scale and therefore he conceals a constant interest in making the analyst behave the way he is accustomed to seeing people react to his misdemeanors. The easiest way is to make the analyst angry. If he could succeed in provoking his therapeutic friend into an outburst of anger then the delinquent could place him in line with other people who had been objects of his attacks, such as father, or teacher or the neighborhood kids. If that happened, the analyst would lose the special position he had held in the delinquent's emotional life. This position, however, is an indispensable prerequisite of the therapeutic situation.

An important and difficult task is to be able to predict the delinquent's behavior. Relapses into manifest delinquency can often be forestalled if the therapist foretells their imminence. Here again an attitude is necessary in the analyst which is different from that required in the therapy of the neuroses in which the analyst's faculty of making predictions is far less taxed. In the analysis of delinquents the analyst must be able to reconstruct large parts of the delinquent's life with the help of only a minimum of information. The delinquent consciously tries to conceal the most important data, particularly of the recent past, and he will test the analyst's ingenuity by watching his credulity. The art of guessing the truth behind the delinquent's falsifications and lies is one of the most important tools with which a positive, though narcissistic, transference can be established. Generally the therapist must be aware of hidden motivations in the delinquent and must make him face the true issue of that part of the personality which he persistently tries to hide from others and partly from himself. The delinquent's attitude toward his new friend, the analyst, is, in spite of the intensity of the attachment, essentially selfish. This means that no matter how numerous and strong the bonds with the analyst appear, the delinquent is indirectly attached to himself, i.e., the delinquent found projected parts of his own ego in the analyst who will succeed in establishing a firm relationship only insofar as he succeeds in giving his patient an opportunity of finding himself in the therapist. The analyst thus must become an only slightly distorted mirror-image of parts of the delinquent's personality. As soon as his behavior deviates too much from that narrow frame the delinquent will go into a panic or will withdraw or aggressively turn against the analyst. The often-claimed "ingratitude" of the delinquent is based on his inability to maintain a friendly contact with a person to whom he had entertained a narcissistic, yet socially acceptable relationship for as soon as his partner does not continue to gratify this narcissistic need the delinquent has no choice but to withdraw. It is remarkable to what extent the delinquent's external behavior may change in terms of a conformity which seems to be an adjustment to the requirements of society so long as he can indulge in a relationship gratifying to his narcissistic needs. Under such circumstances he develops a kind of bondage to the person representing his own self. It seems as if he had become able to bear displeasure and to bring sacrifices for the sake of his fellow men. His environment believes him to have reformed, but the analyst knows that at this stage the delinquent has not changed in his personality structure at all. Psychologically he is still suffering from the same alloplastic disorder despite the essentially new appearance he offers to society. This would become evident at once if the analyst were to vanish permanently from the delinquent's sight. Deprived of his narcissistic love object the delinquent would quickly lose his apparent control over his alloplastic disorder and would relapse permanently into his former condition. He would be cured only if he were able to continue his social behavior independent of any vicissitudes of his positive relationship to the analyst. In order to achieve this goal, the therapist must gradually shift to the second phase of the delinquent's treatment. In this phase the delinquent is analyzed in a way similar to the one used with his neurotic counterpart from the very beginning of the therapeutic effort. His dependency on the therapist now makes it possible to proceed with the techniques which have proved their therapeutic efficiency in the treatment of autoplastic disorders. His narcissistic dependency on the therapist to whom he now concedes that omnipotence which he had arrogated to himself during the time of manifest delinquency, makes him more and more similar to the neurotic. In maintaining over a period of time which varies with the severity of the disorder, a relationship of love, although narcissistic, the delinquent had to repress his aggressions in order not to lose the gratification derived from the love object. In the course of that treatment phase the growth of autoplastic symptomatology is favored and alloplastic symptoms are gradually eliminated. He becomes throughout a neurotic and does not pose any other difficulty in treatment but those ordinarily encountered in the therapy of neuroses.[11]

The alloplastic disorders can be treated. Society's claim and that of a large number of psychiatrists, that the delinquent is a psychopath, unable to learn from experience and therefore not a suitable object for therapy, is essentially false. Such beliefs are not valid statements based on fact, but irrational expressions of ambivalence and emotional biases. True, the delinquent cannot derive that benefit which others do from their societal experiences in regard to value-adequate behavior patterns. The delinquent needs a very special constellation of conditions which will permit an adaptation of his personality structure to the exigencies of his cultural milieu. The special conditions necessary for the delinquent's "learning" do not pose essentially greater demands on man's ingenuity than other exigencies. The greatest obstacle to the abolition of human crimes seems to involve man's unconscious ideation in regard to crime and his obstinate refusal to accept responsibility for its perpetration and consequently, its perpetuation. That solutions can

---

[11] The delinquent who does not possess sufficient autoplasticity to be treated in the way briefly outlined here must be educated. The principles of this educatory process which is not entirely different from the aforementioned therapeutic measures, but different enough to reserve for it a special name, will not be described here.

be found for this kind of tasks becomes evident if the effort is made to apply to the alloplastic disorders the conceptual frame which has enriched our knowledge of the autoplastic disorders. If the genetic history of the delinquent is consistently submitted to analysis in terms of Freud's dynamic and structural concepts, then appropriate therapeutic measures can be evolved from this analysis. Such analysis would ascertain what therapeutic procedures are required in order to enable the delinquent's personality structure to continue its growth and integration. It would find the way to release the development of individuality at those points where a series of severe traumata have either stunted the growth process or driven the formative energies into deviate behavior patterns.

Freud described the processes taking place in neuroses and psychoses in terms of the ego's relationship to id, superego, and reality. In a psychosis the ego first withdraws from a sector of reality, denies its existence, and in a second stage replaces that part of reality by a creation of its own which is a more satisfactory substitute. In a neurosis the ego sides first with reality when the id tries to enforce the gratification of a desire irreconcilable with the demands of reality. The ego withdraws from that particular urge and represses it. When the urge grows strong and succeeds in circumventing repression, it returns in the second stage of the disease to the confines of the ego. Then in a disguised shape it forces the ego into a partial avoidance of that sector of reality with which the original impulse was irreconcilable. In both instances, in the psychoses as well as in the neuroses, the course of the disorder is diphasic. There is a step of withdrawal and a step of restitution. In the neurosis the id is partly restored to its rightful position by means of the neurotic symptom; in the psychosis a new reality is forthcoming partially substituting for what has been lost. Both solutions, neuroses and psychoses, in their particular way of solving the conflict, offer advantages and disadvantages to the ego. In both cases the ego must suffer displeasure although less than it would if the specific psychopathological solution were not at hand. The neurotic symptom does deprive the ego of real pleasure because it grants gratification in a distorted and insufficient way which is not in keeping with the ego's aspirations and desires. The ego fights against the neurotic symptom as it fought against the original urge, but this time it is bound to be on the losing side. In the psychosis the ego must struggle to maintain its newly created reality in the face of the original which consistently threatens to usurp its former place. It is noteworthy that the first phase in the formation of the neurosis and the second phase of the psychosis are model patterns of "normal" behavior. If repression were strong enough it would serve its purpose and keep the ego free of the objectionable urge although at the price of losing energy which could be used productively in other pursuits. By creating a new reality the psychotic does in an ineffective way what the normal does when exposed to a conflict between him and external reality, when turning towards the world and changing it in accordance with his demands and the possible opportunities of reality. The structural relationship of ego and superego in melancholia is less clear. The alloplastic disorders, the delinquencies, combine features which are significant of the other disease entities. They grow out of the same constellation as the latter, namely frustration of the growing child. Then they too take a diphasic course.

In the delinquencies there is a withdrawal from a specific sector of reality, namely from a portion of the representations of prohibitions. The ego refuses to accept the validity of certain behavior norms, but permits the corresponding id impulse to maintain its full force. Thus the second phase is initiated when the ego attempts to change reality in such a way as to provide the id with a real and alloplastic discharge.

Whereas in the narcissistic neuroses (melancholia) the ego is overwhelmed by the superego's interdict and submits slavishly to all superego demands, sometimes to the extent of self-annihilation, the delinquent succeeds in outwitting his superego by devaluating it, and thus denying the existence of its demands. The delinquent's ego then directs the restitutive process towards that part of reality which is necessary for the gratification of the id impulse and which his superego tried to deflate as a source of pleasure. Different variations are possible. The superego may be quite stunted in its development and then the conflict is entirely externalized and takes place solely between the ego and that part of reality which may oppose by force the ego's gratification. Or the moral demand has been internalized and then the delinquent must first escape the superego's interdict which is ever ready to interfere with pleasure-seeking pursuits and thus endangers the success of the ego's assault against reality.

We have said that the delinquent's value representations are a composite structure — some integrated, some not, some represented with full awareness, while others are unconscious. It is from these value representations that the delinquent's ego withdraws and this withdrawal of the delinquent's ego from normative representations corresponds to the withdrawal from reality as it occurs in the psychoses. The assault against reality is the analogue of the process of restitution in the psychoses. Since this mechanism of assault against reality does not lead to a gratification of the original id impulse, the mechanism is similar in this respect to that of the neurotic. Although the delinquent withdraws partially from the original demands of the id, especially as they are directed against his parents, his gratification of id demands is far more satisfactory and less disguised than any the neurotic achieves. Thus the delinquencies must be viewed as composite disorders in which we can study some of the most important mechanisms which are active in other disease entities. Yet despite these manifold resemblances the delinquencies are an original and unique group of disorders which cannot be reduced to a mere composite of other disorders. This outline of the structure of alloplastic disorders will make it understandable why a large number of delinquents may develop neuroses or psychoses when external reality does interfere with their symptom formation. However, it is noteworthy that the alloplastic disorders are the only group in which the ego is not exposed to the internal displeasure which is caused in the autoplastic disorder by a secondary fight against symptoms. The only source of displeasure which a delinquent may have to bear comes from reality's taking over that secondary fight and incarcerating the alloplastic patient. To a certain extent it can be rightly claimed that the delinquent is a distorted model of normal behavior since the pleasure principle is maintained to a degree pleasing to the delinquent without endangering the patient's survival and freedom if he is smart enough to select as his hunting ground one among those in which society permits the free growth of condoned delinquency.

PSYCHOANALYTIC PREVENTION VERSUS THERAPEUTIC PSYCHOANALYSIS

By Paul Federn and Heinrich Meng

(*New York — Basle*)

In the early days of psychoanalysis, Freud recommended this form of therapy only for selected cases of transference neurosis. Since then its realm has become more and more enlarged. He underestimated the therapeutic efficacy of his method but he expected better results as a consequence of progress in knowledge and technique; he was also sure that the popularization of psychoanalysis would have a beneficial effect on mental health in general. He anticipated that the analysand's resistances would diminish and that in consequence, the usual treatment would be shortened because of the analyst's greater authority and heightened suggestive influence. His prophecies were realized sooner than was expected. The most striking change is that conversion hysteria has almost disappeared. Severe obsessional neuroses always were exceptional and rare cases. But there are more neurotics than ever before and today the number of nervous victims of our civilization who need the help of psychoanalysts constantly exceeds the number of analysts being trained to meet these needs.

Of those who undergo psychoanalysis many complain that it is too late. Often this is mainly an expression of resistance. It is never too late to get rid of a neurotic or — if possible — of a psychotic state. From an objective standpoint one would often prefer to have been able to analyze a patient in his younger years. On the other hand, since neurosis is based on a partial lack of maturation, it is accompanied by a prolonged flexibility and plasticity. Therefore, the "too late" refers less to mental rigidity than to the inveterate conditions of life which were built up on neurotic motivations. To the patient, the "secondary gain" of the neurosis as well as the anticipated "secondary loss" through the cure balance the scales against a basic change of attitudes. However, we have successfully analyzed people of all ages, even beyond sixty and seventy, without finding it too late. On the other hand, we discontinued analysis when we found that the neurosis

26

had become an indispensable part of the patient's compromise with his destiny.

The title of this paper suggests the question whether every therapeutic analysis does not start too late. It seems rather an absurd waste of time, money and skill to decide that despite the years spent in neurosis from now on the veils must be lifted which have mercifully obscured an awareness of the pain and disgust, fear and guilt, experienced and suffered in the past. Furthermore the analysand has to be more truthful, courageous and even broadminded than life usually requires of normal people. His analysis involves these demands on him because neurotic mental structures are more resistive to change than are healthy ones. Another immanent difficulty is that the neurotic pattern has to be given up before the normal one is established.

Therefore it seems obvious that prevention is far preferable. This answer is in line with the general march of medicine from therapy to prevention. Medicine learned to immunize with much smaller dosages than those required after the organism was overpowered by an infection. Psychiatry may reasonably be expected to do even more so inasmuch as no alien agent is responsible for functional diseases. It seems to be a commonsense demand that mental hygiene should establish healthy childhood conditions and that child psychiatry should interfere immediately whenever a serious traumatic or developmental mental injury occurs. This demand could be justified theoretically by pointing out the enormous saving of mental energies which such interference would prevent the individual from fixating as cathexes and anticathexes in every manifest or latent neurosis or psychosis. Furthermore, the development fixation of the ego was found instrumental in preparing later severe organ-psychosis. The degree of developmental egofixation likewise preconditions the depth of regression in schizophrenic states, which becomes manifest whenever the adult ego loses its full cathexis. A mental hygiene of the ego during infancy and childhood is, therefore, the prospective aim of a preventive psychiatry of psychoses. There can be no question but that it would be wiser to protect the ego during growth than to have to resurrect and unburden previous ego states through analysis or even hypno-analysis. One might even go so far as to say that adult analysis is necessary only because there was no preventive hygiene. This statement will gain in emphasis if we outline clearly some of the specific methodical difficulties of adult analysis. For in addition to the practical difficulties which are emphasized by its adversaries but which are without scientific interest, there are true antinomies inherent in the method itself.

1) The aim of the treatment is to free the patient from morbid residuals of his development. He should cease to nourish futile resentments and senseless attachments, he should become oriented in the present — yet

the method constantly forces him to dig out the past and to live through it again.

2) The aim is to substitute object-libido for narcissism. Libidinous forces should be channeled away from the ego and turned towards present, external goals. Likewise the manifestations of the death-instinct, aggression and sadness should be diverted from the ego and must be overcome by mechanisms too complicated to be described here. Yet, the procedure makes the patient's own ego the permanent goal of study and of interest.

3) The aim is to overcome anxiety — yet the situation of the analyst sitting behind the analysand creates a constant awareness of an "unseen" and unknown being. This feeling involves anxiety.

4) The aim is to make the patient proceed from psychic to external reality. Yet the whole transference situation renews in a kind of artificial reality, the fantasies and frustrations of his earlier love life.

5) The aim is to integrate the patient's feelings and to enable him to make independent decisions. Yet the transference creates a state of frustrated dependency. It is used to overcome repressions and must be resolved and re-established repeatedly. This does not help integration.

These are not weak points of the psychoanalytic technique but on the contrary, they are its most effective means of getting into conscious, present reality, the patient's fantasies, the past, and the unconscious. In dealing with children on the one hand and with psychotics on the other, the technique had to be changed. There is no reason and no possibility — as far as we see — to make changes in the technique of adult analysis. However, the patient is taught to understand the analytical situation, to keep it apart from his daily life, not to do self-analysis as home work and to postpone any basic decisions until after his analysis — all this within the limits of common sense.

Both serious and superficial reformers have given up one or the other of these procedures in order to avoid the antinomies which they involve. Such reformers who deny child sexuality or the existence of the individual's unconscious ceased to be psychoanalysts. Moreno and other group therapists counteract narcissism by the publicity with which conflicts are revealed. Some change the couch routine, others do not resolve the transference. There is no originality in any of these reforms. Every dynamic approach can release tension, improve the actual impairment and bring relief of anxiety and symptoms — temporarily or permanently. Yet psychoanalysis aims at more than symptomatic help. All functional disease should be removed by functional therapy. Therefore, brain surgery used in cases of severe neurosis means surrendering one's scientific standpoint to expediency. Drastic methods against mental illness are mostly due to the necessity of institutional routine. Psychoanalysis, which in its procedure is the antithesis of surgical intervention, may make practical adjustments to practical needs but not scientific compromises. In many regards the psychoanalyst carries a heavy burden of responsibility, which would be eased if psychoanalytic prevention could take over.

Since the analyst is the instrument of the method, his own mental hygiene must also be considered. It is a problem whether enough individuals have a personality that tolerates the demands of daily psychoanalytic work. There are some professions which are dangerous not in respect to life or physical health but in regard to character-health. Whenever a professional worker constantly deals with people who look up to him, or are dependent on his help and judgment, have absolute confidence in him, or who are inferior in strength, education or are younger than he, he may become seduced into narcissistic inflation. The psychoanalyst is in an analogous position although the effects of the positive and negative transferences to which he is exposed, tend to cancel each other out. However, he has the constant advantage of objectivity, of deeper insight and of previous experience, and the calmness of the expert. His main danger lies in feeling superior and arrogating to himself the right of ultimate arbitration in nearly every problem.

The mental hygienic remedies of a "dangerous" profession consist in being psychoanalyzed oneself; regularly to interrupt one's work, and to interpose periods of work in an inverted relationship to one's fellowmen; the sabbatical year is a wise institution. The main help, however, is one's own insight and some modesty, in view of the importance of one's task. Since the psychoanalyst is compelled by his work to passivity and receptiveness he needs the compensation of some activity and productiveness. This is the reason why nearly every analyst participates in scientific research, in teaching and in discussion.

The difficulties inherent in the method are not a justifiable excuse for replacing adult analysis by psychoanalytic prevention wherever there exist arguments in favor of adult analysis. From a practical standpoint the technique of adult analysis is an established method while psychoanalytic prevention is still in an experimental, albeit, promising stage. Theoretically, there are decisive reasons against generalizing our first dictum that "it is obvious that prevention is preferable". The statement, however, is justified that psychoanalytical prevention[1] will enormously increase mental health and diminish the number of neurotics who today need but cannot attain their psychoanalysis as adults.

A sound prevention, which avoids hypochondrical fear of "complexes", might prevent symptomatic neurosis but it cannot change the conditions which give rise to fixation, repression, ambivalence and incestuous sexuality. These mechanisms are the product of conditions intrinsic to human civilization. Civilization must be accompanied by a postponement of maturation,

---

[1] This was first emphasized by Marie Bonaparte.

by a prolonged fetalism, i.e., infancy, prolonged childhood and adolescence. It means the coexistence of sexuality and ego-drives, since the human species no longer has short periods of sexual heat, well and wisely separated from the individual's struggle for existence. These conditions demand a slow and complicated integration of the ego and the superego. Therefore, even with adequate prevention, there will still remain incoherence, unsuccessful repression, increased investment of anticathexis and libido- and ego-fixations which must be adjusted by adult psychoanalysis. Psychiatry unconsciously acknowledged this fact by calling all kinds of personality disturbances "neurosis". Psychoanalysts unconsciously acknowledged the situation by instituting the psychoanalysis of mature and healthy individuals for the purpose of training them for special professional tasks and also for the purpose of education. Even if the child's ego and superego formation is protected by psychoanalytic mental hygiene, the child still needs its period of immaturity and should not be forced prematurely into the shape of an adult.

Psychoanalysis implies the revealing of the unconscious to the conscious ego. Before the patient can make that "reliable contract" which Freud says is requisite for this purpose, he must have attained the necessary degree of maturity. Child analysis is similar to that of psychotics, in that both techniques are forced to compromise with the conditions offered by the patient's ego. Adult analysis cannot be replaced or made superfluous by child analysis. The cooperation of the patient is necessary. The analytical process proceeds in the main as a kind of mental automatism going on in the patient which is observed but not checked, either by the analysand or by the analyst. This demands a toleration of hardship, an acceptance of responsibility and a degree of insight, which however much it may have been handicapped and incompletely matured in consequence of neurosis is nevertheless only possible in adulthood. Therefore adult analysis still is successful when previous analysis has failed and even a successful previous analysis may need to be completed by adult analysis.

There is still another and more subtle argument in favor of postponing an analysis until after adolescence if it has not been urgent as a medical emergency. It is unfair to influence individuals before they have formed their own judgments and chosen their viewpoints. It was characteristic of Freud's fairness and modesty, of his objective interest without any wish to dominate, that he repeatedly modified the technique in the direction of the neutrality of the analyst. He would have preferred to hold to his early formulation that the patient's ego needs only to be confronted with his unconscious, which is unknown to him. While such a psychological process is possible theoretically, in practice the goals of therapy, training and even education constantly prevent the analyst from maintaining an attitude of absolute reserve. All neurotic reactions are connected with individual, social and scientific viewpoints and values. Even though he does not give advice, the analyst is continuously participating in all the problems of the patient's life by resolving neurotic manifestations. Moreover the analysand himself expects not only a symptomatic cure but also a strengthening and improved integration of his personality. He usually wants more guidance than the methodical analyst offers. However, the "orthodox" method can be applied in training analyses, where therapy and instruction as well as education then result as a kind of by-product of the psychoanalytic process per se. Yet this type of analysis requires even more than the usual degree of maturity. The analysand should have made his choices in love, friendship and professional direction as well as his political and social allegiances, before being purified of the residuals of the conflicts of his past since such a purifying process cannot but involve the influencing of the analysand by the analyst.

On the other hand, one of the great cultural merits of Freud's method lies in the fact that it enables the experience and mental maturation acquired by previous generations to be transmitted to the next without the usual repetitive and wasteful expenditure of energy, resulting in unhappiness and frustration. Thomas Mann recognized the possibility that psychoanalysis as a cultural process may have a developmental value for the whole of mankind. It enables us to hope for a future in which neither illusions nor rationalizations are necessary. The analysis of individuals has demonstrated this result, and thus shown that it is legitimate to transmit a better and deeper understanding to the patient. But this goal is achieved even more manifestly in child analysis and in psychoanalytic prevention. It has always been the aim, if not the achievement, of religious education. Natural science likewise promised its attainment but failed signally to keep that promise until mental hygiene learned in recent years how to improve the methods of bringing up a child to better mental health.

So we may conclude that therapeutic analysis and analytic prevention are not in competition in attaining this goal. Every therapeutic analysis also means the prevention of later illness. Although the two procedures differ in method, they both deal with the same problems, have the same aim and make use of the same knowledge. Nor do they exclude each other in regard to their timing. Psychoanalysis is indicated whenever a neurotic or a psychotic outbreak causes a child unhappiness and hinders his normal education. The above-mentioned antinomies and other difficulties are not yet present in the analysis of childhood and puberty. Whether the immature individual is of the black, yellow or white race, whether he later becomes a moderately religious, an orthodox, or a free thinker, a whig or a tory, a genius or a mediocre citizen, during childhood and puberty the conflicts which need help are the same.

The analysis of a neurotic child does not make later analysis superfluous, but it shortens it, because the development deviation was checked before it was too late. It frees many areas of conflicts if not always completely. Just so does surgery have a better prognosis when its operation is done early or in two stages. Child analysis does not immunize against neurosis, but — to use a frequent though inexact term — it strengthens the ego. It is both, therapy and prevention. As a prevention measure it is incomplete because of the child's complete dependence on his family and school conditions.

After his analysis, the child, like the paroled psychotic, is again exposed to his detrimental surroundings unless the family has been educated to a better understanding and a more enlightened behavior toward him.

When the records of the analyses of preschool children are published, they will constitute a grave indictment of the family, the neighborhood and of society. Every child-therapist is forced to become a preacher — very frequently a voice in the wilderness — as well as a reformer. The help of social agencies is highly appreciated. Yet an adequate mental hygiene of the child and of youth is still not available wherever and whenever it is desperately needed.

Under these circumstances psychoanalytic prevention must also eventually protect the child against his parents, teachers and parent-figures. One might be tempted to have the whole family psychoanalyzed, in order to effect a radical improvement of their attitude in the hope that they will then cooperate fruitfully with the child's analyst. This method is impossible in practice, since even if the several analysts work together to form a mental hygiene team, the situation would be worsened by the fact that all the figures in the drama would become emotionally restive by being analyzed. The more exacting their analyses, the more collisions would be precipitated. It is therefore preferable to have the parents undergo analysis before undertaking the child's treatment. However, whether previously analyzed or not, the parents should be directed and advised by a psychoanalytically trained helper, who has contact with the child's analyst. He will intervene like a social worker, or more like a confessor, will in a friendly manner explain the child's reactions and will allay arising doubts or suspicions. It is seldom advisable or necessary that the child-analyst himself takes over this role, except in very complicated family situations. When the child's analysis is terminated one should not sever the contact with the family. Prevention has to continue.

But the best protection of the child is not to wait until he has become neurotic but to protect him by taking mental hygiene and if advisable, psychoanalytic care of the "neurotic" marriage itself and of the neurotic partners who entered the marriage. In addition to the child, there are always three patients to be cured, the third being the marriage itself. It should be the function of the psychiatric social worker to take over the family part of the mental hygiene teamwork rather than to leave the mental care of the whole family to the analyst, and thus handicap him with the ensuing difficult situations of rivalry and jealousy. But there are also sensible if untrained people whose help can be enlisted so that the main object can be attained of taking mental care of the whole family at the same time.[2]

August Aichhorn was the first to organize psychoanalytic mental hygiene on a large scale and in many teams of which he was the spiritual center and consultant. The greatest group was the consultation center of the Viennese Psychoanalytic Society. Aichhorn introduced two new tasks of psychoanalytic prevention. The one was mental guidance during puberty, the other the prophylactic and therapeutic approach of the psychoanalyst to boys who threatened to become future delinquents.

While the future neurotic may wait till maturity and in some cases might be cured more successfully after maturity, and in other instances may overcome his neurosis without special treatment, the future delinquent cannot wait. His delinquent tendencies must be arrested at all costs and as early as possible. For this reason it is of greatest importance to be able to make a differential diagnosis between the future forms of delinquency and to determine which indicate a neurotic or psychotic basis, which are due to a retardation of development and prolonged states of primitive and aggressive behavior, and which are early manifestations of addiction. Future delinquency offers the greatest as well as the most promising challenge to psychoanalytic prevention. Research and experiments in this field are going on everywhere. Although the social roots of delinquency forbid undue optimism, yet there is no other field in which the advantage of prevention is so great, and in which our appeal for attention and help will be more justified when the good results of prevention and therapy can be shown and compared with each other.

We come to the conclusion that both therapeutic psychoanalysis as well as psychoanalytic prevention have to be offered as emergency help whenever a latent neurosis, psychosis or delinquency begins to become manifest. Prevention should be offered to every one from birth to death. In childhood it is especially necessary in the periods of increase of sexuality, i.e., the preschool and the pre-puberty and puberty years. Every boy or girl should have mental hygiene guidance and be entrusted to a mental hygiene helper. This requires the mobilization and additional training of many pro-

---

[2] Settlement work began fifty years ago to institute appropriate groups or clubs, with a common interest or hobby for every member of the family — father, mother and each child.

fessionals, such as clergymen, visiting teachers, social workers, psychologists and of course physicians, psychiatric nurses and — psychiatrists. Such extended mental hygiene must be standardized without being chained by too much control and overburdened with the detailed clerical work of recording and statistics. Ample opportunity of consultation seems preferable to permanent supervision.

When prevention will have diminished the necessity of therapy, adult analysis will become a modern kind of initiation, based on psychological science and without any ritual. Adult analysis will mainly serve training and educational purposes. At the same time neurosis and future delinquency will be stopped in their development during infancy, childhood and puberty.

THERAPY AND ETHICS IN AUGUST AICHHORN'S TREATMENT OF WAYWARD YOUTH

By Oskar Pfister, Ph.D.

(Zurich)

The name of August Aichhorn evokes in those who know him the image of the kind-hearted, strongminded educator who has succeeded in taming little savages with the magic wand of his intuitive and boundless love of humanity.[1] The man who introduced the psychoanalytic principle into the therapeutic training of delinquents does not belong among those thinkers who are prone to lose themselves in theoretical abstractions. He is not one of those teachers of pedagogy who write a book about the science of education without ever having educated either a child or an adolescent, as two men I know actually admitted having done. Aichhorn's educatory work is inspired by his tremendous will to help. His profound compassion is what has made him a bold pioneer, whose indomitable energy was able to overcome the initial resistances to his innovations. Kindness is the driving power in his education of delinquents just as, according to Freud, a positive transference is indispensable for the cure of a neurosis. "For the patient," says Freud, "transference is the way to success in psychoanalysis as in every other therapy";[2] "psychoanalytic therapy always constitutes an attempt to liberate the repressed love which had found only a meagre compromise outlet in a symptom."[3]

Love, however, the awakening of which Aichhorn conceives as the core of his educational task, must not consist solely in an emotional relation to the therapist-teacher, but must become an ethical driving power of its own

---

[1] I well remember the first lecture I attended of this famous man. What impressed me most was the ease with which he dissolved the tension of a distinguished audience by his informality, only to re-create this tension and to concentrate it on the content of his lecture. What he conveyed to his listeners was the result of serious, pioneering research, but the man who presented it was a simple, jovial, self-confident person in whose company one felt comfortable.

[2] Freud, S.: The Dynamics of Transference, Collected Papers, Vol. II, London, Hogarth Press, 1924.

[3] Freud, S.: Delusion and Dream, New York, Moffat, Yard & Co., 1917.

in the sense of the genuine Christian concept of love. Aichhorn's therapeutic technique which centers around love as the main tool, nevertheless conforms in minute details to Freud's psychological and therapeutic methods.[4] Aichhorn had to modify the method for his purposes; formal analysis was impossible with his subjects because of their psychological peculiarities as well as in view of their large number and the short duration of their stay under his supervision in the training school.

In the following, we shall deal with Aichhorn's therapeutic method only. However, we shall keep in mind that his hygienic measures are, at the same time, largely ethical measures, although ethics always is maintained as a distinct entity, separate from hygiene or therapy. Furthermore, since we shall deal here with education for love, a comparison with the demands of Christian love, and its ethical, therapeutic, and hygienic implications, seems indicated.

I.   THE ROLE OF THE EDUCATOR

Aichhorn hardly ever mentions love. Following Freud, he usually speaks of the delinquent's "positive transference" which he identifies with "the tender feeling" for the educator,[5] or he speaks of kindness, or of the awareness of social obligations. It is easily understandable that both, Aichhorn and Freud, are wary of the use of the word "love," a word more abused than perhaps any other. It refers to the highest and the lowest in the human soul and, in addition, covers any number of indefinite values in the gamut between the two extremes. Our first task is to establish what, according to Aichhorn, is the function of the educator's love in the education of delinquents. For the sake of clarity, let us distinguish between the educator's giving and accepting love in dealing with delinquents.

The giving of love

It is important to note that Aichhorn differentiates in meting out kindness between the needs of those of his charges who were over-fed with love and those who were starved for it. The victims of over-indulgent love who were showered with tenderness without any demands for reciprocity, and therefore were destined to moral failure, must not receive the same kind of consideration as their counterparts who resemble them so much in their external behavior. The latter's waywardness, however, originated in frustration, in the lack of parental love and of the warm, kind sympathy, and supporting interest, for which these boys vainly longed. To the former, Aichhorn pays little attention in the first days after their referral to his school, apart from a brief friendly reception which they share with the latter group to whom, however, much more time is devoted from the very be-

---

[4] Aichhorn, A.: *Wayward Youth*, New York, Viking, 1944, pp. 7f.
[5] *Op. cit.*, p. 235.

ginning.[6] Then only he begins his discussions with whatever type of patient he has and to each he conveys how great is his interest in him and his eagerness to help. Deliberately and according to plan he creates a positive transference and then uses it as his chief instrument for corrective education.[7]

He painstakingly avoids anything that could remind the delinquent of a courtroom. He does not reprimand, nor does he harp on former misdeeds and he never lets anyone feel his disapproval. He is not a judge but a physician, never relinquishing his attitude of helping or treating whatever causes there may have been for the delinquent's commitment. The thief who has been found out and expects strict punishment is handed the sum he stole, the truant who returns anxiously is given a meal at Aichhorn's own table and a bed in his home. In this way he heaps coals of fire on the sinners' heads. He shows them how well he understands them and humbly he even goes to the length of assuring them (and somewhat infringes on veracity for the sake of a positive transference) that he would have acted the same way in their place. His attitude suggests that of a brother rather than that of a father and in fact, he is primarily concerned with avoiding the arousal of oedipal hatred.

Aichhorn says: "The optimistic attitude of the counsellor toward life, the cheerfulness with which he works, create an atmosphere in which remedial work can be carried on without great effort."[8]

With all of these qualifications, Aichhorn himself is richly endowed. More than that; his is a truly positive attitude toward his charges. What he has to give them is not an "as if," not a pretense of love. Certainly, his expressions of emotions are scarce, he avoids sentimentality; yet as an educator he is the personification of the noble and sublimated love, which manifests itself in helping actions.

The parallel to Christian love is obvious although Aichhorn nowhere refers to it explicitly. One crucial difference has to be noted: Christian love originates and culminates in God's love and its reciprocation. Aichhorn conforms with his master Freud in that he acknowledges religion as a therapeutic agent, but he does not concentrate on it. Obviously, however, he agrees with the teachings of the gospels and we shall see that the therapeutic and preventive precepts of both coincide to an amazing degree even in details.

Jesus claimed that love must be dispensed to the sinners and the morally distressed because it is their primary need. He said: "For the Son of man is come to seek and to save that which is lost" (*Luke*, 19:10), and when he

---

[6] *Op. cit.*, p. 89.

[7] Aichhorn himself always kept to the principle he had formulated so well: "First we had to compensate for this great lack of love and then gradually and with great caution begin to make demands upon the children. Severity would have failed completely." *Op. cit.*, p. 172.

[8] *Op. cit.*, p. 152.

was reproached for mingling with publicans and sinners, he said: "They that are whole have no need of the physician but they that are sick; I came not to call the righteous but sinners to repentance." (*Mark*, 2:17).[9]

All this denotes the very revaluation of values that bourgeois society and its leaders never took seriously, but which was realized in innumerable works of love throughout Christendom and realized to the full by a few self-sacrificing individuals. It is noteworthy that Aichhorn who approached the problem from an entirely different angle and who based his techniques on psychoanalysis, nevertheless discovered the indispensability of love and made it the pivotal mechanism of his corrective education.

Aichhorn's rejection of the kind of "judgments" that had been previously customary in education has been anticipated in the Sermon on the Mount: "Judge not, that ye be not judged" (*Matthew*, 7:1). The prodigal son is not reproached upon his return but is given the "best robe" and a ring is put on his hand, whereas the self-righteous grumbling brother is reprimanded (*Luke*, 15:11-32). In Christian education as well as in that of Aichhorn the delinquent is guided to love through an unsentimental kind of educational love. The culprit's conscience, namely, reacts not only according to talionic law but also according to the motive of revenge; whereas the teacher personifies a kind, merciful and yet superior law and power.[10] In Aichhorn's method, there are no ethical demands made until the educator's love has taken strong roots and developed in his charge.

The acceptance of love

In his corrective therapy, Aichhorn freely accepts and furthers his patients' affection for himself. He consciously differentiates his method from psychoanalytic therapy which does not stress the successes achieved through transference. Aichhorn says: "In the analysis of neurotic patients, the transference must be used, not for temporary improvement, but to give the patient strength to complete a special piece of work, to change unconscious material into conscious material and thereby to bring about a permanent change in his whole being."[11] I agree with Aichhorn in the rejection of non-analytic or superficially analyzed transference cures. However, I believe that a positive transference should give the patient the strength not only to gain access to unconscious material but also the strength to recapture repressed emotions and decisions and to rebuild his life on the basis of these newly gained insights.

Whether he wants it or not, the analyst will influence his patient's way

---

[9] In this context, cf. also the story of the one sheep lost out of one-hundred and of the joy when it is found; "Rejoice with me; for I have found my sheep which was lost." *Luke*, 15: 1-7.

[10] Cf. *John*, 3:17.

[11] *Op. cit.*, pp. 235-236.

of life which replaces the one he had led under the sway of his neurosis. If a positive transference is rejected it may easily turn into a negative one, and the analyst must, at certain junctures, prevent any destructive action on the part of his patient. The analyst will find himself obliged to familiarize his patient with ethical norms even though his goal be solely to guide the patient toward becoming a free, independent and socially well adjusted person.

Transference to the teacher by the youngsters who are starved for love plays a far greater role in the education of delinquents than it does in the treatment of neurotic patients. Therefore Aichhorn even grants to a specific group of pupils love as "reward ... as means to achieve renunciation of pleasurable desires."[12] This compensation, however, is bound up with a demand for reciprocation. Otherwise the pupils would continue under the sway of the pleasure principle. Excess of love is rejected;[13] the teacher's as well as the pupil's love is pedagogically necessary and valuable only as a guide to a higher goal.

In their acceptance of, or rather emphasis on the leader-roles, both Aichhorn and Zulliger apply Freud's findings to mass-psychological phenomena. Love of the leader is a means to creating adjustment and thereby to conveying ethical strength.

Termination of transference has no place in Aichhorn's system. On the contrary, he is particularly pleased when the formerly aggressive boys later express feelings of affection for him. However, he makes it clear to his pupils that he expects them to lead useful lives and thus enable him to take pride in them. He overcomes evil forces by good ones, and admits: "Without really knowing what we were doing we worked out what might be called a practical psychology of reconciliation."[14]

Let us point briefly to the parallels in the Christian conception of the positive transference. Jesus was fully aware of the significance of love for ethical rehabilitation. He dispensed love to everyone and tied up his ethical demands with the very love that he awakened and developed by offering his love. Therefore he could say: "Come unto me, all ye that labor and are heavy laden, and I will give you rest ... learn of me; for I am meek and lowly in heart ... For my yoke is easy, and my burden is light." (*Matthew,* 11:28-30).

Aichhorn's struggle with the harsh and strict administrators of reformatories which are conducted like prisons has its parallel in Jesus' woe over the hard Pharisees who "bind heavy burdens and ... lay them on men's shoulders ... but when they have made a proselyte, they make him twofold more the child of hell than they are themselves." (*Matthew,* 23:4, 15).

---

[12] *Op. cit.,* p. 196.
[13] *Op. cit.,* p. 200.
[14] *Op. cit.,* p. 150.

Aichhorn successfully combats relapses by sympathy and forgiveness. This parallels Jesus' actions and precepts. Not "seven times, but seventy times seven" Jesus commanded Peter to forgive his brother who had sinned against him (*Matthew*, 18:22). Crucified, Jesus asked forgiveness for his friends, who had fled, and for his enemies (*Luke*, 23:34). He was the first to recognize the liberating, protecting and therefore therapeutic power of forgiveness that is granted freely, of the gratia praeveniens. Aichhorn demonstrated with his delinquents that it is far more effective than the most powerful threats. By virtue of his position as leader, of his dignity as representative of the ethical norms of life, Aichhorn has assumed the functions of the minister, the personification of the ethical command. By forgiving the offender who felt guilty he abolished the anxiety of guilt, thus, at the same time, alleviating what might otherwise have become a profuse source of delinquency. This is also one of the main tasks of Christianity.[15]

II. THE PUPILS

The administrators of the old reformatories considered delinquents as incipient criminals, as candidates for prison, as it were, "the scum of human society, the rabble that populates the prison a few years later," as a friend of mine, a governor whom I once consulted about a juvenile delinquent, expressed it, when warning me not to send the boy to such an institution.

Aichhorn does not know of scum or rabble, he only knows unhappy human beings, in need and worthy of help. All of them have received too little genuine love, be it in the form of an excess of indulgence with its disastrous consequences (particularly as regards the resolution of the oedipal crisis), or be it through a lack of tenderness and kindness. In either case, the reaction was an excess of hatred and a negative attitude to the social order. They never learned to accept the ethical command of instinctual renunciation with the goal of achieving higher, though delayed pleasure. They are unaware themselves how strong is their desire for love and understanding which they have repressed behind a layer of coldness but which will bloom forth if they are given love.

If Aichhorn initially pays less attention to boys who had become delinquent "due to an excess of love," this does not mean that he has any less readiness to help them or benevolence toward them than toward those whose waywardness originated in a deficit of love. But he knows that even if he were to treat them all alike, it would not be the same. He is just as careful in the quantity and quality of kindness he dispenses to the "mixed" cases who constitute the majority.

Aichhorn's capacity for empathy and his intuition supplement his

---

[15] Cf. Pfister, O., *Christentum und Angst*, pp. 115f, 265-67, 271f, 310ff, et al.

depth-psychological knowledge. Combined, they make him almost a master-detective in the discovery of the causes of delinquency. These methods are just as effective in cases of boys who transferred upon Aichhorn the hatred that originally was felt for their father or mother. Thus, the corrective educator becomes a psychotherapist, in the same way in which Jesus had to take up the vocation of a physician. Their *medicina sacra* is helping and healing love.

III. THE THERAPEUTIC METHOD

To understand Aichhorn's method, two points must be kept in mind: First, he was entrusted only with pupils whose rehabilitation could be expected even though their delinquency might have reached a high degree;[16] secondly they were brought to his training school under duress, compelled by a law-enforcing agency. The task was to create a new ego ideal, strong enough to put an end to the predominance of the instinctual drives over the social demands and to break the defiant resistance against the commands of conscience and society. After the infantile residues had been resolved, re-education could set in and correct what had formerly been neglected.[17] In order to accomplish this, sublimation must occur.

The process is initiated by consistent friendliness and kindness;[18] as mentioned above, demands for achievements are made only after a sufficiently positive transference has been achieved and under painstaking avoidance of brutal severity.[19] Punishment is meted out only on the basis of an accurate evaluation of the psychological constellation and after detailed explanation of its reason and purpose. Unless punishment is wisely and carefully made to fit the "crime," it might easily result in callousness and slyness, and in a stifling of love. The analytically trained educator must be able to dispense ample enjoyment without either lavishing too much love on his charges or denying them due tenderness; he must be able to make attractive the duties that were formerly hated and to adjust them to his pupils' inclinations.

What aroused most hostile comments and resistance was the fact that Aichhorn permitted the aggressive group to abreact their aggressions, that he never interfered, except in cases of acute danger, and that his assistants were not allowed to interfere either. No complaints on the part of the neighbors or even of the police could shake him in his determination to protect these young savages in their destructive activities. The result was amazingly favorable. When these wild boys realized that they were not only not punished but not even prevented from acting out their rage, that, on the contrary,

---

[16] Aichhorn, *op. cit.,* pp. 223-25.
[17] *Op. cit.,* pp. 148f, p. 234.
[18] *Op. cit.,* p. 172.
[19] *Op. cit.,* p. 144-45.

they were being treated with consistent kindness, they felt that "coals of fire were heaped upon their heads" (*Proverbs*, 25:22). The acts of aggression were followed by tears of rage, by a period of emotional instability and finally by acceptable behavior.[20]

That the boys could freely discuss their problems with the director of the institution who represented governmental authority constituted an essential factor in these successful "cures." When they poured out their worries to Aichhorn, they soon found that he understood them better than they understood themselves, that he was a kind helper, not a public prosecutor or a judge. He never enforced a confession but explicitly granted them the right to keep their secrets, making it clear, at the same time, that only honest and truthful statements would enable him to help them. Presently, he would point out desirable goals and chances in their lives which, so far, had seemed hopeless; gradually their trust in and love for the teacher grew. The young rowdies who had first been inclined to take for weakness the non-interference with their aggressive acts, came to realize to their amazement that here was a kind of strength far superior to their own and one to which they submitted willingly in the end. That the teacher who knew their past and the hidden depth of their minds nevertheless trusted them, increased their confidence in him which, in turn, decisively furthered their re-education. This constituted the basis for a strong transference which the leader readily used to impose frustrations of instinctual drives and their sublimation into work. The grouping of the delinquent children from a psychoanalytic viewpoint, i.e., in accordance with the underlying mechanisms of their disturbances, proved to have a very favorable influence upon their recovery.[21]

In every detail these principles are found to be in agreement with the ethical-therapeutic principles of the New Testament. The formation of a new ego ideal which breaks the predominance of the instincts is one of Jesus' foremost demands, which, however, he presents from the religious point of view. His ethics of love and his struggle against the cold, obsessional, legal-minded Pharisees is illustrated by his word: "Repent ye, and believe the gospel" (*Mark*, 1:15). He breaks defiance by his helping love and his ever-compliant forgiveness. That he actually aims at the achievement of an obligatory ideal, follows from his word: "Be ye therefore perfect..." (*Matthew*, 5:48). He does not force his love on those who want none of it: "He that hath ears to hear, let him hear!" (*Matthew*, 11:15) "Give not that which is holy unto the dogs, neither cast ye your pearls before swine" (*Matthew*, 7:6). Jesus has even anticipated the non-interference with aggressive acts, as evidenced in the parable of the tares and the wheat

---

[20] Cf. *op. cit.*, pp. 167-185.
[21] *Op. cit.*, p. 146.

(*Matthew*, 13:28ff). Naturally, there are differences in conception, due to the historical situation; but the basic idea is identical with Aichhorn's.

Jesus granted his disciples individual interviews during which they could discuss their most personal problems and make their confessions. (*Luke*, 19, Zaccheus). He does not enforce admissions, but he fathoms the depths of their souls, as he did Judas Ischariot's intention of betrayal. (*Matthew*, 22:21). Jesus' primary concern, love, and his active assistance go to the poor, ignorant and despised Amhaarez whom he helps in changing their attitudes as Aichhorn helps his pupils. Jesus does not conceal his superior power and proclaims himself the leader; in St. John's Gospel he calls himself the "way, the truth, and the life" (14:6). Deliberately, he headed his community and from the very beginning he practiced community education. From the start of his activity, he accepted human venality and mercenariness as a natural phenomenon; however, he succeeded in sublimating it magnificently into a concept of pure ethics of love and duty, a development which can be pursued throughout the gospels.

In fact, there is not one leitmotif in Aichhorn's re-education of delinquents for which there cannot be found an analogy in the gospels, except psychoanalytic insight which Jesus replaced by his miraculous intuition. Both arrived at closely related therapeutic hygienic principles.[22] Although Jesus based his entire system of ethics and therapy upon religion which Aichhorn as educator and counsellor disregarded, it must also be pointed out that Jesus always emphasized the priority of ethical actions: "Not every one that saith unto me Lord, Lord, shall enter into the kingdom of heaven; but he that doeth the will of my Father which is in heaven" (*Matthew*, 7:21). This is his ethical achievement: "For I was ahungered and ye gave me meat; I was thirsty and ye gave me drink; I was a stranger and ye took me in; Naked, and ye clothed me; I was sick, and ye visited me; I was in prison and ye came unto me ... Verily, I say unto you, inasmuch as ye have done it unto one of the least of these my brethren, ye have done it unto me ..." (*Matthew*, 25:35-40). This kind of helping, rescuing, social love is what inspires Aichhorn's education of delinquents.

IV. RESULTS

Aichhorn's work represents an enormous progress beyond those strict reformatories which, as I know from my own observations, are conducted in a spirit of regimentation and where punishment or threats play the part that psychoanalytically trained pedagogists assign to love. Aichhorn is the

---

[22] Cf. Pfister, O.: *Analytische Seelsorge*, 1927, pp. 20ff; Die psychohygienische Aufgabe des theologischen Seelsorgers, in Meng, H.: *Praxis der seelischen Hygiene*, pp. 111-150.

Pinel of the juvenile delinquents and he will remain their benefactor and a pioneer for a future, better civilization.

He himself is aware that expectations should not be too high. He knows that, no matter how tough are the educational problems presented by his charges, as long as there is adequate constitutional endowment and as long as there was some measure of an early love relationship, the prospects for influencing them favorably are bright.

In his opinion, psychoanalysis is an indispensable tool of social retraining without which all efforts are mere quackery; but he does not believe that psychoanalysis is a panacea of education; he considers intuition an indispensable supplement to the scientific method of analysis.[23] Even in cases that seemed very hopeful from the start, Aichhorn had to admit that he was not always successful nor was he always certain of the duration of the cure although the prognosis in most cases is favorable.[24] But does he not share this predicament with every educator? Has not every educator had the experience that the very pupils of whom he expected most became stymied and their development arrested?

Jesus' ministry differed from Aichhorn's not only in extent and depth, but also in external circumstances. He practiced not as a civil servant nor on social outcasts exclusively; he ministered to an entire people and its most distinguished leaders, to all ages and to all walks of life — but he practiced as an itinerant teacher. Successes were scarce and unsatisfactory, failures were frequent. One need only remember how unsympathetic, cowardly and regressive was his disciples' behavior immediately before and after his death. He was persecuted, scorned and derided as a visionary.[25]

Aichhorn, too, has met with resistance as have, throughout history, all of those who have preached love.

V. REFLEXIONS AND CONCLUSIONS

The great Viennese humanitarian and a true father of wayward youth may well be counted among those most eminent educators whose group is distinguished by the names of Amos Commenius, Heinrich Pestalozzi, and Thomas Bernardo, to quote only a few. Love is his guiding principle, love as proclaimed and lived by Jesus Christ, love that rejects judgment and retaliation in education and aims only at mercifully helping, and curing, at the rescue of those who went astray and became wayward, at the liberation of those in bondage and at a community of mutual brotherhood of all men. This community of friendship, veracity, mutual esteem, social and political

---

[23] Aichhorn, *op. cit.*, pp. 9-10.

[24] *Op. cit.*, pp. 128 and 178.

[25] Cf. *Matthew*, 11:2ff; *Mark*, 23:37-39; *Luke*, 3:34f, *Matthew*, 23:24f: Jesus upbraiding the cities of Chorazin and Bethsaida for their unrepenting attitude.

solidarity corresponds in its ethical content to the Christian concept of the kingdom of God, of the rule of God. This is independent of any explicit reference to a transcendental origin of the desired new psychic structure of men and of their external social, cultural and political order. I gladly admit that I find much more genuine Christian ethics and much more genuine Christian love in August Aichhorn's principles of re-education of juvenile delinquents in which no explicit reference is made to religion and Christianity than in innumerable books by theologians. The latter primarily derive callous, dogmatic theories from the gospels of the New Testament and turn these theories into a tiltyard for theologians who battle each other with hatred and bitterness; the God of the gospels thus is turned into a wrathful dogmatist who casts dogmatic errors into sufficient reasons for eternal damnation and for hatred of heretics. The result is a pitiful distortion of the core of the gospels and of the commands of Jesus Christ.

Freud's psychoanalysis is the formative principle underlying Aichhorn's pedagogy, and we have stressed above how indispensable a scientific tool it is in his work. However, we may ask, is Freud's teaching really no more than a formative principle in Aichhorn's work? Is not Freud's ethics an essential factor in Aichhorn's pedagogic art, as in all psychoanalytically oriented educatory methods, applied to patients, to children, to adult criminals, and to pastoral wards? It is true that Freud nowhere mentions love as the dominant principle in ethics and that under certain circumstances, he is sceptical of positive transference and rightly so. On the other hand, he states explicitly that cure of a neurosis is dependent on positive transference. The ethical content of his analytic therapy coincides completely with the genuine Christian one, with the exception of two points:

1) Jesus arrived at his ethics not in an empirical-scientific way but intuitively. He based his *Weltanschauung* philosophically on the ultimate reasons for existence that is, on absolute values, while Freud as a positivist rejected all philosophy, particularly ontology.

2) Freud conceives of his task only in a negative sense: his goal is reached when knotty unconscious maladjustments have been rectified and the neurosis has been eliminated. He is not concerned with his patient's subsequent way of life; he considers it beyond the analyst's province to influence its morality or immorality.

In the latter point, all of Freud's pedagogically oriented disciples[26] have adopted a different view. Much more than their master, they consider the individual as a social being, and the establishment of sound social relations as an essential element of therapy. This conforms to Jesus' goal. Freud's method is Christian inasmuch as it applies hygienic measures that, by their very nature, are ethical norms. The founder of psychoanalysis does not judge,

---

[26] With the exception of Melanie Klein.

as no doctor should; he does not condemn or punish, but rather tries to help and rescue; even in the debauched or neurotic never-do-well or scoundrel he sees a human being who should be raised to a higher level of existence; he forgives if he is offended and insulted in the course of negative transference, he is patient, he masters his own anger and affects. Though he strictly refrains from counter-transference, he acts as if he were driven by kindness. Possibly he suppresses conscious love out of kindness. Aichhorn nowhere explicitly favors counter-transference. That he occasionally succumbed to it is revealed by his emotion at the reconciliation of a father and son.[27] How to utilize counter-transference therapeutically with children who suffer from a complex of abandonment, was illustrated convincingly in a paper by Violette Jequier.[28] Jesus, on the other hand, strongly emphasizes love, even makes a commandment of this ideal, yet simultaneously divests it of the character of a commandment.

It is not our task here to decide which is preferable therapeutically or ethically: either to refrain from integrating the individual into the social or cosmic whole or to initiate this very integration as Jesus did in his social demands and in his religion. This decision will depend on whether one is more individualistically or more socio-universally oriented and it will also depend on the trend of the times. There will always be periods in which "the individual and his property" (Max Stirner) are deified, and others, in which this isolation is considered a calamity and the cause of the most horrifying catastrophes; this results in a flight of the individual from isolation. At times, this flight ends in nationalism which then again is rejected. At others refuge is taken in social, humanitarian, universal, transcendental, religious ideals, or in a new religion which devaluates the world of man, or in a different religious conception in which the world of man is glorified by the light of eternity, and destined to be expanded into a cosmos, that is, into a great, well-ordered unity and thus endowed with a more profound and humanly richer meaning.

In his writings, Aichhorn, like Freud, shows himself a positivist. In the transposition of his theories into action, however, he realizes Jesus' ethics. Like his master Freud, he gives proof of the fact that the exact science of mental hygiene and therapy leads to those very results that Jesus attained intuitively. While I cannot and do not wish to infer a direct causal connection, I yet wish to point out that Aichhorn has bridged the gap between Chistianity and pedagogy by introducing an empirical point of view, thus lending support to the opinion I have expounded for years, that ethics must be built upon an accurate knowledge of human nature and the character of

---

[27] Op. cit., p. 136, German edition. Omitted in translation.

[28] Violette Jequier, Le complex d'abandon; Beno, Bersot et L. Bovet, Les enfants nerveux, 1946, p. 106.

man as a political animal.[29] In contrast to my own work, Aichhorn did not deal with the philosophical foundation and elaboration of ethics. In his book on delinquency, he was not concerned with this aspect of the problem which some scholars sarcastically classify as just a hobby of individual eccentrics. There cannot be any doubt, however, that Aichhorn does not share such sarcasm. Despite his tolerance he does not allow his pupils to make disdainful comments about religion and he only eliminates misunderstandings about religion that are psychologically injurious.[30] The basic principles of education that Aichhorn postulates for delinquents are applicable in the same way to the socially well-adjusted, to the so-called normal and "good" children. The writings of Anna Freud, Fritz Wittels, Hans Zulliger, Madeleine Rambert and others, contain a wealth of pedagogic wisdom and are in full agreement with the basic principles of Christian teachings — a fact that cannot be emphasized strongly enough in this Christian world of ours.

However, there are further implications in Aichhorn's work. Paul Reiwald has derived from it his basic ideas for the treatment of criminals. In the face of our totally unsatisfactory current penal law, it would be highly desirable that Reiwald's suggestions for future treatment of criminals be given full consideration and a practical test.[31]

Another problem area that, unfortunately, has as yet been given hardly any attention at all is that of the hygiene of nations or as I would not hesitate to call it, the therapy of nations. One of the most burning questions of the times is: how should one treat delinquent nations? Nobody can deny that there exist such nations which must be considered delinquent or sick in regard to their inner political life or their social relations with other nations. It is an immeasurable catastrophe of our days that we still know far too little in the field of the hygiene of nations to put a stop to this kind of waywardness. As early as 1928, I discussed the urgency of developing a science of the mental hygiene of nations[32] and pointed out that such a science could only be built upon Freudian depth psychology. Even previous to this, I had published a little paper on the human strivings for unity.[33] In it, I contrasted Kant, the rationalist, with Freud, the Columbus of the Unconscious. Furthermore I stated that collective neuroses, among them above all war, fanatical national hatred, slavery, and the like, could prophylactically and therapeutically be adequately treated only on the basis of psychoanalytic principles. Only in this way could the pathogenic forces of the unconscious which threaten to devour mankind, be overcome and a re-

[29] *Psychoanalyse und Weltanschauung,* 1928.

[30] Aichhorn, *op. cit.,* p. 163.

[31] Reiwald, Paul, *Die Gesellschaft und ihre Verbrecher,* Zurich, Pan Verlag, 1948.

[32] Voelkerhygiene, *Buersche Volkszeitung,* January 31, 1928.

[33] Die menschlichen Einigungsbestrebungen im Lichte der Psychoanalyse. *Imago,* vol. 12. 1926.

integration through love be achieved. Freud, in his paper, "Why War?"[34] has declared himself unable to make practical suggestions for the prevention of war. In fact, we might well despair of utilizing psychoanalysis for the prevention of war since Freud himself does not indicate any means for prevention or cure of war-bent delinquency except love in the sense of pure object love and identification, and cultural development which he unfortunately does not consider as based on ethical-hygienic norms.[35]

Aichhorn's magnificent cure of many delinquents who had previously been considered incurable offers the most encouraging example for the way in which Freud's heritage should best be administered in his spirit by the conquest of new areas of life with the help of depth psychology. It is not only wishful thinking but a well-founded hope that this will be a means more successfully to tackle collective neuroses than has so far been done by the incredibly primitive psychology of statesmen, and thus to create a lasting peace based upon the needs of nations. Both Freud and Aichhorn — the latter much more emphatically than the former — have characterized love as a spiritual force of the first order; Freud has specifically called it the means to overcome war. Jesus Christ was the first to elevate it to the rank of a norm and he used it as such. For the purpose of a hygiene of nations we shall have to realize this love in its functions as a norm whereby we shall transcend, to a certain extent, psychoanalysis which abstains from setting positive goals, but shall open up an enormous and extremely valuable field of action to our science. Aichhorn has demonstrated conclusively that the liberation of delinquents is not only a liberation from bonds but also a liberation for a more pleasurable way of life, for which purpose the setting of a more positive goal in life is needed. Without such positive goals, further deviations into neurotic maladjustments will be as unavoidable for nations as they will for individuals. Christian ethics, originating in the pastoral care of publicans and sinners, of depraved and perverted social outcasts, has

---

[34] Freud, S.: *Why War?* Paris, Int. Inst. of Intellectual Cooperation, 1933.

[35] Freud does not differentiate "culture" from civilization. By it, he understands "all phenomena by which human life has risen above its animal conditions and whereby it differs from the life of animals" (*The Future of an Illusion*). This concept of culture, I disputed in my amicable refutation, "Die Illusion einer Zukunft" (*Imago*, vol. 14, 1928). According to Freud's concept, the atom bomb, the hypocritical kind of diplomacy which is guided by national egotism or national hatred, mammonism and innumerable other products of the human mind of which animals need not be ashamed must rightfully be considered elements of culture. I also refuted the messianic character of science which is independent of ethics and allegedly aims at the betterment of human existence. In the meantime, what Freud optimistically called culture, what I, however, consider a pitiful mixture of culture and non-culture, has expanded tremendously in scope. We have witnessed the barbarous, devastating second World War with its implied judgment on purely intellectual culture. Everyone has become acutely aware and wary of the fact that scientific and technical progress does not offer the faintest protection against the diabolical destruction of the highest human values, but rather that it constitutes the most terrible danger unless the development of humane, social-ethical attitudes keeps pace with it.

spread all over the world and through all subsequent centuries and has attempted to penetrate ever more spheres of life. In this process, it has undergone many a distortion, but it has also effected a great amount of good. Let us hope that Aichhorn's work of rescuing wayward youth also may include ever more groups of those in need of help and may bring them help. May it stimulate an ever further development of Sigmund Freud's life-work. May it propagate the spreading of the ethical, therapeutic, blissful love that appears new, yet is age-old and which found its original representation in Jesus Christ.

CLINICAL PROBLEMS

SUBLIMATION AND SEXUAL GRATIFICATION IN THE LATENCY PERIOD OF GIRLS

By Lauretta Bender, M.D. and Joseph B. Cramer, M.D.*

(New York)

The Children's Ward of the Psychiatric Division of Bellevue Hospital of New York City accepts problem children (usually under twelve) for observation, recommendations and therapy from social agencies, courts, guidance clinics, pediatric services and other sources in the community. Any child whose behavior is disturbed enough to warrant in-patient care, or whose problem cannot be adequately understood on an out-patient basis, is accepted.

Among the girls admitted during the six months period at the end of 1947, there were five who were charged with delinquency and who were remanded by the children's courts. Of these, two presented clinical pictures and mechanisms of sufficient uniformity and distinction to warrant special interest. The delinquency charges against both centered around their sexual behavior patterns. Asocial acts on the part of both included illicit sexual relations with an adolescent or adult male.

Actual living out of sex drives is not at all uncommon in girls from deprived homes, especially where asocial or antisocial behavior is the family pattern. It is common, too, for "institutional" children whose relationship problems interfere with maturation, and for psychotic or brain damaged children in whom greater dependency exists. In all these, however, the infantilism extends into all aspects of the personality, and immaturity or defect of patterning is not only obvious in the area of sexual behavior, but also manifests itself in an inability to adjust to any new social situation, especially school.

School adjustment is considered to accompany the repression of infantile sexual strivings and quiescence if not solution of oedipal problems (5).

Ordinarily, girls in the latency, pre-puberty and puberty periods who

---

* From the Psychiatric Division of Bellevue Hospital and New York University College of Medicine.

53

are making an adequate school adjustment do not find their way to our children's service. Almost all girls of normal intelligence between eight and twelve admitted routinely for various behavior disorders and personality deviations are referred directly by the schools or indirectly because of school maladjustment.

The unusual aspect of these two nine year olds was that they were doing so well in school concurrently with their uninhibited sexual activity. In fact, they were considered outstanding school pupils, especially with regard to conduct. Instead of the sexual drives having been "sublimated" to allow success in school, acting out and "sublimating" existed side by side.

Shirley S., nine years and ten months old, was remanded on her mother's complaint that she had been having intercourse with a twelve year old boy from the neighborhood. There was no truancy or other school difficulty. The complaint was instigated after Shirley had told her story to the Catholic Big Sisters, a social service organization. She had been taken there one evening when she complained of abdominal pain while wandering alone in the street after dark. Investigation proved the truth of the story of her "rape" which she told without urging, though one month before, the story had been dismissed as fantasy by her mother when examination failed to give evidence of sexual intercourse.

When Shirley's mother learned that the story which Shirley had made no attempt to hide from her, was in fact true, she sought, through the courts, her daughter's immediate removal to a corrective institution.

Shirley's mother, thirty-nine, a small, thin woman with a high-pitched voice, infantile speech and a general aspect of immaturity, was intensely self-righteous about her position with respect to Shirley's misdeeds and showed open hostility to the child. She complained that Shirley's stepfather, to whom she had been married for a year-and-a-half, was unnecessarily lenient and had attempted to forestall her taking Shirley to court. She herself had had a child out-of-wedlock by her first husband, Shirley's father, two years before their marriage was forced, against his wishes, by her family. This child, Shirley's sister Lorna, five years Shirley's senior, had, five months before Shirley's admission, given birth to an out-of-wedlock child by a thirteen year old schoolmate. Shirley knew about the pregnancy before her mother did. At the same time her mother was pregnant. The mother's child and the sister's child were born within a month of each other, at about the time Shirley's affair with Robert began. Shirley's mother not only made a home for Lorna and her baby, but welcomed the young father into her home after the baby was born as she had before.

Shirley's mother said frankly that Shirley was bad, but that Lorna was essentially a good girl who had made a mistake for which she should not be punished. Though the physical resemblance between Lorna and Shirley was striking, their mother believed Lorna was like herself, and Shirley like her father.

The disparity in the mother's treatment of her two daughters was difficult for Shirley to understand or accept. She was unaware of the manifold differences between herself and her demure, grown-up older sister.

Despite her fear of her sister and her hostility toward her, she idealized her sister's lover. She complained that she was not allowed the same privileges as Lorna. In reality Lorna's attitude toward Shirley was a reasonably wholesale one. Yet Shirley described several fantasied episodes of physical torture at Lorna's hands and resented the fact that Lorna used her own motherhood as an excuse for preference and authority. Shirley was closely attached to her real father, who had been a cardiac invalid at home for two years before his death. He died when she was seven, at the time her period of latency ought to have been established. Though she was fond of him and was his preferred daughter, he was nevertheless a frightening figure to her. "She jumped when he spoke." His death had no marked effect on her overt behavior, and she grieved for only a short time.

A year later, her mother married a young-looking, easy-going, passive man whom Shirley soon came to adore. The second marriage was a much happier one for Shirley's mother.

There was a younger brother, Richard, aged six, to whom Shirley showed much affection. From the age of six, until the birth of her half-brother and her sister's child, she had played with him and mothered him. They slept in different beds in the same room. Shirley had a habit of taking Richard into bed with her. When reprimanded, she would reply, "I didn't make him. I just asked him", or; "He was there when I woke up." Despite repeated threats she continued this behavior.

In early childhood, Shirley was friendly and active. Her development was normal. She was bottle-fed and weaned without difficulty, at about a year. She had been successfully bowel-trained before two and had rarely smeared. Occasional wetting at night stopped at three. There had been no regressions. Masturbation had been continuous from the age of two and had been excessive as compared with her sister, who stopped at five. Though she had never been a nail biter, she had recently developed a habit of clicking a long thumbnail against her front teeth when anxious. Her speech which had become increasingly infantile during the two years since her father's death, showed considerable pressure under stress. At the time of her admission this pressure was accompanied by a spurt of activity and flight of ideas seldom seen in a child and quite up to the standard of an adult hypomania. These traits as well as some occasional facial grimacing diminished during her hospitalization, recurring only when she was frustrated, usually by insufficient attention from her doctor.

In her relationship with other children, Shirley showed a strong need to dominate their play. Her infantile "omnipotence" enabled her to organize the activities even of older and larger girls, who were helpless before her driving, unrealistic push of language and activity. Frustrations in sibling situations on the ward and neglect by parent substitutes were responded to with temper tantrums sometimes of intolerable duration. Yet in the ward school, even with the same children, she was cooperative and showed the ability to tolerate a give and take relationship. She did more school work than was asked of her and after school could often be found in a corner with a book which she had borrowed from the teacher or one of the nurses.

A first impression of Shirley was more that of a pert, precocious five year old than of a child almost ten. She was undersized, with thin arms and legs and small bones. Her wide-eyed, questioning look added to the immaturity of her appearance. She walked with an exaggerated swaying of the hips. Eschewing rouge, she painted her nails inexpertly and wore her dresses long but she always looked like a little girl play-acting the role of her mother. She was rather uninterested in her appearance and dress and careless of her hair and personal cleanliness. Her use of big words was incongruous in the presence of her lisping speech and high-pitched voice.

Despite good achievement in psychometric testing, her thinking was concrete out of proportion to her good vocabulary and general intelligence. She carried over her feelings toward her mother and sister onto their children, fondling and caring for her mother's six months old Michael and rejecting five months old Patrick, Lorna's son. Her family relationships were distorted and unreal. In school she was a model child and had received "A" in conduct without exception. She loved her teachers and respected them. At home when disciplined and asked "Will you promise not to do it again?" she replied, "How can I know what's going to happen tomorrow, tomorrow isn't even here yet?"

Whenever negative feelings toward her mother were mentioned she would start off by saying, "I love her". She would then become anxious, negativistic and evasive and in a few moments would develop a tantrum that sometimes lasted several hours.

At four, when in bed with a slight fever, she had suddenly cried out, "Mummy ain't got no head". She complained of animals climbing on the wall, and a man under the bed. The illusory fantasies of people without heads were persistent but had undergone a meaningful alteration. "I used to see people—everybody but my mother. I saw everyone with their heads cut off and a horse's head on them. I used to see Lorna that way. She would come in and stand by the bed and her head would be off. But not my mother".

Her art showed good form but was primitive in projected symbolism and content. She drew a very large, personalized sun (father symbol). If a house or a boat (mother symbol) was drawn, it was small, windowless and cut off at the edge of the paper. The penis symbol was absent from her drawings. (1, 2).

She had only one dream. It recurred nightly. It consisted of "blood, blood, blood,—just a whole bunch of blood. It pours and pours. Like there are two rocks and the blood pours over it. The blood just piles up high and I see pitch red in front of me. Then I wake up screaming and crying and I hold onto the bed."

She spoke freely about her "rape". Though she had protested against being questioned about it, she regaled the night nurses voluntarily with the "true story" and expressed her glee at fooling the doctor about having been frightened and unwilling. Shortly after her discharge to a girls' shelter pending permanent placement, a propitiary note was received in which she wrote: ". . . and tell Dr. C. that lots of the girls here like to get raped and they play with themselves."

Anxieties at the age of four were manifest in her fantasies of the headless mother. The fact that Shirley identified Lorna with the hostile mother was brought out in her dreams, her fantasies and her "acting-out". All the attributes of the "bad mother" were displaced onto the older sister as a defense against rejection. At the same time she identified with Lorna. This confusion of identifications was an important factor in her failure to solve

her oedipal problems. In the specific area where the tendencies of her own
mother and older sister were asocial, Shirley failed to develop inhibitory
capacities. There was a pressing need for gratification which escaped compromise. E.g., when she was three, her brother was born. Her motherly
attitude toward him did not prevent his becoming a sexual object for her
curiosity and infantile sex play at the phallic level.

Despite Shirley's legitimate birth, her mother showed a preference for
the older sister Lorna who had been born out-of-wedlock. Shirley was supposed not to know about her sister's out-of-wedlock birth. Our studies
revealed no evidence that she was aware of it. Their mother's identification
with Lorna was obvious.

The incongruity of her mother's punitive and rejecting attitude in view
of the mother's own experience and that of Shirley's older sister give some
explanation for the lack of inhibition in Shirley's sexual activity. She had
no guilt about her "rape" and projected responsibility for her actions. Her
strong identification with both mother and sister made her unable to comprehend why she was punished for them.

At six she was still acting-out her identification with her mother in such
a way as to suggest pathologically poor reality appreciation. She answered
"you can do it, why can't I", when, at seven, she was caught hanging around
street corners with sixteen year old girls wearing lipstick and smoking.

When Shirley was seven her father died. She was already doing well
at school. His death had no effect on her school adjustment. True indifference to the death of the male parent would be a rare reaction indeed for
a girl whose oedipal conflicts were scarcely past their zenith. That she did
not mourn is not surprising considering her identification with the much-
wanted mother who was relieved rather than grieved at the death of the
husband she did not love. But Shirley's sexual activity itself may well have
been a part of a manic behavior pattern and elaborated as a defense against
depression, so clearly seen at the time of admission, even though it was not
until the mother's remarriage and the pregnancies of both mother and sister
that the affair with Robert began.

Such school success as Shirley achieved, consistently and despite her
identification problem in the traumatic home could hardly have supervened
without superego development. The lack of sexual inhibition can be considered a product of the moral standards and sexual patterns of the relevant
female figures in the home, her mother and Lorna. Whence, if the sexual
impulses continued to be acted out, came such unusual interest and drive in
school? Could it be if instinctual needs are not inhibited and energy is not
wasted in unsuccessful attempts at repression, that school success, though
deprived of its value as a sublimation, is still possible through another mechanism? If her identification with mother and particularly sister allowed

Shirley her uninhibited sexual gratifications and made repression unnecessary despite threat of punishment, then the excellent school work could not have the significance of a compensation or atonement. This concept of the mechanism underlying her sexual activity might explain, however, her guiltlessness and the superficiality of her denial. "She could not have her mother, so she *was* her mother."

The sequence, masturbation, sex play with her brother Richard, and the affair with Robert indicate that the latter was an object choice mainly for instinctual gratification and of little discriminatory significance. Nevertheless the unresolved oedipal conflicts point to Robert as a substitute for the idealized stepfather and the sister's lover. If such was the case, the acting-out was completed with little guilt or anxiety concerning the act itself. The acting-out could account for Shirley's anxiety about her hostility to her mother, and the displacement of this hostility onto Lorna. Another aspect to be considered is that of a "constitutional" deviation with pathologically strong sexual impulses as evidenced by the early and excessive masturbation.

Even the formulation which would explain the good school work on the basis of identification with the "good mother" seems inadequate. In the first place, Shirley showed no excessive need for approval and support in school and none of the attention seeking behavior toward the teacher always resorted to by other girls with infantile characters. Furthermore, it seems unlikely that the ability to conform to the social situation in school and the motivation for good schoolwork should have commenced "ex cathedra" upon starting school, whether the teacher was kind and sympathetic or not. The potentialities for this adjustment must have existed much before the age of six and must have been developed along the uninhibited sexual activity.

Freud (6) reported a fragment of a case in which a boy continued masturbating and still made a school adjustment. At the same time he developed a fetish and a symptom involving his two small toes which was the expression of the castration fears and which kept these fears from interfering with his sublimation in school. Such a "split" was effective also for Shirley yet the mechanisms remain obscure.

In pre-puberty, Deutsch (4) speaks of a "thrust of activity" and a "turn toward reality" with renunciation of infantile fantasy life through a search for new object relationships. She believes that "the thrust of activity represents not an increase of aggression but an intensive process of adaptation to reality . . . made possible by the development of the ego . . . the source (of this activity) lies in the inherent drive of the ego toward growth and independence . . . a certain degree of ego strength must be attained before the offensive can begin . . . and the activity . . . serves to build up an ego strength. . . ." Deutsch further feels that the need to be recognized as an adult is great and is all the more painful because of a need for protection and an unconscious desire to remain a child.

Even Shirley's conflict between growing up and remaining a child was acted out with poor reality appreciation. Her desire to remain a child seemed almost conscious as did the acted-out fantasy of womanhood and motherhood which she could not renounce. She retained her infantile fantasy objects and found a way to make them real. Because the environmental situation permitted it, the incest taboo failed to function in the employ of repression and the oedipal fantasy could be acted out.

In discussing the problems of pre-puberty, Deutsch also stresses the effect of nebulous and poorly formed identifications and mentions identification with the "sexual mother". The effect of such normal mechanisms when manifested in pathological degree is demonstrated by Shirley's failure to grow or mature psycho-sexually. One part of Shirley's ego seemed to have no real drive to grow up. Was it fixated by the need for continued erotic gratification at the oedipal level, or did gratification persist because of an already existing constitutional fixation of unknown genesis?

Regarding normal children, Susan Isaacs (9) emphasizes the testing of reality in the latency period. "The child has come to the point where he dares to look at what other people are really like—because he has already had some degree of real proof that they are not altogether hostile. The importance of this is seen very clearly in people who lack it because they have had to construct romantic and idealized figures of parents who have no hostility. They dare not acknowledge the reality of hate in others because any signs of this open up the whole world of the child's fantasy of dangerous destructive parents." Though such a formulation is accurate and is useful to explain Shirley's partial failure to mature, it fails again to explain her school success.

The other allegedly delinquent girls observed during the same period formed an effective and adequately homogeneous group for contrast and clarification. In this latter group, the behavior disorders were clearly manifestations of failure of the ego to cope with multiple problems of puberty and adolescence. Despite similarities in age, and in the economic and cultural milieux between the two groups, in the second group were indications of definite latency periods, during which sexual interests had been minimal. They were physically precocious and their delinquent behavior followed the pattern of older, more clearly adolescent girls, with truancy, school difficulty and running away from home as prominent symptoms. Illicit sexual activity was a factor in each case, but in none was it the sole cause for the delinquency charge and hospitalization. Their puberal sexual conflicts found expression in many areas.

Theresa C., eleven years of age at the time of remand, was ten when her behavior disorder began. At that time she was hospitalized for study because of seizures. She had periods of irritability and over-activity and panic states during which she mewed like a cat. Since the onset of her spells, she had fought with her fourteen year old sister and had frequently wandered away from home.

Our studies revealed at that time that she had epilepsy and she was discharged for out-patient care. Only incidentally during hospitalization it was found that she had been having intercourse with the husband of a friend of her mother's. She felt that he had not seduced her, that she liked him and enjoyed intercourse with him. She displayed marked anxiety in recounting the episode and great relief at having gotten it "off her chest". She accepted responsibility for the asocial nature of her acts and knew they were wrong. She spoke of the adventure as though it was past and done, despite the fact that the affair was interrupted only because of her hospitalization.

The present study occurred following a court remand a year later. Her mother had complained that she was aggressive and disobedient beyond control, that she ran away from home frequently and stayed out all night, truanting from school. Despite the fact that the spells had not recurred since anticonvulsant therapy had begun, Theresa was "worse than ever". No mention was made of overt sexual activity but Theresa "had much information regarding sex" and her mother was suspicious that she "went with boys when she stayed out all night".

Theresa's sister, Olga, three years her senior, was obese, phlegmatic and well behaved. She looked like her mother who identified with her and preferred her to Theresa. The brightest by far of six siblings, Theresa found little stimulation in her relationship with these two and her conflict with both mother and sister arose partly out of obvious sibling rivalry. Mrs. C. frequently contrasted the two to Theresa's disadvantage and displayed little insight into Theresa's problems.

Theresa masturbated until the age of six and then stopped. She was a nail biter under stress. As a child, despite the presence in the crowded home of older and younger male siblings, there had been no evidence of unusual sexual activity or interests.

From six to ten she had done well in school despite a language handicap. Her bickering with Olga was not extreme.

At the time of observation Theresa was a well-developed, tall, eleven year old. She was in good contact and respectful and was able to get along well with the staff and the other children among whom she rapidly became a leader. She used makeup cleverly and displayed a good sense of style in clothes, altogether appearing more like a fifteen-year-old. She took considerable pride in her dress and her appearance.

In early interviews she was depressed and suspicious. She had much anxiety when sexual problems were broached, especially in connection with an episode a few months before when, at a carnival, she and another girl had approached a man "for money", and he had "touched" the other girl. She since then had feelings of being followed by the man whose intent was to kill or rape her. "He followed us, me and my girlfriend. We hid in a place. He seen us, he grabbed her, hurting her, twisting her arm. Then he done—he, he, he, touched her. I tried to get away. He threw a knife at me.

He was going to touch me when some girls came. Later I seen him again at the carnival. I ran to the cop. The cop got him. He had a big dog. They woke us up at night cause another man touched two little girls. We went to court. The girl was so scared. They let the man go. Later I saw him in St. Mary's Park. He looked at me. He almost came near me so I ran and told my mother. Since that day I used to feel that somebody was following me. A man. It could be that man. Maybe he is trying to get me cause I told on him. I got him in trouble. He'd kill me. He might touch me. He might be dressed up in a disguise."

She was reticent and shy about her liking for boys and blushed when talking about her boyfriend on the ward. On this admission she denied the affair with the neighbor but it was recalled under pentothal with much anxiety. This pentothal interview was followed by a considerable period of tension, depression, irritability and apprehensiveness.

She was modest and self-conscious with her doctor. Her attitude toward men in general was that they were aggressive potential attackers. She was well aware of her conflicting attitudes toward her mother. She recognized her dependency and desire for acceptance, at the same time expressing a desire to be different. Her dream life was filled with aggression especially toward her mother and herself. She also expressed an obsessive fear that her mother would be killed in an accident. She was afraid of cats and remembered an episode in early childhood when a cat had been killed by a car and she had been blamed for its death. She also felt that she had once strangled a cat in a fit of rage but was not sure that she had not dreamed it.

Many of her dreams and fantasies symbolized typical adolescent sexual problems. She dreamed of her brother digging a hole in the ground and putting a big snake in it. Her art work, too, was richly symbolic. She drew a girl tied down to a burning stage being rescued by a little man from the flames.

She dressed in boys clothes frequently for dramatics or even for routine play on the ward, and evidenced a rather considerable problem in sexual identity. She often described spontaneously the advantages of being a boy.

She had a rather exact knowledge of the anatomy and physiology of reproduction but discussed it only after confidence in the examiner had developed and with much shyness.

We have seen few Shirleys but we have seen many Theresas.[1] What we wish to emphasize here is that Theresa underwent a period of latency during which her social development accompanied a quiescence in sexual activity— even though she lived in a slum neighborhood where opportunities for delinquent behavior were manifold.

There were multiple factors which contributed to her behavior disorder. These included physical precocity, a language handicap, poor understanding and little stimulation in the home, sibling rivalry, and epilepsy. It has been our experience that few puberty girls develop asocial behavior patterns which include illicit sexual activity, under the pressure of only one or two threats

---

[1] We are aware of the presence of serious psychopathology in both girls. We feel that it is just this seriousness that points up mechanisms which are not so clear in less disturbed children but are qualitatively similar.

to the ego. Even when precocious physical development and social opportunities combine with the sexually re-awakened, advancing id against the not-yet-ready ego of the ten or eleven year old, it takes more traumata to break down the inhibitions. This breakdown may be followed by many other manifestations of asocial activity.

As Deutsch says, "one [girl] tries to take the heterosexual path though she lacks the necessary psychological preparation. She easily falls into confusion, and this may have unfortunate results, the nature of which will depend on the girl's social milieu. Many acts of gangsterism, prostitution or criminality in very young girls are a consequence of a violent interruption of pre-puberty, with its harmless homosexual attachments, in favor of a heterosexuality for which they are not yet really ready. In my opinion, the real dangers of this period of life lie in any anachronistic behavior. Either the young girl is retarded in her psychologic growth by her own excessively infantile emotional ties, guilt and fears[2] or, conversely, premature experiences produce disturbances in the development of her whole personality."[3] Bender and Blau (3) have illustrated with many interesting case reports the latter alternative.

The real puberty girl who has recuperated through latency from the strife of the oedipal conflicts, faces their resurgence, even if the advance of the id at puberty is premature, with an ego that has demonstrated the capacity for sublimation and has had the experience of integration. In this respect are the Theresas different from the Shirleys.

Clinically the two girls differed markedly. Shirley was nine, looked no more than seven and acted like five. Theresa at ten, looked, acted, spoke and dressed like fifteen. She was almost grown up. When she tried, she could achieve a mature appearance. Shirley's nail-polish, speech and walk were caricatures which served only to emphasize her infantilism. Theresa took pride in her appearance and was clean and fastidious. Shirley was careless and untidy. Theresa was modest and soft spoken, Shirley loud and exhibitionistic. Theresa got along well with children her own age and when she dominated their play it was because of her ingenuity and real leadership. When Shirley dominated her playmates, she simply pushed them about until they protested.

Theresa had some conflict over her sexual identity, even occasionally wearing boys clothes. Shirley said: "If I was a boy, I suppose I'd rather be a boy, but I'm a girl, so I'd rather be just like I am." Theresa's occasional temper outbursts were aggressive and followed by guilt, Shirley's were negativistic and usually occurred when the world failed to cooperate in her attempts to live out magically her own omnipotence. Theresa feared men

---

[2] Cf. Shirley.
[3] Cf. Theresa.

as potential sexual attackers. For Shirley, all adult males were cast in the mold of her ideal image and she had no fear of them. Her actual object choice was as indiscriminate as her masturbation, though it may have represented oedipal fantasies acted out. Shirley was oedipal in the first edition, Theresa in the second. Theresa wanted to be less like her mother than she was afraid she was. Shirley *was* her mother.

Shirley had little fantasy life. She needed none because she was living it. Theresa had a rich and highly symbolic fantasy life which was not quite enough for her to settle for.

Theresa's guilt and anxiety emphasized the compulsive nature of her illicit sexual activity and the asocial behavior which had the same connotation. Shirley was anxious only about her aggression toward her mother and her mother's toward her. Though Theresa's problems were not unusual, though despite her many handicaps she was bright and made good human relationships, she could not get along in school—could not conform to the demands of this social situation because of the recrudescence of her sexual problems.

Shirley, whose contact with reality was no more than tenuous and whose relationships were poor, was nevertheless able to do excellent school work and ask for more throughout all of her experiences.

Healey and Bronner (8) indicate that the peak incidence of juvenile delinquency as defined by the courts is between the ages of fifteen and seventeen. They state, however, that histories reveal in many cases that the first delinquent behavior was at eight or nine. The Gluecks (7) in their study of five hundred delinquent women found that although less than 8 per cent of the girls studied were under fifteen at the time of their first arrest; at the time of their first known delinquency, 10 per cent were eleven and twelve years of age, 5 per cent were nine or ten, 3 per cent were seven or eight and more than 2 per cent were under seven. Illicit sex life began (for those girls in whom sex activity was a factor in their delinquency), for almost 20 per cent between eleven and fourteen, 2 per cent were between six and nine at the time of their first illicit sex experiences.

These findings indicate a not inconsiderable number of girls whose earliest illicit sex experiences begin in the latency period. That their delinquency does not lead to arrest until much later indicates the possibility that many, like Shirley, had infantile sexual patterns, expression of which did not lead to difficulty because it did not interfere with learning or school adjustment.

After all, of forty-eight children under twelve charged with delinquency at the Manhattan Children's Court of the City of New York,[4], during the

---

[4] These statistics were obtained through the cooperation of the Honorable Justice John Warren Hill, Presiding Justice, Domestic Relations Court, New York City.

last six months of 1947 (the period used for the above study) only three were girls. Two of these were the nine-year-olds we have discussed.

REFERENCES

1. Bender, Lauretta and Wolfson, William Q.: The Nautical Theme in the Art and Fantasy of Children. *Amer. J. Orthopsych.*, XIII, 3, 1943.

2. Bender, Lauretta and Montague, Allison: Psychotherapy Through Art in a Negro Child. *College Art Journal*, VII, 1, 1947.

3. Bender, Lauretta and Blau, Abraham: The Reaction of Children to Sexual Relations with Adults. *Amer. J. Orthopsych.*, VII, 4, 1937.

4. Deutsch, Helene: *Psychology of Women*, Vol. 1, New York, Grune & Stratton, 1944.

5. Freud, Sigmund: Three Contributions to the Theory of Sex, in: *The Basic Writings of Sigmund Freud*, New York, Modern Library, 1938.

6. Freud, Sigmund: Splitting of the Ego in the Defensive Process. *Int. J. Psa.*, XXII, 1941.

7. Glueck, Sheldon and Glueck, Eleanor T.: *Five Hundred Delinquent Women*, New York, Alfred A. Knopf, 1934.

8. Healy, William and Bronner, Augusta F.: *New Light on Delinquency and its Treatment*, New Haven, Yale University Press, 1936.

9. Isaacs, Susan: *Social Development in Young Children*, London, George Routledge and Sons, Ltd., 1946.

THE ETERNAL DILETTANTE

A Contribution to Female Sexuality

By Kata F. Levy

(*Budapest*)

The present paper is a report on some observations made during analysis, of a specific type of female development whose outcome in social life is dilettantism.

In his basic study of the female castration complex, Abraham (1) recognized among its various manifestations, certain specific types. These types develop as reaction formations when the female first becomes aware of her anatomy. He described them as the wish-type, the fulfillment type and the revenge-type, depending on the denial or acceptance of what the girl believes to be the discrimination involved in her anatomical structure.

As early as 1925, Freud (6) pointed out the little girl's preoedipal attachment to her mother, and in two later papers (7 and 8) he emphasized its importance. In these papers he describes the three possible trends in female development in the crucial period after the little girl has relinquished her first love object.

In order to achieve femininity, the little girl must exchange her primary mother-object, she must reverse her primary activity into passivity and she must substitute for her hitherto dominant penis-wish the wish for a child. To accomplish this, the cathexis which had previously been invested in the clitoris must henceforth be displaced to the vagina. It is the narcissistic injury of discovering her lack of a penis which, as a rule, furnishes the motive for giving up clitoral masturbation.

If this optimal development of changing from an original masculine attitude (corresponding to that of the little boy) into complete femininity does not succeed, it may result in a characterological masculinity, with continuing clitoral masturbation and may finally lead to homosexuality. Or this failure may lead to a renunciation of the mother-object, the avoidance of all sexual activity, the giving up of clitoral masturbation and eventually to a blocking of all activity in real life. In such instances the result will be either sexual inhibition or a neurosis.

In analyzing women, we frequently find cases whose development does not entirely fit into any of these schemes but who nevertheless have a sufficient number of these developmental features in common to justify grouping them together for consideration. After experiencing a strong preoedipal mother-attachment and a positive oedipus-situation, these girls do not attain real femininity but continue clitoral masturbation despite vehement struggles against it. They neither develop a masculine character nor are they able to sublimate their masculine strivings into any sort of activity. Despite their regression to the primary love-object, and the perseveration of the mother attachment, they do not solve their libidinal object conflict by recourse to manifest homosexuality. Nor, finally, do they show the third development trend which leads to complete sexual inhibition. Instead such women vacillate between two developmental trends with certain characteristic and concomitant psychic fluctuations which we wish to describe in some detail.

Let us investigate further what prevents these women from developing in one of the three well-established directions and whether we are justified in considering them a particular developmental type.

But first we must turn our attention to a conspicuous peculiarity of their social life, namely their manifest tendency toward a dilettantism which is obviously of a neurotic variety.

In ordinary usage the term dilettante is applied to those who pursue an activity as a hobby, be it scientific, artistic, or social, or of any other kind, without practicing it as a profession. The term also implies a lack of professional training and knowledge. At this point we would emphasize that dilettantes of the type to be discussed here seem to have the characteristic of never schooling or preparing themselves for a profession and then wanting to master it without training. They have a predilection for attending accelerated courses which promise to teach them within a month or two what otherwise must be learned in three years of study or practice. By such methods, they will "learn" a handicraft, graphology, psychology, or dancing, or become actors, or journalists. There are many who would like to become psychoanalysts in this way. Often they change their profession repeatedly, without finding satisfaction in any. When asked why they shy away from regular training, some of them may point to actually existing financial difficulties, but most of them will offer all sorts of rationalizations. We believe two answers to be typical: "I am unable to tie myself down." And: "It is too late for me!" But why it has become too late, why these people frequently have missed the best years of their youth for their training as a consequence of their inability to tie themselves down, why they sacrificed the continuity of their careers and thereafter had to make desultory attempts to fill in what they had missed, can none of it be explained by their conscious motivations.

Frequently their feelings of incompetence and inadequacy are quite conscious—therefore their abrupt attempts to reach a final goal are all the more surprising. In a conversation, Aichhorn once said of such types that they always want to *be,* but never want to *become* something. What is most characteristic, however, is the behavior of such a person when the irrationality of their actions or the improbability of such sudden success is pointed out. The ensuing reaction of guilt feelings is comparable to that of a thief who is being caught red-handed and drops the loot. This is more than a mere comparison. Feelings of inferiority and inhibition then emerge and persist for quite a while.

We were struck by this type of dilettantism as an attendant symptom of various forms of neuroses in men as well as in women. It also seemed to be a characteristic feature of a group of neurotic delinquents. The following study will be limited to the psychosexual development of women who behave socially in the manner described above. Their typical neurotic syndrome seems to be hysterical conversion symptoms accompanying a phobia.

It is often difficult to decide whether the dilettantism of women who choose a profession without any previous professional training is due to external circumstances, conditions of life or the prejudices carried over from a former era, or if—as analysis can sometimes establish—a will free from ambiguity could have found a way to the fulfillment of the desire to learn and to work. We find the same neurotic and characterologic types of female today as existed in the time when women were excluded from professional opportunities.

I became particularly aware of this situation during the analyses of two young girls with inhibitions and difficulties in the choice of their professions.

The two young girls—whom we shall call A and B—were in their early twenties when they began their analyses because of hysteric-phobic symptoms. Both were timid and feminine in their appearance and behavior, and had above average intelligence. The common feature of their career histories was that each had been unable to make use of the training opportunities which opened up before her and in their later years, both devoted themselves to the education of children without previous professional training.

After graduation from high school, Miss A could neither decide to go to college which at that time she could easily have done, nor could she make up her mind to take a job, a decision which would have been well advised because of the financial circumstances of her family. She was unable, as she explained again and again, *to tie herself down.* Since she felt particularly handicapped in the choice of a profession through her phobic difficulties and in order to escape her relatives' nagging, she had finally taken a job, after a brief training period. During her psychoanalytic treatment, she exchanged this exquisitely feminine trade for an educational activity. The interpretation of this professional choice as an identification with her analyst hardly scratches the surface of the problem. She had always refused to do the least bit of domestic work. Toward her new profession she assumed a conspicuously reserved and theoretical attitude. She started a school and used this as a framework within which to satisfy both her organizational and intellectual strivings. For this purpose, she moved into the office of her father who had died a short time before, and from his desk "administered" the institution. This procedure, however, aroused her guilt feelings which were followed by tendencies to self-punishment. She made hardly any effort to master the requirements of her new profession by adequate studies. On the other hand, her auto-didactic attempts also met with peculiar inhibitions. Instead she demanded that her analyst instruct and advise her in her work. She found herself unable to read an excellent paper on pedagogy but had a compulsive desire to take home from the analyst's waiting room a magazine with a trivial article on education. This apparently unimportant wish could be interpreted as a symptom. She had a tendency immensely to overrate a certain category of intellectual women—especially her analyst. She began to produce fantasies, referring to her own circle of professional colleagues as well as to psycho-analysts, in which she eclipsed all those persons whom she habitually over-rated. Her original wish to become an analyst which she had repressed for a long time, manifested itself in the same, peculiarly ambiguous way. She entrenched herself behind her phobic difficulties when she ought to have taken a training course, but she herself wanted to conduct such a course. She wrote popular papers on education for journals, then seemed to be frightened by her success and again succumbed to unsurmountable inhibitions. To every interpretation of her acting-out she reacted as if it had been a prohibition, compelling her to guilty renunciation and even to denial of her desires. Two phases could be distinguished in her behavior: an active one, characterized by the striving to acquire abilities on the spur of the moment, and an inhibited one, characterized by a renunciation caused by guilt feelings.

Her struggle against masturbation had not ceased up to the time of her treatment. She practiced clitoral masturbation in spite of her fear of having injured herself and her idea of having an abnormal genital: "something was hanging down from her genital." Not even the narcissistic mortification of her lack of a penis was able to spoil her enjoyment of masturbation. However, this narcissistic mortification manifested itself, by means of displacement, in her enhanced desire for physical attractiveness. Her reaction to her successes with men revealed the return of the repressed desire, since to excite a man, to awaken expectations in him and then to leave him unsatisfied, was a way of attaining power over his masculinity (16).

The patient's strongly repressed desire for masculinity which was hidden behind an impregnable mask of delicate femininity and childlike timidity manifested itself in her greed to obtain and to take away. This propensity referred not only to men against whom her active castration wish directed her behavior, but it also referred to the masculine woman whom she over-rated, obviously on the basis of the infantile idea of the "woman with the penis".

This wish was the source of her guilt feelings which attached them-

---

16 Rotter found that the little girl derived her fantasy that the penis belongs to her from her ability to provoke an erection of the boy's organ.

selves to her sublimated strivings for masculinity and which made her react to every success as to the realization of her wish to appropriate a penis. It explained both the suddenness with which on the one hand she tried to grab success, and on the other, was ready to renounce it.

It is obvious that Miss A does not fit into any of Freud's developmental types. Tendencies of two opposite developmental trends were operative in her alternatingly. Despite her constant efforts to overcome her inhibitions and to attain sublimated masculinity, her guilt feelings prevented her from ever reaching her goal. Again and again she had to succumb to passivity and inferiority feelings. In this state she sought the help of psychoanalysis, but, as it turned out, only in order to gain support for her masculine tendencies.

The analysis of Miss B, the second patient, revealed, behind her passivity and indecision, her repressed striving for activity. This striving was characterized by the impatience with which she wanted to *be* at a goal immediately, coupled with her inability to submit to any kind of discipline or to take examination. The conscious reason for her refusal to graduate from high school or to train for any occupation was defiance of her father's wishes. The analysis showed it to be the "defiance of the castrated". She supported her negative tendencies by illness which she herself learned to recognize as attempts at flight. Concomitantly, however, these illnesses served the purpose of exhibiting to her father her physical inferiority. She stubbornly refused to comply with her father's wish to attend a commercial college or to learn some simple, feminine trade. By chance she had the opportunity to replace the owner of a children's home and as she proved herself efficient, she was entrusted with a responsible position in this institution. She took over some of the work of the physician, was put in charge of the dispensary and of the finances, and was made the head supervisor of the children's group, etc. She felt in her element in whatever organizational and executive work her position required. But it is significant that she hated supervising the kitchen. Through her analysis she came to understand how much the former type of activities gratified her masculine strivings.

The outbreak of a grave hysterical condition drove her out of this haven she had found for herself. Anxiety forced her to avoid most of her activities. After a partial recovery she restricted herself to the instruction and supervision of the children which she carried out under anxiety and with difficulty. A new profession upon which she embarked after an accelerated preparatory course during her analysis succumbed to the same fate: after a period of enjoyment and success in her work, difficulties set in. In both work situations it could be established that the same external event was responsible for her failure. A man had entered her professional orbit who roused her jealousy and envy. In the first breakdown her aggression manifested in the form of an intra-psychic conflict, caused the outbreak of hysterical and phobic symptoms. The same conflict forced her in the second instance to retrench her activities. In the first experience the conflict was converted into symptoms; in the second it manifested itself spontaneously as anxiety related to her aggressive desires and her injurious tendencies directed against the objects within the orbit of her work. Her unconscious aggression led to compensatory apprehension in regard to the children in her charge and resulted in great insecurity in the performance of her duties.

The analysis revealed grave traumata in her instinctual life. A traumatically abrupt weaning and the loss of her wet nurse at the age of three months, resulted in an apparently insoluble oral fixation. Her incessant, unsatisfied searching with mouth and hand which was very conspicuous at that time, later manifested itself in her clitoral masturbation and in her fantasies which clearly revealed their origin from and connection with the nipple. The patient seemed fully to confirm the hypothesis that clitoral masturbation is a substitute for the loss of the nipple (6), and that this loss has the same effect as a first castration experience (17). In this sense the patient elaborated a concept formed during her latency period from mutual exhibition and from touching the penis of a playmate. She felt that the penis was something that could be taken off, something made from rubber, like the teat of a feeding bottle. Life in a boys' boarding school where she had this experience made her so devastatingly conscious of her physical inferiority that she became enuretic. "Urethral accidents" (14) and difficulties in regulating her urinating urge were still present as derivatives of her castration complex when she started her analysis in the course of which these symptoms were dissolved.

Miss B recalled that she had not been much disturbed as a child by being forbidden to masturbate. She did not let the long nightgown into which she was tied up interfere with her self-gratification. However, in the course of time extreme measures were resorted to. She was tied to her bed and eventually her father spanked her with a stick, all of which did not fail to have traumatic effects. The result was that from the beginning of puberty she masturbated, under phobic avoidance of her hand, by means of her blanket or of a little pillow. This voluminous object conformed even better to the image of her mother's breast which she fantasied bringing into contact with her genital.

The loss of her mother before the onset of the latency period acquired the meaning of a repetition of her primary deprivation during her weaning. The experience was repeated once more when her father who, as she expressed it, had been father *and* mother to her, remarried and she thus lost him to her stepmother. Through the births of three brothers, she also re-experienced her role as the only girl in a group of boys. Penis envy and sibling rivalry re-enforced each other in their effects upon her castration complex.

These disturbances of her object-libidinal relations, her experience of aggression and anxiety, the memory of her mother's suffering under the impact of her father's violently aggressive outbreaks, all contributed to her anxious rejection of an identification with her mother. A regressive mother cathexis occurred in the form of a series of *revenants*. The patient's relations to these objects as revealed in her dreams and wish fantasies were manifestations on the pregenital level, both active and passive, aggressive and tender, and they completely dominated her adult life. She wished to be loved and fondled like a little child and was full of longing for her mother's breast. On the other hand, she was also preoccupied by fantasies of obtaining or possessing a penis.

---

14 One of her earliest wish fantasies was to have a *real* penis which would hang down like a hose from her bed into a pail and would freely drain off her urine.

She produced the typical oral and anal fantasies of acquiring a penis. She also fantasied that the small labia had been a penis which had been cut in two and which the analyst should sew together for her. She wanted to tie her own nipples together and to swallow them. She wanted to urinate into her mother and thus beget a child. In another variation of the same fantasy, she herself wanted to be this child.

It was characteristic of her psychosexual experiences that she described her physical sensations during masturbation as a "sensation of compactness", which in the oral sphere was attached to the image of her mother's breast filling out her mouth, and to the feeling that her tongue was swelling up. The same sensations also appeared in displacement onto other parts of her body. They were revealed to be equivalents of an erection (11).

The patient reacted to these sensations with grave guilt feelings and anxiety, since they originated in fantasies of acquiring a penis by violence and in oral castration desires. The latter caused typical hysterical conversion symptoms, particularly vomiting. A characteristic feature of this "sensation of compactness", as the patient described it, was that it came and went in rhythm with her clitoral sensations, as though she alternately did and did not have a penis. This gave her the illusion of two alternatives regarding her sex and threw her in doubt about her own anatomy. Her overwhelming anxiety prevented her from examining herself and thus reaching a decision; and her tendency to "deny unpleasant reality" contributed to her confusion.

These fantasies threw light upon her inhibitions of activity which developed from her sensations of possessing a penis, her desires to appropriate a penis by violence, and her subsequent guilt feelings and anxiety.

In connection with her phobia of manual masturbation, she associated the custom, in a Negro tribe, of cutting off a thief's hand and added that this tribe also practiced castration. After this analytic session she went to the bathroom and had one of her typical "urethral accidents" in which she wet her slip. She rolled it into a sausage at the pack, pinned it fast and then walked home, cringing and humiliated as though she carried a poster marked, "Stolen goods". Occasional minor cleptomanic temptations were fugitive symptoms of her desire to appropriate a penis by theft.

Her inhibition of activity was reinforced by the fantasy of ensuring her possession of an imaginary penis by concealing and never making use of it. This could be termed a masked masculinity.

In addition, her renunciation of masculine activity had the meaning of soliciting love. The associations she produced in this context confirmed the findings of Lampl-de Groot (12) that repeated submission to the punishment of castration is to be understood as solicitation of love.

Before an interruption of the analysis due to vacation-time, she dreamt that a tooth extraction which in reality she dreaded had already taken place. In the dream she exclaimed: "I sacrifice the tooth on your altar. It shall be extracted—I don't want to be abandoned!" She was ready to give up her favorite fantasies of having an independent profession as long as the analyst

---

11 Several of Isakower's patients reported bodily sensations before falling asleep. These sensations corresponded to the situation at the mother's breast, whereby the mouth was full of "something that was not a foreign body" and the hand performed movements as if kneading dough. The phenomena were recognized as the cathexis of very early ego-attitudes.

did not abandon her. Her behavior in that session was characterized by a similar giving away of everything; i.e., she gave up her silence and her reserve, attitudes by which she always had tried to keep "something" for herself. Miss A, the first patient, was similarly inhibited in her professional work by the idea that the woman who was her superior resented her success. She said: "I'd rather be completely stupid than have her be angry with me!"

The following, probably more or less typical, motives for avoidance of activity were revealed by Miss B's fantasies:

1. Activity is tied to the idea of the possession of a penis, an idea which in turn is created by the positive penis sensation in clitoral masturbation. Since masturbation is forbidden and must be kept secret, the positive sensation of possessing a penis must also be kept secret, being just as forbidden and threatened by punishment.

2. One becomes active and masculine by appropriating the penis by violence, for which crime one is punished by castration. To be active is therefore equated with being aggressive. Impulses to injure can also be displaced to specific activities and so may lead to avoidance of these or of all activity.

3. The prohibition of active masculinity stems from the prohibition of the wish to play the active role with the mother. These wishes are prohibited for two reasons: a) because they are of a pregenital nature and thus clash with the standards of education, habits of cleanliness or modesty; b) because the rivalry with the father rouses anxiety.

These reasons for the prohibition of activity could be observed in patients who did not give up masturbation even after the discovery of their lack of a penis and the subsequent narcissistic injury.

Temporarily, Miss B would renounce the gratification of her desires for masculinity which concomitantly led to the cessation of all forms of activity. These periodic renunciations were caused by her feelings of guilt and anxiety, and they led to a condition of infantile craving for help and love. Women analysts frequently have the opportunity of observing, in the transference, this vacillation between the desire to conquer in the role of the man or to be fondled and loved as a child.

The patient's psychic make-up is entirely different, however, when renunciation is based upon the narcissistic injury and its ensuing inferiority feeling of being unable to compete with the man. The symptoms in such cases will consist in a demonstration of castration, in complaints about emptiness, in a defiant failure which can be interpreted to mean: "If I have been brought into the world in such a deficient state, you can't expect anything of me." Regression to prephallic stages of libido organization, frequently coupled with urethral incontinence, neglect of cleanliness and of appearance and with depression occur in both types of cases.

To a certain extent, both motives are probably operative in every case. However, prevalence of the one or of the other will characterize the symptomatology while in the course of the analysis both themes in the form of a repetition of the primary experience, may also appear alternatingly. Anxiety and guilt feelings were found to be the decisive factors in this development.

What kind of anxiety is it which initiates this restriction of functioning? Freud (9) raises the question whether castration anxiety should be considered the only lever setting in motion those defense mechanisms that lead to neurosis. He also points out, however, that while there is no doubt of the existence of the castration complex in women, it was not correct to speak of castration anxiety in the literal sense of the word where the castration is, so to speak, a fait accompli. Freud considers that the fear of the loss of love is the specifically female characteristic and is the content of female castration anxiety.

Lampl-de Groot (13) investigated in detail the disappointment which is caused by the discovery of the lack of the penis and the ensuing anticipation of failure in the solicitation of love. She found the fear of this narcissistic injury to be so overwhelming that she considers it to be as effective as the three great ego-anxieties and that it constitutes an equally powerful motive for restriction of ego-activity.

We found that women who have undergone the above-described development and who have experienced clitoral sensations so intensively that they have built their entire personality upon this fantasy of the secret possession of a penis, also experience the fear of the loss of this imaginary organ as real castration anxiety identical with that of the man. Anna Freud (5) has most pertinently termed this condition "fantasied objective anxiety". The very fact that the sensation of possessing a penis is a fleeting one probably contributes to the formation of castration anxiety. But even this anxiety is dominated by the fear of loss of love as the case of Miss B clearly showed. The moment she became active, her superego anxiety, guilt feelings and the neurotic mechanism of "failure by success" were released.

Let us now discuss the reasons for this atypical development. It will not be necessary to enumerate all the factors which—in addition to a bisexual constitution—may impede the development of true femininity. Inhibition is the only resource left to the woman whose path toward masculine activity leads her into aggression and therefore is blocked by anxiety. This inhibition, however, is counteracted by that remnant of her activity which manifests itself in recurring clitoral masturbation and the fantasies and impulses of masculinity. This is the most outstanding feature of the alternating phases of activity and inhibition which characterize the women of this type.

Freud accounted for the vacillation between two attitudes which had been observed by many analysts, by pointing to the complications which result from the inevitable disappointments from the father. These complications may drive the child into a regression to the previous mother attachment or, in the course of a woman's life, to a frequent alternation from one attitude to the other (7). He states: "In many women we actually find a repeated alternation of periods in which either masculinity or femininity has obtained the upper hand." Freud considers this alternation "the signs of bisexuality in female life" (8). Miss B presented a special case of these "complications". Vacillation was no longer a manifestation of bisexuality, of alternating masculinity and femininity, but rather was a neurotic alternation of sensations of masculinity and inhibitions. The positive periods of aggressive acquisition and momentary possession alternated with the negative phases of renunciation and the state of being castrated. These fluctuations seemed to be a reflection on the psychic level, of the sensations of clitoral masturbation; i.e., they corresponded to the feelings of having and not having a penis during masturbation.

The conception of self-reliant masculinity implied in the clitoral sensations helps us to understand the autodidactic tendencies of the female dilettante. To illustrate this point, I should like to quote a classic child analysis by Berta Bornstein (2). When her little five-year-old patient was found in her bath, studying her genital with tense interest, the child said: "There is something and sometimes it isn't there. And nobody can help me, I must find out everything by myself." At this time, the little girl developed an ambition clandestinely to learn to read and to write. Suddenly, however, this child who hitherto had stubbornly and patiently succeeded in acquiring knowledge, dropped this interest in reading and writing. Her ambition had become distasteful because she would never be able to catch up with the boys. Bornstein interpreted this to indicate that the child must have been conscious of clitoral sensations, that she took the erected clitoris for an organ equivalent to the penis and that she could not understand how it could sometimes vanish. The child showed transient symptoms of cleptomania and enuresis.

Both symptoms can be found frequently in dilettantes. The tendency to stealing or plagiarizing, the delight in gambling are based upon the self-delusion to possess or to appropriate by violence something one does not possess. These tendencies which have been observed in other, similar cases are related to the aggressive phase of masturbation, whereas enuresis is related to the inhibited phase, characterized by feelings of incapacity, of incompetence, and of being castrated.

In his brilliant study of the female castration complex, Abraham (1) emphasized impatience as a conspicuous character trait of his subjects. In these cases, the inability to bear tension, the tendency to insist upon immediate gratification which is also characteristic of masturbators, refers to the immediate fulfillment of the wish for the penis since the hope of obtaining a penis by gradual growth has been destroyed. The impatience not only expresses a tendency to speed up the realization of their active castration fantasies; it also refers to their passive castration wishes as if to realize them were a salvation for the eternally vacillating creature who is continually uncertain about her sexual role. Miss B expressed this feeling unmistakably when she said: "If there is little of something, then I'd rather have nothing at all. If something has to come to an end, I'd rather have it end abruptly."

The inability to tie oneself down proved to be determined by multiple factors. In general, it reflects the inability to bear tensions, and likewise the fear "of missing something" (the fantasied wishfulfillment). Finally it turned out that to tie oneself down, to accept coercion was also the equivalent of submission, with the acceptance of the feminine role. To tie oneself down would then mean to renounce the wishfulfillment.

In summarizing, we may state that the investigation of female dilettantism has drawn our attention to a complex of interconnected psychic mechanisms which do not regularly manifest themselves as dilettantism, from which, however, the neurotic type of dilettantism described in this paper derives. These mechanisms constitute a type of development which differs from the three developmental types postulated by Freud (8). The deviation occurs at the crucial point of the little girl's psychosexual development, when she relinquishes the primary mother object. In our cases, too, this relinquishment led with a thrust into the oedipus situation, but optimal development of real femininity failed. The desire for a penis was not transformed into the desire for a child. The dilettante shares with her opposite, the type who exaggerates masculinity, only her stubborn clinging to the penis-wish and to clitoral masturbation. In the dilettante the development either to masculinity or to femininity has been hampered by overstrong sadomasochistic tendencies with corresponding castration anxiety. The resulting grave inhibition of active strivings and the typically feminine inferiority feelings indicate a trend to complete passivity and inhibition. However, it soon becomes clear that these subjects have remained arrested in a continual vacillation between the two trends of masculinity and inhibition, and in their defensive struggle against masturbation. Characteristic clitoral sensations constitute the basis of psychic occurrences which manifest themselves in an alternation of inferiority feelings and over-estimation of self, of inhibition and masculinity. There is no development from the one to the other, only a leap which is bound to fail. This is the origin of the symptom of dilettantism. The narcissistic injury has compelled the totally inhibited woman to give up masturbation and frequently to renounce any kind of activity. But the female dilettante uses this same experience of clitoral masturbation as a confirmation, albeit temporary, of her masculinity, and thus has become fixated to this method of gratification.

REFERENCES

1. K. Abraham: Aeusserungsformen des weiblichen Kastrationskomplexes, *Int. Ztschr. f. Psa.*, 1921.

2. B. Bornstein: Kleptomanie und Enuresis als passageres Symptom, *Ztschr. f. psa. Paed.*, 1934.

3. H. Deutsch: The Significance of Masochism in the Mental Life of Women, *Int. J. Psa.*, XI, 1930.

4. ——On Female Homosexuality, *Psa. Quart.*, 1, 1932.

5. A. Freud: *The Ego and the Mechanisms of Defence*, New York, Int. Univ. Press, 1946.

6. S. Freud: Some Psychological Consequences of the Anatomical Distinction between the Sexes, *Int. J. Psa.*, VIII, 1927.

7. ——Female Sexuality, *Int. J. Psa.*, XIII, 1932.

8. ——Psychology of Women, *New Introductory Lectures on Psychoanalysis*, New York, W. W. Norton, 1933.

9. ——*Inhibition, Symptom and Anxiety*, New York, W. W. Norton, 1936.

10. ——Some Character-types met with in Psychoanalytic Work, *Coll. Papers*, vol. IV, London, Hogarth Press, 1924-25.

11. O. Isakower: Beitrag zur Pathopsychologie der Einschlafphaenomene, *Int. Ztschr. Psa.*, 1938.

12. J. Lampl-de Groot: The Evolution of the Oedipus Complex in Women, *Int. J. Psa.*, IX, 1928.

13. ——Hemmung und Narzissmus, *Int. Ztschr. Psa.*, 1936.

14. K. Levy: Vom Bettnaessen des Kindes, *Ztschr. f. psa. Paed.*, 1934.

15. J. H. U. Van Ophuijsen: Maennlichkeitskomplex der Frau, *Int. Ztschr. Psa.*, 1934.

16. L. Rotter: Psychologie der weiblichen Sexualitaet, *Int. Ztschr. Psa.*, 1934.

17. A. Staercke: Der Kastrationskomplex, *Int. Ztschr. Psa.*, 1921.

LES "ENFANTS TERRIBLES"*

By Margaret Schoenberger Mahler, M.D.**

(New York)

The title of this paper was taken from a book by the French author Jean Cocteau. In his book: Enfants terribles he depicts children who do not restrict their passions. These passions are the same passions of love and hate that adults feel but exaggerated and not amalgamated. In fact, the youthful actors in Cocteau's book are held together by masochistic infatuation, self-sacrifice, and tender adoration as well as by sadistic aggression and brutal subjugation. In other words, Cocteau has chosen as a literary theme a fact, self-evident to psychoanalysts, that children and adolescents are moved by the same erotic and aggressive cravings as are adults. The children of his novel inflict physical and mental torture upon each other. Their ego condones the breaking down of the barriers against direct expression of the instinctual impulses set by the superego. Their grossly aggressive and erotic pursuits are not challenged by the grown-ups. The youthful actors rely upon, and anticipate an adult prejudice namely the superstitious, stubborn and traditional belief in the innocence of children. Because they are children, their obviously and grossly sexual and destructive actions and relationships are not recognized as such. The children rely on this prejudice. They love and hate in entirely adult fashion before the eyes of the adults. But the adults, entrenched in their complacent superstition, do not believe this conduct to be motivated by adult-like passion, and can be fooled all the time.

Jean Cocteau's Enfants terribles thus are products of a peculiar emotional interrelationship between infantile and adult society. The same elements in a conflict described in Cocteau's novel with dramatic exaggeration are contained in every day "enfant terrible" phenomena occurring between children and their parents. The dynamic elements of these every day phenomena, however, appear mitigated in quality and quantity by the operation of the economic principle of the comic. In fact, the most generally accepted

---

* Paper read at the Meeting of the New York Psychoanalytic Society on December 9, 1947.
** Associate in Psychiatry, Columbia University (New York City).

concept of *enfant terrible* behavior can be formulated as follows: A person —
usually a child — pretending innocence and naivety, shocks adults by a
deliberately embarrassing remark or gesture.

A father, who was a psychoanalyst, used to amuse his friends from time
to time by telling them each new crop of his small son's cute remarks and
questions. The curiosity of the little chap had obviously centered upon his
father's professional pursuits. He wanted to know what his father did with
the patients behind the closed door of his office. He wondered whether he
beat them up, etc. It was a mystery to him why he was forbidden to join his
father even for a minute when the men and women could take up all his
time. In fact, he was not even supposed to know the names of the ladies and
gentlemen who came to pay such long visits to his daddy so regularly. He
was strictly forbidden to talk to the patients—these mysterious creatures, who
to his mind were surrounded with an utterly exaggerated immunity. The
curiosity and resentment of the little boy grew until one day, when coming
up the elevator with a gentleman who, as he had discovered, was one of
these creatures, he suddenly burst out: "Are you perhaps a patient?"

In the minds of children whose mothers are analysts these emotions
which this small boy indicated are even greater in intensity. An analyst mother
one day overheard her little daughter shouting all over the house:
"Mooommmy, come out of the bathroom, hurry up, the patient has arrived!"

Another woman analyst's seven-year-old son gives us a more obvious
example of aggressive phallic behavior. He felt frustrated and irked by having to share his mommy with all those patients. So, one morning he waited
till the patient entered the hall, and with perfect synchronization opened the
bathroom door, popped his head out, and shouted a mocking and spontaneously invented rhyme about his mother: "Mrs. E. G. is a piggie!"

Seven-year-old Pete, while in analysis, was taken for a check-up to his
beloved pediatrician, a very tall and imposing looking man. Upon leaving
the office he raved about what a wonderful doctor uncle B. was, etc. Whereupon his mother, in her concern for Pete's "transference" to me, said to him,
"But you know Margaret is also a doctor", whereupon Pete with condescend-
ing and understanding innocence retorted, "Oh sure, Margaret knows a
lot about penises."

And finally there is the example of the two sons of another analyst.
They entered the elevator just in time to meet one of their mother's woman
patients going up to her hour, and with the most innocent expressions they
nonchalantly wiggled a snake they had just caught before her horrified eyes.

I took these examples because such and similar incidents are familiar
to all of us.

If we examine the immediate genesis of such *enfant terrible* manifestations as these cited, we can see that frustrating exclusion from the mysterious and enticing community of adults over a period of time augmented
the youngster's curiosity and his erotic aggressive wish to participate, until
the impulse gathered enough momentum to cast off the lid of educational
pressure. The first little boy pretends naiveté to asking the forbidden questions, "Are you perhaps a patient?", whose identity is kept from him. The

little girl achieved even more with her pseudo-naive vocalization. She embarrassed her analyst mother. By her loud broadcast she revealed, "unmasked" as it were, her mother as a human being in the midst of intimate family life. By admonishing her to hurry to her professional work she put comical emphasis upon the urgency of attending to her patient — a deliberate reversal of the child's own, opposite emotions. She achieved a two-fold revenge on her mother and on the patient. In the third instance, the child actually exposed his mother in a frankly erotic, aggressive, mocking way, calling her a piggie. He was thus sure of interfering with the patient-analyst relationship. The two boys by suddenly displaying a phallic symbol quite effectively shocked the woman-patient.

And finally, in Pete's case, from my intimate knowledge of his actual emotional situation I know that by the pseudo-naive remark with which he replied to his mother, he ridiculed and minimized the importance of women around him: the doctor, mother, sister, etc., who allegedly know so much about penises but who, when "unveiled", are merely vulnerable, penisless creatures.

The children of analysts, utilizing the generally accepted pretence and privilege of children to be considered cute, innocent and naive, transgressed the barrier of adult rules. In fact, they interfered effectively, if only for a moment, with the daily analytic procedure. Thus, they actually reversed the power position between child and adult. In these episodes they managed to usurp adult superiority by the very weapon of being a child.

Hence, the *enfant terrible* whom I should like to present today, turns out to be a counterpart of that specific type of pseudo-imbecile child whom I described in a paper in 1942 (18). Such children hide under a magic hood of apparent stupidity, and thus manage to participate undetected in the erotic life of the adult world. The *enfant terrible* on the other hand, by virtue of his subtle or bold but swift erotic aggressive attacks, succeeds in taking the adult by surprise and disarming him by throwing him off balance, and unmasking the adults' pretence of superiority.

The child with the magic hood of pseudo-stupidity manages to transgress the border of adult life by means of his disguise of invisibility. The *enfant terrible,* in contrast, overwhelms the sentinel by the abrupt exhibition of his naiveté, charm and acuteness. He takes the risk of being castrated for mocking the adult, but relies upon the disarming magic, which the "irresistible baby", the naive child, exerts upon the average adult, over whom he thus triumphs.

I am aware that the *enfant terrible* whom I shall describe uses motility more than does the traditional *enfant terrible*. The latter depends more preeminently on his verbalizations as a weapon.

In age *enfants terribles* are not confined to the period of childhood.

The person whom we call an *enfant terrible* may be an adult who utilizes
the mechanism of pseudo-naivety for a similar purpose or dynamic effect.
The expression *enfant terrible* cannot be accurately translated into English.
It expresses a bipolarity and contains a comical paradox. The epithet, *terrible,*
is bestowed on the diminutive human being as an attribute pertaining to
the strong and powerful adult. Thus, the French expression contains in a
nutshell the principal dynamic and economic elements involved in this
phenomenon.

As we have seen, *enfant terrible* behavior may be regarded as a special
form of erotic aggressive unmasking and provocation of the adult in order
to force him to let down for a fleeting moment the time-honored barriers
between the infantile and the adult world of experiences. I shall apply
Freud's fundamental concepts of *Wit and its Relation to the Unconscious,*
and refer to Ernst Kris' (14) (15), Edith Jacobson's (13) and Annie Reich's
(21) important work on comic phenomena and laughter, in summarizing
what seemed to me essential in the dynamics of *enfant terrible* behavior.
The behavior of the *enfant terrible* shocks the adult audience's superego and
disarms it. It carries away and seduces, as it were, the adult's ego into fore-
saking, albeit for a short span of time, its serene and austere reality standards,
so that the adult regresses with the child into the abandoned carefree
impulse-indulgence of childhood. The adult's ego, realizing immediately
its uncontestable superiority dissolves the initial shock into an amused smile
or laughter. In turn, the child playfully experiences provocation of and
deliverance from the danger of castration.

Inasmuch as the *enfant terrible* mechanism is a social phenomenon, I
believe we shall investigate genetically both the infantile and the adult
partner's roles in this phenomenon.

Parents are thrilled to tell about the shocking and cute remarks and
deeds of their small fry. This contains both an element of narcissistic exhibition and a desire to share such delightful experience with their adult friends.
The parents usually take for granted the other adult's libidinous readiness
for participation. Normal adults usually promote, with friendly condescension, their children's struggles and competitive effort at playing adult. Fairy
tales make abundant use of the pleasurable effect of following up to victory
the audacious efforts of a little boy or a youth against obstacles, which seemed
threateningly insuperable. There the little chap's triumph over the ogre
contains the immortal topic of overcoming castration fear. In fact, the
children's playful struggle in the growing-up process is an inexhaustible
source of amusement to adults. This is due to their identification with the
child's efforts to overcome castration fear, which the adult once experienced,
and over which his ego achieved mastery. We know by observation that

those adults who habitually tease children, are those whose sublimation of castration fears is not solidly established.

Children, particularly boys between five and six, frequently resort to a play of hiding behind doors or underneath furniture, and startling the adult by jumping up like a living Jack-in-the-box. They expect the adult to display shock and at the same time to show delight at the sudden emergence as a kind of happy reunion with the lively little man. This behavior belongs to normal phenomena of the phallic stage of development. It does not seem difficult to recognize in this sudden dashing up movement of the boy's or girl's body as a whole, the playful dramatization of an erection. Here, I think, traces of an identification of the whole body with the father's phallus can be detected as a normal transitional stage of development in both boys and girls alike. The same gestures and actions, however, may become connected with and be the expression of a conflict, and lose their playful quality through endless repetitiousness and exaggerated intensity. Incidents of the type quoted of the analyst's child evoke pleasurable reactions in the adult audience only if the aggressive element is not too prominent and if repetition does not so increase the nuisance value of such behavior as to decrease the pleasures of comic condensation.

There are numerous economic and dynamic shifts in this *enfant terrible* behavior phenomenon which vary all the way from the occasional mischievous manifestations of the analysts' children to harassing and continuous trickery. We can readily see how the quality of the terrible in behavior of this type may increase to such an extent that the *enfant terrible* ceases to be considered funny. Finally, the phallic aggressive nature of the *enfant terrible* behavior may become so intensified as to betray to the analyst by the very quality of its exaggeration its character of a *pathological defense mechanism*.

As illustration I should like to describe a child patient, six and one-half year old Maxie. He remained a diagnostic enigma to me until I understood the meaning of his conspicuously phallic, aggressive behavior. Before his treatment and during the first part of his analysis, Maxie succeeded in scaring away innumerable nurses whose departure had a comic quality of flight from a highly desirable position, because of a six year old urchin, hardly three feet tall. The only employee who stayed for any length of time was a rather old, and matriarchal cook, whom Maxie's provocative behavior neither challenged nor seduced. This woman, resolute and firm, had known Maxie from infancy, and dealt with his aggressive advances by instinctively adopting his own methods of teasing and throwing him off balance by surprise actions. He was frankly scared of her, as he was of his father, a handsome, vain and despotic young man, who seemed to lack any sense of humor. The mother was a brilliantly talented young artist, a sculptress, sensitive and narcissistic, and filled with a sincere wish to reconcile her turbulent professional, social and marital life with her role as a mother. She felt threatened not only by Maxie's unmanageable conduct, but particularly by the increasingly apparent rivalry between her son and husband for her favors, a rivalry which she unconsciously instigated and maintained. Whereas earlier in life the little chap's precocious and pertinent remarks and gestures had filled the mother with delight, even if their timing was inopportune and embarrassing, lately Maxie had developed into a little tyrant in the home, whom neither his mother's bribes nor his father's hardness could bring to order. The youthful father's competition with his son was quite overt. He tried to suppress and subdue Maxie with his teasing, roughhousing and brutalization—including beatings. On the other hand, the boy challenged his father's privilege as his mother's erotic partner. He offered himself to the mother as a constant source of pleasure. He continually kept awake and satisfied this mother's narcissistic needs by his exhibitionistic display of his conspicuously gracious movements, by his unusual artistic skill both in drawing and in music, and by his precocious, witty intellectual brilliance. As a result, the mother considered Maxie's smile "irresistible as far as any woman was concerned". This and similar comments were characteristic of her attitude toward him.

The mother's infatuation with her son was obvious. She was one of those mothers who regard their little sons as part of their own persons (a penis) and treat him as though he were emotionally a part of her own ego even if physically separate. When the analyst once carelessly asked: "What is our child doing?", the mother was annoyed and angry.

The attitude of that type of mother and father towards their offspring is strikingly identical with the libidinous attitude which children maintain toward their own sexual organ as described by Ferenczi in his book *Thalassa* (7), and also in his paper "Gulliver Fantasies" (8). Ferenczi pointed out that the sexual organs, penis and clitoris, because they are reservoirs of pleasure for the whole individual, are cherished as a kind of second personality, which Ferenczi called the libidinous ego. Ferenczi also reminded us of the fact that frequently the male organ is given pet names of a very personal character as if it were an independent little personality. Bertram Lewin in his paper "The Body as Phallus" (16), gave numerous illustrations of this tendency, among others how a phallus was portrayed clad as a little man.

It is a rather common occurrence for an adult to transfer to his child his own infantile libidinous overvaluation of the genital, especially his phallic exhibitionistic tendencies. To this erotic overvaluation the child reacts, according to the quality and quantity of the parent's attitude, and according to the stage of his or her libido and ego development. One of the possible transient results is that the child for a while indulges in the previously described body-erection play to his own and his parents' pleasure.

Maxie, at four and five years of age, was a typical *enfant terrible*. For example, when his parents had company at night, Maxie would get out of bed during the party, sneak into the living room undetected, hide behind a large chair and when the party was at its height, he would seize the most inopportune and embarrassing moment to suddenly make his appearance with a funny gesture or noise, shocking and throwing both hosts and guests off balance. He would say to Mr. X.: "You look just as funny as your necktie", referring to something which his parents had discussed disparagingly in his presence. His charm and pseudo-naive curiosity were so disarming, however, that the company felt genuinely amused by the little chap.

The older Maxie grew, however, the more annoying and the less tolerable became the repetition of such and similar behavior. The previously comical exhibitionistic behavior had changed by the time I met Maxie to a pathological defense mechanism.

My thesis is that a certain type of *enfant terrible* behavior *represents a defense mechanism in which the eroticised body* — the entire libidinous ego in Ferenczi's sense — *is identified with the threatening phallus of the father and is used to ward off overwhelming fear of castration.* This "defense by offense" reminds one of the defense mechanisms of "identification with the aggressor", described by Anna Freud (9). I believe that the crucial failure prompting this particular mechanism of defense is a fixation of libido at the phallic stage of development. We studied in adult women patients such failures in concentrating and organizing the libido under the primacy of the genital organ because of intense castration fear. In the genesis of this mechanism, two equations seemed of paramount significance, namely, for the child, the equating of body with phallus, and for the parent, the equating of child with phallus. It would be challenging to speculate why in so many cases identification with the aggressor is used as a defense, while in my cases "pars pro toto", i.e. the erotic weapon of the aggressive male, was selected for identification.

About Maxie's early life the following could be elicited: He was a very much wanted and planned for child. Pregnancy and delivery were uneventful. He was not breastfed, because his father did not want the mother to be tied down so much and because he wanted her to preserve her youthful figure. The mother reiterated that Maxie got too much love and had his way too easily. Feeding and habit training were normal. He was showered with toys, shown off to the many guests who came to the house, almost from the day of his birth. He entered kindergarten before he was three and exerted himself to keep up with much older boys — an ambition which Maxie maintained ever since. However, there never seemed to have been any attempt to meet the child's emotional needs on his own level.

Instead he was pushed rather precipitatedly into an intense oedipal situation and his libido development was thereby accelerated toward the phallic phase. His father expressed affection by roughhousing, wrestling and using his superior strength on the boy "in a teasing way". In this area the father dealt with the boy as if he were his sibling, but on the other hand he expected his immediate obedience to abrupt commands, interrupting whatever the boy was doing. He tolerated no opposition and enforced his views by sheer physical power.

While the child was only four or five, Maxie's exhibitionistic behavior was enjoyed and tolerated. But as soon as the child used this mechanism to ward off his intense castration fear, it became intolerable to his environment.

I learned to know Maxie as an overly smooth, wiry and yet babyish-looking boy with peculiarly undifferentiated facial expression. His motor coordination, graceful movements and acquired bodily and manual skill were striking. His verbalization and all other kinds of performance ability were far ahead of his chronological age. Maxie considered his muscular strength and his *swiftness* as his main assets, and he had learned to combine this strength and speed with the startling effects of abruptness and suddenness into an unusually effective weapon. In school his scholastic records were outstanding.

After a very short period of appearing at his best in the analytic situation, Maxie played the role of the rude, sophisticated master, who orders around, abuses and overpowers people whom he considers in any way weaker than himself. He was a bully. He accompanied his orders by shouting: "Make it snappy!" One had the feeling he was copying, trying out and mocking, as it were, his father's methods of dealing with him.

Soon one trait became strikingly apparent in his analysis: He would play dominoes, or occupy himself with drawing in a most absorbed, calm way, and then suddenly, and with no transition, and without external cause or provocation, he would jump up with lightning speed, a living Jack-in-the-box. He would start to throw things about and to work himself up with scolding and shouting. The arresting feature of such *spells* was the *complete detachment* of the child's person, which remained peculiarly aloof. Even as he proceeded in his erectile behavior, working himself up into violence, one had the impression that *his ego was not participating*. Affects came into this procedure only if he had to be restrained. Otherwise he would go back to some quiet occupation and then start the cycle all over again. The behavior strikingly suggested a dramatization of phallic erection by means of the whole body. The erection, that is jumping up, etc., appeared a quasi automatic gesture detached from the rest of the personality.

At times, he definitely preferred exhibitionistic but *solitary* occupation. He drew and modelled. He forbade with great ado any glancing at his productions while they were in the making. When he had finished, he would jump up triumphantly and show them to me for a minute, and then usually would quickly destroy his work.

Two motives appeared in the first phase of his analysis: competition with the analyst, in which he settled any issue in his own favor either by provocative, open cheating or by "brute force."

The second apparent motive was a peculiar, erotic, aggressive provocation. Suddenly, during the treatment, in the course of some building, bombing and water play, he abruptly turned to me and said: "Undress!" In a series of sessions he would threaten and plead to see the analyst in the nude. Maxie's passionate pre-occupation with nudeness seemed primarily motivated by his confusion about the anatomical sex difference. It was obvious from the analytical material that he had never accepted the fact that his mother had no "Mr. Wee-wee" as he called the penis. According to him it was hidden, under the pubic hair. In this connection he also revealed his admiration for his mother, whom he considered much more efficient and clever than his father, and most of whose interests he shared including her artistic talents. At this point he fantasied with glee, but with an unmistakable intensification of excited apprehension how he would surprise me while I was taking a bath. Thus he had to search another woman for a phallus, in order to deny castration. He was told again and again that women did not have a penis, and was given the assurance that what he needed was not to see men's and women's bodies but to tell and understand his worries about their bodies and his own. Thereafter his effort to impress me changed in the following way: His peculiar aloofness vanished. Instead he tried to sneak under my skirt or to tickle me. He would try with a great display of charm to seduce me into giving the proof he craved which would reassure him about being a man in the face of his *desperate denial of castration*. He built himself up to a veritable miniature roué, bragging about his sexual exploits with the intention of seducing me. He lay on the floor and dreamily recited a little parody of a poem, which went like this: "The night was dark and hazy, and the Piccadilly Daisy Took off her clothes, in front of me." His behavior at this point could best be described as that of a puppy in heat.

Maxie's perplexity in sexual matters *seemed intensified* by the following dilemma: The art studies which his mother generously shared with her little son, gave him an opportunity of looking at photographs of nudes, at Greek statues, etc. Here big men were represented with the genital organs of a little boy's size, and women with only a mons veneris and then again there were statues with a fig leaf which looked to him like pubic hair. His parents were progressive people who did not conceal their bodies in the bathroom, to which Maxie had free access. Maxie therefore had the opportunity of seeing and of observing his father's genital which in size could not be compared with the organ he saw on statues, or with his own. He had ample opportunity of observing erectility — tumescence and detumescence phenomena.

Dr. Greenacre in her paper, "Vision, Headache and the Halo" (11), pointed out the traumatic visual impression of the phallus which is at the root of the anxieties and clinical symptoms of certain patients. It is interesting to note that not only in Maxie's case but also in other cases, particularly in adults who showed the mechanism of identification with the aggressive phallus, there were unexpected visual and particularly tactile experiences of the motion and erectile tumescence of the membrum which seemed to have been the crucial traumatic factor.

Maxie tried to impress me by exhibiting his muscular strength, skill, and fastness in *acrobatic stunts*. He began the following repetitious game: he piled up all the furniture in the children's room in a huge pedestal, and with cat-like grace and rapidity climbed up, stood for a while and then toppled down. I was supposed to admire his ability to perform this stunt. His dramatization of himself as a huge erect penis was even more obvious.

At this time I heard from a relative of Maxie's how direct was his curiosity about the adult male genital and its size. He wanted to surprise this man in the bathroom, and to be present when he urinated. The same male relative related that one of Maxie's favorite games with his father, for which he asked again and again, was piggie-back riding. He rode on his father's or uncle's neck and revelled in that elevated position. He would get quite excited and at times unmanageable. When I tried to discuss this topic with him Maxie warded it off violently. But finally he listened to my interpretation. Thereafter he began to change this manifestation and would come into the room with his fly open and a tumescent penis. He no longer needed to use only his whole body as phallus.

I now made use of a little monkey puppet to represent Maxie and started to move the monkey on my fingers. Maxie passionately tore it off my hand, and from that day on kissed and petted it as if it were something very precious and living. He came back to it for several days in the same affectionate way until he finally destroyed it by decapitation and threw the headless rag away. It was an amazing display of the little Narcissus Maxie loving the puppet-phallus. But he also castrated, and made the Maxie-monkey into a limp rag. Maxie brought out other material which revealed that he was worried about erection and detumescence and masturbation. He played with fire and showed considerable fear. His castration fears were now more clearly demonstrated.

At this time, one of his series of nurses had fainted in Maxie's presence just after she had warned him that she could no longer stand his tormenting. This and his father's ensuing anger started Maxie off on a phase of fantasies of phallic violence in his analysis. The way in which he would break into the treatment room if the doors were closed, made me fully realize that there was a graver pathogenic agent in his life than the one represented by his interest in nudes, and that while he could not see it clearly, he surmised it. It was not the bathroom, but his mother's bedroom, shut only when the father was home, which challenged Maxie. He liked to hide under his mother's bed, and despite his father's anger, he could not bear to stay hidden, but would shock his parents by suddenly appearing. It was evident from his material in the analysis that he witnessed intimacies and the primal scene.

Also in the analysis his movements were utterly unpredictable, and because he was so small he could force his body in between and under furniture from which he would suddenly dash out. If he was held down bodily, he would yell and scream that the object of such attacks had injured him. Interpretation resulted in ferocious fantasies like the following: "I shall bring my Mexican knife, and I will cut off your head and then I will undress you." In later sessions he would declare, "When I grow up, I'm going to be a doctor" (and the analyst thought that a good sign) . . . "but I will not do doctor's work, I will undress people and pinch them, and I will be undressed myself."

This child, who developed from a charming *enfant terrible* into a little tyrant with a compulsion to shock people could no longer conceal his own anxiousness and his tendency to being excessively startled by any sudden and unexpected noise or motion. At such times he could not conceal his intense fright.

At the same time his overt sexual aggression toward the analyst changed and he began instead to fantasy about her. These fantasies he communicated to his mother. They dealt with the topic of the analyst being castrated. One day the mother called me up, utterly puzzled by Maxie's statement, "Dr. Mahler has lost an eye". This was a projection onto me of his repeated observation of one of my adult patients who had lost an eye and pointed to Maxie's fear that I was castrated and moreover that he was responsible.

In the analysis his corporal erotic aggressive attacks on the analyst were abandoned and replaced by stealing toy soldiers and other things from her and showing them off to his mother. He was told the meaning of such acts; that because I did not show him what he wanted to see, he took away my equipment instead. He reacted by beginning to play with the scissors, cutting out things and provocatively announced that he would steal the scissors. When the analyst told him he could have them, he turned on her and exclaimed, "You are a liar", meaning, "You do not have a penis". He dashed to a desk fountain pen set and stuck the pen into the container with such fury that the point broke off.

Maxie brought out material which showed that he believed that by his magic power he had damaged all the nurses who left so suddenly. This was revealed through his fantasies about the analyst's being crippled. The episode of his nurse's fainting formed the basis of Maxie's fantasy that he could drive people crazy, make them faint and almost die. He asked me questions about death and about "being nuts", and pretended to be nuts himself. Women were castrated by the attacks of men. But in turn Maxie was afraid of the phallic woman. This became evident when Maxie fell ill with mumps and overheard or sensed concern about his testicles. He was then still behaving like an erectile phallus, abruptly jumping up and attacking people. But when confronted with an abnormally tall nurse, he gave up this performance and became subdued. After this his castration fear could be worked through in his analysis and he became calmer.

I have deliberately omitted the contributory oral and anal material in order to simplify the presentation of the specific mechanism which I wished to describe.

In concluding I would say that when Maxie's oedipus conflict reached its peak, its solution and partial repression was destined to failure because of the obstacles which stood in the way of his identifications with a desexualized image of his father, because of his intense fear of castration by him, and finally because of his mother's phallic seductive attitude. His strong identification tendencies with his mother added to the conflict. He had to resort to a fixation at the phallic level, using his entire body. This erotization of his entire body as phallic symbol was the result, as mentioned before, of special and traumatic visual, kinesthetic and tactile experiences of tumescence-detumescence which occurred at a crucial stage of his development when latency should have set in. Narcissistic encouragement of his phallic exhibitionistic tendencies by his mother, including his ego talents, and corporal teasing and brutalization by his father, made Maxie identify not with the desexualized image, but with the sexual aggressive organ of the father and with the fantasied phallus of his mother.

Annie Reich's unpublished paper on "The Grotesque-Comic Sublimation" describes an attempt at a solution of the castration complex through denial of castration by an exaggerated display of a damaged, and disfigured body in lieu of the genital. In the mechanism here described denial of castration is attempted by an exhibition of the erectile potency of the adult male using the body as a phallus.

In summary I would say that Maxie's case seems to illustrate with special clarity the clinical picture of those children whose latency period has been deferred because, as Aichhorn pointed out, for specific environmental reasons they were unable to identify with the desexualized ego ideal of the parent of the same sex.

Maxie also belongs to that large group of problem children whose mechanisms of defense are expressed through the function of motility (of acting out). His overt behavior when he was first referred for treatment, was such that for six months I was uncertain whether or not it indicated a possible psychopathy. To the environment the persistent motor aggression of these children has a nuisance value so acute that the ensuing reaction reminds us forcibly of Aichhorn's dictum that the term "delinquency" is more a social epithet than a considered psychiatric diagnosis.

In Maxie's case, however, the analysis of his aggressive behavior soon revealed the deep-seated anxiety for which his noisiness was a compensation. His case, therefore, might be said to have shifted from Aichhorn's category of neurotic delinquency to that of potential (latent?) delinquent neurosis as the ratio of alloplastic to autoplastic elements in his behavior changed during treatment.

Today Maxie is a well adjusted youth, attending high school where he has maintained a satisfactory record of excellent scholastic and social performance.

This history may serve as a simple illustration of a whole group of cases. It is a clinically verifiable fact that a large number of such children, who show noisy and aggressive conduct during an extended pre-latency period, in later school age, develop a neurosis and not delinquency. Or else, if they undergo a successful child analysis, they later may make a good personal and social adjustment.

REFERENCES

1. Aichhorn, August: *Wayward Youth*. New York, Viking Press, 1944.
2. ——Erziehungsberatung. *Z. f. psa. Paed.*, VI, 1932.
3. ——Erziehungs-Beratungs-Seminar. *Z. f. psa. Paed.*, VII, 1933.
4. ——Zur Technik der Erziehungsberatung. *Z. f. psa. Paed.*, X, 1936.
5. Cocteau, Jean: *Les Enfants Terribles*. Transl. by Samuel Putnam. Norwood, Mass., Brewer & Warren, Inc., 1930.
6. Fenichel, Otto: Die symbolische Gleichung Maedchen-Phallus. *Int. Z. f. Psa.*, XXII, 1936.
7. Ferenczi, Sandor: *Thalassa*. New York, Psa. Quarterly, Inc., 1938.
8. ——Gulliver Phantasies. *Int. J. Psa.*, IX, 1928.
9. Freud, Anna: *The Ego and the Mechanisms of Defence*. New York, Int. Univ. Press, 1946.

10. Freud, Sigmund: *Wit and Its Relation to the Unconscious.* New York, Moffat, Yard & Co., 1916.

11. Greenacre, Phyllis: Vision, Headache and the Halo. *Psa. Quart.,* XVI, 1947.

12. ——Conscience in the Psychopath. *Am. J. Orth.,* XV, 1945.

13. Jacobson, Edith: The Child's Laughter. *The Psa. Study of the Child,* II, 1947.

14. Kris, Ernst: The Psychology of Caricature. *Int. J. Psa.,* XVII, 1936.

15. ——Ego Development and the Comic. *Int. J. Psa.,* XIX, 1938.

16. Lewin, Bertram: The Body as Phallus. *Psa. Quart.,* II, 1933.

17. Mahler, Margaret Schoenberger: Discussion of Dr. Silberpfennig's paper: Mother Types Encountered in Child Guidance Clinics. *Am. J. Orth.,* XI, 1941.

18. ——Pseudoimbecility: A Magic Cap of Invisibility. *Psa. Quart.,* XI, 1942.

19. ——Ego Psychology Applied to Behavior Problems, in: *Modern Trends in Child Psychiatry,* N. D. C. Lewis and B. L. Pacella, Editors. New York, Int. Univ. Press, 1946.

20. Olden, Christine: Headline Intelligence. *The Psa. Study of the Child,* II, 1947.

21. Reich, Annie: On Grotesque-Comic Sublimation. Unpublished.

22. Silberpfennig, Judith: Mother Types Encountered in Child Guidance Clinics. *Am. J. Orth.,* XI, 1941.

INCENDIARISM *

By Ernst Simmel[1]

The crime of incendiarism can have various causes. The incendiarist may be a feeble-minded or a psychotic individual; he may set fire as an act of revenge, or in order to collect the fire insurance. However, it is generally agreed that there is a particular form of incendiarism called pyromania, which is pathological. These pyromaniacs cannot explain why they set fires — they act under a compulsion and we are entitled to assume that even among the incendiarists who think they know, there are genuine pyromaniacs who only rationalize their unconscious drives.

Some years ago I was called in by a judge of a Superior Court to act as a psychoanalytic expert in a case which was unquestionably one of pyromania. The subject was a twenty-one year old boy, whom we shall call George. I interviewed George twice and by applying my general psychoanalytic knowledge and interpretation of symbolic actions I arrived at some conclusions, at least in this individual case of pyromania. I gave my report to the judge and the boy was not sentenced to jail but put on probation.

The criminal act was repeated incendiarism. The defendant George was accused of setting fires to fields of dry grass on five different occasions. This is a very serious crime. The defendant pleaded guilty. On being questioned by the court psychiatrist, as to why he had committed these incendiary acts, George's reply was: "I don't know — except for the thrill." The psychiatrist concluded: "George is not insane in either a legal or medical sense. I believe that he has told us all he knows as to the motivation of his offenses: that he committed them for the thrill he derived from setting fire to grass fields and helping the fire department to put them out. This, in my opinion, is a case in which only a psychoanalytic diagnosis could serve as a guide to other than the usual, conventional action by the authorities in dealing with him."

Before investigating the criminal acts, I should like first to acquaint you with George's personality and development. George is a middle child;

---

* Paper presented before the San Francisco Psychoanalytic Society, Spring 1944.

[1] The editors are deeply indebted to Mrs. Ernst Simmel for her assistance in carrying out the late author's intention to contribute this paper to the present volume.

he has an older sister and a younger brother. His parents are living, but were divorced before his memory begins. George's personality reveals an obvious disturbance of his sexual development. In this respect he appears to be absolutely immature. In spite of the fact that he is twenty-one years old, he has had no sex life whatever. For the past four months he has had an affectionate relation with a "nice" girl. However, he abhors the idea of having sexual intercourse with her. In the course of the interviews he revealed that he actually is afraid of intercourse. He went so far as to say that he would never have intercourse with this girl, even in marriage, because "no one can tell, after all, whether or not she is sick. . . . Intercourse is too *dangerous.*"

In George's physical contact with this girl, he never experienced an erection. He never masturbates. He never has had an ejaculation, not even in the form of a pollution as the result of a dream. Only when he feels an urge to urinate, whether at night or during the day, does he notice an erection and relieves this by emptying his bladder.

He recalls a temporary period of masturbation when he was eight or nine years of age. Asked whether he remembered any bed-wetting as a child, his answer was that he did not.

To summarize: he is capable of loving a person of the opposite sex only by excluding every wish for genital contact with her. He suffers from a neurotic inhibition of his sex instinct, which is based upon fear, the origin of which is unknown to him. He rationalizes the unconscious motive of his fear in a typical neurotic manner. He believes that the female sex organ is dangerous and can injure his penis.

We may assume that George had to meet unusual emotional difficulties during the first six years of his life. During that period, his parents' marital relations were so inharmonious that they were finally divorced. This occurred when he was about six years old. He has absolutely no recollection of ever having lived with his parents and his siblings. His first recollection of childhood dates back to the moment when his grandmother took him up the steps to her apartment. He lived with his grandparents until he was eighteen. Later in his childhood he learned that his parents were divorced when he went to his grandmother and that the whole family, consisting of the parents and three children, were separated. His mother remarried, but George cannot recall when this happened. His younger brother went with the mother and her new husband. The elder sister accompanied the father to California, where the latter subsequently remarried.

George was the only child who lived with the grandparents. He remembers that at their home he felt very unhappy. They were very strict and disapproved of his playing with other children. In recalling his life with his grandparents, George had the feeling that he suffered intensely from their lack of warmth, love and understanding. The bright days in his life came once every two weeks, when he was allowed to visit his mother and his younger brother.

It can be assumed that those visits to his mother's home aroused definite mental conflicts in the boy which he could not solve. On the one hand, he suffered from the loveless atmosphere in his grandparents' home; and on the other, he experienced the love of his actual mother only at definite intervals and at the same time had to face the fact that his mother no longer belonged to him, but to two other persons — her new husband and his younger brother. We can assume that the divorce of George's parents determined a significant break in his mental development. He was forced to give up his mother completely to others at that time when he was in need of her to resolve his oedipus conflict. He had to renounce his mother as his love object and had to take as a substitute for her the strict unaffectionate grandmother whom he hated. There is no doubt that at that time George must have suppressed feelings of envy and aggression against his happier rivals.

Like other children in similar situations, George took refuge in masturbation to comfort himself. The aim of such masturbatory acts is not only the enjoyment of pleasurable sensations but even more, a mental economic one. The attempt to achieve genital satisfaction serves the purpose of alleviating the mental tension brought about by the suppression and repression of frustrated love demands as well as aggressive tendencies. In this way the infantile individual releases autoerotically, or rather autoplastically, tendencies which strive for a contact with a definite object in the surrounding world that is denied to him. The child's masturbatory act actually avoids collision between the child driven by instincts and his object. In this way, the infantile masturbatory act can also be described as the first social deed of the child's weak immature personality. Masturbation provides him with a release of incestuous and aggressive, instinctual tendencies, through which otherwise he would collide with the object of his conflict.

George indulged in his masturbatory activities when he was eight or nine years old — until he was caught by his grandmother. Once when he was supposed to be asleep, she found him sitting on his bed masturbating. She scolded him severely. This frightened him. The following morning, both his grandparents came to his bedside and announced in a serious and solemn tone of voice that if he ever masturbated again they would cut off his penis. George recalls that the period immediately following this prohibition was very hard for him. He continued masturbating. As a consequence of the castration threat uttered by his grandparents, he was overwhelmed by feelings of anxiety and guilt after each masturbatory act. George was convinced that they would carry out their threat if they ever caught him again. For months, he was shaken by this mental conflict. His fear was evidently stronger than his desire, for he stopped masturbating completely and has never started it again.

At the time of these inner conflicts, George was afflicted with a serious illness. He had to be operated on for a ruptured appendix, which resulted in general peritonitis. George informed me, in my interview with him, that he felt sick at that time and had severe abdominal pains and that, as a remedy, his grandmother gave him an enema. We know that this enema signified to him a hostile attack by his grandmother and may indeed have been responsible for the serious character of his appendicitis, since the appendix ruptured.

I think I am not mistaken in considering it not a mere coincidence that George was stricken with appendicitis at a time when he had to suppress the masturbatory impulses because of his grandmother's castration threat. It was an attempt of his organism to dispose inwardly of his aggressive destructive tendencies, which he could not discharge either autoplastically by masturbation or alloplastically against the grandmother. I am inclined to assume that George's ruptured appendix marked the time when he definitely repressed his entire infantile genital and aggressive instinctual demands, a repression which later on precipitated his incendiary impulses. This infantile instinctual repression was traumatically increased during adolescence. His sexual impulses reawakened and he then wanted to associate with girls as other boys did. But here again he came into severe conflict with his over-religious grandparents. They considered all forms of social intercourse with girls inappropriate for a boy — before the age of twenty-five. With threats of punishment, they forbade him to associate even with his boy friends when any girls were present.

Both these great traumata were disastrous for his development *because they were associated in his mind with the trauma of the previously mentioned threat of castration*. This castration fear made it impossible for him to satisfy autoerotically, *on his own body,* his desire for the love of his mother and his repressed aggressive reactions against his grandparents.

Of particular significance for the psychoanalytic elucidation are George's compulsive acts in his relation to his father's second wife — his step-mother. During the past two years, he has been living with his father and his step-mother. George and his step-mother became very friendly and he was devoted to her. When I asked him why he was so fond of her, he replied that she "explained so many things to me," things pertaining to sex, and that she gave him instructive books on sex to read, such as *What a Young Man Should Know.* Obviously, she had noticed his immaturity in matters relating to sex, and thought that she could help him through intellectual enlightenment. I do not think it improbable that through his step-mother's encouraging attitude he was able to overcome his timidity toward the opposite sex and thus to make the afore mentioned affectionate contact with a girl.

We may conclude that his step-mother became a really adequate mother-substitute for him. But she was the direct opposite of his first mother-substitute, his stern grandmother. The harshness of the grandparents, especially of the grandmother, and their threat of castration had caused him to repress all sexual desires. The barrier of repression was now loosened by the fact that the new mother-stubstitute alleviated the effect of his grandmother's prohibition. It is quite clear that he transferred to his step-mother the unfulfilled love demands which he had to suppress in relation to his own mother, and which he tried in vain to transfer to his grandmother.

When he now lived with his father and the latter's second wife, the situation which existed during the first six years of his life was repeated. But there was one significant difference between the two situations. The home atmosphere was harmonious, and now he was the only child of his new mother. Old repressed incestuous wishes must have been revived in his unconscious. It was probably as a defense against these wishes that he transferred his love from his step-mother to his girl friend. Typical of the pattern of relations that come about in this way, by simultaneous displacement and defense, George could have no sexual feelings toward his love-mate, because in his unconscious that girl represented a mother-substitute or, more accurately, a step-mother substitute. Therefore his girl friend was sexually taboo.

Psychoanalytic experience has shown that in such situations repressed infantile masturbation impulses become reawakened in the unconscious. These impulses, however, are immediately inhibited since they tend to satisfy forbidden incestuous desires, the more so if, as in George's case, they are paralyzed by the threat of castration. These unconscious autoerotic tendencies therefore had to strive for a substitute gratification. As we remember, there was an intimation of at least latent sexuality whenever George felt the need to urinate. At such times he experienced an erection which disappeared when he emptied his bladder. From this we may conclude that under the threat of castration he had regressed *from the level of genital object love to that of urethral autoerotism.*

I consider George's incendiary acts an unconscious compulsive attempt to find a substitute gratification for his reawakened and again repressed infantile masturbatory impulse. Due to the blockage of genital libido, this impulse had regressed to the level of infantile urethral autoerotism. I was led to this assumption by evaluating the actual occurrences which preceded George's incendiary acts.

I might remind the reader that George, on his father's invitation, had come to live with him and his second wife. During the years preceding his incendiarism, George had been employed as a night clerk in a hotel. He was in the habit of going home every morning and having breakfast with his step-mother and his father. It was on one of these mornings that an abnormal exaltation was aroused in him for the first time by the sight of fire.

After breakfast, he had gone to the rear of the house and had seen a grass fire in a vacant lot some distance away. He was overwhelmed by the danger of the situation and thrilled with the prospect of putting out the fire. He ran to the telephone and called the fire department. When the firemen arrived, George eagerly helped them to extinguish the fire. He could not understand why he felt so elated. The experience was so exciting that afterwards he could think of nothing else but to experience it once more. The fact that this first fire was in an empty lot — where no one else was present — impelled him to look about for isolated lots which he could set on fire, unobserved. He had the feeling that this would still his unrest.

He did not drive back to the hotel that afternoon, but felt impelled to search for empty lots. He found one that suited his purpose, set fire to it, and immediately was overwhelmed with feelings of anxiety and guilt. He could only think: "What will happen to me now?" He ran away and hid nearby. As soon as the firemen appeared, however, he rushed back to the scene and worked furiously to help put out the fire. This activity relieved his mental strain. In all, he repeated his incendiary act five times. And in every instance his procedure was the same: he first looked about for a vacant lot where he would be unobserved, then set fire to it. Again the subsequent reaction was one of dread and guilt and the feeling of relief when he was able to assist in extinguishing the flames. In each instance, however, he managed to get close to the fire chief. His presence at all these grass fires was observed by the chief, who became suspicious and had George taken into custody.

There was no doubt that George *unconsciously* wanted to be caught, for in all the repeated acts of incendiarism he also used his father's automobile to drive to the vacant lots. This car was painted red and was very conspicuous. He drove the car onto the lot, set fire to the dry grass, then drove away from the lot, called the fire department and waited near the fire for the firemen. Naturally not only he personally, but his car as well became conspicuous. The fire chief discovered the traces of car tires on the lot, measured them, compared them with those of George's car and George was trapped.

I have no doubt that George's whole attitude toward his incendiary act is a repetition of his former conflict about masturbation. It is typical of persons suffering from an unconscious masturbation complex to become excited when they find themselves unobserved in isolated places. This situation invariably revives the temptation to do something that is forbidden. For George, the incendiary act — a symbolical representation of masturbation — became compulsive, just because it was against the law. This nameless fear which overcame him after setting fires corresponds to his earlier castration fear. His efforts to make himself noticed by the fire chief in helping to extinguish the fire can be interpreted as an unconscious wish to atone for his sin and to regain the love of a father image.

In conclusion we can say that George repressed his impulses toward genital masturbation out of his fear of the threatened castration. He sought an inner escape from this conflict by regressing to the urethral phase of his libidinal development. Whenever his bladder was full, he produced an erection, which was relieved by urinating. Now in a symbolic repetition of this process George felt the compulsive need to splash water on the fire, thus to extinguish an excitation which he himself had kindled.

The sympathetic, or may we call it, the seductive attitude of the step-mother, had reawakened in George the impulse toward genital masturbation; psychoanalytic experience permits us to assume that the actual situation which was associated with the precipitation of George's pyromaniacal impulse must have been of particular symbolic significance in this respect. He was sitting at the breakfast table with his father and his step-mother. Then he saw the fire. Eating together with a couple very often has, as we know from dream symbolism, the unconscious connotation of taking part in the primal scene, i.e., the sexual relations between the parents, and with oneself as spectator. Seeing the fire behind his father's house and becoming aware of the power of destruction this fire had, George was also immediately overwhelmed by the idea that he could extinguish by water the destruction which threatened him and the others. The excitement and relief he felt at the same time was due to the fact that the danger is external which can be met. This excitement and release associated themselves with his experience that sexual tension (erection) can be released by urinating.

Therefore the act of incendiarism can only be considered as genuine pyromania when it is considered in its entirety, to set the object on fire and also to extinguish the fire. This gives the pyromaniacal act the significance of a masturbatory act, projected into the outside world. What is the thrill which George told us impelled him to repeat the incendiary act? In my opinion, the sensation of thrill reflects the triumph of extinguishing the fire through water, i.e., urine; a discharge of sexual tension is possible, a discharge which is socially accepted and for which one cannot be punished because it neutralizes the possible damage. Setting the grass on fire must have meant to George kindling his sexual excitement, and extinguishing it by water must have provided him with the sensation of an organic discharge, which he could not find as a child because of his grandparents' interference and later on because of his inhibitions.

As far as the unconscious content of the masturbation fantasies are concerned which he released in his incendiary acts, we are entitled to assume that they represented his oedipus situation. The grass lot symbolized his mother, as well as his step-mother, and also his grandmother. By using his father's car to drive onto this lot, he identified himself with the father and his powerful penis, performed the act of incest on his mother, but at the same time attempted to destroy her, particularly when she assumed the image of the grandmother as a frustrating love object. The fire chief symbolized the father, as well as the grandfather, by whom George was afraid of being castrated and to whom he had to prove that he had no incestuous intention toward the mother object.

This is the extent of the material I gathered from the two interviews with George. I felt entitled to assume that a pyromaniacal act was a substitute for a repressed act of masturbation and the connection of this act with urethral erotism, which counteracted the object-destructive energies, gave the pyromaniac his specific opportunity to re-extrovert his repressed oedipus conflict. However, from the viewpoint of psychoanalytic theory, one important part of the development of this pyromaniac remains unclear. This is that George remembered his childhood masturbation so well and the castration threat which, as I had reason to infer, made him repress and forget the masturbation tendencies. This is contrary to all our psychoanalytic experiences. We would have expected that a castration threat in childhood would have effected a complete repression of the masturbatory impulse and would have caused the castration threat itself to be repressed and forgotten. We know how difficult it is in our analyses to make conscious this whole repressed conflict of the forgotten masturbatory tendencies.

Perhaps we may discover by comparing this case with other cases, that it is characteristic of pyromania and differentiates it from a neurosis that the castration threat does not become repressed. In this way the fear of an external danger can be displaced to the destructive element of fire. The other problem which seems to contradict psychoanalytic theory, namely that this pyromaniac had not repressed his infantile masturbation conflict, found some clarification through information given me by the probation officer to whose care George was entrusted.

Very fortunately this probation officer was a student of psychoanalysis and decided to try to help George to become aware of and to understand his problems as much as possible. This officer, because of his own psychoanalytic knowledge and because of reading my report was not satisfied to merely watch George to see whether he would set fire to another empty lot and try to persuade him not to do so. The probation officer decided to try to help George to uncover the unconscious roots behind his compulsion. In these interviews he also made use of the technique of interpreting dreams, on the basis of George's free associations.

Surprisingly, George told this psychotherapist that he had lied to me about his sex life; that he had masturbated, not only in childhood but also later on, throughout his life and that he had had several affairs with girls, among them real intercourse. The reason for not telling me about these sexual debauches in the first place seemed to be the fact that I was a man representing the court. His dreams showed that the judge and his grandparents and I were all one person and from this person he had to conceal his sexual strivings because of his castration fear. Therefore, in lying to me, he seemed to be repeating his experiences with the grandparents during his childhood. He had lied to them for fear of being castrated and he expected the same punishment from the judge and me.

At first sight, George's confession seemed to shake the whole ground on which the structure of my conclusions was built. However, in the period of his treatment afterwards, it turned out that George had lied to the probation officer and not to me. The probation officer had become to George's unconscious the image of his younger brother, whom he had hated because he could live with the mother, and George admitted that he had invented his sexual exploits — that he had wanted to shock him, and that he had wanted to brag to him of his sexual potency.

There was one point however, on which George *had* lied to me, and this point, in clearing up the puzzle of George's unrepressed castration threat, actually proved a confirmation of my psychoanalytic theoretical assumption. George now had to admit to the probation officer that he could not remember anything about having masturbated during his childhood or having been punished for masturbation.

Had the defendant been a student of psychoanalysis and not, as a court psychiatrist described him, "of dull mentality", we might have thought that he invented the classical masturbation conflict with its accompanying castration threat, because he knew about it from reading case histories and had used it to fool the judge; but he was a truck driver and no student of psychoanalysis.

There was another lie, implied in his interview with me, which I consider closely associated with this invention of the masturbation conflict in his childhood. When I asked him about bed-wetting, he denied any recollection of such experiences. In his treatment it came out that he had again felt compelled to lie, because he was afraid of me. He really remembered that during his whole childhood, up to the time he had his ruptured appendicitis, he was suffering from enuresis. This was the real castration threat, but he was never threatened with castration by the grandparents for masturbation — rather he was threatened with castration for wetting his pants and his bed. Once his grandfather showed him a knife with which he would cut off his penis.

The experience he mentioned in his interview with me, of his grand-parents one morning holding some kind of a solemn trial with him, he con-firmed in one of his psychoanalytic sessions, when he remembered more material, namely that his grandparents had arranged some sort of court session with other people present, to make it appear similar to a real judicial procedure. This pseudo-court at that time condemned him to castration, but put him on probation. However, as he later verified, this was not for masturbation, but for bed-wetting.

George brought up some childhood material which showed how his enuresis conflict brought him in contact with fire. At the time when he stopped bed-wetting, after the castration trial and the appendicitis, he developed a great interest in the village fire house. A dream and associations showed that this fascination was stimulated by his admiration and love for one particularly large fire engine which appeared to him like a person, because it had lots of water inside of it. The engine he saw in the dream and particularly the nozzle of the hose attached to it, reminded him of a penis. Projecting himself into a fire engine helped him to keep repressed the urge to urinate against his grandparents' prohibition. He also remembered that at that time he had fleeting fantasies of being able to put out fires, just by urinating. Moreover he reported remembering that around this same time he had the idea that intercourse between women and men consisted of their urinating into each other.

The analysis showed that he also identified the fire engine and its big hose with his father's and grandfather's penises. We now understand why he used his father's red truck when he drove onto the grass field and com-mitted his incendiary acts. His father's red painted truck was a substitute for the loved fire engine of his childhood. The emotional relationship which George built up as a boy to this one fire engine, had a similar value to that described by Erikson in the play configuration of children.[2] By identifying himself with the fire engine with the big hose, which everyone admired not in spite of, but just because of the fact that it eliminated a great amount of water, he could overcome his fear of his protracted enuresis and imagine that his bed-wetting was an act of great social valor. Bed-wetting obviously had for him the meaning of urinating on his mother out of erotic desires, but it also meant the discharging of his pent-up destructive desires against his grandmother. These aggressive destructive desires against his sadistic grandmother again proved to be of a devouring character. And finally the analysis of this incendiarist served to assure me of the correctness of my theory of the devouring instinct.

---

[2] Hamburger, E. H.: Configurations in Play—Clinical Notes. *Psa. Quart.*, VI, 1937.

The patient had the following dream:

> He was in his grandparents' home in the East, and a small
> bull-dog was let loose and ran up the stairs toward a
> woman who was crouched on the first landing. The woman
> called for help. He looked and saw that the dog had a
> tailor's measuring tape tied around its mouth so that it
> couldn't bite.

Of his associations, I mention only that the woman on the staircase was his
grandmother, whom he hated, and of whom he was afraid. She deprived
him of all pleasure and had particularly humiliated him for his bed-wetting.
Therefore in his dream he let the dog loose against her but then became
frightened and had to tie its mouth with a measuring tape. The patient had
the feeling that he was in a similar mental condition when he lit the fires.
He first unleashed this destructive element and then, afraid of what would
happen, he tried to ameliorate the effect. The fire becomes identified with
the devouring dog and the patient also identifies himself with the dog.

Another dream:

> Patient is driving a truck down a steep grade. It is going
> fast and at first he is very happy. All of a sudden one of
> the front tires blows out, the truck goes over an embank-
> ment and the cab of the truck burns up his right side in
> the vicinity of his appendix. He is taken to the hospital and
> treated for his injury. Afterwards the highway patrol takes
> him back to the scene of the accident and he must explain
> how it happened.

I shall omit mentioning all of the patient's associations to this dream
and state only that the dream represents a symbolic condensation of the
criminal act of incendiarism, his appendicitis and appendectomy. Going
down a steep grade is a well-known symbol of the act of autoerotism. The
injury to the front wheels indicates an identification of this autoerotism with
the act of self-destruction, by turning the erotic energies against oneself.
The self-injury manifested in the right side of his abdomen, his appendix,
is caused by the fire which he had brought about himself. The surgeon is
his grandfather as well as the judge. The place of the accident is the empty
lot, the hidden place where he performed autoerotism.

This dream and its associations show that I was correct in assuming
that George's psycho-physical organism attempted to consume the repressed
hatred against the grandmother by displacing it from the mouth, which in
the symbolic dream about the dog he had tied with a measuring tape,
to the deeper inner strata of the gastro-intestinal system, the region of the
coecum.

Was I really wrong when I interpreted these furtive acts as a substitute for an act of masturbation? I do not think so, but here we can only

conjecture. We know that the enuresis complex, manifested relatively late in a boy of eight or ten, means regression to an earlier stage of libido development and a retreat from the phallic stage to the stage of urethral erotism. Usually the urethral erotism is revived when the phallus, which children of that age believe is common to both sexes, is threatened by castration. Therefore we are entitled to assume that George must have reacted to the separation from his mother with early infantile masturbation, to compensate for the loss of his mother. I have reason to believe that this must have been between his third and sixth year of life. George, as you may remember, told me that he came to live with his grandparents when he was six years old, because at that time his parents were divorced, and that he did not remember anything about the first six years of his life. However, his father testified in court, that he was divorced when the boy was three years old and that was the age at which the boy went to live with his grandparents. What he completely repressed therefore, were the first three years of his living with his grandparents. I assume that the complete amnesia for these three years is due to the fact that at that time he was caught playing with his penis by his grandmother, was punished, repressed the masturbation impulse and replaced it with bed-wetting.

This looks like a screen memory and the proof of my assumption is that the patient in his treatment remembered with great joy and in detail a little toy wagon which was his favorite toy in his grandparents' home. He recognized in his analysis that this little toy wagon represented to him his lost mother. I think we are also entitled to assume that this little toy wagon found its imaginary resurrection in the big fire engine with the imposing hose, a personalized object with which little George attempted to identify himself and which also represented his mother, whom he could not have, the phallic mother, by whose existence the reality of castration is denied.

DELINQUENT MECHANISMS IN A
FOUR-YEAR-OLD GIRL

By Editha Sterba, Ph.D.

(*Detroit, Mich.*)

August Aichhorn's theory of the libidinal structure of the neurotic delinquent, which he formulated and illustrated in *Wayward Youth* twenty-three years ago, continues to illuminate our understanding of the behavior problems of such cases.

We wish to present the following report on the delinquent trends shown by a little girl at the unusually early age of four, because they demonstrate so clearly the mechanisms which Aichhorn pointed out as characteristic of youthful delinquents.*

Sally Green and her mother were referred to the social worker by the management of the housing project in which they lived because the neighbors had complained of the child's sexually perverted activities.

In the first interview Mrs. Green was extremely defensive and answered all questions slowly and reluctantly. She admitted that during the previous summer she had several times found Sally with her clothes off, playing on the stairs with some little boys. She had seen these boys exhibiting themselves and believed it was they who had taken off her clothes. Her limited understanding and rigid methods of dealing with the child were illustrated by her procedure after these incidents. She kept Sally indoors all the time, was very strict but never discussed the episodes with her.

She was much upset by having been referred to the social worker for help with Sally and very defensive in stressing that she had never had any trouble with her other children, a nine-year-old boy and two girls, aged ten and eleven. The social worker therefore advised her to ask for more details from the neighbors who had made the complaints.

Mrs. Green did so and they told her that they had several times seen Sally sucking the penis of one of the little boys. She spanked the child and

---

* This case was treated under the close supervision of the author by Miss Anna Katz, an analyzed and analytically trained social worker, to whom the author is greatly indebted for putting at her disposal this material for publication.

102

told her that she had done something very naughty, and Sally cried and promised never to do it again. This promise she repeated spontaneously thereafter every time she left the house.

Mrs. Green then again brought Sally to the social worker and furnished a few meager details about the child's developmental history. Sally had been breast-fed for two weeks only, after which she was given a bottle because the mother had no milk. It was very difficult to find a formula for the child, who vomited considerably and developed rickets, which required a special diet. As a result of the rickets, she did not walk until she was sixteen months old. She talked at normal age and sucked her thumb slightly. Sally slept in her parents' bed until she was a year old and then shared a bedroom with her sisters. Her toilet training seemed to have been completed when she was three years old but she still wet the bed about once a week, which her mother considered merely a sign of being overtired. Her mother also reported that Sally did not get along well with her siblings, that she was easily irritated and cried a great deal.

Mrs. Green admitted reluctantly that her marriage was unhappy. Her husband drank constantly, was unfaithful and she had often considered divorce. She had recently changed her mind, however, and was trying to console herself by strict observance of the rules of the Baptist Church. They had always been poor and unable to meet the needs of the family.

Sally was an attractive and very lively child, normally developed for her age, but tense in her mother's presence. She was neither shy nor fearful when her mother left the room nor did she mind her leaving. She ate an orange which she had brought with her, then cleaned herself meticulously and began to play with the dolls. She betrayed her main interest immediately by commenting that the boy and girl dolls had their pants on. She wanted to undress all the dolls and began by taking the pants off the boy doll. While doing so, she repeatedly asked permission, saying constantly, "Can I do this? Is it all right? Isn't it bad?" She played that a boy had thrown a girl down and that the girl had got hurt after which she spanked the boy for being "bad".

Certain themes appeared repeatedly in these games. A baby doll was constantly ill, suffering from a fall or a stomach ache. The worker had to be the doctor and take care of the doll. Frequently the baby doll was put to bed between the two larger dolls, or Sally herself would crawl into the doll bed, pretend to be "Mamma", put the doll on top of her genital region, and then go to sleep. In putting the dolls to bed, she sometimes interchanged their sexes, pretending the boy was a girl and vice versa.

The mother had told us that she never allowed Sally to go out alone or to play outdoors. Sally now complained to the worker that her mother never let her play with boys. She often played a game of "going bye-bye", in which she became very excited and once climbed out the low window of the treatment room. The social worker had to climb out too and Sally immensely enjoyed playing out of doors with her. This game was repeated and each time she became more active, daring and restless when she was outdoors. During the treatment hour, whenever she saw a boy playing outside, she would say: "There's my boy friend." During this same period she once succeeded in slipping away from her mother at home. She ran away with a two-year-old boy, and was later located by the police who had been called by the boy's parents.

After the first four weekly interviews an attempt was made to evaluate Sally's problems. It obviously was not possible at this time to verify the story of Sally's alleged sex offenses.

The other mothers had used Mrs. Green as a scapegoat by shifting the blame of their own children's sex play because she was too timid and too inflexible to be able to cope with them.

But the interviews indicated the effects on Sally of her mother's rigid regime with her. Her tenseness and her constant game of "going bye-bye" clearly referred to her lack of freedom and of all normal play outlets at home. We foresaw that the tension due to these inhibiting methods could only create fresh difficulties when it was released by Sally's going to school. We therefore hoped to prevent Sally from developing more delinquent symptoms by working with the mother to change her attitude and understanding of the problem.

Sally had frankly expressed her liking for the worker in these exploratory interviews and with this good relationship established, we decided to begin intensive treatment through weekly interviews with both the mother and the child.

In the weeks preceding the summer vacation these interviews with the mother brought only slight results. She did modify her regime to the extent of allowing Sally to play outdoors under supervision. She relaxed her extreme standards of cleanliness by now allowing her to play with sand. But she refused to consider putting Sally into a nursery school for the summer months.

Her capacity to understand any explanation of the child's problem remained primitive and she countered all such attempts to bring her insight by insisting that it was the other children who had tried to seduce Sally.

The meager details of her own history which these interviews elicited caused her such tension that she always managed to skip the next appointment after revealing any. She had married at seventeen, and had always been shy and unable to assert herself and gave the impression that the slightest freedom of expression was unbearably threatening to her.

In a following treatment hour, Sally was given plasticine to model with.

She liked it very much and while playing with it began to talk with great excitement about "sucking the pee-pee" (her name for the penis). When the worker asked her whether she had ever taken a boy's penis in her mouth, she denied ever having done it, and covered her face, saying, "It's not nice! Not nice." But in the next interview she brought a small bottle filled with water and made a great fuss about sucking from this bottle and letting the baby doll suck it.

As mentioned before, in her play the dolls were constantly supposed to be sick, or to have suffered from falls. At the same time Sally bruised herself repeatedly by falling from swings or slides. She admitted for the first time that she was anxious, and pretended that boys hit or pushed her. Once when a boy approached her on the playground and touched the swing on which she was sitting, she said, "It's mine," ran to her mother for help and cried excessively. Afterwards she complained that her eyes had been poked out, and that the eye doctor had to poke them in again. She mentioned her father rarely, but said that he had made her right arm sore, and also that he shot her, but refused any explanation of what this meant. In direct connection with the fantasy of being hurt by the boys she fantasied extensively about snakes. She pretended that a huge limb of a tree in front of the treatment room was a snake, and that it was going to bite her. She made snakes out of clay, put them in bed, and wanted to take them home with her. Once she flattened out a snake by stepping on it, and told the worker that she wanted to flatten it out and eat it. But then she stopped and said, "It's not nice". When the worker asked her why, she was suddenly blocked and said that she could not talk, that her throat hurt her.

She played many games in which she pretended to kill the worker, who had to let her head hang down as if she were dead. When she played that she killed other people at this time, it was always a man who was the object of her attacks.

Her conflict and her confusion about the role of the male and the female also became apparent. She often put boy's clothes on the girl doll and vice versa, and even called some of her drawings, "boy-girl".

She referred voluntarily to her bed-wetting by suddenly saying to the doll, "Don't pee in the bed". When asked why she herself sometimes did so, she answered proudly and happily, "Because I want to".

Her relationship to the worker continued to be a very positive one. She emphasized how much she liked to come to play and although nothing had been said about the reasons for her coming, she seemed to accept the routine without question. When the worker asked unwelcome questions, she would simply start to play and say, "I can't talk".

In the Fall, Sally started kindergarten. She went to school alone which at first she did not like but she soon went without difficulty. We decided not to make any contact with Sally's school in order to avoid drawing the teacher's attention to Sally's conduct. It was also decided not to press the mother for any material which she did not offer voluntarily.

During these first weeks of kindergarten, Mrs. Green was very relieved that the school had made no complaints about Sally, but she reported to the worker that lately Sally had begun to fight back when attacked. She added in this context, that she had always interfered in her children's fights in the home but had to admit that her interference greatly increased the fights. For the first time she was willing to talk a little more freely about the hardships of her daily life.

Although Sally seemed inhibited in the first interview after starting school, and was afraid to talk about boys, she showed slight changes reflecting the increased aggressiveness which her mother reported. She took the initiative in asking for scissors to cut out paper dolls. She still maintained that boys were hitting her. Once when she came home stained with paint, she boldly told her mother that the boys had pushed her into the paint. When the worker would not allow her to take home a toy, she said for the first time that she did not want to come back again, that she was mad at her and pretended to whip her.

When playing with a boy doll in overalls, she said that she was a boy because she had overalls too. She took off the doll's clothes, pretending that he had to go to the toilet, tentatively put her finger in his crotch, and when the worker made no comment, she pressed it harder, saying that this was his butt, and then made him go to the toilet. After this she wanted to give the boy doll a ride on a stuffed horse, and became absorbed in the latter, commenting on his tail and name. She became quite wild, calling the horse "dog" and "horse" alternately, and made barking and neighing noises as she turned the horse against the worker to bite her. Sally then began to bite herself on the arms, saying that she liked this, put the horse's mouth against her body, pressing it against her own nipples and putting it in the crook of her elbow, as if trying to make it bite her in these places. She kissed the horse and caught his mouth in a fierce bite, which she held for several seconds. Sally abandoned herself completely, was almost beside herself with excitement, and concluded this scene by turning the horse over and kissing him with a long kiss in the place where the genitals of a stallion would ordinarily have been.

In her interview the mother reported that Sally often told stories about having been hit by a boy, which were completely unfounded. Interestingly enough, the mother said at this point that she herself had always preferred the company of boys, girls seemed noisy and silly to her, boys more quiet. She could always talk with her father, but it was difficult for her to talk with older women.

The mother again tried to minimize the importance of Sally's bed-wetting. She had not wet the bed during the summer, had wet a little during the Spring, but now wet the bed once or twice a week, though irregularly. She herself had never punished Sally seriously for this but her husband had recently whipped the child. None of her other children had been a bed-wetter except the boy who had wet occasionally when he was four years old.

She mentioned her husband rarely but now admitted that he had a violent temper. It was hard for her to stand up to him when he was angry, even when she felt she was right. Lately he had tried to control himself. She added that his outbursts did not seem to affect the children particularly.

She was concerned over the kindergarten teacher's report that Sally had to be kept occupied all the time because she got into mischief when left to herself. Her behavior had changed, she no longer got on so well with the other children and hit them. She was also trying to slip away from her mother to play outdoors. This intense desire disturbed Mrs. Green who wished at all costs to prevent Sally from being exposed to further sex play with boys.

Since Sally steadfastly refused to talk on all topics connected with boys, the worker now pressed the mother to admit that she had told Sally not to talk in the interviews. She said that she had often told Sally that God would punish her if she engaged in sex play and that she had frequently told her she was a bad girl. Her father had also hit her because of what she had done with boys. She finally realized that her threats may have been very frightening to the child and her attitude made Sally afraid to discuss anything with her and that she must try to change.

The worker made use of this bit of progress to obtain the mother's reluctant permission to talk to Sally about the difference between boys and girls. It was hard to convince her that Sally needed this enlightenment. She had enforced the utmost modesty in her household by keeping her son and daughters completely separated. She finally admitted that she herself had been given frightening explanations of sex as a child and that most of her information before marriage had depended on guess work. The only information she could give her oldest daughter about menstruation had been a religious one; that Jesus had placed a seed in her body which some-times would develop into a baby, and she would become sick regularly as all women did.

The worker's offer to talk to the older daughter at last seemed to convince Mrs. Green of the advantages of accepting the worker's help in such matters.

During the next interviews, despite Sally's unwillingness to talk freely, she nevertheless revealed new material. When she saw the boys in the adjoining school, she said she was afraid of boys, that they could hit her, that they could pull her drawers down and poke her eyes out. When asked what she had done or wanted to do with boys, she refused to talk anymore, said she had a headache and that her throat was sore. Finally, after much reassurance, she admitted that her mother had forbidden her to talk of such things, and that she would begin to bleed if she talked. She showed her vaccination scar and called it an injury. During one of these talks about what boys can do, she actually did cut her finger with a knife and seemed very gratified by the resulting attention and bandaging. When her mother came, she exhibited her cut and asked to have a tooth pulled. In the next appointment she wanted to cut herself again.

She was given repeated reassurance that nothing would happen if she talked about the bad things she had done. She repeated that she was afraid her arm would start to bleed if she talked, but nevertheless she showed that she had accepted the assurance that she could talk without ensuing punishment by saying that she did not need the knife to cut herself anymore.

In the next interview, for the first time Sally brought her own scissors and magazine to cut out. As soon as her mother left, she announced that she could talk. She then emphatically stated that her father was dead, and that her mother had killed him, but, as usual, she refused any further explanation.

After this Sally started undressing the boy and girl dolls and interchanging their clothes. All of a sudden she tried to put on the boy doll's overalls, saying that she was a boy, and found it hard to accept the fact that they were too small for her. At the same time she began to talk about Johnny, the little boy with whom she had chiefly been engaged in sex activity: she did like him, she said, and she did not like him.

For several interviews after this Sally did not want to take off her leggings. She insisted that she had to keep them on, and dragged them around unfastened for as long as twenty minutes. She was told repeatedly that she wanted to keep her leggings on because she wanted to be a boy, and that she was afraid that taking them off would show that she was a girl.

When she saw a jeep among the toys she showed great interest in it. She said her brother had received a toy jeep for Christmas, but she had not, because she had been bad. She had wet in her bed because she wanted to. She admitted that she had done it because she was angry at her parents. In all her games with the dolls at this time it was always the boy doll who wet the bed. She wanted to punish and spank the doll, and then said with glee that he wanted to wet the bed. But it was interesting that she always made the boy sit on the toilet like a girl, and that when he wet himself he had to put on girl's clothes.

The repeated interpretation that she wanted to keep on her leggings because she thought that wearing leggings would make her a boy made her gradually give up wearing them during the treatment sessions. She took them off at the beginning of the interview and would proudly display her skirt to the worker. Finally she even refused to put them back on at the end of the interview.

The leggings also served a protection purpose. In one hour in which she again refused to take them off, she showed great fear of a piece of candy with a red filling. She called the red filling a worm and acted as if it had blood on it. She said she was afraid of the worm, which she called a snake, because it would bite her. When asked where, she pointed to her genitals. When given the interpretation that she was afraid the snake could bite off the penis, which, as a boy, she pretended to have, she took off her leggings at once.

Her aggression against boys now became quite apparent. Not only did she talk and play that she was hitting and kicking boys, but she again made plasticine snakes and excitedly flattened them out and stamped on them. She also threatened the worker in her games and attacked a boy doll whom she had named after the worker's brother.

She now said that she was mad at her father because he had cut off her mother's head with his tongue and had knocked off her neck. She also played games in which the father was killed in a car accident.

Another form of aggression against boys was biting. Once when expressing feelings against a boy she put clay on her forefinger and began to bite it savagely. Here she was told again that she wanted to take his penis away from him and destroy it because she envied boys this possession. As first she rejected this interpretation, then began to chant loudly, "I did bite it! I did bite it!"

The repeated interpretations given in these hours brought about a change in the material. For the first time she said it was not "nice" to wet her bed. Though her mother had always minimized the importance of this wetting, she did admit that she always picked Sally up at eleven to take her to the bathroom and that recently the child had wakened by herself and asked to be taken to the toilet.

During this period some of Sally's fears took a new form of expression. Although she had always been an excellent eater, she now said that she had to throw up, which her mother confirmed. Sally's only explanation was that she had swallowed orange pits. After repeated interpretations that she did not want to be a girl, she suddenly asked the worker to look down her throat, saying that there was a little belly button (the uvula) in the opening. She pretended the pits might turn into a baby and that the doctor who had come when she was vomiting, had made her very sick and had given her a pill and a doll.

With this change in material, there was a corresponding change in her whole attitude. She talked less about hurting boys and more about girls. The mother also reported that there had been no return of the original problem and no complaints from the school. Sally was getting along much better with the other children and had even acquired some girl friends who often called for her, and who seemed to like her. Sally was also beginning to be more cooperative in helping about the house and she seemed noticeably less tense and more settled.

At the beginning of spring another of Sally's symptoms, however, became more conspicuous. During the previous summer her mother had mentioned quite casually that Sally often took other children's bicycles and rode off on them without any apparent sense of wrongdoing. Now Mrs. Green brought a bicycle to the session which Sally had brought home from school, refusing to say from whom she had taken it. Sally was not ashamed of having taken it, only angry with her mother for wanting to return it. Mrs. Green admitted that this bicycle-stealing had already been a problem in the previous summer but as always she had never discussed it with Sally.

Since these stealing episodes were now becoming more frequent, we decided to interpret this behavior to Sally as one of her ways of gratifying her wish to take something away from boys. At the same time the worker suggested that Sally be given her brother's skates.

She reacted to this interpretation with a flare of aggression against the worker. She called her names, said she hated her and made a wolf out of clay, who bit the worker. Although she was still storming when her mother came, and began to say she did not like her either, she abruptly switched this remark back to the worker. Only in her fantasy play did she dare to pretend that she was killing her mother. But now she admitted that she feared boys would hit her in retaliation for stealing their bicycles.

During the interviews prior to the summer vacation, Sally showed definite improvement. Only once did she slip away to visit with a girl cousin of her own age whom Sally's mother considered very dangerous company, because, as she said, this little girl had tried to play with herself. Once she took change from her father's purse in order to buy candy, and another time stole some potato chips from a store.

Sally now seemed to accept her female role. She showed much interest in her clothes, often tried to comb her own hair and complained because she sometimes had to wear her brother's cast-off clothing.

She had been told repeatedly that nothing could change her into a boy, neither eating candy which she was given in her hours, nor stealing things, and that despite her complaints about her injuries, that nothing had been taken away from her because nothing had been there in the first place. During one of these sessions, while playing with clay, she said very pointedly, "Look, I have a hole". It was interesting to note that after this period, her marked oral greediness diminished considerably.

The mother was very pleased with Sally's improvement. She was no longer afraid of her father, liked him a lot and wanted him to stay home from work to take care of her. She no longer stole bicycles but was getting along well with other children who let her use their bicycles. When she played house, she not only took the role of the mother, but also let a boy playmate be the father, which she had never done before. There had been no bed-wetting for a long time, and she was getting along well with her siblings. The mother admitted that she had babied Sally too much, and that she was now trying not to. Mrs. Green herself seemed more relaxed in these interviews, and better able to manage her children.

Since there was no change in her good adjustment during the two weeks before the summer vacation, and Sally had been seen for a year and a half, it was decided not to resume treatment if the summer brought no relapse. In the Fall, Sally and her mother came to report that she was still well adjusted and the treatment was concluded.

Discussion

In discussing the course of Sally's treatment, we may assume that her delinquency syndrome was undoubtedly present at the time she was referred to the worker. This syndrome was expressed in her stealing bicycles, her running away, her attempts to seduce and undress other children, the sex play with little boys and taking their penises in her mouth, her continuous fighting with her siblings and other children and her bed-wetting. Her mother's extreme defensiveness made it impossible to know exactly how much of Sally's delinquent behavior was manifest at the time she was referred to us.

Sally's case material seems to us to present exceptionally revealing insight into the structure of her libidinal development, especially in regard to the preoedipal mother fixation and its complex ramifications. It also provides unusually undisguised material illustrating the transition from her mother fixation to a father fixation with its manifestations of penis wish and envy. And finally it gives us insight into the development of her superego at this stage.

At the beginning of her interviews Sally clearly identified with her mother in the preoedipal relationship. She plays the mother role in all her games, gives her doll a mother's care and is as meticulous in sweeping and cleaning as is her mother in the home. She also shows that she identifies with her mother's standards in her constant asking permission to play her games and in her judgments that this or that is "not nice". Her identification even made her stop her play and become stiff and rigid like the mother as soon as the latter came to take her home. Her refusal to talk which persisted throughout the greater part of the treatment was not only obedience to the mother's orders not to talk about sexual matters, but also an identification with the mother's own great difficulty in expressing herself in general as well as about sexual matters in particular.

Mrs. Green's own upbringing was not only responsible for her own inflexibility but made her set exacting standards for her children's conduct and left her without any understanding of their emotional needs.

In regard to the stage of Sally's libidinal development we find that her fixation to her mother was predominantly oral. We would expect strong oral tendencies in this child, quite apart from the possible constitutional element suggested by her father's alcoholism. She had reacted to weaning with extreme vomiting and since there was prolonged difficulty about the formula, this experience was possibly very traumatic. She displayed the same oral tendencies both in her play and in the undue greediness of her demands for candy during her hours, and obviously in her oral sexual practices for which she had been referred to us.

It may be that the strict modesty maintained in Sally's home deprived her of any opportunity to satisfy her curiosity concerning the difference between the sexes. The mother may also have overlooked Sally's early play with boys on the streets since she herself had preferred to play with boys as a child.

Although we know that sexual curiosity is a sign of the beginning of the phallic phase, and although Sally seemed really confused about the difference between the sexes, we nevertheless feel that her constant interchange of the sexes expressed her own ambivalence about which role she should accept.

Throughout this oral stage she was unable to express any aggression toward her mother. However, we consider her fear of bleeding if she talked a manifestation of oral aggression turned against herself.

But as the treatment progressed her material showed evidence of the beginning of the phallic phase and here her aggressions became more overt. Her fear that boys would hit her changed. She began to hit and attack them. She wanted to castrate them as she showed when she pressed the "butt" (penis) and when she wanted to bite off the boy's penis. The clay snakes which she made now were bitten and flattened out and these sadistic impulses toward the male sex culminated in her death wish against her father when she stated that her mother had killed him.

Her pretended ignorance in regard to parental sex relationship was disproved when she claimed that her father had cut off her mother's head with his tongue. This might be a sadistic interpretation of a fellatio observation.

During the period of penis envy, her aggression towards her mother was more nearly overt. She expressed it in several ways; by wetting the bed because she was angry at her for not having made her a boy, and by outbursts of rage against the worker when confronted with the interpretation that she was pretending to be a boy by wearing her leggings.

This interpretation was followed by the symptom of stealing. One should remember that she stole not only bicycles, but money from her father's purse and food from the store. She attempted to obtain by force what the interpretation prevented her from obtaining by fantasy.

Throughout all such manifestations of her aggression, she showed many masochistic tendencies in her propensity to hurt herself in minor accidents, in wanting to have a tooth pulled and even in deliberately cutting herself during treatment. This masochism reflected her mother's submissive attitude toward her choleric and intemperate husband, and further corroborated Sally's identification with her mother.

Diagnosing Sally as a case of waywardness may seem hardly justifiable at her preoedipal level of development. Most girls show slight tendencies to steal and to attack boys during the phallic phase. It was the continuous and impulsive character of Sally's symbolic play during treatment which made us consider these symptoms a sign of abnormal libidinal development.

Sally's anamnesis presented all the features characteristic of the early history of juvenile delinquents. The father was alcoholic and had a violent temper. The mother was rigid and inhibited. There was serious conflict in the marriage and little agreement about educational methods. The mother was herself ambivalent in her treatment of Sally. She babied her to stop the inconvenience of her bed-wetting but was too repressed to show her any affection.

Sally's insatiable pleasure craving and her demands for immediate gratification are also typical, as are her early feeding traumata and the resulting oral fixation.

At four, Sally's superego formation already showed the defects characteristic of juvenile delinquents. She constantly repeated her mother's strict demands without letting them inhibit her from satisfying her irresistible pleasure drive.

That Sally's symptoms of running away, sex play, and stealing did not assume the proportions we find in juvenile delinquents was only due to her age which made her mother's complete restriction possible.

But the unusual amount of material, the irresistible urge, and the complete freedom of expression with which Sally acted out her symptoms in play, convinced us that she would have done all this in reality had she been older.

Sally's age makes it understandable why the treatment was so successful in spite of her unfavorable home conditions. Since the mother cooperated very little and the father not at all, the home influences remained unchanged. But as Sally was only four, acting out her waywardness in the treatment sessions gratified her impulses to an extent impossible with an older delinquent. This acceptance of acting out as a substitute for reality seems to explain the unusual amount of undisguised material she produced.

We realize, of course, that many problems remain unsolved at this point, despite the fact that Sally's symptoms had disappeared and that she seemed well adjusted even to her mother's exacting demands.

Although Sally's penis wish and envy, her fears and her wetting were thoroughly interpreted, there were several elements which were not worked through in the treatment. The oral fixation in particular was not worked through, and we therefore see oral constituents in her positive oedipus complex, when she wants her father to stay home and take care of her. Although she was given repeated enlightenment we cannot tell whether or not her fantasies had progressed to the genital level.

The aim of the treatment had been to cure her syndrome of waywardness. The technique therefore had the effect of singling out specific parts of the material for this purpose.

The therapeutic results of this treatment illustrate the value of analytically trained social workers and suggest the need for increasing the number of workers so trained. It also points to the need for institutions where young children with symptoms of incipient delinquency could be placed whenever the home environment would make such treatment impossible.

SOME IMPRESSIONS FROM CLINICAL EXPERIENCE WITH DELINQUENTS

By S. A. Szurek, M.D.*

(San Francisco, Calif.)

"Thus every type of delinquency requires a special type of treatment. In all cases, however, the treatment must concern itself with the further development of the ego-ideal, and we must put the question thus: how can we direct social retraining in order to bring about corrections of character in the individual?"[1]

That "delinquency" is a term both too broad in its implications and lacking in precision is well known to those psychiatric clinicians who deal with children. This is a fault which often characterizes psychiatric terms and concepts. By lack of precision and breadth of implications — in a psychiatric or scientific sense — one means that it includes large variety of "personality structures", of persistent patterns of interpersonal behavior—the results of different combinations of "constitutional" and social determinants. In its widest sense, the term "delinquency" refers to a child's or adolescent's failure to conform to more or less generally accepted standards of behavior and to a positive rebellion against these standards. These cases usually do not manifest any associated, very obvious evidence of either "mental" or "somatic" disorders, or any combination of both. It is not our purpose in this paper to delineate the complex symptomatic factors of delinquency. We are all familiar with the varieties of maldevelopment of character, the failures of personality integration, the various constellations of family and social settings, the types of life histories which are or may be included in this concept of delinquency. Let us leave the conception in all its vagueness and assume some understanding of the general field of human behavior it implies. We believe that the most useful contribution to a symposium such as this is some summary record of personal, professional experience in the area so vaguely defined. We therefore offer a few specific examples of such experi-

---

* Langley Porter Clinic, University of California Medical School.

[1] Aichhorn, August: *Wayward Youth*. New York, Viking Press, 1935.

115

ence and some general remarks and impressions, drawn from almost a decade of participation in the work of psychiatric clinics and hospital wards for children.

A well-dressed, rather handsome boy of sixteen was brought by his distraught father to the clinic because he had several times forged the name of the father's former employer to checks which he cashed. In his interview with the clinic psychiatrist the boy was quite at ease, frankly answering questions about himself, his family and the reasons for his being brought to the clinic. There was no marked evidence of guilt or anxiety when he stated that he had committed the forgeries, that he had had other minor troubles with the police for stealing in the past years and that he did not like or want to go to school. He could not say he had any definite, or strong ambitions, but he "had thought of" joining the Marines. He gave other facts regarding his past, when asked, without lengthy elaboration, and he seemed indifferent and almost bored. He shrugged his shoulders and said he did not know why he forged the checks. He just needed more money for dates and fun, and his father had recently had to take a less lucrative position when the war had reduced the business of selling automobiles. He returned to the waiting room after the interview and slumped indolently behind a magazine.

The father in his interview, on the other hand, poured out his story with much tension and with little need for encouragement or questions. He was utterly baffled as to the reasons for his son's acts and as to what to do about it all. The whole affair had made the mother too sick and nervous, as she was so often, to be able to come to the clinic. After a torrent of speech lasting a considerable period, it was possible by gradual questioning to obtain much information from which we give the following brief summary. The mother was eager to have a daughter, but had had three miscarriages in the first few years of their marriage. To assuage her extreme disappointment during her recovery from the last of these miscarriages, the father went to a private adoption agency and brought her a child — this son. Within the next few years they adopted another child, a girl, and finally a boy was born to them. The mother was often dissatisfied with her husband because among other reasons he seemed not to share her eagerness for the kind of recreation she enjoyed, especially dancing. The oldest son had always been a problem to them in various ways. He took up with bad companions; he showed little interest in, and was a truant from school; and he had been in several stealing scrapes with the police, from which the father had to extricate him as best he could. Yet the father liked the boy. He himself had been rather "wild" in his youth and had run away from home to join the Marines at sixteen by falsifying his age. He had made a good record in his two "hitches" in the service and he had brought up his son "on the Marines".

Some six months before their visit to the clinic, after the father had been forced to take a job as a guard in a defense plant, the boy announced that he would like to leave school and go to work, and somewhat reluctantly his parents agreed. Weeks went by and although he had made some efforts the boy was still without a job. The father became impatient and finally insisted on dictating a letter of application for several jobs advertised in the want ads. The boy soon had a job but was discharged after one week. Two weeks before the visit to the clinic the father was notified by his former employer that several checks amounting to forty-five dollars had been forged and cashed. The evidence pointed to his son who admitted it. In a serious effort to impress the boy with the gravity of his offense, the father demanded that the son sign three legal-looking documents. He told his son that one of these would be sent to the bank, another to the employer and the third to the judge. If there were any repetition of forgery the son would thereby be automatically remanded to the authorities. The son signed the documents. The father then became desperate and, upon the advice of friends, brought the boy to the clinic.

In the ensuing discussion it became evident to both the father and the psychiatrist that in the last forgery the boy had called his father's bluff. The father felt "licked" and helpless. He had thought of permitting the boy to join the Marines but he was afraid the boy would damage his reputation in this branch of the service. He asked pleadingly for advice or suggestions. The psychiatrist wondered at this impasse whether there was anything left to do except for the father frankly to admit to the boy that he felt helpless, bewildered and defeated. The father anxiously asked whether he should do this, to which the psychiatrist replied he could not urge or advise any course of action upon the father which he himself did not feel he wanted or could undertake. It seemed to the psychiatrist that since the boy had checkmated his father, and since the father had done everything except to treat the son like the man he wanted him to become, and had not been able to admit his defeat to his son, the next move obviously seemed to be up to the boy. Perhaps the father could ask his son what *he* wanted to do. The father seemed much eased by the discussion, and suddenly decided this was all he could do and that it was what he wanted to do.

A week later the father returned to the clinic alone, looking much happier, and enthusiastically reported the events of the week. On the way home from the previous clinic visit father and son had had the most serious conversation they had ever had, during which both were very much moved. The boy wept a little and suddenly announced he was going to get a job. A day later he was at work and seemed a changed person. He was too busy to come to the clinic and the father also felt it was unnecessary either for the son to return or for himself to continue coming for further visits. He himself felt as if a tremendous load had been lifted from his shoulders. His colleagues at work had spontaneously remarked at the change in him. He looked so different, like a new man, and so much more relaxed and happy. The father was very grateful and promised he would come again if difficulties even began to appear. He was never heard from again and because the psychiatrist soon left the clinic and the city for military service, it was impossible to learn the further events of this father and son story.

On another occasion the psychiatrist was consulted by a young male social worker, a member of the staff of a denominational welfare agency of the city, regarding a sixteen-year-old boy. The boy had appeared at the Juvenile Court repeatedly following episodes of truancy from home and school and numerous burglaries of homes and stores. The Court was almost decided to commit the boy to the state reformatory when the agency, extremely eager in its effort to keep children of its religious denomination out of the reformatory, urgently requested the court to grant the boy a probation period in the community under its auspices and guardianship.

Although of good intelligence and in good physical health, the boy appeared to the worker to be a doubtful prospect because of his longstanding indifference to his family, and because of his family's sense of resignation and defeat, if not indifference toward him. The worker asked the psychiatrist what help the clinic could offer. Could the clinic arrange for a staff member to give the boy psychotherapeutic interviews?

The psychiatrist, recalling his many failures in attempts at direct psychotherapy with adolescents of this sort from just such homes as this one, was dubious of the value of this approach. Such boys rarely responded to psychotherapeutic interviews. They rarely seemed troubled or under any inner stress. They had little to say and acted as if they were more interested in doing things and having fun instead of "just talking" to a psychiatrist. Occasionally, if they became attached to the therapist and continued their visits to the clinic for more than a few weeks, they began insistently to demand that he intercede for them with the agency caring for them, or with their own parents or with school authorities for more money, privileges, gifts or special changes of curriculum. Then, they might come late or at odd hours for their appointments or ask for rides in the psychiatrist's car or to be allowed to see him at his home on weekends. The slightest disappointment of these wishes, no matter how unreasonable, often prompted them to discontinue their clinic visits and often were followed by some delinquent act. Because of such experiences the psychiatrist told the worker he was doubtful of the value of psychotherapeutic clinic interviews in such a case.

However, the psychiatrist had been impressed with the more fruitful results of the short, weekly recreation trips on which social workers of the clinic staff had taken several moderately impulsive preadolescent or adolescent children of the same sex as the worker. During such trips the workers made no suggestions that the child discuss "his problems", but received such confidences as were offered spontaneously during activities of the trip. He asked the agency worker whether, since he would be responsible for finding a foster-home and a school placement for the boy and would be supplying his spending money, he would also be willing and able to find the time to work with this impulsive youth. The psychiatrist offered to be available for repeated and regular consultation hours regarding his experiences with the boy. The worker agreed hesitantly and asked what his general attitude toward the boy should be.

In the following discussion it was decided that, above all, the worker would be as thoroughly honest as possible with the boy about everything in the situation between them. This would include not only re-emphasis of the fact that this was the boy's last chance to stay out of a reformatory and that neither the Court nor the agency could again intercede for him, but that the agency, and especially the worker himself, would not feel justified in doing so. It would also be necessary to make it quite clear to the boy that the worker, although willing to do all he could for the boy's welfare and comfort insofar as the resources of the agency permitted, first of all, doubted that he could immediately satisfy all his needs and wishes, and second, that he doubted whether the boy and he could really "hit it off" together and eventually feel each could trust the other. Because the worker knew the boy had for many years felt distrustful of anyone's sincerity towards him and had impatiently done what he could to satisfy his impulses, he knew, too, that there was perhaps not much chance the boy could restrain himself long enough to give either of them time to learn whether things could be different. That part of it was almost entirely in the boy's hands. There was no reason for either of them to trust the other at the outset, but although the worker was frankly skeptical about the chances of either of them being successful at what they were about to try to do together, he was willing to try.

This was somewhat against the worker's principle of not using "threats" with children. But he nevertheless agreed that only frankness regarding the boy's social reality as well as regarding the psychological reality between himself and the boy, promised an atmosphere in which the worker — and therefore perhaps the boy — could begin their relationship.

There followed a period of over eighteen months — before both the worker and the psychiatrist left the city for military service — of interesting collaboration. The worker found a home — several of them were necessary in this period — for the boy. He provided him with spending money, and went with him on a number of occasions for various forms of recreation. He made himself available at his office or on the phone for visits from the boy as often as his time permitted. He listened to his requests considerably, granting those within his power and regretfully denying others. Several school placements, despite conferences between the worker and school counselors, were such failures, because of the boy's poor achievement and because of some truancies, that it was decided to let him go to work. Within a year after he began to work, the boy had found a job as a messenger for a firm and was carrying over $10,000 at a time to the bank. Eventually there was — undirected as far as the worker was concerned — a gradual spontaneous rapprochement between the boy and his family and he finally returned to live with them.

The worker and the psychiatrist — who never saw the boy — met at first at weekly, later at less and less frequent conferences, to discuss progress and the details of the worker's experience with the boy. Occasionally, especially during some crises, there were discussions between them by telephone. In these conferences it became clear to the psychiatrist and then to the worker that the worker quickly came to feel a good deal of spontaneous warmth and admiration for some of the qualities of the boy's personality.

Eventually, as the rapport between the worker and the psychiatrist increased, the former would mention casually that he could understand some of the boy's feelings toward adults in authority because of his own memories of adolescent experiences. But although this empathy between the worker and boy, which early showed itself in a degree of frankness and directness on the part of the boy, often surprising to the worker, was the basis for the generally favorable direction of the boy's readjustment, it was likewise the source of some of the difficulties and crises. On several occasions the boy failed to keep appointments or to carry through on some courses of action he had apparently decided upon with the worker. Repeatedly, in such instances, the psychiatrist and the worker uncovered the fact that the worker had had some inner doubts, hesitations and uneasiness regarding the matter being discussed with the boy. For one or another reason — often because he was not clearly aware of his own conflict — the worker had not voiced these divided feelings to the boy. Almost inevitably a failure or crisis in the boy's adjustment followed.

The worker finally became convinced that the boy at such times responded in terms of the worker's own unspoken and unacknowledged feelings toward him and nothing less than the full expression of his own attitudes would serve to help the boy choose the path leading to his own best self-interest. This meant telling the boy, whenever the worker felt it, that he was angry, disappointed or regretful about the boy's behavior or impulses. It meant telling him at times that the worker felt skeptical about the truth of some story the boy told, or that perhaps, on another occasion, he felt some admiration for the boy's rebelliousness even while he felt he should demand that he submit and conform. It meant even admitting to the boy in the later period that the worker's quite egocentric pride was now involved in "succeeding" with him even though the worker knew that the boy might prefer to do something else than the worker thought "best" for him, such as choosing work rather than an education. Finally, it meant telling him quite frankly whenever the boy made him feel worried, uneasy or frightened for whatever reason. The worker thus learned that when he could say some of these things out loud to the boy, he felt easier and more able to consider the boy's impulses from the boy's point of view, and the result was usually that the boy responded in a way which allayed the tension of both of them.

Again, circumstances prevented a later follow-up to learn of the eventual life adjustment of this boy. It is probably too much to expect that such a relatively short period of work with a boy of such character structure and relations with his family, would be finally decisive for his later life. But the experience was an illuminating one for both the psychiatrist and the worker.

Other clinical experiences have suggested the need for a very flexible approach. This is especially true in the problem of children or adolescents whose relations with other persons are characterized by impulsive self-gratification, inadequate restraint of their sexual, revengeful or exploitative impulses, and whose durable loyalties and interests show a relatively poor integration. Perhaps the factor of major importance in determining the type of therapeutic effort is the presence or absence of some degree of parental affection and warmth in their lives. One is tempted to assert that, other things being equal, the less the child has experienced of this essential and spontaneous interest in his welfare and wishes, the more difficult will be the therapeutic problem. However ambivalently his natural or adoptive parents may feel toward him, the treatment of such a boy will still be less difficult than of one who has had no parents. This is often because there have been numerous failures in foster-home placements by the time the clinician is consulted, and the agency caring for the child is generally dubious of being able to find another home willing to try again, or one any more likely to succeed.

If such a child is still under ten years old, the agency often insistently requests that we attempt treatment within a psychiatric hospital ward for children or some other residential treatment center before they try to place him in a foster-home. If we grant such a request, the hospital staff usually finds itself in great difficulties because of the demands on its time and emotional resources made by such children. The staff's available time is diverted from the more inhibited — the psychoneurotic and psychotic children. These impulsive and neglected orphans, if thwarted in even minor ways, promptly respond with hostile destructiveness and aggressiveness and direct their response in various individual ways. They may make use of other children whom they have intimidated or they weld the other children into gangs allied against the personnel or weaker children, or are destructive of hospital property. Their insatiable demands for affection and for durable security are more difficult to meet than those of other children whose parents visit them and give them at least some semblance of a sense of "belonging" to a family.

Placement of such parentless impulsive children in other public institutions such as juvenile "detention" homes is generally very temporary. Yet the prolonged residence provided by state funds is undesirable because there is little educational or recreational provision and too few in staff for the numbers of children admitted. Such staffs are perforce often, and perhaps in spite of themselves, more apt to be more generally repressive and punitive in attitude than guided by any rational therapeutic principles. Such adolescents, after discharge from these state schools, frequently present problems to their parole officers who then in turn consult the clinic staff about the inevitable crises which arise when they try to restore them to community life in foster-homes. If such parole officers are not overburdened with large case loads and if the clinic staff has the time, it may be possible to help the officer. Such help is perhaps more often fruitful if it is offered by way of conferences regarding his contact and work with the adolescent and his foster parents, than by direct psychotherapy of the adolescent in clinic interview sessions.

There are at times many misconceptions on the part of some psychiatrists attached to Juvenile Court clinics as well as of some parole officers in regard to the prospects and possibilities of direct psychotherapy in the outpatient clinic.

Few of these psychiatrists and parole officers appreciate the difficulties involved in the hospital care of such impulsively aggressive children or adolescents. One source of such misconceptions on the part of parole officers is their overestimation of the effectiveness of psychiatric treatment — specifically of psychotherapy. Such overestimation is in part the product of their own deep sense of helplessness in regard to their professional burdens and problems. But unfortunately the psychiatrists themselves at times increase this overestimation by implied and unrealistic promises of the results of psychotherapy. There is of course also the opposite and older attitude among such parole officers, namely, skepticism regarding the value of any psychiatric treatment. Although this may be based only on insufficient knowledge it may also perhaps stem from repeated disappointments. Another source of minimizing the difficulties of hospital treatment is at times the strong desire on the part of both parole officers and court psychiatrists to keep a particular — often a young, attractive and likable child — out of public institutions. In these situations their pressure upon the psychiatric clinic to assume the responsibility may stem from several origins. Aside from whatever personal feelings they may have developed for the particular child's qualities, they are often fully aware both of the gross inadequacies of their own residences and services and of those of the state institutions.

Court psychiatrists also are occasionally prone to these misconceptions about treatment because their inadequate clinical experience with this category of psychopathology makes them unable to correctly diagnose this type of case. Now and then a child is seen at court who seems "anxious" to them, when actually he is thoroughly frightened of the possible consequences of his activities. This "anxiety" when studied in a psychiatric clinic shows itself to be not genuine anxiety arising from an internalized conscience or superego, but chiefly fear of the external, impending punishment for transgressions. The child only serves to deepen such errors of diagnosis, if when asked for the reasons for his behavior, he persistently denies any knowledge or awareness of his motivation. Since he often is not fully aware of them, or, in his frightened state, is unable to state those he is clear about, he may convince a relatively inexperienced examiner. The examiner then concludes that such "unconscious" motivation is sufficient indication for dynamic psychotherapy. Such inexperienced psychiatrists may be further misled by statements in the literature regarding the "psychodynamics" of the "neurotic" character which they may take to imply that a dynamic or psychoanalytic treatment has been or can be successful. They overlook the fact that the staffs of psychiatric clinics for children rarely have many or even any therapists who are fully qualified to do psychoanalytic treatment. Even if there were more such therapists we would be doubtful of their value with these cases for two reasons. The first is the question of the time involved. Few therapists or patients would have the time to meet for the frequent therapeutic sessions which classical child analysis requires. The second is that we are doubtful that psychotherapeutic sessions, whether by play or by the interview method, are the effective approach in these cases. The psychotherapeutic method seems to us to be contraindicated for several reasons. Psychotherapy in general aims and is primarily devised to reverse the psychoneutric process of repression. Its goal is to aid in transforming and integrating such repressed impulses into ego attitudes which are in harmony with such self-esteem as the patient has already integrated. But the impulsive child in contrast to the psychoneurotically inhibited patient, suffers from the lack of restraint of impulses.

We believe that such a child needs to be provided with the experiences previously denied him. He needs the spontaneous ungrudging warmth of an adult, given to him as a person and not merely as a reward for conformity. He needs this warmth for the prolonged period necessary for him to develop that essential sense of security. He also needs frank, unyielding firmness. This firmness must be coupled with uncompromising fairness and justice. The therapist must be sufficiently self-aware to be able to recognize the many forms which the patient's distrustful, unmodified egocentricity and revengefulness may take and yet not be swayed from his therapeutic goal by them. We admit that this is extremely difficult at times and often it is impossible to consistently provide such attitudes. However, at least an approximation of these conditions may offer a chance that such a child will become attached to the adult, and *if the relationship is continued long enough,* begin to identify with the adult's ideals, the adult's wishes for his own welfare, and to acquire a new sense of his own worth as a person. In short, he may be able to integrate the beginnings of a new self-respect, of a conscience or more conscience, and of more self-restraint. At the same time the basis of his egocentricity, his distrustful impulsiveness and his revenge-fulness may gradually be liquidated as this experience counteracts his former experiences with people.

Aichhorn was quite clear about this point when he wrote: "Our work differs from that of the psychoanalyst in that we use the transference to accomplish an entirely different task. . . . In remedial training we cannot be content with transient results which arise from the emotional tie of the dissocial boy or girl to the worker. We must succeed, as in psychoanalysis, in bringing the wayward youth under the influence of the transference to a definite achievement. This achievement consists in a real character change, in the setting up of a socially directed ego ideal, that is, in the retrieving of that part of his development which is necessary for a proper adjustment to society."[2]

These goals require not only adequate financial support but also, and that is even more necessary, parent substitutes (either in our institutions or outside) who have at least some of the qualities described above. Only such parental surrogates may be able to give some of the time and feeling requisite to redress the balance. Some selected cases may in addition need direct psychotherapeutic treatment at the clinic, and the parental surrogate may require concomitant help for his own conflicts during the inevitable times of crises. In many other instances it may be feasible to plan to have the

---

[2] Aichhorn, *op. cit.,* pp. 235-236.

parole officer or child placement agency worker give the foster mother the support and advice she needs and then to have these agents in turn be briefed by the psychiatrist in regular conferences at the clinic. In an institution the parental surrogate in the person of matron, cottage father, nurse or attendant might similarly benefit from repeated regular discussions of their particular difficulties with a given child with a dynamically oriented and trained psychiatrist. The writer is familiar with the reports from such institutions on "forced therapy" with the child by the psychiatrist. This may be an important technical addition whenever there is sufficient psychiatric personnel, adequately trained for the peculiarities of this type of psychotherapy.

By now it is probably clear why the writer wishes to emphasize the imperative need for treating the natural parents of such an impulsive child when they are present in the family picture. This treatment should be clinically as adequate and therapeutically oriented in the same way as that of the child and should be conducted simultaneously. The question of the importance of treating or dealing with the parents is so great that its adequate discussion would require a great deal more space than is here available. A very few comments must suffice. Our theories of delinquency rest on the implicit assumption — supported by our clinical experience — that the child has failed in certain essential areas of integration. These areas are the integration into his ego-organization of attitudes of confidence that by and large his essential needs will be gratified. Since he has not integrated such attitudes of confidence he is driven instead to defiant, either open or surreptitious, aggressive and egocentric pursuit of these gratifications. The emphasis is, of course, on the egocentric nature of the pursuit, i.e., with disregard for the rights of others and without consideration for their needs or feelings. This can result, according to this view, only if the earliest experiences at the hands of others were similarly characterized, namely, without much regard for the child's needs, feelings and welfare. Such handling of the child stems from a variety of attitudes of his parents. There may be gradations of difference toward him in one or both parents, or one or both parents may have serious conflicts either internal or between each other or in regard to the child, but all of these difficulties have a similar end effect on the child. Moreover psychotherapy with the parents will be effective only if their conflicts produce inner suffering and anxiety in them. Only by offering the parents psychotherapeutic help in solving their own conflicts will the child's welfare eventually profit. In other words, it is essential for both parents and for the therapist himself to be aware that the work is *not* carried on merely *for the sake of the child*.

Admittedly helping such parents to accept therapeutic assistance for their own internal conflicts is often the crucial difficulty.[3] During a crisis following pressure from police or Juvenile Court authorities for some delinquent act of the child, parents are often ashamed and chagrined by the threat of possible social ostracism. At such times genuine anxiety and guilt may be mobilized and sufficiently increased so that one or both may be willing to participate in clinical work towards a solution of their common family problem. Such participation means, ideally, separate therapists for the parent and the child. Occasionally, such parents do seek clinical assistance before the child has actually been arrested, driven perhaps by their own anxieties over early indications of his rebelliousness. In these instances the prognosis for successful therapy is likely to be the best. But such family situations are rare among those most frequently seen in Juvenile Courts. When parents show relatively less anxiety about their status and self-esteem, and perhaps more resignation or indifference with regard to the child and his behavior, the prognosis for even beginning therapy is less good. The difficulties of treatment in these cases approach those in the case of the parentless child. In the more favorable instances — in which parental anxieties are high — the therapeutic plan may vary from direct treatment of the child and one parent (the more available and emotionally involved) through treatment of both parents and the child by separate therapists, to therapeutic effort with one parent only. It sometimes happens that after work is begun with one parent and the child, the anxieties of the other parent lead him to request help as well. It is natural to ask whether the treatment of one parent only is not then adult and not child psychiatry, especially when the child may have been seen for therapeutic purposes at the beginning and then drops out of treatment because of, or without improvement. This is a matter of definition depending on the nature of the psychopathology within the family. It becomes difficult to define only if one adheres too rigidly to administration or "specialty" classifications instead of following the clinical indications of the problem.

In conclusion, the writer is tempted to condense and oversimplify his clinical experiences (with children who have parents) into a dictum. This dictum, which should perhaps be discussed separately and with the appropriate clinical facts to justify it, would read: "The psychoneurotic parent is likely to rear at least one psychopathic child."[4] Space does not permit us to discuss here all of the factors or variables or their quantitative interrelation which are necessary to produce such a result. The writer has been

---

[3] For somewhat further elaboration of the difficulties encountered by therapists in the treatment of such children and their parents, see Szurek, S. A.: Some Principles of Child Guidance Practice, *The News-Letter of the American Association of Psychiatric Social Workers,* 16:119-120, 1947.

[4] For further elaboration of the basis for this thought, see Szurek, S. A.: Notes on the Genesis of Psychopathic Personality Trends, *Psychiatry,* 5:1-6, 1942.

impressed with the fact that among many such factors may be the ordinal position of the child in the family, e.g., a middle child coming soon after the first-born, or the youngest child coming late after the older siblings. This factor by itself is perhaps insufficient. The emotional state of the parents, perhaps more often of the mother, the result of increasing dissatisfactions in her life at the time of the child's birth and early years, are probably among the essential determinants. An additional factor which comes readily to mind may be the sex of the child, or some physical qualities, such as resemblance to someone else, which may help to arouse and specifically intensify ancient conflicts of the parents toward that particular child. In any case, the content of this dictum has been stated in an alternative or more generalized form: "The most overt symptom of a parental personality disorder is the behavior of the child."

Where a natural parent shows such a personality disorder (and in the writer's experience this occurs frequently, if not invariably) then the plan of treatment is determined by what adequate psychotherapeutic skill is available. In view of the fact that such children and adolescents are, however, ambivalently attached, and emotionally as well as economically dependent upon their parents, therapeutic work with the parents is often the most direct approach and often the most economical use of the clinician's time in solving the problems and needs of the child. All this does not exclude in every case the careful evaluation of the accessibility of the child to treatment by *psychotherapy* and even offering such direct treatment for the child as a means towards this evaluation. But all this is an effort to emphasize, or perhaps only to re-emphasize, the advantages of concomitant therapeutic effort with the parent to assist him in the resolution of the conflicts which were etiologically important in the child's personality problem.

An equally important factor which determines the success of such clinical efforts was not touched upon in this discussion, that is, the personality — as well as the trained clinical skill — of the child's therapist. It is extremely important for the empathy and the development of rapport with such aggressive children that the therapist's attitude be infused with elements arising perhaps from his own early experiences which he has resolved and integrated, but which are not unlike those of the impulsive child. In this matter, too, Aichhorn was clear and emphatic when he wrote: "I cannot close this book without once more stressing the great importance of the personality of the workers in this field. You have seen that a character change in the delinquent means a change in his ego ideal. This occurs when new traits are taken over by the individual. The source of these traits is the worker. He is the important object with whom the dissocial child or youth can retrieve the defective or non-existent identification and with whom he can experience all the things in which his father failed him. With the worker's help, the youth acquires the necessary feeling relation to his companions which enables him to overcome the dissocial traits. The word 'father-substitute', so often used in connection with remedial education, receives its rightful connotation in this conception of the task.

"What helps the worker most in therapy with the dissocial? The transference! And especially what we recognize as the positive transference. It is above all the tender feeling for the teacher that gives the pupil the incentive to do what is prescribed and not to do what is forbidden. The teacher, as a libidinally charged object for the pupil, offers traits for identification that bring about a lasting change in the structure of the ego ideal. This in turn effects a change in the behavior of the formerly dissocial child. We cannot imagine a person who is unsocial as a worker in this field. We assume therefore that the ego ideal of the child will be corrected through the worker's help in bringing him to a recognition of the claims of society and to participation in society."[5]

---

[5] Aichhorn, *op. cit.*, pp. 234-235.

TECHNIQUE AND THERAPY

THE USE OF THE PSYCHOANALYTIC PRINCIPLE IN CHILD GUIDANCE WORK

BY JOHN M. DORSEY, M.D.*

(*Detroit, Mich.*)

> "His treatment of his charges had its source in a warm sympathy for the fate of these unfortunates and was rightly guided by his intuitive understanding of their psychic needs".
>
> From Freud's Foreword of *Wayward Youth*.

Clinical Perspectives. Freud's discovery of our psychoanalytic principle, our mind-integrating procedure, laid the foundation for our enabling ourselves, scientifically, to assess the worth of man in full measure. And truth itself is a matter of full measure. Our greater self-acceptance gives us an understanding of the greatness of humanity that is more than theoretical, that rather is based upon our feeling more greatness in ourselves with all of the evidence of natural fact.

In the following pages the attempt is made to indicate how the contributions of psychoanalysis to the understanding of psychology and psychopathology are utilized in the operation of a child guidance clinic serving some fifteen hundred children a year. So far only five of the staff of thirty members have had psychoanalytic training experiences. However, the aim is taken for each worker to practice systematically the extension of his consciousness of self.

Established principles of developmental psychology are used to arouse and guide sentiment in the interest of the child's mental health. *Clear thinking about the dignity of every and any human being is the chief source of helpfulness.* Instead of "taking it for granted" we aim to take, and prescribe the value of being human as our sovereign remedy. Experience teaches that serving with this cause offers the most solid benefit to child and parent.

What we represent is not new, it is as old as time and as common as space: Attention to human being. We define specific psychotherapy as the disciplined use of the human element as therapeutic agent. We hold that

---

* Chairman and Professor, Department of Psychiatry, Wayne University, College of Medicine. Director, Child Guidance Division of the Children's Fund of Michigan.

the most eligible way of life leads us to growing respect for the great human values, truth and charity. This is our doctrine of mental hygiene. We find that this special kind of clinical sense fixes the true point of human welfare and accounts for all that is fundamentally therapeutic in our efforts. *To that end* we aim to keep clear in our minds the one big idea: *psychic determinism.* In so far as we have cause and effect relationships to depend upon we can claim divine protection. Endowed with cause and effect thinking, our God is with us, not just waiting for us. Scientific man can collaborate in the shaping of his own destiny. Determinism includes individual man as an agent in the causal series. It is Fatalism that omits him from the causal sequence.

Freud revealed the most formidable weapon against human error of every kind to be the reach of attention. Our mental discipline helps us to discover that even the very reaches of our attention that seem furthest from our concept of self are nonetheless the enlarged view of the self. Attention, the great tribunal, bounds the melioration of our common lot. So frequently commonplaces are the hiding places of influence. The strong mind extends its attention to conceive respect for humanity as reverence, and as wholesome self-respect. For each one of us selfness is the great truth, so great that it needs the greatest light to reveal its essential goodness. In our clinic staff's efforts at psychological treatment, we methodically attempt first of all to observe our own misbehavior, to attend to it. The art of medicine is the art of eschewing hypocrisy. Only solemn reverence for truth, that is, for everything existing, can give sense to our life and transform misunderstanding into enlightenment, can make the joy of living more than an empty phrase. The feeling of well-being, by itself, is not trustworthy; in fact it constitutes a chief symptom of one of our most common forms of mental illness. Only the truth seeker can afford to feel well-being.

If we ask ourselves, "What do we, the people, need most of all?" we cannot avoid the reply, "Attention". To be out of attention to each other is to be out of charity with each other. For the most part we are dangerously free of the understanding of this basic significance of attention. Attention is the breath of wholesome mental life, but our restricting necessities require of us that we strive against such tolerance. Only by means of our attention can we get our psychological bearings. The untouchability, invisibility, and inaudibility of our mental structure deprive us of our most trusted reality checks upon our mental tissue. Since our attention functions for our mental self much as our perceptions do for our submental self, it pays us to learn to trust the self-evidence it reveals. What we are unable to attend to goes on exerting itself, unobserved though it may be. *Mark* acknowledged: "For there is nothing hid which shall not be manifested; neither was anything kept secret, but that it should come abroad". As long as we are unable to apply our attention, we must employ ourselves as blind guides who strain at a gnat, and swallow a camel. To pay attention is to care; to deprive of attention is to abandon to misuse. August Aichhorn's word for the dissocial youth, *"verwahrlost"*, literally scores the delinquent youngster's illness of self inattention, self neglect.

It is by means of our attention that we take hold of everything, meaning "take hold of ourselves". What we cannot attend to, we cannot make serviceable. We have had to learn how the "uncaring" child may be defending himself against directing his attention to his needs for his infantile clinging dependency, how the reckless child may be defending himself against directing his attention to terror he has invested in his fantasy directions, and how the "irresponsible" child may be defending himself against directing his attention to his taut guilt feelings. Mindful of how unpleasant it is to attend to many thoughts and feelings, it is little wonder that we so often put ourselves to the question, "What's the use?" Only by adding our attention to anything can we find its use.

Our staff in-service training is set up on the principle that every human being of wisdom concludes finally that he is his own everything. To tell a child, or a childish adult, that he is his own everything (and let it go at that) can lead to nothing but misuse of this eternal truth. It will travel like lightning seeking conduction that will permit it the least resistance, and the child will try to bend his External World to his childish content. In our human relationships we are living in too much of a childish world as it is. Through rejecting the meaning of evidence as self-evidence, attested to by everything without exception in our External World, we have been able to maintain some wild systems of psychology.

Helping the parent to think and to feel in terms of a psychological level of the body reminds us of nothing so much as of the missionary's efforts to convince the infidel that he has a soul. Religion has needed its defenders too. There never was an educator, or re-educator (reformer), whose contemporaries did not accuse him of trying to abolish the then established moral virtue. The teaching of ideals is comfortable only to those already possessing them. The inertia of the masses to mental health forces is dangerous. They rise up against them exactly as if they were being required to accept a false god.

For example, much as we have begun to recognize the importance of paying attention to the developing child's psychosexual expressions, even greater is the need to attend well to his expressions of hostility. We find that the parent is seldom aware of the great aggression represented by the addition of another human being into the house. Husband and wife suffer too much unawareness of their jealousy and ignorance to govern their children well. The invasion of the home that results from being born, the infant's original transgression of forcing entry into an already mentally crowded family, is rarely acknowledged as such. The parent's charity, that is, his insight regarding the advantage to himself in being able to share, is rarely well developed. Experience deriving from the privileged opportunity to study many families suggests that it is well to consider to what extent the infant is born into a human environment that is hostile. In this direction of caring for the child's welfare oversight is exercised most commonly without full insight regarding its double meaning.

For parents who are ready for such insight, perhaps our staff accomplishes its greatest good through educating them to understand that their child's growing mind requires, first of all, their attention and sustained interest, whenever safe *without interference*. Thus their child keeps bringing to them new self uses characteristic of each succeeding step in his mental development. All of a sudden these new self expressions are with him, on his mind, and he does not know what to do with them, how to mind them. The contributions of psychoanalysis have demonstrated for us how he brings his waxing thoughts and feelings to his parent as if inquiring, "Here is something new and strange to me. My attention has a new access. Will you help me to apply it to, rather than against, my mental health account? Will you help me to understand this growing part of my human nature so that I can learn, in time, to employ it beneficially rather than harmfully? I will not hurt myself unprofitably if I am able to attend to the real meaning of my behavior. Only the anaesthetic hand rests on the hot stove, you know. Will you help me to learn, in time, the safe and sane use, the mental hygiene, of fear, guilt, hostility, jealousy, love and curiosity, so that my self-management will be wholesome, useful, self-fulfilling and self-possessing? I do not need your other reasoning about it right now. Right now, I do need a more mature mind's experienced attention to reinforce my own mind's efforts to consider these strong forces within me and to notice their consequences. Your attention is the cure for my own mind's inability to attend to what demands expression, and what will ail me without attention. Whatever of my human nature that is thus demanding my attention will either be attended to as well as proper attention provides or it must be lived out by me as a kind of charade. To be, is to be expressed, well or ill. I can only fear my self uses whose gainful employment I am not helped to attain. Credit me with the ability to learn other meanings and their important consequences, in time. When I am actually getting into serious trouble, and you *must* interfere besides pay attention, please interfere with insight as to what you are finding it necessary to do to me."

Most of the time parents are already overwhelmed with mental burdens and it is essential that our workers direct first efforts towards relieving their minds rather than towards heaping extra responsibilities, in the form of other accumulations of wisdom, upon them. For them we consider that we may be accomplishing our greatest good as friendly heedful listeners. We are able to be of very real help in guiding their attention, most respectfully, where they are unable to extend their consideration themselves. Particularly with regard to this latter group of parents, innumerable opportunities for "practical" suggestions are constantly presenting themselves.

As a rule the parent comes to us offering as his chief complaint his child's problem. The child offers as his chief complaint the parent's attitude toward his problem. Study usually discloses that interpersonal relationships of the child and parent are troubled by the circumstance that each is speaking a language foreign to the other. When each is helped to understand the other's necessities, a common ground for improving their relationships is provided. Hence, in a deeply meaningful sense, our workers function not just as interpreters, but also as teachers of foreign language.

Just working with the "why" of the parent-child misunderstandings, just the letter of the truth, does not deliver either member of the family from the misuse of his antipathy towards the other. A first tendency for each opponent is to use such new found knowledge to build up a stronger case *against* the other. The purpose of "working with the why" is to discipline the mind in the understanding of the role of necessity, to imbue the mind with the spirit of the truth. Both the letter and the spirit of the truth are required to provide the useful motivation for bettering human relationships. For everyone the spirit of the truth is the acceptance of its self meaning, its self reference. Experience in a child guidance clinic, and in reviewing child guidance literature, leads us to consider soberly how difficult it is to attain and maintain this insight. Our council is embarrassed by such a multiplicity of aspects we risk losing sight of our main issue, humanity. Of necessity so much of the material deals in the importance of explanation itself, that the importance of human being gets lost in the shuffle. *Caveat emptor.*

Therefore our staff training objective revolves systematically about the preventive and curative benefits of the practice of human decency, of good breeding in human relationships. As the developing child is helped to growing self respect, through being respected, he can be interested in conceptions and disciplines of democratic living that guarantee his safe self unfolding and self realization. Parents and teachers are the child's first guardians of his mental health. The future of human relationships is in their power.

The publicized incidence of sociopathic behavior may tend to distract attention from misbehavior that is a developmental necessity for every infant and child, as well as a necessary imperfection characterizing all human nature. The illusion that there is juvenile behavior that does not necessarily express the immaturity of the child is tempting.

It is the nature of every child to be a delinquent, to be found wanting in his duty to society. Juvenile delinquency is a matter of degree. A child is not mature enough to "be" and "have" himself well. To *"behave self well"* is a large order involving both self being and self having, self expression under the aegis of self possession. Indeed, according to its full definition well behavior is rare in all adults.

An insight for parents and teachers to develop is the recognition that the child is unable to act to his own best interest but may be capable of learning such action, in time. A certain amount of misbehavior is characteristic for the healthy youngster. All of us have had to learn that there is no such thing as a "good" normal child. The wholesome attitude to have towards his straying from the path that pays is not one of just blaming him, or of just furthering his conviction of the effectiveness of whimpering, but more one of helping him, in time, to see how it had been *necessary* for him to act in his disadvantage and how essential changes will have to occur in him before it will be possible for him to act in better ways. Helping him requires loving him and expertly attending him in direct proportion to his injury.

The more a child misbehaves the less attention he is *able* to invest in his welfare and the more he needs real understanding about his child necessities; certainly the less he needs a whipping or scolding, however good the intentions of the lasher may be claimed to be. We have not inherited our virtue. Virtue is a plant of slow growth. Only a strong adult mind can manipulate the full meanings of virtue without getting hurt by them. A common reason why so many adult minds cannot use the wholesome values of virtue well is that they were forced to try to operate these powerful meanings before they were strong minded enough to do so and their minds were irreparably hurt in the process. We do not demand that the three-year-old behave like a little man as far as carrying a heavy weight on his back is concerned.

A thought provoking definition of criminality was offered by a woman suffering schizophrenic behavior: "Why Doctor, you ought to know that a criminal is a golden-haired, blue-eyed, red-cheeked child at play." Although inherent in all of us, delinquency and its older sibling criminality are commonly unpleasant to identify with and hence are seldom recognized for their potential value to the advancement of civilization. Yet they are most usefully conceived as valuable aids doing for the social "body" what pain does for the human body and what fear does for the mental part of the human body. Study of delinquency usually discloses its meaning as a danger signal, as a warning to us that something is wrong that needs our attention and further help. Thus, we learn to understand ill manners as the worst form of illness. We discover misdeeds to be one of the products of our culture and the human being who has had to misbehave as the butt of circumstance. As a people our criminality counsels us to consider our course and to mend the error of our ways. Divinity in rascality.

Delinquent behavior *is* the hurt child's cry for help. Any other conclusion about it is delusional, propagating the hurt law enforcer's vicious play of "cops and robbers".

The. Role of Punishment in Education. Every home and school are asking: What is the healthful attitude towards the question of the punishment of the miscreant? Psychiatrists are asked by educators, "Do you believe in punishment?" A correct reply is that suffering is real, is with us, and is best faced squarely rather than by-passed. The child's long hard road of growing up, from one stage of development to the next, is a series of punishments. Weaning hurts, but beneficially. Gradually accepting the truth about our human nature is a life long weaning procedure.

Truth can hurt and goodness can have an edge to it. It is necessary for the mind to attend to its punishment if it will grow to, and hold to, maturity. It is beneficial to endure the mental hardships of changing a narrow mind into a broader mind and of maintaining the greater breadth of mind. Enduring can be a synonym for curing. In our training program involving the *practice* of our understandings we observe regularly how vexation regarding the mental material itself is displaced upon "the monotony of repetition". The whole problem, therefore, is not one of getting rid of punishment but of suffering what it pays to suffer.

The punishment felt upon extending one's awareness of self may be likened to the removal of an anaesthetic from a painful area. Many mental regions are extremely sensitive to the touch of awareness. Yet with help, this kind of hurt may be economically sound. Psychoanalytic treatment is a procedure of "making conscious what is unconscious". There exists an universal anosognosia for the universal human malady of depersonalization.

It pays to develop, in time, to become able to endure the "growing pains" necessary to attending self. However, hitting a child, in every instance, even in self defense, constitutes for every child an attack of illness which calls for immediate psychological treatment of the most expert kind available. The same observation holds for the mistreatment of adult misbehavior. The remedy for any one of our public or private offenders is friendly considerate help to a human being in trouble. Claims of greater efficacy for forces other than charity and skill are delusional. In fact, the degree of our comprehension of our tormentor's unfortunate plight in having to be a tormentor, is the indicator of the degree of our preparedness to help him.

What about the punishment-as-a-deterrent policy? It carries the bad risk of creating hypocrisy, of forcing the terrified child to deny to himself that he even wants to misbehave. The hypocrite cannot understand misbehavior in others because he is forced to deny his own tendency toward it.

All mental illness is an expression of hypocrisy. All mental health is an expression of sincerity.

Mentally well leaders entertain the fuller, more useful, opinion of both well and ill man. For the treatment of the antisocial character, what weighs most with the well mind is the insight that only his slow and gradual emergence from the dangerous suspense of self negation will raise his level of morality. The spirit of striking back at our attacker, our necessary primitive illusion of easing our pain through trying to project it upon our opponent, if extended to a national scale becomes the war like spirit. The motive and object of returning blow for blow is the undisciplined mind's primitive strategy for displacing its pain to a part of itself where it is not aware of feeling self: its repressed "others". That area of our mind that represents those with whom we refuse to acknowledge an identification joins the property of our rejected death and destruction tendencies, unavoidable consequence of our false self measure, of our disconnecting principle. For the sake of self deception, all for supposed convenience we tend to cut off our nose to spite our face. Who cannot identify with his opposition is not fit to work at reducing it. An individual who denies his comprehensiveness is always a seat of secession, a focus for civil war, often sanguine in ambition, and never a peaceable man.

Law-abiding citizens who favor mistreatment of the evil-doer are not able to be aware that they are espousing the lost cause that two wrongs will make a right. The most potent corrective to apply to the avenger is to help him to be able to consider thoroughly how he would like to have to be a wrong-doer, to consider clearly how crime *is* punishment. Who wants to have to be like a criminal?, is the question that sobers us of our intoxication for vengeance. But natural repugnance to self hurt can function only narrowly for us as long as we are only autoerotic and narcissistic.

The affairs of self promotion and of general promotion are inseparable. A man has a right to be only what he is, his own individuality. He has no right to be anybody or anything else, despite the fact that he uses his perceptions of everybody and everything else more commonly as repression. His interest in his fellowman is motivated rightly only by the meaning of his fellowman for his own welfare. Our psychoanalysis has discovered for us an educational principle the application of which leads to sincerity, and the withholding of which misleads to hypocrisy.

Renunciation and repression are two contrasting techniques for training the mental organ, the strategy of renunciation making for strong mindedness, the machination of repression making for wrong mindedness. We have two ground plans, or curricula, for infant and child training, one of which systematically turns out well citizens, the other of which systematically turns out sick citizens.

Growing up to live in the world requires that the mental organ of the infant and child, in due time, be changed by experiences to endure, and beneficially employ, increasing tensions. These stresses, first felt as distresses, insure that the person's demands for instinct gratification will be compatible with social demands that have been set up, presumably, to provide that each individual receive as much respect as possible in community life. For controlling the narrowly selfish needs of the infant and child, the strategy of renunciation accepts the naturalness of our wishes for antisocial behavior. Thus, the parent practicing renunciation makes it clear to the child (1) that he understands the naturalness of the child's primitive needs, (2) that it is essential for the child to continue to be able to be aware of such primitive "rights" within himself, but (3) that despite all of his other temptations the child must learn, in time, to *prefer* a course of self expression that is socially permissible. The child is asked to renounce, rather than commanded to repress, "the devil and all his pomps". We express the difference between educating to mental health and misguiding to mental illness as simply as that. The old gospel of renunciation and work is as good as new.

For controlling these same narrowly selfish needs of the infant and child the machination of repression forces the child to deny the existence of great uses of his human nature. The insistence upon repression teaches a pharasaical psychology claiming that only "other people" want to do evil. It forces the child to stop undesirable social behavior, by deceiving himself that he still has any wish to be antisocial. The beginning of evil days, of a fool's paradise. Then throughout his lifetime the one requirement necessary for his being antisocial is that he not be aware of the antisocial meaning of his misbehavior. This adult person "succeeds" in being narrowly selfish by calling his inhumanities accidental, by claiming that his fellowman is not entitled to any need to misbehave, by continually apologizing for his own continuing mischief. Self uses that we disown can never be used as identifications, but only as fig leaves. And what we cannot identify with we must deal with unjustly. The good life is inseparable from the well life and, as Herbert Spencer put it, "the first requisite is to be a good animal". Repression points the way to an impractical ethic that can never permit our pleasure principle to grow up to become our reality principle.

It pays us to suffer the truth that we cannot teach what we, ourselves, do not have, and that we must teach what we do have. We educators impart what self help, what genuineness and hypocrisy, we have. If we are able to want to do a better job we try to improve ourselves as the means. We citizens of today are the product of the complexities of civilization, and for us to see ourselves truly is hard work indeed. The machination of repression is abetted by the crude impulse of primitive nature, observed strikingly in animals, to jump on a fellow who is down. Habit renders it easier for us to go in the direction we are going in, even though that direction be that of blind self misuse.

Of the somewhat punitive term "discipline" we may say: Only that discipline is beneficial that can be subsumed by the term "education". Nothing happens except through the application of force. Education, itself, is a force tempered by understanding of the role of necessity. For example, psychoanalytic experience offers the understanding that the time for education is when feeling is self-contained both in teacher and pupil. When feeling is running too high to permit self composure the indications are essentially those of nursing care, involving temporizing, isolating, and understanding forbearance while effecting the restraint required.

Much misuse of punishment in child training is traceable to the mistaken idea that the child "ought to be able to" behave himself "like a man". Parents and teachers frequently say that all the misbehaving child needs is to have "the devil knocked out of him". This attitude toward treatment characterized medieval medicine. Many educators know better now. They recognize the truth that misbehavior of any kind *is* self-punishment. Since misbehavior is *not acting to one's own best interest,* it necessarily represents self-punishment. Once this insight is minded, we see that it does not pay to punish a child blindly because the child has punished himself blindly. *Nemo bis punitur pro eodem delicto.*

Weaning the child from misbehavior to behavior that pays him more is a beneficial distress inflicted by his minding of three facts:

(1) that his behavior does represent punishing himself unwisely,

(2) that under the circumstances he was forced to indulge the misbehavior,

(3) that if he does not, in time, renounce his misbehavior, he must be denied social privileges.

We understand that these three facts are painful to the misdoer because only the acceptance of all of them will confront him with the necessity for mental growth. As long as he can lull himself with the opium of opprobrium into the false security of believing that he did not have to do what he did, he will not have to consider the necessity for a change. Changing our mental organ so that it can soberly consider possibilities that are new to us, means development to be aware of additional mental stress. Insight about the necessary conditions of human nature is not deliverance from them. Shakespeare prescribed: "To willful men, the injuries that they themselves procure must be their schoolmasters."

The goal of all wholesome education is the acquisition of fuller measures of self possession. In our democracy, we call it the development of independent thinkers, free agents, young men and women who are able to stand up on their own feet, follow their own noses, and yet belong to the human community of purpose and effort. It takes a long time to cultivate this kind of person, and in the human family many years of training in gratification and renunciation are provided for. But if the parent and teacher are immature they are forced to demand instant obedience without enjoying insight about the greater value of agreement. We hear much about the child's dependence upon the father and mother. It is equally true, however, that the father and mother must depend upon the child's cooperation in training. Only the father or mother who is aware of his dependence upon his child senses the necessity for collaboration with him. The respected youngster renounces for his parent's sake. What respect parents are paid by their youngsters is earned through their respecting him. What we cannot identify with we are not prepared to work with. Where the parent's unfitness for educating the child is involved, that child steals whose parent either steals or has repressed his wish to get something for nothing; that child fights whose parent quarrels or has repressed his hostility; and so on.

Every human being wants what he wants when he wants it. This tendency continues throughout life. What we can do about it is to become aware of its possibilities, develop insight relative to it, and attain healthful employment of it. It is evident that most of the events in life cannot happen just when we want them to happen. The event known as the child's cooperation is one of these.

At times obedience is necessary because immediate compliance is essential for safety reasons and the child may be incapable of agreement. In such instances it is most helpful for the educator to enforce obedience with keen appreciation of the superiority of agreement. When the technique, obedience, is resorted to consistently, the result is either the dependent, sheep-like type of child, or the antisocial, rebellious one.

Character Formation. Character has been likened to a steering mechanism for the person. Facts about its early formation in infanthood and childhood are readily observed in the child guidance clinic. All education is character education. We find that a person is being steered by *all* of the forces within him. His dislikes and his likes and whatever he learns about the world guide him. A human being is actually in one piece, with the mental level of his body his highest level of integration. Integrity of this highest level furthers his being "at one", rather than "at sixes and sevens", with himself. The truth *is* out, always. It may or may not be recognized. The fact that we are individuals absolutely guarantees self-possessed citizens of mankind's continued march of progress in their direction, despite temporary meanderings. His solitary confinement is man's greatest asset, it is his identity. Until he finds it he gropes around, a lost soul, a weak world citizen.

There are thousands of terms describing character. We can sum up in a single word the qualifications of the superior one. That word is "genuineness", a synonym for truthfulness. All education worthy of the name is character education because it is education to truth, to reality. Truth is the *only* proper antagonist to error and to ignorance. The mental organ, ill or well, cannot be helped by any other means. Psychopathology is the study of imposture.

The character that is genuine is as wholesome and vital as it can be. It is ready to be wounded in the cause of respect for individuality. It is the prerogative of man to *be*. To be, means to count. To ignore being, is to bear false witness. Any civil state that ignores one man is treasonable to human nature. Any man who is disinterested in any of his observations is out of character.

The genuine character lends itself to understanding and to being understood and thus represents the best working basis. A person who is genuine enjoys all of the economic advantages of directness, of candor. He is not given over to false fronts, ghosts, and other neurotic constructions. Character education may be defined as the development of the individual's ability to consult the best interests of his whole self for determining his conduct.

Effective character education (1) defends the pupil's right to have no better use of his self than he has, at any given time, and (2) helps the pupil to be able, in time, to make fuller use of his self. For the advancement of the young one's understanding, the way in which each new experience is presented to, and attended to, by his mind is a most telling force.

Our understanding of justice is derived from the way in which we have been helped to mind our novel experience. For example, through misguidance of our experiences we develop the weak kind of character that forces us to feel that we are exceptions to the laws of nature and of man; or forces us to "expect" from life justice that is "favorable to us"; or forces us to court injustice.

The genuine character is developed and sustained during the first years of life through timely experiences that are genuinely adaptable to the nature and needs of the growing mind. Justice is founded securely on the insight that *acceptance of necessity* is mental health's first law. To take upon our self this theodicean orientation to truth is to stop playing God foolishly, and to start working at it wisely. Considering the responsible function of the mind as the highest level of integration of the body, and considering the great lack of integration in this integrating level, itself, it appears likely that even our most enlightened medical educators are just beginning to realize the disordered mind's etiological role in infant mortality and in all diseases.

Education To Mental Health. Education to mental health is essentially a gradual, time-consuming, process of helping our growing young one, first of all, to discover and use himself, and later, to discover how to use himself best in terms of others. *If* the educator can share with the infant, or child, to the extent of granting him, first of all, his right to be only the way he is forced to be for the time being, then the condition of truth is ordained for educating that child, in time, to share with the educator the benefits of greater selfism. Every other educational technique drills the growing child in magic thinking. Inconsideration can be ruination to the mental organ. As the child experiences the parent's inconsideration his sense of power becomes allied with the cause of slavery.

Education's responsibilities are two-fold: to accept, temporarily, the growing individual as he is, and to provide him in due time, with the graduating self experiences that are necessary for his increasing self emancipation. In our child guidance center our *most* consistent finding is that well meaning parents begin their efforts to help their infant, or child, by disrespecting his temporary need to be only the way he is.

The parental contribution to the child's unacceptable behavior is made either through (1) the parents' indulgence or (2) intolerance of the same kind of behavior. Both parental examples are derivatives of repression. The "indulgent" parent represses by the way of his inattention to the ordinate necessities deriving from his External World. Depending upon whether the behavior involved is erotic or hostile he conducts either as a libertine or as a nihilist. The "intolerant" parent represses more evidently by way of his inattention to the ordinate necessities deriving from inner erotic and hostile impulses, and, depending upon whether the behavior involved is erotic or hostile, conducts as a prude or a coward.

Investigation usually reveals that the child is unconsciously used by the parent for the expression of the parts of the parent's ego that represent weakened areas. The child of the "indulgent" or "intolerant" parent will either repeat the parent's pattern *or its opposite,* depending upon whether the identification with the parent is positive or negative.

Adults who have repressed their immature behavior systems have thereby broken essential lines of communication with all infants and children. There is no healthful training of a child, or full measured rapport with an adult, that does not employ remote infantile and childlike self uses. Our attempts to help parents to help themselves, and, hence, their children, are blocked most by two widespread illusions:

(1) the popular misbelief that a strong mind does not have weaknesses to contend with. For example, that mental composure means being composed of no passions or "heady" emotions.

(2) The widespread misconception that certain feelings should be reserved only for certain people. For example, that the person who is loved should not represent a potential object for hate or other "unsympathetic" feelings.

It takes a heap of fortunate living to realize that the growth of our capacity to love compensates us for our increasing acceptance of our capacity for hate. The mature mind is forced to the understanding that the only way to conquer his enemy is through helping him, and that the only way to win the victory more quickly is through improving his ability to help him.

Our clinical data show that the child's mind is shaped by "impersonal" influences such as illnesses and accidents, as well as by the pressure of the more readily recognized psychic influences of the personalities around him. It frequently happens that a child who has obvious difficulties with his hate has mentally mature parents who had not been forced to use him in the service of their hate. The health history reveals, however, that other life circumstances had been no such respecter of his person. There are inevitable violations of the infant's mind through illness and accidents. All the more reason to protect the baby from human misuse.

Usually parents do not know of the biological roots of mental growth. Misguided weaning and later habit training, based upon parental ignorance of the baby's violent reactions to the *human* element, misshape the mind of the infant and child. The child is very much a psychological being and all of the training of its natural functions (such as its eating, sleeping, and elimination) has tremendous significance for the development of its mental organ. The unhealthy personality of the parent ignores this significance and thus injures the young one's mind.

We find the parent disrespecting the truths of developmental psychology by insisting that the child (1) act "older than his years", and (2) stay "a baby". The parent usually vacillates between these two fantasy systems, violating the truth of the youngster's real mental age. Only to the degree that the child is capable of self respect can he be interested in guaranteeing his best interest. Only respect begets respect. As his real nature and needs are respected, so he develops a true sense of dignity. We are born individuals but we are born without the awareness of our individuality. Discovering the comprehensiveness of our individuality through our expressions of self use is the process of psychic integration. In his education, to the extent that *his* necessities are not consulted, the youngster's individuality is violated. Insofar as he is not studied soberly and helped considerately, in terms of his requirements, he suffers the consequences of human oppression and is weakened within himself in the direction of mental illness. The growing youngster, in modifying his instincts and feelings so that their expressions will be acceptable in society, needs the help of *mental* adults.

Psychological growth, like all growth, has its own rate of occurrence. All wise education has made itself as familiar as possible with this tempo of development in order that two awful pitfalls might be avoided: (1) that premature demand will not be made, and (2) that opportunity for *timely* self advancement will be offered. We educators are gradually learning better the importance of selecting from all that is eternally true just what is also currently good.

If we human beings do not live right during our first four or five years on this earth we go through life in a kind of purgatory until our adolescent years. Then if we do not mend our ways we suffer hell on earth. What is the most beneficial infant and child behavior? and, How can the infant and child be helped to behave himself? remain very difficult and very useful questions. Our greatest educational opportunity is to prepare experts in right (fullest) living to benefit the young who are to inherit the earth.

In our child guidance clinic our workers can see for themselves who constitute the most oppressed minority on earth, the most unrecognized of all minorities, our babies. Fathers who are oppressed by their mentally unhealthy community forces, in turn, oppress their mates at home, who, in turn, oppress their infants and children. However degraded a man might be forced to become, his wife is usually dependent even upon him. But at the very bottom of the social and family heap is the infant. *Violated individuality is the only cause of mental illness.* It is only fair that the misused mind turn to misuse. So much of medical practice deals with babies and women. Men need community mental health improvements, in order that they can partake of, *and thus pass on to their families,* greater opportunities for more wholesome selfhood.

Teachers are being helped by our staff to find out that society is in trouble because actual wrong conditions seem practical, and idealized right conditions seem impractical. Teachers well selected and well trained are society's great hope. Inequalities of mental health hopelessly handicap our people in their fight for human rights. Contrasting mental health conditions among our people mock our Constitution.

Mental Health and Morality. Particularly as a consequence of our release of atomic energy, scientists are becoming more usefully impressed with social responsibility. Freud's discoveries bearing upon the release of human energy shoulder us with moral responsibilities of the highest order. It is human nature to escape if possible from unpleasant situations. As we mature mentally, we strengthen our mind so that it becomes ready and looking for situations that challenge its ability. We can live, and help live, to no nobler purpose. A man of this resolution secures for himself all of the right thrills of miracle, mystery, prophesy, and revelation through his own honest employment. Profound thought. By definition, our highest and best ideals are a source of our mental strengthening. To have to turn from them is to have to spurn mental nourishment that is indispensable to wholesome mental growth.

Our government is our overall instrumentality for living together well. For us to treat each other well is truly to act civilly towards each other. It is possible for us to know *how* to be good to each other to the degree that each knows the other's needs. We find that it pays us to take nature for our guide. Thus there is no basic difference in our treating a strong-minded man, or a schizophrenic patient, or a delinquent child well. The psychotherapeutic and moral indication is to respect each of these human individuals. The essential difference in our treatment of them lies in the fact that it is far more difficult to know *how* to be effectively humane in terms of the needs of our schizophrenic patient, and of our delinquent child. We can expect to fail our necessary amount in our office as guide to our fellow man. But our position is founded upon a new hope springing from the encouraging discoveries of Freud that counsel us more and more in terms of what is possible.

The growth of mental health in the land, that alone can account for the extension of self respectful living among us, is necessarily slow and must be conceived quite as the blessings of the fathers visited upon their children for generations to come. The root of our social evil is the root of our individual's evil, that is, mental illness. Few of us would deny that we are sinners, but our clinic experience shows that most of us shy away from the implication that there is anything wrong with our mind. Our folly is to arrogate to ourselves a rank of mental health to which we are not entitled. We pose a part that is not natural, and it is common knowledge how the poseur withstands integration. We have not yet reached the level of mental health as a society to be willing, that is, able, to assail the principle of mental illness in its true proportions.

Healthiest morality is founded upon knowledge of the truth about ourselves. It consists in our respecting our own and, hence, each other's, individuality, quite as we observe *things* behave in relation to each other. Principles that stand the trial of self-application are the only wholesomely conscientious ones. The only true testimony we have is self testimony. False testimony is that which we cannot apply to ourselves. Our faith in God can mean only our best possible expression of self confidence.

Healthiest morality is not just a matter of doing the right things. It includes doing the right things *for the right reasons*. It is the sign of a weak mind, immature or ill or both, that it must be offered more than the real reason for socially acceptable behavior. The real reason for behaving ourselves is that it is to our greatest advantage to do so. Man's wickedness consists of his degree of not knowing any better than to hurt himself unprofitably, his degree of having to neglect his own gain. Man's *summum bonum* is self possession.

For every human being all of his experience is self experience. It is the nature of the mind to appropriate all it meets. The injunction "to know the world" means to encounter many a self collision. Every new lesson that a person learns turns the pages upon himself, helps him to "cut his eye teeth". We can measure a man's mental health only by his mind's ability to express itself in the best interests of his whole self. As the person grows, he discovers more of his whole self and, by this cumulative power, he is enabled in time to express himself in ways that are most beneficial to his whole self.

Can we offer the adult any specific information about how to fit a person to be entrusted with himself, how to help the child's mental organ to develop? Our psychoanalytic experience has trained us in the all important considerations: properly introduce the child to what he is ready to meet in himself, meanwhile also respect his ignoring, temporarily, whatever of his human nature he is not prepared for.

Every one of a person's observations is weighted with self meaning so that he is incapable of taking it or leaving it. He *has* it. It *is* he. He may or may not be able to acknowledge the self-meaning of his observations, depending basically upon the help he gets from his educators in developing a changed idea of himself in keeping with the changes that his observations effect in him. As Robert Browning found it out: "When the fight begins within himself a man's worth something."

As might be expected from the regularity with which it is ignored and misunderstood, the ideal of "individual liberty" is hardest of attainment. It is most difficult to safeguard our growing child's sense of his right to his individual liberty, to persevere in our furthering his learning the austere lessons of helping, rather than hurting, himself under his own power.

All of our scientific advance in our child guidance clinic is acknowledged to be based upon the accumulation of each individual's self observations. It is because scientists have not always been able to ask themselves, "What has this to do with me?" that so many unhealthy consequences of science have eventuated. Our External World is a teacher who carries his own credentials. He says to us: "Here I am. Indeed, you are part of me. I am self-evident." Thus, the fortunate ones of us learn from the example of our External World to assess truly the value of self possession. To be mentally well from the years of our full growth on through our old age, it is required of us that we become accustomed to taking ourselves wherever we go and to becoming our every new experience.

There is only one method for becoming more way-wise in helping our fellowman, the same method that forced us to be as kind to him as we now are: self improvement.

All that we perceive is self use. Who are forced to conclude otherwise suffer sheer ignorance and sham. That understanding is weak, because it is illusionary, that teaches man nothing of himself. We can give to others only what we can take for ourselves. Our benevolence towards our fellowman grows with this comprehension of mankind; and shrinks with any other.

Dependable learning does not consist of a knowledge of "people" and of "things", but rather of a knowledge of "self". Any consciousness of our existence is our own uniquely human brain-child. It is our greatest concern that it not strangle in the womb of self respect. Newly born dignity. As those of us who grow up learn to identify with our External World and strive to assume its quality of self possessiveness, so the first necessity of the child is that of striving to assume the manifestations of the adult's power. Our task is to not become lost in our imitations. The kind of "advantage" to be derived from stunting and cutting down the learning, self growth, of our fellowman through the illusionary interpretation of self sacrifice is the most short-sighted "advantage" of all. Mutual benefit is the principal link in the chain of mutual love.

Our staff aims at practicing the understanding that what we cannot take the trouble to call self is what troubles us, misuses us. Self defense necessitates our allowing for, excusing, our identifications. It can only be a loose morality that is not based upon self acceptance. It is self betrayal to study anything without the intention of owning up to it as an individual, without growing equal to it, without growing to call it self.

No previous experience of the "people" has prepared us for understanding the exclusive efficiency of mental health forces for producing well individuals, and hence, well society. The contributions of psychoanalysis have brought understanding of the role of necessity to bear upon the inability of moral virtue to govern the world.

Resistances to accepting the truths of mental health have their rightful place. These resistances, like all else, have their usefulness. Well disciplined minds cannot but consider that if all of our people, by a miracle, could see the extent of our mental illness, the disgrace of human nature, and our slim chances for recovery, we would then be confronted with such undisguised human wretchedness that we would cry out for the ease, or disease, of our former ignorance and inattention.

Summary. In psychoanalysis Freud discovered a reliable means for systematically advancing mental integration and hence establishing solidly in the human individual's self observation the true measure of human worth. Respect for the dignity of the human individual attained a new access.

It is essential that mental health education gradually work its way into home life and politics. As Juvenal claimed: "A single house will show whatever is done or suffered in the world". To bring forth the divining rod for straight thinking, the mental instrument for smashing pretensions, the concept "individuality" has been carried to its farthest bound. Man is poisoned by an improper belief in his own importance. As a human orrery he must use or misuse his power to begin a world all over again. The necessity that each generation learn to do the same job of developing individuals counsels us that it will pay us to learn the best means of communicating what we know.

For those who have had the experiences that make it necessary to respect individuality, full explanations for respecting it are superfluous; for all others explanations are impossible. Public opinion shows its illness in destructive inattention to the parent who lacks self possession. This parent suffering from self dispossession develops the compensatory illusion that his offspring belongs to him. A child belongs to himself and to no one else. When our government guarantees rights to individuals these rights extend to infants and children. Children who are not helped constantly in assessing their self importance find themselves seeking this acceptance in all kinds of substitute ways such as boasting, lying, stealing, cheating, complaining.

We examine the minds of the child and of the parent and observe that they are all *on the verge* of all that is great, but held back invisibly into what is small because they are unacquainted with the truth that their whole world is theirs. Weak-minded people speak of their "betters" or of their "inferiors" without the slightest conception that they are speaking of themselves, of their own undiscovered powers. Dishonored humanity. Our fellow man is unredeemed from self darkness, unable to assume the leadership proper to self, consigned to a living death, because there are so many aspects of his own mind that he cannot use except with the handle "others". Self forgery.

Unless teaching represents gradual education to the full meaning of human individuality, progressive self introduction, it is vicious. Only self reference gives everything it values to self. Mental discipline offers superficial diffusion of knowledge when it is not attended by the instruction that it is self experience. Investing our attention and then accepting our observations as self experience is the essential wisdom inherent in the age-old counsel: Let nature take its course. Scientific research is a matter of letting nature take its course. Whatever is, is natural. No less than gain of self possession is our compensation for assuming the act of observing what is happening in our mind.

Civilization is the culture of citizens, each living self expressing individuality only. Know thyself, and discover thy world, are one idea. Truly to know self is to be able to feel wonder. When listening to a speech cannot mean hearing our own voice of self it is better not to have been among the audience. The spirit of truth is not in it. Using our senses, accepting the evidence of our world, means losing our minds if it does not mean gaining our minds.

DECEIVING THE DECEIVER

By Willie Hoffer, M.D., Ph.D., LRCP.

(*London*)

In one of his publications August Aichhorn (1936) describes the initial interviews of a number of adolescents, whose overt characteristics are imposture, lying and stealing. They often display brilliant qualities in their social activities, but their unceasing thefts, their selfishness and unreliability prevent any firm attachment to a social unit, be it the family, school, workshop, club or friend. The psychiatrist classifies them as psychopathic liars and swindlers who lack response when interviewed and, when their acts of stealing are examined more closely, occasionally intelligence as well. From Aichhorn's description of the background of these boys one cannot but imagine that in a few years the adolescent impostor (*Hochstapler*) will turn into the fully developed impostor, whom Karl Abraham (1925) so vividly described and Sacha Guitry impersonated so convincingly in his film, *Le roman d'un tricheur*.

But those who have listened to Aichhorn's lectures and have worked with him at the Institute of Psychoanalysis in Vienna are reluctant to apply psychiatric nomenclature to these cases. Because of the emotional response Aichhorn has been able to evoke and to utilize in treatment, they believe that this group of adolescents should be studied more closely and their final prognosis not assessed until a greater number of cases has been treated. On the other hand it would be premature to conclude from a small number of successfully treated cases that the prognosis of the whole group of psychopathic personalities should be as favorably judged as the group of adolescent impostors. Aichhorn himself has never made such a claim.

The story is told that at the beginning of this century a charitable restaurant was opened in the city of Prague, where poor people, among them students from the provinces, were served with hot soup for luncheon. Instead of plates, hollows were carved out in the table, the spoons were chained to it, and a waiter went round pouring soup from a big syringe into the hollow after each guest had placed a copper coin on the table. Failure to do this was followed by the return of the soup to the syringe. It is further said that before long none but the most honest of folk came to the restaurant.

The Prague method seems excellent for sorting the honest from the dishonest, the hungry from the adventurers, those who are not out to take risks from those who are. But that is all that this plan achieves, and the same may be said of the many corrective methods which have been invented to save the juvenile impostor from imprisonment. He will never be found in a place where there is absolutely no chance for him to display his skill.

Psychologists have resorted to the opposite course. They refuse to use chains and locks, sometimes even alertness and caution. They believe that such measures are partly responsible for the evil, and must be given up completely. Unfortunately this is not true in the case of the delinquent of the impostor type.

Aichhorn tells of many instances where psychoanalysts have failed with juvenile impostors because of this attitude. But psychoanalysis as a form of treatment cannot be blamed for such failures. The psychoanalytic technique was devised for people of a quite different kind. The only concession to psychoanalysis which the hard-pressed juvenile impostor can make, is to pretend to be a patient; he will never really feel that he is one. To him the idea of an internal conflict is quite absurd, although he may accept such a suggestion pro forma. Internal tensions and needs exist for him only in the form of imperative desires, which, as in the case of an addict, neither yield to reason nor to substitute gratification. His actions resemble perversions in which regard for another person merely spoils the pleasure and is felt to be a weakness. No evidence has yet been adduced to show that transference interpretations or any other interpretations on whatever level can pave the way for a deeper analysis of the adolescent impostor's actions and their roots. This does not mean that the impostor is incapable of appreciating the analyst's effort, skill and helpfulness. His admiration may be great even to the point of a fantasy to become a psychoanalyst himself. But it means no more to him than acquiring a new mask. It cannot prevent frequent and unexpected acting out, with the analyst himself as the victim. It constantly endangers the analytic work through interference by other victims and eventually by the police. Being imprisoned may gratify the adolescent's need for punishment, but does not affect his impostor-fantasies. The prison itself becomes the stage for clever deception.

All this has long been known to August Aichhorn. Within a research project the application of psychoanalytic technique may reveal new and interesting facts. Alexander and Healy described such facts in their book, *Roots of Crime;* but as a therapeutic approach it will prove inadequate as far as the juvenile impostor is concerned.

According to Aichhorn the juvenile impostor is not able to form a transference relationship, not even one comparable to the transference produced in the narcissistic neuroses. "As a rule the adolescent is not in the psychological state in which we would like to have him. He is negativistic, often hostile, insecure, irritable; he feels superior and pretends a still greater superiority; often he is not interested in what we can offer him and very rarely does he expect, that the hours with us will serve a useful purpose".[1] The therapist has therefore to add something to his technique in order to evoke in the impostor a positive response and an interest in the therapeutic work. Such an addition is alien to the classical psychoanalytic technique (Freud) which we use with the neuroses and allied states. The therapist must assume something at which the impostor has himself been aiming and which he then unconsciously recognizes in the therapist. Thus the therapist becomes identified with the juvenile impostor's own ideal of himself. And this has to be achieved in such a way that the adolescent does not become aware of what is going on in his mind. The change in his attitude towards the therapist must come to him suddenly and as a surprise. It is a "narcissistic relationship" in which the impostor "loves" the therapist as if he were part of his own self and not an object in the outer world from which he gains some advantage.

The aim of the initial stage of treatment is therefore the establishment of a narcissistic transference. Temporarily the adolescent wants to be like the therapist; the latter's cigarette box or other valuables do not interest him. How does Aichhorn achieve this change? One can hardly describe it except by saying that it is through a series of tricks, the result of skilfully applied psychology. Aichhorn's main device seems to be arousing surprise without causing fear, exhibiting strength without threatening, pretending to attract without promising anything. He utilizes any weakness the adolescent may show, outdoing the impostor's tricks in cleverly conducted fantasies à deux. It is no doubt dangerous to play with the patient's secret belief in magic, but if successful it is most effective, since it takes a long time before one can rely on reasoning. As a result, the adolescent feels in awe of the man who can treat him as he has treated those to whom he felt so superior. He now suspects that Aichhorn's mask of friendliness conceals his own weapons of arrogance and lack of interest. He feels in the position of those whom he has cheated and that Aichhorn has taken the role of his former self or the self he would like to be. This is not a relation based on authority or respect or anything that can be described in terms of interpersonal relationship. The fact is that for quite a time no such relationship comes into being; but something that in terms of modern psychology is hard to describe and that it has not yet integrated. It is more closely related to mental processes during

---

[1] *Loc. cit.*, p. 65.

hypnosis than to anything else that is aimed at in the modern methods of psychological treatment. It works only if the therapeutic methods are highly flexible, and breaks down as soon as standardized methods, such as free association, transference interpretations or interpretations of resistances, indispensable in other forms of treatment, are applied or too often repeated. There are times when the therapist and the adolescent's surroundings are put to a severe test when the impostor tries again to break out into acting out. Often this is caused or facilitated if the therapist is not fully concentrated to the highest pitch, if, for example, his mind is occupied by another case or by his own problems. The neurotics live their own lives, although these will be deeply affected by the transference during treatment. For the juvenile impostor in positive narcissistic transference the therapist is part of his life, an extension of his ego or ego ideal to which he returns compulsively, sometimes disregarding fixed appointments or the lateness of the hour. Woe to the therapist who needs a Sunday off from his impostor and does not make provision for a surprise visit or a ring when he is out of town! For weeks or months it may be just an exploration on the part of the adolescent as to how far the therapist's "counter-transference" goes, whether it is serious or merely one of these detestable, stupid attempts to convert him to something in which he will never believe. He is rarely aware of the fact, but if he were he would frankly state that the distinction between good and bad, honest and dishonest is hypocritical and has no basis except in our wishful thinking. If one refrains from arguing about this and gives him a chance to prove his belief, he elaborates ample subjective evidence that from his experience he is right. One must not, of course, approach the impostor with this knowledge. He cannot stand being pitied or "understood" or "helped"; he carries a deep grudge in his unconscious mind against the oedipal figures, like an unhealed wound which he treasures, or a souvenir for the purpose of auto-erotic masochism. From childhood on it has become part of his unconscious ego.

So far Aichhorn has shown us two stepping-stones to the understanding of the juvenile impostor. First, that he is liable to a peculiar form of transference of the narcissistic type. He can be made to slide into an internal situation in which the therapist is a part of his ego ideal, which is the true instigator of his impostor-like behavior. Without it he may be a manifest homosexual, a passive-feminine character, or a psychopath of any description. The content of his ego ideal is to be invincible and above everyone, free from emotional ties to any individual or society.

The second fact we have established is that the impostor is highly sensitive in his ego, vulnerable and grudging. He lives for his ego ideal so as to avoid facing his scared ego. The former is a reaction or defense against the latter, and we wonder why this defense became necessary.

Admittedly there is as yet no empirical basis for answering this question. The ego ideal has its roots in the narcissistic needs of childhood. Self-preservation, self-love and self-respect are the main regulations of the child's emotions and act as the sparks which kindle internal conflicts. The child's dependence on his parents is like a constant threat to his narcissism, an obstacle to his omnipotence. To this he reacts either by withdrawal into fantasies or by idealization. The latter is also a form of denial of reality but in contrast to fantasy it impels the child to change reality according to his ideals. In his fantasy he turns disappointing parents into satisfactory ones, in idealization he denies what is disappointing without withdrawal from the objects. It contributes to the child's ambition and inventiveness. In some boys tied strongly to their fathers no idealization takes place. In some the father is idealized but remains the ideal father, and no identification takes place which would lead to the formation of an ego ideal. With the impostor we must tentatively assume that idealization and the formation of an ego ideal occurs too early, the formative influence of reality and of the oedipus situation ends too soon. The developing ego does not take notice of a threatening, castrating father-competitor. It has fallen in love too early and too deeply with an idealized father, probably to ward off active castration wishes and passive ones rooted in the passive-feminine disposition of the little son. The ideal father does not become depreciated and enters the ego ideal unchanged. The oedipal struggle with its active and passive castration threats remains in suspense.

No evidence can be offered in support of this attempt at reconstruction except Aichhorn's therapeutic approach. He knows that the juvenile impostor is convinced of being himself as his unfailing father was in his childhood. Much as he may have suffered as a child from the father's untruthfulness, deceptions and lies he nevertheless believes in him, and he himself can do the same, because father did it. He cannot admit having once been threatened with castration and having been deceived. There is therefore no need for him to react as other boys do with contempt, aggression and feelings of revenge. All the feelings connected with the castration complex are repressed and the impostor's activities testify that repression works well. Aichhorn's approach aims at intrusion into this ego ideal. He unmasks it by proving its inferiority through his own superiority. Posing as a superior impostor he shows that he can see through the mistakes and omissions of the other's behavior and thus unmasks his ego ideal. But an ego ideal which is not proof against such discovery, is of no value and therefore no protection to one's threatened narcissism. Castration no longer appears impossible and the fear of it leads to meeting the stronger therapist halfway. To the delinquent, lying and stealing are not dangerous unless one is caught and the therapist now appears as the person from whom one may learn. This approach makes

Aichhorn acquainted with the details and secrets of the impostor's ego ideal. Once anxiety has entered the picture, the impostor trusts himself less and less, he feels less safe and more dependent on the therapist than ever before. The day comes, Aichhorn says, when the impostor realizes that the therapist is not really part of himself but a person in his own right. But now he has ample proof that this other person (the therapist) is really superior, himself skilful in deceiving and very difficult to deceive. His predictions are often like oracles, he reaches the highest ideals of one's own childhood, and if there were still a choice to make it would be difficult to turn away from him. As in the transference neurosis of the neurotic the ego ideal has been reduced to the ideal father, and that image has been transferred to the therapist.

The juvenile impostor now believes absolutely in the therapist's invincibility, and not only feels complete dependence on him, but also arranges his life on that basis. His own former ego ideal has become depreciated; he feels critical about the influences which acted upon him in childhood. He is able to admit anxiety and talks about it. He has become human, but not mature; he is rather like a neurotic. He is in a state of transference neurosis in which everything that seemed powerful and potent in childhood is now embodied in the person of the therapist. He cannot believe that he overrates the latter. He has made him the God he once believed himself to be. He has completely given way to the therapist's deception, has changed his active role of deceiver into the passive one of being deceived. He likes to seek the company of those who are prepared to share the illusion of the therapist's omnipotence and love. He has become a child again, and soon under the pressure of the transference neurosis will show the infantile emotions of fear, jealousy, curiosity, love and hate, and thus will manifest the infantile neurosis which for twenty years or so had been latent.

REFERENCES

Aichhorn, August: Zur Technik der Erziehungsberatung. Die Uebertragung, Chap. 5, Die narzissistische Uebertragung des "jugendlichen Hochstaplers". *Zeitschr. f. psa. Paedagogik,* X, 1936.

Abraham, Karl: The History of an Impostor in the Light of Psychoanalytic Knowledge, *Imago* XII and *Psychoanalytic Quarterly,* IV, 1935.

Alexander, Franz and Healy, William: *The Roots of Crime,* New York, A. A. Knopf & Co., 1935.

DIFFICULTIES ENCOUNTERED IN THE PSYCHIATRIC TREATMENT OF CHRONIC JUVENILE DELINQUENTS

By Hyman S. Lippman, M.D.

(St. Paul, Minn.)

A child who has lived in an atmosphere of delinquency for many years, and who has developed a dissocial attitude towards life, finds it difficult to change his way of living especially when — from his point of view — the reward for changing carries with it the need to give up satisfactions and to accept new, unpleasant responsibilities. When such a child is referred for study to a child guidance clinic, he probably feels surprised at the attention and concern given to his behavior which is no different from that of so many of his associates who have not been called in. Rarely, if ever, does he come because of a wish for help. A social agency has become interested in his family, learned about his delinquent behavior, and convinced the family that something should be done about it; or, he has been referred by school personnel who have found him difficult to manage, and a harmful influence to the other students; or he has been apprehended several times, and has been referred to the clinic by the Juvenile Court. He passively complies by coming to the clinic with no intention of exerting any effort to change his behavior. It is not surprising, therefore, that many difficulties are encountered in the process of psychiatric treatment with him, the success of which depends on a real give and take between the patient and therapist.

The child who is chronically delinquent largely because he has lived in a delinquent setting where there is little emotional pathology, does not present the serious problems of the larger percentage who have been brought up by parents with serious emotional conflicts. The result is that when this latter group are first seen by us, they are conflicted youngsters with serious character disturbances, distrustful of adults, and suspicious of our motives. Frequently they have deeply set patterns of behavior which have as their goal getting pleasure with a minimum of effort and without delay, and these youngsters are openly hostile to any study that will upset this status. This kind of resistance may soon disappear if they recognize the therapist as accepting and non-punishing. They recognize this attitude without being told, through long-continued experiences with adults, for they must be able to distinguish friends from enemies to be successful delinquents.

This article cannot include all the various types of chronic delinquents seen in child guidance practice. Rather, it is the intention of the writer to touch lightly on many interesting clinical observations made in the course of years of experience with delinquents. This interest was stimulated largely by work done with Aichhorn from 1929 to 1931 in Vienna. These clinical observations, however, are not derived from psychoanalytic study of these delinquents — for which there is, unfortunately, very little opportunity in child guidance work.

Most of the children whom we see and who have been delinquent for many years, are neurotic. Their delinquency is either a result of neurotic conflict or is kept active because of conflict. In almost all instances many environmental factors of a non-neurotic nature complicate the picture. One might suppose that since so many of these chronic delinquents are neurotic, they would be anxious for treatment that promises to lessen their neurotic suffering. Unfortunately, however, this is not the case. They have little conscious insight into the fact that they are conflicted, and rarely suffer from severe anxiety as do the inhibited neurotics. Only if they have been apprehended so many times that they are afraid they may have to spend their lives in institutions, may they actively seek help to change their behavior. Apparently their delinquent behavior yields them deep satisfactions in the form of substitutes for unconscious drives or serves to punish those who have deeply offended them. There must be some unconscious mechanism operating that justifies their delinquent behavior to them sufficiently to prevent an outbreak of anxiety. Anna Freud once described to the writer a delinquent boy whom she had in analysis, who was doing a good deal of compulsive stealing. She succeeded in getting him to exert a great deal of effort necessary to control his stealing for a few days, just to see what would happen. The result was that after a few days of no stealing the boy developed marked feeling of anxiety. In his case, therefore, she concluded that the stealing served as a defense against anxiety. We know that the neurotic symptom often succeeds in preventing an outbreak of anxiety. This is best illustrated in the obsessional neurotic who suffers from anxiety and panic when he is unable to carry out his ceremonials.

If it were possible to convince the neurotic delinquent child that back of his delinquency lies anxiety which, if not gotten at and removed, would cause serious disturbances in later life, our therapeutic work would be much more effective. To do this, however, we would have to break down the suspicion and distrust, and this would require frequent visits over a long period of time. Therapy would then begin after the relationship was established, and it would require psychoanalytic therapy to get at the underlying, unconscious factors. Such intensive therapy cannot at the present time be undertaken at a child guidance clinic because of the many demands made on the staff by the large number of children under treatment. There are always a few chronic delinquents who relate themselves to the therapist with greater ease, and in whom it is possible to effect a change through the development of insight. This is particularly true with children who have stolen for many years in an attempt symbolically to regain the affection of which they have been deprived.

Fortunately, some of our chronic delinquent children can respond to treatment which is not psychoanalytic. This applies particularly to those who have been seriously rejected and who have had little opportunity for recognition, with the resulting impoverishment of the ego structure. They are able to commit all types of delinquency without any obvious feelings of guilt or remorse. They are bitter, defiant, and cruel. I would like to present, briefly, a case that was once described to me by Dr. Stanley King, formerly of the staff of the Institute for Child Guidance in New York City.

For a number of years Dr. and Mrs. King accepted an occasional seriously delinquent boy for foster home care. They were challenged by the severity of the problems and had succeeded in socializing delinquents who had been given up as hopeless. Dr. King told me this story about twenty years ago and, although the details may not be accurate, I believe the important facts are correct. They accepted a boy about fourteen years old, who had been rejected by his family, and who had been delinquent for many years. He was told at the outset that they would do what they could to give him a home and make him happy, but because of the laws of the State they would have to insist on his being in every night, and going to school. They welcomed him to their table, but told him he did not have to eat with them if he did not wish to. For quite some time he would take his food to a corner of the room where he ate it, or more accurately, devoured it. He was defiant, abusive, and secretive. They left small sums of money around which he consistently appropriated. He was not punished, and his difficult behavior was overlooked; they continued to accept him in a kindly manner, looking for ways in which to make him more comfortable. A few months after he had been with them Dr. King overheard him telling some boys who were standing on a corner in front of the house, that he was cruelly treated by the Kings, frequently beaten, and denied food. Nothing was said to him about this conversation. After he had been with them for many months, he began to eat with them, but made no overtures of friendliness, and rarely spoke. I do not recall what took place at school but know that he continued to go to school during this time. Nor do I recall the steps of the improvement which was very slow. After he had been in this home for close to a year, he surprised Dr. King one day by asking him if he was going downtown and said he would like to go down with him. Dr. King told him he would be glad to take him along, but made no attempt to engage the boy in conversation, preferring to let matters take their own course. Shortly after this it was obvious that the boy was trying in his own clumsy way to become more friendly with Dr. King, and finally began following him around like his shadow. Within a short time he began to speak about some of his past experiences. This was followed by a marked urgency to speak about his past, and Dr. King said that he had never been so clearly aware of the extent to which a delinquent child can suffer in a vicious environment. The boy brought out his hostility against his family, schools, agencies who dealt with him, the police, court and others who had been part of his life. Dr. King explained to him that his resentment was understandable, and was able to show him that a good deal of his suffering was due to his own attitude and behavior which had come from his earlier suffering. The delinquency stopped. He continued to live on with the Kings, and completed his high school and college education. He was adopted by the Kings, as were several of the other delinquents who had previously lived with them. It was my understanding that at no time did more than one of these boys live in the home with them.

The treatment of this boy has many aspects in common with the experiment that Aichhorn described with the aggressives in his book *Wayward Youth*. As I recall Aichhorn's description of this experiment in his seminars, he waited until the aggressive delinquents developed a state of confusion and anxiety when they were no longer able to find an outlet for their hostility. When this occurred he found them to be amenable to treatment, and proceeded to work with them — presumably to analyze them. In Dr. King's case, the therapy was limited to the relationship that was established between the boy and his foster parents. Apparently the understanding acceptance and affection resulted in an ego strengthening. Having lived with them, it was possible for the boy to prove hundreds of times to his own satisfaction that the Kings were sincere and could be trusted. It was safe to behave differently with them only after all possibilities of disillusionment had been ruled out. One may assume that during this time, through identification with the Kings, he was able to develop a superego that could now handle, with some degree of success, the modified instinctual demands. Repression of earlier drives was possible by the strengthened ego. Sublimation was possible and a certain amount of gratification was granted to instinctual drives. These are the processes which occur in healthy individuals.

It will be seen that no interpretation of underlying, unconscious conflicts had been given to this boy. Nor were any of the other techniques used in psychoanalytic treatment applied in his case. His outpourings to the therapist were all conscious conflicts.

Although this case is quite extreme, it illustrates that to do effective therapeutic work with children who are conflicted and have been delinquent over a long period of time, the therapist must be able to give them affection, tolerate attacks made against him, have tremendous patience, and be in a position to be helpful at all times. To some extent this is possible in child guidance clinic work with the less seriously involved children, providing that the community will tolerate repeated acts of delinquency during the process of treatment.

It would be helpful if we could have a transcription of all the things that took place between this boy and the Kings, or if we could know what there was about Dr. and Mrs. King's knowledge, experience, behavior and personalities that in the end sold themselves to this boy. Social workers and psychiatrists show great variations in their ability to relate themselves to delinquents. The analyzed individual who has worked through his own delinquent drives is less likely to be threatened by anything that the delinquent says or has done. Aichhorn repeatedly stated that the therapist must accept the fact that the delinquent is always right in his behavior, in the sense that he could not have behaved otherwise. Without the right philosophy of delinquency, the therapist is blocked at the outset in his ability to develop a tie to the delinquent — a tie indispensable for therapeutic work.

Many of the delinquents we are asked to treat have been traumatized beyond repair, or have developed attitudes that are so deeply ingrained that no direct case work methods in themselves other than psychoanalysis can change their behavior. One must be careful, however, not to come to the conclusion that this is the case a priori, for there may be a therapist, with attributes of which he is not consciously aware, who can exert a more positive effect than have the others who tried. Also, it may be that peculiar circumstances within the recent experiences of the delinquent may prepare him at any given time to react favorably to therapeutic attempts which had previously been unacceptable to him. The delinquent will be quick to recognize the therapist's feeling of hopelessness about him, which would be fatal to any further attempts at therapy.

One of the greatest obstacles to effective psychotherapy with seriously delinquent youngsters is the narcissistic defense which they have set up. This narcissism is very likely due to early profound rejection, and the secondary rejections which result from the behavior occasioned by their early trauma. Attempts that are made to provide affection for these children in foster homes fail because of their inability to relate themselves to others. The same difficulty occurs when an attempt is made to give them psychiatric treatment. In severe cases this is so marked as to lead one to suspect that these narcissistic delinquents show some of the characteristics of the psychotic reaction.

The clinic is often called upon by other social agencies to study emotionally conflicted children rejected by their parents, who have lived away from their homes for many years and whose chronic delinquent behavior has resulted in their being moved from one foster home to another. The case worker in a placement agency, who works with such a child, is usually so burdened with a large case load that she can do little more than deal with the emergency problems that arise in the foster home, school and community. It is not surprising that the child thinks of this worker as a law enforcer whose responsibility it is to punish him for his misbehavior. The agency worker would be an unusual person if she did not react with annoyance to the trying situations arising from her client's difficult behavior which are so time consuming and make her efforts so unavailing. Our clinic[1] social worker is in a more favorable position to deal with these children who have been conditioned against their social agency, because she is further removed from the child's day by day problems and does not have to be the denying and, therefore, the punishing person. She can spend more of her time in building up a warm relationship to the child until he can accept her. She can then try to help the child to see the reasons for his distrust of his foster parents, school teachers and others, and the danger in continuing in this manner. She also may be able to get the child to see that the worker (and her agency) is really deeply fond of him but have been forced into the denying role because of situations outside of their control, and which often make them just as unhappy as they do him. Later on, this child may be returned to the agency worker who may then be able to continue with the case work. If for any reason at this point, this particular agency worker finds that the child continues to be resistive to her, and uncooperative, an attempt must be made to refer him to another case worker of the same agency — presuming that it is the worker and not the agency whom the child is fighting. In our clinic, if a child, who needs and seems to want treatment, shows an aversion to any member of the staff, an attempt is made to have the treatment taken over by another staff member toward whom the child may not have a similar negative conditioning.

If to the direct treatment of seriously delinquent individuals are added the negative factors associated with attempting to do case work with the parents and family of these delinquents, the reasons for the many failures in treatment are more apparent. One should not be surprised at the lack of willingness or ability on the part of the parents to sustain the prolonged interest and sacrifice necessary during treatment, since it was largely due to the parents' chronic lack of interest in their child that the problems of delinquency developed. Several years ago a graduate student in social work made a study of the interest displayed by parents of delinquent children in institutions, in order to develop a plan of treatment within the home in preparation for the delinquent's return. She was appalled by the indifference of the parents towards working out a constructive program, their placing the responsibility for their unhappiness on their child's delinquency, and in many instances their expressed wishes that he never return to them. Along similar lines, one of our state institutions for delinquent girls decided, that

[1] Amherst H. Wilder Child Guidance Clinic, St. Paul, Minn.

with few exceptions, the delinquent adolescent girls under their care should not be returned to their own homes and immediate neighborhoods. These families, when treated by family agencies, fall largely into the group that fail to respond to case work treatment. In our child guidance clinic work the social worker dealing with the parents of the seriously delinquent child rarely is able to effect a significant change in the relationship between the parents and their child, in spite of the anxiety experienced by these parents. Unfortunately, the anxiety is less often related to the welfare of the child than to the effect his delinquency is producing on the other members of the family.

To be sure, there are exceptions to this situation and occasionally case work can be successfully accomplished with lasting results. This occurs particularly in those cases where the difficulty was the result of other factors than chronic pathologic character changes in the parents. If there is enough stability in the parents to make it possible for them to come in for interviews over a long period of time, and if they are intelligent enough to gain insight into the role their conflicts have played in the development of the child's delinquency, something of value may be accomplished in a program of therapy.

Over the years there have been very few cases in our clinic of chronic delinquency in children due to organic diseases of the central nervous system. In the few cases we have seen it was not organic pathology per se that caused the problem but, rather, concomitant emotional factors.

Thus, an adolescent boy, known to the Clinic several years ago, was referred because of uncontrolled behavior which culminated in threats on the lives of his foster parents. He was suffering from general paresis, and both parents had died of this condition in a psychopathic hospital where they had been committed because of their uncontrolled behavior. In our study we found that this boy deeply resented removal from a former foster home where he had lived with his brother — his only living relative. He had been removed from this home because of attempted sex play with the daughter of the foster parents. Case work with these foster parents resulted in their giving him another trial in their home, and the behavior which had been staged for the purpose of making himself unbearable in the second foster home, disappeared.

The community must share a good deal of the responsibility for our failures in doing effective work with chronic delinquent children, for they have failed to keep up with the advances made in the studies of the emotional factors in delinquency. These studies demonstrated the needs for early recognition of those conditions within the home that could not help but develop dissocial behavior in children. There have never been sufficient funds for highly trained staffs who could work intensively with families and children when pathology in the home was first recognizable. In spite of urgent demands for the development of small institutions for the study and treatment of children who early showed patterns of delinquency, these were never obtained. In spite of proving beyond a doubt that children needed individualized care and treatment in their school work, the demands for improved school conditions have met little adequate response to date. Classes became larger rather than smaller. Tutoring programs were not supplied, and special classes that might have offered so many children an opportunity for accomplishment, have not been developed. Nor was school personnel discarded after they had evidenced the fact that they were emotionally unsuited to deal with the complex problem of educating growing children. Such relatively simple matters as adding courses in mental hygiene factors to the curriculum of student teachers, or screening out students temperamentally unfit to become teachers, were adopted by very few teachers' training schools. The need for mental hygiene clinics for adults was disregarded. Institutions for the treatment of chronic delinquent children could not obtain the teachers, social workers, psychologists and psychiatrists specially trained to deal with disturbed adolescents, without which little constructive work could be accomplished.

It is as though the community continues in the pattern of rejection of the delinquent child, and, in spite of giving lip service to newer methods of dealing with delinquency, prefers to retain the older punishing methods. Aichhorn predicted that in America it would be little different than in Austria, and that although the community would be willing to spend money for the handling of delinquency problems after they occurred, it would not spend the money necessary to a program of prevention. This has been demonstrated over and over again in our work. Lay people become acutely aroused about the severity of the problems which result from the neglect of carrying out procedures which would lessen the problems. Committees are formed by agencies; executives or high public officers form lay committees to deal with problems of delinquency. But enthusiasm soon wanes and disappears both because of the many other urgent problems facing the individual committee members which affect them more vitally and because of the demands for money which never seems to be available in sufficient amounts to carry out a comprehensive program. This has been interesting to me because the same business executives who are on these committees, spend considerable time in working out long range programs that will eventually yield profit for their ventures, and yet it has been impossible to show them the obvious fact that money is saved by programs for preventing delinquency. An executive whom I interviewed in Moscow in 1935, told me that they selected for their personnel in their institutions for delinquents the top men of the classes in the schools for social work — those who were most intelligent, had the greatest histrionic ability and the warmest feeling for people.

At the present time our institutions for delinquent children are used as a last resort in a treatment program, when all measures for direct psychiatric treatment and environmental manipulation fail. Ideally, the institutions should be used early, particularly for treatment of many of the chronic young delinquents who would welcome an opportunity to live in an impersonal setting in which they are not expected to develop an emotional tie to parents, and where therapy with them could be carried on. It would be well, also, to use the institutions early for many of the aggressive delinquent youngsters who for a number of reasons have failed to control their instinctual drives. They are uninhibited, defiant, and contemptuous of any case work methods. Before their aggression and attitudes are modified, it is unavailing to place them in foster homes because few, if any, foster parents are able to deal with the punishing behavior of these aggressives. Supervised treatment for a year or more in an institution may be sufficient to help them to tolerate frustration of their aggressive drives, accept the authority of others, and live socially in a community. Their problem is much more one of control and restraint, than a resolution of inner conflict.

The vastly greater need of undertaking psychotherapy with disturbed adolescent delinquents in such an institution would make it an invaluable resource to agencies in formulating an enlightened treatment program. Neurotic delinquents remain in institutions from one to three years during which time psychotherapy could be, but is not, given them, and this is particularly unfortunate since many of them, even if granted an opportunity for psychotherapy outside of the institution, could not take advantage of it. There are too many opportunities for gratifying aggressive drives in the community, and those gratifications seem to lessen the wish to continue treatment. Added to this is the fact that in many instances the neurotic delinquent is threatened by the discussion of the emotional factors that have produced his delinquency, and he may react with further aggression to this stirring up of conflict in order to avoid the ensuing anxiety. Within the institution this anxiety, instead of being left to express itself only in aggression, could be used as a motivating factor in treatment. The delinquent in an institution, whose outlets have been taken away from him, may welcome the interest and friendly concern of the therapist whom he might reject in the community.

We have failed in our responsibility to educate the proper authorities to the needs of these disturbed delinquents within the institution, and to their rights as sick individuals to get the treatment necessary for their recovery.

Until we can be provided with the basic needs for handling the emotional factors which are an integral part of delinquency, we will be denied the opportunity of learning much that we need to know, in order to solve a major social problem.

PSYCHOTHERAPY IN A
RESIDENT CHILDREN'S GROUP

By C. P. Oberndorf, M.D.

(*New York*)

When August Aichhorn published his notable work, *Verwahrloste Jugend,* in 1925, a great many psychoanalytic observations on the conduct of small children had been fully described and investigated, especially by H. von Hug-Hellmuth[1] in her pioneering study of the emotional life of the child. In her preface von Hug-Hellmuth defends publishing another book on the psychological aspects of childhood where so many excellent works already existed on the ground that the previous authors had ignored or omitted the sexual elements in the child's development and maintains that these play no less a role in childhood than in the life of the adult. Later in this same book she comments that "the need for joining and participating in groups, with comparisons, is so deeply rooted in people, that it already becomes apparent in very earliest childhood. Satisfying this urge manifests itself as one of the strongest influences in the character development of the human being."[2]

I have quoted freely the above from von Hug-Hellmuth because I believe that this latter characteristic of children is one of the most valuable forces which we have for the correction of conduct deviations in childhood. This desire for inclusion manifests itself in a child's activity early through imitation and soon may be converted into one of the many aspects of identification, a mechanism first investigated and described by Freud. Identification is not conscious imitation but is essentially an unconscious process based upon the emotional tie of the individual to an object outside himself. In due time such identifications become substitutes for such libidinal object-ties and finally, to quote from Freud,[3] identification "may arise

---

[1] von Hug-Hellmuth, H.: *Aus dem Seelenleben des Kindes.* Franz Deuticke, Vienna, 1913, p. V.

[2] *Ibid.* p. 138.

[3] Freud, S.: *Group Psychology and the Analysis of the Ego.* London, Hogarth Press, 1921, p. 64.

with every new perception of a common quality shared with some other person who is not an object of sexual instinct".

Of course, a very close connection exists between our conscious and unconscious actions and often no line can be drawn. However, I am inclined to think that when identification has once been established it leads especially in the formative years, to imitation to a greater extent than imitation leads to identification. In later years characteristics initially acquired through identification may be deliberately integrated in the person through conscious imitation. Sometimes when identification has not been too successfully attained by the individual he may attempt to substitute himself for the desired person even though he had been unable to achieve a satisfactory identification with him. To that extent imitation and substitution are identical. Each represents an attempt at being like another object but in both substitution and imitation there is still need for conscious effort.[4]

In any group whether it be so small a group as two children near the same age living in their own household and family, or in a congregate institution, one finds not only imitation and substitution but true identification as well. One of the very important effects of identification is its powerful influence on the formation of the ego category of the personality of the child and equally important, of the quality of his slowly developing conscience (superego). Inasmuch as conscience is the force that directs, supervises and attempts to control the instinctual drives of the child, there is a need on his part of desirable patterns of moral and ethical standards which influence his behavior but which are not too far removed from his own level. With these patterns the child can more readily identify himself. Therefore it is desirable wherever feasible not to segregate completely children who are emotionally disturbed but to attempt to alter their deviations while keeping them within a group considered healthy and normal.

To illustrate this I should like to present the experiences of the Staff of the Child Guidance Department of the Pleasantville Cottage School for dependent children at Pleasantville, New York, a unit of the Jewish Child Care Association of New York.[5] When the experiment with the psychiatric care of children at Pleasantville originally began in 1925, the number in the institution was over three hundred but today there are about two hundred children. The decrease in the population of the school is partly attributable to the decrease in the total number of children under the supervision of the Jewish Child Care Association and partly to the placement of a greater

---

[4] de Saussure, R.: Identification and Substitution. *Int. J. Psa.*, XX, 1939.

[5] The School was formerly known as the Hebrew Sheltering Guardian Society which merged about 1940 with the Hebrew Orphan Asylum and other Jewish child-caring agencies in New York City and is now known as the Jewish Child Care Association of New York. The writer initiated the psychiatric service and has since been continuously in charge of it. The staff changes over the years have been numerous, and the clinic has served as a training center for many physicians and social workers.

number in foster homes. Now, as before the merger, a percentage of the children at this institution suffer from very serious problems and disturbances but they have not been adjudged delinquent. Their deviations have a qualitative resemblance to those which Aichhorn studied and described in his work. They differ in being of a milder degree and in the circumstances under which their particular asocial conduct arose or was detected. Children of subnormal intelligence are not admitted but are cared for in a special school, Edenwald, also a branch of the Jewish Child Care Association.

The Pleasantville Cottage School, as its present name (since 1942) indicates, is conducted on the cottage system and each cottage houses about fifteen boys or girls who range in age from seven to sixteen years. Up to the present we have not attempted the experiment of housing children of the opposite sexes in the same cottage although from time to time this has been proposed. A cottage mother presides as the head of each cottage and we attempt to approximate the family set-up. However, in each of the boys' cottages there also resides a male worker who psychologically represents a cottage father. The house mother encourages active participation in the management of the cottage as a constructive influence which stimulates a group solidarity akin to family life. Each child is given an opportunity to work, play, study and compete with others of his own age and to recast his former unsatisfactory home ideals.

The Psychiatric Department consists of an attending psychiatrist, two associate psychiatrists, six psychiatric social workers, one administrator of the case work department and one case supervisor. The above psychiatric group is engaged in the treatment of approximately one hundred children. Every child who enters the School, whether or not his history indicates neurotic tendencies, is given psychological, educational and vocational tests. The major function of the Department, however, rests in psychiatric therapy of appropriate intensity for those children where it appears desirable. In addition to the care of specially selected children, the cottage mothers and supervisors often consult with the Department about children, either "normal" or under treatment who they feel need more expert direction than they themselves can give. When a child is referred to the Department the psychiatric social worker discusses the situation with his cottage mother, teachers and supervisors. After the psychiatrist has obtained a full medical and social history he decides upon the amount of treatment indicated and outlines a plan of therapy.

The location of the Child Guidance or Psychiatric Clinic on the grounds of the School makes it possible for children to avail themselves of its services whenever they feel the need. In addition, the fact that the children can be reached at all times and the general staff of the School has become accustomed and attuned to psychiatric thinking, facilitates the task of the Department in carrying out any therapeutic program which it has devised to assist the child in his adjustment to himself and the group.

Even at the beginning, before psychiatry had permeated social work as it has today, no difficulty was experienced in inducing most children to consult with the psychiatrist. Indeed, the psychiatric program gradually came to be accepted by the general staff as an integral part of the daily routine of the institution. In many cases children seem to take considerable pleasure in their contact with the psychiatrist and some have felt slighted because they had not been invited to see the doctor. When this feeling comes to the attention of the Clinic, usually in some indirect way, the offended child is asked to come for at least one interview.

During World War II the activities of the Psychiatric Department were appreciably curtailed because of the dearth of psychiatrists, and incidentally, their absence was felt by the Administration, but at the present time the Clinic is again adequately staffed.

The developmental history of the majority of institutions, whether they be schools, dependency institutions, general or mental hospitals, is likely to reflect the standards which are accepted currently by the community at large and progressively reflect the more significant changes in social attitudes. A comparative survey of the population changes in the Pleasantville Cottage School corroborates such functional interrelationship. Most striking is the almost vanishing so-called natural orphan and the increasing number of what is commonly known as the problem child who so often is the product of a disrupted home.

Social changes involving marital relationships and the increase in legal separation and divorce have augmented the number of emotionally distressed children whose needs are often best met by residence in the right type of institution. This may be an expensive boarding school or a free school, such as Pleasantville, especially designed to assist the children in meeting the handicaps of being in the exceptional social status which fate has assigned them. It is such hopeless, maladjusted children who are least likely to adapt well in foster homes and for whom institutional placement is often prescribed as a most satisfactory solution for their difficulties.

The need for a new type of service for such children resulted in the inauguration of the Child Guidance Department at the Pleasantville Cottage School in 1925. At that time about 25 per cent of the children in residence were considered to present severe behavior disorders. Today the proportion of severely emotionally disturbed children approximates 50 per cent of the total population, partly because of the acceptance of the psychiatric approach by a greater number of judges and social workers, partly as a result of changing social conditions, and also because of the favorable reputation which the Clinic has developed.[6]

The child's maladjustment may manifest itself in symptoms ranging from inability to mingle with other children, prolonged school truancy, persistent running away from home, temper tantrums, habitual lying and stealing, to alarming suicidal tendencies. Others present perverse sexual tendencies, obsessive fears and compulsions, aggressive and destructive behavior which in one or two instances had resulted in arson. Some of those admitted are children who had not found contentment in one or more foster home placements.

Where the difficulties of the children have brought them to the attention of the court the responsibility for their plight has been shifted to the parents or guardians where it justly belongs and these children have been referred on a charge of neglect and not delinquency. Through such disposition by the court children who might otherwise have been committed for delinquency escape such a stigma which is apt to stay with them through life, in coming to the Pleasantville Cottage School. A considerable number of the children in the School have had contact with the courts, currently about 20 per cent and in some years this number ran between 40 and 50 per cent. In some cases they have shown such alarming psychological difficulties that they had been under observation at the Children's Ward of Bellevue Psychiatric Hospital or at the New York State Psychiatric Institute and Hospital.

Any therapeutic program designed to assist such asocial and anti-social children to a solution of their emotional conflicts must investigate the pernicious influences to which they have been exposed in their homes. Among our cases it is customary to find marital discord and conflict, illicit sexual activities on the part of parents of which the children are well aware, conviction of one or both parents for crimes, also mental disease in the parents which had resulted in temporary or permanent commitment to a hospital for the mentally ill.

To a very appreciable degree residence and participation in the orderly, well-organized routine of an institution acts as a stabilizing influence to the bewildered child whose previous terrifying experiences at home have forced him to develop behavior habits unconsciously formed as a defense against the insecurity, unfulfilled promises, frustrations and disorganized living of his previous environment. In addition to the sense of safety and of security which identification with and incorporation into a large social unit provides, whether it be the Boy Scouts, a school or a college, the child at Pleasantville receives a consideration and recognition psychiatrically planned to counter-

[6] For this estimate and other comments upon the current work at the School I am indebted to Dr. Norbert Bromberg and Dr. Gerard Fountain, Attending and Associate Psychiatrists, respectively and to Miss Julia Goldman, Director of the Department of Child Guidance of the Jewish Child Care Association.

act his previous exposure to rejection, abandonment and abuse. At least this is the ideal which the Child Guidance Department attempts to attain. Bettelheim and Sylvester[7] in 1947 reported essentially the same conclusion of the effect of group living on children, all of whom were emotionally disturbed, at the Orthogenic School of the University of Chicago.

Another aim which the cottage system attempts to provide is a new emotional attachment for the child through sympathetic understanding on the part of the cottage parent while at the same time the cottage group may offer a stimulating ideal to replace the confused one of the child's former home. As a resident in the institution, and particularly in his own cottage, the child is subject to group pressures which serve as effective mechanisms in preparing him for the subsequent competition which will confront him in the community. In this respect the situation is analogous to that which parents hope to attain for their children, especially boys, in sending them to boarding or military schools away from home.

Among other advantages in institutional life are opportunities for occupation which revolve about psychologically influenced group activities. The close relationship between the social worker, the teacher and the psychiatrist within a planned and regulated environment, which may be manipulated and controlled as the situation demands, offers a particularly advantageous setting for research and study into the deeper-seated problems of the child. Also, the fact that the child remains for some time in one environment (the average length of stay in the Pleasantville Cottage School is one and a half years) provides opportunity for continuity of psychiatric treatment and an unchanging philosophy of psychiatric pedagogic approach. Children who seem most in need of a stabilizing environment often stay two years or more in the institution.

The therapy has been psychoanalytically oriented from the inception of the Clinic. The limitations of time and personnel have seldom allowed an orthodox child analysis in any case but always the therapy is undertaken on the basis of the physician's knowledge of psychoanalytic mechanisms and the dynamics operative in the child-parent relationship. Thus, the psychoanalytic interpretation of aggression is a guide in the handling of that omnipresent and troublesome reaction — namely, that the hate which leads to anti-social acts in multiform manifestations is due to a feeling on the part of the child that he is unloved by one or both parents, or that he has been given love which was not primarily intended for him but has been displaced upon him by a parent who is not loved by the mate.

The working methods, although always based on psychoanalytic thinking, are necessarily eclectic and include advice, consultation, persuasion,

---

[7] Bettelheim, B. and Sylvester, E.: Therapeutic Influences of the Group on the Individual. *Am. J. Orth.*, XVII, No. 4, 1947, p. 684.

indulgence, temporization, changing of environment from one cottage to another, directed activity in work, art and play, these last intended to sublimate the aggressive and other instinctual drives. The psychiatric therapy is directed to the specific needs and personality of the child, always keeping in mind the basic and often unconscious determinants which underly the child's conduct. By such eclecticism at times the psychiatrists have avoided too great an absorption with psychoanalytic technique and too deep probing and also the tendency which, it seems to me, sometimes attempts to fit the patient to psychoanalytic technique rather than the technique to the patient.

An important aspect of the work is its advisory function to all children in the institution, and its aid to the social worker in her role as an integrating force in the life of the children and in the attitude of the institution staff. Much valuable help is given outside of the clinic rooms during walks on the campus where the child is encouraged to discuss his immediate problems and his reaction to group activities. Guidance workers are thus always available for conference and assistance.

Since it is our belief that much of the maladjustment stems from the home, another important part of the program is to help parents develop a better insight into the problems of their children and to establish more satisfactory relationships between the parents and children. This is accomplished through frequent interviews by the social workers with parents either at the School or in the city. At the same time an effort is made to interpret the family to the child.

One of the original changes brought about by the Psychiatric Department was a relaxation of the rigid rules concerning visits of children to their parents or relatives in the city and to nearby towns. It was felt desirable not to isolate the children too completely from outside associations and also to make as few prohibitions within the school community as were compatible with workable living conditions.

As the Child Guidance Department at the Pleasantville Cottage School became more widely known it was necessary to exclude a goodly number of children so disturbed as to be near psychotic or older, hardened delinquents. However, with the influx of more difficult cases during the past decade there have been times when both Staff and Directors were apprehensive as to the assimilability of these cases in a normal group. It was not unreasonable to suppose that these unruly, often destructive children might disrupt the orderly routine of the institution. Of graver and more far reaching significance was the possibility that these children would permanently contaminate their hitherto well-behaved cottage mates with the anti-social traits which characterized their own behavior.

Up to the present time no evidence supports either of these suppositions. There has been no need for increased custodial care, indicating that the routine of the institution has not been threatened. Nor have we had any indication of the continued influence in undesirable conduct of any normal child because of contact with the problem children. As yet we have not experienced any serious wave of stealing, lying or destructiveness although inevitably with the children we treat, individual instances of these types of transgression occur sporadically throughout the year. Further, we have seldom been confronted with any mass hysterical outbursts through identification such as Freud described as occurring in boarding schools in *Group Psychology and the Analysis of the Ego*.

Problem children at the School have never been segregated in special cottages from the normal boys and girls who also are in residence there. In the past it had been definitely determined that the presence in residence of as high as 50 per cent of problem children of both sexes mingling freely does not undermine the general morale of the institution provided that sufficient attention is given to the unruly child. As previously stated, the percentage of problem children admitted has been raised considerably from the originally estimated 25 per cent with no apparent deleterious effects. Presumably at neither the recently established Orthogenic School of the University of Chicago, already mentioned, nor at the residential home of the Children's Service Center at Wilkes-Barre[8] has the mixture of the normal with the deviant children been attempted.

In general, psychiatric experience and observation would certainly confirm the theory that identification of a well-adjusted child with the individually maladjusted child does not occur readily, probably because he recognizes that most of such traits are regressive. Private boarding schools which often view with alarm social deviations of their pupils would probably find on investigation that their normal children are not apt to be greatly affected by the contacts provided that the deviating child received adequate psychiatric assistance which is today rarely done.

In contrast to the negative influence on the normal child through contact with the deviant, it would seem that a definitely salutary influence is exerted upon the deviant from his close association with the normal group. From time to time we have noted a valuable trend towards social rehabilitation given to the pathological child through identification with his normal associates and older leaders, and that the influence of normal children upon maladjusted children is a potent factor in assisting the latter to the formation of desirable ideals and goals. We have observed that the rebellious child aided by psychiatric help eventually comes to appreciate that the normal individual attains greater happiness and contentment through conformity to society than he can possibly achieve by his antagonism.

---

[8] Robinson, J. Franklin: Resident Psychiatric Treatment with Children. *Am. J. Orth.*, XVII, No. 3, 1947, p. 458.

The Pleasantville School is not an institution for delinquents. We feel that whatever contribution it may be able to make to the clarification of conduct disorder would be vitiated should it become one. Nevertheless, it would be possible to select from our records numerous complicated cases which under certain circumstances might have been sent to reform institutions and who appeared quite hopeless on admission but who have been gradually restored to cooperative attitudes. Perhaps one of the best proofs of the satisfactory results is the willingness of the lay Board of Trustees to meet the high and ever-mounting costs of the psychiatric work at the School.

Genetically, juvenile delinquency, as Aichhorn so brilliantly pointed out, and a large proportion of adult crime are symptoms which may be traced to the same motives as conduct disorders in early childhood. As we have indicated, behavior difficulties in children, like many of the shocking murders featured in the daily press year in and year out, are symptomatic of emotional and psychic disturbances. Our experience shows that great and apparently enduring changes have occurred as a result of the dynamically oriented psychiatric treatment of adolescents burdened with internal conflicts and external handicaps. The whole program indicates that adequate therapeutic attention to such children at an early age may prove one of the best agents in the prevention of future criminality.

The approach and plan of treatment in this resident institution closely parallels that which Aichhorn described twenty-five years ago in *Wayward Youth*. It differs — and in that sense it is perhaps unique — in that it was and is being applied in an institution where at least 50 per cent of the children are getting along satisfactorily without any psychiatric help whatsoever. The patterns of normal conduct which, the child eventually realizes, lead to easier accommodation to living, also include those of essential normal leadership and in the School, as in society, the state or in the army, identification with the leader is necessary for successful individual adaptation.

THE ANALYTIC TREATMENT OF MAJOR CRIMINALS: THERAPEUTIC RESULTS AND TECHNICAL PROBLEMS

By Melitta Schmideberg, M.D.

(*London-New York*)

The great majority of offenders who come before the courts do not differ much from the average person: they were prompted by need or temptation, acted under financial or psychological stress or just behaved foolishly. Many of them are somewhat below par, physically, psychologically or intellectually and hence less able than the ordinary person to cope with life. Others just have hard luck and live under too difficult social or personal conditions. Even if they continue to repeat their offences, this is no proof of their basic abnormality, but rather of the fact that they have not been adequately helped when first they broke down and that punishment only aggravated their problems. Though this type constitutes the majority of offenders it presents no inherent problem that could not be solved with some commonsense, humanity, financial or social help and expert guidance.

There is, however, another type of criminal, sometimes called "major", "habitual", "professional", "real", or "dangerous", "tough", "hardened", or "callous", who differs fundamentally in his psychological make-up and general outlook from the ordinary "accidental" offender and who, though relatively small in numbers, represents a serious danger to the community. Few reformers or even psychiatrists care to tackle these men except by repressive measures, and those who have tried and failed speak loudly of their wickedness. The persons anxious to help juvenile delinquents and sympathetic to ordinary offenders often advocate special harshness for these "real" criminals who they claim cannot be rehabilitated.

For the purpose of the present contribution I am listing as "major criminals" those who have (1) fundamentally anti-social attitude and criminal associations; (2) whose offences are either particularly serious or repeated and in most cases carried out with considerable skill or at least deliberation; (3) who live mainly on the proceeds of crime and do no steady work. Psychiatrically this group consists mainly of psychopaths, some of them borderline psychotics or even psychotics, made worse by their isolation from ordinary society and their penal experiences. Just as a neurosis of long standing becomes more intractable, owing to the accumulation of "secondary factors", so the "secondary" factors in the life of a criminal — society's reaction to him, the social, personal and family consequences of his crimes, his prison sentences and the ensuing social ostracism — make his abnormal personality still more abnormal.

Case 1. This case was considered a "tough guy" and a "dangerous criminal". He was an American, aged twenty-eight, the child of immigrant parents, from a broken home and otherwise bad social environment, convicted for hold-up. He had been delinquent from childhood and was sent to a reformatory at the age of thirteen. There his initial defiance was broken, he decided to make good, and by the time he was discharged, had become a star pupil. After his discharge he was for some time under the guardianship of a social agency whose report of him was excellent. However he could not hold a job, because he remained a "hobo" and finally became a "gamster", and he was convicted twenty times for minor offences. At twenty-one, he received indeterminate sentences up to eighteen years for "more than thirty-two armed hold-ups". Though he thinks he committed double their number, he served six and one-half years and was paroled for the twelve. He claimed that there is no crime he did not commit with the exception of murder, counterfeiting and cheating at cards. For example, he would cohabit with a homosexual and then, when he was asleep, hit him over the head with a bottle and rob him. He was unusually intelligent, and was very successful in his hold-ups so that as leader of his gang, he enjoyed quite a reputation. He managed to escape on many occasions and was arrested only when he was asleep after he had been denounced. Before any hold-up he was so excited that he used to vomit. He had intense feelings of inferiority and neurotic difficulties in working. Though trained for many jobs he had never been able to keep a job for any length of time and had been extremely restless. He came for analysis some months after his discharge from prison, was seen about fifty to seventy times during a few months and after that continued to keep in touch with me although irregularly. Now he is settled, contented, a good father and husband, has good sense of values and is socially adapted.

Case 2. An American in his late twenties who had been a professional criminal since childhood. When fourteen he had pushed a man from a train so that he was killed. He specialized in very skilled types of robberies and was arrested twenty-two times although sentenced only once: He was sent to a reformatory for one year, where he was very violent and claimed to have dominated the reformatory, and that the others went about in fear of being stabbed in the back. There is no record of definite lawbreaking activities but since he left the reformatory he was unable to work. I analyzed him for some months and have kept in occasional touch with him since. The treatment straightened out his marriage difficulties. He is now a good husband and father, goes straight, works, has more initiative in a socially adapted way and feels well.

Case 3. An American in his late twenties who is a friend of the previous case. They used to "work" together. His record is similar. He was the son of poor and almost illiterate immigrants, and had an unhappy childhood. His father used to thrash him savagely, yet he claimed to feel no resentment, but was sorry for the old man. He was a professional criminal since childhood, often charged but "had many lucky breaks", and was sentenced only once to a year in a reformatory. He has now been on probation for several years. He was very skilled at his exploits and used to work steadily and conscientiously at crime, e.g. the thought of having failed in robbing a purse because he was clumsy would keep him awake at night with self-reproaches. He had a very friendly, trusting manner, and would do anything anybody asked of him. He could not kill a cockroach, and would feed baby cockroaches with meat. He was a very affectionate father, but used to beat his wife savagely though he was attached to her. He gave up crime when he went on probation and worked steadily but was poorly paid, and unable to manage his affairs, was restless and harassed. He earned $30 a week, while by crime he used to make $400 per day and in consequence his wife threatened to walk out on him. He was helped by a philanthropist. He suffered from depressions, crying fits, and fears of suffocation, which were alleged to date back to anesthetics given him before an operation in childhood. He was very restless, slept poorly and drank too much. There was improvement after his treatment in that his marriage improved; he felt less anxiety and slept better. The treatment was not completed.

Case 4. A man in his middle forties of English nationality who emigrated overseas in his late adolescence. He was a hobo for some years and his first sentence was at twenty-one for a bank robbery. He served altogether eight years of his long indeterminate sentences in the United States and was then deported to England. In England he served a three-year sentence in Dartmoor (the most repressive convict prison in England for specially selected offenders) and received twenty-five "strokes with the birch" (rod) for "robbery with violence" against a bank. He had committed other types of offences as well, e.g. confidence tricks, bootlegging, and the like. He considered himself a failure at his criminal activities because he was too easily caught and too easily cheated by fellow criminals. He had certain confused grandiose ideas about reforming society, and felt strongly on these matters yet nevertheless used these ideas for his confidence tricks — and by means of them succeeded in making contacts with many well-known persons. He made a point of robbing only banks and not individuals (though there have been exceptions to this self-imposed rule) ; and looked down on petty crime although he sometimes stooped to it. The thought that he owed somebody one shilling would keep him awake at night. He took the blame for an offence committed by his wife, though it had much more serious consequences for him. While he was at Dartmoor she ran away with a man, taking all his clothes.

He was a depressive schizophrenic with intense depressions, depersonalization and overwhelming feelings of disgust. His claim to rob only impersonal institutions reflected the impersonal object of his sadism and was an expression of his depersonalization. He suffered from impotence (partly an after-effect of prison), and very deep inhibitions in work.

His mental condition struck the attention of the prison authorities and he was given a psychiatric examination to see if he was fit to undergo flogging. After flogging, he had a compulsion to pick up, put down and touch again every object in the cell to regain some contact with reality and to assure himself that he had not lost his reality sense. When he came out of Dartmoor he looked, and was, dangerous; he used to walk about at night, hoping somebody would bump into him accidentally, and give him an excuse to knock him down. Once before entering Dartmoor he almost killed a fellow worker on a sudden impulse because the man tickled him. Once in an American prison a visitor asked him what he wanted most and he blurted out "to have a machine gun and mow everybody down" with such hostility that the man was deeply upset. When he came out of Dartmoor, a philanthropist promised to support him until he was able to work, on condition that he be analyzed. When this support came to an end after two years he lived for a time on the earnings of his girl friend, a prostitute, and perhaps by other shady means. He has since settled down fairly well, is now working for his living, and has kept out of trouble for five years. He seems generally better adapted but still looks somewhat strange.

Case 5. An Irishman of thirty-two with white hair, who came for treatment straight from a ten-year sentence in Dartmoor for blackmail. His social background was very poor and the family life was unhappy. He saw his father sober only twice. At eighteen he was fined for "assaulting" a girl (this does not necessarily mean with violence); and at twenty-one he received a sentence of three years hard labour and twenty-five strokes for "robbery with violence". He claimed that a hernia resulted from his effort to control himself while undergoing the flogging. Before this prison sentence he had practiced blackmail on homosexuals in an "amateur" way but in prison he learned the professional tricks and when he came out he "was determined to be a rotter". He committed many crimes and mean acts and was given a ten year sentence for an attempt to blackmail a homosexual for 10,000 pounds. When he came out of Dartmoor he was determined to go straight for the sake of his wife who had waited for him, and his child, but found to his horror that he was unable to do even simple factory work, though he was an intelligent man. He could not understand the reasons for this inability but realized the likely consequences and got into a panic which made it still more impossible for him to concentrate. In despair he wrote querulous letters and begged for help from all and sundry till a philanthropist referred him to our Institute. I got him some financial help and exemption from both work and the Army (this was during wartime) in order to give him a breathing space. As a result of this help and the treatment, he began to feel more secure and this enabled him to take up work, although at first with some difficulty, with an unusually sympathetic and tolerant employer. On several occasions in times of stress he indulged in both hetero- and homosexual promiscuity, though he was devoted to his wife. On some of these occasions he had serious criminal impulses, but he has kept out of trouble for four years and has worked steadily. He is more settled and contented even though for persons with such experiences it often takes years of normal life and social and financial security to become like other people.

Case 6. This was a friendly old man of sixty who came to the United States in his childhood. His sentences for robbery totalled fifty years, of which he served over thirty, seven of them in solitary confinement. He was referred to me soon after his discharge from prison. I saw him only three to four times, listened sympathetically to his story and practical troubles, commented on the resentment he must be feeling, and sent him to an aftercare worker for help with his practical problems. I heard two years later that he was doing well, and both the worker and the patient thought that I had helped him to settle down. The patient was particularly impressed with the fact that I, as a woman, talked to him on equal terms and was not afraid of him even though I knew his record. I have helped several other criminals who were very disturbed just after they came out of prison and were helped by just a few analytic talks, to settle down and tackle their personal problems. This is a particularly rewarding service.

Case 7. An Irishman in his late twenties was sent to me by his family. He had never worked, but lived mainly on his family and used to pawn his father's clothes, steal or get money from him under false pretences or by threats, and the like. He also committed many offences outside the family but was only charged three times before the court. He was court-martialled for "striking a superior officer" but managed to get acquitted. He drank heavily and was prone to violence. He became engaged to a girl but quarrelled with her continuously and refrained from intercourse. At the same time he slept with many other women, but had no more than the physical relation, and never went back to them a second time, for fear of being held responsible for any possible pregnancy. After several months' analysis he was deported for a minor passport offence. Since then, in the last three years he has settled down, studied, passed an examination and is earning his living. He has gone straight and is happier and has discovered that he is attached to his fiancée and means to marry her. He also gets on better with his family.

Case 8. A school teacher, about thirty, American of immigrant parents. He twice set his school on fire, "in order to have a holiday with pay". He made elaborate arrangements to make it appear that some anti-Semites were responsible who wanted to get rid of a Jewish teacher (himself); and did so by writing threatening letters to various persons including himself. He was sentenced for incendiarism and for "sending threatening letters by mail", and served three years. He had intense feelings of inferiority as well as social and sexual difficulties. Now he leads a strictly law-abiding life, earns his living and is studying for a degree. He shows some personality improvement since his treatment which is not yet concluded.

Case 9. An English girl, aged twenty-four. She was a particularly skillful shoplifter, who had committed thousands of offences but was caught only once, and then only because the sum involved (£5) was "too small to bother about". She came from a respectable middle class family. Her parents were devoted to each other and attached to their daughter. She had been very difficult from early childhood, unusually precocious and pathologically greedy. She was brought up in good convents. She suffered from intense anxiety, depressions, feelings of isolation and depersonalization and from self-hatred. She had an intense hatred of men, and excessive guilt feelings about sex. The only thing that gave interest to her life were mad champagne parties and driving at 80 miles an hour. When she was twenty-one, the family lost their money. She felt cheated, and bitterly resentful that she should have to work. The only thrill she got out of life from then on was from shoplifting, which mitigated her resentment. She could not take an interest in a job unless it gave her a chance to steal. She had hundreds of jobs. She began to make friends only with "shady" persons. She used to daydream and boast about her stealing exploits to her confidants, yet she carefully concealed it from others, in particular from her parents. Her attitude to these acts repeated her masturbatory experiences. She had several years of analysis, about three times a week, and about fifteen to twenty minutes each session. She improved greatly and now works for her living, has a boy friend with whom she gets on well except for occasional scenes and is on the whole contented. The case was followed up for two years.

Case 10. An English girl, aged twenty-four. She was an illegitimate child brought up by very religious, narrow-minded foster parents who were attached to her in their own way. She stole and lied since childhood and ran away at fourteen. She was put in various charitable institutions and later was sent to Borstal,[1] with four prison sentences for theft. She had never been able to keep a job, and spent any money she had, however much it might be. At nineteen she had an illegitimate child who was taken away at birth. She never showed any feeling for him. She became a prostitute and gave her earnings to her boy friend. She then became a member of a gang (there are very few of them in England). At the recommendation of our psychiatrist she was put on probation with the condition that she undergo treatment. She suffered from anxiety, depressions, lack of initiative, neurotic fear of people, nervous headaches and general insecurity. In the institution in which she was placed she proved very difficult and behaved like a child of fourteen, e.g. was afraid to go out by herself. After six weeks of treatment, while I was on a holiday, she ran away and stole 5 pounds from a member of the staff who had befriended her. Two years later, however, she returned, made good the theft and told me that she lived with an older man whom she meant to marry, was supporting herself by honest work and was for the first time in her life contented.

Case 11. This was an English woman in her middle forties, who had served fifteen sentences for misrepresentation and theft. She was the daughter of a clergyman, who had spent some time in mental hospitals. Her brother, a doctor, was an alcoholic and eventually committed suicide. Her mother and sister were also unbalanced. She herself had been abnormal since childhood, and oversensitive and very conscientious till late adolescence. In her twenties she committed many irresponsible acts, and according to her family cost them 5,000 pounds. She was sent to a number of psychiatrists who diagnosed her as a "psychopath" and refused to treat her. She had married, and had two children; but the marriage was not happy. Her husband was irresponsible, never worked and often fell back on her for financial support and she had several unsatisfactory episodes with other men.

---

[1] Village in Kent. *Borstal System,* in Great Britain and colonies, a method of treatment of juvenile delinquents up to twenty-one years of age, by an association (*Borstal Association*) established by act of Parliament (1908). Its chief features are a special form of detention in a *Borstal Institution,* and a highly organized supervision after dismissal. (*Webster's New International Dictionary,* 1947).

She first appeared before court when she was about thirty and from that time on was continuously in and out of prison. She was referred to our Institute[2] by her prison visitor when she was serving her twelfth sentence but the patient failed to come until the eve of her next appearance before the court. The Institute for the Scientific Treatment of Delinquency managed to persuade the magistrate to give her another chance but almost immediately she committed another offence. I kept in touch with her while she was in prison and when she came out she came to see me regularly. She seemed to improve till she committed a further offence and received a sentence of eighteen months. I went to see her in prison, and asked her what she did with the money she had stolen. Now at last she confessed that she was being blackmailed by three people who knew that she had killed her illegitimate baby at birth fifteen years ago. One of the blackmailers was her former lover, the father of the baby. Her appearance before the court dated from that time. I continued to keep in touch with her while she was in prison and helped her to solve her practical problems when she came out by sending her to a solicitor who advised her how to behave should she be blackmailed again. Though at first she was still unstable she has not been in trouble for over three years and is stabilizing increasingly since she had some security and a normal life and has cut herself off from her former prison associates. She has a steady job and says she is contented and happy and looks very much better.

It must be stressed that this patient's troubles were not caused but merely aggravated by her being blackmailed. It was important to protect her future against such further attempts. But it was the fact that I stood by her repeatedly and went to this trouble, instead of letting her down as had her family and many others, which was of such therapeutic importance.

To evaluate these therapeutic results let us now compare these specially selected cases of "major" criminals with the statistics of ordinary criminals. The statistical records of criminals after discharge are merely negative, simply stating whether or not the man has been rearrested, but there is no indication as to the personal fate and psychological condition of the individual, nor whether he really obeyed the law or merely managed to evade it.

In England "Dartmoor men" constitute a group of their own, since only those convicts who are regarded as the most hardened and dangerous criminals are sent there. This is the official explanation for the fact that 90 per cent of the men discharged become recidivists (the remaining 10 per cent presumably die) ; but the very harsh treatment meted out in this prison is a further factor that makes subsequent social adaptation difficult, if not impossible. For this reason results achieved with Dartmoor men, or with criminals who have undergone flogging, are to be regarded as more important than with ordinary offenders.

On the other hand the results here described should not be overestimated. It would be absurd to claim 100 per cent results for any type of

---

patient; eleven cases is a much too small number from which to draw any conclusions, except to say that the results are encouraging.

The English patients and the one Irishman were treated under the auspices of the Institute for the Scientific Treatment of Delinquency in London. They were referred to the Institute; one by her probation officer, one by a social worker, one by her prison visitor and two by a private citizen who took an interest in the patients' welfare. The American ones were sent by social agencies and aftercare organizations. In the latter case the selection depended on the referring agency: two agencies would ask me to see patients only in emergency situations whenever the aftercare worker felt that psychiatric help was needed, while the third agency selected the patients in whom they thought I would be most interested and prepared them for analysis. Nobody paid for the treatment of these patients except for the one treated in private practice and most of them were helped in a financial or in a practical way while undergoing treatment.

It is comparatively difficult to get major offenders for treatment in England — partly because there are not so many of them. Most patients are referred to our Institute by Magistrates' Courts and probation officers who deal only with, or are more ready to see, the need for treatment of minor offenders, and in particular of juveniles. The English aftercare organizations and prison visitors rarely send us cases. In New York there are many agencies that are only too willing to send any type of criminals for treatment, if they could only find the psychiatrists ready to take them on.

I have not treated any patients while in prison or living in a regimented institution, and I have misgivings about doing so. It is difficult to serve two masters: either you are on the side of the prisoner and then you are likely to get into difficulties with the prison authorities sooner or later, or you are on the side of the latter and then cannot win the trust of the inmates who are always likely to suspect the prison psychiatrist of being a spy. Also, if we treat a patient in the restricted, and in its way, sheltered situation of prison we have no means of judging how he will adapt himself when he comes out and is faced with the manifold difficulties of liberty, family life, or lack of it, the task of finding and holding a job and the innumerable hurts and disappointments he is sure to encounter.

It is particularly important to treat patients immediately after their discharge from prison. An important factor in recidivism is the fact that when the criminal comes out of prison he is not psychologically in a fit state to settle down or to take a job or to cope with his innumerable (family and other) problems. Really good aftercare would radically reduce the problem of criminality. In England, official aftercare is niggardly, the ex-prisoner being given a small sum of money, and maybe a suit. Sometimes he is found a job. But these jobs are often offered by employers who take advantage of the man's position, while the man who comes out of prison physically and psychologically below par would need a particularly lenient and sympathetic employer to make good. If as a result he throws up the job, or is sacked for inefficiency or "impertinence", he may drift in and out of two or three more jobs, getting increasingly discouraged or hostile and hence less able to give satisfaction until he eventually finds himself back in prison again.

The New York agencies with whom I worked were very much more generous; they tried to give the men not only material help but a feeling of friendship and support, and some help in sorting out his personal problems. But for a seriously disturbed man, as so many are after a long sentence, even that is not enough. Sometimes as little as two to three analytic interviews with me helped the men to settle down; this does not mean of course that radical changes were effected, but such aid may mean the difference between the man going back to prison or leading a fairly normal life. In the treatment of criminals, more than with any other patients, I have been impressed with the tremendous difference even a little help may make to a man's future life. There is a world of difference between a man who is still neurotic and unstable, and yet able to support himself and lead a fairly normal life, and one who is compelled to commit crimes that make him spend the rest of his life in and out of prison. The difference is still more marked from the point of view of society, which is either hurt by the criminal when free or has to maintain him while in prison. Generous and humane aftercare combined with psychiatric help upon discharge should therefore be among the first considerations in combatting criminality.

I treated some criminal patients for their neurotic symptoms. Two of the patients referred to me had not been involved in any lawbreaking activities for several years, but they were not able to work for their living adequately, which of course always means the danger of a later relapse. The purpose of analysis was to remedy their work inhibitions and their difficulties in coping with life, to adjust their marital difficulties and to remove their anxiety and other neurotic symptoms. But such patients must be handled carefully lest as a result of the analysis and the removal of their neurotic inhibitions and the making conscious of their repressed hostility, they embark again on criminal activities.

The majority of the patients enumerated here (eight out of eleven) were treated with a view to achieving a character change, i.e. of modifying their antisocial outlook and enabling them to cope adequately with life within the law. All of them suffered from a deep-rooted neurotic work inhibition and from sexual difficulties. A poor man with a neurotic work inhibition is likely to turn criminal, for how else is he to support himself? Such patients do not know of course that they suffer from a neurotic reaction; and the authorities are only too ready to assume that they are "lazy". Reluctance to work is a breach of the conditions of probation or parole and may itself be a reason for the man being sent back to prison. Difficulties in work may take the form of restlessness, changing from job to job, of "inefficiency", for which they get sacked — a fact that increases their difficulties and sense of inferiority. Sometimes they just throw up their job without knowing why. Often after having changed their jobs frequently, mostly without giving notice, they become vagrants, and from that to drifting into crime is only a small step. The more enlightened authorities are aware of the need to enable delinquents to earn their living. One of my patients who had been to a progressive reformatory, under the care of a progressive social agency, and in a progressive prison had been well trained for at least half a dozen jobs, yet was unable to keep any job for psychological reasons, until analysis cured him.

To cure a criminal's work inhibition is a most important aspect of the treatment and one of the tests as to whether he will settle down satisfactorily.

The prognosis in these cases depends on many factors:

(1) *Clinical psychiatric considerations.* It may be more difficult to achieve results with a psychotic petty offender than with a major criminal who has a fairly normal personality or only minor neurotic traits.

(2) *Criminal record.* We must distinguish between fact and appearances; no experienced criminal is ever caught for every offence. Case 2 was charged twenty-two times but sentenced only once. Several months had passed before it occurred to me to ask why he had not been sentenced more often: he merely commented "cash is 90 per cent of the criminal law". He had always succeeded in buying his way out, except the last time. His friend, Case 3, also commented on the "many lucky breaks" he had had. But of course, even being charged twenty-two times bears no relation to the actual number of crimes committed in the case of men who habitually and professionally practised crime all day and every day for many years. In England, where the enforcement of the law is more effective and where once a man is charged, justice is incorruptible, the criminal record bears more relation to a criminal's real activities. But English sentences are much shorter, e.g. an American patient of mine received a ten to twenty years' prison sentence at the age of seventeen (as he said, "because I did not know the ropes") for being accessory to an act of burglary. In England the worst that could have happened to him would have been a three years' Borstal sentence, of which a considerable part would have been remitted for good behavior.

But though enforcement of the law is more effective in England, Case 9 managed to evade the law for years; as she put it "if you have a confident manner and some money in your pocket and are well dressed when you steal you are likely to get away with a lot". In the case of more serious crimes, however, such as holdups, the offender is usually quickly caught.

But in no country of the world is every offender arrested every time, nor ever charged with all the offences committed. Often it is an indication of the skill and the dangerous character of the offender that he is able to get away with so much. Again social factors play a role. In England there is probably less class injustice than in most countries, and once a man is charged neither money nor influence will make much difference to the sentence. But background and money do make a difference in keeping the offender away from court.

Case 7 committed money dishonesties, but owing to the fact that he lived on his family and committed his dishonest acts, if possible, at home, he had less need to commit crimes in the outside world and on many occasions his family helped him to straighten matters out so that he was not charged or could get off lightly. Similarly Case 11 is supposed to have cost her family £5,000 before she ever came before a court. It is impossible to estimate the number of upper class criminals who live on their families and friends and escape both detection and being charged through the help of their families.

(3) *The family situation.* Probably the strongest inducement for a criminal to go straight is a law-abiding wife and a happy marriage, or his concern for his children. It is all important whether a wife stands by the man when he is in prison. Personal and family factors exert as great an influence in the cases of criminals as in those of neurotics, but social factors are more important.

When considering the family situation of criminals attention centers almost exclusively on whether the other members are criminals or not; yet all the factors relevant in the background of neurotic patients such as ambivalence, lack of love, neurotic anxiety or any special complex on the part of the parents are just as important with criminals. When my gangster patient (Case 1) settled down, worked steadily and was for the first time in his life happy, his mother got into such a state that she went to the parole officer and denounced him, with the intention of sending him back to prison. When an adolescent psychopathic delinquent became normal as a result of the treatment, his father, who had claimed that his only aim in life had been to see the boy get well, for which purpose he had sacrificed very large sums, had a nervous breakdown. The mother of a delinquent girl was good to her only when the daughter was in trouble and she, the mother, felt herself a martyr and the object of pity. Is it surprising, in any of these cases, that the children had become criminals?

(4) *Social conditions.* You can redeem criminals only if you are able to offer them decent conditions of life within the law. Contrary to the official slogan "crime does not pay", it does in fact — at least for a short while and when a man is desperate he considers only the immediate present.

In recent years, it has been easy to get jobs for ex-criminals and for all and sundry; but what will happen if there is a depression? All those who are somehow below par — and therefore are in particular social and psychological need of a job — will be the first to be fired, and the consequences of losing a job for these men are particularly serious.

(5) *Penal experiences and social ostracism.* The criminal is isolated by his law-breaking activities and associations from respectable society and ordinary standards, even if he is not discovered and punished. Case 9 took a great deal of pride in her skillful stealing and had no conscious compunctions about it. She lived out her masturbation fantasies that way. Yet she had overwhelming guilt about the latter which she felt made her different from everyone else. The guilt over sex and the displaced unconscious guilt over stealing accounted largely for her self-hatred, feelings of isolation and depersonalization. She was devoted to her parents and she realized how distressed they would be if they knew of her stealing. She achieved better relations with people when as a result of the treatment she eventually gave up larceny, and in turn, these better personal relations enabled her to work, i.e., to take her place in society and to give up her solitary, anti-social (masturbatory) thieving.

There is no criminal in our society who is not at least ambivalent in his attitude to his crimes, and has neither conscious or unconscious guilt about them. He may displace the latter onto irrational anxieties, e.g., hypochondriacal worries. This psychological isolation from the rest of society, which is largely conditioned by anxiety (frequently of a paranoid type) and guilt, in conjunction with the actual social ostracism throws the outcasts together and this constellation of factors plays an important role in the formation of gangs.

Penal experiences are as a rule the next step in the development of a criminal. In no case I treated have I yet seen any beneficial effect from imprisonment. This is not a subject to be dealt with in a few lines. Briefly, the abnormal life in prison and in particular the sexual frustration intensifies any existing abnormality. Flogging (whether in England by order of the court or in America in the form of beating up by the police, or illtreatment in prison) intensifies hate more than any other experience. But even ordinary prison experiences, including the so-called "progressive" prisons, had similar effects — namely the intensification of anxiety and hostility. This anxiety as a rule led to an increase in antisocial tendencies. For persons who have spent years in prison these experiences have become an integral part of their lives; the associations formed with their fellow criminals are usually their main attachments. The prison sentence often breaks up their marriage or family life; they have difficulties in getting a job, and would be ostracized by decent people were the truth known. To hide the truth continuously is a great psychological strain and creates a gulf between them and the rest of the world, and whenever their attempts to settle down socially fail, it is an additional incentive to falling back on their criminal associates with whom they can at least be themselves.

In spite of an apparent toughness these criminals are extremely sensitive, for the "toughness", largely based on depersonalization, is only a defence. Especially in England where there is no glorification of crime, it is sometimes pathetic how much a man who tries to go straight suffers from fear that an accident might bring his criminal past to light. Therefore it is particularly important for the ex-convict to have friendly contact with an analyst who often represents the man's only link between his criminal past and respectable society. A patient explained this to me, when he asked me out to tea. I accepted his invitation. I make a point of shaking hands with some of these patients as often as possible but of course make sure that my attitude does not seem patronizing or oversolicitous.

Many psychiatrists fail with criminals because they are biased against them. We must see things from the patient's point of view, realizing not only that he has wronged society but that society has also wronged him and owes him something. Such patients often behave in a very obnoxious manner, partly because they hate being under an obligation to the analyst, partly because of the hostility and oversensitivity created by their past experiences and by the insecurity of their present position. A great deal of patience is required in dealing with them. More important still, the analyst must have some knowledge and feeling for *their* world which differs so radically from our safe and respectable one. A criminal, in speaking about a certain policeman said "he was quite a criminal himself", and in answer to my question, added "you could talk to him about his children and wife, he was quite human, he was like one of us". To him being "human" was synonymous with "criminal". Hardly surprising, since often all reactions these men encountered from respectable society are retaliation and inhumanity, or at best patronizing charity and moralizing hypocrisy. I believe, one must have one qualification for this type of work: one must be fundamentally unimpressed by our social set-up and take a very matter-of-fact view of our society and the slogans propounded by it. One must also keep an open mind when listening to the views and experiences of any type of patient. This unbiased approach goes a long way towards making contact. What I learn from one criminal about social conditions, the police, prisons, courts, etc., I use in the analysis of the next one; with the more intelligent I discuss these issues objectively. This makes them feel that I treat them on terms of intellectual equality, and through their increased communicativeness I learn a great deal.

The more difficult patients test you out, again and again. As one said to me with a smile: "I am a bit of a psychologist myself." Of course they are. They are bound to be, it is their only means of survival. After having been so often let down or disappointed or hurt by people who professed good intentions, they naturally are distrustful. They not only judge your actions but sense your attitude. I play fair with them: I do not try to trick them into admissions, nor into anything else. Above all I will not betray them. I often have to deal with the officials in charge of them or with their landlords, families, or the like, and sometimes try to straighten out situations; I am, however, very cautious not to say anything that might be used against the patient. In one case, however, I did inform the father of my patient of the fact that he was getting more and more involved with dangerous criminal associates and discussed the best way to handle the situation; and on another occasion I warned him that the patient was coming home carrying a broken bottle and was in a dangerous[3] mood — but in this case I knew the father well and could rely on his discretion and on his handling the situation sensibly.

As I said, the reality of these patients is usually so complicated that it is necessary to help them to cope with problems they cannot solve by themselves; but apart from that it is often of therapeutic value to do so. Analytic theory regards neurosogenesis from the point of view of instincts, and in more recent years to some degree in terms of affects; but antisocial development and psychopathy is, in my opinion, largely due to a disturbance of object relations (rather than of the superego). "Standing by", showing forebearance again and again helps the patient gradually to acquire a sense of security, makes up for the love and security he missed in childhood, and enables him to gain a social attitude by identification. This mechanism explains the sometimes remarkable results good English probation officers achieve even with difficult cases. But with many criminals this is not enough: they must be analyzed. However, the attitude just described is the precondition for analyzing them, as well as part of the therapy. Analysis must be modified to meet the psychological as well as the practical needs of these patients who are excessively ambivalent and particularly unstable. They must be analyzed in such a way that they do not get upset, as even a temporary increase of anxiety and the consequent "acting out" might have the most serious social consequences. I only give them interpretations which diminish anxiety and do not even temporarily increase it; I also give a great deal of reassurance and practical help. I analyze the latent negative transference yet at the same time encourage to some degree the positive one. It is essential to interpret hostility in such a manner that it is not felt as a reproach and to give due credit to their "good" impulses. My spontaneous

---

[3] By heating a whisky bottle it cracks irregularly and is then used as a dangerous weapon to lacerate the face of an opponent.

and unprofessional manner helps to break down their depersonalization which is an important defence mechanism of the "callous" criminal. I often give interpretations in such a way that the patient does not notice them, and I may use any pretext possible to get him to see me. (Hardly any criminal attends regularly.) Our social worker informed me that a patient of mine who had stopped treatment three years ago was involved in various dubious situations of which she wished me to know nothing. I got in touch with the patient under the pretext of asking her to procure for me a certain article in short supply. When she came, I had a chat with her about things in general until her anxiety gradually diminished. Then she told me about her difficulties and the situation she was involved in, and I unobtrusively made a few interpretations based upon my previous knowledge and the social worker's information. We parted on very friendly terms and I made her promise to come to me if she should get upset and not wait till things deteriorated too much. Another criminal patient telephoned me in great excitement two years after he stopped analysis, because a friend of mine who had formerly employed him had, he said, refused to give him a reference. I asked him to see me, and we discussed the matter in detail. I promised to talk to my friend and then inquired how he was. In this one talk I did more analysis than I had done during several weeks of regular treatment previously. It is essential to see these patients immediately when they get into a bad state, and if possible within a few hours, because their state of mind is so explosive. While with an ordinary patient the worst that would happen is a bad spell of anxiety, these cases might commit a serious antisocial act on the spur of the moment under the stress of anxiety, accentuated by resentment at not seeing the analyst when they most needed to.

If a patient gets himself into further trouble I continue to stand by. If it is reasonably possible I stand bail for him, attend his trial and may give medical evidence on his behalf. I keep in contact with him while he is in prison and help him to manage his affairs during this period. Unfortunately, the English prison regulations do not allow me to visit an offender in prison, unless I use one of the few visits allotted to the family. This is a great pity as the seclusion of prison and the fact that the analyst takes the trouble to visit him in prison makes the convict more responsive and more communicative. Two patients confided to me on such an occasion important facts that they had kept from me during several months of treatment. I continue to keep in touch with patients even after they stop treatment and encourage them to turn to me in emergencies. I promised my Irish patient (Case 7) after he was deported to persuade his family to help him, but after several attempts I had to admit that I had failed. I expressed my regret but added in my letter that he would do better to start to stand on his own feet — and he did. I expressed my sympathy when things went badly and my satisfaction and appreciation when they went well. Altogether we have only exchanged about half a dozen letters during the last three years but they were an important factor in inducing him to settle down satisfactorily and to start work. I try to introduce other people (e.g. colleagues of mine) into their lives so that they have somebody else to fall back on when I am away or when they feel angry with me. It gives them more security to have several people they can ask for help, and it is wise to let them act out their ambivalence towards me in a way that is harmless, as it may otherwise burst out in antisocial acts.

In this article I have only touched briefly on a few aspects of this vast subject. It is important to realize how very little we know about it yet. For fifty years many hundreds of analysts have treated tens of thousands of neurotics, people who as a rule come from a similar background and have a personality similar to that of the analyst. Yet how many criminals have been studied as yet, and how far can we disassociate ourselves from an inherent social and moral bias? How little do most of us know even about the conscious personality of the criminal, the world he lives in and the experiences he is subjected to? There is a temptation to build up a theoretical construction of "the criminal" and be led in our practical approach by such preconceived notions, instead of first gathering ample empirical material before we lay down rules and generalizations.

ETIOLOGY AND DEVELOPMENT

CERTAIN TYPES AND STAGES OF SOCIAL MALADJUSTMENT

By Anna Freud

(London)

Social Maladjustment Based on Early Disturbance of Object-Love

August Aichhorn, in the introduction to his book *Wayward Youth* emphasizes the pathogenic significance for social maladjustment of faulty ego and superego development. Internal and external factors which prevent the normal growth of the various ego functions act as a hindrance to the "primary adaptation to reality" which Aichhorn regards as the indispensable basis and background of a development on social lines. Internal and external factors, on the other hand, which interfere with the emotional development of the child and prevent him from attaching his feelings to permanent love-objects (the parents or their substitutes) prevent as Aichhorn explains, the second step in social development, i.e. adaptation to the cultural standards of the community of which the child is expected to become a member. Where normal emotional ties are missing, there is little incentive nor is it possible for the child to model himself on the pattern of the adult world which surrounds him. He fails to build up the identifications which should become the core of a strong and efficient superego, act as a barrier against the instinctual forces and guide his behavior in accordance with social standards.

Since the recording of the observations which have led to this first tentative explanation of dissocial behavior, many workers and authors in all countries have confirmed and extended Aichhorn's theories. Separations of children from their parents, prolonged absence, or death, of the parents, loss of affection for or of confidence in the parents, repeated change of foster home, institutional life without provision for the development of personal attachments — all these have, in accordance with Aichhorn's findings, been emphasized as the factors most frequently discovered when investigating the histories of dissocial and delinquent children. Among these findings special recognition has been given to the factors which concern the

193

relationship of the small infant to his mother. The first year of life is the crucial phase in which the all-important step from primary narcissism to object-love should be taking place, a transition which happens in small stages. By means of the constantly repeated experience of satisfaction of the first body-needs, the libidinal interest of the child is lured away from exclusive concentration on the happenings in his own body and directed towards those persons in the outside world (the mother or mother substitute) who are responsible for providing satisfaction. In those cases where the mother is either absent, or neglectful, or emotionally unstable and ambivalent, and therefore fails to be a steady source of satisfaction, or in cases where the care of the infant is insufficient, or impersonal, or given by changing figures, the transformation of narcissistic libido into object-libido is carried out inadequately. There remains a stronger tendency for all future life to withdraw libido from the love objects to the self whenever the object-world proves disappointing. The body and its needs retain a greater importance than normal, as shown by stronger emphasis on auto-erotic pleasures (rocking, sucking, masturbation, etc.). The blunting of libidinal development which results from these early deprivations leads further to an inadequate binding of the destructive urges in the child.[1] Normally, the destructive impulses ally themselves with the child's manifestations of object-love on the pregenital levels of infantile sex development and thereby lend force and vigor to the preoedipal attachment to the mother and to the manifestations of the oedipus complex. Where the child's love-life is deficient, the destructive urges remain more isolated and manifest themselves more independently in various ways, from merely overemphasized aggressiveness to wanton destructiveness, i.e. in attitudes which are in themselves the most frequent sources of delinquency and criminality.

There is, thus, a wide variety of social maladjustments which are based essentially on very early disturbances of the development of object-love and the consequent weakening of the ego and superego functions. These maladjustments usually make their appearance at the beginning of the latency period, i.e. at the time when the child's behavior begins to be mainly dependent on the inter-relations between the agencies within him, and when his aggressive actions begin to direct themselves to the wider environment, outside the immediate family circle.

OTHER TYPES OF SOCIAL MALADJUSTMENT

Theoretical and practical work on the behavior problems which are built on this pattern has, in recent years, deflected interest from other forms of social maladjustment which are of different origin and significant though

---

[1] See the author's, Aggression and its Relation to Emotional Development, Normal and Pathological, *Psychoanalytic Study of the Child*, Vol. III.

they arise at approximately the same time (the first half of the latency period) and show a similar symptomatology. These other disturbances of social functioning, which form the subject of this paper, are based, not on the early stunting of object-love but on conflicts which belong to the normal realm of the child's emotional attachments, especially to the attitudes of the oedipus complex of which they are derivatives and distortions. They do not originate from a weakening of the ego functions and identifications though secondarily their existence may harm the integrity of the ego. These social maladjustments are, therefore, in their content nearer to the neurotic than to the common dissocial abnormalities. But they cannot, on the other hand, be classed with the neuroses since their manifestations are not, like the neurotic symptoms, compromise-formations designed to hold the inner balance between id and ego forces, but rather irruptions of more or less undistorted libidinal and aggressive material into the sphere of the individual's dealings with the real environment.

An approach to the understanding of this variety of social maladjustment is best made by way of those imperfections and failures which appear during the development of the child as normal transitional stages.

The Period of Normal Social Maladjustment

We do not, ordinarily, apply the term dissocial to the emotional upsets which occur between the young child and his environment, even if these upsets consist of disorderly and disruptive behavior that is extremely disturbing to the family, i.e. to the first social community to which the child belongs. The child cannot be said to respond either in a "social" or "dissocial" way before he has acquired some ability to perceive and understand objectively his surroundings and the rules governing them. While he is still developing his sense of reality,[2] it is normal and inevitable that he should misunderstand and distort what he perceives of the external world. The child passes through stages when he *identifies* elements of the external world with his own person or body, when he *projects* unwelcome inner urges into the outer world, and when he perceives and thinks in accordance with his own wishes, not in accordance with objective realities. While identification and projection, wishful thinking and magic omnipotence dominate the functioning of his mind, he can see the environment only subjectively, not objectively. The child thus reacts to what he feels to exist in the outer world rather than to an actual reality. His consequent unwillingness to accept restrictions, to renounce or to postpone wish-fulfilment, his over- or underestimation of his own powers (feelings of grandeur, sense of inferiority), all these constitute the young child's inherent social maladjustment which gives

---

[2] See Ferenczi, "Stages in the Development of the Sense of Reality", in: *Contributions to Psychoanalysis,* Boston, R. G. Badger, 1916.

way gradually — as the sense of reality develops — to a growing social adjustment.

Where these infantile modes of mental functioning (remnants of the primary process?) persist beyond their normal time, the behavior based on them is then classified as dissocial.

One of these instances, namely the distortion of reality owing to the projection of the individual's own inner urges into the external world, and the consequent hostile, aggressive or anxious behavior towards the external world has been studied and described in detail by Melanie Klein and her followers.

TRANSFERENCE OF THE FAMILY SITUATION AS A SOURCE OF SOCIAL MALADJUSTMENT

Transitory maladjustment to the environment arises further from the child's tendency to displace libidinal and aggressive attitudes from the emotionally important people in relation to whom they have arisen to less important or even indifferent persons. It is normal for the young child in the first two or three years to look at the whole world within his reach as an extension of his family. Primarily, young children endow in their imagination all adults with the same qualities with which they have become familiar in their parents and expect from them the same treatment which they receive at home. As the child makes more contact with people outside the family, there is a constant overflow of emotion from the crucial preoedipal and oedipal relationships to the child's relationships to comparative strangers. Viewed from the side of the family, this acts as a relief of tension which, especially in small families, may otherwise rise to unbearable heights. Viewed from the point of view of the environment, the displacement of emotion (transference) creates in the child an unrealistic attitude to the environment which acts as a barrier to adjustment. In normal cases the child learns by experience to differentiate between adults standing in a positive or an indifferent relationship to him and this realization gradually reduces his tendency to transfer emotion indiscriminately. Instead of merely displacing feelings and conflicts which in the environment act as a constant source of friction, the child then becomes able to make new and different contacts, to meet people on their own merits, not as new editions of the parents, and to profit from this extension of his emotional life.

This step in development from the family circle to a wider community is not taken where the preoedipal and oedipal attitudes are too violent and remain unresolved. In such cases the environment is merely — throughout the latency period and sometimes for ever — an extended battleground for the fighting out of family conflicts.

In this difficult task of growing beyond the family relationships the child receives varying, often insufficient, help from the adults who are responsible for his upbringing.

Many *parents*, especially middle class parents, are in the habit of teaching the young child that adults, no matter how superficially met, are "uncles" and "aunties". They find it difficult themselves to accept the fact that the child who is precious to them is merely tolerated by strangers and often considered a nuisance. In these instances parents and child are thus moved by the same impulse: to treat the whole environment as an extension of the family.

The old-fashioned *kindergarten* or nursery of former days was based on the same principle of merely widening the family circle. To say of the nursery nurse that she was a kindly, motherly person who succeeded in establishing a warm family atmosphere in her classroom was intended as high praise. In some countries the nursery nurse was officially addressed by the children as "auntie" (*Kindergarten-Tante*). The disadvantage of a system which invited the displacement of family reactions to the new surroundings, would have been still more obvious if the formal methods of discipline and occupation, which were in use in those times, had not suppressed all spontaneous emotional expressions of the individual child and thus obscured the issue.

Modern nursery schools are built on completely different lines. The adult in the nursery behaves as a teacher and deliberately refrains from playing the mother-role. She restricts bodily contact with the pupils, avoids, wherever other help is available, assisting the child with his bodily functions, does not handle the child's body, or pet him, take him on her lap, etc. Instead of affection and kindliness only, she offers the child interesting and fascinating occupations of a more subtle, indirect (sublimated) kind. Where a nursery school is organized in this manner, the behavior of the children differs considerably from their behavior at home. In response to the new atmosphere and the new approach to their faculties they react in new ways. The nursery school teacher takes the place in their life, not of a mother substitute for the gratification of unsatisfied emotions, but of an ideal figure, farther removed from instinctual life, with whose sublimated interests and demands the child can identify himself.[3]

---

[3] War work with homeless children (Hampstead Nurseries 1940-1945) has afforded experimental proof of this statement. In *Infants without Families* (Dorothy Burlingham and Anna Freud, New York, Int. Univ. Press, 1944) the authors write: "It is of the greatest interest to watch the difference of behavior shown by the children in these intimate relations with their chosen foster-mothers on the one hand and with the group teacher in the nursery on the other. We are in this respect often reminded of the difference of behavior which children, who live with their families, show in the day-nursery. They are sometimes perfectly good and social in the nursery and extremely difficult at home. This is not — as many nursery-school teachers seem to think — due to the fact that the mother does not know how to handle the child whereas the teacher does. It is due to the difference in the emotional response to mother and teacher respectively . . ."

Schools for latency children have, in this respect, developed in the opposite way. Schools of the conventional type used to take so little notice of the emotional life and conflicts of the child that, especially in boarding schools, the sudden transition from the family atmosphere to a completely new and more impersonal group life acted as a shock and retarded inner adaptation to the new surroundings. There were no outlets and no possibilities for transference of feelings for adult love-objects and hence arose the risk of libido, used formerly in relationship to the parents being withdrawn into the self, used to over-emphasize auto-erotic activities or turned too violently to contemporaries. Modern progressive schools for the same ages are attempting to remedy these faults but seem to overshoot the mark in the opposite direction. Instead of forcing the child to fit into the environment, they aim at fitting a flexible environment to the needs of the individual child, so as to give the pupil's abilities the widest possible scope for expression. In many cases children use this scope, not to develop their faculties, but to displace and transfer the loves, hates, jealousies, anxieties and conflicts which are the residues of their unresolved family relationships. Where this happens the result is a lack of adjustment to current reality. The child is then unable to make use of the opportunities offered to him by the modern school. His development goes in circles instead of progressing and deteriorates into a series of repetitions of emotional experience.

Transference of Fantasy as a Source of Social Maladjustment

Teachers are better able to understand their pupils in the light of understanding the psychological mechanism of displacing emotions and thereby transferring the attitudes of the early mother relationship and the oedipus complex to the school surroundings. Behavior which seems meaningless and unexplainable as a reaction to the real school environment, and the actual educational methods of the teacher, makes sense when seen in terms of the child's home surroundings. By watching the children in school the teachers learn to draw conclusions as to their homes, and to confirm their suppositions by contact with the parents. The knowledge gathered in this manner may, in many instances, provide the key to the pupil's maladjustment in the class, his over-active or excessively passive behavior, the inhibition of his intelligence, his aggressive or oversubmissive attitude to teachers and classmates.[4]

---

[4] Many children of nursery-school age completely change their behavior towards their classmates and become jealous, uncooperative and resentful when a new baby has been born in their family. — Fear of an excessively strict father is expressed as fear of the teacher. — Quarrels between the parents, divorce of parents, almost inevitably create a tendency to play out teacher and parents against each other.

See also in this connection Hertha Fuchs' paper Psychoanalytische Heilpaedagogik im Kindergarten, *Zeitschrift für psychoanalytische Paedagogik,* VI. Jahrg., Nr. 9, in which the wildly aggressive behavior of a boy of nursery-school age is traced back to his witnessing scenes of violence and of sexual intercourse between his parents.

On the other hand, teachers should not rely too confidently on these interpretations of their pupils' behavior. The conclusions drawn as to the home life of the child are as misleading in some cases as they are accurate in others. Many children appear cowed and miserable in school though they are not maltreated at home. Many are overanxious in their relationship with the teacher, inhibited in their work and afraid of bad marks or criticism, though no undue pressure is put on them by the parents. Others feel suddenly rejected by classmates and teachers without anything having happened at home to explain their changed attitude. The emotions with which the child responds in the community are, in these instances, transferred, not from actual family life, but from the conscious and unconscious fantasies which accompany the development of his object-relationships. The aggressive and destructive images of the oral phase, the sado-masochistic fantasies of the anal level, exhibitionistic fantasies with the defense against them, fantastic castration fears, the family romance with the feeling of being isolated and unloved — all these distort the child's picture of the teacher, as they originally distorted the picture of the parents. Transference of these fantasies to the school cannot but act as hindrance to social adjustment. Instead of responding to the actual environment and benefiting from the opportunities which it may offer, many children live for long periods in a painful and, from the point of view of normal development, unprofitable, self-created fantasy world.

It may be taken as a danger-sign when children, without obvious reasons, persistently complain that they are discriminated against and badly treated by the teacher or not liked, or ridiculed by the other children. A change of school, in these cases, makes little or no difference. Usually, after a short interval of comparative adaptation, the transferred fantasies reassert themselves and, as before, disturb the child's relations with the new environment.

The disturbances of social adjustment which are based on this transference of preoedipal and oedipal fantasies are deep and far-reaching but do not, as a rule, lead to violent dissocial outbreaks. They color the child's attitude to the environment, make him moody, anxious, resentful, inhibited, and apparently unresponsive. But these repercussions affect primarily the inner emotional life of the child and only secondarily his dealings with the outer world.

ACTING OUT OF FANTASY AS A SOURCE OF SOCIAL MALADJUSTMENT. PSYCHOPATHIC BEHAVIOR

It is a further step in social maladjustment when the fantasies, displaced to the environment, do not remain in the realm of thought and feeling but lead to direct action. The environment is, then, not merely understood in terms of fantasy but treated on the same basis. Life, in these circumstances, is a form of psycho-drama with the child concerned acting as stage manager and as the central figure. The other members of the community, adults as well as children, are used by him as actors on the stage who have to play prescribed roles according to his dictates.

Children who, in this manner, act out *passive-feminine,* or *masochistic fantasies* in school actually succeed in being punished more often or more severely than others. They provoke the teachers by behaving insolently or aggressively, or by failing conspicuously in their work, or by managing to be found out in all the small current misdeeds which, normally, remain unnoticed. They invite the dislike of their classmates to such an extent that they become the butt for their aggression and even persecution. In day-schools, it is no rare event to see such a child running home breathless with a whole horde of pursuers at his heels. In boarding-schools, the persecutory actions of the others may reach their height at bedtime or in secret scenes of bullying. The maltreatment may be focused in one teacher or one especially strong and active classmate, or may come more diffusely from all teachers and a vague group of children.

In the absence of personal persecutors the maltreatment may be ascribed to impersonal factors. Such children run to school breathless in the morning, pursued by the idea of being late; they constantly feel oppressed by the lack of time for finishing their work; by feelings of incapacity and inferiority; by the pressure of work in general, etc. They live at home, in school and in the wider environment as in a world peopled by oppressors, and in fact they succeed in being treated with unkindness, severity, suspicion, hostility, etc.

The corresponding *sadistic fantasies* are usually acted out with either animals or younger children as objects. Maltreatment of animals has always been observed in boys during the latency period. When this urge is directed toward small insects, as for instance flies, etc., it may take the form of deliberate and intricate torture. (For instance: to turn insects on their back and enjoy their hopeless efforts to right their position; to pull wings off flies and watch their helplessness; to permit an insect to escape, only to haul it back to renewed torture at the last moment.) With bigger animals, such as dogs, cats, etc., a fear of retaliation usually accompanies the sadistic actions. The victim is less helpless and is expected, at any moment, to scratch, bite, etc., in self-defense. This fear of a counter-attack seems merely to heighten the boy's pleasure in hurting the animal. Some children take special pleasure in scaring animals (e.g. chickens); others are fascinated by the idea of drowning animals (kittens), and are delighted to watch their struggles in the water. Many boys are fascinated by the idea or sight of pig-killing. Similar sadistic actions are directed towards weaker children in the form of bullying.

Sadistic fantasies may also be lived out in the role of onlooker, when other children are criticized or punished. Some teachers believe that such scenes appeal to the pupils' sense of justice and serve to establish moral values, the distinction between right and wrong, etc. They act as they do in ignorance of the fact that punishment in front of the class serves as a stimulus to certain *scoptophilic* attitudes in fulfilling a fantasy where the child is witness to a sadistic scene which is enacted before his eyes. Where these fantasies play an important role in the child's emotional life, such scenes of "crime and punishment" may for the child be the high lights of his school experience.

Community life in a classroom offers special opportunities for the acting out of *exhibitionistic fantasies*. Some children succeed in continually concentrating the attention of the class on themselves, either through excellent performance in work or games, or through heroic behavior of some kind, standing up to the teacher, fighting bullies, defending the rights of the weaker ones, by showing themselves indifferent to danger, to bodily pain, to punishment, etc. Where the expression of direct exhibitionistic fantasies is inhibited, the exhibitionistic aim is pursued in a disguised manner. Instead of being the hero in his class, the child may persistently play the fool, invite ridicule instead of admiration, and thereby concentrate attention on himself as effectively, although in a negative manner.

The acting out of positive exhibitionistic fantasies may fall into social channels and thus serve the aim of adjustment to the community. (Heroic, unselfish behavior, good performance of difficult tasks, etc.) Even then, there is a socially disruptive element in the fact that it is compulsive. Whatever the circumstances, under the pressure of this fantasy, the child has to excel at all costs, his interest is primarily concentrated on being conspicuous; the activities which help him to achieve his aim are of secondary importance.

In a similar way, children become involved in continual battles with their environment when an *observation of intercourse,* or fantasies concerning intercourse between the parents, have had a traumatic effect on their sexual development. Influenced by his own crude pregenital urges, the young child conceives that intercourse is a violently aggressive, sadistic act which is continued until one of the partners, or both, are severely damaged. The fantasies expressing these ideas are then displaced on the environment and acted out. Such children impress the community as belligerent, truculent, quarrelsome, always up in arms against something or somebody, ready to pick a quarrel about points of minor importance and relentless in the pursuit of their quarrels. They readily come to blows with other children and get involved in endless verbal fights with adults. It is significant that they do not avoid their enemies or attempt to rid themselves of them in some other manner. Their hate-relationships are as important to them as love-relationships are to normal children, i.e. the hated enemy is for their unconscious the representative of the sexual partner.

When surveying the range of fantasies which are acted out in the environment in this way (masochistic, sadistic, scoptophilic, exhibitionistic, fantasies of aggressive intercourse), we recognize their content as that of the well-known, ubiquitous masturbation-fantasies of the pregenital phases.

While the child is passing through the oral, anal and phallic phases, he normally develops these images and fantasies, which represent, on each subsequent level, the main trends of his instinctual life. The child's ego normally rejects these fantasies, and as a result they become repressed from consciousness, projected into the external world, turned to the opposite, displaced, sublimated, etc. By the time the child has passed the climax of the oedipus complex and entered the latency period, all that is left of them is one single image or fantasy into which the whole past era of infantile sexuality and aggression has been compressed. The nature of this fantasy varies according to the main fixation-points in the child's instinctual life, i.e. according to which of the early satisfactions, frustrations and traumatic experiences has had the strongest influence on his development. This residual pregenital fantasy thus survives the first period of childhood and becomes its embodiment and secret representative. It is, from then onwards, the sole carrier of the child's sexuality and finds its bodily outlet in phallic masturbation. It does not, at this stage, lead to acting out, nor does it disturb adjustment to reality in other ways. Indeed, it manifests itself so little in the ordinary ego-activities that it is impossible to guess the contents of a child's masturbation-fantasy from watching his behavior.

But this state of affairs alters with the child's attitude towards phallic masturbation. The struggle against the need to masturbate begins earlier but usually comes to a climax at the beginning of the latency period. It is, as we know, based not only on prohibitions from without but on inner conflicts. The instinctive wishes which find their outlet in masturbation are, in many instances, incompatible with each other. Death-wishes against the parents, destructive images, clash with desires for sexual possession, etc. The whole underworld of fantasy, in its crude and primitive nature is unacceptable at the levels of ego- and superego-development which the child has reached. The child's ego therefore adopts a defensive attitude against the masturbation-fantasies and the bodily activities which are connected with them.

Psychoanalysis has always stressed the role of the masturbation conflict in neurotic development. In normal development, the elements, the stages and the variations of the conflict are powerful factors in determining character formation in the latency period. In the development of social adaptation certain aspects of the masturbation conflict play a specific part.

The child's struggle against masturbation is directed on the one hand against the content of the fantasy, which as a result may disappear from consciousness, on the other hand against the bodily act itself, a battle which has been followed and described in many analyses of adults and children. The inner prohibition may concern the use of the hands in stimulating the genitalia. (This leads to many inhibitions in the use of the hands, to neurotic clumsiness, to obsessions concerning contact by hand, obsessional precautions against dirtying the hands, etc.) Or the prohibition may be directed against the place of stimulation (penis, clitoris) so that the masturbatory activity becomes displaced to another part of the body. (This is the origin of ear-pulling, nose-picking, nail-biting, rhythmical rubbing, etc., as masturbatory equivalents.) But normally this struggle against masturbation, whatever direction and form it assumes, is at least partially unsuccessful. Throughout the latency period the need to masturbate reasserts itself periodically as a powerful urge. At such moments, the ego-defenses are over-run and, accompanied by conscious or unconscious fantasies, bodily relief is achieved through voluntary or involuntary phallic stimulation. (The latency-child's reactions to these involuntary breakings-through, his consequent guilt-feelings, self-punishments, depressions, etc., are familiar.)

In certain cases, on the other hand, this struggle against masturbation is abnormally successful. The ego then, and usually under the influence of castration-anxiety, inhibits even the occasional, relieving, masturbatory outbursts. As a result, the masturbation-fantasy is deprived of all bodily outlet, the libidinal and aggressive energy attached to it is completely blocked and dammed up, and eventually is displaced with full force from the realm of sex-life into the realm of ego-activities. Masturbation-fantasies are then acted out in dealings with the external world, which become, thereby, sexualized, distorted and maladjusted.

The acting-out of fantasies (passive or active, sadistic or masochistic, exhibitionistic or scoptophilic) is, therefore, a derivative of phallic masturbation and, in these cases, its substitute and representative. This origin explains certain characteristics of this special form of social maladjustment. The driving force behind it, which makes adults and children in the environment join in the acting-out, is the full force of infantile sexuality; the monotony and repetitiveness of the child's behavior corresponds to the endless monotony of the crude fantasies which accompany masturbatory acts; the compulsive and periodic character of the acting-out corresponds to the periodic need for masturbation which arises from the id and appears in the child's ego as an unrelated foreign body.

SUMMARY

Certain types of social maladjustment should not be understood as the consequence of early disturbance and consequent weakening of object-love, but as happenings within the realm of the child's normal emotional attachments. A first phase of normal social maladjustment is brought about by the

use of certain primitive mechanisms of projection, introjection, magic thinking, etc., as regards the object-world.

A second regular phase of social maladjustment can be traced back
to the child's tendency to displace (transfer) his object-relationships.

A grave disturbance of social adjustment is to be traced back to the
complete suppression of phallic masturbation and the consequent flooding of
the ego-activities with sexual content. This sexualization of ego-activities
produces certain familiar forms of psychopathic behavior.

LATENT DELINQUENCY AND EGO DEVELOPMENT

By Kate Friedlander, M.D., D.P.M.

(*London*)

In 1925, Aichhorn (1) introduced the concept of "latent delinquency" into psychoanalytical literature. This is, in my view, one of the most decisive contributions to an understanding of the personality deviations of offenders. Aichhorn recognized that delinquent behavior is often released by experiences which are in themselves not traumatic and he realized that these experiences lead to antisocial behavior if a disposition thereto already exists. He saw this disposition in an arrested personality development. He maintained that the ego of the delinquent is still under the dominance of the pleasure principle and that for this reason impulses are acted out more easily than with a personality whose ego is governed by the reality principle.

This conception is of importance from various aspects. It is fully recognized that a decisive change in delinquency figures can only result from an effective program of prevention. Therefore, if there is a disposition to antisocial behavior and if this disposition is to be found in the personality structure rather than in inherited characteristics, the factors contributing to this development must be understood before effective preventive measures can be devised. From the point of view of treatment, only methods which deal with the underlying disposition will eventually effect a cure.

The conception of "latent delinquency" has not been given the attention it deserves and it therefore seems justified to show its implications in some detail. Aichhorn himself, although working with this hypothesis, never studied the early disturbance in itself, but only stated its implications.

I should like to examine further the hypothesis that environmental factors lead to a disturbance in early instinct modification and object relationships, which results in what I have called the "antisocial character formation". (5) The findings of those cases which have been analyzed as well as the findings of a larger number of cases which have been examined, seem to show that this character deviation was the result of a disturbed ego development. This occurs when for various reasons the modification of primitive antisocial instinctive drives has not taken place, or has only partially succeeded. During the first three years of life, a process of education takes place which is more far-reaching than any other educational effort later on, although normally it comes about almost unnoticed. Owing to the child's absolute dependence on the mother and the strong emotional tie which unites them, the mother's demands are fulfilled without undue stress, even though each of them imposes a frustration on one or another instinctive drive. Changes in two different directions are being brought about by this early handling. First, the child learns to wait for the gratification of instinctive drives and does so even in the most lenient environment. Secondly, it learns to accept substitute gratifications, and, slightly later, a deviation of instinctive energy into reaction formation takes place. All these factors are essential for ego formation. We assume that the first distinction between the ego and the non-ego occurs when gratification is not forthcoming and tension rises and causes unpleasant feelings. Each further frustration, if administered by the person whom the child loves and if handled in a way the child can easily endure, contributes to a deviation of energy from the instincts to the ego.

Any factor which interferes with the establishment of a firm mother-child relationship and with consistent handling of primitive instinctive drives will hinder this process of ego development. Separations of any length of time before the age of three, lack of interest or lack of time on the mother's side, personality defects in the mother which make her inconsistent during the periods of feeding, weaning and the training for cleanliness, all may lead to a disturbance in ego development, which will be the more severe, the graver the environmental defect and the stronger the child's instinctive drives. This disturbance in ego development runs parallel in the disturbance in establishing object relationships. The relationship to the mother is highly gratifying and this gratification leads to an outward flow of libido and thereby to a strengthening of the object relationship. If the gratification derived from the love object is insignificant or followed by too much displeasure, the self remains cathected to a much larger extent. We observe this result constantly in counselling mothers of children under the age of three. The mother of a one-year-old child, for instance, is exasperated because her child will not eat, and she feels that all her efforts are in vain. She has no influence over the child. The child's needs are explained to her and this effects a change in her way of handling him. In the majority of cases she comes back after a fortnight very happy not only because the child now eats but because she feels that the child's relationship to her has changed, not necessarily from hostility to love but from withdrawal to interest.

Normally the child's ego at the age of three is strong enough to enable him to endure a certain amount of tension and to cope with primitive instinctive urges, the expression of which is not favored by the environment. Object relationships also have to some extent become more important than direct instinct gratifications, at least at certain times and when there is a conflict between the two.

In cases where this early education has failed, a three-year-old child cannot stand tension and easily withdraws to autoerotic activities if the object relationship becomes frustrating. The child then freely expresses undesirable urges, such as aggression.

If a child enters the oedipal phase with an ego thus undeveloped, and, as Aichhorn points out, still more or less fully under the dominance of the pleasure principle, it is very unlikely that this phase can pass without further disturbance. The most important outcome of the decline of the oedipal phase is the consolidation of the superego by a process of internalization and desexualization, which together lead to the oedipal identifications. This process of identification is based on the *slow* renunciation of oedipal desires. These wishes have to remain active and unrepressed for some time and the ego has to be sufficiently strong to stand the tension of ungratified desires and castration anxiety. If the ego is weak, castration anxiety is unbearable and the oedipal desires are quickly repressed. But such an ego is not strong enough to maintain an effective defense. The tension of ungratified desires becomes unbearable and the instinctual drives then seek gratification by regressing to a pregenital level. In contrast to the mechanisms at work in obsessional neurosis for instance, this defective ego permits the gratification of these desires without building up new defenses against them. The relationship to the parents or other adults remains sexualized, usually on the anal-sadistic level and as a result of this the superego is defective. Contact with adults outside the family circle does not lead to the usual identifications of the latency period, which enrich the personality, but remains on the same level as the sexualized relationship to the original love objects. The people in the environment are loved as long as they gratify and hated as soon as they frustrate. The usual reaction of the latency period to the demands of adults is lacking. Since there is no functioning superego, there is no internal demand and consequently no tension between ego and superego to produce guilt feelings. The child's actions are governed by the pleasure principle, so that only direct prohibition of instinctive drives is successful, and that only temporarily. Although there is intellectual insight into the result of actions, there is no emotional insight. The pleasure of the moment is more important than the threat of displeasures in the future.

This character formation is identical with what Aichhorn called the state of latent delinquency, and our understanding of the antisocial personality has greatly gained by it. I believe that basically it is this character formation which determines whether a person reacts with neurotic or delinquent behavior to inner or outer stress. (5) The unconscious conflicts which we find in neurotic or delinquent children and adults are identical and so far no specific conflict constellation has been described to explain why one particular person becomes delinquent and not neurotic and vice versa. Even the conflict underlying the actions of the "Criminal from a Sense of Guilt"[1] is found in masochistic character disturbances without antisocial tendencies. Elsewhere I have made a classification of delinquent behavior on the basis of this underlying character disturbance. (6)

I believe that the age at which the delinquent behavior becomes manifest and the form in which it expresses itself depend both on the degree of this character disturbance and the degree of the neurotic admixtures. There are many delinquents whose behavior is based solely on this disturbed character development. There are others, of a later age, near puberty, who show this character disturbance with an admixture of neurotic conflicts which color the picture. This category includes the cases of obsessional stealing, or wandering, or incendiarism. Here the superego functions in relation to certain instinctive urges but not with others. And finally this category also includes those cases of antisocial behavior whose conduct is the result of an emotional conflict of recent origin. The conflict is much easier to unravel in these latter cases than in those with a neurotic disturbance, but, the recent conflict is not the sole determinant of their behavior. It was the basic character deviation which prevented the delinquent from making a further elaboration of the conflict and drove him instead into immediate action.

If we are correct in assuming that it is an antisocial character formation which is the basic disturbance underlying delinquent behavior, we should expect to find in the early history of delinquents those environmental factors that are apt to cause the specific disturbance in ego development.

In recent years some observations have been made which seem to confirm the correctness of this assumption. The authors (4) of a statistical investigation, carried out in this country for the purpose of finding the significant environmental factors contributing to delinquent behavior, concluded that their data can only be understood if a "susceptibility" to delinquency exists before it becomes manifest.

Of more significance are Ophuijsen's (8) observations. He states that in his cases of "primary conduct disorders" antisocial behavior starts very early in the form of unmanageableness at home, truancy from school, lying and pilfering. In all those cases he finds gross disturbances in the early family setting, resulting in rejection and neglect of the child. According to his findings, children with conduct disorders are characterized by "abnormal aggressiveness, absence or defective development of guilt feelings and narcissistic self-evaluation". He connects the absence of guilt feelings with a

---

[1] See Freud, S.: Some Charactertypes Met with in Psychoanalytic Work, *Collected Papers*, Vol. IV, London, Hogarth Press, 1925.

defective superego development, again due to adverse environmental influences. Ophuijsen described another type of delinquent behavior which is related to the influence of one particular person or displayed in one situation only, as for instance at school. These cases, especially the ones in which the delinquency first manifests itself at puberty, have a different pathology, according to Ophuijsen. Their etiology lies in a disturbed oedipal development or in neurotic conflicts. I should be inclined to a different interpretation of the causation of these delinquencies. When antisocial behavior is manifest from the age of four or five onwards, the character defect is very pronounced and superego formation is therefore correspondingly defective. In such cases the environmental disturbances are always obvious. In other cases where delinquent behavior occurs only in relation to certain persons, the character defect is less pronounced and a partial superego development has taken place. When the delinquent conduct does not appear until puberty, the character defect is slight and normal or abnormal conflicts lead to antisocial behavior instead of to neurotic manifestations. I have usually found that the conflicts leading to the antisocial manifestations are the usual ones met with in adolescence; severe frustrations of the desire to be grown up, events in the home which tend to increase incestuous desires, such as the birth of a sibling and so on. Despite the fact that the home environment of these cases is not a severely disturbed one, nevertheless we usually find typical antisocial rather than neurotic reactions in their early histories.

Lauretta Bender (2) describes "psychopathic personalities" among children seen at Bellevue Hospital, whose main characteristic is their inability to fit into any community. Her own investigations and those of her co-workers confirm the fact that this personality development predominates in those children who, up to the age of five, were unable to establish object relationships because they were separated from their mothers and were in institutions, or foster homes where there was frequent change of the adults in their environment. Lauretta Bender maintains that the disturbance occurs very early, before the oedipal phase, and that it is closely linked to separation from the mother at this early age.

Bowlby (3), investigating the early family setting, with special emphasis on the mother-child relationship, of forty-four juvenile thieves, found that in a highly significant number of cases there were early separations from the mother with a subsequent disturbance of the establishment of object relationships, while in his control group of otherwise disturbed but non-delinquent children this factor played a very minor part.

A recent study at a child guidance clinic of the home backgrounds of delinquent children and adolescents showed that of thirty-four cases, twelve had been separated from their mothers before the age of four, or had never known them, and were living in institutions or foster homes. In all these cases

there was a frequent change of adults in the child's environment before the
age of five. In a further series of twelve cases there were gross disturbances
in the family setting before the age of five, such as psychotic mothers, deser-
tion by the father, separation from the mother and living away from home
after the age of six, illegitimacy and so on. In ten cases only were the children living at home and had not been separated from their mothers, and of
these homes only two could be regarded as stable. In these two cases the
delinquent behavior became manifest in adolescence for the first time, under
provocation, and disappeared after management of the environmental and
inner disturbance. The factor common to the other eight homes was the
lack of interest in and the inconsistent handling of the child, a lack of tradition in the home and frequent changes of residence, which is rather rare in
the rural population of the clinic district. In most of the cases we had difficulty in getting a detailed social history covering our essential data of the
first five years, not so much because the parents were uncooperative,
(although this factor played a part as well) but also because the mother did
not remember what was to her quite unimportant. This attitude is in great
contrast to that of parents of neurotic children, where with very few exceptions the parents are as interested in providing us with facts of the early
history as we are in receiving them.

The same contrast exists in the actual home background. Out of thirty-
three cases of neurotic children, thirty-two cases showed a stable home background and an uninterrupted mother-child relationship.

In recent years the study of the early mother-child relationship has
received such attention, and it is to be hoped that follow-up studies of
children observed during the first years of life will contribute substantially
to the elucidation of this problem. Spitz's (7) investigations have already
shown the relationship between ego development and the presence or absence
of the mother or a mother substitute during the first year of life.

A further confirmation of the basic character disturbance in delinquents
can be found both in the treatment results and in the recommendations for
treatment of those who deal with large numbers of delinquents. Aichhorn (1)
has always maintained that the first step in the treatment of delinquent personalities was the establishment of an object relationship, and he draws
attention to the difficulties of doing so because of the delinquent's inherent
inability to form relationships which can endure frustrations. Ophuijsen (8)
states that in all cases of "primary conduct disorder" the treatment plan consists in the establishment of a relationship with the child. He maintains
that this may take a long time but that it must be the essential part of every
treatment plan. We would expect that a character disturbance of the type
described can only be rectified by a process of re-educating the child by
means of an emotional relationship to an adult who represents a parent
substitute.

If the assumption of a basic character disturbance is correct, the result of this process of re-education will depend on the age at which the child is diagnosed as being antisocial, regardless of whether treatment is undertaken by working with the parents, with the child or with both, or whether it is being done in a foster home or an institution. Naturally, treatment can be more effective before or at the beginning of the latency period than at any later time.

We are all familiar with the picture of the antisocial child during the late latency period and prepuberty, with his narcissistic self-evaluation, his impulsiveness and his inability to establish object relationships which endure frustrations. It would be valuable to be able to diagnose the disturbance at a much earlier age, between four and six years. This may appear difficult, as at this age both normal and neurotic children are also still narcissistic and impulsive. But the history of the primary antisocial child even at this early age is very typical. The parents complain that such children have always been disobedient, destructive and unmanageable. They lie with unconcern, pilfer, run away and tend to stay out later than is permitted. In addition to this there may be other behavior disorders, but it is the combination of the unmanageableness with lying and running away, and the attitude of the parents towards the child which point to an antisocial character disturbance.

In most cases the diagnosis can also be established by examining the child. Between the ages of four to six, the difference between a neurotic and an antisocial child is rather striking, especially if the diagnostic procedure includes observation in the treatment situation, either individually or in a group.

I should like to illustrate certain points regarding early diagnosis by a short case history which is typical of the early manifestation of an antisocial character formation.

We first heard about Peter when he was five and one-half years old. His mother had come for advice about the feeding difficulty of her second son, aged one. After a few weeks when this had disappeared, she confided to us that she was also worried about the older boy, whom she had previously described as perfect. He had started school but was having reading difficulties although he appeared to be intelligent.

At this stage the mother did not admit any difficulty at home and it was not until much later that we heard about certain behavior disorders which had existed ever since early days. He was dry and clean before eighteen months, but at that time he began smearing with faeces. Threats and punishment succeeded in putting a stop to this habit but nothing could prevent him from being destructive. Toys were so promptly destroyed that the mother no longer bought him any, and he could not be left alone in a room for fear he would damage everything in it. In further interviews with the mother it appeared that the destructiveness had not disappeared at the age of four, as she told us at first, but that he still had phases when he would destroy his own toys and everything else he could lay his hands on. He had always been very disobedient and his behavior had now reached a stage where neither friendliness nor strictness was of any avail. His behavior had become more difficult at four-and-a-half after the birth of a younger brother.

We also learned in time that the teachers were not so much concerned about the boy's inability to read as about his behavior in class. He was a disturbing influence in the group because he prevented other children from learning either by drawing attention to himself or by being aggressive to them.

When Peter was first seen at the clinic, this information was not available and therefore his difficulty in learning to read (he had an I.Q. of 140) appeared from the description as a neurotic learning inhibition.

During the first interview the boy gave the impression of being a friendly uninhibited child. He came into the room with great pleasure and without any embarrassment, and immediately concentrated on the toys, talking quite freely while doing so. He did not settle down to any play activity, but investigated everything in the room, as is not unusual in a first interview. The only salient features during this interview were that his free and easy behavior, his lack of embarrassment and his free talk did not fit into the picture of a neurotically disturbed child and that his talk and behavior were on a superficial and social level, and had no relationship to the interviewer. During the following interviews he displayed two different attitudes. During most of the interview he was friendly on a very superficial level and talked freely, revealing fantasies and ideas about religion which were very much in the foreground at that time. He maintained that ghosts urged him to be naughty, but that he was always very good. At the end of the second hour he suddenly decided that he wanted to take one of the toys home with him, and when it was explained that toys remained at the clinic he became aggressive and threatening, saying that he would not come again if he could not have it. He admitted that this was the way in which he behaved at home, but he took the toy with him when he left, without my noticing it. This aggressive behavior repeated itself during the following sessions, appearing sometimes at the beginning, but more often at the end of the session, when he declined to leave. On many occasions he would empty the content of all the toy-shelves on the floor in one quick sweeping movement, usually after he had helped to put the toys back. Invariably when it was time for him to leave he would invent many things which he had to do before going.

While there was still no relationship to me during his friendly behavior, the first sign of an object relationship revealed itself in these brief episodes when he became aggressive and unmanageable.

It was months before Peter established a relationship to me which was genuine and not intended to deceive me. When that stage was reached the mother stopped his coming. Half a year later we heard that he had stolen outside the home.

During the interviews we were able to observe closely the boy's behavior at home and at school, his relationship to his parents and brother, as well as the other inter-family relationships, and could confirm the diagnosis which was made after the third interview before the pertinent facts of his history had been made available. The diagnosis was based on this failure to establish an object relationship as well as on the way he behaved toward the instinctive desires aroused in the treatment session, namely to take home a toy. This desire is universal in children who come to the clinic, but only antisocial children express it in this way, by stealing what they cannot get by bribery. Sometimes, during the course of treatment, neurotic children may insist on taking something home with them, but they are then easily satisfied with a substitute and their reaction relates only to material brought forward in one particular session.

The attitude of children with a pronounced degree of antisocial character formation is so typical even at an early age that we have postulated a definite diagnostic entity for them, namely that of "Primary Antisocial Conduct". In some cases, especially with children under the age of five, there are still doubts about the future development. These we would classify as "primary behavior disorders with antisocial traits."

Although Peter's home background was one of the least disturbed, in our group of cases, it was not difficult to understand how the boy's ego development had been disrupted.

His mother was a young and attractive woman, with little emotional control. She had a good relationship with her husband, who shared her attitude of unconcern about the children whenever their own emotions were involved. They had both very much wanted the oldest child and were glad that he was a boy. But the mother's handling was very inconsistent from the beginning. She smothered the child with affection one moment and was very harsh with him when he was tired or when he annoyed her. Her husband had grown up with a very strict stepfather and his only interest in the boy was to punish him. Both parents had high ambitions for the older boy until the younger child was born. Then the father openly preferred the baby and Mrs. X had very little time to spend on Peter. She also told him that now he would not be able to go to the university because there would not be enough money for both of the children.

Mrs. X's attitude toward the clinic was also rather typical. She was superficially co-operative and did not break appointments as long as she only came for advice about the baby's feeding difficulty. But as soon as Peter started to come regularly, she was late for her appointments and often failed to come. She was more interested in showing off the younger boy than in giving information about the older one, and it became clear that she was quite unable to avoid having scenes with Peter. She was insincere with us and induced the boy to lie for her. In the end she kept the boy away just when he had established a relationship with me and was himself very eager to come and frightened that he might not be allowed to continue. Half a year after the end of the observation, when the boy had stolen from a neighbor and the school became aware of his pilfering, the headmaster informed us that the mother had rejected his suggestion that she should come to the clinic but had asked him whether he could see her regularly. He agreed, but she never came again.

The relationship of this mother to her child was not one of simple rejection. She certainly had a strong emotional relationship to him, but one which was based first and foremost on her own narcissistic needs. She was not only unaware of the child's needs, she disregarded them as soon as they ran counter to her own desire of the moment. The father's relationship was very similar to hers, with the added difficulty that he openly preferred the younger child. The mother's relationship to the younger child was the same as that to the older. She showed him off as part of herself and was impatient when he presented any difficulty. Peter was, of course, very jealous of his younger brother, but this acted only as an aggravation of his already existing disturbance.

Under these conditions the early instinct education could not proceed satisfactorily because of the constant oscillation between too much frustration and too much gratification, which disturbed the ego development. The correspondingly defective superego development is shown in the boy's inability to conform to rules at school and at home, and in his lack of guilt feelings when he was destructive. Peter could not learn because his interest was still centered round the direct gratification of pregenital instinctive drives.

In summary, I should like to emphasize that Aichhorn's conception of "latent delinquency" has directed attention to the study of the underlying basic disturbance in the delinquent personality. The most important result of these studies is the elucidation of the effect of gross environmental disturbances on the child's ego development, and the subsequent disturbance of superego function. Studies of the early home background of later delinquents have already given ample proof that the cause of the antisocial character formation lies largely in the environment. Any effective program of prevention will have to make use of these observations, and plans for treatment should be based on the idea of helping the offender to establish a relationship with one adult who can then undertake the process of education which has not taken place in infancy. In those cases where there is a neurotic admixture as well, the treatment of this condition will have to be deferred until after the education process.

One rather interesting conclusion could be tentatively drawn; namely, that the idea current in the literature of delinquency that constitutional factors play such an important part in the development of antisocial behavior may be fallacious. We can point to the early environmental factors responsible for the faulty development underlying delinquency with even greater certainty than to those which cause neurotic disturbances.

REFERENCES

1. Aichhorn, A.: *Wayward Youth*. New York, Viking Press, 1935.
2. Bender, Lauretta: Psychopathic Behavior Disorders in Children. In: *Handbook of Correctional Psychology*. New York, 1947.
3. Bowlby, John: *Forty-four Juvenile Thieves. Their Characters and Home Background*. London, 1946.
4. Carr, Saunders and Mannheim, Rhodes: *Young Offenders*. Cambridge, 1942.
5. Friedlander, Kate: The Formation of the Antisocial Character. *The Psychoanalytic Study of the Child*. Vol. I, 1945.
6. ——*The Psychoanalytical Approach to Juvenile Delinquency*. New York, Int. Univ. Press, 1947.
7. Spitz, René: Hospitalism. *The Psychoanalytic Study of the Child*. Vol. I, 1945.
——Anaclitic Depression. *The Psychoanalytic Study of the Child*. Vol. II, 1946.
8. van Ophuijsen, John H. W.: Primary Conduct Disorders. In: *Modern Trends in Child Psychiatry*, ed. by N. D. C. Lewis and B. L. Pacella. New York, Int. Univ. Press, 1945.

SOME POINTS IN THE TRANSFORMATION OF
A WAYWARD TO A NEUROTIC CHILD[1]

By Margaret E. Fries, M.D.

(*New York*)

All major social problems may be approached in diverse ways. No single approach is all-inclusive but, viewed relatively, some are more productive of results than others. Such are the procedures initiated by August Aichhorn many years ago. His successful handling of juvenile delinquents through judicious group living (1) has long served as an example for group therapy in camps, boarding schools and individual recreation groups.

He has described in detail his handling of individual cases. His preparatory stage in treating the wayward is in his own words: "The treatment of neurotics we have learned from Freud. However there appear in growing children attempts to solve situations arising from inner conflicts which do not express themselves in the form of neuroses but which appear as *schwer Erziehbarkeit* (behavior problems) and *Verwahrlosung* (waywardness). There is no method of direct treatment for this type of disorder. If a treatment is successful in making it impossible for the child to express his inner conflict in this form, he will then have to resort to expressing it in a neurosis. The resulting neurosis can then be treated by psychoanalysis and in this way the problem of treating wayward children is solved."[2]

He makes it clear that while it is possible to take time to build up an object relationship in the case of a neurotic child, this is not possible when handling a wayward child for it is essential to protect the juvenile delinquent from repeating his asocial acts so that he is not sent to a reform school. This requires building up an extremely strong transference in a very short time. The relationship to the analyst is a narcissistic one rather than an object relationship. That is, he experiences the analyst as an individual cleverer than himself, who can outwit him, and therefore he accepts him as a leader. The child stops his asocial behavior not out of insight derived from analytic

---

[1] The term "wayward" is here used in the sense in which August Aichhorn employs it.

[2] Personally dictated by August Aichhorn to the author in 1932.

procedure because that would take too long, but out of love towards the analyst to whom he has developed this extremely strong transference and whom he would not wish to disappoint. Aichhorn emphasizes strongly the importance of going along with the wayward child into his fantasy and following it to its logical end rather than going against his symptoms. In the wayward type there have been difficulties in the development of the superego.

A brief illustration of how this procedure takes place is shown in the following report of Tom, eight years old, who was referred because he was unable to play with other children on the street or adjust to public or private school, and who had then been treated for five months in a psychiatric hospital with only slight improvement. While at home for the last five months he attended a child guidance clinic weekly. At a staff conference when interviewed before a group he attacked the physician and was quite uncontrollable. The mother complained particularly about the child's negativism, hyper-activity, and sudden uncontrollable outbursts of hostility. She was afraid that during the adolescent period he might live out his fantasy and become a sex pervert or a criminal.

The father had died of tuberculosis when the child was four years of age. Previous to the father's death, the mother noted that the child had already shown disturbances in development. He had an insatiable appetite. At nineteen months he threw toilet paper rolls at people, had a phobia about the moon, and was very anxious after a tonsillectomy at two years of age. He was extremely jealous of his father's attention to his mother saying: "Leave my mother alone." The mother felt the marriage relationship began to deteriorate at the time of the child's birth. The father resented the child, paying no attention to him. During the last two years the father drank and displayed reckless behavior, although he never actually beat either the wife or the child.

The first interview really started in the waiting room where Tom was sitting in the largest available armchair. As I approached to greet him, he violently pushed a small table across the room at me. Feeling that he was testing me out, I asked him at once to please replace it. This he promptly did and willingly followed me into the office. When asked what I could do for him he replied "Find me a school. . . . I was thrown out of the last one for tricks I did. I stuck adhesive on the desks and threw clay at the walls. . . . I fought the teacher. It was such fun." When I indicated that this was a very difficult situation for me to help him find a school when he really did not desire to go to one he said: "No, but I must go otherwise I would be sent to a truancy school and I don't like that." (Aichhorn points out how treatment is facilitated in such cases because the authority of the state threatens the child and therefore the child is more willing to work with the analyst.)

At once the problem of the child's transference was discussed in terms of his pushing the table in the waiting room. He was defensive when asked why he had pushed the table. "It didn't kill anyone, did it?" When I indicated that he also had a desire to fight with me and then asked him what I had done he replied, "Nothing", but he continued to say that he had missed his radio hour, that he had never wanted to come at all, but that his mother had insisted. However, when I referred to the reason why he had come he immediately answered: "Yes, I came to get the name of a school. I made myself come." We discussed that he certainly was in a difficult spot since he must be fighting himself and that I, too, was in a difficult spot for whether I got him a school or not, part of him would be irritated at me. And finally when I said, "You seem to have a hard time since you can never do what you want to and therefore have to fight", his defiant attitude changed and he looked sadly out of the window saying, "I can't eat as much ketchup as I want. My mother stops me and says it upsets my stomach. Nor as much mustard as I want."

He then saw the building blocks with which he played for a short time and when told there were five minutes more for tidying up he said, "Oh, I can throw them in quickly." When told that this was not possible for they would break, and that he could verbalize but not do such things here, he tidied up at once in a very orderly fashion.

In the following two hours he continued to test me out. He threw clay and put pins in the door bell. However, he responded quickly to firm but unemotional prohibitions of such acts and cooperated when encouraged to act these desires out with blocks and a nest of dolls. He constantly showed his oral fixation by putting things in his mouth, describing his hunger and his great need to be loved.

By the third hour he sat quietly, drawing and verbalizing his fantasies. He divided himself up into the good and bad Tom, or cop and robber or wrecker and fixer. He played with blocks for only a short time and changed to drinking water from test tubes. (Aichhorn never uses toys but the children he treats are usually older. Nevertheless using his technique it is possible to resort to toys and play less than might otherwise be anticipated.)

By the fifth hour (after two and one-half weeks of treatment) the mother reported that the child was more depressed, crying more instead of being so revengeful. By the following week he had quieted down considerably, had no more fights, and cried instead of breaking objects when he could not accomplish things he attempted. He started making friends on the street and said, "I have such an itch — to break things. I must hold myself back. But I am keeping myself back and making friends."

From that time on the treatment of this child was for the major part of the time similar to that of any other neurotic child (2).

The question presents itself whether this type of change in a child from a delinquent who has irregularities in the development of the superego to a neurotic individual cannot also occur in the life of children, independent of analytic treatment. The case of Harold who showed early asocial behavior is a provocative example. He was one of a group of children observed by the author in a research study begun at the New York Infirmary in 1928 (3-9). In a clinical paper such as this, a few important facts will be presented very briefly while the entire material, its theoretical implications and the motion picture of the child, will be published at a later date.

Harold was a second child, born six years after his sister Gertrude. Sociological factors played a vital role in the development of these children. The mother was born abroad, left her native country at twenty-two and came to the United States in her twenty-fifth year. She had left school at thirteen years and after helping to raise her siblings she worked in a factory and as a domestic in private homes. She continued to work until she married. The father, a Hawaiian, came to the United States in his twenty-first year. He worked as a civics instructor and studied law at night. At the time of Harold's birth the mother was thirty, the father thirty-three years of age. Because of segregation due to the mixed marriage, the family was limited in its choice of living quarters. They lived on the boundary of white and negro districts. Harold's family was also limited in social contacts. The mother claimed that the father was more self-conscious than she in the matter of discrimination, and as far as could be ascertained, she dealt with this either very realistically or at times by denial.

Even prior to Harold's birth this marriage was fraught with difficulties. Not quite a year after Gertrude, the sister, was born the mother left the husband and with her daughter spent ten months visiting her relatives abroad. She claimed that her husband would not accept "any job", to earn money for the family and that she had learned he had a wife and children in Hawaii. Her parents paid for the trip. On her return she discovered that the husband had been involved in several affairs with other women. Through the Family Court she had Gertrude placed in a foster home and she and the husband separated. After a time a case worker effected a reconciliation and the family came together again. Harold was born a few years later.

The father was very sadistic and brutal, while the mother was less so. She was more in touch with reality, and capable of being very warm and outgoing. She was genuinely interested in the development of her children. She consciously cooperated with the hospital's research study and even after the family left New York City in Harold's ninth year she kept up a correspondence with the psychiatrist.

As the family lived a considerable distance from the Infirmary, Harold was born at another hospital. At six weeks he was registered and examined for the first time by the research group, where the physician was both pediatrician and psychoanalyst. He was organically healthy and had an Active Activity Pattern (5). He was breast and bottle fed. He showed some early vomiting, but had an excellent appetite even when ill.

During the first year a sadistic trend was perceived in the mother-child relationship. The mother rationalized her aggressive behavior saying, "Harold pulls my hair while nursing, and so to teach him not to do this I pull his in return". Her aggressive attitude was again expressed when Harold was two and one-half years old: "When he bit I just bit him on the arm so he would know what it felt like. I have had no further trouble." According to the mother, Harold "bit" before his first year. At twenty-one months he threw objects at others and held his breath when he cried. The mother said he had stopped biting and for a time pinched instead. He also displayed tremendous activity and defiance. The mother spanked him for throwing objects and in general perpetuated the child's resistant behavior. Nevertheless, she was also affectionate toward him and gave him ample opportunity for exploration and play, for she herself was a jolly person.

The father was totally involved in his own problems and incapable of giving Harold any warmth or security. The marital conflict increased with his unemployment. He was unable to meet the scholastic requirements of the law schools and he became embittered by social and intellectual limitations. The father's attitude toward the children was characterized by petty and aggressive tyranny. He disciplined Harold by compelling him either to walk up and down the hall carrying two bags, weighted with such items as books and shoes, until he was fatigued, or he made him kneel for a period of time. This form of punishment was particularly inflicted on Harold when he was about three and one-half years old. The mother was ambivalent toward the father's mode of discipline, but Harold obeyed only the father. Although he was reported to fight and scratch a great deal, his behavior was nevertheless considered "much improved". His sister said: "Even when I hit him so hard his skin is red, he only smiles." Whether this change can be considered favorable for his future personality development is questionable.

The sister, Gertrude, developed surprisingly well. She was given a house key early and treated as an adult. When the father finally opened a pool parlor in which the mother also had to work, Gertrude assumed responsibility for cooking her own lunch and rearing Harold. She saw to his dressing and punctuality at school, fed him and was his close companion. Although Gertrude objected to corporal punishment by the parents, both emotionally and intellectually — she told the psychiatrist, "You know, Harold and I listen to the radio program, 'How to Bring Up Children.' They disapprove of spanking" — she nevertheless pushed her brother around when his aggressive behavior interfered with some of her own goals. However, she was far more tolerant toward him than either of the parents.

At two and one-half years Harold, whose Binet Test rating was 97, was affectionate and outgoing. He was well liked by the neighborhood children and adults. Yet his underlying emotional conflict was typified in the following traumatic incident that occurred at three and one-half years. While he was still enuretic the father introduced an untrained puppy into the household. The mother, irritated by its messing, announced to her husband in Harold's presence that either the dog had to go or she would leave. Upon her return from marketing she missed the puppy. Harold denied any knowledge of its whereabouts. After searching every closet the mother noticed an open window and glanced into the courtyard where she saw the dog, lying dead on the pavement below. What really had occurred was that Harold had walked into the dog's faeces and then thrown him out of the window. Although the mother understood that Harold had thrown the puppy out of the window through fear, she spanked him mercilessly — not for throwing the dog out, but for denying the act. She even told the physician, sardonically, that she had done so because he had been untruthful. At this time Harold's responses to the Controlled Play Test administered in the clinic indicated hostility toward the father and great castration anxiety. In his free play with blocks and dolls his anal-sadistic sexuality was noticeable, and he showed a fear of being locked in the bathroom. His death wishes toward his mother were acted out with the female doll as he said: "The lady goes with no clothes on and she stands up here on top of the tall house and then she falls down and is dead."

It is significant that two months after this incident Harold displayed marked symptoms of repression and inhibition in his clinic examination, in the clinic playgroup and in the Controlled Play Test. He no longer struck anyone who attacked him, but took possession of the slide, climbing up and coming down as slowly as possible and obstructing the animated play of the other children. When asked to undress for his physical examination he dawdled, and when his mother urged him to hurry he raised his arm, but refrained from striking out.[3] This gesture became a characteristic response to many frustrating situations; and those in the clinic who dealt with him were impressed at the resemblance his facies and bearing had to that of Hitler. One day he and his sister related how they played "Hitler" together and demonstrated with a piece of black paper as a mustache, that Harold was the image of Hitler. Also evident at this time was Harold's poor posture, the great difficulty he had in verbalizing, and his facial expression which, when not rigid, was often inappropriate to the situation. By three years, eight months, to gain his mother's approval he had to deny his true position in the family as the baby, since this was equated with being a sissy.

His Controlled Play Test[4] responses showed that he felt his father to be a castrating figure and felt that his mother, when called upon, took his part by counter-attacking. He tried to solve his own anxiety over death wishes toward both parents by hiding. His infantile concepts of sexual differences were confused. At times he expressed the idea that both sexes were the same, while at other times that the female has a penis inside.

Throughout Harold's childhood he had enuresis, although there were periods when he remained free of the symptom. When he was one year old, his mother for a time had held him over the pot every hour and also spanked him to enforce bladder-training; although in later years she said of the symptom, "It's my fault if Harold wets — I wet the bed until I was eleven. I was stopped by cold showers from the waist down."

During Harold's first dental examination he handled his anxiety by standing at a distance, and peeking out from behind a pole at the other children. He finally submitted to the inspection in the manner common to such children — arms akimbo and with an assumed air of bravado. In a Binet Test he was intensely interested in knocking down the cubes, and when the examiner deviated from the routine test to build a tower of cubes he knocked them down with the spontaneous delight of a much younger child. Such situations showed the extent of Harold's aggression and his relief at being able to express it in a permissive setting. In the schoolroom Harold conformed and did satisfactory work.

----

[3] See movie film, "Psychological Implications of Behavior During the Clinic Visit" for this behavior as well as his neurotic act of aggressively striking out and hurting his arm against a table, following which he tries to comfort himself by soothing his arm.

[4] For details of use, value and interpretations of Controlled Play Test see (4). This playtest is patterned on the Oral Test of infancy. A family of dolls, father, mother and a little doll representing sex of child being tested, plus a lollypop are presented to the subject. The examiner gives the frame of reference by acting and saying the mother and father give the child a lollypop and what does the child do? Except in very disturbed children, the child states, "sucks or eats it". Then the examiner says the parents take the lollypop away and again the child supplies the subsequent act. As a third part of the test, the examiner offers the child all the props and suggests he play with them as he wishes. After the above is completed, the lollypop is offered to the child.

In Harold's Bomb Test[5] he acted out his death wishes towards both parents but then restored them to life. He became the "big shot — a sailor" (in real life this manifested itself as bravado and strutting. The movie film during dental examination shows his arms akimbo, legs apart, nod of head when he gives the dentist the signal to start).

His free association wandered afar from the setting of the test and acted out the oedipus situation by first placing the mother face down on the father; then after the mother is up the child, now a sailor boy, knocks her from behind and then with tremendous force starting from a distance he pushes the father down.

His behavior in general was far more friendly and cooperative.

From the clinical data on this child it appeared reasonably certain that the lack of an acceptable father figure with whom he could identify and his disillusionment in his punitive mother were seriously undermining Harold's capacity for sustaining positive object-relationships. However, a change began to take place in the family situation in his fourth year. The father left home and also enlisted in the army. Shortly thereafter the mother took in a boarder with whom she had a very satisfactory sexual relationship and whom she later married when Harold was nine years old.

By five years Harold's behavior had noticeably changed. Although aggressive in his Bomb Play Test he was far more controlled and less impulsive than before. His depression over the father's departure was evident. His verbalizations and play with the snakes he moulded, in clay, established the fact that he had reached the phallic phase, and was still very aggressive.

From Harold's fifth year his emotional development began to improve and it became apparent that "Uncle Joe" had taken over the role of father to the two children. He was never seen at the clinic, but guidance was given through the mother. Of greatest importance was the fact that this man was far more mature than their own father had been. He also provided financial assistance, and the economic tension was reduced. He was proud of being the head of the family and actively tried to win the affection of Harold and Gertrude. For the first time there was marital harmony, to which the mother responded with lessening of anxiety and tension.

Harold's transition from an asocial child to one capable of accepting social and parental authority was noted particularly in his sixth year. Quick mood changes, overt sullenness, quietness and talkativeness were present. He resented promptings to be polite, but was pleasant and cooperative in social relationships. He expressed aggression verbally and was less interested in physical destruction. "Uncle Joe" did much to channelize the boy's aggressiveness into acceptable, masculine channels of behavior. He taught Harold

---

[5] During the war a variation of the Controlled Play Test was given. The examiner tells the child: "An enemy plane is approaching and is being pursued by one of our planes. They are over the house in which the family lives." *Scene 1:* "An air raid alert is sounded. What does the family do?" *Scene 2:* "A bomb is dropped on the roof of the house. What happens?" (Examiner demonstrates Scene 2, letting a piece of paper represent roof of house and dropping a small ball of clay on it from above. She holds paper on a slant [slanting roof]. Child may thereby select one of two solutions: either the bomb may be fantasied to roll off, injuring no one, or it may be fantasied as going through the roof or otherwise doing damage.) *Scene 3:* The child is encouraged to act out fantasy alone, in free play.

to box and encouraged his participation in sports. With a father figure who showed both love and firmness Harold was able to identify with a male through love, rather than through fear of the aggressor.

Prior to "Uncle Joe's" entry into the family, Harold had been so preoccupied with his own fantasies that he did not mingle very well. For instance, during the clinic playgroup while standing on top of the slide while other children were awaiting their turn, he shouted to the church clock "Stop those bells". In his seventh year he became more spontaneous and joyous and started to enter actively into all kinds of human relationships. He was already freer in his total behavior except for his gait. He everted his feet saying he could walk with them more parallel but, "tough guys walk this way and I am a tough guy", thereby indicating that his specific gait was a defense mechanism against his castration anxiety.

For the first time he reported his cooperation with the neighborhood gang. The boss who had made up the gang was no fighter and had appointed him guard because he could beat up all the boys. The major activity was the fighting between the boys over taking the girls to the park. He indicated his preference for the girls over the boys in, "they have pretty faces, nice hands, shoes, feet and dresses, we have dirty clothes", but he ended up by saying, "boy clothes were better as they were warmer".

His sex conflict evidenced itself also in the Controlled Play Test where he stated: "The boy she is in bed." "The boy she gets under the man." However, in handling the parent dolls he placed the man on top of the female in bed. In his free associations he still continued far afield from the original scene of reference, an indication of serious emotional disturbance.

During his last interview at nine years he was more at ease and uninhibited in verbalizing his aversions and preferences and displayed great ability at establishing rapport with others. His mother, however, reported that he had recently visited the dentist where he had one tooth pulled; this was followed by an acute anxiety attack in which he fantasied that all his teeth had been pulled. His tendency toward much purposeless motor activity persisted and he handled his castration anxiety by threatening others verbally. Some phobic mechanisms of a verbal and visual nature were present; he explained that he would not use a certain word because the correct pronunciation sounded "affected" to him, and also that he had a black building block toward which he had developed such an intense aversion that he had it in the bottom of the toy drawer so he would never see it. It has not been possible to follow Harold's development for some time, as his family have moved to another city where the stepfather holds an excellent position.

In this brief summary of one child's life from seven weeks to nine years it is possible only to highlight a few salient points that seem significant in relation to the problem of juvenile waywardness. The way Harold was handled during the preoedipal phase of his life as well as his manifest behavior would seem to augur future asocial behavior of the wayward type. With the benefit of a change in the father figure and improved marital relations of the parents, Harold was able to establish object relationships more satisfactorily and he became neurotic rather than wayward.

Conclusions

These two cases represent changes in the total personality with emphasis on the modifications in the superego. The question was raised: can the beneficial effect of the change in the father figure in a growing child who is passing through the oedipal stage be compared to the therapeutic role of the analyst in an older, wayward child during treatment?

REFERENCES

1. Aichhorn, August: *Verwahrloste Jugend,* Vienna, Internationale Psychoanalytische Bibliothek XIX, 1925.
2. Freud, Anna: *The Psychoanalytic Treatment of Children,* London, Imago Publishing Co., 1947.
3. Fries, Margaret E.: Interrelationship of Physical, Mental and Emotional Life of a Child From Birth to Four Years of Age, *Am. J. Dis. of Children,* 49, 1935, pp. 1546-1563.
4. ———Interrelated Factors in Development (A Study of Pregnancy, Labor, Delivery, Lying-in Period and Childhood), *Am. J. Orth.,* VIII, 1938, No. 4, pp. 728-752. (With Beatrice Lewi.)
5. ———Psychosomatic Relationships Between Mother and Infant, *Psychosomatic Medicine,* VI, 1944, No. 2.
6. ———Importance of Continuous Collaboration of all Agencies in Dynamically Handling Each Child, *The Nervous Child,* 3, 1943-44.
7. ———Child's Ego Development and Training of Adults in His Environment, *Psychoanalytic Study of the Child,* II, 1946.
8. ———Diagnosing the Child's Adjustment Through Age Level Tests, *Psychoanalytic Study of the Child,* II, 1946.
9. ———Film studies of the children may be obtained through the New York University Film Library. These include: I. Some Basic Differences in Newborn Infants During the Lying-In Period. II. Psychological Implications of Behavior During the Clinic Visit. III. A Psychoneurosis with Compulsive Trends in the Making: Life History of Mary from Birth to Seven Years.

    (Film I and II are supplied with guides; Film III is supplied with case-history guide from birth to eleven years.)

    Other case history films are in preparation, including that of Harold.

SANCTIONS FOR SUPEREGO LACUNAE
OF ADOLESCENTS*

By ADELAIDE M. JOHNSON, M.D.

(Chicago)

The problems discussed in this paper are not peculiar to adolescents, although most of the material will be drawn primarily from my experiences with that age group.

It is essential to define the character problems involved: those of adolescents in conflict with parents or some other external authority because of an acting out of forbidden, antisocial impulses. There is rarely a generalized weakness of the superego in the cases under consideration but rather a lack of superego in certain circumscribed areas of behavior, which may be termed superego lacunae. For instance, a child may be entirely dependable about regular school attendance or honesty at work, but engage in petty stealing or serious sexual acting out. Frequently, mild or severe neurotic conflicts accompany such superego lacunae.

I shall attempt to illustrate that the parents may find vicarious gratification of their own poorly-integrated forbidden impulses in the acting out of the child, through their conscious or more often unconscious permissiveness or inconsistency toward the child in these spheres of behavior. The child's superego lacunae correspond to similar defects of the parents' superego which in turn were derived from the conscious or unconscious permissiveness of their own parents. These conclusions are the result of the collaborative study and treatment of the significant parent as well as the adolescent patient as reported briefly by Szurek in 1942 (17).

The literature reveals a variety of descriptions and discussions of the etiology of such superego defects. Reich (13) was the first to introduce the term "impulsive character" into psychoanalytic literature. Alexander (2) introduced the concept of the need for self-punishment as a motive for "acting out". Other authors stress the patient's receiving insufficient love and warmth so that a strong identification with the unloving parents is impos-

---

* Paper given at the Chicago Psychoanalytic Society on March 25, 1947.

sible. This lack of love is commonly considered the basic cause of superego defects.

Schmideberg (14) believed that people who act out their conflicts have a greater constitutional inability to tolerate frustration than the more inhibited persons. Greenacre (7) reported in some detail a number of cases of psychopathic personality but without concomitant study of the parents. She found that the fathers of such patients were usually ambitious and prominent, and the mothers usually frivolous and superficial, giving little attention to the home. She discussed the interrelationships of such parents with the child in respect to its superego development, but did not speak of defects in the parents' superego.

Aichhorn (1) and Healy and Bronner (9) stated that some antisocial children have identified themselves with the gross ethical distortions of these parents. These observers saw the gross pathological correlations but apparently did not stress the implications in the subtler cases with which we are concerned in this paper. Healy and Bronner attributed the child's inability to develop a normal superego to the coldness and rejection of the parents, so that one child in a family may steal and another will not, depending upon the one being unloved and the other loved. Even granting that unloved children may not develop a "normal superego", it does not follow that coldness of parents alone can lead to the superego lacunae under discussion. Some very cold parents create such great guilt in children that a punitive, hostile superego is developed. On the other hand there are warm parents whose child may act out antisocially.

At the Institute for Juvenile Research our collaborative therapy of purely neurotic children and their parents revealed certain unmistakable but subtle parent-child interrelationships in which one provided the other with an unconscious impetus to the neurosis. The confusing literature on delinquency and the dissatisfaction with our results in treating delinquent children stimulated a research into the subtle family relationships for a clue such as we had found in the purely neurotic cases. It seemed logical to seek some hidden links between the superego of the parent and the child, even in cases where the parent himself did not act out.

Szurek (17) stated the problem briefly and brilliantly in an understandable and simple way for both the gross *and* the subtler pathologies. Due to limitations of space he could not present the large amount of available evidence for his thesis. He saw the problem as a defect in personality organization — a defect in conscience:

"Clinical experience with children showing predominantly behavior which is a problem to others and *concurrent therapeutic effort with the parent* leaves the impression that the genesis of some of the human characteristics included in the definition of psychopathic personality is no greater mystery than other syndromes in psychopathology. Almost literally, in no instances in which adequate psychiatric therapeutic study of *both* parent and child has been possible has it been difficult to obtain sufficient evidence to reconstruct the chief dynamics of the situation. Regularly the more important parent — usually the mother, although the father is always in some way involved — has been seen *unconsciously* to encourage the amoral or antisocial behavior of the child. The neurotic needs of the parent whether of excessively dominating, dependent or erotic character are vicariously gratified by the behavior of the child, or in relation to the child. Such — neurotic — needs of the parent exist either because of some current inability to satisfy them in the world of adults, or because of the stunting experiences in the parent's own childhood — or more commonly, because of a combination of both of these factors. Because their parental needs are unintegrated, unconscious and unacceptable to the parent himself, the child in every instance is sooner or later frustrated and thus experiences no durable satisfactions. Because the indulgence or permissiveness of the parent in regard to marked overt hostility, or to some mastery techniques, for example, is uncertain, and inconsistent, control over the former or acquisition of the latter by the child is similarly uncertain and confused. If a discipline of the parent is administered with guilt, it permits the child to exploit and subtly to blackmail the parent until the particular issue between them is befogged and piled high with irrelevant bickerings and implied or expressed mutual recriminations."

The astonishing observation emerging repeatedly in our studies was the subtle manner in which one child in a family of several children might unconsciously be singled out as the scapegoat to act out the parent's poorly integrated and forbidden impulses. Analytic study of the significant parent showed unmistakably the peculiar meaning this child had for the parent and the tragic mode in which both the parent and the child were consciously, but much more often *unconsciously*, involved in the fatal march of events. As therapists we could not avoid feeling sympathy for these consciously well-intentioned parents whose unconscious needs were unwittingly bringing disaster down on the family. This was strikingly illustrated in several families that had an adopted child as well as one or more children of their own. The acting out of the parent through the adopted child was always rationalized as inherited behavior.

Although not emphasized by Szurek, another fact that became obvious was that not only was the parent's forbidden impulse acted out vicariously by the unfortunate child, but this very acting out, in a way so foreign to the conscious wishes of the parent, served often as a channel for hostile, destructive impulses that the parent felt toward the child. In many cases, parents may reveal blatantly the child's acting out to schools, family friends and neighbors in a way most destructive for the child's reputation. This becomes one of the greatest sources of rage in the child. The press recently reported a young adolescent girl hanging herself because her mother, missing $10.00, telephoned the school authorities to search the girl's purse.

Thus the parents' unconscious condoning of the acting out of asocial impulses by the child may serve the two-fold purpose of allowing the parent vicarious gratification of forbidden impulses as well as the expression of hostile destructive impulses felt toward the child.

Similarly the child consciously but more often unwittingly exposes the parents to all degrees of suffering through acting out. This acting out may often be an exaggerated picture of the unconscious impulses of the parent.

We must first understand the behavior of a well-integrated parent, and the subtle conscious and unconscious ways in which this behavior directs the child's superego development in order to be able to recognize the evidences of such destructive sanctions in less integrated parents. To be sure, the dissolution of the oedipus conflict puts the real seal on the superego, but it is well to be aware of all the preoedipal and oedipal subtleties in the family which are part and parcel of this development. To the child in the early and middle latency period there may be alternative modes of reacting on an ego level, but when the superego is involved the child normally is reared as if there could be *no* alternative reaction in regard to the suppression of the impulses to theft, murder, truancy, etc. The well-integrated, mature mother issuing an order to a child does not immediately check to see if it has been done, or suggest beforehand that if it is not done, there will be serious consequences.

Such constant checking or such a warning means to the child that there is an alternative to the mother's order and an alternate image of *him* in the mother's mind. Identification with the parent does not consist merely of identification with the manifest behavior of the parent. It necessarily includes a sharing by the child of the parent's conscious and unconscious concept of the child as one who is loved and honest or sometimes unloved or dishonest. It is essential to appreciate this fact if we are to understand the etiology of superego defects and plan a rational therapy. Angry orders or suspiciousness or commands colored by feelings of guilt convey to the child the doubtful alternative image of him in the parent's mind. The mature mother expects the thing to be done, and later if she finds the child has sidestepped her wishes, she insists without guilt on her part that it be done. The mother must have this undoubting firm, unconscious assurance that her child will soon make her intention his own in accordance with her own image of him. This, however, produces a rather rigid and inflexible attitude in the young child. As Fenichel (5) says: "After the dissolution of the oedipus complex we say the superego is at first rigid and strict . . . and that later in normal persons it becomes more amenable to the ego, more plastic and *more sensible.*"

In adolescence the superego is normally still fairly rigid and the child is greatly disturbed when adults express doubts about it. Nothing angers adolescents more than to be warned about or accused of indiscretions of which overtly they were not guilty. Such lack of good faith in them threatens to break down their repressive defenses and lowers their self-esteem and feeling that they would do the right thing. It suggests an alternative mode of behavior which at that age frightens them.

With these simple basic concepts in mind it becomes relatively easy to see what is happening in some rather simple cases of superego defect and to present the evidence for what Szurek stated in his article. It should be made clear that it is not within the scope of this paper to discuss the multiple determined types of character defenses which the child may evolve and use. Nor can the particular mode of therapy dealing with such character defenses be here included. These topics have been discussed in previous papers (6) (7).

Let us return to our simple cases of superego defect. How is truancy initiated? It is not just that parents are cold and rejecting as so many authors imply. How does the specific idea of leaving home originate? At six the little girl may say angrily: "You don't love me — nobody loves me — I hate you all." Quite often the child will receive such replies as: "Well, why don't you just pack your bag and go live some place else if you think we're so awful?" We know that some parents even follow this up by packing the little one's suitcase which at first may terrify the child. The suggestion to leave home comes more frequently from inside the home than outside, for not many small children tell others at school that their parents are mean or get suggestions from other children to leave home.

If little children (especially up to the age of eleven or twelve) let the thought that they are unloved come into consciousness at all, they then do not express that thought outside the family circle from feelings of both guilt and pride.

When we carefully examine the cases of a first or a repeated running away, we often find that it was the parents who unconsciously made provocative suggestions from a variety of motives such as hostility, or a need of vicarious gratification or both.

As, for example, six-year-old Stevie, who had been running away since he was four. His father seemed to know an inexplicable amount of detail concerning the boy's episodes of exploration. He reported that during these same two years he himself had been unable to continue his work as driver of a transcontinental truck, a job in which he revelled. Instead his present job confines him to the city. It was striking to observe this father with the little boy. He asked Stevie to tell of his most recent running away. When the child guiltily hesitated, his father started him on his way with an intriguing reminder. As the boy gave his account, his father was obviously fascinated — even occasionally prompting the child. Toward the end the father suddenly and angrily cut the child off saying, "That's enough, Stevie; now you see what I mean, Doctor?" Stevie could not help but see his father's great interest and pleasure when he told his tale each time he returned home, even though at the end of his account he received his whipping. The father was a kind, well-intentioned man who rightly feared for his little son's safety, but he was quite unconscious of the fact that the stimulus of his own thwarted need to travel was easily conveyed to the small, bright boy of whom the father said: "Stevie's really a good kid — he would follow me around the top of a wall 50 feet high."

No better example of how an adult can initiate such running away can be found than the story of how Aichhorn (1) deliberately resorted to such provocation as a technique of treatment. In handling the transference he consciously used a simple provocative mechanism to get a boy to run away from the institution, since he could not make any positive contact with the adolescent. This very narcissistic boy, with no positive feeling for Aichhorn, constantly complained about the institution. Aichhorn made subtle suggestions about the attractiveness of the outside world and an hour later the boy ran away. As Aichhorn had anticipated, some days later the boy returned, having found the outside world uninviting and then entered at once into a positive relationship with Aichhorn.

Let us now attempt to discover how stealing is initiated.

One of my patients, a woman, who had been in analysis for nine months, came in very angry at her nine-year-old daughter. The reason for the anger was that the child had been found stealing some money from the teacher's desk the day before. The patient stated that she knew Margaret had taken nickles from her purse off and on since she was six or seven but had said nothing, feeling that "she would outgrow it". When I asked why she had said nothing, she said it was never serious, so she had felt the less said the better. It was stated earlier in this paper that the mature mother does not anticipate trouble nor check up constantly on her child. On the other hand, neither does she let something amiss go by when she observes it, but instead handles it promptly without anxiety or guilt. She can neither be the nagging, checking detective, nor the permissive, lax condoner. During this hour, my patient told me a dream she had had over the weekend. In the dream she went into Saks and stole a beautiful pair of slippers. In the discussion I commented that I was struck with the fact that in her dream she did not even project the theft onto someone else and wondered if possibly her mother had been permissive with little thefts. Then my patient told me, for the first time, of numerous thefts all through her childhood and adolescence and that her mother had always protected her. For instance, during one year of her adolescence she had stolen at least two dozen lipsticks from stores. The prohibitions which had been so poorly integrated in her own life were unconsciously permitting and condoning her daughter's stealing. It was a revealing experience for my patient when three months later her mother came for a visit, to observe her mother's little deceptions and permissions with the two grandchildren, such deceptions as my patient had herself hitherto ignored. She did what she could to stop them and decided to limit long visits from her mother until the children were much older. In a very short time her daughter stopped all thefts as my patient, through her analysis, was able to make a definite stand without anxiety or vacillation. The child, formerly so unhappy and unpopular later became an outstanding pupil in her school.

We see in this mother's behavior an attitude commonly found among parents of children who steal. The parent whose own superego is defective is the one who will say "he will outgrow it", and often the parent who is not involved in the acting out is the one who finally insists upon bringing the child to treatment. "He will outgrow it" is the permissive protective attitude that keeps the problem active.

There are many such parents whose own poorly integrated prohibitions permit them to let slight offenses go by, only to react with sudden and guilty alarm at the first signs of criticism from outside the home by then angrily accusing and punishing their child. The child, confused and angry, in turn feels betrayed, and may in his own mind review his parents' similar deceptions. If he has the courage and is not too ashamed, he may point this out to the parent, and in this way the vicious circle of hostile, mutual blackmail and corruption is started.

The fantasies, hopes and fears which parents express in reaction to some behavior of their child is one of the commonest ways in which a child is influenced toward a healthy or a maladapted career. The horrified comments or anxiety over some behavior of the child are well-known to everyone. How commonly we hear the parent of the little child, caught in some minor offense, angrily say, "You are beyond me — I can't handle you any more — if this doesn't stop, you will end in the reform school." Or the child who is just beginning to misbehave is likened to his uncle who came to a bad end. We become "good" or "bad" depending upon our parents' fantasies about us.

A professional worker recently told me that seventeen years ago she visited her friends who had a nine-months old baby boy. The worker took the little boy on her lap and when he reached up and put his hands around her neck, the child's mother with a really frightening expression said, "I hope my son won't be a killer." The worker told me that by the age of fifteen years that boy had committed murder.

However, I do not intend to use evidence here of the more tragic cases, which have come to our attention, but will confine the discussion to fairly simple examples.

In *Psychoanalytic Therapy*, written by the Staff of the Institute for Psychoanalysis of Chicago, I reported the case of seventeen-year-old Ann who suffered from great anxiety and whose mother had written fraudulent excuses for the girl's absences from the school. The girl refused treatment and I treated only the mother. It was possible to analyze not only much of the mother's destructive hostility to Ann, but also in the transference, to manage and thwart the mother's attempts to corrupt the analyst and pull her into the vicious circle. Two years later, Ann is in college and making an excellent adjustment.

Another case is that of a sixteen-year-old girl who came to treatment because of several years of severe depression and the occasional idea that she was being poisoned at the school cafeteria. As her depression subsided and her anger toward me came out, she went home one day and told her mother she was so angry at the therapist, she was going to kill her. The mother said, with horror, "Oh, Marion, don't bring any more tragedy on the family." Marion rushed back to me greatly frightened saying, "My mother actually believed I would murder — what is wrong with her?" At that point I succeeded in also getting the mother into treatment with another analyst. It was fortunate that I did so, for Marion's father had died psychotic, and the maternal grandmother had been promiscuous, so Marion's mother was acting out ominous impulses through this girl, and blaming them all on Marion's heredity from her father.

When one parent advises a child to keep something from the other parent, it is a frequent and destructive factor in creating deceptions and stealing. "Here, I'll give you $2.00, but don't tell your father." One could list an endless array of such sanctions. In treatment these children will always try to get the therapist to lie to the parents. The parents' "more sensible superegos" unconsciously overlook the fact that to the rigid superego of a six- or nine-year-old, this does not look "sensible" but dishonest.

If we break a promise to a child without a sincere statement of the facts and a regretful apology, we undermine his ability to identify with us as adults of sound integrity.

In work with neurotic adolescents and young people, all therapists at times unwittingly ask questions which the child interprets as a permission. For instance, one frequently hears of analysts in a consultation with a twenty-year-old ask, "Have you ever had intercourse?" One young colleague told me he learned only too well the unwisdom of such a question. In the initial interview he asked a nineteen-year-old college student if he had had intercourse and the patient said, "Yes". Several months later his patient confessed that at the time the therapist had questioned him, he had *not* had intercourse. He felt guilty that he had lied and ashamed that he was so unmanly, so he had sex relations to undo the lie and prove his manliness. Probably all therapists unwittingly make some of the same errors in the treatment of children which some of the parents make to a greater degree. It is just these errors that led me to consider carefully Freud's meaning and intention when he made his suggestion for offsetting "acting out" in analysis, by interpreting and warning ahead of time.

Some analysts, dealing with cases of perversions or even more serious antisocial behavior, warn the patients ahead of time that they may have the impulse to act out in some manner. Certainly, *this* was not Freud's thinking on the matter. When he spoke of revealing to the patient, at the correct time, the possibility of his acting out and the meaning of it, he had in mind the so-called "acting out" of the neurotic patient on the couch who was repeating in the transference the salient episodes of his earlier life. This is an entirely different matter from warning a patient about some antisocial impulsive behavior. In fact, if I understand Freud correctly, he warned analysts against mobilizing and interpreting too rapidly any impulses that might be dangerously expressed outside the analytic hour — particularly sadism. A loose and unclear concept of what is meant by "acting out" has led a number of analysts to carry over Freud's suggestions about transference "acting out" to the "acting out" in a serious antisocial way. A warning to a patient with defective superego can act as a destructive force, disrupting what one has attempted to build up, namely, the patient's belief in the therapist's ethical concept of him. Any warning or questioning without factual justification may be interpreted both as a humiliation and a permission.

There is an additional etiological factor in these cases which is puzzling. In work with adolescents from all social strata, I was impressed, as was Szurek, with the fact that sometimes the child's parents had a similar partial superego defect, that is, the mother was promiscuous or the father committed some thefts, etc. But there are other cases in which the parents had never actually done any of this acting out so far as we could find, and yet we could see them unconsciously initiating this with the child. These parents, let us say, had some neurotic conflicts about thefts, promiscuity, etc., like many of us, but why did such parents permit themselves to act these conflicts out through the child, while many neurotic parents do not? With this question in mind, whenever I had a parent in treatment, I explored the relation to her own parents very closely.

Where did the parent get the permission to act out through the child? Since the parent did not act out herself, she must have had a fairly strong conscience. Yet what caused this poorly integrated prohibition to appear in the next generation?

I frequently found that the present parent had gone along for years developing a good conscience, was secure about controlling her own impulses and then something arose that led her parents to surprising suspicions and accusations. Since the parent under treatment already had a good conscience, he or she could not respond to this permissive accusation by acting out, yet was enraged at the injustice and defamation. The rage and the permission would then come out unconsciously by being displaced onto the daughter or son. The parent's acting out through the child may also occur when the parent, with a well-developed conscience, *later* observed dishonesty, erotic acting out, or some other disturbing behavior in *her* parents and felt much pain and confusion about their actions. Our parent in question already had a good conscience and too much guilt to do likewise herself, but the confusion, anger, and permission cannot be normally integrated into her personality and appears later through her own child. For several years I have found increasing evidence to substantiate this statement, but I am not satisfied that this is the final answer.

With this understanding, it could be seen more clearly why at the Institute for Juvenile Research we had failed so repeatedly with even relatively mild cases of acting out, although we had seen some of them frequently (four to five times a week), for one or two years. We had given a great deal of consistent warmth and affection, but the child continued to steal or act out sexually. Any guilt developed toward us with regard to an act was met with unconscious permission at home and the child was only confused and frequently became more fearful toward us and finally stopped coming. We succeeded with even mild cases only if we could get the significant parent into treatment or could remove the child from the home during the therapy. Treatment of such parents whose role is so often unconscious, is a miserable ordeal for them and the greatest sensitiveness and skill is necessary in carrying them through. Many break away in spite of our best efforts to go slowly. Where the sanction was perfectly conscious on the parent's part, treatment of him was almost always futile. If neither treatment of the parent nor placement is possible, then any treatment in a severe case is not only futile, but often dangerous, because the parent can unconsciously act out through the child and make the therapist "responsible", just as parents make heredity the scapegoat in some adoptive cases.

My first experience with such a serious hazard came a few years ago. A young woman therapist who did not share our conviction of these dangers insisted on trying treatment of a ten-year-old boy who stole and had set a few fires three years earlier.

Neither parent had been interviewed with the idea of considering treatment. A few weeks later a serious fire occurred at the home. The mother particularly was enraged at the therapist. To relieve the tension and clarify the situation I talked with her. She told me that she had been downtown shopping; that she was a woman who trusted her premonitions and she had become uneasy about something vague and hurried home. A few blocks from home she heard the fire department and, "I just knew it was our house." When I asked her why she should have been so uneasy and certain, since there had been no fire for three years, she flushed, stiffened and maintained, "I always trust my hunches." I asked her if the boy had mentioned fires at any time recently. She thought for a while and then told me that he had become angry at his little sister a few days before. When the mother interfered, he shouted that he hated them all and would kill them or burn them all up. This is a frequent threat of many angry children and the average parent pays no attention to it. This mother had told him then that if he tried anything like that, he would end in the reform school. Like most of these threats by parents of antisocial children, they are not carried through and the child knows the parent will protect him until he does something far worse. I spoke reassuringly of our interest in helping in some way, but she angrily withdrew herself and child entirely from the treatment situation, blaming the child's therapist.

In treating younger children and adolescents with conscience defects, one of the great errors commonly made is that of too energetic attempts to liberate the child from the permissive parent, especially by telling the child that the parent is dishonest, or sexually unstable. These children often know these facts consciously, but it is a frightening and humiliating thing to the insecure young patient to be told such things. If he is not conscious of such facts, this knowledge early in treatment is devastating to the child and utterly cruel to the parent who is unconscious of the implications in his or her permissive behavior or attitude. When the children become more secure in handling their own impulses, these patients if they observe them, bring up these tragic facts themselves and they can be discussed at that time.

I wish to emphasize certain facts about the treatment of the young and older adolescents who are not too seriously handicapped. With the exception of one girl who lied and stole, all were able to develop a fairly *positive transference* within a month or two. To be sure some were seen five and six times a week for the first few months and were permitted many additional telephone contacts. I spent over a year developing a good relationship with one girl. There were two girls and one boy whom I never saw, but whose mothers I treated — one by psychotherapy for nine months and two in analysis. All of these cases were adolescents who in certain areas of behavior had excellent conscience formation but nevertheless showed other symptoms of defect such as stealing, lying, cheating, running away, or sexual acting out. I cannot emphasize too strongly that the successes I have had are not with very severe cases such as the highly narcissistic children with widespread superego defects. Also, when I have been successful, the parents have been cooperative and well enough to enter treatment themselves or allow me to place the adolescent in a school or a club.

To make for a simpler presentation of some of the principles of the direct treatment of an adolescent with a conscience lacuna, I shall confine the discussion more or less to one group, namely those children in whom stealing was the essential problem. I can think of none whom I have treated who did not also have neurotic conflicts which likewise had to be resolved when the time was propitious.

In the literature such brilliant therapists as Aichhorn and Schmideberg speak of more or less long periods of education and re-education of such children preparatory to analysis or along with analysis of their neurotic symptoms. This preparatory "educational" phase apparently has to do with strengthening the superego, but I have always wished they would write in more detail of the therapeutic technique which brings this about. Aichhorn deals rather extensively with the need to change the urge for living by the pleasure principle into a more realistic attitude, but there are few specific details of the ways and means he employed.

Aichhorn never began by asking a child to give an account of his misdemeanors because he felt quite sure he would only weaken the relationship by forcing the child into more falsifications. Many therapists, however, approach an adolescent boy who steals by trying to get him to give an account of his misdemeanors and difficulties. When they are asked why they force the child to recount these facts, they reply that it is to see if he has "insight" into why he is brought for therapy. Usually he would not give a frank confession, but even if he did, this has nothing to do with "insight". If he were deeply deprived early, then the therapist might say he hopes to help the patient to see some connection between the consciously or unconsciously permitted stealing and his emotional deprivation. But by proceeding this way their patients' thefts usually increase for reasons which will soon be clear.

How does the patient react to such an approach? By evasions, rationalizations and outright falsifications and the ensuing anger, fear and humiliation will now present an even greater obstacle to therapy.

The primary difficulty is a partial superego lack — a lacuna. If a normal superego is developed through identification with mature parents who automatically believe in and are certain their child will have integrity, then it would seem logical that the correction of such a lacuna (even at so late a period as adolescence) must proceed by having the therapist assume that there are the same potentialities for identification with himself as he would see in his own child. This attitude is essential or all the warmth in the world will not repair a conscience defect in the child. I cannot emphasize too strongly that this attitude and a deep feeling of respect for the adolescent are absolutely basic in the treatment of these cases.

I have no great optimism about success with a very severe superego defect, but with the milder lacunae, the success of our treatment depends on our understanding of the child's relationship to the therapist.

At the initial interview, regardless of the transference, I do take into account a factor which Aichhorn does not elaborate. Since the adolescent for a long period probably has been consciously or unconsciously protected and his conduct ambiguously condoned by his parent or parents, he has therefore developed a definite pattern of expectation of some degree of whitewashing from other adults. As soon as the therapist gives in to that, the vicious circle of blackmail begins. Therefore, at the initial interview I merely say I know he has had these misunderstandings and difficulties about money which we need not go into but that I have the feeling as he becomes more sure of me, and we understand each other this will eventually subside. I feel that the child must be spared humiliation and given hope for the future without burdening him by excessive standards of good behavior. His past must not be held against him yet too great a whitewashing of his conduct would be permissive.

Let us remember that the battle at home has gone on through mutual corruption and blackmail, albeit often subtly. This is true in stealing, having the parents write false excuses, lying, etc. Keeping this in mind, if the therapist begins by asking for an account of past misdemeanors, the patient will at once be humiliated and angry. Every patient soon tests the analyst over and over to see if he is corruptible, and if the therapist begins by humiliating him, that testing out will come much more quickly and often more seriously and the whole case may get out of hand before it is well started.

The first thing that should be verbalized casually to the child is the therapist's confidence that with the growth of mutual understanding, all of these old troubles in time will subside. Doubts, accusations or warnings that the child may be tempted to steal will rapidly destroy any possible identification with the adult's superego, the therapist's good understanding of the patient's potentialities notwithstanding.

If a therapist cannot sincerely feel that this child can eventually become thoroughly honest in relation to her without at the same time burdening the child with therapeutic expectations, no improvement will occur no matter how hard she strives to follow the suggestions given here. Many workers will say: "How can I have confidence in the child when he has stolen for years or set several fires? I shall feel duped if after months of treatment, I find he was pulling the wool over my eyes all along." This is a very real counter-transference problem. The therapist, without conflict in this area, would not mind if he finds he has been fooled for a time. Resistance and relapse are to be expected in the analysis of a neurosis, and similar lags and relapses are to be expected in treating superego defects. If despair or annoyance overwhelms the therapist at these points, all is lost. Misdemeanors should be neither overlooked nor whitewashed but be frankly discussed with the patient.

In several instances I have come into the picture after a crisis when the parents were terrified by the risks of the child's future and the child knew this. Feeling that for once an adult had to express to the child a sound expectation of him, I have casually but definitely and in the child's presence, expressed my complete assurance of success.

I remember the cases of a boy and a girl who precipitated near tragedies in the home by setting fires just before they were to leave for summer camps. I think the fact that the parents expressed their doubts in the children's presence and that I answered promptly and with conviction, made it possible for the children to feel safe. There was little time to develop strong contacts with these adolescents before camp, but the summer was successful. This is not to say that the task of the treatment had gone beyond a mere beginning. Many therapists may feel that in such a situation the child may "call your bluff" for his parents have usually threatened him with punishment for future misdemeanors only to give ground when the child put them to the test. The difference in these two cases was that I made no threats and said nothing to invite a threat.

Treating these cases calls for the greatest flexibility. At the beginning I may see them five or six times a week and answer their telephone calls every night for months. Especially with the narcissistic child it may need many hours a week to stir up any positive feeling. Broken appointments are frequently followed by a friendly telephone call from the therapist, and this may go on for weeks and months. So much flexibility and time for unpredictable calls and appointments are necessary that I avoid carrying more than two or three of these adolescents at a time on my schedule.

All analysts know how carefully and frankly they must deal with the ego problems of a paranoid patient. Similarly, a great amount of care must be taken with these patients, to avoid any possibility of the patients seeing the therapist as deceptive or evasive in any way. I make it clear that if anyone should ever talk of him to me, I shall tell him at once and if possible get his permission before talking to anyone about him. As an adult in these matters, I do not display the "sensible superego" of Fenichel but to many of my colleagues may give the impression of being child-like in my care to have everything above board. I am extremely careful about promises since to a small child a promise is part and parcel of the whole matter of superego development. Some of these adolescents will beg you to promise they can go home in three months — but I use great care in never over-promising just to ease temporary pain.

I make it a point to catch little off-color dishonest things immediately, even though a good positive transference may not yet have developed. The child so often, consciously and unconsciously, makes these little slips early to test the therapist's corruptibility. I try to do this before many of these events have occurred or before the child has too much tension about seeing where I stand. This has to be done in a very comfortable and friendly manner. During the war the commonest technique was to offer to get me extra ration stamps. My own response was to smile and comment that I guessed I could stand the government regulation without dying. At first the patient may be wary about lying and cheating since he knows that is the reason for coming, but often he unwittingly lets slip some matter about cheating because there is little guilt.

Twelve-year-old Jerry had been in to see me about four times and had quickly developed a strong attachment. One day as he was leaving he said,

"Well, I'm off to the movies. Sure lucky I'm little and can get by at half price." I laughed and said, "It isn't the size you know, Jerry. When you are twenty-one years old, whether you are six and one-half feet tall or five feet tall, you will get to vote. The law goes by age, not by size. But, by the way, speaking of age, when you became twelve, did your Social Worker increase your allowance since at twelve, by law, you have to pay more for movies and street cars?" Jerry said, "No, should she?" I replied, "I'm sure she would have if she had thought a minute, for it's the only fair arrangement for boys and girls when they become twelve. Let's try to telephone her about it now and get her O.K. to my lending you the extra today and when she sees you Saturday, you can repay me." He was eager to call her and, of course, she agreed. A few weeks later Jerry said, "The kids think I'm a sucker to spend double for movies." He was silent a while and then said, "I crashed the gate last Saturday with the kids, but it's no go. No more of that."

I never moralize nor act too grave about the matter but comment casually and good-naturedly that I guess we had better stick fairly closely to the rules of the game. Very early, they watch you closely for any slip. I recall a young social worker, just beginning treatment of an adolescent girl who stole. The worker parked her car by a "no parking" sign. When she stepped out of her car and saw this, she commented that she would have to move the car. The girl said, "I noticed the sign and wondered what you would do." There is often a decrease in anxiety and increase in positive feeling when one of these small episodes has been handled definitely and good-naturedly. Complicated character defenses magnify the therapeutic problem greatly, but a therapist's own guilt or anxiety in dealing frankly with the child can frequently greatly intensify the child's defensiveness.

In her second hour, an adolescent girl who had been stealing and who lived in a boarding club, showed me $5.00 which she had just received from her mother and said, "I'm not going to turn this in to my Club Mother." I asked her to describe the set-up at the club, and she explained that the girls turned in their money and then asked for it when they wanted to spend it. I merely commented that it sounded similar to the arrangement I have with the bank which I found very satisfactory and safe. The girl said that she was going to spend 50c and not report it, to which I replied the rules probably irked her somewhat, but that it was a simple matter to report spending the 50c. She then asked if I would report it, and I casually answered, "Why should I, you will report it, and let's drop the subject." The next hour she asked if I had checked up with the Club Mother; I appeared rather blank for I had forgotten the incident. She reminded me and then added: "Well, I turned in the report."

But suppose the child returned and defiantly told the therapist she had not reported the fifty cents? What is the therapist to do then? My own experience has been that if I then became an accomplice, in the end the child's need to test me further would drive him to increasing excesses and I would lose the patient. Therefore, my own procedure is again casually to try to work with the patient toward making a collaborative report as well as talking over her basic uneasiness about whether I will protect her in small or large misdemeanors.

A twelve-year-old boy once said to me," That new foster mother of mine won't work out." When I asked why he replied, "She has no respect for me — she's a snooper. I told her I was going to the 'Y' and that I would take the bus. When I was waiting for the bus, I saw her following in her car, so I slipped into a building and later went out and got my bus to the 'Y'. She told me I didn't go to the 'Y' and when I asked her how she knew, she said she had a seventh sense. She's just tricky and it won't work."

I would rather be deceived for a time than raise such doubts of my belief in the child. I have seen foster mothers give great warmth only to ruin it all by such doubting.

As soon as the patients consciously or by a slip give me facts of misdemeanors or facts come to me by other routes I take them up with the patient frankly at once. When the therapist lets little things go by, and this is observed by these patients, their anger at the seeming treachery of being severe only when a serious misdemeanor arises, is justified. This is exactly what happened at home in their past experience where they were protected in small deceptions. If the first attempts to corrupt the therapist are handled correctly, then very soon one may begin to see more superego strength in the patient. I find that handling such attempts along with warmth makes for a more rapid, confident and positive transference. I think that this has been one of the greatest obstacles and pitfalls in the therapy of these patients. Either its real meaning is overlooked at the beginning or it is mishandled. I have had to deal with several mothers with relatively good superegos in certain areas who nevertheless made attempts to corrupt me. It took only a few hours to work through these attempts with firmness. The change in their child, whom I never saw, was striking enough for others as well as the mother, to report it.

It is important when a relapse occurs that every effort be made to help redress a wrong to someone else, but at the same time to maintain the patient's confidence in his growing strength. I usually help the patient to see that some lack of security may still be leading him to thoughtless and impulsive behavior but that a large part of him would prefer to avoid this. In returning stolen goods or adjusting some wrong, I make it clear to the adolescent that we must return the article with as little fuss as possible, for I do not want the patient to suffer unfair and exaggerated criticism. It is important to help the patient with regard to correcting any injustice done to someone. No young child and usually no adolescent should have to go back to the store alone to return some stolen article or to adjust some serious infringement of a rule with the head of a boarding school. However, if the therapist is willing to help in such situations, the child might take it as suspicion on the analyst's part that the child will not carry through and this must be watched for and reassurance given. The therapist's position has to be one of helping to make amends to the injured party even though punishment may still come about in contrast to the parent's attitude. Yet the therapist should make clear to the patient that she will do everything possible to help the authorities to understand the plan of therapy. Many times the young child or adolescent will agree to do this. What if they do not agree? The therapist may feel afraid that the patient will turn against her if she exposes him. If, however, she maintains silence, she certainly has laid herself irrevocably open to blackmail by the patient and may never undo this. This course would be similar to the vicious family circle of mutual evasion and permissive protection where the parents give in to the child's promises or threats of suicide. Aichhorn writes in detail of this giving in by the parents and of his own capacity to avoid being overwhelmed by such threats. If the therapist is frightened of taking a stand here out of self-protection sooner or later she will lose the patient who will try to push her into a worse situation in his vain attempt to find someone who has the courage to set limits to his forbidden impulses. I believe that the craving to have limits set to their forbidden impulses is often why children and adolescents arrange things so they will be caught. This reason, I believe, to be more often determining than the motive of guilt.

By this time it has become clear why any questioning of the patient or any accusation without facts, or any warnings of possible impulsive acting out of antisocial nature will weaken that confidence the patient achieves from the therapist's confidence in him. If this occurs, then the adolescent for instance, feeling hurt and spiteful will react rapidly and try to enmesh the analyst quickly in the old family net of attempted corruption. Unless he is alert the therapist very soon can be pulled into an embarrassing and destructive situation by the angry child. Then the less experienced therapist is apt to be corrupted by his own anxiety and guilt and the fat may be in the fire.

I recall one gifted social worker who had been making splendid progress with a sixteen-year-old girl who had been stealing for years. No stealing had occurred for nine months. The girl was on a clothes allowance. One day the worker irritably told the child she should not have bought an article of clothing without asking her. They were walking in the suburbs and in two minutes the patient had the worker picking some flowers inside a private yard. The worker soon got hold of herself and said it was not the thing for them to do. Now the girl pitifully tried to excuse the worker, for she wanted her worker to be honest and said there were not any "no trespassing" signs. The worker, however, made it clear that she had been doing wrong even if there were not any signs forbidding trespassing. The girl agreed, "That is right — people do not have signs in their homes saying 'do not take the furniture'." The worker also made it clear to the patient that she (the worker) had no justification for being so incensed about the articles of clothing, since the girl had her own budget for clothes. Actually the worker had for a moment succumbed to the girl's spiteful corrupting influence because the worker was guilty over her irritable outburst toward her patient.

After a therapist has put a great deal of effort into the treatment of one of these difficult patients, one can see how she might over-react to a report that the child has been stealing for months while the therapist had believed things were going well. Some therapists are so hurt and humiliated that they see themselves as "duped". One young man therapist said to me: "I feel like a soft fool taken in by that kid." We usually do not react with any such feeling of abuse in the analysis of a neurotic if our patient has a serious relapse after long and hard work with him. This male therapist had overlooked many small signs of ominous import before this major evidence shattered his self-esteem. His personal need to do so had been sensed by his patient, who had been well aware of the small ways in which he was getting by before he acted out more dangerously. This is one of the great hazards in treating such patients, namely, to avoid accusations without good evidence, but to see little off-color things when they *do* arise and to handle them immediately with frankness and without anxiety on the part of the analyst.

It is important to stress again the adolescent's reaction to feeling that his therapist has a deep respect for him. He must gradually see himself as a personality endowed with the many facets which his therapist has spread before him. A ragged eleven-year-old boy came in beaming one day. I asked him why he was so happy and he said, "I love my new teacher, she respects me". Therapists must not overlook the many small opportunities for stressing their confidence in their neurotic or delinquent patient's sense of good taste and correctness. That adult who can sincerely make an insecure adolescent feel that his ideas have significance, can hope for success in his treatment.

Handling transference and counter-transference problems involved in treatment of the partially developed superego is extremely complex and relatively little explored. I have touched on only a few aspects of our experience with such cases.

In most of these cases there are also neurotic problems that must be analyzed. One should analyze only that transference neurosis which interferes with therapy until the particular defect in the superego has been strengthened. If the latter is not achieved before the therapist begins intensive analysis of the neurotic conflicts, the acting out of the mobilized deeper impulses will get out of control. While our experience in treating these cases was still limited, this mistake occurred often.

Suppose one is dealing with a sixteen-year-old girl who stole and who had too much responsibility for the care of younger siblings. To begin analyzing this girl's dependency needs before the superego had been strengthened with regard to property would lead to such a flood of stealing as to defeat any therapeutic efforts. After this patient's intense guilt about her hatred of her younger siblings had been analyzed, we could see how the mother's unconscious condoning of the stealing had made possible this less painful mode of expressing both her hatred and her own needs. When stealing is an acting out of the oedipal conflict, if one starts to analyze the conflict before the prohibition about stealing is fairly firm, the problem will certainly get out of hand as I saw happen all too often in my early IJR days.

This is the sort of "insight" I think many therapists have in mind when they begin therapy by saying "let us see why you take things", and the more they probe, the worse matters become. But it is true that these conflicts often boil up too rapidly even before the analyst made any attempt to mobilize them, so that treatment is extremely difficult if not impossible outside of a controlled environment. Treatment of the adolescent always involves his total family and environmental relationship. When he is secure enough in his own self-esteem he will, himself, come to the more painful aspects of his parents' personalities which confuse and shame him. When this happens, the therapist must avoid both permissiveness and any moralistic condemnation. I usually stress that this seems to be the parent's problem, that it is not an innate defect, but that had the parent had an easier life and been more secure with his own parents, and had had a helpful counsellor outside the home, matters might have been different. I speak of my regret that one of us could not have helped long ago to make this parent's life a little easier. Although this approach makes the young patient more guilty toward the parents and more neurotic, in such cases this is better than to cut him off from the parent.

In summary I should like to state briefly the significant features in this paper:

1) I aimed to elaborate on the evidence for the etiology of conscience defects as presented by Szurek in 1942.

2) More detailed clarification of the subtleties involved in preoedipal and oedipal and latency superego formation was given with the emphasis on the child's seeing the parent's concept of himself as part of the mother with whom he is identifying.

3) Using this concept as the basis for treatment, the doubting, accusations and policing of the child's developing superego were seen as illogical to any rational therapy. I have emphasized the difference between the warning given in the analysis of a neurosis, the acting out of the transference and the effects of warning a patient about antisocial behavior involving a superego defect.

ADELAIDE M. JOHNSON

4) I have enlarged upon the therapist's role in setting the limits of permissible behavior as soon as test situations arose in the treatment. I have pointed out that his own unanalyzed guilt feelings can prevent him both from quick recognition of such situations and deftness in meeting them. It was stated that it is necessary to set definite limits regardless of threats by the patient in order to avoid repetition of the mutual blackmail and permission of the family constellation. An attempt has been made to depict a few of the details of how certain incidents in the relationship with reference to the superego were handled. This represents only a limited amount of material, should not be accepted dogmatically, and represents possibly only the manner in which certain therapists might operate.

5) The cases reported where the treatment was successful were not severe maladjustments. They were patients who were able to develop some positive transference, fairly soon, whose superego defect was not widespread, and whose significant parent could cooperate by also entering treatment or by permitting the child to be removed from the home during treatment.

1. Aichhorn, August: *Wayward Youth*, New York, Viking Press, 1935.
2. Alexander, Franz: The Neurotic Character, *Int. J. Psa.*, XI, 1930, p. 292.
3. Alexander, Franz, French, Thomas, et al.: *Psychoanalytic Therapy*, New York, The Ronald Press Co., 1946.
4. Bromberg, Walter and Rogers, Terry C.: Authority in the Treatment of Delinquents; *Am. J. Orthopsych.*, XVI, 1946, p. 672.
5. Fenichel, Otto: *Problems of Psychoanalytic Technique:* Psychoanalytic Quarterly, Inc., New York, 1941. Chapter V, p. 71, Comments on the Analysis of the Transference; Chapter VI, pp. 80-81, Working Through and Some Special Technical Problems.
6. ——*The Psychoanalytic Theory of Neurosis*, New York, W. W. Norton, 1945, pp. 468-469.
7. Greenacre, Phyllis: Conscience in the Psychopath; *Am. J. Orthopsych.*, XV, 1945, p. 495.
8. Hacker, Frederick J. and Geleerd, Elisabeth R.: Freedom and Authority in Adolescence; *Am. J. Orthopsych.*, XV, 1945, p. 621.
9. Healy, William and Bronner, Augusta: *New Light on Delinquency and its Treatment;* Yale University Press, 1936.
10. Johnson, A., Szurek, S. and Falstein, E.: Collaborative Psychiatric Treatment in Parent-Child Problems; *Am. J. Orthopsych.*, XII, 1942, p. 511.
11. Johnson, A., Falstein, E., Szurek, S. and Svendson, M.: School Phobia; *Am. J. Orthopsych.*, XI, 1941, p. 702.

12. Orgel, Samuel Z.: Identification as a Socializing and Therapeutic Force; *Am. J. Orthopsych.*, XI, 1941, p. 119.

13. Reich, Wilhelm: *Der triebhafte Charakter;* Internationaler Psychoanalytischer Verlag, Wien, 1925.

14. Schmideberg, Melitta: The Mode of Operation of Psychoanalytic Therapy; *Int. J. Psa.*, XIX, 1938, p. 314.

15. ——The Psychoanalysis of Asocial Children and Adolescents; *Int. J. Psa.*, XVI, 1935, p. 22.

16. ——The Treatment of Psychopaths and Borderline Patients; *Int. J. Psychotherapy*, I, 1947, p. 45.

17. Szurek, Stanislaus: Genesis of Psychopathic Personality Trends, *Psychiatry*, 5, 1942, p. 1.

NEUROTICS, DELINQUENTS AND IDEAL-FORMATION

By Jeanne Lampl-De Groot, M.D.

(Amsterdam)

It is a pleasure to contribute a paper to this volume in honor of the work of August Aichhorn who opened new ways to our understanding and treatment of youthful delinquents.

His famous book, *Wayward Youth,* is an invaluable source of practical experience in dealing with problem children but it is also our first psychoanalytic orientation in the etiology and theory of delinquency.

Some problems in this field of theoretical considerations will be the subject of this paper.

Aichhorn considers delinquency the result of two types of faulty development in the child's libido structure. The first type occurs in the process whereby the pleasure-principle is converted into the reality-principle. The second is a malformation of the ego ideal. Both are problems of ego development.

According to Aichhorn a characteristic symptom of the dissocial child is his inability to meet the demands of reality. His ego cannot give up the pleasure-principle and he meets such demands of his environment with obstinacy or revolt. This is the result of two extremes of faulty training either of which may prevent him from an adjustment adequate to his age level. If he is treated with either excessive indulgence or excessive severity, the result may be the same. Our own clinical experience confirms this claim. Delinquent children all show the same inability to give up immediate gratification and almost invariably they have been brought up by someone (parents or guardians), whose methods were extreme. Either they were too severe and did not compensate the child for frustrations of love or other gratifications, or they spoiled the child until it was incapable of bearing any disappointment, or they oscillated between both attitudes so that the child was too confused to be able to make any adequate adaptation.

But since these parental behavior patterns are found not only in the histories of delinquents but also in those of neurotics, the question arises what determines whether a child becomes neurotic or delinquent?

There has been much discussion of this point. Although psychiatric literature generally classifies waywardness and delinquency as psychopathies, a clear and uniform definition of this term is still lacking.[1] It is very difficult to give such a definition because delinquent (psychopathic) behavior almost always reveals evidence of neurotic trends, and because both kinds of symptoms, delinquent and neurotic, show similar developmental disturbances.

H. G. van der Waals in his studies on the problem of the psychopath[2] distinguishes between "dispositional" and "developmental" psychopathies, though he admits one must always allow for a supplemental series of factors (Freud: "Ergänzungsreihe") in these as in the case of the neurotics.

Although many psychiatrists tend to regard the neurosis as an acquired, the psychopathic state as a congenital disturbance, van der Waals concludes that "it is probable that the genesis of the psychopathic condition is identical in the main with that of the neurosis".

I agree with this author. The study of both neurotic and problem children usually reveals that their parents used faulty educational methods because of their own difficulties or neuroses. Therefore we tend to consider them responsible for the child's pathological development. Yet we sometimes meet cases of both categories whose parents were obviously normal and whose training was both understanding and free from the errors of extreme severity or indulgence. In such cases we are forced to postulate an abnormal disposition, although we must still be cautious lest we have overlooked some influences of earliest childhood.

We would therefore say that the genesis of both neurotic and dissocial disturbance lies in the interplay, in varying mixtures, of dispositional factors and environmental influences.

Yet this similar genesis should not blind us to the striking differences between neurotic and delinquent behavior. We must still be specific about these differences and attempt to find their causes.

Both neurotic and delinquent children show the same inability to harmonize their instinctual drives with the demands of their environment. We realize that in both cases it is a symptom of their faulty ego development. But the neurotic tries to solve the conflict by repressing id impulses while the delinquent ignores the social demands and acts out his primitive desires as far as possible. He refuses to give up immediate gratification and rather than do so prefers to jeopardize his relation to his environment. In contrast, the neurotic's anxiety prevents him from risking a conflict in his relationship

---

[1] Cf. Rümke, H. C. and Carp, E. and D. E.: In the Psychopathie number of the Dutch Journal *Psychiatrische en Neurologische Bladen,* No. 5, 1947.

[2] van der Waals, H. G.: Aanleg en Ontwikkeling (Disposition and Development) in *Mensch en Maatschappij* No. 19, 1943, No. 4, and same author on the Rorschach test in *Psychiatrische en Neurologische Bladen* 49, 1946.

to his environment and therefore to him the pain of giving up direct gratification becomes bearable. To restate, the delinquent's object attachment is
not strong enough to act as a barrier against his instinctual needs and therefore his ego cannot achieve an adaptation to reality, whereas the neurotic
is too dependent upon his object to permit the id more than a limited degree
of instinctual satisfaction. Needless to say we are using these quantitative
terms in a relative sense only.

The delinquent who has made himself relatively independent of his
environment is then proportionately more dependent on the gratification
of his instinctual drives.

Since the neurotic is able to free himself to some degree from the imperative demand for immediate gratification, he, in turn, is correspondingly
more dependent on the love he receives from his environment. Thus we see
that the neurotic's ego is strong where that of the delinquent is weak and
vice versa.

Let us at this point return to Aichhorn's second type of faulty development in the child's libido structure, the malformation of the ego ideal.

During the course of its development, one of the functions of the
child's ego is to take over the demands and prohibitions of its parents. It
thus begins the development of the superego, later to become a part of the
ego-organization by introjecting these parent images. This introjection is
theoretically completed and the superego established with the beginning of
the latency period.[3]

The foregoing description of the neurotic and the delinquent's reactions
to his environment are now further complicated by the demands of the
superego. An inadequate or disturbed relationship to the parents also dis-
turbs the development of the superego, which manifests itself in a defective
social adjustment.

Aichhorn (who uses the terms ego ideal and superego interchangeably),
describes the various types of delinquents whose behavior was the sign of
their inability to form a socially acceptable ego ideal. He describes two groups.

In one group, the mechanism of the superego, or ego ideal, functioned
well but the introjected parental norms were dissocial ones, that is the
parents were themselves criminal, so that the child who formed his standards
from them, inevitably came into conflict with society.

In the second group, it was the early relationship to the parents which

---

[3] Lampl-de Groot, Jeanne: On the Delevopment of the Ego and Superego, *Int.
J. Psa.*, 28, 1947. Following a proposition of Hartmann and Kris in the *Psychoanalytic
Study of the Child*, Vol. I, 1945, I shall, in order to make the terminology more
precise, use the word "maturation" instead of "autonomous development" and reserve
the term "development" for the processes of growth predominantly dependent on the
environment.

had been disturbed, so that the process of ego ideal formation could not take a normal course but resulted in dissocial behavior.[4]

Let us specify at this point, parenthetically, that we consider an ideal social adaptation one in which the inner equilibrium between ego, id and superego enables the personality to realize its own needs and capacities without preventing others from doing the same. Since individual needs often differ from the interests of a group or society this adaptation is often hard to achieve.

Aichhorn, then, in discussing his second group of dissocial personalities enumerates various situations in early childhood which can cause faulty development of the ego ideal. Such is the case if a child is an orphan or semi-orphan, or an illegitimate child who is placed in a succession of institutions or foster homes. It therefore has no one to whom it can form a sound and stable attachment or with whom it can make a real and lasting identification. In such cases there is either no way of establishing an ego ideal or it is defective and too weak to regulate conduct in later life.

Aichhorn describes other abnormal family situations that can have similar consequences, but they all demonstrate the same formula, namely, a defect or absence of object attachment causing a defect or absence of an ego ideal. Both a normal object relation and a sound ego ideal are necessary for an adequate social adjustment, and where either factor has been abnormal, delinquency may result.

Let us examine these same processes in neurotics.

The anamneses of neurotics also show disturbances in object cathexis and ego ideal formation. It seems probable that neglected children, who have not had a mother's (or parent's) love seem more predestined to delinquency. Though my own experience with delinquency is too limited to justify an opinion, I am sure that lack of motherly love and severe frustrations can lead to a neurosis.

But this still does not illuminate our question about differential factors since most of the cases we meet show a combination of symptoms. The delinquent reveals neurotic trends, and our neurotic patients show tendencies toward more or less dissocial behavior. Therefore we are reduced to the quantitative aspect in making our diagnosis. Where the dissocial behavior predominates we speak of a delinquent with neurotic symptoms, and where there is a reversed balance of factors, we speak of a neurotic personality with (often concealed) delinquent features.

Although it is difficult to separate abnormal psychic manifestations from each other, careful observation sometimes enables us to gain insight

---

[4] Here I should like to stress the fact that social adaptation is not identical with uncritical submission to every passing demand of a given society. There can be and often really are circumstances in society which require a condemnation of prevailing norms and a rebellion against them.

into the origin of our patients' different behavior patterns.[5] Aichhorn
describes types of delinquents who commit their dissocial offenses because
of a need for punishment (an unconscious sense of guilt). Such cases force
us to assume a severe superego.[6] Yet we repeatedly observe that a too severe
superego causes neurotic symptoms. Can we discover what factors determine
whether a strong and cruel superego leads to delinquency or to neurosis?

Since a punishing superego (like punishing parents in early childhood)
makes one suffer, individual difference in the capacity to endure suffering,
pain or discontent must play a role in the problem. A person who cannot
bear such tensions, not only develops an inadequate adaptation to reality
but, unlike the neurotic, he will not endure self-punishment. He tries to escape
it by mobilizing his rebellion against the outer world as a means of acting
out the tension of his punishing guilt feelings.

Why does the neurotic not do likewise? Perhaps his ability to endure
suffering is greater, yet this means of relieving it would benefit him also.
Must we conclude that his punishing superego is greater than that of the
delinquent? I do not believe so. The delinquents whose offenses are due to
a sense of guilt show an intensity of purpose which hardly justifies this conclusion. It seems to me that another formulation may afford a deeper insight
into this problem.[7]

Up to this point, I have used the terms ego ideal and superego interchangeably as does Aichhorn. I now propose to make a distinction between
them, as have Alexander, Flugel and others.[8]

The superego is established through a dual process of development.
The infant identifies itself very early with both parents and wants to be or
to become like them. The child, however, forms an ideal which in later
maturation takes over norms and ideals from the wider environment. ("I
want to be like my parents and have their ideals.") At the same time the
child also takes over his parents' orders and prohibitions, and by introjecting
them builds up the inhibiting (and punishing) part of the superego. ("I must
or must not do this or that.")

The ideal-formation in the ego of the young child has a special function apart from that of social adjustment. It might be said to enlarge the

---

[5] Needless to say that we must always realize that clinically these various phenomena overlap and merge. Perhaps it will prove to be true that in each individual,
whether "ill" or "normal", some trends of delinquency (psychopathy) are to be found.

[6] Cf. Freud's Criminal from a Sense of Guilt, Some Charactertypes Met with in
Psychoanalytic Work, *Collected Papers,* Vol. IV, London, Hogarth Press, 1925.

[7] Cf. Lampl-de Groot: On the Development of Ego and Superego, *Psychoanalytic
Study of the Child,* Vol. I, 1945.

[8] In the English translation of Aichhorn's book, *Wayward Youth,* the translators
also mention this tendency in psychoanalytic literature.

ego. These ideals serve the child as compensation whenever it feels hurt or incompetent in comparison with older children or adults. They strengthen its self-esteem by counteracting narcissistic injuries and frustrations. During maturation these ideals expand into all kinds of social, ethical, religious and scientific norms. Even for adults, high ideals, if not exaggerated far beyond the personal level of attainment are of great value to their self-esteem.

The young child's judging superego has the function of supervising his instinctual gratifications and curbing his passions through punishment whenever they threaten to conflict with external demands. This function of the superego, therefore, often injures the narcissistic position of the ego and hurts its self-esteem.

Where there has been a harmonious development, both parts of the established superego work together toward inner and outer equilibrium and finally form a unity. But if the development of either the ideal-formation or the punishing part of the superego is disturbed, the two may diverge. We can understand this process better if we study the forces behind them.

We know from Freud that the severity of the superego does not correlate exclusively with the parents' attitude. The cruelty of the superego corresponds more closely to the strength of the child's own aggressiveness. During the period when the child's superego is being established it uses that part of the child's aggressiveness which is turned toward the self. This takes place after the period of active instinctual life has terminated with the ending of its last phase, the oedipal situation.

When development is normal, this part of aggressive energy is turned toward the self and serves to secure the fulfillment of the ideals and in so doing strengthens the ego's self respect. The remaining part of free, aggressive energy is used for mental, intellectual and bodily activities in the outer world, for learning, adapting to or changing the environment. It is "sublimated" into activity.

Unfortunately this difficult, complicated and dual process is frequently disturbed. Often too much aggressiveness is turned toward the self. This aggression then becomes sexualized and the whole relation between superego and ego ceases to be a judging, regulating function in the service of normal adaptation. Instead it becomes a sado-masochistic relationship. The result is an obstinate drive for self-punishment, an arrest and restriction of ego development and also of the formation of the ego ideal.

On the one hand the ego is threatened by the cruel superego which has become as "triebhaft" as the id, and on the other the ego receives no support from the ego ideal because this ideal-formation has been both damaged and restricted.

Moreover when the two processes of the formation of an ego ideal and of a sadistic superego diverge, this divergence is itself another inhibiting force to the growth of the total personality.

When the aggressive energy used for developing normal activities cannot be adequately sublimated still another disturbance results. Either repression and inhibition are increased or the aggression is expressed in a direct, primitive manner. If it combines with sexual energy it can lead to various other forms of abnormal development.

Neurotics as well as delinquents may show a driving need for self-punishment. I now claim that the differential factor between neurotics and delinquents is to be found in a developmental difference of their ego ideal and superego formations.

Where there has been a strong ideal-formation in early childhood which later was disturbed by an oversevere superego its effect is to inhibit ego development and prevent it from sublimating aggressive energy into activity. The strong ideals forbid the expression of any aggression toward the outside world and it therefore turns toward the self. The result is the well-known vicious circle of the neurosis.

If in the young child there has been weak ideal-formation which later is disturbed by a sadistic superego, the result is self-punishment and also defective ego development. But in such cases the weak ideal-formation is unable to prevent the aggression from discharging and the sadistic superego is acted out against the environment. This results in dissocial behavior or delinquency.

There are interesting instances of mixtures of these two processes. Thus, for example, one may observe persons who, in one area of their lives have high ideals to which they may either be making a good adjustment, or if blocked in attaining them, react with neurotic symptoms in this special field. But in other areas they may be utterly lacking in ideals and norms and behave quite dissocially. Careful examination of many delinquents often reveals a similar mixture in their personalities, with a few areas dominated by high norms and fine social feelings.

The ideal-formation which begins in early childhood and uses the mechanism of identification, is probably a difficult and vulnerable process.

Since it would seem that almost everyone, be he as "normal" as possible in ordinary life, has a small "neurotic" nucleus and sometimes an almost undetectable "personal delusion", he probably also has a minor "psychopathic" spot in his makeup.[9]

---

[9] Lampl-de Groot: *Op. cit.*

I regret that the scope of this paper prevents me from presenting illustrative cases. Instead, I should like to discuss here two additional problems.

What are the prerequisites for a sound and lasting ideal-formation? What is the source of this overpowering and ungovernable aggression which partly threatens the self and partly the external environment?

I would say that there are two prerequisites for ideal-formation. There must be a capacity for identification, innate and capable of being stimulated by experience. There must also be the right objects with which the child can identify. If these are lacking or inadequate the process is correspondingly difficult.

There are children who succeed in building high ideals and norms in spite of having either no parents, or unsound or unstable parent figures. It may be that this astonishing achievement of some unloved children is the result of their need to compensate for the narcissistic injuries which this lack of adequate object-gratification caused them.

But when a child is not loved in its early years the more frequent result is an impaired ideal-formation. The child's narcissistic needs are then doubly frustrated through lack of love as well as through imperfect ideal-formation. This formulation brings us once more to an awareness of the importance of a child's first love objects.

To return to our second point, namely, the source of the overpowering aggression: Observation of children convinces us that even a young child's aggression can be and generally is mobilized by the frustration of a bodily or mental need or wish.

The same is true in regard to sexuality. The infant at first seeks gratification of his sexual urges through his own body (thumb-sucking, friction, anal play, masturbation, etc.). It is the mother who introduces the child to sexual pleasure. By offering her breast and by caressing the baby while nursing it, she excites the baby and provokes its libidinal attachment. We know how important for the sexual development this maternal "seducing" proves to be and how an excess of "seduction" may cause a variety of disturbances. It is true that in normal development the baby's discharge of aggressive energy by means of its own body is seldom noticed. The normal tendency toward the preservation of life ordinarily masks the signs of these aggressive urges. But occasionally these aggressive urges reveal themselves unmistakably in cases of self-damage (by scratching, etc.).

In obviously pathological cases, however, severe self-mutilation has been observed.[10] But we hold to the truth of our previous statement, namely that acts of aggression are in the main provoked by "frustration" as are

---

[10] Cf. the case in W. Hoffer's paper on Mouth, Hand and Ego-integration.

sexual ones by "seduction". These facts guide our educational procedures and make us say: A child needs love but too much gratification is seduction and can be as harmful as lack of love.

Our knowledge that frustration stimulates aggression leads us to say: the child must have opportunities for discharging a part of its aggression, but stimulating its aggression by too much frustration will have damaging results. All of us who deal with children are aware of this danger of steering from Scylla into Charybdis.

Since too many frustrations provoke an excess of aggressiveness the child must be compensated by love so that it can make a sound love attachment and a tenable ideal-formation.

There seems a tendency in the literature to neglect the topic of aggressive, instinctual urges in life, because of the fact that we only notice the aggression which follows frustration. We would be in a like position were we to ignore the need for sexual object attachments, because they arise only after seduction. The fact that some authors have never observed acts of genuine aggression hardly justifies this omission. In the same way, in the early days of psychoanalysis, the existence of infantile sexual urges was indignantly denied by the pediatricians, educators and parents who had never observed them. Although the analogous observation of aggressive urges is far more difficult, it seems possible that further investigation will broaden the observer's views.

Some authors seem to neglect this topic of instinctual aggression because of their doubts in regard to Freud's theory of a biologically founded death instinct. In my opinion, biology has not yet gone far enough either to affirm or deny Freud's hypothesis. Should it be proven erroneous, psychoanalysis must discard it. This would leave us without an answer as to the origin of aggressive energy until we can formulate a new and more tenable hypothesis. But meanwhile we cannot afford to overlook the manifestations of both sexual and aggressive drives in mankind.

From the social point of view it is vitally important that mankind does not deny the existence and intensity of genuine aggressiveness. Denial always leads to blindness and therefore to disturbed reality-testing and adjustment. Some people seem to have a deep rooted fear of admitting their own aggressive drives and therefore deny them in all human beings. Not until the role of the aggressive instincts in the individual and in society has been accepted can we conceive of finding ways and means of overcoming the menacing manifestations of aggression and destructive behavior in mankind.

Among the major purposes of any educational program must be the aim to provide compensating love, constructive ideal-formation, and suitable methods for sublimating aggression into fruitful activities.

In one chapter of his book,[11] Aichhorn describes an attempt to re-educate a group of juvenile delinquents in an institution. Their aggressiveness was so overwhelming as to segregate them from all other groups. Though he himself points out how, in his handling of this group, he was still groping for technique, and though today he might have used other methods, one is nevertheless struck by his intuitive understanding of their problems.

And we can recognize in this pioneer attempt at group re-education his awareness of the balance of factors and his redirecting of the processes which have been the subject of this paper.

•

---

[11] Aichhorn, August: *Wayward Youth,* New York, Viking Press, 1944, The Aggressive Group, pp. 167-185.

THE EGO OF THE ADOLESCENT

By Fritz Wittels, M.D.

(New York)

Let us begin this study of the adolescent ego by recapitulating what we know from observing the baby in his nursing stage. It is through this act of nursing that his first experience of ego is obtained. It is a mother-child ego. We might say that the first experience of an ego comes from without — it is sucked in. This discovery of his own ego is one of the definitive experiences of a child's psychic life. Terminologically we may say that the birth of the ego is the beginning of narcissism, because the concept of narcissism pre-supposes the existence of an ego. We therefore speak of the pre-ego period as of the auto-erotic stage.

Many authors have attempted to describe how the child makes this discovery. By the third year the child is almost overwhelmed by the growing awareness of possessing a self which is like that of those who surround him. This self-awareness is all-important and indeed becomes the center of the child's universe. Despite this ego-centering, however, and even at later stages, we know the people surrounding us, particularly those needed for our support, better than we know ourselves. These supportive people we group into the "yous" separating them from the more or less dreaded "he, she, and they." The infant feels a gap between these yous (mother, nurse) and the alien "theys". Later this sense of gap between the newly born self and all other people deepens.

The infant is too weak psychologically to function without help and therefore includes in his new self a considerable part of the "you". His supporters form a part of this self and this initial certainty that they are a part continues until cumulative experience shows him more or less definitely that there is quite a difference even between his mother and himself. This experience forces him to depend on himself as though he reasoned, "If I do not take care of myself, who will?"

The newly acquired ego is unfathomable. We see a child look at his own reflection in the mirror (I believe, Lauretta Bender calls it the mirror phenomenon) and kiss it. He has decided to realize the enigma by loving it.

256

I once saw a girl of about three look at her reflection and when I asked her: "Like yourself?" she answered with deep conviction: "Yes".

The child attempts, at least in his imagination, to be independent of all these more or less unreliable supporters outside of him, by increasing his personal power. A good example of such attempts is the little boy cited by Anna Freud who possessed an imaginary lion. This lion was his inseparable companion, a totem animal of which he had no fear. On the contrary, the lion was the expression of his omnipotence. I knew a little boy who insisted on carrying around a piece of pink cloth, which was his fetish, without which he refused to go to bed and later even to the Kindergarten. To the child this fetish, which he called "pinky", had supernatural powers and courage and also took over all the naughtiness that training forbade the boy. Pinky became the bulwark against frustrations. The ego of the child is and becomes more and more a narcissistic world of its own.

The following conversation is characteristic of the child's situation. A three year old boy asked his nurse: "Do you like me?" — "I like you very much." — Do you *always* like me?" — "Always." The boy, after a pause for thought, said with faltering conviction: "I *am* a good boy." He knows that he has to be a good boy in order to be liked. Beyond this he is not interested in civilization nor in the object called nurse. He yields to force. In a similar conversation later in life he would not say, "I am a good boy", but "you are a good girl", and, maybe, "I love you".

The beatitude of the narcissistic ego is in a precarious situation. It is hard for a little fellow to insist on being the centre of the universe. Reality proves all too often that he is not. However, the little hero fights for his position against older siblings, other children and even against parents, who may assail this position. Their attacks make it evident that he is small and weak. Even his own mother is not completely satisfactory, since her role, as Freud said, is dictated by destiny. She has to train the child against his will. Reality which, like a creditor, demands an accounting, pierces his beautiful narcissistic armor early in life. The child is forced to respond and to give something which resembles love, in order to save the bulk of his self from damage. But in normal training the child gets all the support, tenderness, and protection *unconditionally,* even if he gives very little in return.

The structure of the child's ego is very different from the ego of the normal adult. Juvenile courts often are startled by misdeeds which can be explained only by a completely different structure of the offender's ego, strangely devoid of any compassion for his neighbor's suffering. About a year ago, a thirteen year old boy hanged an eight year old playmate just for the adventure. Another fourteen year old "sitter" strangled the baby in his care and the court psychiatrist succeeded in convincing the jury that even at that age the youngster's ego was too narcissistic to permit him to realize his deed. When crimes of such extreme cruelty occur later in life, psychiatrists suspect an epileptic equivalent, which is a pathological regression to this profound narcissism, oblivious of human ethics.

Under normal circumstances, the child does not conquer reality before the end of adolescence. We can almost see him struggle to preserve his narcissistic paradise when confronted with the attacks of fate. Many intrusions break through the child's protective barriers. Usually, the child is drilled rather than educated by his trainers. If these trainers have a sympathetic understanding of the child's ego, they spare the child's mechanisms as much as possible. There has been considerable progress in education as well as in educators in this respect. However, fate cannot always be gentle and all kinds of abnormal family conditions may work inimically further to retard the slow progress of ego development. Loss of parents, and their replacement by step-parents leave indelible impressions. We see such effect not only in real orphans but also in the so-called "social orphans", children who have their parents nominally but not in reality. Many events in a child's life prematurely force it out of its narcissism. Among such factors are prolonged and particularly painful diseases, sexual shocks, and precocious sex life. Sometimes such precocious sexual life is the result of constitutional factors, but more often it is caused by external circumstances which forced sex upon the immature child.

The child's answer to all these attacks may be anxiety, neurotic repression, isolation, or annulment, in short all the defense mechanisms available to the human ego. In such cases the ego of the child is crippled by tasks beyond its age and assimilative power which would demand qualities belonging to a later age.

*   *   *

Puberty brings an increase in instinctual demands and consequently also a corresponding advance in the ego's defenses. We may speak of a second edition of the phallic phase with its castration anxiety. Some youngsters show this anxiety consciously, they feel scared by a danger to their genitalia. I have not found in the literature any reference to a second phallic phase at the start of puberty, but it is so obvious that we all know it whether or not we call it such. The first period of the original phallic phase as we know it in childhood is still free from anxiety. Fear of castration comes only in the second phase. The simplest example is that of a child around its fifth year, who masturbates without anxiety at first, and later does so with anxiety. In contradistinction to this sequence, the pubescent return of the phallic phase begins with considerable anxiety. We may lay down the rule that all pubescents feel anxiety on the occasion of their first orgasm even if the act is no more than masturbation. It is the pressure of the unknown pushing them on, which arouses their drive for self-preservation. To this is added the returning castration anxiety, all of which combines at first to destroy pleasure. Such storms will be raging for a number of years.

All authors describe the ambivalence, the swinging pendulum that characterizes pubescence. Rebellion versus blind submission, cynicism versus idealism, optimism versus pessimism, may serve as examples of that polarity, which has so often been described in detail by various authors even before Freud. That polarity is the expression of the tendencies of the id versus those of the ego: wish versus fear, often defiance versus anxiety. Some youngsters cling to childhood, denying the signs of maturity as long as possible. These adolescents appear to have no interest in the other sex, they play the part of care-free children but nevertheless betray their anxiety. I observed a girl, not quite fifteen, who had remained particularly childish. Boys did not interest her. Though her contemporaries were chattering about beaux, using lipstick and attending dances, she was unmoved and preferred the company of six year olds and reading fairy tales and other children's books. Her mother was congratulated on having so "chaste" a daughter. One day this girl told her mother that a man in the crowded city park had touched her obscenely and then pursued her until she managed to hide in a ladies' room.

A week later she had to leave town by train, travelling alone. The same man, she said, boarded the train in a small station. She stared at him petrified, becoming restless until the man asked whether anything was wrong with her. She answered: "You know". At that the man rose to his feet and left the car in a hurry. We can understand his reaction. The story hardly needs comment. Anxiety permeated the girl's psychology because of the fear of and desire for rape.

Other youngsters, like swimmers who dive into the cold water because they are afraid of entering it gradually, anticipate adulthood by giving themselves to early flirtation and puppy loves. More often than not those two phases, the retrograde phase and the anticipation of love co-exist, e.g. in our college girls. On school days they wear mocassins and dirty slacks and insist on looking as unattractive as possible, but at week-end reunions they appear in splendid regalia and dance cheek to cheek.

In the midst of all this turmoil, as Anna Freud described it in her two superb chapters on adolescence,[1] a deep change of the child's ego is prepared slowly. Love and protection are no longer unconditionally given to the growing youngster. What he needs now, is a sex partner, a need that is biologically initiated with the mature functioning of the sex glands, although for social reasons it is inhibited in aim for some time to come. That partner is a *tu*, if we might use the Latin word as the complement of the Latin word ego. The tu has demands which have to be acknowledged; the relationship

---

[1] *The Ego and the Mechanisms of Defence*, New York, International Universities Press, 1946.

is no longer exclusively one between a maternal person who gives and a child who receives. The expanding demands of the adolescent ego would be unfulfilled if it were not coping with a tu which also demands and gives only on condition that such demands are gratified. Thus a new reality appears on the horizon: *The* reality, Freud's third "creditor" of the ego, the enemy of narcissism.

It seems to me that psychoanalysts are too quick to accept the statement that adolescence creates nothing really new. So Fenichel says: "All the mental phenomena characteristic of puberty may be regarded as attempts to *re*-establish the disturbed equilibrium." He should have said: to establish a new equilibrium. Anna Freud emphasizes that while the id does not change in puberty, the ego does. What she means is the different arrangement of the ego's defenses. The main difference, which probably is realized by all of us but not described in detail, is the change from narcissism to *tu-ism,* which makes man capable of love. We remember that the child's ego grew out of the tus by which the growing baby was surrounded. In adolescence and post-adolescence, the ego feels that it has to return to the tu what it has taken from the tus of perhaps ten or twenty years before. We can see that sometimes very slow, in other cases explosive process in the magnifying glass called love. Freud says that lovers lose their ego by pouring it into the other ego, the tu, of a beloved person. In this way they impoverish themselves, become humble and would constantly feel their loss, were it not for a kind of megalomania that goes with the projecting and introjecting mechanisms of love which more than compensate for the humility of the lover: he serves with pride.

Even without that ecstatic phenomenon called love, the maturing ego, actively standing in the current of life, feels the necessity of devotion, of surrender, and of renunciation. All three of these emotions are alien to the narcissistic ego of the child. The principle of reality, only partly recognized in childhood, definitely enters the pleasure-displeasure mechanism. Naturally, the recognition of reality is not completely absent in childhood, nor on the other hand is it realized without resistance in later years. We speak of narcissistic types. They do not sufficiently recognize the rights of the tu, they cannot love.

It may be that all recognition of reality is accomplished in the image of the tu. It may be that men love their property as they love a tu, e.g.: I and my books, which I hold in my hands, sometimes almost caressingly. An I and a tu. Here we have reached one of the borderlines of psychoanalysis: the inner experience (*Erlebnis*). However, we are on firm psychoanalytic ground when we describe the ego's change in the maturing man from narcissism to tu-ism, recognition of the love object, recognition of the world outside ourselves. We need objects for our completion, sex objects and others. In our understanding of reality lies the main difference between childhood and maturity. Here indeed, something new is added to the development of man, so that we no longer can say that all the psychological phenomena of adolescence are second editions of previously settled problems. With the maturity of the sex glands comes the maturity of the ego, both of them new in the growing body and mind. We have learned from Freud that "the ego is primarily a body ego". We may add: reality outside of our ego is primarily a body reality also. Adolescents and adults alike need a body, as a rule one of the other sex, for seizure and union. That body is the prototype of reality originating in the id. The ego has to "realize" it.

*　　*　　*

The process of accepting reality probably never ends. However, a relative lull follows the storms of adolescence. When? The law pronounces the age of twenty-one as responsible maturity. This is too early in most instances and too late in others. We know that higher education begins at about the eighteenth year when it can utilize the relative peace of a kind of second latency period, mainly due to the desexualization and sublimation of the ego-tu problem. Apprentices have finished their apprenticeships and are sent out into the world as journey men. They are supposed to come back from their journeys as young masters. Neuroses and particularly the first depressions of a circular psychosis frequently break out at the age of eighteen. The second latency period is shorter than the first, and less sharp in outline. Yet such a lull does occur before the tides of life submerge all attempts at classification.

We suggest the following four phases as subdivisions of adolescence.

(1) A second phallic phase with outspoken anxiety as defense against pubescence.

(2) The often described phase of ambivalence, the fight between advance and retardation, in the main a subterranean struggle between the id and the superego. Reality, the third creditor of the ego, seems to be the loser in the struggle. The adolescent cannot decide what to do and that is why his clinical picture is sometimes reminiscent of an incipient psychosis. The psychotic in his initial stages feels at sea and is fearful and perplexed. But in his case the end is different. He tries in vain to regain something that was lost, whereas the adolescent is struggling towards a goal, something he has not yet possessed. Educators agree that we cannot help him very much in his struggle and should not even try to interfere in

the struggle of all these growing and shifting strata as long as there is no immediate danger.

(3) A second latency period, preparing the post-adolescent ego: tu-ism in the place of narcissism.

(4) The mature ego, emerging from both the phase of ambivalence between advance and retardation and the second latency period, into the phase in which it is capable of love and of understanding the world outside the ego.

THE CHILD'S MORAL DEVELOPMENT

By M. Woolf, M.D.

(*Tel Aviv*)

Kant taught that the moral categorical imperative is transcendental and innate in man. His teaching seems confirmed by the belief in the "innocence of little children", which has been taken as axiomatic for a long time, and which seems to refer chiefly to their alleged innocence regarding sex. Today, however, we realize that this belief is a prejudice which is overwhelmingly contradicted by facts. The question is therefore forced upon us, whence came this firmly rooted conviction of the child's innocence? The Bible tells us that Adam and Eve lived in innocence until they ate the forbidden fruit of the Tree of Knowledge of Good and Evil, and it was this knowledge of good and evil that robbed them of their innocence and resulted in their expulsion from Paradise. Their innocence therefore consisted not only in their ignorance of evil but of good as well.

But ignorance can be neither positive nor negative in a moral sense. It is simply the absence of morality, and an uncorrupted child who knows neither good nor evil is still merely amoral.

How, therefore, does the child's moral development proceed from this stage? The only way is to teach it the precepts of morality, that is, the precepts of both good and evil. One has to change its amorality by ending its ignorance of good and evil. We can only make a child moral by imparting to it the concepts of both "good" and "evil", not only the "thou shalt" but also the "thou shalt not", as do the ten commandments, the foundation of our morality.

The reality of this paradoxical situation whereby we have to enlighten and thereby "corrupt" the child in order to make it moral and wherein the child's moral development must pass through immorality has long been recognized. A Russian proverb says: "He who has not sinned does not know repentance and atonement." A poet attributes to Czar Ivan the Terrible, one of the greatest sinners of history, the thought that only he who sunk deeply into the abyss of sin, can know the sublimity of repentance and penance.

263

That genuine salvation comes only through sinning is also the conviction of that combined genius, moralist and potential criminal, Dostoevski.

This observation would seem to confirm our hypothesis of the development of cultural morality in human society. Freud claimed that human civilization stems from the original sin of parricide and that from the ensuing reaction of repentance for this primeval crime, arose religion and our moral code.

The child too must travel this same road of overcoming its primary urges and this path also leads him through the experience of sin, guilt and repentance. A child's early mental life is governed by the pleasure-displeasure principle. He seeks the gratification of his pleasure everywhere and in everything and soon encounters moral prohibitions. The temptation to trespass these prohibitions is natural and the child finds it difficult to resist and to obey the moral code.

Two impulses eventually move the child to decide in favor of morality; the fear of punishment and feelings of guilt. Usually both impulses act simultaneously but their effect is not the same. Fear alone cannot produce morality. Education based only on fear may lead to a mental breakdown resulting in a neurosis or psychosis. Those whose urges are stronger, react to education through fear with obstinacy and defiance, bitterness and seclusiveness which defeats all pedagogic influence. The way to criminality is then wide open.[1] But if ever a bright ray of love enters the embittered, intimidated soul of such a child — even if it occurs rarely — the child opens his heart to that educator's influence and feelings of guilt develop. These feelings of guilt, associated with trespassing moral prohibitions, strengthen the child's inhibitions toward the seductive experience of pleasure.

We thus conclude that the child's moral development takes place through the experience of sin, repentance and the feeling of guilt. The child must have time and experience for this process. He cannot immediately comply with all the demands of morality, any more than he could learn to eat, talk and walk all at once. The educator must therefore have patience and be indulgent.

Moreover, guilt feelings can arise only as a reaction after a sin has been committed, a prohibition transgressed and the evil of the deed has become conscious. Thus sin is a step toward morality, a point which the educator must not overlook.

We are then faced with the question, what is the psychological mechanism of this moral development? When, how and at what stages of his growth does the child learn to know repentance and feelings of guilt?

Let us briefly recapitulate the phases of a child's emotional develop-

---

[1] We would point out that defiance which is rarely a motive for crime in adults. is a frequent motive among juvenile delinquents.

ment: with the beginning of the oedipus complex the child feels rivalry toward the other members of the family and develops hatred, jealousy and anger. Even though these feelings are also turned against the mother, nevertheless the child's love for his mother is not destroyed. On the contrary, that love increases and eventually spreads to the formerly hated rivals. This conflict of love and hate inevitably arouses guilt feelings and these very guilt feelings determine the struggle between love and hatred. Either the hatred is overpowering and triumphs, or the guilt, speaking as the voice of conscience, grows louder and love triumphs over hatred, morality over sin. For in the last analysis, all morality is the codification of love.

The boy's first love for his mother (like the girl's for her father) is intermixed with sensuality. This infantile sensuality seeks its gratification in all the various pregenital activities, oral, anal, voyeuristic, exhibitionistic, etc. The educator often fails to understand the sensual nature of these activities and therefore not only fails to limit or avoid them but may even further them because he himself enjoys them unconsciously. Sooner or later, however, he draws the line and rejects them as "shameless" and "immoral". In fact, the more indulgent the educators (mother, father, etc.) have been at first, the more rigorously and harshly, as a rule, do they reject and suppress these practices later on by punishment and intimidation. These forms of gratification then often become a second source of guilt feelings which in turn lead to exaggerated sexual morality and prudery.

Since infantile masturbation is the easiest of all forms of gratification, as well as the most persistent and least detectable, it becomes the focus of guilt feelings. The real cause of these feelings, the prohibited incestuous emotions and desires towards the parents, is soon repressed from consciousness and the feelings of guilt which they roused are shifted to masturbation and thereby rationalized. This accounts for the curious and otherwise incomprehensible fact that masturbation, in itself completely innocent and harmless, is regarded as a severe moral offense, a "dirty" sin, alleged to have all sorts of horrible consequences.

Suppression of the hatred and sensuality of the oedipus complex leads to sublimation of the loving emotion towards the parents and its transformation into pure childlike fondness. The child gives up the hope of gratifiying his sensual love but his mental dependence on his parents and his susceptibility to their influences increases during the latency period.

Thus the parents' rules, prohibitions, moral and esthetic demands take deep root in the child and the soil is prepared for the cultivation of the child's ethics, for the development of moral forces as a part of his ego.

Psychoanalysis has called this constellation of moral exaction the superego. It corresponds to the moral demands and prohibitions which the child has received and is the image in his mind of the parents' or educators' moral personality. We then say the child has identified himself with his parents' standards of morality.

But there is an important exception. If the child previously had a good relationship with his parents, one based on mutual love and esteem, the parents' influence is accepted and such identification results. But if in their emotional relations there was hatred, fear and embitterment on the child's side and indifference, intimidation, brutality and more or less unconscious hatred on the parents', the child's moral development inevitably turns in a direction opposite to their intentions and aims. Their attempts to influence the child rouses his open or furtive defiance. The demands of morality and their commands and prohibitions only rouse resistance if not opposition or even revolt, and the child's ethical development is hindered or seriously disturbed. This is true irrespective of his overt conduct — whether good or bad, submissive or resistive.

Lying and stealing are the two main offenses characteristic of childhood. The child is taught that he must not lie but must always tell the truth. Up to his fourth year the child cannot comply with this demand because he does not know what truth is. For truth is the statement of reality and before the age of four a child cannot differentiate external reality from his own inner experiences, desires, fancies and aspirations. He is inclined to believe that the occurrences of his mental life, what he perceives, feels, thinks, imagines and desires are reality. A child of this age does not lie, even when his assertions contradict facts, because he believes in the reality and truth of his experiences even when he invents them.

After the fifth year the child develops a clearer differentiation of reality and is now more or less able to discriminate between external reality and the products of his fancy. The conception of lying becomes clearer and the child at this age already knows the conscious lie. Therefore the demand not to lie and always to tell the truth can now become a matter of conscience.

This demand is repeatedly and seriously made by the educator. But woe to the child who takes this demand too literally. It may become the source of vital disappointments and of the most bitter experiences.

A mother told me the following story of her four-year-old son. The family were expecting a young girl and her fiancé to call. The child overheard the comment that while the fiancé was nice, he had an ugly long nose which spoiled his looks. In the evening, when the couple was sitting in the drawing room with the family, the child approached the fiancé with a stick in his hand and said as he touched the young man's nose with it: "This has to be cut off." The little boy behaved with calm and assurance and without the slightest awareness of the embarrassment caused by his unsuitable veracity. He was later enlightened, in rather an awkward manner, about the possible negative consequences of truthfulness in real life. His veracity was described to him as insolence and terrible rudeness, and this new point of view was confirmed by suitable "educational measures".

What education really demands and teaches the child is to know when not to lie, when not to tell the truth and when a lie is necessary. This statement may seem to be exaggerated but may I refer to the philosopher Georg Simmel who taught that certain kinds of lies are a necessary feature of our social life and that our society simply could not exist without them. Let me also quote the testimony of the Prime Minister of a country proud of its democracy who, on hearing an influential politician accused in Parliament of lying, exclaimed indignantly: "But gentlemen, if I always told the truth, I could not stay here for ten minutes!"

The question is only one of how and in what way the child learns the art of lying. There is one sphere of life in which our society is particularly and obviously mendacious, namely, the sphere of sex. There is even a saying to the effect that a gentleman in love is permitted to lie. But to lie to the loved one is the most destructive of all lying, for it is an insult to trust and violates the deepest and most intimate confidences in a manner which causes indignation and suffering to the one betrayed. Yet love-lies accompany man throughout his whole life from early childhood on.

The axiom that the child has no sex-life and no sexual emotions is itself a lie. But this lie was believed until fanatics of truth, like Sigmund Freud, undertook to destroy it. None of his great psychological discoveries has caused such an uproar and met with so much resistance as his refutation of this axiom. From his first months of life, the child feels sensual stimulations whose kinship to sexuality are beyond doubt to any impartial and unprejudiced observer. After about the third year of life, the child has an uncertain presentiment, an instinctive knowledge of sex-life, an "organic" unconscious knowledge which is deeply rooted in the urges of the organism, the same kind of knowledge that animals and all of living nature seem to have. From the age of three to five, the child is deeply excited by presentiments, dark sensations, impulses the sexual nature of which, although felt, cannot be understood by his undeveloped consciousness. He begins searching, exploring, observing, perhaps asking questions. In this matter that affects him so deeply and strongly, and incites his interest and drive to explore, the child soon perceives that all the adults are lying obviously, and with the intention of hiding everything from him. Soon the child begins to understand that he is expected to do likewise: to simulate innocence, that is ignorance, to behave as if he knew nothing, saw nothing, understood nothing; then he also begins to hide his experiences in this sphere, his knowledge of sex, and he begins to lie. If the child does not grow up alone, but in the company of other children, two strictly separated social circles soon develop around him. One is the circle of adults in which the child simulates, lies or hides his sexual knowledge and activities and pretends to be naive and innocent. The second is the circle of children who secretly discuss all the interesting matters of sex, exchange their sexual knowledge and experiences, undertake explorations together, and play the well-known sexual games.

The province of sex is the ground on which children learn and practice the art of the "necessary social lie". This is done under the guidance of adults, the child's educators, parents and teachers. From here, the practice of the social lie spreads to other spheres according to the child's needs and the influence of his environment. Thereafter, little is left of the original demands for truthfulness and of the prohibition of lying.

The question may be raised here how it may happen that there are people in whom veracity is so deeply rooted, that they are quite unable to lie, and that they become fanatics for truth in the face of every sacrifice? In such cases specific factors of that individual's fate, the influences of his education and of his experiences were decisive. Because those are individual phenomena, it would lead too far afield to discuss them here.

From his sixth year of life, the child lies for about the same motives as adults, namely, for the sake of convenience. Unfortunately, he has ample incentive to do so, because he feels small and weak and lying — as everyone knows — is the defense of the weak and discouraged. But the advantage occasionally to be gained from lying is not the only motive which induces the child to lie. Sometimes he resorts to lying in order to ridicule or to dupe the adult, to take revenge and to prove his own superiority and cleverness.

A boy of five, whose family was in comfortable circumstances, but whose father was away in the army, one day set himself up at a street corner and started begging from passers-by: "My father has gone to war, my mother is ill in bed, I am all alone." He roused compassion and in a short time, collected a sum of four shillings. At home, there were strawberries and whipped cream for supper, a delicacy of which he was very fond. While eating, he suddenly laughed and said, "Mummy, I wonder what all the people who gave me money, would think if they knew what I am eating now!" He triumphed over the people he had deceived.

Finally, children lie in order to comfort themselves for the things they have to give up and for their suffering in life. These are lies which — if only for the moment — give them a feeling of happiness like that which artistic achievement gives an adult.

The second typical offense of infancy is "stealing", the crime against property. This leads us to examine a child's concept of property.

It is obvious that our interest here is not the conception of property as an abstract idea, but the sense of property, the feeling of something belonging to one's own "ego". This sense of property can often be observed in children at the beginning of the second year, perhaps even earlier. When the child can barely pronounce a few words, even this very limited vocabulary contains the word "my", and the child's whole behavior shows unequivocally that the word is used in the sense of "belonging to me". But up to the third or fourth year this sense of property must be understood according to the law of the jungle: "What is mine is mine, and what is yours is also mine."

Observation of infants points to the mother's role in the development of this sense of property. Perhaps it is weaning which first gives the child the bitter feeling of the loss of something dear, important and belonging to it. In any case, separation from the mother is a source of great suffering, torment and fear for the infant and this trauma sets the pattern for all the child's later experiences of being deprived of something beloved and dear, of whatever affords pleasure.

Another important component of the sense of property develops very early from changes in the anal drives. With the inclination to hold back the bowel movement there develops the urge to retain, collect and not to give away the desired objects which provide pleasure, but to keep them as one would property. In this way, the characteristics of covetousness and greediness develop, which become important components of the sense of property and intensify it.

Up to the third or even fifth year of life — depending on the general state of the child's mental development and the influence of education — the child clearly shows a sense of property, sometimes intensified by covetousness and greediness in relation to all the objects he likes or desires. The fact that these objects may belong to somebody else is beyond his comprehension. After this age, the child gradually begins to understand that he often cannot or is not allowed to appropriate what he craves, that, for example, he may be forbidden to take a desired object home or may even not be allowed to touch it because it belongs to someone else. In the beginning, the child cannot comprehend the full significance of this new situation and conceives of it only as of a temporary obstacle to the fulfillment of his desires. In other words, the urge to appropriate desired objects is not diminished by understanding that there is a prohibition against doing so. The child only tries in a more or less naive manner to possess the desired object anyway, and carries out actions which may have all the characteristics of stealing and cheating.

So long as the pleasure-principle dominates the mind, temptation is great and the superego is weak even though the intellect may whisper softly: "Stealing is forbidden." It takes a long time for the ego to grow strong enough to be guided by the intellect, and to be able to resist temptation. It is no wonder therefore that, in analytic treatment, one seldom finds a patient who cannot recollect having stolen at some time in his childhood. The claim that theft is a misdemeanor typical of childhood, like masturbation or bedwetting, and that every normal person has stolen in his childhood is no exaggeration. The question is only one of circumstance and motive.

I have so far mentioned only one important factor — lack of resistance in the face of temptation. Another striking characteristic in many cases of infantile theft is the fact that it is often carried out by groups. Moreover, even if the deed itself is executed by a single child, the pleasure and the profit derived from the booty are enjoyed in groups. The spoils are distributed among playmates, frequently with a special hint that they were stolen, apparently to enhance the pleasure.

A child usually tries to appear as "good", "moral", "obedient", in the presence of adults. When alone, his games, fancies and desires yield to the urges of the pleasure-principle. This is most evident when children in groups play their games unobserved or in secret. The game is then almost always something prohibited, tabooed, or opposed to the demands of morality; it most often deals with sex and secondarily with thefts. Thefts by groups of children are extraordinarily frequent and in these groups even the most honest, decent, and morally well-developed child (or youth) easily loses his strength of resistance and succumbs to temptation. The following story told by a teacher is a typical example.

"Some years ago, when our school moved into a new and spacious building, many pupils from other schools were transferred to us. Among the pupils added to my class was a boy who soon attracted my special attention. He was eight years old, quiet and reserved, intelligent, sensible and of quick understanding. He had a good knowledge of literature and distinguished himself in composition. One day during a quarrel, his best friend called him a thief. I was surprised, questioned his former teacher and learned that at his former school an organized group had formed under the leadership of an older pupil, and that this gang systematically robbed the neighborhood shops. My new pupil belonged to the gang and as he was a quiet and good-looking boy, he could easily dupe the shopkeepers. One day, the gang was caught and handed over to the police. The police officer, an intelligent and understanding man, informed the director of the school, and the whole affair was closed in a simple pedagogical manner without any publicity. During the investigation, the children stated that they had intended to buy a yacht and to found a sports club with the proceeds of their thefts."

Another story told me by a highly esteemed and successful woman doctor dealt with her own childhood.

"A group of children in our section of town founded a secret criminal organization and I was their leader. Our aim was not only to play games but to carry out real crimes, particularly stealing from our neighborhood shops. I cannot recall what we did with the booty, it was not important, neither was it important what we stole. The main thing was to plan an attack on a shop, to organize it and to carry it through without being caught. Therein lay our great pleasure and satisfaction. Why did we do it? It was the secrecy, the danger, and the pleasure of law breaking, I might say, and the proud consciousness of having done something terrible and forbidden."

These words contain a truth that is not always fully appreciated. Children and primitive people enjoy the experience and adventure of a crime, the carrying out of a forbidden deed for its own sake. It is the stolen fruit that tastes sweetest.

To this is added the enhanced self-assurance of having outwitted clever and powerful adults, and of thus having proved one's own superiority. In this way thieving may develop into a peculiar sport of children and youngsters. Bets are made and a successful theft is celebrated as a victory over grown-ups. One brags about the theft instead of keeping it secret, and one tries to get together the largest possible group of children to enjoy and distribute the spoils of the deed. In this way one also makes accomplices of the largest possible number of friends which partly relieves one's conscience. Compared with this adventurous aspect of stealing, the profit of the deed, the utilization and the value of the stolen goods rarely play more than a secondary role. All this shows how slow is the development of a moral personality.

Nor is this all. There is still another important motive of theft in children, particularly in the latency period, before puberty. The following are illustrative cases.

A boy of eight took piano lessons from a young and pretty teacher. He was gifted, industrious and made good progress, and her affection and respect made her slightly indulgent. The boy reciprocated this affection to the point of adoration.

One day, the teacher observed that some coins were missing from a box on the table in the lesson room. It did not even occur to her to suspect the beloved pupil. But the thefts were repeated, and it struck her that money was always missing just after this boy's lessons. Although she dreaded the disappointment of such a revelation, she could not disregard the facts and decided to watch the boy closely. And indeed, she soon had the opportunity of seeing that the moment he was alone in the room, the boy approached the box and removed a number of coins. She was distressed and shocked, but what followed increased her astonishment. For the boy did not go home with the money, but into the garden, where he dug a hole and buried it. The teacher decided to say nothing but to watch the boy further, and the performance was repeated at the next lesson. She finally called the boy to account in a cautious and inoffensive manner. The lad confessed, with tears, went into the garden, dug up the money and gave it all back. When he was questioned why he had done it, he gave the following strange reply: "I wanted to have something of yours, I do love you so."

Those who cannot appreciate the boy's answer, should remember that our moral code allows a gentleman in love to steal a handkerchief, a glove or even a photograph of his beloved. As is so often the case in pathological stealing, the theft of such articles still belongs to the permitted and normal, and differs only in quantity from the pathological; it is, in fact, a transition to the pathological, to kleptomania. The psychological motivation consists in the urge to appropriate an object that, to the unconscious, represents a "substitute" for a lost object of love. Such was the case of this boy. After the lesson, when he had to leave his beloved teacher, he was driven to take something from her and to keep it in secret, as a substitute for her love.

This is often the meaning of theft in little children, especially during pre-puberty. One steals sweets or money only from beloved persons; especially from mother or father. This is "stolen love", for the child misses love. Money and gifts are often proofs of love or substitutes for love, no matter whether they were given voluntarily or stolen; and a gift returned is interpreted as a refusal of love.

This psychological meaning and these psychic features of stealing make the educator responsible for the difficult and serious task of investigating the meaning of each case of theft. Only then will his pedagogic measures be both expedient and successful. But the most important point to keep in mind is that not every appropriation of other people's possessions is theft, and not every child who has taken other people's property is a thief. The error of the educator who brands a child as a thief for a first offense is worse than the child's crime. For indulgence toward a single theft will not make the child a criminal, but branding it as a criminal may indeed do so. Words like "theft", "thief", "criminal" simply should not be used with a child. We must not give the child the idea of being degraded. Once put into the inferior position of an outsider, he not only feels himself cast out from the honest and decent society of "good" children, but also freed from their morality, their prohibitions and the duty of being honest. "Now that I am a thief, I am allowed to steal." One fact must be clear and must never be forgotten: children are not thieves, they are only weak personalities disturbed in the course of their moral development (chiefly by external influences). Any child may find himself in this situation, for his moral development can only be regarded as completed several years after puberty. But children can be made into thieves if they are treated as such. This statement does not refer to neglected children whose description we must leave to another paper.

SOCIAL PSYCHOLOGY

THE OBJECTIVITY OF CRIMINOLOGICAL SCIENCE

By Paul Bergman, Ph.D.

(*Topeka**)

This paper owes its existence to my wish to contribute my bit in honor of August Aichhorn's seventieth anniversary. As I have not worked with delinquents or criminals for quite a few years, I looked around for a topic which would — even in a distant way — give testimony to the teaching I had received from Aichhorn. I had the feeling that respect for the values inherent in the delinquent's personality had always been present in Aichhorn's work. I wondered how the approach of others compared with it. I decided to review the main theories of crime in order to examine them from this angle. I found, after review, that it was hard to take an unequivocal stand on these problems. I then chose a form which, I hope, allows me to express views which are no doubt dubious, but may serve to bring a certain aspect of the problem more sharply into relief. I imagined the text of a speech given by a scientist to a group of organized criminals, on "The Objectivity of Criminological Science". To be sure, I do not really think that any organization of criminals would be interested in listening to such a speech.

—P. B.

MOTTO:

> Son: And must they all be hanged that swear and lie?
> Lady Macduff: Every one.
> Son: Who must hang them?
> Lady Macduff: Why, the honest men.
> Son: Then the liars and swearers are fools; for there are liars and swearers enow to beat the honest men and hang up them.
>
> Shakespeare, Macbeth, Act IV, Scene 2

Mr. Chairman, Ladies and Gentlemen:

I want to express my deep appreciation for the honor you bestowed upon me when you chose me to be speaker at the scientific part of your annual meeting. The topic which I have chosen, and which I hope will meet with your interest, is "The Objectivity of Criminological Science". Science of course, by definition is supposed to be objective. But, unfortunately, not

---

* The Menninger Foundation.

everything is as it is supposed to be. Rays of light are supposed to be propelled in ideal straightness, but Einstein has shown that they, too, bend under the influence of the gravitational field. Criminology, as a science, would be supposed to be unbiased, to send its rays of examination straight to the naked facts. It is our contention, however, a contention for which we will try to proffer as much proof as can possibly be pressed into the frame of this address — for which you generously allowed time taken from most important practical business — it is our contention, we say, that criminology has, understandably enough, become somewhat bent in the field of powerful social gravitation that, for better or worse, centers around the "honest men". You, distinguished members of this organization, know as well as I do to what amazing degree the honest men are fictional, how much hypocrisy goes into the making of the average "honest man", how many of these individuals who from the cradle to the grave pretend to be honest, really should be one of you. But we have to accept facts which have not changed since the time of Macduff's son, and which may never change, though with such a prediction, we must admit, we are already leaving the firm ground of scientific observation and method. The facts are that social prestige and the power that goes with it in our society are with the honest men. We should therefore not be astonished to find science, sometimes consciously, perhaps more often unconsciously biased in their favor. Science is made by scientists. But scientists are human beings, fallible and self-deceiving, just like you and I.

Enough of preliminaries now. It is time to discuss the subject itself. It can be easily divided under three different headings, corresponding to the type of approach to the topic of the criminal used by three different sciences, namely, biology, sociology and psychology.

A. *The biological approach.* Here we may be brief. For the biologists' attempts to characterize the criminals as a distinct group have long ago broken down, have been thoroughly discredited and no longer hold a conspicuous place in the thinking of contemporary scholars. It would be wrong, however, to neglect them, for they hold a valuable lesson for us. For here the tendency of men of science to identify the criminal with or by some trait that is considered inferior and bad, emerges into an almost glaring light.

The most famous theories of this class, which dominated the field for generations, may be considered representative of the whole group. There were scientists who maintained that the criminal was a distinct biological type, carrying stigmata of atavism and degeneration on his body. Recently, some late follower of these theories has again come out with a modernized version of this biological slander on the criminal. Mr. Chairman, Ladies and Gentlemen! In your rich and varied experience you have undoubtedly met fellow criminals with unusually receding chins, low foreheads, queer-shaped ears, etc., etc. But how do these scientists proceed to prove that there is a correlation between unusual physical characteristics (which, by the way, they gratuitously call degenerative or atavistic) and the criminal way of life?

First, as a sample of their criminal population they invariably choose the inmates of some penitentiary. It is as if one sampled businessmen from among those appearing at a bankruptcy court. You would see there the most incompetent, inferior types, and also, no doubt some poor fellows suffering from physical handicaps. The typical criminal of our times is not to be found in the penal institutions. He comes, like the ladies and gentlemen in this hall, from smoothly functioning organizations that maintain close and mutually satisfying contacts with politicians and with members of the judiciary. He keeps himself and his colleagues out of trouble.

Secondly, the scientists either chose no control group or one that is unfairly selected; as for instance, the recent scholar who included in his control group firemen and a company of militia, men screened by thorough medical examination, whose standards would be well above the average of the total population.

Another point that one could raise would be, of course, that of the social situation of those unfortunate individuals who are visibly stigmatized from birth. The "honest" people turn away from them, distrust them, do not employ them, do not buy from them. One reason for this is their prejudice that the stigmata are signs of inherited criminal disposition. And let us be honest, you yourselves tend to prefer to keep your organizations clear of types that attract unfavorable attention. No wonder that these individuals get into trouble, are arrested and punished.

Another type of theory advanced by biological scientists maintains that the criminals differ from honest people by the functioning of their endocrine glands. The pith of this contention seems to be that the criminal's body is chemically disturbed, ergo in the face of a tempting situation he cannot wait, his moral judgment succumbs and he steals, rapes, murders, etc. (We will find an essentially identical view, only couched in different language, when we examine psychological theories.)

It is, of course, not up to us to say that there are no cases of this kind. But the average criminal, yea, even the average juvenile delinquent, can probably stand as much or more frustration than the honest citizen. What a slander on you, Ladies and Gentlemen, who are planning your strategies over the spans of months and years, postponing action time and again in keeping with the warnings of your seasoned judgment, to declare that you "cannot wait". Or consider the truant juvenile, who suffers cold and hunger for days and weeks; should we assume that he cannot wait as well as his brother who gets anxious when he has to go without his supper and the reassurance of sleeping in his bed?

We need dwell no longer on this group of theories tonight. The fact is that, in this country at least, even the scientists themselves do not give them much credence. Even the responsible endocrinologists consider that their science is still far from being able to offer statements of the kind described. To us all these theories are of interest only as examples of the bias in scientific investigation into crime. Has endocrinology, e.g. even considered the possibility that the criminal (or some criminals) may have an unusually stable endocrine system that would enable that individual to withstand anxiety, dependent needs and the like?

B. *The sociological approach*. Let us examine some theories to be found in the fields of social science. The theory of race factors in crime may offer us a convenient transition from the biological sphere, for race can be studied both from the biological and the sociological angle. Neglecting a number of minor variants, we may choose as an example the theory of the Negro's special inclination to crime, a theory widely accepted in this country. In fairness to the social scientists, however, we must state that they have almost unanimously objected to this kind of thinking. Therefore we need not expand this point beyond calling it to your attention that popular prejudice, when it makes theories of crime, involves the same kind of technique as that of the scientists: It links crime to a trait it considers inferior or bad. It does not occur to the prejudiced mind in this country to construct a racial theory on the fact that our Japanese population have an exceptionally low crime rate.

Let us take a fleeting glance at the theories which in one form or other make poverty responsible for crime. Sometimes the accent is on actual frustration of vital needs, at other times on lack of education, unemployment, uncongenial work, crowded living conditions, etc., etc. Ladies and Gentlemen, in spite of the deep respect in which we hold these factors we cannot totally silence our criticism. First, the impression that there is a great statistical preponderance of crime amongst the poor classes of the population is likely to be misleading. The wealthier classes commit different types of crimes and are generally better able to keep their deeds beyond the ken of statisticians. The authorities are related and allied to the people of wealth in a thousand ways. Some of you probably know from your own experience how relations to magistrates differ when one of you has no money from other times when he has. But we do not think that we should base our mental reservation concerning these theories solely on the lack of statistical reliability of the crime ratio among the poor and the wealthy. No, for we would protest just as strongly against the tendency to view the criminal with the pity and condescension which inevitably creep into any theories of poverty. These are merely the reverse side of the coin we already know well enough, namely inferiority and viciousness.

The same, we are afraid, must be said about the theories that establish a link between the spirit of capitalistic competition and crime. The scientists who see such a link are, of course, invariably critics of the capitalistic system and consider it to be very bad. You, Ladies and Gentlemen, who in your organizational and business practices follow the patterns of monopolistic capitalism most closely, will have no difficulty in appreciating the kernel of truth in such theories. There is, e.g. hardly any difference between the pennies the housewife is over-charged on each bag of groceries by the monopoly which cornered the wholesale market and the pennies she is over-charged for your monopolistic "protection" of the distributor. You are, and have to be, monopolistic in your pattern of organization if you don't want to have your profits cut to the bone, just like the honest men organizing a "corner". On the other hand you will agree with me that the spirit of competition contributes an important factor to your efforts. Of course, you want to make as much money as possible, with the least trouble, in the shortest time, just like everyone else.

But again we must look closer. Do the facts, which we do not dispute, mean that modern crime is caused by capitalism, or only perhaps that crime always takes its particular form and spirit from its contemporary environment, in our case from capitalism? Unfortunately, it would be impossible to discuss within the allotted time all the evidence for and against these two views. Instead I beg your permission to state briefly and summarily that crime has existed and exists in many non-capitalistic societies. Furthermore we might ask those who insist that to abolish crime we ought to change our economic order, how they explain the fact that in the countries where monopolistic capitalism instituted a dictatorship, such as fascist Germany, crime was far less a problem than in our republican and democratic United States. What prevents them from suggesting the hypothesis that crime is caused by the democratic way of life?

C. *The psychological approach.* Turning our attention finally toward what the psychologists have offered as scientific views, we encounter first an older trend represented by those who concentrated upon the evaluation of intelligence and a more modern trend of the psychodynamic school.

The old idea — today discarded by all psychologists of repute — was that the criminals were predominantly recruited from feeble-minded stock. How could such a theory ever gain a foothold in the thinking of scientific workers? Any thorough examination, not of the successful criminal, mind you, but even of the prison populations would show that their intelligence is at least equal if not better than that of their contemporaries. In a conciliatory mood we may accept as a possibility that feeble-minded individuals are perhaps more easily seduced into committing petty crimes — anything ranging from the stealing of a watermelon to the molesting of a young girl. But the social importance of this kind of crime is negligible. If you will permit me to express a hardheaded businessman's view, I would say, it does not account for one ten-thousandth of the alleged many-billion dollar bill which crime presents to this nation each year. We would probably also not be mistaken in assuming that some provinces of contemporary crime — watering stocks, number and gambling rackets, levies on stores, restaurants, night clubs, etc., in brief the "white-collar crimes" are predominantly in the hands of individuals of superior intelligence. These are, of course, the socially important provinces of crime. Do not expect, however, to hear men of science come out with the theory that superior intelligence is a factor in crime, and recommend that bearers of such intelligence should be sterilized, which would be the logical analogy to their attitudes in regard to feeble-mindedness. The scientists' eyes look only one way: namely, where they expect or hope to see a link between crime and an inferior trait.

Let us finally turn our survey to the opinions of dynamic psychology. Many people, especially in this country, consider modern psychiatrists, whose tools of thinking are the concepts of dynamic psychology, to be the most unprejudiced individuals of our times. What have these gentlemen whose words will be met with such great expectations, to say about the criminal?

Let us begin by presenting the simplest of all the theories offered in this field. Unfortunately it is not uncharacteristic of the rest. According to this theory the criminal is essentially a discouraged person. From his earliest youth, so they say, he could not tolerate the torture of feeling himself inferior to others. But he did not then and does not later have the courage to see that only a feeling of community with the rest of mankind could solve his problems. Instead he builds his life (like other maladjusted individuals) upon a guiding fiction of his superiority which in his case he hopes to attain through crime.

This is a very fascinating theory indeed, uniting as it does pity for the poor discouraged criminal with contempt and condemnation for his fictional life goals. It rests, of course, upon the assumption that there is a correlation between courage and acceptance of social values. Unfortunately — for the theory — there is little proof for it, unless you assume that every individual wants to be socially good and helpful by a kind of natural gravitation until something discourages him and drives him to get his security by other means. We will readily agree that such a process can occur. But the opposite also occurs, namely that a child (or even an adult) is aggressive and antisocial, until something discourages him and makes him look for security in goodness. The assumption of man's innate "goodness" is unconfirmed by scientific observation. In fact, the opposite assumption has found some important support, namely that hate and hostility is the affect quality which the very young child experiences when he first differentiates between himself and the outside world. Anyway, we should insist that psychiatrists define their concept of courage operationally. We may be confident that after such a definition they will have more than a little difficulty in proving that it is the criminals who are the discouraged ones. For instance, what if one decided to use the way individuals meet death as a test of their courage? Where would one find the anxious, desperate ones, those who complain, beg, cry, or lie to themselves? I wonder whether on the average it would not be the criminals who come closest to the old but still admirable stoic ideal of suffering and dying without uttering a word.

The psychiatrists' reasoning about such a point often follows still another line. They cite the quasi-experiment of the therapeutic situation. Take a delinquent child, they argue, give him a decent environment, which gives him love and encouragement, and you will see him change his delinquent ways into honest ones. True enough, but do not the psychiatrists overlook the possibility that the whole experiment might also be reversed? Take a "good" child, give him a criminal environment, which gives him love and encouragement, and in all likelihood also you will see him change his honest ways into delinquent ones. If that be so, the therapeutic experiment fails to prove that the delinquency was based upon discouragement.

Among the psychodynamic theories on the market in our times, those of Freudian psychoanalysis enjoy a particular reputation. As far as criminality is concerned the theory offered most insistently maintains that an unconscious need for punishment due to unconscious guilt feelings is the motive that leads the criminal to his style of life. The more cautious psychoanalysts say that they so describe one type of criminal, the more reckless ones think that the formula of the need for punishment may explain all criminal behavior. One of the latter group even offered the suggestion of establishing a clinical entity "criminosis", in line with the accepted clinical diagnoses of "neurosis" and "psychosis".

We cannot and do not have any intention of doubting that the psychoanalysts have correctly observed and interpreted a number of cases before they came to their generalizations. There are criminals driven by an unconscious need for punishment. But how important is this observation in explaining temporary crime? According to the best available surveys of the field, probably less than 2 per cent of the crimes committed amidst the population of this country receive punishment. And, make no mistake, not all of these 2 per cent by any stretch of the imagination come to punishment because of their need for it. After all, as you know, there are unfortunate circumstances which at times may thwart even a perfectly planned plot.

A recent psychoanalytic theory maintains that criminality develops on the basis of a young child's characteristic ego qualities which the theory calls "anti-social character". How are we supposed to recognize the anti-social character? I am afraid that the first answer the theory offers does not yet make its meaning clear. This answer reads: The anti-social character "results from the failure of the ego to develop toward the reality principle". You might object at this point that many a delinquent child and many an adult offender seems to have no difficulty taking into account and mastering physical and social reality. The delinquent child frequently succeeds in maintaining his existence under conditions in which other children would be destroyed. The capable criminal, as you well know, many times and in many social constellations creates a better chance of survival for himself and for those whom he supports than does the average honest man. But this is not exactly what the theory means. It explains "failure to develop towards the reality principle" by inability to wait for satisfaction. Here we have, of course, again the idea which we previously discussed when it came from the endocrinologist. In its psychological wrappings the theory is no better. The majority of criminals can wait as well or better than the honest citizen. You will agree that the discipline in your organizations is as perfect as in any police force. I know that you would execute any member of your corporation who, e.g., would dare to kill on his own initiative or for his own profit. There is no evidence that inability to wait for satisfaction is characteristic of more than a few of the petty criminals.

Psychologists and psychiatrists — no different in their prejudices against the criminal than other scientists — have failed to examine the possibility of establishing links between criminality and any traits which, in harmony with their cultural environment, they consider valuable. Nobody e.g. has ever investigated the hypothesis that the criminal by maintaining the original hostile defiance against the frustration of man's environment may be able to achieve a higher degree of integration than the average honest citizen, who also has in his unconscious the same fundamentally hostile attitudes, but overlays them with a variety of "social" substitutes. Nobody has investigated the values inherent in crime for the individual's self-expression or for the realization of his idealized image of his self. There may be creativity and even genius in crime unless you give creativity and genius a narrow moralistic definition. And many an abyss of self-contempt or apathy toward life may be overcome through the criminal deed. Nor has anybody examined what personality assets are buried when youngsters who might find harmonious fulfillment of their unique individuality in a criminal career are at all costs and with all imaginable pressures led towards an honest way of life. It would not be difficult to propose a long list of similar suggestions.

Whether such investigations would yield much or little we do not pretend to know. This kind of research, wherever it may lead, is in our opinion indispensable to counterbalance the socially conditioned one-sidedness of the criminology of today. This criminology still bears too clearly the marks of its origin in the old demonology. The difference is only that the criminal instead of housing a demon of badness as of old, now houses a variety of symbols of badness and inferiority ranging from bad genes to poor development towards the reality principle.

It is not the business of science to direct propaganda against the criminal way of life nor to control morals. Science should give an unbiased understanding of the phenomena, and if it can, also say by what means morals are improved or impaired. Then, let society act on the basis of this knowledge. The next move will then be yours, Ladies and Gentlemen. Thank you for your attention.

TWINS — AS A GANG IN MINIATURE

By Dorothy T. Burlingham

(*London*)

There is a certain type of dissocial children who fall in with bad company, are influenced by these lawless individuals and soon become one of a group, forming a gang.

When these dissocial children once belong to a gang, that is when they have taken over certain characteristics of the group performing aggressive acts, stealing, etc., it is impossible to get them to desist from such acts or to give up their wild behavior with any of the usual means of education. They appear to withdraw from all influence except that of the gang.

While in contact with several pairs of twins over a number of years in the Hampstead Nurseries it was possible to observe in two pairs of twins certain forms of behavior which showed characteristics common to some specific types of dissocials.

These twins at certain times would form a pact of mutual understanding and agreement. Nothing else interested them, they were occupied exclusively with each other. If disturbed by the outside world they combined forces against it. While together it was impossible to influence them in any way.

Bill and Bert, a pair of identical twins came to the nursery when four months old. They had lived with their mother until then. While in the nursery the mother visited them regularly several times a week, later not more than once a week. They were exactly alike in appearance, and in everything they did they were mirror images of each other. They appeared quite normal until their second year, when they seemed overactive and as they grew older became more and more erratic. They started copying each other from the age of fourteen months. Bert started copying Bill but soon it was Bill who copied Bert, then both copied each other. This behavior developed into a game. Bill would throw himself from a sitting, kneeling, standing position onto his back. Bert would copy him. Bill would make funny clownish faces, Bert would copy him. Each of these games was accompanied by uproarious laughter from both of them.

As the twins grew older, the games became more and more complicated but were always accompanied by outbursts of laughter. They took turns copying and being copied, provoking each other with new ideas until the games became so violent and uncontrolled that they gave the impression of an orgy. The twins became more and more absorbed in each other owing to these games. If anyone tried to interrupt them, they grew violent and aggressive towards the intruder. It was quite impossible for anyone to get their attention or to influence them at such times. They withdrew into a world of their own which was most pleasurable for them and they cut themselves off from everything and everyone else. This does not mean that at other times they were not aggressive towards each other. Bill was the aggressive one, biting, scratching and attacking Bert until the latter became very frightened of him, but during these games all fear disappeared.

The similarity between the behavior of these twins at two and three years and the dissocial behavior of some gangs of children at the latency period or pre-puberty lies in the same complete loss of interest in everything except the gang, in their single-mindedness in carrying out delinquent acts, and in their not permitting any distraction or interruption and resorting to violence if interfered with.

The second pair of twins, Mary and Madge, came to the Hampstead Nursery when they were three and one-half years old. When ten months old they had been evacuated to a nursery to avoid the air raids. The parents had only been allowed to visit them once a month and the twins had become estranged from them, calling the mother "lady" when she visited them. They returned home when they were three years and three months old. But they could not form a satisfactory relationship to the parents and remained as estranged and frustrated as they had been during the time of separation. The parents could not manage them, and the twins defied them in every possible way, fighting, kicking, swearing and refusing to go to bed, they would lie screaming on the floor. Finally they ran away from home together.

In the Hampstead Nursery they continued this same behavior refusing to do anything that was expected of them, hitting and kicking the nurses and children, swearing and masturbating from morning until night. Everything they did was in absolute union, as a team, and they never left each other's side.

This wild behavior continued about six months. They had been put in charge of a nurse who very gradually was able to make contact with them and from then on she was slowly able to gain an influence over them. Whenever she left for a day or was off duty for a few hours or when the parents disappointed them by not visiting them as planned the twins relapsed into their former behavior.

This identical behavior, their revolt against their parents, their nurse and the world about them was an expression of their dissatisfaction. Both had had the same experiences, separation from the parents at an early age with the resulting disappointments and frustration of affection. Both reacted in a similar manner in answer to the emotion of dissatisfaction which was alike in both. It is likely that one of the twins first behaved in a certain way in answer to the emotion that had overcome her, and that the other twin then fell in with this expression of emotion, which was similar to her own, by a contagion of feelings.

It may be that one of the reasons why children are drawn together to form a gang and then perform acts of delinquency is because they are attracted by some common emotional factor, i.e. early disappointment and frustration in their relationship to their parents. They then combine forces and defy the rest of the world by committing acts of delinquency which are an expression of revenge. The pleasure found in these delinquent acts may be compared to the games of the first pair of twins, Bill and Bert, described above. The gang is exclusively occupied with its own absorbing activities, interest is withdrawn from the rest of the world except where it is part of these doings. In some way the delinquent activities are symbolic expressions of the personal needs of each member of the group, as well as a revenge, which is displaced from the personal parents to the community as a whole. The dissocial acts express the dissatisfaction common to the gang.

The individual members of the gang are able to withstand all the efforts made to influence them because they are completely engrossed in each other and in these symbolic activities. The superego of each individual cannot be reached at the moment, it is overwhelmed by the power of the emotion which has found an outlet and which is reinforced in each member of the gang through the contagion of feeling.

When the twins, Mary and Madge, had become attached to their nurse, they gradually made friends with the children in the nursery and were friendly and pleasant with the rest of the staff; they adapted to their surroundings.

After the twins had been ten months in the nursery, Madge contracted ringworm and had to go to a hospital and only returned after seven months. The separation of the twins caused them great unhappiness and Mary appeared often to be in a state of mourning. She continually hoped for Madge's return and as the time drew near for her to be back she made many plans to welcome her. During this period of separation Mary had continued to improve in her behavior and became a most charming and well behaved child. There was little information obtainable about Madge's experiences in the hospital. It was evident that she had been handled strictly and that she had not developed favorably. She was delighted to return to the nursery and was very pleased to be with Mary again. But very soon she relapsed into her former behavior. She screamed, had temper tantrums, was rude and aggressive. Mary looked on much perturbed, would often cry when Madge cried and when asked why she was crying she would reply: "I don't know why, but I must cry when Madge does." Everything was done to help Mary keep up her good conduct. She herself tried hard to influence Madge, and to be a good example. But no matter how hard she tried it was impossible for her to resist Madge. She became more and more unhappy and dissatisfied, cried a lot in a distressed way, and was in a dreadfud conflict. She showed Madge her great affection for her and protected her. But soon Mary slipped back, too, into her former behavior and was even more difficult than Madge. The two had become a team of unruly children, quite out of control and impossible to influence. Madge's behavior had an attraction for

Mary that she simply could not resist. She struggled valiantly against this attraction, often turned against Madge saying she did not like her ways, criticized her and once at a time of tension cried out that she wished Madge had never come back from the hospital.

Why was it that Mary could not remain the well behaved child she had become, and why should she not keep to the stage of development she had acquired? Everything was done to help her maintain and to strengthen her superego and to give her pleasure in her superiority over Madge.

Mary found herself in a conflict of emotions when Madge returned. Her attachment to Madge had not lessened during their separation, it had rather increased. But her relationship to her nurse had also developed and for the first time in her life had made it possible for her to establish a positive bond with a parent substitute, to overcome the past frustrations and therefore develop her social adaptations. Madge's return brought for her a conflict of relationships and loyalties. Without Madge, Mary could have remained the well balanced child she had become. Madge on the other hand under the influence of her new separation had had a full revival of all the negative emotions of her past with the resulting bad behavior. Mary without being conscious of her own reasons regressed to Madge's state, on the basis of her strong identification with her, which was rooted in their twin relationship and their common unhappy experiences of the past. Mary cried as she watched Madge, but was unable to say why. Her identification compelled her to abandon the nurse, to answer to Madge's expression of strong emotion and to be drawn back to a state similar to her sister's.

The individual members of a gang may experience a similar conflict of loyalties. They feel the tie to the parents as well as to the gang pulling them both ways. As with the twins, there exists a strong identification with the members of the gang which is based on old, often unconscious disappointments, conflicts, and frustrations in the relationship to the parents. The gang activities which express the reaction to and the symbolic revenge for these disappointments have an irresistible attraction for them. The loyalty to the gang because of this underlying identification with its members has a greater claim on them than the relationship to the parents and thereby to the social community.

It would be an interesting subject to investigate whether the adherence to the gang always presupposes the existence of a strong relationship to a child companion, with whom the child has shared the first disappointment in the parent relationship and who is then replaced by the later comrades of the gang.

SCAPEGOATS OF SOCIETY

By Ruth S. Eissler, M.D.

(New York)

"The punishment of a crime cannot be just (that is necessary) if the laws have not endeavored to prevent that crime by the best means which time and circumstances would allow."[1] This quotation taken from *An Essay on Crimes and Punishments,* by Beccaria, written more than one hundred and fifty years ago, leads us directly into the problem with which this paper attempts to deal. The prevention of crime is one of the most puzzling social psychological problems today as it was hundreds of years ago. Although the content of laws has been changed, and punishments have been made somewhat less severe, at least in democratic countries, little progress has been made in the prevention of crime. This is the more baffling since, during the last fifty years, the knowledge, gained through psychoanalytic investigations, that criminality or delinquency belong in the field of psychopathology has become widespread, at least among psychologically oriented groups. Yet whereas scientific findings in other fields speedily led to practical application, be it in natural sciences, medicine or technology, progress in psychological understanding has not shown any such results where crime and crime prevention is concerned. Beccaria's words loom like an inescapable accusation against modern society which, with all its dazzling technological progress, has not been able to protect itself from individual or mass aggression against property or life. Must we assume that this helplessness is accidental and has no psychological basis? It would be strange if the inability to cope with a foremost psychological phenomenon should not itself have psychological roots. Granted that many other factors beyond the scope of the psychologist may play a role, nevertheless I think that we have the obligation at least to try to investigate how great a part psychological factors may have in society's failure to prevent crime.

Were we to apply occidental moral standards to infants and children we would have to call them criminals. Originally the human being is steered

---

[1] *An Essay on Crimes and Punishments,* translated from the Italian of Beccaria, p. 126, London, printed by E. Hodson, 1801.

288

by the pleasure principle and desires only to gratify his instinctual drives without consideration for realistic consequences. Every individual has to undergo a process of socialization which involves sacrifice of inacceptable gratifications or postponement of immediate gratification for the sake of reality adjustment. By the time adulthood is reached there remains only a certain percentage which has developed into individuals who act out these original asocial impulses. That means that in the process of their development from infancy through childhood and adolescence to adulthood something enabled this particular group of individuals to continue behaving in a specific way once common to all human beings as a phase of their development. They actively carry out what had to be given up by the others for the sake of adjustment to the demands of society and acceptance by society. It is not the intention of this paper to discuss the psychopathology of delinquency or criminality in detail, but I wish to recall the fact that people are not born either as "moral" beings or as "criminals" and that the full grown criminal is the product of internal and external psychological constellations and requires many years of specific development. During these important years he is exposed to the attitudes and reactions of his environment, which essentially consists of parents, teachers or other persons who take care of him, siblings and playmates. This environment has to deal with the delinquent tendencies of the future criminal, and it is the interaction between the environment and the delinquent individual which is the center of our interest.

My attention was first drawn to this problem, many years ago, by an experience in the treatment situation of a delinquent boy. The twelve year old patient was the only child of a widow whose deceased husband had been an embezzler and confidenceman. He died when the boy was about seven years old. Not long after the death of his father the child developed symptoms of delinquency: lying, stealing, truancy, rude and aggressive behavior. When he was referred to me for treatment these delinquent symptoms were in full bloom. He was a very lonely child, without friends and with scarcely any other relationships than that with his mother and an aged uncle. During his treatment it was evident that the mother in a markedly competetive manner tried to establish contact with me, frequently asking for appointments for herself and thus interfering with my attempt to establish a relationship with the boy. This went on for a while until it became noticeable that whenever there was a period of improvement in the patient's symptoms something occurred that threw him back into delinquent behavior. He did not steal for a while and suddenly his mother's purse lay on the table, or money was left lying about, or a cabinet, which contained valuables was not locked. Invariably the patient gave in to the temptation and stole whatever was within his reach. Since these incidents repeated themselves in a stereotyped way every time an improvement in the boy's condition occurred, I could not regard the mother's forgetfulness as merely accidental and had to find a method of investigating these episodes. Therefore I sent the mother to another psychiatrist in order to gain insight into the interrelationship between mother and son. It now became evident that whenever the boy abandoned his delinquent behavior pattern the mother became depressed and it did not take very long before she arranged some situation in which the child was tempted to act out again. As soon as he gave in to the temptation the mother's depression disappeared. To be sure, she was not at all aware of these connections nor did the boy's delinquencies hinge entirely on the opportunities she offered him. He unconsciously reacted to his mother's depression and by stealing re-established the psychological equilibrium between them. Without doubt the delinquent actions of the son were a safeguard against the mother's depression. Apparently she herself had an urgent need for delinquency which was satisfied by her husband and after his death had to be carried out by her son. When this need was not satisfied she fell into depression.

From the viewpoint of therapy the situation was not favorable at all, since any gain made in the therapeutic situation was reversed very soon after. At the time I was not aware of the fact that we were dealing with an essential situation, typical for the psychopathology of delinquency and when through external circumstances the treatment had to be discontinued I remembered my experience with this individual case, but my therapeutic optimism regarding the treatment of delinquents was not impaired. However, during the years which followed and with growing experience in treating juvenile delinquents, whether in private practice or in institutions, and by watching similar experiences of other therapists, I became aware of the stereotype occurrence of such "external" interference with the treatment of these cases. Finally any concept of the accidental nature of these interferences had to be discarded. There was some pattern inherent in the situation which had to be realized and understood. To be sure the relation between the delinquent symptoms of the patient and the pathological condition of another family member does not become so drastically evident in all cases as it did in the one mentioned above. Usually one could only guess at the underlying motivations for interference, interruptions or discontinuation of the treatment. But in general it became obvious that by treating the delinquent member of the family, the family's emotional equilibrium was disrupted and by the resulting removal of the asocial acting-out of the patient the significant family members, usually one or both parents, had to re-establish this equilibrium by interfering with the treatment situation. Two cases which I will sketch briefly, may illustrate this point.

A boy of eighteen was referred to me for treatment after numerous delinquent actions, mostly thefts, embezzling and drinking. His symptoms had already been noticed during the latency period and lasted through pre-adolescence and adolescence. He had been sent to a Military Academy. His school record was fair but his asocial behavior increased rather than diminished. After graduating from the Military Academy, he attended college. But here he even neglected his studies and abandoned himself to drinking, stealing money from his stepmother and his father. He came from a wealthy middle class family, was the only child, and the central figure in his life was the father, a successful businessman who — on the surface — showed great interest in and understanding for his son. The sincerity of his conscious intentions to help his son could not be doubted. However, it was evident that unconsciously he fostered the asocial behavior of his son however and wherever he could. After a few months of treatment, when the boy showed signs of a positive transference relationship to the analyst and for the sake of this relationship abandoned his delinquencies, the father decided to send him, during his summer vacation, to a resort where he was supposed to earn his money as a bellboy. This job exposed him to many situations of temptation such as gambling and drinking. This interference was counteracted by the analyst and for a while the treatment was continued. The boy improved considerably but had not yet reached a condition of stability in which he could battle his impulses without therapy. Quite suddenly the father discontinued the treatment, securing a job for the boy in which he had the opportunity of handling large amounts of money. No amount of remonstrating with the father had any success. Very soon the boy stole some of this money and passed out false checks. Only his father's social influence saved him from the penitentiary. He was pressed to enlist in the army, where the last I heard of him was that he got himself into severe trouble and was to be court-martialed. Significant of the father's history was that he had a younger brother who was a drunkard and for whom the father felt deeply responsible.

The second case pertains to a girl of fifteen who was committed to an institution for delinquent girls for stealing. Her stealing was compulsive and showed the earmarks of a sadistic perversion, the fantasy behind it being that she killed her mother in the act of stealing. She was a completely isolated individual who suffered from excessive conscious guilt feelings, unusual in delinquents, and who could not tolerate being separated from her mother. The father had deserted the family when the girl was about four years old; there was a brother, a few years her senior, whom the mother delegated to punish the patient by severe beatings for her misdemeanors. The patient's mother, who lived in straightened financial circumstances, was a peculiarly infantile personality with shallow affects and a superficial cheerfulness quite inappropriate to her realistic situation. She professed great concern for the daughter and was willing to make the greatest sacrifices in order to have her treated. The sacrifices were not accepted, but the child started treatment after her discharge from the institution. As long as the child declined to see the psychiatrist or resisted any help the mother insisted on her treatment. But after a while the first signs of a positive transference showed and the youngster improved temporarily, i.e. she ceased stealing. The mother immediately interfered by insisting that the patient wanted a job. She promised that she would call the analyst at once if there was the slightest sign of trouble. The next I learned was that through the mother's provocation the girl had had a temper tantrum and the mother had called the police and had the daughter confined to the State Hospital. She notified neither the analyst nor the social worker. But she took the child back soon and, although she complained to the social worker and the police she nevertheless seemed to be satisfied to have her daughter continue to steal.

As I mentioned before, these experiences in the treatment of delinquents are shared by many therapists. The family equilibrium seems to be threatened by any therapeutic success, be it because one or several or all members receive vicarious gratification by the acting-out of the delinquent or be it that the member in question needs the acting-out to safeguard his own stability. In any case the delinquent will be supported in his asocial acts.

I will make use of August Aichhorn's permission to quote his views about this problem from a recent communication by letter: "My formulation is: the intrafamilial libidinal equilibrium is maintained at the expense of the child who, overburdened by it, defends himself and according to the given circumstances develops into a delinquent or a neurotic. The delinquent and his defects must never be viewed per se: One must view him and his libidinal relationship as enmeshed within the family group, for if the libidinal equilibrium is maintained at the expense of the child, it will be necessarily disrupted by the cure of the child. The child defends himself against the libidinal overburdening and the family member who misused him for his own needs will break down neurotically."[2]

This psychological interaction between the acting-out delinquent individual and his environment deserves further investigation, and the case in which the mother reacted with depression to the improvement in her son's condition might well lend itself for this purpose. It certainly strikes us as strange that a parent becomes depressed when the child ceases to steal. From a commonsense point of view just the opposite would be expected. We might be tempted to explain it by saying — if we disregard any possibility of coincidental occurrence — that the mother's depression is not directly connected with the discontinuation of her son's delinquent symptoms, but is the consequence of the mother's feeling of inferiority in respect to the analyst; an expression of guilt or shame that she could not deal with her son's problems and had failed, whereas a stranger was able to help him. This element of rivalry may have played a role; however, it does not adequately interpret the stereotype interaction, which almost looks like a conditioned reflex on the son's part. Also there is to be considered the history of the mother's marriage to a delinquent individual and the development of the child into a delinquent after the father's death. From all this it certainly appears that the mother has the need to associate intimately with an individual who acts out his asocial impulses. Apparently she receives a vicarious gratification through the delinquency of another person.

This mechanism of vicarious gratification may remind us of the mechanism of identification in hysterical conditions. However, in hysteria the identification with the ambivalently loved object typically results in either

---

[2] August Aichhorn: Letter to the author, summer 1946. Translated by the author.

identical action or physical symptoms with preservation of the object relationship. In depressions the relationship to the object, which essentially is of a narcissistic nature, is given up and the ego replaces the object. The ego is exposed to the cruel treatment of its own superego which finds its expression in self accusations, feelings of inferiority and unworthiness. Usually the depression occurs when the individual meets with frustration by the love object and the resulting aggressive impulses strive for complete annihilation of the object.

In the above-mentioned case of mother and son, the mother was free of depression only when the son, or previously the husband, behaved in a delinquent fashion and evidently felt frustrated and disappointed whenever her love objects refused to act out, to which she apparently reacted as if it were an act of aggression directed against her. This leads to the conclusion that her own asocial impulses, which she could not permit herself to satisfy directly, but which were symbolized in the act of stealing were realized in actuality by their delinquent actions. The aggressive and asocial behavior of the love object thus served three functions: 1) The object satisfied her own inacceptable impulses by carrying them out in reality; 2) She secured a masochistic gratification which served as a punishment and relief of her guilt feelings; 3) She could use son or husband as a scapegoat, pointing at them as the criminals, and thus reassuring herself of her own innocence. As soon as the love object no longer served this triad, the conflict which had been carried into the external world, by proxy so to speak, again became internalized and shattered an equilibrium which had been based on the continuous reassurance furnished by the misbehavior of an ambivalently loved male object. In the patient, on the other hand, the loss of his mother's love stirred up unbearable anxiety which consequently made him again gratify her unconscious needs in order to regain the security of her love.

If on the basis of our experiences with individual cases of delinquency we come to the conclusion that the above mentioned constellations are typical we should broaden our viewpoint in regard to the general attitude toward delinquency. So far we have considered only the immediate environment of the young delinquent and have assumed that this environment has vested interests in the asocial behavior of the delinquent. But the third function of the described triad seems to be of particular importance. The institution of a scapegoat plays an important role in ancient and primitive cultures and furnishes the background for the Christian religion as well. Since our Western civilization is based on Jewish and Christian religious and moral concepts, the idea of the human scapegoat has never been abandoned although human beings are no longer sacrificed in undisguised religious ceremonials. To indulge in such a ritual would be offensive to our conscious moral demands and beliefs. However, the more civilized man becomes, the stricter the social demands are, the more intensive will be the conflict between the aggressive impulses of the individual and these demands. This means that modern man despite all his cultural achievements has to live in a state of constant tension, produced by external and internal pressures. This discontent in our civilization has to find outlets.

"Culture has to call up every possible reinforcement in order to erect barriers against the aggressive instincts of men and hold their manifestations in check by reaction formations in man's minds. . . . With all its striving, this endeavor of culture's has not so far achieved very much. Civilisation expects to prevent the worst atrocities of brutal violence by taking upon itself the right to employ violence against criminals, but the law is not able to lay hands on the more discreet and subtle forms in which human aggressions are expressed."[3]

Man, in order to become civilized has to renounce his instinctual drives, sexual and aggressive ones, to a great extent. Freud in *Civilisation and its Discontent* points out that with the frustration of sexual drives the aggressive impulses mount and in consequence, they either have to be satisfied in relationship to other objects, or they have to be turned inward and are experienced as guilt feelings, leading to the need for self punishment. To a certain extent the Christian religion provided a relief from this inner tension by identification with Christ. Based on the ethos of the Jewish religion it presented mankind with the dualistic moral values of good and evil. But the acceptance of these moral standards demands a sacrifice of instinctual drives and the recognition of guilt which only can be atoned by identification with Christ. The acceptance of his supreme sacrifice assures redemption but on the other hand it increases the inner conflict through awareness of one's own unworthiness and inferiority compared to Christ and through acceptance of the fact that a divine being had to be sacrificed for one's own salvation. This inner conflict has to be externalized lest it lead to complete self-destruction. The dualistic system of values actually provides for this externalization. If there is an absolute Good there necessarily must also be an absolute Evil. God and the devil belong together inseparably. If one can renounce, that is, sacrifice the devil, or whatever belongs to him, the relief of inner tension, produced by guilt feelings, is certainly more complete than by the sacrifice of an absolutely good, that is, a divine being. In former times when the conscious belief in magic was ubiquitous, the persecution and execution of witches satisfied this need, at least to a certain extent. However, progress in civilization no longer permits this outlet. Racial or religious discrimination still provides an outlet especially at certain periods when aggression mounts to a high peak. But this gratification of aggression is in direct

---

[3] Sigmund Freud: *Civilisation and its Discontent.* London, Hogarth Press, 1939, pp. 86-87.

contradiction to the moral demands of religious as well as liberal humanitarian beliefs. War, of course, always remains the solution par excellence, for a tremendous discharge of aggression. But since it involves so large an element of self-destruction, man will resist it so long as he retains any tendency toward self-preservation.

Thus for society in general there remains only one justifiable outlet for aggression, which can be rationalized on the basis of morality and which can provide the desired relief by externalizing inner conflicts without creating conscious guilt feelings. This is the persecution of the wicked, the criminals, that group of individuals who commit violence, who break the laws and who do not conform to the demands of society. But if this is the case, if society needs criminals as scapegoats, then what are the chances for a rational prevention of delinquency?

If we take the standpoint that society needs its criminals in the same way as the mother of my delinquent patient needed his delinquency, then we understand the puzzling problem of the inefficacy of the methods used in the fight against criminality. We would then also understand the existence of two general tendencies which serve to assure the preservation of delinquency. The first is the seduction of individuals into criminal acting-out. The second is the interference with or the prevention of anything which promises to prevent delinquency. And thirdly we will have to establish proof of the vicarious gratification which the "noncriminal" group derives from the actions of the criminal group.

If we start with the assumption that society needs its criminals and if we are agreed that a full-grown criminal does not fall from the skies but is the result of a long process of interaction between the individual's instinctual drives and the attitude of his environment, it might be most illuminating to investigate society's attitude toward the juvenile delinquent. The child, naturally dependent on his environment for care and affection and love, is more pliable than the adult and certainly a more hopeful object for therapeutic procedures. On the other hand, since his character-structure is not yet rigidly established, that is the external demands have not yet been definitely internalized to make for a reliable superego, the child is also a more susceptible object for seduction into asocial behavior.

It is true that modern democratic societies during the last century have created laws to protect children and have established special courts and institutions for dealing with the delinquent child. In the United States, e.g., there is a law against contributing to the delinquency of minors. Let us quote as one example the law of the State of Illinois. It is set down as "an act to define and punish the crime of contributing to the delinquency of children" (approved June 25, 1915; L 1915, p. 369).

After defining what constitutes contributing to delinquency, it continues: (the following is not penalty, but determination of guilt) "Any person who shall knowingly or willfully aid or encourage any male under the age of seventeen years or any female under the age of eighteen years to be or to become a delinquent as defined in section one, or who shall knowingly or willfully do acts which directly tend to render any such child so delinquent and who when able to do so, shall willfully neglect to do that which will directly tend to prevent such state of delinquency shall be deemed guilty of the crime of contributing to the delinquency of children."

This law, rationally interpreted, means that any adult person who deals with children has the duty of preventing those children from becoming delinquent and if he neglects this duty he is punishable under this law. Parents, educators, child-agency personnel, and institutions for children alike are bound by this law. Modern psychological investigations have established the fact that delinquency or criminality belongs in the field of psychopathology, although it cannot be disputed that economic conditions and the sociological structure of the community may be serious contributing factors. This would mean that in order to prevent or to cure delinquency, psychological and sociological methods must be applied. Slum areas should be abandoned, living conditions should be changed to comply with the sociological demands, and wherever delinquency exists psychiatric treatment should be made available. But, when has the law against contribution to the delinquency of children ever been enforced because of the neglect of these primary and rational demands? Or against whom could this law actually be enforced?

In my experience with agencies and institutions for the care of delinquent children, I encountered a situation very similar to the one pertaining to the parents of delinquent children, described above. The psychiatrist, who has been welcomed as consultant and therapist, is led to believe that the personnel of institutions and agencies are sincere in their efforts to obtain his help. But as soon as he recommends changes which promise real success, whatever they be, a wall of bland resistance arises which defeats both his previous efforts and his further progress. Very rarely is the psychiatrist in a position to enforce his suggestions and whoever counteracts them is not called upon for a reckoning. If in a hospital the doctor's prescription is not carried out either by nurses or administrative staff, the hospital is responsible for the damage inflicted on the patient by the neglect. I never heard of an institution or an agency which assumed a similar responsibility for the care of delinquent children. The damage inflicted upon children is of a psychological nature and therefore intangible.

In the early part of the last century the Boston House of Correction for Juveniles had as superintendent a man who ran the institution on modern principles, showing deep insight into the needs of the children, anticipating the self-government of juvenile reformatories and applying liberal and humane methods in dealing with his charges. This Mr. Wells, although showing remarkable results and attracting favorable comments from travelers and visiting authorities, was soon dismissed by the Common Council of the City of Boston. Apparently the community could not tolerate a future without criminality.[4]

In most institutions for delinquent children the emphasis is put on discipline, routine and cleanliness. Since the delinquent child usually failed in just these areas in his home environment, showing himself completely unable to tolerate the more or less rigid demands put upon him, he is thus exposed to even more severe demands in the institution while at the same time he is deprived of any compensatory features and the possibility of using his previous methods of outlet for tension. Even common sense psychology can foresee the result: the accumulation of aggression and in consequence the active or passive shifting into even more delinquent activities. The untrained personnel, who frequently take advantage of their position, and the company of more experienced delinquents, make it easy for the child to identify with the stronger objects, who commit acts of violence or brutality. In these institutions society has indeed produced effective breeding places for criminality.

We do not deny that an occasional institution does show sincere strivings toward dealing rationally with the problem of delinquency. However, the counteraction then usually occurs through the community which shows itself unable to tolerate any slight misdemeanors or is unwilling to provide funds for "experiments" or, as I observed in one case, the unconscious conflicts of an otherwise willing and understanding personnel lead to acting out with detrimental results.

In this particular case the superintendent was above average in understanding, training and talent and showed remarkable intuition in her contact with the children. She went a long way with the psychiatrist, enthusiastically trying to change the aspect of the institution from a punitive setup into a friendly and humane atmosphere. She was even successful in gradually converting the overaged members of the governing board to liberal views. When it became necessary to employ more professional help she chose an excellent social worker, who soon gained the children's respect and love and who was able to relieve her superior of part of her various responsibilities, especially the therapeutic interviews. This brought the social worker into close contact with the psychiatrist who paid recognition to her achievement and skill and became aware only too late of the superintendent's enormously jealous reaction. One day the superintendent spontaneously told a dream of the previous night: She had cut off the hands of the psychiatrist and the social worker respectively. In telling this dream she was giving an alarm signal, but

---

[4] John L. Gillon: *Criminology and Penology.* Revised edition. New York, D. Appleton Century Co., 1925.

too late to be of any use. What she announced in her dream she proceeded to do in reality by counteracting everything the psychiatrist suggested, reversing her attitude toward the children, siding with the authorities, becoming punitive and intolerant and permitting the institution to go to pieces. On the basis of her jealousy she apparently identified with the delinquent children and their impulses to asocial, hostile actions. As defense against these impulses she had to identify with the punitive authoritarian attitude, using the children as scapegoats; and finally by destroying the means and methods of curing their delinquency she gratified simultaneously her aggressive impulses against them, the psychiatrist and the social worker. The children became incurable delinquents and she could point to them to silence her own guilt.

Again we are reminded of the same psychological configuration which we discussed before; the ego-inacceptable, destructive impulses which create an unbearable inner conflict. If a scapegoat can be found, the conflict can be externalized and the inner tension will be relieved. If it were not for this tremendous need to externalize the inner conflict and to achieve vicarious gratification through the misdeeds of others we scarcely would find the press, the movies and fiction constantly offering us crime reports, crime thrillers and detective stories. Murders and various types of crime appear on the front-page and frequently as headlines in newspapers and are avidly read, discussed and reacted to by the majority of the literate population and the market for crime stories in fiction, picture and radio broadcasts has evidently grown immensely. Aside from the vicarious gratification which the law-abiding citizen receives in this way, we must also consider their influence on children. Probably children whose relationship to their environment, parents, siblings and parent substitutes is not essentially disturbed will not be dangerously affected by these productions. However, children who have no stability in their relationships are exposed to impressions which may well lead to increased anxiety and to identification with the aggressor, regardless of consequences. This may be the more so since in recent years, in fiction and in the movies the hero is not distinguishable from the criminal. Detective and criminal have become interchangeable and the only thing that matters is victory by brutal force. The child who, at first, is the victim of anxiety stemming from the conflict of his own aggressive impulses is soon led to believe that the important factor in life is to be more aggressive and more destructive than others in order to succeed, and will justify his asocial behavior by his admiration for the strong and ruthless hero. From this point of view crime stories are certainly a means of seducing minors into crime.

But while fiction and movie production use the crime story as entertainment and usually do not distinguish too greatly between the actions of hero and criminal up to the end, which for reasons of convention must be moralistic, the newspapers play up real crime, preferably murders, doubtlessly in order to furnish scapegoats for society. This purpose becomes the more evident the younger the criminal is. To become a civilized social individual, man has to undergo a process of development from birth to adulthood. When he reaches that age we may expect to find him, at best, in control of his worst destructive impulses which by that time he may have sublimated and channeled into socially acceptable outlets. Or he may have repressed them severing them from his consciousness without ever having been able to cope with them adequately. The child or the adolescent is still in the process of development, still not master of his archaic impulses and may be victimized by them at certain occasions. The younger the child the more archaic are these break-throughs apt to be. Therefore a crime, especially a murder, committed by a young individual will necessarily show archaic features, namely unmitigated cruelty, savage attack, mutilation of the body, etc. But strangely enough, if the newspapers report such a crime, these features are played up as especially incriminating and unnatural, something not reconcilable with the age of the criminal. The need to cling to the belief in the sweetness and innocence of children stemming from the denial of one's own cruel impulses either remembered or repressed, equals only the need to punish the youngster who dared to act them out and in this way threatens to disturb the self-righteous attitude of those who renounced the gratification of direct action. One receives the impression that the young criminal is not only accused for the deed he committed, but for the fact that he committed the crime as a young individual, namely in a more archaic way, almost as if these very features were privileges of the adult and the child or adolescent had usurped rights reserved for the grownup. A reaction of horror and hatred against the youngster is created and the vindictiveness of adult society contributes an important factor to the trial and punishment of the young criminal. Mercilessly the newspapers usually drag out facts which stir up anxiety and, in turn, hostility, especially if the crime can be linked to sexuality. Here, too, the young offender trespasses into the territory reserved for adults.

In June 1946 the seventeen year old college student William Heirens was arrested in Chicago after an attempted burglary. He was identified as the murderer of six year old Susan Degnan, who had been kidnapped and dismembered early that year, and of an ex-Wave who had been brutally killed in her hotel apartment. Also a third murder, that of a woman, was proven to have been committed by him. The killings had been savagely brutal, the bodies mutilated; on the wall in the apartment of the young ex-Wave a message was written in lipstick: "For heaven's sake catch me before I kill more; I cannot control myself." A ransom note had been left in the room from which the child had been taken; parts of her body had been found in various sewers and drains. The citizens of Chicago were horrified by these murders, particularly because the police showed itself powerless to identify the murderer.

William Heirens' arrest was accidental. He was intercepted by a policeman off duty when he tried to make a getaway after an attempted burglary.

It turned out that the boy had a police record, having been arrested for burglary at the ages of thirteen and fifteen. He also was arrested for carrying a gun when returning from rifle practice at the university. This occurred after the perpetration of the murders; but at that time his record was not checked and he was dismissed as "just a kid with a gun" and was told to register the weapon.

At the age of thirteen he was apprehended by the police, trying to break into a basement storeroom. Subsequently he admitted nine burglaries during the preceding six months. He was committed to a reformatory school for boys where he stayed for about a year. Two months after his release from this school he was again arrested. In Juvenile Court the judge acceded to the wishes of the family, and the young criminal was placed on probation and sent to a Catholic Academy at Peru, Illinois. He showed a satisfactory school-record, was in no way conspicuous in his environment and showed himself a devout Catholic, going to confession regularly and becoming a member of a Catholic club. He visited home frequently and his probation was terminated in January 1945. In September 1945 he entered the University of Chicago where he shared a room with an older student in one of the dormitories. During the weekend-leaves from the Academy and during the time he stayed at the dormitory or at home he committed innumerable burglaries and three murders without his environment being cognizant of anything strange or conspicuous about him. The loot of the burglaries was recovered in part from his room at the dormitory and at his parents' home. The burglaries were committed usually after a certain pattern. He climbed over the fire escape into a window and frequently completed his criminal action by defecating or urinating at the place of the crime. He did not sell any part of the loot but just cached it away. According to his own story he felt sexually excited before his burglaries and found a sexual release through breaking into strange apartments. When he was discovered in the act of breaking in, he had to kill. Apparently he then got into a panic since he could not make use of his usual outlets and the primitive archaic impulses were gratified by the killing and then dismembering or mutilating of his victims.

He was the older child of a middle class Catholic family with a brother a few years his junior. Neither from the newspaper reports nor from a paper by Foster Kennedy, Harry R. Hoffmann and William H. Haines[5] published August 1947, do we learn anything of the family interrelationship.

The case of Williams Heirens is reported here for several reasons: 1. The attitude of his environment up to the time of his last arrest, 2. the public reaction general and specific after his arrest, and 3. the reaction after his conviction.

It must indeed seem most strange to us that a young boy from the age of thirteen to seventeen has committed innumerable burglaries and three murders without anyone in his environment becoming aware of any indication of this youngster's psychopathology. It seems almost incredible that his parents, teachers and priests had no suspicions after his first two arrests and his commitment at the Catholic Academy. From the age of twelve to fourteen

---

[5] Foster Kennedy, Harry R. Hoffmann and William H. Haines: A Study of William Heirens. *Am. J. Psych.*, 104, No. 2, 1947.

he was very eager to earn his own money and took odd jobs. He did not spend much money on himself. However, he made expensive presents to his family out of proportion to his earnings. But apparently this fact did not arouse his parents' suspicion. Neither did anyone question the origin of the objects cached away in his room at the dormitory and at home. He was described as a likeable fellow but somewhat withdrawn; apparently he did not have any close friends although he participated in social activities of his club and had dates with girls. How was it possible that nobody sensed anything pathological in this severely sick boy? There is only one remark allegedly made by his mother and reported by one newspaper which, if true, may indicate that her unawareness of Heirens' criminality was only a seeming one. After the discovery of the murder of Susan Degnan, she is supposed to have asked her son: "You would not have done such a terrible thing, would you?" How could such a question come to a mother's mind regarding a son of whose murderous impulses she is not aware?

The newspapers played up the murders to a high degree before the identification of the murderer, pointing to the helplessness and inefficiency of the police and arousing a near panic in the population of Chicago. With every wrong arrest the apprehension and terror grew. After Heirens was arrested and his handwriting showed similarity to the one on the ransom note the general concern seemed to be to elicit a confession from the boy. This confession seemed to be of tremendous importance and was finally obtained by methods which, too, are of interest in connection with the subject of this paper. The newspapers reported that Heirens had been subjected to an injection of sodium pentothal (truth serum) by a psychiatrist in the presence of the State's Attorney and that under the effect of this drug he confessed to the three murders. This report was never repudiated or denied, thus there is a strong possibility that it is correct. This would mean that confession of the murders was so important that, although a confession induced by a drug is not admissable in court according to American and British law, this method was nevertheless applied. After that a tremendous relief was expressed in the daily press and the subsequent reporting of the Heirens case for a while showed an almost sympathetic tone. After the drug-induced confession however, when the murder suspect refused to give a voluntary, written confession, the attitude of the newspapers changed into one of great hostility and vindictiveness and again showed signs of apprehension and alarm.

To explain this reaction I will use material gained from an individual case under psychoanalytic treatment which seems to me significant for the understanding of these changes in public attitude.

At the time when the murder of Susan Degnan was committed and the newspapers reported every detail of the crime, a patient of mine showed himself completely oblivious to these reports, pretended not only a lack of interest in the murder but absolute ignorance as to the fact that the murder had occurred. He did not read the newspapers and evidently avoided any discussion of the subject in his analysis and outside of the analysis. After the arrest of Heirens and his identification as the murderer, however, the same patient reacted with extreme compassion for the murderer, cried for hours out of pity for him, read everything available about his case and showed himself very well informed about every detail of the murders of which

Heirens was accused. In his dreams of that period the patient identified with the murderer, committing similar crimes. The analysis of this material showed that the patient was convinced that he himself had committed a murder in the past and that his entire life had been lived under the pressure of this fantasy so that he even went so far in attempting to change his identity to have had a cosmetic operation done on his face. He had lived like a fugitive from the law without being conscious of the cause for his anxiety. The unconscious guilt for the murder which he believed to have committed was stirred up by the murder of the little girl and the gory details pointing to archaic destructive impulses. As long as the murderer was unknown the patient on the basis of his fantastic guilt feelings could not be sure that it was not he who had committed the crime. Therefore he had to pretend ignorance of the case, since the slightest display of interest might have betrayed him as the murderer. But when Heirens was identified as the criminal the patient experienced a tremendous relief and felt so grateful that he could show his identification with Heirens by feeling pity and compassion for him. He had a compulsion to know every minute detail of the crimes, receiving vicarious gratification on the one hand which he now could safely enjoy since, on the other hand, by knowing as much as possible about the crimes and the criminal he could make quite certain that someone else had committed the murders.

Although the denial of the facts of murder during the period when the murderer was yet unknown was specific for the neurosis of this patient his relief about the identification of the murderer was shared by the public and in many instances, in particular in the newspapers, resulted in a reaction of compassion and sympathy for the young murderer even if only for a short time. When it became uncertain again that Heirens would give a written confession the identity of the murderer again became uncertain and the anxiety caused by this uncertainty expressed itself in violent newspaper attacks against the boy. Finally after everything was settled and the boy had been convicted the press celebrated orgies of vindictiveness and pointed in particular to the fact that now Heirens would be only a "number" completely deprived of his identity which for all practical purposes signifies death. With the deprivation of his identity he ceased to exist and by this one act the terrifying crimes were simultaneoulsy denied as well. The public conscience could be reassured that since the criminal no longer existed, no crime had been committed.

In William Heirens, although he was declared sane according to the letter of the law, we see an individual who, from the viewpoint of psychopathology, suffered since early childhood from a mental disease which led to his own and several other individuals' destruction. For all practical purposes we may compare his case to that of a person suffering from a contagious disease which, not being adequately treated, will infect other people and cause their death as, f.i., in a case of tuberculosis. In early boyhood Heirens showed all the indications of a severely disturbed child. What means were employed to help him? Arrested after his burglaries he was sent to a reform school, dismissed after a year, he was again exposed to his home environment which necessarily must have had some part in the development of his pathology. He promptly resumed his delinquent acting-out, was arrested and on the insistence of his family was placed on probation and sent to a Catholic Academy from where he was able to continue his criminal career. There is no mention of any attempt to have the boy treated adequately and his environment professed not to have been aware of any pathology. He enters college and still receives no help. The collection of stolen objects in his rooms must have been conspicuous. Is it really credible that a young boy can be so clever in deceiving his environment to such an extent without the persons next to him having any part in this deception?

The writing on the wall after the murder of the ex-Wave "For Heaven's sake, catch me before I kill more; I cannot control myself", seems to be a genuine cry of despair of an individual who never received any help and is unable to turn to anyone. Certainly he is not the first case in history of crime to commit murder after murder where the environment was oblivious to the situation in spite of many indications of the reality of these crimes.

As one illustration I refer to the case of Belle Gunnes who lived on a farm outside of the small community of La Porte, Indiana. She killed eighteen or nineteen men who were lured to her farm by marriage advertisements and never left the farm again. The community was aware of these men visiting Belle Gunnes; several of them even mentioned the purpose of their visit. The strange character of Belle Gunnes was known, she was conspicuous enough in her hostile, unneighborly and secretive behavior; and yet although her visitors never showed up again the community never investigated and for years she was permitted to go on killing her victims. The famous case of H. H. Holmes, who in the last decade of the nineteenth century killed scores of women and who was a conspicuous and questionable member of the community of Englewood, Illinois, shows the same incredible feature of obliviousness on the environment's part.

One cannot help but come to the conclusion that this unawareness serves a certain purpose. Denying any awareness that crimes have been committed permits an unconscious, prolonged and vicarious gratification from them and at the same time secures reassurance by denying the existence of both crime and criminal. As long as no corpses are displayed, the crimes, for all practical purposes, have not been committed. However, as soon as the unmistakable evidence of murder, namely, the body of the victim, is found, it becomes vital for everyone to have the murderer identified, since according to the unconscious impulses and fantasies the murderer can be everyone, oneself or one's next of kin, enemy or friend. The many false arrests, denunciations of innocent people and self-accusations after a murder prove the state of general alarm and insecurity.

To return to the case of William Heirens, soon after he was apprehended

and suspected of the murder of Susan Degnan, the need to interfere with
any future rational attitude toward criminals and crime prevention demonstrated itself, coming this time from quarters on which the hope for rational
application of modern psychological findings is based; namely, psychiatry.
The psychiatrist who allegedly conducted the sodium pentothal experiment
which induced the confession, acted, I am sure, *bona fide*. As to William
Heirens, no more harm could be done to him anyway. The purpose of the
experiment might have been a scientific one or it might have been a social
one, namely by a quick confession to reassure the public. Whichever it was,
it neglected any consideration of the effects on psychiatry's role in crime
prevention or in dealing with criminals. If psychiatrists either take over the
part of the prosecutor or actively help the prosecutor, especially by using
methods which are contrary to the ethical standards of society, the chances
that any delinquent or criminal will trust a psychiatrist are slim. And yet
the only way to obtain information regarding the psychopathology of criminality is by honest communication from the criminal to the psychiatrists.
Insight into the psychopathology of criminality is the prerequisite for and
the only means of preventing crime. A criminal cannot be expected to reveal
anything incriminating about himself, e.g. to be completely honest with the
psychiatrist, if the psychiatrist has voluntarily become a part of the prose-
cuting authorities whether police force or State attorney's office. As to
William Heirens, not only was the question of rehabilitation through prolonged psychiatric treatment never raised, but the profession even gave up
any chance of gaining valid scientific information which might bear on the
future possibilities of dealing with similar cases. The newspapers triumphantly reassured the public that William Heirens, convicted and sent to
prison to the end of his natural life, had become a number and would never
again become a member of society. However, for our purpose, one of the
most interesting news items in connection with this case is that Heirens'
family not only changed their name but that William's parents separated
accusing each other of being responsible for their son's criminal career.
Granted that other explanations for this situation are possible, we may yet
think it probable that the marriage of William's parents was preserved and
safeguarded at the expense of his criminal acting-out, and that after the
scapegoat was sacrificed and no longer existed, the family equilibrium was
disturbed to such an extent that the family unit disintegrated.

The Heirens case was selected for the purpose of illustrating the three
features of the irrational attitude which society employs toward delinquent
children and young criminals: It fosters delinquent acting-out by its osten-
sible unawareness of the criminal impulses and acts. It seduces individuals
into criminality by providing them with the opportunity to continue their
delinquencies. And it exhibits vindictiveness against the juvenile criminal

after arrest and finally achieves the annihilation of the criminal. In this one case society paid by the sacrifice of four lives: the criminal's and the three victims', and one receives the impression that the ritual sacrifice of a few selected human scapegoats in pre-Christian primitive societies was more effective and less expensive for society.

In myth, folklore, legends and fairy tales the sacrifice of the child is an ever-recurring motif. The laws for the protection of children in modern society have done away only with the more obvious signs of destructive impulses against children. Every young generation seems to be hopelessly exposed to these impulses of the older generation as is most evident in the case of war where the young men of a tribe or a whole nation are sacrificed.

This hostility against children seems to stem from two main sources: the oedipus situation and sibling rivalry. The child is unconsciously regarded as the avenger for one's own murderous impulses against one's parent, and is the reminder of that ancient guilt and at the same time he represents the younger sibling who was the object of jealousy and envy because of the care he received from the parent.

If the child can be induced into acting-out of asocial criminal impulses and is punished for it, he satisfies at the same time both these unconscious hostile impulses and the superego demands of the parent generation. He then represents the scapegoat by whose sacrifice the rest of society hopes to attain redemption, forgiveness for their own sins and reconciliation with God or their own conscience. However, society's attitude toward its criminals reminds one of Oscar Wilde's novel, *The Picture of Dorian Gray*. Dorian's portrait reflected his sinful life, and in that way he himself could preserve an appearance of innocence. But Dorian could not bear to look at his portrait and finally tried to destroy it with the result that he killed himself. Society by using its criminals as scapegoats and by trying to destroy them, because it is unable to bear the reflection of its own guilt, actually stabs at its own heart.

THE PRIMAL CRIME AND THE UNCONSCIOUS

By Martin Grotjahn, M.D.

(*Los Angeles*)

Mankind has finally found the fulcrum which Archimedes promised could turn the world from its course by leverage.

The urge to destroy is a psychological problem but it was not recognized as such until Sigmund Freud transferred the topic of original sin and guilt from the realm of religion and art to that of science, to make them the subject of psychoanalytic investigation. It is now within the power of mankind to actualize this age-old fantasy of total destruction.

THE PRIMAL CRIME ACCORDING TO FREUD

In his autobiography,[1] Freud summarized briefly the hypothesis about the original crime, which he formulated in more detail in his great book, *Totem and Taboo*.[2]

"However, the sons came together and united to overwhelm, kill and devour their father, who had been their enemy but also their ideal. After the deed they were unable to take over their heritage since they stood in one another's way. Under the influence of failure and regret they learned to come to an agreement among themselves, they banded themselves into a clan of brothers by the help of the ordinances of totemism, which aimed at preventing a repetition of such a deed, and they jointly undertook to forego the possession of the women on whose account they had killed their father. They were then driven to finding strange women, and this was the origin of the exogamy which is so closely bound up with totemism. The totem-feast was the commemoration of the fearful deed from which sprang man's sense of guilt (or 'original sin') and which was the beginning at once of social organization, of religion and of ethical restrictions."

The evidence of psychoanalysis confirms what art and religion have claimed since man formed society, namely that the primal crime is the patricide. The findings of anthropology, psychology and archeology seem to support this conclusion. The *"Mea Culpa"* of the Church proved to be a

---

[1] Freud, Sigmund: *An Autobiographical Study*. London, Hogarth Press, 1946.
[2] Freud, Sigmund: *Totem and Taboo*. New York, Dodd, Mead & Co., 1918.

306

fact substantiated by scientific research. Clinical evidence shows that the primal oedipus complex forms a part of the development not only of every neurotic but of all human beings. Some of this clinical evidence will be given later.

Freud in *Totem and Taboo* and later in *Group Psychology and the Analysis of the Ego*[3] has laid the foundation for an understanding of patriarchy. He himself was influenced by the androcentric bias of his time, and perhaps of his own psychological make-up. It may also be that the great clinician was satisfied with an explanation of the œdipus complex which advanced the scientific understanding of man beyond any point previously attained. Freud was fully aware of the problems posed by the phenomena of matriarchy, feminine deities, the symbol of the Sphinx and man's hostility toward the woman who gave him life. He was aware of the reign of the mother before the coming of a patriarchy, but he never described this in the scientific terms nor with the almost seer-like clarity with which he described the existence and clinical importance of the oedipus situation as a phenomenon in the history of mankind. Freud preferred to stop at the oedipus level rather than go further and make the still deeper interpretation that matricide antedated patricide. His theories met with such resistance in his time that to have gone even further might have quashed psychoanalysis at birth.

It is unlikely that Freud was guided in this restraint by motives of strategy or politics but rather that his intuition told him how far he could advance.

Clinical observation, anthropology and the analytic interpretation of literature, all show clearly that there is a "preoedipal phase" in the historical development of mankind as well as in the development of each individual. There is a "pre-Totem and Taboo" phase in the history of social groups. Before the Gods of the "Great Father" type were created, the more primitive "Great Mother"[4] had to be destroyed. In the development of the individual we observe that the infant has to turn from the mother before he can discover the existence of the father.

Lester W. Ward[5] characterized the male as "an afterthought of nature" when formulating this development of a matricentric organization into a patriarchy.

The earliest crime to be discovered both in the history of the race and in the development of the individual seems to be patricide. But the crime

---

[3] Freud, Sigmund: *Group Psychology and the Analysis of the Ego.* London, Hogarth Press, 1922.

[4] Weigert-Vowikel, Edith: The Cult and Mythology of the Magna Mater from the Standpoint of Psychoanalysis. *Psychiatry,* I, 1938.

[5] Zilboorg, Gregory: Masculine and Feminine. *Psychiatry,* VII, No. 3, 1944. Quotes and discusses Lester W. Ward's lecture at the Six o'Clock Club in Washington 1888, *Pure Sociology.* New York, Macmillan, 1914.

which antedates it — on an historically older level and even more deeply repressed in the unconscious of all of us—is the murder or rape of the mother. The mother, whom Oedipus finally possessed after slaying his father, is *not* the all-powerful, all-knowing true woman, but she is already the woman of the patriarch episode, already dethroned and degraded to the status of the father's chattel.

The mother of the preoedipal era is the woman who gives life and who can take it away. Her dominance is absolute and man fears her mortally and eternally. In the East she is symbolized as the Great Goddess. The struggle against her is symbolized, for instance, in the fight of the Greeks against the Amazons.[6] Before the oedipus situation can arise and be resolved to make way for the later development, there must be the struggle with the mother. The hatred of man against woman is a mixture of retaliation, fear, and envy. Man succeeded in dethroning the mother in reality, but not in his mind. Zilboorg states: "It is not penis envy on the part of the woman, but woman envy on the part of the man, that is psychogenetically older, and therefore, more fundamental."

It is possible that the mother image of this deepest unconscious level was not murdered like the father on the oedipal level. She was dethroned, degraded, stripped of her power by other means, by the first rape. This probably was less a sexual act, and showed very little, if any, tenderness and love. It was an act of power, hatred, and animal conquest. In other words, it showed all the features of pregenital organization. The phallus was used as an aggressive, destructive, demonstrative organ. Only the dethroned mother could be loved with the kind of love which Oedipus had for his mother.

Before Freud, but unknown to him, the research of Johann Jacob Bachofen[7] claimed that matriarchy and matricide were historical events antedating patriarchy and patricide.

Johann Jacob Bachofen was born in Basel, Switzerland, in 1815, where he died in 1887, little known even in the German speaking countries. He is responsible for the theory that patriarchy is based upon and evolved from matriarchy. He was the first to discover and investigate the culture of that "prehistoric history" of which we have no written documents. He interpreted material taken from archeology, mythology, paleontology and even poetry to reconstruct a vast span of remote history. Bachofen's methods are closely related to the psychoanalytic methods of Freud. The scientific world either ignored or rejected his claim that there had been a chthonic matriarchial

---

[6] Schulz-Engle, Bernice: The Amazons in Ancient Greece, *Psa. Qart.*, XI, No. 4, 1942.

[7] The interrelation between Freud and Bachofen is instructively summarized by Turel, Adrien: *Bachofen-Freud: Zur Emanzipation des Mannes vom Reich der Mutter.* Bern, Hans Huber, 1939.

period. His theory was too foreign to the common concept of remote antiquity. Mankind is unwilling to face the thought of its maternal origin and dependency.

The foundation and starting point of Bachofen's theory is his analysis of Aeschylus' *Orestes,* especially the third part of the trilogy, the *Eumenides.* The Erinyes are the priestesses of the matriarchy who defended Clytemnestra. They are opposed and attacked by the young deities, Apollo and Athene, who represent the beginning of patriarchy and who defend Orestes. According to the old *matriarchal law* Clytemnestra was not the murderess but the lawful executioner of Agamemnon. According to the new patriarchal law Orestes did not murder his mother but avenged his father. The matriarchal principle of maternal pregnancy and birth is opposed by the spiritual idea of paternal procreation culminating in the cephalogenesis of Pallas Athene. The fight between matriarchy and patriarchy, the fight of Theseus against the Amazons, the fight of the old culture of Asia with the new culture of antiquity in Athens and Europe is the essential meaning and importance of Greek history. In this time of evolving patriarchy, the Erinyes are still powerful but they become the childless mothers of the night. They live in the darkness of the earth as the deities of love and fertility who have been vanquished and drawn into the darkness by Zeus — the new ruler of the patriarchal Olympus.

These problems and conflicts are clearer and franker in Sophocles' *Oedipus* than in the tragedy of Aeschylus. Shakespeare's *Hamlet* is more closely related to Sophocles than is his *King Lear* to Aeschylus.

In the Oedipus tragedy the fight between matriarchy and patriarchy is no longer the issue. This conflict is settled so far as the unchallenged predominance of the patriarchy is concerned. *Oedipus, Hamlet, Don Carlos,* all picture the same incest conflict and differ only in the degree of consciousness.[8] What was a deed in *Oedipus,* was a conscious wish in *Hamlet* but a wish already repressed in *Don Carlos.* All three dramas could have been written by the same Sophocles growing older and more Christian: Man's desire to conquer the mother, and the woman is not only a problem of libido but also a problem of power and of achieving recognition of the male, for he cannot forget the time of gynaecocracy and the fact that he was once forced to submit to the frightful passage "under the yoke".

THE SYMBOLIZATION OF THE TWOFOLD PRIMAL CRIME IN DREAMS

The clinical evidence that the primordial rape of the mother and the later slaying of the father is living truth in our own unconscious can be found in two different observations. These experiences are disguised and,

---

[8] Rank, Otto: *Das Inzest Motiv in Dichtung und Sage.* Leipzig, 1912.

of course, show that the original desires are deeply repressed in our time. They remain unconscious and can be studied only in their derivatives.

Such derivatives are our dreams and fantasies, and they show what mankind always knew — that we all are sinners. Only a few act it out in the actual crime of rape and murder.

In our patients' dreams it is more difficult to detect the importance and the struggle with the primordial mother than the more obvious and genetically so much younger struggle with the father.

The following dreams are not reported because they are in any way unusual nor shall we relate them to any neurotic symptom or psychosomatic syndrome, or to any character trait. They are given as illustrations of unconscious tendencies which are universal, and are quoted from different parts of one analysis.

The patient, aged forty-six, was in analysis because of a mild chronic depression. In general it seems to be easier to penetrate through the level of the oedipus situation to the level of the primordial mother in the age group of forty, than in the younger age groups. It may be that certain unconscious aspects of the oedipus complex are worked through to relatively satisfying results during the process of maturation, and especially during the social adjustment to our form of democratic patriarchy. This then in turn facilitates the analysis of the underlying levels of development.

The following is part of a dream as reported by the patient — ". . . In a little town in southern France the people got together in a kind of revolution. I was their leader and showed them how to get into the castle overlooking the village. I also showed them how to get to their leader or king or somebody running the affairs of the city. When we finally got there I was alone and did not know any more whether I was myself, the leader, or one of the revolutionaries . . ."

The meaning of this almost undisguised oedipus dream was nearly conscious to the patient, who had first rebelled against his father then followed in his father's footsteps and finally outdid him in many respects.

Twelve months, or approximately two hundred analytic hours later, after having worked through the oedipus situation, the patient had a dream, which signified the change in his analytic situation.

". . . I passed a dying man lying half concealed in dirt and straw. Then I saw a woman who looked almost like my mother, but bigger, standing in a window or a shop, like a butcher shop. She was exposed or partially exposed, as if a crime had been committed. I went away from there and had to climb up a steep wall or mountainside. I could hardly make it and got out of breath. . . ." Another dream — from this analytic period — gives a variation of the same motif. ". . . I saw the vice-president of our company and our woman advertising manager sitting at a long table with many people. I only saw these two distinctly. They sat at the head of the table. I was sitting at the other end. The woman ate little silver fishes with great delight. The whole thing happened on an open street and heavy traffic, people and cars, were going by, but nobody paid any attention. I think I was serving the woman, like a waiter. . . ."

The last dream to be reported here from a still later period of analysis, approximately the four hundredth hour, was reported while the patient went through a rather deep depressive episode:

". . . I don't know whether this is a dream or a recollection of something I learned in school, or whether I made it up while half asleep. It was as if the earth opened, or as if I were in a basement without a cement floor. A big hole opened and I backed my car or a truck into it. I must have once heard a story of people who were threatened by an ever-deepening and widening canyon or splitting of their land. Finally the bravest of their sons in full armor and on his best horse, sacrificed himself and hurled himself into the canyon to his death. The earth slowly closed over him and the people were saved. . . ."

We will not discuss here the therapeutic use of these dreams, their relation to the central issue of transference neurosis, nor their meaning in terms of the patient's depressive condition, nor have we reported these dreams to prove scientifically that the rape of the primordial mother (last dream) was older than the patricide (first dream).

They are offered only as an illustration of the theory from clinical observation. The patient had worked out well the passing of the oedipus complex and had succeeded in life and in his profession. In his oral sadistic desires, he remained frustrated and later said that he felt he did not get anything out of life.

As a rule the derivatives and symbols of the early stages of the preoedipal development are vague. Frequently anxiety and guilt are not bound to any object. They are felt as panic or horror. It is also significant that these dreams are rather uniform, that they could have been dreamt by almost anyone and are stripped of individual symbols. From the content alone it is often not evident whether they were dreamt by a man or a woman, since women also go through a phase of liberation from the mother and this phase of both sexes occurs at an age level before there is any awareness of sex differences. The main psychological differences between the sexes become apparent more in the results of this liberation than during the process of it.

As a rule these early feelings of trying to fight the mother, or denying the fact of having been born of the mother, these feelings of the struggle for independence from her, are expressed in affects almost beyond the possibility of verbalization.

"There was a disaster or something. I was running my car over a body in a crouched position," or "I killed a dog, and I did not know what to do with the corpse. It was terrible." Or, "I kissed my wife, and then I saw my mother's face in the window. She cried and I woke up." Or "A bat flew in the room, and I did not want it to bite anybody, so I tried to catch it and it turned into my hand. It had to be taken off and it was horrible."

These dreams are not necessarily dreamt by psychotics. They may be dreamt by almost anyone sensitive enough to allow his dreams to arise out of the depths of the unconscious, and to be noticed before they again sink down into repression.[9]

Sometimes such dreams are actually acted out, and then the fateful step from a dream state to a psychosis or a crime is made. This was the case of the psychotic veteran who disemboweled his dog, "the promiscuous and sniveling bitch", as a last attempt to symbolize the matricide. He was then swept away by this break-through of his impulses and with tears streaming down his cheeks, stabbed his step-mother through the heart.

The regressive, schizophrenic matricide is at the same time a symbolic rape. The schizophrenic attacks whom he would have loved if he could love at all. The social counterpart is a mob lynching. It is regressive in its cruelty, its lack of rationality, its almost demonstrative denial of justice. The lynching is schizophrenic in its symbolism, and in its implied homosexuality. After the mother has been raped, the culprit is murdered and the brothers can live in peace again.

REALITY MANIFESTATIONS OF GUILT

Our interest in crimes as reported in the newspapers or in murder mysteries, in movies and in books, is another proof of these criminal desires of long forgotten times which still live in us, but have been laboriously controlled. It is easier for us now to participate as an onlooker of other people's crimes and punishments than to look into ourselves and to discover them within ourselves and so to suffer all the pain of guilt and shame.

Intolerance is the projection of guilt; tolerance is the identification or at least the partial identification and acceptance of one's own part in every crime. Tolerance means a recognition of common features between anyone's crime and one's own desires. In the tragedy this is enacted before our eyes; it may be in real life or on the stage. "Entertainment", which is quite different, but still related to art, denies the identification with the criminal or the hero of the tragedy, and finally denies the existence of tragedy by means of the happy ending.

The movie thriller and the mystery story play a peculiar, teasing game with guilt and the deliverance from it. The thriller, too, invites identification, but does it in the form of splitting the on-looker into two parts: one part identifies with the murderer and goes through all the agonies of the chase; the other part identifies with the detective, policeman or prosecutor, and insists that the crime must be solved and punished. The unsolved crime is a threat, causing a feeling of the uncanny. As long as the murderer is

---

[9] For a more detailed discussion of this aspect see: Fromm, Erich: Sex and Character. *Psychiatry*, VI, No. 1, 1943.

among us it could be my brother and it could even be "I", namely, that part of me that I do not know.

The peculiar thrill of the mystery story is based on a teasing game with the collective guilt. Before the criminal is found everybody is suspected, and sure enough, everybody turns out to be guilty in one way or another, at least guilty in the psychological sense. This almost goes so far as to include the reader or the movie-goer even before he starts to identify. The thrill depends on making use of everyone's conscience.

The term "teasing" is used here in order to show the difference between the true identification in the tragedy and the deluded identification in the movie thriller. The identification is a testing one, as if the onlooker were only asked: Maybe it was you? In the tragedy the onlooker goes further: in his identification with the hero he is willing to atone by suffering, but the movie-goer stops his identification with the murderer at the moment when suffering and punishment begin and changes to an identification with the prosecutor. In this righteous identification he insists on the punishment of the "enemy", his former self.

A few years ago a peculiar murder case caused sensational interest all over the country. According to all newspaper accounts, the evidence was clearly against the defendants. It seemed that the accused young girl, together with her fiancé, had bludgeoned her parents to death and then dynamited the sailing yacht where the crime had been committed. The proceedings dragged on for weeks, and the appointment of a jury alone took more than a month. The defendants steadfastly denied their guilt. They were shown the receipt for the purchased dynamite which had been found in one of the defendant's cameras, which bore his own signature. The entire crime could be retraced step by step almost like a movie taken during the real act.

A stanchion was found which fitted perfectly into the victims' wounds. Blood, hair, and flesh were found on the defendants' clothes. Several notes written by the male defendant amounted, at least psychologically, to a confession. The facts were obvious from the newspaper accounts. The courtroom atmosphere was clearly against the defendants. The defendants' own family gave an unmistakable expression of their opinion, almost condemning the defendants.

The whole mounting interest no longer focused on whether they did it but changed to the question: will they get away with it? Interestingly enough, the question *why* they did it was easily settled in everybody's mind — greed and lust, which was both true and false. Nobody noticed that life here repeated the tragedy of Orestes and Electra.

Then at the end of the whole trial, the unbelievable happened. The jury, as it seemed to the reporters peeping through the windows, was deadlocked from the beginning with a majority for condemnation and only one dissenting vote. Finally the jury informed the judge that a decision had been reached and he admonished the public that no demonstration would be allowed, and court attendants were stationed all over the courtroom. When the verdict of "not guilty" was read, bedlam broke loose. Everybody cried, laughed, shouted, kissed everybody else, including the defendants. The jury joined the accused, and some of the jurors were photographed with the acquitted girl. The crowd behaved as if not the two young people had been accused, and had been set free, but as if they, the innocent onlookers, had been accused, had felt their guilt, but had still been proved innocent. Before everyone's eyes, and in actuality, the guilty unconscious was declared free of guilt and criminal punishment set aside. It was a total absolution of everybody concerned.

Something similar seemed to have happened in the collective mind of the jury. They felt that circumstantial evidence could not be accepted, because it seemed possible to use it against everybody with a guilty conscience. They freed themselves by not accepting anything but confession or "objective" proof.

THE RETURN OF THE REPRESSED AS THE POSSIBLE ULTIMATE CRIME

It would be fantastic and no longer scientific to compare the analysis of the primal crime against the mother with a total destruction of mankind in a future war. The primordial mother was cruel, and most mother goddesses have been cruel and cannibalistic. The mother could give life and could take it away. The primordial mother was lawless and promiscuous. It was the organized brother horde which decreed law, order, rational thinking, property, and orientation in time and space. The same man who felt so inferior to the life-giving mother, who denied his dependence upon her, created out of his fear of being a parasite time and space and finally the machine. All this he achieved by sublimation and repression.

But the return of the repressed may result in re-creating the primordial situation. This would be the situation before the first crime, before the Garden of Eden, even before time: When There Was Chaos.

THE PHENOMENON OF CONTAGION AND "SHOCK EFFECT" IN GROUP THERAPY

By Fritz Redl, Ph.D.*

(*Detroit*)

The phenomenon of "contagion" is not new to the social psychologist. In fact, the "spread" of behavior from one person to another or to a whole group has been described in connection with studies of "mass behavior" in most textbooks and publications on social psychology. Riots, panic situations, incidents of "mass hysteria" furnish good illustrations for this purpose.

However, group psychologists as well as the students of individual behavior have so far neglected this phenomenon when it occurs in small face to face groups, or even in larger groups with well structured organization. The practitioners of group leadership, teachers, recreation leaders and others are familiar with the event referred to, but are ill at ease when challenged to explain it. The educator has been inclined to a general theory of "germophobia" — the idea that one bad apple might make the whole classroom rotten has deterred many a principal or teacher from trying their hand on Johnny or Mary when they were suggested as additions to their groups. The psychiatrist has neglected the phenomenon for other reasons, mainly because to him it seems obvious that the real reason why contagion can take place at all is to be found in latent trends within the individual.[1]

If Johnny begins to steal under the contagious influence of Bobby in the same group, there must have been something in Johnny to respond to Bobby's seductive wiles. Since before the recent development of Group Therapy, psychiatrists were mainly limited to the operation in a two person

* Wayne University, School of Public Affairs and Social Work.

[1] The observational data underlying this paper were collected in the framework of the clubs of "The Detroit Group Project", in the Detroit Group Project Summer Camp which operated from 1943-47, and at Pioneer House, founded in 1946. The "Detroit Group Project" and its Summer Camp is an agency for group therapy with disturbed children and Pioneer House is an all year round Group Therapy Home for delinquents on a residential basis. All three organizations were started and are directed by the author of this article, are affiliated with the School of Public Affairs and Social Work, Wayne University, and are supported by Community Chest and Private Funds, especially the Junior League of Detroit.

consultation situation, the actual domestication of contagion-behavior was no problem to them.

I.

With the development of Group Therapy the picture has changed, and the phenomenon of contagion deserves, to my mind, the foreground of our practical as well as theoretical interests. For, no matter what the basic explanation may be, the following phenomena can be established beyond doubt:

1. Sometimes the behavior of one group member is being "picked up" nearly "automatically" by other members of the same group or by the majority of that group. This "pick-up" takes place through rather mysterious channels, it is not even necessary that conscious or unconscious intent is present in the person who commits the "initiatory act".[2]

Example: Eighty rather disturbed children between the ages of eight and fourteen are in a large camp mess hall. Johnny, in a fit of temper against one person at his table, throws a plate at him. A minute later, plates fly all through the air, and the place is in an uproar, even though Johnny neither contemplated nor planned such an effect, and is otherwise a rather inconspicuous figure at the camp, without any leadership role.

2. Sometimes, there is an equally puzzling absence of such an expected contagious effect of one group member upon another or on a larger part of the group, even though previous experiences with the same group might suggest that it would occur.

Example: The same camp mess hall situation; a child throws a plate; nothing happens; it remains an entirely isolated incident without any relevance to the wider group situation.

3. Sometimes, the addition of one child with an openly expressed area of clear cut problem behavior to a smaller group of others who had never previously shown this behavior, may make overt in all of them what previously had only been present as a dormant possibility or as a trend on the fantasy level.

Example: George is added to a group of children, who are all hesitant to form positive relationships to adults in general, who have begun to form a positive attachment to their specific group leader. Upon George's arrival, his open defiance and hateful sneer against everything the adult suggests or does is immediately "picked up" and the other children show similar behavior, to the leader's and their own surprise.

4. Sometimes, again, the addition of a child with an openly expressed area of specific problem behavior has no direct effect at all on the behavioral trends of the others as far as imitation goes.

Example: Mary was added to a group of preadolescent girls who have a wide assortment of behavior problems from sex delinquency to stealing and so

---

[2] See: Fritz Redl, Group Emotion and Leadership, *Psychiatry,* V, No. 4, 1942, p. 580.

forth. Mary's open display of wild, close to paronoiac fantasy life including mainly accusations against adults, remains ineffective upon the otherwise not easily manageable group. The other children do not use her "example" to pick up similar behavior; in fact, they run to the adult for protection and develop scapegoat formation against the newcomer.

With these phenomena in mind, it seems highly relevant to find out just what determines whether such "contagious" influence from one group member to others or to the whole group takes place or not. The psychiatric explanation that contagion presupposes the existence of similar trends within the imitator seems acceptable, but inadequate. For practical purposes, it makes quite a difference whether your group member only daydreamed about stealing, or actually began to steal after the advent of that other child.

We do not know the answers. The United States Health Service just gave us a grant[3] for a two year study of these phenomena, considering such study as essential to more effective work in therapy groups. However, on the basis of rich if not systematic observations in our previous work, we should like to set forth a number of *tentative hypotheses* which suggest themselves from what we have seen.

II.

It seems to us, that the factors which decisively determine whether or not contagion takes place, can be classified into two categories: those of the psychology of the group and those of the psychology of the individual. Needless to say, we assume that most incidents of contagion are the result of a cooperation of both types on a sliding scale.

GROUP PSYCHOLOGICAL FACTORS DETERMINING CONTAGION

1. *Group Status of the Initiator*

If we mean by "initiator" the person whose behavior is being imitated, then it seems to us that, other things being equal, the trend toward contagion is higher if the initiator enjoys high status in his group, while contagion is less likely to occur if the initiatory act comes from an individual of low status. *Example:* In a group of toughies who hated adults, the obvious and recognized ringleader, the toughest of them all, was the first to make open advances of friendship toward the adult leader. His behavior worked like a charm (positive contagion). From now on the other youngsters gave way to their own beginning desire for leader acceptance which they hitherto had not

[3] Research Project on "The Use of the Group Medium for Clinical Work with Disturbed Children". Two year grant by the U. S. Health Service, Division for Mental Hygiene, Washington, D. C. Principal Investigators: Fritz Redl, Wayne University, and Dr. Ronald Lippitt, Research Center for Group Dynamics, Massachusetts Institute of Technology, Cambridge, Mass. Director of Research, Mr. Norman Polansky; research center at Wayne University, Detroit.

dared to express, for fear of being considered "sissies." If another child in the same group tried similar advances toward adult affection before, he was exposed to ridicule and contempt.

2. *Affinity of the Behavioral Area to the Group Code*

Other things being equal, it seems that behavior that is related to items which have a high value rating in the group code is more easily contagious than other acts by the same individual.

Example: Jack's attempts at getting other members into sex play are warded off effectively by everybody in the group. On the other hand, whenever Jack becomes tumultuous in a situation where the whole group is supposed to be quiet and listen to somebody else's announcements, his behavior has immediately contagious effect. Needless to say, the group is one of preadolescent boys with not too strong a trend toward sex precocity but with a high degree of pride in mischievous pranks. The things that "count" in this group are whether you are openly daring against adults. Sexual precocity is left to individual differences, and carries less weight in determination of group status.

3. *Communality of Basic Expressional Trend*

Other things being equal, behavior which is liable to give vent to the suppressed needs of the largest number of group members with high group status will be the most sweeping in its contagious effect.

Example: On the day when one child's plate throwing found such promiscuous imitation, there was a suppressed mobility and wildness present in practically every member of that group, due to a sequence of rainy days and the nature of the preceding program, which had involved passivity and listening.

It seems to us, that this item of communality of basic expressional trends determines spread rather than the actual occurrence of contagious effect.

4. *Size, Structure, Organizational Pattern and Nature of the Program of the Group*

If we lump these factors together under one heading, we do so under the pressure of space limitation. We realize that each one of them constitutes an item of great independence from all others and of great variability. But this chapter must limit itself for the present purpose to a summary of the following observations:

It seems that the factor of the *size* of the group has some bearings on the occurrence of contagious events. We would not be prepared to say, however, that large groups automatically make contagion easier. Depending on the behavioral item in question and other factors, we found both that sometimes the larger and sometimes the smaller group size was favorable to contagion. For instance, the spread of *group mood of a ritualistic nature* around a camp fire seems easier in larger than in smaller groups. The spread of a group reaction against the adult seemed more effective in the smaller group, provided, of course, the structure in both cases remained the same. In other cases the *"structure"* of the group certainly makes a considerable difference. For instance, if a group is clearly substructured into well definable group units within itself, the spread of contagion is minimized, as compared to a group without subgroup formation. Strong *organizational* dependence on an adult "leader from above" seems to favor contagion in certain areas, as compared to democratic group organization. The degree of *program absorption,* too, functions as an insulational layer against contagious effects of the negative type, while it fosters the effect of "positive contagion" in terms of "enthusiasm-spread".

The most obvious fact we could notice is a peculiar reaction of groups to certain combinations between structural and organizational factors. Thus, for instance, contagion of one clown's behavior in a huge dormitory (organizational regimentation in a large group with its substructures submerged through routine pressures) is much greater than the danger of spread of mischief or noise from one four kid room to another. Or, the discipline problems resulting from contagion on "tense" days will be much greater in a detention home with a chow line and long table and bench arrangements, than if the children and (group-related) adults are seated at smaller tables in a skilful distribution based on natural subgroup formations.

5. *Group Atmosphere*

The "sum total of the feeling tone prevailing among the group members, among the members toward their leader, toward the things they do, and toward the image of their own group" constitutes another variable in this problem of contagious effect. By and large it seems to us that behavioral incidents which have a high affinity to the present "group mood" will have more contagious possibilities than others. In an "atmosphere" of happy, mutual acceptance and cheerfulness of all members toward each other, including the leader, even a recognized toughie's rebellious pranks may pass by ignored. In an atmosphere of "resentment of punitive pressure" even the chance clowning of an otherwise inconspicuous group member will be "picked up".

PERSONALITY FACTORS DETERMINING CONTAGION

Important as they are as variables in determining contagious effect, the above group psychological factors alone seem to us insufficient to explain the phenomenon as such. In fact, we have a strong suspicion that they determine more the "when" and "how far" of contagious effect, than the "why". However that may be, the clue to the basic process of contagious effect seems

to us to lie in the same principle which we have described six years ago in
Group Emotion and Leadership.[4] Instead of referring to that publication,
however, I would rather modify that formulation on the basis of more
recently observed examples.

Example: A cabin of six preadolescent boys with quite a strong trend toward
destructiveness. There had been a considerable number of incidents of
window breaking. For a while a good tie between the children and their
adult group leader had been developed and the incidents were well handled both individually and in group discussions. Nothing further happened
for some time. One morning, however, one of the youngsters who was sweeping the floor, picked up the broomstick and with a war-whoop charged
against the windows full force. Like a flood everyone else's destructiveness
was set loose and an orgy of destruction followed.

In analyzing this situation, the mere mention of what the instigator did
was not enough to explain the event. More detailed knowledge of everybody
involved and of previous events suggests the following analysis:

Five of the children were filled with suppressed destructive desires.
Their newly developed "group conscience" forbade destructive acts within
their own group, which they would have to pay for by guilt feelings. The
instigator, in this case, was a clearly psychopathic youngster, a type for whom
even the controls defined by the group code have little meaning, and if so
for only a short time. What really set loose the wild imitation pattern was
not the pattern of destruction by itself

If another child had done the same thing, they would have jumped on
him for breaking their promise and "getting them all in trouble". The present
instigator, however, did more than just start it off. His mannerisms when
charging at that window, as described by the children and as subsequently
acted out by himself, were most intensively suggestive of a most reckless,
devil-may-care mood. His whole pattern of gestures as well as that gleam
in his eye, suggested that he was entirely *free of fear or guilt* while doing
it. It seems to us from this and innumerable other similar incidents, that
this is one of the conditions for contagious effect.

Because of our limitation of space, we shall try to condense into a list
the steps which we think are involved in the production of contagious events,
as far as "personality factors" are concerned.

1. *Existence of an acute conflict area* within the imitators: strong impulse urge toward fulfilment of a vehement need on the one hand;
   on the other, sufficient pressure from ego or superego forces to keep
   it down.

2. *High degree of lability of this "personality balance"* in the area concerned: impulses strong enough to press for release, controls only
   just strong enough to prevent that release. If they were somewhat
   stronger no contagion would occur, if impulses were stronger or

---

[4] See: Fritz Redl, *op. cit.,* p. 392.

controls just a little weaker, they would not have to wait for some-body else's "initiatory act".

3. Existence of a *similar type of strong urge* toward impulse expression along the same line in the initiator. His urge must lie in the same direction as those of his imitators (destruction in this case).

4. *Open acting out* in favor of impulse satisfaction by the initiator, with equally open display of an *entire lack of fear or guilt*.

In short, what the initiator really does is this: he shows the fulfilment of the others' desire, also shows that it can happen without fear or guilt. What happens inside the imitators can be formulated as follows: the sudden visualization of fearless and guiltless enjoyment of what they really wanted to do sways their own labile balance between desire and control in favor of the former. Their own potential conflict is being resolved into open action along the line suggested by the visualized behavior of the initiator.

It seems to us that sometimes it is not even necessary for the initiator to go the whole way: strong and open gestural and physiognomic expression of his own lack of guilt and his fearlessness about an impulse gratification may be enough to sway the rest ("The Bad Example").[5] In other cases, direct visualization through the initiatory act is essential for the effect ("The Seducer").[6]

Needless to say, that contagion can also take effect in the opposite direc-tion, in which case we might call it "positive contagion".

Example: In a cabin of delinquent thieves who took great pride in their code, using rough language and swearing, one of the youngsters suddenly knelt down, when the bugle sounded "taps", pulled out his rosary, and started his evening prayers. Amazement temporarily paralyzed the rest of the group. Since our religious hero also happened to be one of the most openly delin-quent representatives of toughness and the delinquent philosophy of life, he was suddenly joined by three others who also knelt down by their bunks, while the rest simply stared in open-mouthed surprise.

Analysis: Open religious devotion would be considered sissy stuff according to the group code of these children. Yet they were all labile about this code and really felt somewhat guilty after their blasphemous orgies. The clear cut "solution" which their pal presented them by throwing his fear of ridicule aside and openly obeying the religious dictum of his superego, suddenly made it possible for the others to overcome their shame at letting their con-science openly triumph and they abandoned all further urges to ridicule or blasphemy.

III.

INDIRECT CONTAGION AND SHOCK EFFECT

In the previous illustrations, "contagion" always led toward imitation of the behavior of the initiator. We think we should pay attention to two other phenomena, which seem to us based on the same principle, even though

---

[5] See: Fritz Redl, *op. cit.;* p. 581.

[6] *Op. cit.,* p. 580.

direct imitation is not involved. By "indirect contagion," we refer to a situation like the following one:

Example: The "Spitfires" were a group of eleven to thirteen year old boys who had about a year of intensive club work around an adult leader who had unusual skill in developing a style of "democratic" group leadership and a pattern of "group expression" of feelings and thoughts related to their group life. When faced with conflict or problems, these youngsters would have a "gripe session", bring their complaints against each other or the leader herself out into the open, and show a remarkable group pride in an attitude of frankness and an ability of "taking it without offense". I have to mention this in such detail so as to show how the subsequent events were quite typical for this group. It was into this very "friendly" group that Al was placed, when the whole gang came to camp. Al's insertion into the group was well prepared, camp director and group leader had explained to the youngsters why an addition of another member was necessary, and had handled the youngsters' feelings about it extensively. The stage for Al's entry was as carefully prepared as could be, the group attitude to him one of most favorable cooperation.

It didn't last long. We knew that Al had considerable tendencies toward masochism. That was exactly why we tried placement in a group so leader-cooperative and self-expressive in case of conflict. After a few days, the group was in an uproar. Al's bid for being chased, wrestled with, pushed, was so strong, that the youngsters lost all self-control. They would begin in a spirit of fun, but Al would invariably be so coaxing that he always lured them into more sadistic satisfactions than they could foresee. After about a week, the group could hardly be recognized; they were like a bunch of sadistic bullies, became defensive and alibi-wise in their group discussions, started to bicker and fight with each other, and became aggressive and restless in their relationship to the adult.

From a great "gripe session" about all this as well as from the individual interviews, the basic structure of the event became unequivocally clear. The children complained that they knew they shouldn't give in, but "he just does something to us" — "he always makes us chase and hit him and then complains". They had no comment when asked just how he "made them hit him" and admitted that this statement was, literally taken, incorrect. It was obvious, however, what they were trying to say: Al's mere display of extreme masochistic desires "stirred up" within them more sadistic pleasure temptations than they could cope with. Needless to say that the wrath over their own lack of control finally accumulated as an additional cloud of rejection over Al's head, and that the "intangibility" of the whole process blocked their former skill of free group expression. The guilt over their own behavior into which they were lured became a collective motivation for real scapegoat formation against the "source" of all this, and they finally wanted Al "out".

What we want to show by this example is that something like "contagion" was happening here. Only, it does not mean that the other children began to "imitate" Al. It means, however, they were stirred into falling into the reverse side of his satisfaction pattern (**sado-masochistic temptations**).

The basic principles seem to me clinically the same, even though it is not an "imitation of behavior". We might, for lack of a better name, call this phenomenon "indirect contagion" until we learn enough about it to give it a name of its own.

The phenomenon of *"shock effect"* is of even more concern to the clinician. An illustration may show what we have in mind:

Example: "The puppeteers" were a group of eight year old boys and girls, all referred because of their basic fear of self-expression. They were all "shy and withdrawn", they were all "afraid to express themselves" and so scared they could not even use finger paint or other media which are messy. A few weeks later, the leader's efforts had taken effect, only by this time it became obvious that these children were alike in symptom only, not in the level of repression of their forbidden urges. For all but one by then not only used finger paint freely, but they also produced drawings with the most fantastic content, and indulged openly in oedipal and other fantasies and games while they did so. This was too much for one of the girls. Janie dropped out. Her case worker reported that she was quite upset, and a closer examination of the total situation showed clearly what had happened: The open visualization of so much material which for Janie was "repressed" more severely than for the others, had thrown her into an anxiety phase. Instead of "imitating" the more open expressiveness of the rest of the children, their behavior only caused her to reinforce her own reaction-formation against self-expression.

Briefly, comparing this case with the analysis of contagious behavior in the previous pages, it looks as follows:

1. Some desire for self-expression in Janie, but a very heavy reaction-formational taboo against it. Balance less than labile, rather in favor of repressional taboos.
2. Open visualization of "conflict solution" of the other children, who expressed wildly and freely (and with leader approval) without guilt or fear, what Janie did not dare to accept.
3. Discrepancy between Janie's range of self-acceptance and that of the other children much too great for imitative enjoyment.
4. Therefore, visualization of the others' self-expression did *not* solve the problem along the line of impulse expression, but rather forced Janie into more efforts toward reaction-formation, or at least threatened her original conflict solution and produced anxiety.

Not always is the result the production of fear or increased reaction-formation, sometimes it goes much further than that and has quite serious group psychological consequences in its wake.

Example: The intensity of Aileen's hatred for Martha assumed proportions which were hard to comprehend. Not only did she go out of her way to hurt, tease, offend, embarrass and torment her cabinmate, but she went to great pains to make vicious propaganda against her with Martha's boy as well as girl friends. And there seemed little on Martha's side to account for this reaction. Martha kept out of Aileen's way whenever she could, and was unusually decent and tolerant of the leader's effort to help Aileen rather than punish her for some of her quite outrageous exploits. Things came to a point where Aileen had set every girl in the group against Martha, and made her into a real "scapegoat".

An analysis of the case showed this situation: Aileen was big for her age (thirteen), physically overdeveloped, but the case worker and the school assured us she was really not yet interested in boys, and that we need not be worried at having her in a co-educational camp. She lived in a slum neighborhood where most girls of her age openly brag about their promiscuity, and where sex and boy friends are the constant topic of discussion and gossip. She lived with her aunt, who was a most virtuous woman, and who wanted to make sure that Aileen would not become "the kind of woman her mother was". To make a long story short, Aileen was threatened by the open talk and bragadoccio that went on in her group at camp, and Martha was the greatest threat to her. For Martha had no conflict about her interest in one of the boys, and enjoyed her courtship in such a way that Aileen could not simply "despise her" as a "bad girl". To express one's erotic wishes and have no guilt feelings about them and also to have success in accepting sexuality without a conflict threatened to weaken her own tremendous task of repression.

Her "balance" was threatened, and it is not enough to increase her own reaction-formations against her sexual wishes. She had to destroy or eliminate the person who caused all this, in the good old style of a witch hunt. . . .

We might briefly summarize these two and other forms of "shock effect" in form of the following list:

FORMS OF REACTIONS TO "SHOCK EFFECT"

1. *Diffuse Anxiety*

   Children having to live in the same group with one who is threatening to their id-ego-superego balance, have often shown nightmares, fear of a particular child without actual threat; displaced anxieties: fear of the woods, snakes, psychosomatic symptoms, homesickness, etc.

2. *Temper Tantrum Attacks*

   Children thus threatened in their personality balance through the visualization of unacceptable behavior have sometimes had a sudden increase in their temper outbursts, or have shown fits of rage which could be clearly traced to anxiety attacks.

3. *Increase in "Goodness"*

   Sometimes they have to become temporarily "good" because of this shock reaction and this may easily be confused with real improvement. Actually this transient effort to accept group values is only a counteragent against the threat to their inner balance. They are threatened by observing the fearless and guiltless enjoyment of others and this necessitates an intensified reaction-formation.

4. *Avoidance and Withdrawal*

Some children, under the impact of "shock effect", begin to "avoid" certain other children, want to be regrouped, sent home, run away, or they drop out of activities they previously enjoyed, or take refuge in daydreaming and reading instead of play action.

5. *Hostility and Scapegoat Propaganda*

If pushed too far, they have to go beyond all this, to the length to which Aileen had to go. Only the exclusion or destruction of the one who threatens their precarious personality balance can solve their problem. Thus, you may find them engaged in real political machinations against this or that child or leader, or in an attempt to get the group to establish punitive rules against certain offenders or offenses, or they turn themselves into a gossip mill, solely in order to eliminate the threat to their virtuous but unstable equilibrium of a strong urge and an implacable superego.

The question, what determines in a similar situation whether the reaction is contagion or shock effect, is a fascinating one, and I wish I knew the answers. Tentatively, I could only venture the following suggestions:

Contagion will take place if (other things being equal):

1. The "balance" within the recipient is strongly loaded in favor of impulse expression to begin with.
2. The *degree of freedom from fear and guilt* shown by the initiator is just strong enough to relax the imitator, but not so extreme that it frightens him into a fear of all loss of control.
3. The area in which contagion is to take place is relatively free of other problems.

Shock effect will take place if (other things being equal):

1. The "balance" in the recipient is strongly in favor of a solution in terms of superego triumph, especially if the suppressed urges are threateningly strong, so that even temporary enjoyment would involve a great risk.
2. The initiator's freedom from fear and guilt is so great as to threaten the recipient beyond the momentary issue by jeopardizing his basic principles and superego control.
3. If the area in which contagion might take place is in itself a much too conflict and taboo ridden ground, so that much too heavy counter forces would get into motion for even a little bit of "sin" . . .

IV.

PRACTICAL IMPLICATIONS

No less interesting than the question of when and why contagion or shock effect take place, is the problem of determining why they fail to work when we might otherwise have expected them. The group leader especially needs this knowledge, for it is obviously of greatest importance to be able to control this phenomenon. Specific technical suggestions must be left to future research. On the basis of our previous observations, we could venture the following tentative clues:

1. The Importance of Group Composition

It obviously is not feasible to group people together on the basis of such simple criteria as age, "interest", I.Q., or the like. Somewhere, sooner or later, other factors come into play which may decide whether the type of group atmosphere developed in a certain mixture of individuals will be favorable or unfavorable, and just who will influence whom in which way.

We have been increasingly impressed with the multitude of criteria which has been offered for "hygienic grouping". But this is too elaborate an issue to be dealt with in this place. Suffice it to say that it is through the ways of grouping that we can sometimes prevent Johnny or Mary from exerting either an excess of contagious or shock effect on the rest of the group.

2. Group Psychological Insulation

Since subgroup formations and group structure as well as factors of organizational control seem to play an important role in the process described above, the following observations might offer leads for further investigation.

Example: Sometimes contagious or shock effect can be limited by having children in different cohesive subgroups, while still living in the same over-group. Thus, for instance, Cabin 7 was composed of youngsters who were wild and had delinquent leanings, but could not be compared with the elaborate and near to professional toughness of Cabin 4. Johnny, who was somewhat less delinquent than the rest, could live happily with them. What he knew about the behavior and goings on in Cabin 4 excited him somewhat, but since he was imbedded in the emotional ties of his own group, it had little meaning beyond that. He would, together with his pals, occasionally give vent to his indignation at those "awfully tough kids over there" and question my wisdom in letting such youngsters come to camp at all, but he neither had to imitate them nor develop exaggerated shock reactions. This would have been different had we made the mistake of putting him into Cabin 4. Exposed to the same group code and group emotional relationship pattern as they, he would either have had to imitate in order to attain prestige, or he would have been thrown into an emotional tailspin out of fear of loss of self-control. Also, he could hardly have forgiven his group leader for showing the same acceptance to the "bad" youngsters as to him, and would have developed a diversified hysteric display.

Example: Children who come to a large group entertainment with their counsellor and come in by cabin groups, are usually much easier even when exposed to the program pressure of sitting still, than if they all crowd in topsy turvy, the way they happen to arrive. Reason among others: behavior (clowning) visualized by somebody who is not a direct member of their subgroup, while their subgroup surrounds them, is not half as contagious as it is otherwise.

3. Specialized Leader-Handling

Contagion or shock effect are really unavoidable in the life of any group. The problem is not to avoid all of it, but to handle incidents of this sort wisely, so that their effects can be counteracted. Knowing the "contagion potential" and the "contagion area" of Johnny and his group will go far to help a leader anticipate and handle group developments and individual incidents. Shock effect, too, can be dealt with up to a certain degree by increasing the direct and indirect support the adult leader gives the child. Individual interview, group discussion of the expressional type, and other ways can be used as additional techniques.

4. Implications for Intake

Many of the hitherto rather "mysterious" phenomena, like the increased irritability of whole wards or groups because of the addition of a new member, or the restored manageability and relief after the expulsion of an old one, begin to assume a new meaning. It also seems obvious that both the addition or elimination of group members has strategic implications far beyond the consideration they are usually given.

THEORETICAL IMPLICATIONS

These phenomena raise anew the question, what are the processes going on in groups, when we follow the fascinating paths of observation such as we have described. Even though we hope we adequately delineated for the purpose of this study what we mean by "contagion" and "shock effect," we are far from knowing what it is. The following seem to be the most urgent speculations that force themselves upon the theorist's mind:

1. Where is the difference between this and other forms of member-member influence?
2. Does contagion only take place between group members, or is the same principle at work if we say a group leader really "swayed" the atmosphere of the group, or of individuals? Same question for shock effect.
3. By what subtle means do people communicate such things? How does Johnny know that Bob is really guilty and fearless, when I read his whole case history and still am not sure? How does Aileen know the depth of Martha's sex-acceptance? How does a whole room full of people sense the implication of one gestural act (plate throwing) as a potential for impulse release, when other opportunities are passed by. The intuitive precision with which group members seem to "convey" meaning way beyond the reach of ordinary language and signs, baffles us.
4. What gives an act such "signal function?" Would any behavior along the same line have similar contagious or shock effect or is there something specific in the way or in the intensity with which Bob acted, which effected the result?

5. Does the same principle hold for situations of intentional influence? Can it be learned, and taught, and does it perhaps underlie many other influence situations which so far we have too glibly interpreted as being entirely based on direct verbal or gesture connotations?

6. How is it possible that the mere "visualization" of an "unconflicted superego situation" has such an effect over somebody else's "conflicted one?"[7]

7. How could we translate such phenomena into measurable units so that they may be scientifically investigated and perhaps taken from the realm of intuitions based on observation and experiences based on hunches?

Well, the purpose of this little study was not to solve this problem, but to raise it. More people working with groups in which more is known about both the constituent group members and their backgrounds, as well as the dynamics which actuate the group, may finally answer these questions. For the present, we would conclude with a strong plea in favor of research into group dynamics which combines the disciplines of psychoanalysis and sociology.

---

[7] See: Fritz Redl, *op. cit.*, p. 582.

ON SOCIAL RESPONSIBILITY

By Gregory Zilboorg, M.D.

(New York)

Like every medical endeavor, psychoanalysis was first and foremost pre-occupied with symptoms and with the ways and means of removing them. Like any healing art, it was first and foremost interested not in how good or how bad a person the given patient happened to be, but primarily in how sick a person the patient happened to be. Like any scientific discipline, psychoanalysis was interested in the problem of how the given patient became ill, regardless of whether the cause of the illness were humble or lofty, clean or dirty. Like any scientific method, the psychoanalytic method was from the outset a method of empirical, cool, objective investigation, and as such it braced itself against any feeling of horror, disgust, shame or anxiety which might overcome one when dealing with human aberrations. Not that as a human being the psychoanalyst is devoid of these feelings — any more than a pathologist while doing an autopsy is devoid of the usual fear of death. But like any scientific investigator, the psychoanalyst learned to proceed with his assignment without swerving and without diffidence, regardless of which side of its face human nature chose to turn to his gaze: murder, falsehood, theft, incest, intrigue or chicanery. All was, as it should have been of course, grist to the mill of psychological study.

The results of over half a century of psychoanalytic labors were grati-fying in many respects and disappointing in others, but on the whole it is accurate to say that the influence of psychoanalysis has been greater than its overall therapeutic performance. We are still groping for thorough and permanent therapeutic results in such conditions as severe obsessional neu-roses or depressions, and we are still puzzled by the riddle which the schizo-phrenias present. But we abound in theoretical diversities and adversities, and the historian, the politician, the sociologist — not to mention the lady at the dinner table, the **free-lancing intellectual, or the psycho-**somatologist — all claim psychoanalysis as a basic set of premises for many of their respective preferred beliefs. Even Hitler, who had burned Freud's books and wanted to abolish psychoanalysis as a purely Jewish science, reverted in one

329

of his speeches to psychoanalytic free-lancing; he tried to explain why the Jews and the democracies were so aggressively proud of themselves, and he pointed out their unconscious sense of inferiority and their overcompensatory social and historical ebulience.

But psychoanalysis — as it stood on the foundation of the Freudian method and principles — remained strictly scientific: that is to say, objective, cool, rational, un-moralistic, non-political, equally indifferent toward and equally curious about social passions and political upheavals. Wars made one, even a psychoanalyst of course, sad. But it appeared to a psychoanalyst more interesting to find out the psychological dynamics which are set into play when men kill each other in droves and in a well-organized way, than to discuss whether wars in general, or some special wars, are right or wrong. As a person, a psychoanalyst is not at all immune to the torment of such inner queries, but as a psychoanalyst he had to remain Olympian and care not much about the immediate sources of wars, revolutions, or economic strife in any form.

World War I left psychoanalysis rather intact in this respect. We came out of it discussing some of the ego reactions in war neuroses, we extended a little our understanding of traumatic neuroses. But as Freud stated to Ernest Jones: "I refuse to assume responsibility for the follies of mankind." And as Ernest Jones, reminding the writer of this *mot* of Freud's stated (in a letter to him), the sense of embarrassment which the writer felt at the thought of the plenty in which Americans lived and the want, austerity and despair of many Europeans "wants analyzing", because there must be some sort of neurotic sense of guilt in this embarrassment, and because: "I refuse (i.e. *I* too should refuse) to assume responsibility for the folly of mankind."

On the other hand, World War II, with its staggering mass murders and mass executions by the vanquished and of the vanquished, and with its aftermath of constant aggressive contentions all over the world, involved a number of psychologists, sociologists, psychiatrists and psychoanalysts in the maelstrom of social and political strife. A great eagerness arose to find a legal basis for practicing a form of *lex talionis* on the leaders of the Nazis and some of their underlings. In the search for this legal basis, rather paradoxically, a medico-psychological basis was also sought to justify formally that which our all too human hostility made us do. This was but a reoccurrence of a phenomenon which even almost five hundred years ago was condemned by many an enlightened mind. But the legal authorities of the day brand the enemies as criminals, and the medical psychologists brand them as mentally ill — ill enough to be dangerous to mankind, not ill enough to escape execution at the hands of their victorious enemies. The lawyer wants gallows erected in sufficient numbers to save the world, while the medical psychologist would make the same world an insane asylum with the psychiatrists as the sole custodians properly equipped to deal with the situation. Freud's rather casual excursion into psycho-sociological parallelism reinforced some psychoanalysts' gullible acceptance of the amateur's mass diagnoses of mass neuroses and of mass psychoses.

Psychoanalysts thus found themselves involved despite themselves as it were, and in some as yet unanalyzed way they found themselves unable to rid themselves of some sense of responsibility for the follies of mankind. This is perhaps an indirect way of saying that the psychoanalyst found himself taking his sense of social responsibility more seriously than his own science prepared him for. And, too, he seems to have been forced by the very harshness of world events to assume that what is socially evil is psychologically pathological, and that it is his, the psychoanalyst's, duty, (i.e. responsibility) to prevent the universal mental disease called war or fascism, and to cure universal psychoses in order to achieve peace and democracy on earth. All this is of course a departure from the fundamental tenets and traditions of psychoanalysis, and one wonders whether this departure denotes the failure of psychoanalysts or the failure of psychoanalysis itself. One wonders, also, whether the whole problem may not have been so badly simplified as to offer analysis only the choice between total indifference to social issues and active medico-psychological and sociological partisanship.

The problem is actually more complex. The physicist and the astronomer may remain totally indifferent to social problems — the third law of thermodynamics and the sideric parallaxes do not change with the change of political regimes or of the economic structures of society. But the level of neurotic reactions and their ideational content do change. Moreover, unlike physics or general biology, psychoanalysis assumed from the very outset a special attitude toward the individual and society. It always favored the individual, and always looked upon society with considerable suspicion and even hostility. The unchallenged postulate of psychoanalysis is that there is a constant and unavoidable conflict between the individual and society. Society, according to this almost affirmed tradition, is strictly speaking the confirmed enemy of the individual, *the* big reality that thwarts his freedom and development.

It is of no importance just now to discuss the truth or untruth of this contention; what is important at this juncture is to bear in mind that by direct assertion or unconcealed implication psychoanalytic theory emphasized the restrictive influence society has on the individual's instinctual life, and almost never failed to affirm the hostility with which individual and society treat one another. The permissive aspects of social life and the variety of sublimations which society and culture offer were not overlooked, of course, but Freud's emphasis, at the beginning at least, was on what society forces us to repress rather than on which forms of sublimation society offers us for that which we repress. Human relationships were viewed more from the point of view of relationships between individuals than between molecules of the body social. The American rather popular (but rather unfortunate) term "interpersonal relationships" reflects this fundamental aspect of psychoanalytic theory. The term "anti-social behavior" applied in cases of delinquency or neuroses, reflects the same attitude. The same is true of the less known term "social anxiety". Even the dissident groups in psychoanalysis, who undertook to prove that culture is the main source of the conflicts leading to neuroses, have unbeknown to themselves accepted the early Freudian postulate of individual versus society.

No wonder, then, that problems concerning the psychology and the essence of social responsibility seem not to have attracted the psychoanalyst's attention. Just as the term "reality" was and is being used by psychoanalysts in the broadest and most general sense, without much if any regard for the philosophical or semantic meaning of it, so is the word "social", or the term "social adjustment", used in the loosest possible sense to cover anything from group formation to unquestioning conformism.

As if further to complicate or confuse matters, the term "society" has been somewhat unwittingly used by psychoanalysts as psychologically equivalent to "group", "mass", or "crowd". Group psychology and mass psychology and social psychology became all automatically equated.

It is difficult to explain the real reasons for this confusion in psychoanalytic thought. On the other hand, since the center of psychoanalytic attention has been from the beginning the person as an individual, and the ego-psychology in a social setting rather than the social psychology of man, we became accustomed to focus our eyes on what the individual's ego loses, or on what ego forces one is compelled to give up, in a social setting, rather than to inquire what happens regardless of the possible losses or gains of the individual ego.

Even a cursory glance at the problem would convince one that there is something more to social psychology than merely a gratification of the herd instinct or the sacrifice of a part of one's self on the altar of an avaricious aggregate called society. As long as psychoanalysts continued to be thus oriented, they were unable to solve the real problems of social psychology, because the great and profound and humanistic individualism with which psychoanalysis is permeated when followed too literally and too one-sidedly was bound to defeat its own purposes and become a sort of anonymous personalism. We thus fell into the error of assuming that the ego's behavior in a group *is* group psychology — an error of greatest methodological importance, and one fraught with rather sorry consequences. For in order to understand such sociological phenomena as anti-Semitism or racial prejudice in general, or Fascism or political psychology in general, we began to claim that the individual, *clinical* manifestations of anti-Semitism and Fascism *are* the psychology of these phenomena. We began to assume that persons are anti-Semitic or Fascists, because they have certain psychopathological quirks which make them anti-Semites and Fascists. We thus became inclined to view anti-Semitism and Fascism and Communism as social phenomena, in this individual light and to think we could find out precisely what type of personality is more prone to become a Fascist or a Communist and thus formulate a *psychopathology* of these, and perhaps a *psychotherapy* and *prophylaxis*.

It is not to be denied that these contemporary as well as age-long problems have imposed themselves upon us by the disturbing impact of world-shaking events. But it is also not to be denied that this impact has derailed us scientifically and made us put our own scientific armamentarium in the services of the prevailing prejudices, in favor of the scientific technology and rapid-fire pragmatism with which our industrial civilization is afflicted. For, if it were not for this derailment we would have escaped involvement in the prevailing social strifes. Yes, as members of society we cannot help but become antagonists or protagonists of various ideologies. Yes, we could do this and remain to a great extent psychoanalysts, as we could do this and remain carpenters, chemists or physicians; we could be psychoanalysts and be or remain democrats, socialists, communists, Lutherans or Roman Catholics. But it is doubtful whether we can remain on the foundations and on the level of scientific psychoanalysis if we enter the field of social strife as active combatants under the flag of modern psychopathology, with all our individual passions duly aroused and enlisted and the panoply of our scientific terminology equally mobilized as adjuvants in the passionate struggles of wars and revolutions.

I am not advocating even by implication any sort of studied indifference in the name of an ivory tower called science, psychological or natural — we cannot become indifferent to social issues, any more than we can stop breathing and remain alive. But I do own to the inclination toward a clear-cut differentiation between ourselves as interested, civic-minded individuals and as detached psychological investigators of social phenomena. If we fail to make such a differentiation, we are bound to fail in our social responsibility by making our science serve our transitory or permanent social prejudices, and to founder in our scientific responsibility by infusing our social prejudices into our scientific work.

As a matter of fact, we ought to have the courage to admit to ourselves that Mussolini's castor oil treatment and Hitler's crematories are but facets (horrible, nauseating facets) of the universal trend of the twentieth century's socio-scientific utilitarian pragmatism, of a century in which the terms science, technology and immediate achievement seem to be semantically synonymous. It is readily admitted here that during periods of intense social crises we easily regress to the old tradition which made us call insane or crazy or evil everything that hurt us, or our side. Therefore, it is understandable how we fall into the old trap of condemning as pathological that which we consider bad; thus we tend to re-establish, quite unwittingly of course, the centuries-old equation between sickness and badness, between moral failure and mental illness.

This is what actually happened to a number of psychiatrists and psychoanalysts who would "cure" the world of anti-Semitism or Fascism, which they want to classify as "psychopathic". If we as scientific contemporaries are to pass judgment on every contemporary social crisis in terms of our civic reactions clothed in the cloak of our own scientific training, much of that which is positive, creative and permanent in our science is bound to be tarnished, as so much of the human spirit was tarnished whenever scientific knowledge was made to serve the immediate ends of social crises. This mistake is a dangerous error which little helps our civic performances (except formally) and hurts a great deal our scientific performance and capacity.

One wonders what the world would be today (and a frightfully dead world it might have been) if we had been spared the "psychopaths" of the French Revolution or the Renaissance, if we had been spared Socrates, or Julius Caesar, or Peter the Great, or Napoleon, or Leonardo da Vinci, or St. Paul. One also wonders whether we would not be on much more solid psychological and sociological ground if we said that in times of wars and revolutions it is natural for psychoanalysts, like some physicists, to become involved as individuals, as members of society in the passionate struggles raging around them. It is also natural that in the heat of these struggles we should grab at our psychoanalytic pitchforks even as a farmer would in his despair grab at his pitchfork to defend his house against an invader. But sooner or later we ought to become aware that psychoanalysis is as ineffective against social strife as the farmer's pitchfork is against a submarine gun. Pitchforks are excellent tools to pitch hay; psychoanalysis is an excellent tool for investigation of psychological phenomena. Neither can stop an invading army. Neither can solve the basic sociological issues which are involved in the mass tragedies of wars and revolutions.

As scientists we cannot exist unless we do stand *au dessus de la mêlée*. If we find ourselves unable to stand above the battle, we must give up our scientific position. There is no choice — *tertium non datur*. For there is no socialist physics or capitalist algebra, Soviet astronomy or Fascist biology; and there is no American psychoanalysis or British psychiatry. Science remains universal and cosmopolitan, as it always has been, or it is not science. Even now, when the world speaks so many different philological, economic and ideological languages, science remains unitary and universal as it was when it had but one language and one dominant faith.

That this leads us to an apparent cul-de-sac is impossible to deny. That this situation requires a clear definition of the psychoanalyst's attitude toward issues involving social responsibility is beyond any doubt. That a direct, concise and immediate answer to the question is desirable is beyond any doubt. That such an answer cannot be directly arrived at is perhaps regrettable, but true.

In search for an answer we may recall that Roger Bacon would have contributed little if anything had he not been able to rise above the battle — yet Roger Bacon was not a man of indolent temperament and of indifference to public issues of his day. He was a true "scrapper" throughout his life, in and out of prison. One also recalls the immense intellectual performance of Condorcet who, condemned to death by the French Revolution, certainly could not be considered indifferent to the public issues of his day. Yet Condorcet would contemplate the march of human progress as if he had not been in hiding and threatened with detection, apprehension and execution at any moment. Apparently there *is* a way of meeting one's civic duties or combating civic injustice and yet preserving one's scientific perspective unmarred and undimmed. The achievement of this state has its own psychology. It is admittedly given to a very few, but it is a state to be striven for by every scientific mind and particularly by psychoanalysts. What we should not do, what we should avoid in order not to cut ourselves off from this desirable state, has already been stated above. What is it that should be done in a positive way?

Let us turn for a moment to consider the attitude of psychoanalysis toward criminals. It so happens that psychoanalysts consider criminals anti-social people, and also psychologically sick people. We do not consider *criminality* but the *criminal,* and while we call his criminal acts anti-social we do not consider them psychopathological *because* they are anti-social, but because psychologically they are not normal regardless of whether the acts are anti-social or not. When a man rapes and kills a woman, or when a woman kills her child, we consider them psychologically abnormal not because the law calls them criminals, but because the capacity to love in such individuals is perverted: it is associated with death instead of life; it is not genital but anal-sadistic, primitive, archaic, infantile. Any criminal, or if you wish most criminals, *are* deeply neurotic, infantile persons who are physiologically and otherwise seemingly mature, but who psychologically proceed only in the direction of their narcissistic impulses, sadistic or sado-masochistic. Such individuals should be treated, of course, instead of punished. This attitude of psychoanalysis might be formulated as follows: The criminal is an anti-social person who acts violently against society, but society is hopelessly wrong, cruel, foolishly revengeful in its attitude toward this anti-social person; society has no right to kill its killers, but it has a duty to cure them.

This above attitude has developed in the past twenty-five years or so under the influence of psychoanalysis, and one cannot stress too much that the mere fact of the criminal's being anti-social is not considered in itself to be a psychopathological phenomenon, and that even if it were society is charged with the duty to rehabilitate the delinquent. The question of the delinquent's moral responsibility for his act is not considered here at all. As a psycho-biological phenomenon he is a sick person.

This being the case, the question of social responsibility, whether it be in the field of politics or economics, can be solved if we consider and assess in every given case the contribution society makes toward the growth and development of the individual; beyond the recognition of this contribution and reciprocating for it, the individual does not owe society anything in the strict sense of the word. Political and economic struggles, bloody wars and revolutions are not sicknesses due to some psychological failure of certain individuals. Popular unwritten conceptions of history would wish of course to place the responsibility for every social calamity on some given individual. "Roosevelt got us into this war," "Stalin is sapping the strength of European democracy," "Churchill saved England," etc. Any historian, even the one who is devoid of any psychological insight or even intuition, would know better and seek for the multiplicity of factors which make up historical crises.

The psychoanalyst cannot afford to do less. He cannot fail to consider that every historical phenomenon has its psychology, but it is not alone the psychology or the psychopathology of the individual but it is the group as a whole that determines the course of a given society on the path of history. The various psychopathies which we observe in great men and during great historical crises are resultants and not causes of these historical crises. These psychopathies do require special study, but one's sense of social responsibility can hardly be discharged by the appeal to cure the so-called mass psychopathies. Our own sense of social responsibility might reflect an unhealthy insecurity which would lead us to want society to take us under its protective wing and to allow us to live out vicariously the sense of revenge and destruction. This is the psychology of the prosecutor or the executioner and of every member of society who is proud of the society's punitive efficiency. In other words, in the thrill of playing the role of vicarious executioners, we do not identify ourselves with the victim, and whatever identification there might be, it is hostile; non-loving, non-genital. We might in this our condition invoke the highest moral principles and ethical rationalizations, but fundamentally we are on the side of sadistic narcissism. Consequently this our state does not reflect true social responsibility, and it does not serve any positive, genital purpose.

This is why it appears to me both dangerous and not in conformity with true social responsibility to label a destructive social phenomenon both bad and neurotic and then proceed to believe that we could cure the given neurosis, that is, social badness — for in this attitude we assume the role of protectors of society, and as the psychological agents thereof we would descend upon the especially designated individuals with all the weight of our psychoanalytic enlightenment in order to "socialize" or "democratize" them. As agents of society we become unable to identify ourselves with those culprits, and therefore we are bound to fail both as healers and as sociologists, because one cannot heal and cure anyone unless one can identify one's self with the sick person in question, with the culprit in question, with the guilty one in question. That is to say, one must be capable of a positive, genital, non-hating identification, and thus become the psychotherapeutic agent of the person and not of society. Even in a non-psychological field, like public health, the same principle prevails. We want to have a clean city not for esthetic reasons but in order to prevent persons from becoming sick. We want the people to be healthy not in order to protect an abstraction called community, but in order to have a lot of healthy individuals who thus will make a healthy community. The center of attention and endeavor is and remains the individual person.

Therefore psychoanalysis, which is based primarily on humanistic individualism, both methodologically and psychologically has no other way (cannot have any other way) than the way of positive identification with the given individual and enter an active request from society to help this individual. It is obvious that such problems as social and political reform might lie within the province of the psychoanalyst, but only in the light of his service to the individual. This being the case, the psychoanalyst's sense of social responsibility is in danger of being dislocated unless this service is borne in mind. He has no other way of discharging this responsibility. His sociological perspective can be broad and deep, and his performance creative and extensive only if his identification is with the person to be served and not with the disindividualized aggregate called society or history. This is not a matter of choice for a psychoanalyst; this is the essence and the inherent, postulative psychology of his specialty.

The whole problem of the sense of social responsibility thus appears much more complex than the simplified views which would see in psychoanalysis a tool for influencing large masses of people, and would thus make of psychoanalysis an added technological tool to our civilization of disindividualized, technological pragmatism.

PENOLOGY

OBSERVATIONS ON THE PSYCHOLOGICAL EFFECT OF IMPRISONMENT ON FEMALE POLITICAL PRISONERS

By Edith Jacobson, M.D.

(New York)

During the last decades increasing attention has been given to the psychology of criminals. Of psychoanalytic authors Aichhorn stands out among those who have been concerned with this subject matter. While his work has been devoted mainly to the psychoanalytic study and treatment of juvenile delinquents, Alexander and Staub have turned their interest to the investigation of adult criminals. In this connection they have discussed the fatal effect of penal servitude on the unconscious trends underlying criminal activity. Otherwise, however, not much literature has been published on the psychology of imprisonment — other than psychiatric descriptions of severe mental syndromes resulting from captivity.

My paper will deal with this problem but from a different perspective than that of Aichhorn, Alexander and Staub. It will present observations and psychoanalytic interpretations of characteristic reactions which the normal average — not criminal — personality type develops under the influence of prison confinement. Such an approach is not only of theoretical interest. It leads back to the practical problems of therapy — or re-education respectively — of criminals. In fact, it is from such investigation rather than from the observation of criminal convicts that we are able to draw conclusions on the educational effectiveness of present-time correctional methods.

This paper has definite limitations. It is not the result of systematic broad investigations but presents and interprets some impressions gained from a group of about a hundred female prisoners during two years of common life in cells and collective confinement in the state prisons of Nazi Germany.

I will begin by describing the emotional experiences of these prisoners, the changes in their personality structure during imprisonment, the emotional atmosphere of prison and the mentality of prison officials.

341

In his extensive psychological essay which is based on prison memoirs R. Sievers (1) correctly points out the difficulty of getting valid general statements about the influence of captivity because of the diversity of exogenous as well as endogenous factors. By this he means the variations arising from the specific prison conditions in different countries and times, on the one hand, and from the different mental conditions of prisoners on the other. From this point of view, the scope of this paper may even appear too limited. The whole group of prisoners who were observed had been sentenced for the same offense, that is, a political crime, and lived under the same conditions. All of them served their term in the same Nazi State Penitentiary, under supervision of the same officials, partly in cells, partly in workrooms and dormitories assigned exclusively to political prisoners. In contrast to the criminal convicts most of the prisoners who were examined according to their histories presented average normal (i.e. neither delinquent nor conspicuously neurotic) personalities.

Such material may appear to be too uniform and one-sided to give generally valid information on the psychological effects of captivity. Objections may be raised because of the exceptionally harsh prison conditions in an authoritarian country as compared with those in democratic countries. This issue must not be overrated, for the following reasons: the period of observation stretched through the first years of the Nazi regime (1935-38). Contrary to the situation in concentration camps which were under the control of the Gestapo, the conditions in City- and State-Prisons at that time were not yet essentially different from those in democratic countries. To be sure, political prisoners were treated with much more severity than criminals. They could not expect a fair trial. Favors which the criminal convicts enjoyed were refused them. Every possible restriction was imposed upon them — though not beyond the legal regulations which had not yet been abolished in these years.[1]

Other limitations with regard to the material and the peculiar situation of the observer, which was, indeed, not favorable for scientific research, were actually of great advantage to the study even though they may reduce the value and the validity of the findings in some respects. The fact that the observer shared her life with the group of prisoners offered a rare opportunity to observe first-hand and to watch the psychic reactions to prison confinement more closely than is possible under any other circumstances.

The true psychopathology of prison confinement will not be dealt with in this paper. Severe syndromes of prison psychosis ("Haftpsychose", Kretschmer (2)) which includes all kinds of neurotic and psychotic reactions to

---

[1] This, of course, does not hold true for the first questionings and cross-examinations by the Gestapo who applied all variations of mental and physical torture to wrest confessions from their victims.

captivity according to the individual disposition were not observed in this group of prisoners.

So far it has been emphasized that the prisoners subject to observation presented average normal material. Yet, certain differences and exceptions must be pointed out. The group consisted of women between twenty and sixty years of age. About 90 per cent of them came from the upper labor and lower middle class: wives or daughters of highly trained laborers and craftsmen, etc. One to two per cent of these women had a history of criminal offenses and one of them was a prostitute. About 10 per cent of the group had a higher middle-class background. Their education was that of the daughters and wives of business men, engineers, doctors, journalists. Some of them were professional women with university degrees: economists, physicians and teachers. Among this latter group there was a greater percentage of neurotic personalities — the reasons for which we will discuss later on.

THE TRAUMA OF ARREST

Prison confinement starts with a traumatic experience: arrest. According to Sievers, arrest often hits the average type of criminals "like a flash of lightning". They are apt to repress any thoughts of consequences of their action, much more so than "professional" criminals or political prisoners do. Most political prisoners observed here had indeed visualized the possibility of an arrest. Yet the severity of the penalty, its consequences for the prisoner and his whole family were rarely anticipated.

Apparently, in some prisoners the dangerous situation preceding the arrest had not increased their inner defense against anxiety. In others the strain of underground political activity had mobilized infantile anxieties which were fused with fully justified realistic fears. Outstanding among all types of individual defense mechanisms which were thus acquired, was the frequent reaction of fearless levity. It originated in a protective magic fantasy of omnipotence: "Nothing can possibly happen to *me*" — the type frequently found among war heroes, racing motorists, air pilots, etc. In neurotic persons — with severe unconscious hostility and corresponding guilt-feelings — the tendency to do careless over-heroic work could easily lead to their arrest. When this finally happened it would take those persons — consciously at least — by surprise and frequently provoked panic reactions.

Here is an example:

A very neurotic student, a girl with a severe moral masochism whom I had observed before her arrest had been sent abroad by her political friends when her arrest was imminent. She managed to convince her friends abroad that she was not endangered. Consequently, she went back into the danger zone as a courier and was taken into custody at the frontier. Here she immediately committed suicide.

Clear anticipation of the consequences of illegal activity had not protected any of the prisoners from the tremendous trauma of arrest which Sievers compares with a catastrophe in nature or a sudden bankruptcy. He describes correctly the initial state of "helpless stupefaction" with "blurred feeling and thinking," "anxiety and restlessness" and its "transition to depression".

These symptoms are the outcome of a complicated psychological process which will be analyzed according to impressions gained by questioning prisoners. In the foreground stands the sudden violent attack on the narcissistic safeguards of the captive whose personality is threatened by the executive power of the state. Associated with this severe shock is the devastating effect of the sudden isolation from the object world, particularly if the prisoner is immediately put in solitary confinement.

The dreadful change of surroundings, the restriction of normal everyday activity and the severing of all object relations mobilize the hostile instinctual powers from within. Unexpectedly struck, the ego of the prisoner has to face a fight on two fronts: against the outside as well as against his own inside world. The throttling of any normal discharge of libido and aggression just when it is most urgently needed necessarily leads to a fatal blocking of libido. Under such circumstances the ego is prone to collapse. With the impact of this crushing blow at its structure which destroys its essential defenses, the weakened ego succumbs to the assault of intruding instinctual drives. Thus we observe a transient inundation of the ego by wild impulses and eventually a paralysis of its functions, not unlike the outbreak of a psychosis. This brings about that half-waking state of stupefaction and confusion with fidgety restlessness, haunting thoughts, violent anxiety attacks and desperate revolts. The stupor of the ego can even lead to temporary loss of the sense of time and locality. Next the prisoner tries hard to collect his thoughts in order to prepare himself for the all-important interrogations. For some time he may manage to get a clear picture of the situation and to prepare a clever and plausible statement. Then he may relapse into a chaotic jumble of feelings, succumbing to a quickly changing series of images (like the projection of a motion picture or of a rigid and obsessionally recurring succession of thoughts). In psychoanalytic terms, the "secondary process" (Freud) is to a large extent substituted by the "primary process". During questioning the prisoner is exposed to a realistic frontal attack which he is better able to withstand than his internal dangers. Hence the stupor often recedes during the questioning by virtue of the ego's gigantic effort in its struggle to recover its functions. Previously stable personalities may temporarily even strengthen their ego functions when being cross-examined. They may make their statements with cold logical detachment and with complete repression of affects — in the manner of obsessional defense mechanisms.

It was a striking fact confirmed from many sides that female prisoners faced cross-examination more easily than men. By means of their specific feminine structure they seemed to be more capable of dealing with the male Gestapo officials. Even when they were beaten they behaved more cleverly and cunningly and were mentally more stable than male prisoners who were frequently overwhelmed by infantile fears of father figures (castration fear) when attacked by their own sex.

Far reaching changes in the libidinous structure accompany the breakdown of the ego. These are the result of the sudden damming up of the libido, a damming up caused by the enforced separation from former surroundings and the utter loneliness in which the prisoner is submerged. All at once, quite unexpectedly, he sees himself deserted by the whole world, a small helpless child, clinging to what is left of his ego in order to escape from the threatening primitive reactions. Partial or extended regression from the adult to the early infantile stage of instinctual development inevitably takes place. Temporary disintegration of the genital organization and a breaking through of anal and particularly oral impulses occur in all prisoners during the first days in prison. This finds expression in intestinal disturbances, such as anorexia, nausea, vomiting, disgust at the sight of food, diarrheas or constipation. The sudden change of diet and the deprivation of smoking naturally help to bring about these symptoms. The degrading treatment, certain measures like the taking away of personal belongings, especially glasses, aggravate the anxiety and promote regressive processes. The fear of being left alone and helpless during a great calamity, of losing precious, irreplaceable years revives unconscious childhood anxieties: castration fear and the earliest infantile fear of loss of the first love object, the mother. There were women who on their first day of captivity would cry incessantly for their mothers, others who would moan for their deserted children, frequently in transparent unconscious reversion of their own infantile wish for protection. Bjerre (3) reports on the same experiences. He writes about a murderess:

". . . And so she clung with desperate strength to her mother and tried to hide with her and to forget about herself just like a small child frightened by something incomprehensively hostile and powerful."

The "shock syndromes" (Sievers), i.e., explosive actions, such as panicky attempts to escape or blind active resistance happened rarely among this group of prisoners. One rather neurotic professional woman whose arrest was due to particular carelessness, jumped out of the fourth floor window when facing the entering Gestapo. She sustained only a minor spine injury.

Closer investigation showed a severe guilt-conflict with regard to her schizophrenic brother. Her action was a masochistic identification with him who had tried to jump out of the window. He was held back by her but he died from his illness soon after.

Two other prisoners — chronic depressive personalities who had occasionally felt suicidal impulses before imprisonment — tried to cut their wrists during the first week of captivity. Both rightly anticipated long terms of four to five years and, when arrested, had been exposed to unusually grave traumas. What was characteristic was that their suicidal attempts occurred soon after arrest. According to Baer (4), thirty-five out of seventy-eight suicides in prison happen during the first fortnight after arrest.

After some hours or days the chaotic state of mind changes to one of desperation, and, later on, to a quieter depression in the course of which the personality recuperates and gets reorganized to some extent. Naturally, the prisoner regains his composure more quickly if he is brought together with fellow-sufferers with whom he can talk about mutual experiences. But even when in solitary confinement, he gradually adjusts mentally to his new situation.

IMPRISONMENT PENDING TRIAL

Most of the political prisoners spent the first days or weeks after arrest in the tiny cells of the police-prison, with rare and short recreation periods, on an exceedingly bad diet, and under pressure of continual cross-examinations. Later on, they were moved to the State Prison where the conditions were better.

They lived in fairly spacious cells. Except for serious offenders they were permitted to get additional food, to see visitors, to talk with their lawyers, to write and receive letters and to do manual or intellectual work.

Of all the privations, lack of correspondence seemed to be the worst. Prisoners live on letters which are their bridge to the outside world, even more than personal visits, which are too upsetting. Especially in the penitentiary, which establishes firm identifications among the prisoners, letters are common property: they are exchanged and enjoyed together.

The period spent in the State Prison up to the trial may — schematically speaking — be subdivided into two emotional stages: the phase of adjustment to the prison routine and to the ever recurring interrogations and the phase of preparation for the trial. During the first stage of imprisonment pending trial the prisoners still suffer from the consequences of the shock caused by their arrest. Even those who have never had a manifest neurosis are haunted by frightening fantasies which may develop into phobias and obsessional symptoms. Temporary claustrophobia, fear of fire, compulsive brooding and similar transitory neurotic conditions were generally observed. Almost all prisoners showed a readiness to react to any kind of excitation with anxiety or anxiety equivalents, such as weariness, sleeplessness, irritability and disturbances of the vegetative nervous system. A conspicuous general symptom of prisoners is their forgetfulness with respect to names, streets and persons. Its deeper psychological root is probably the desire of concealing damaging facts; the intention to suppress the latter pushes such data into repression along with other irrelevant knowledge.

What stands out among the pathological methods of adjustment to the changed condition of life is the tendency to mental flight reactions. Some women spoke of experiences which must be defined as phenomena of depersonalization. Even after their ego had recovered its normal functions, they felt occasionally "like not being themselves", like "dreaming". One prisoner used to touch her body when she would suddenly wake up frightened in the middle of the night. She would feel "as if her body did not belong to her" and "as if her face were pulpy". She remembered having had such sensations in her childhood when she had run high temperatures.

Such conditions are obviously reactions of the threatened ego which defends itself by denying the reality of the situation: "It cannot be true that such awful things are happening *to me*. I refuse to believe it."

As long as the questioning lasts and later, for instance, when new damaging evidence turns up, or when reading the charge, the prisoner is exposed to renewed experiences of shock. During these days severe anxiety attacks will occur again. In this connection the frequent endocrine disturbances of prisoners must be mentioned. Observation shows definitely that they are not physical consequences of captivity (diet, etc.) but psychosomatic phenomena.

All the prisoners who were investigated had developed functional endocrine disturbances in varying degrees and of different types. They were promoted by excitement of the sympathetic nervous system and originated in severe shock experiences of the first period of imprisonment. In some prisoners the vegetative syndromes (clammy hands, urticaria, quickened pulse rate and respiration) developed after some weeks of confinement in consequence of repeated experiences of shock. In any case, vegetative symptoms would usually precede the endocrine disturbances. The latter are less conspicuous in male prisoners than in women whose menstrual cycle is regularly affected by imprisonment. Some prisoners showed thyrotoxic symptoms, and there was one case of a severe disturbance of the whole endocrine system. Although precise studies could not be made, it was found that in many women menstruation would not occur during quieter periods. After upsetting experiences, such as cross-examinations, or talks with the lawyer, menstruation would often occur unexpectedly, while after the sentence the regular cycle would be re-established if the term was not too severe. In many prisoners with long terms, menstruation would stop completely — possibly under the additional influence of lack of vitamins. Frequently, however, menstruation would come back shortly before their release which left no doubt about the psychogenetic origin of their disturbance. The correlations between the types of menstrual disturbances and the emotional reactions to captivity — in particular anxiety and defense against it — are striking. As soon as acute anxiety flares up as a result of shocks intense bleeding may start suddenly. In periods of warded-off anxiety and quiet depression, menstruation may stop. If the sentence brings relief from anxiety or the release is imminent the period recurs. If a long severe term is given the menstrual cycle may be interrupted or very irregular for years, particularly in chronically depressed persons.

One of the prisoners presented an especially interesting psychosomatic problem. This is her history:

She was just menstruating when she was arrested. The period stopped immediately. The next day she developed an acute *acne vulgaris*. It got worse and could not be cured for nearly two years. Her menstrual period did not come back although she was treated at once with hormone injections and X-ray by a physician interested in psychosomatic medicine. When questioned by the author, the girl said that she had been extremely fearful that the Gestapo might find out certain facts which would severely involve other persons. Since then she could not get rid of this fear, although the investigation of her case had long been completed. She suffered from nightmares that "everything would come out" which used to disturb the whole dormitory.

Since the prisoner could not be studied thoroughly, the author could only make conjectures as to the unconscious background of the girl's illness. The shock of arrest had evidently mobilized specific infantile conflicts. It seemed that her fears centered around the temptation to betray her comrades and a corresponding need for punishment.

The girl suffered excessively from her facial acne and was preoccupied by it. She made it worse and called attention to it by touching and picking her face incessantly. Her masochistic exhibitionism suggested that unconscious wishes to confess and betray and to be punished as well as deep exhibitionistic tendencies may have contributed to causing amenorrhea and to the formation of the facial skin disease (erythrophobia).

The weeks preceding the trial can be looked upon as a phase of tormenting uncertainty and chronic tension, because the prisoner expects the charge and wonders about the extent of damaging evidence against him. After the first shock of the charge is over and the date of the trial is set, he enjoys a short period of relief, even if he anticipates a hard sentence. When this phase is over, the prisoner becomes wholly absorbed in feelings and thoughts concerning the procedure of the trial and its outcome. While his anxieties and other neurotic symptoms of the first period after arrest are transitory and easily reversible, his emotional condition now gives evidence of increasing conflicts within the ego. In the foreground is his fight against severe guilt-feelings, which are mobilized by anticipation and fears of the impending punishment. The prisoner is mentally very unsteady and restless and prone to sudden changes in temper. Fits of desperate depression or meek resignation give way to severe irritability and aggressive outbursts. They may be followed by periods of happy confidence and optimism which is even less in keeping with reality. When depressed, the prisoner is tormented by inner arguments. He worries about the consequences and broods over the sense or senselessness of his deed. He furiously accuses those whom he regards responsible for his captivity or he suffers from harassing guilt feelings in view of the unhappiness he has brought onto himself, his relatives and friends. Invariably, these self-accusations are worst with respect to those friends or members of the family to whom relations have always been ambivalent.

Thus one prisoner could not free herself for years from self-reproaches toward her mother with whom she had had a complicated relationship while she never felt guilty toward her husband, with whom she had lived very happily.

With most political prisoners the feeling of serving a cause helped to relieve guilt feelings, to restore their self-esteem and to regain a collected, composed and courageous front. A seriously repentant attitude naturally cannot be expected from political prisoners. But even with criminals it is very rare according to Sievers. Among his forty-five life histories, only one, Wilde (5) says: "Whatever dreadful things the world may have done to me, what I have done to myself is far worse."

As far as the inner relation to the deed and its consequences are concerned differences were found between those political prisoners who were mentally healthy and those relatively few who had been inspired to their illegal activities by neurotic motives. The differences in the attitudes toward the political crime appeared to be definitely related to the social background of the prisoners. To make such general comparisons means an intrusion into the field of mass psychology, the methods of which should not be applied to such a small group. In nevertheless venturing a rough typological confrontation, I am fully conscious of its superficiality.

On the whole, neurotic illnesses may be equally distributed among all social classes. Among these political prisoners, as mentioned before, middle class and intellectual women were more often neurotic than those from the laboring classes. The political convictions of the latter were mostly rooted in political family tradition. They regarded their illegal activity as socially necessary and imprisonment as unavoidable under this regime, and as a step toward future victory. Through identification with their whole class, with its past and its future, they obviously accepted and enjoyed the political fight as an incentive and felt pride in being champions of the future. Their pugnacious attitude was in accordance with traditional ethical codes. As the aggressive components of infantile origin were integrated in their personality, their expansive alloplastic ego seemed better protected from guilt-feelings and masochistic mechanisms. This enabled them to bear their fate without complaints, exaggerated self-accusations, self-pity or indulgence in suffering.

A number of prisoners with a higher social background had definitely been driven into political activity by the influence of undigested infantile conflicts. Even though most of them were highly intelligent and had developed excellent valid rationalizations, their *Weltanschauung* did not equip their ego with sufficient strength for such traumatic situations. Analysis of individual cases does not interest us here and was not possible for obvious reasons. On the whole it appeared that childhood rebellion was displaced to a private individualistic revolt against the ruling regime, which was released in political activity without a sufficiently stable group identificaton. As far as could be investigated, these types belonged to the moral masochistic type of character. They consciously tried to identify themselves with the suppressed part of the population in its fight against the state, but unconsciously they wanted to share its sufferings as their conscience caused them to side with the "humiliated and offended". These prisoners had an inclination toward political martyrdom and enjoyed their sacrifices in humble submissiveness or shone in the glamor of political importance. Others, in varying mental phases, stood up against their fate or against their own convictions. Suddenly they became doubtful, overcritical, or severely depressed, believed their sacrifice to be senseless and were ready to desert their past ideals. They usually recovered from this neurotic unsteadiness during their term as convicts under the influence of confinement and of the collective attitude of their fellow prisoners.

After the dreaded trial, the anxious tension under which the prisoners had spent their time, relaxed. Many of them — even after receiving a heavy sentence — returned from the court in a gay mood. The sudden lifting of an emotional load: the fear of the sentence — and the certainty of a definite fate — bring about a feeling of tremendous relief. "Now it has happened, nothing worse can come after this." This often leads to a short hypomanic state (such as is sometimes felt immediately after the loss of a loved one) which is usually sustained during the transfer to the penitentiary. Many prisoners relate how "amusing and gay" their trip, lasting for days, had been and how, laughing and joking, they had exchanged previous prison adventures. The beginning of the sentence puts an end to this euphoric state fairly quickly.

PSYCHOLOGY OF PRISON OFFICIALS

To gain insight into the practice of correctional methods and their psychological effects on convicts it is not enough to study only the external conditions in penitentiaries. One must know the emotional atmosphere in these institutions as well as the psychological background of the person in whose power the culprits are placed.

It is beyond the scope of this article to delineate the problems of correctional methods. This would require the discussion of too many social issues. However, detached observation of the changes of personality and mentality effected by convict institutions will lead to a judgment of modern correctional methods, from a psychoanalytic point of view. This will be summed up and discussed at the end of the paper. At present, I shall restrict myself to preliminary statements.

There are today far-reaching theoretical differences of opinion regarding the sense of prison detention and the function of punishment. In some countries the theory of punishment is that it serves primarily as a deterrent; in others it is considered and used chiefly as a corrective method. In these institutions, not only in different countries but even in one country, the uses of punishment vary to an astonishing degree. But it is not really important whether the infliction of punishment in one country is, by principle, more lenient than that of another country, one institution more modern and generous than another, and one warden more humane than another. The psychological attitudes toward the convict as well as the views on the sense and aim of punishment are to most prison officials still dependent on traditional social conceptions and are clouded by affective resistances. Therefore, the treatment of convicts seems to be more or less the same in practically all these institutions.

This attitude is reflected in the personal traits and behavior of an average official employed in such institutions. The selection of these people and their training in most countries is still less than adequate. The wardens of State prisons in different countries usually have a higher social and professional background. The lower officials: stewarts, captains and guards, are members of the lower middle class and start their practical work unprepared and untrained.

These lower officials — especially the captains and guards — decide the policy followed in these institutions. The warden in most countries is an administrative official who runs the prison according to the state's regulations though in a rather independent way. He is also the arbiter of all offenses against house-regulations and responsible for prison procedures. The warden may rule, according to his personality and former occupation, in a strictly disciplinary or a more humane manner, but he will rarely discharge lower officials because of rude behavior toward the prisoners. Thus it is the guards who, as executives, actually apply the corrective measures. In many prisons it is they who make the final decisions of putting the prisoners into cells or into collective confinement and of assigning them to rooms and occupations. They have to maintain discipline. They provide the information upon which disciplinary punishment is meted out. They can chicane or favor the prisoners, shout at them or treat them kindly. This makes clear the infantile situation in which the prisoner is placed.

What are the psychological characteristics of these guards, their attitudes toward their job and toward the prisoners? Of course, they can be described only from impressions gained by very limited experiences in one particular German State Penitentiary. At first glance, the average guard seemed to be dominated by the same fundamental concept that the — often caricatured — teacher of former times had about naughty school children. The convicts deserve punishment for having done what is forbidden to civilized adults. They are a danger to society that must be fought and kept down. These concepts imply that the guards fear and therefore hate the convict. On closer observation, however, their attitude appeared to be much more complex. Their singular relation to the prisoner seemed based on a strange ambivalence which came to the fore especially toward the criminals. The infantile impulsiveness of the delinquent apparently shakes the defenses of repression in the official, stirs up his own primitive, antisocial tendencies and thus means a dangerous, though unconsciously longed for temptation. That is why this ambivalence was less often found in young, happily married officials than with the older, unmarried and unsatisfied ones. Among the latter there were many "old-maid" types: definitely crotchety and odd characters who gratified in this job their own warped instinctual desires. These women not only vented an unbelievably refined sadism against the prisoners; they were also inclined to establish strange personal homosexually tinged relations with the consciously despised convicts particularly with those who had lived in jail for many years. Such relations offered a partial sharing in the forbidden instinct gratifications in which the prisoners presumably indulge without restraint. Such identification — forbidden by their moral codes — naturally provoke guilt-feelings of which they can rid themselves again by the legitimate rude treatment of the prisoner. Thus at times there existed an incredibly intimate tone between the guards and certain criminals while, on other occasions, they would discipline those same people more than the other convicts.[2]

There was sufficient occasion in the rooms of the political convicts to study these complicated human relations. The captain was notorious throughout all the state jails as an obsessive and sadistic person with an irritating talking compulsion. She showed her ambivalence by a grotesque attitude toward the convicts. By her tyranny she drove them to the verge of despair, at the same time treating them as "children in her care" and interceding obstinately for them if she believed them unjustly treated by others. Her attitude — that of a domineering tyrannic mother — had become a definite part of her personality through her many years of work.

The attitude of most officials toward the "politicals" was less ambivalent than toward criminal offenders: either very hostile or kind, according to their political opinions. No such complex latent homosexual relations could be built up because of the lack of the above described instinctual identification.

---

[2] Probably the hatred of most people against criminals is partly induced by such components. They have a fundamental influence on the attitude of society toward offenders and the defensive measures taken against them.

For these reasons the best object for study were the relations of the guards to a woman who was serving a life-term for having killed her husband. So far she had spent fifteen years in jail and was put with the political prisoners as a kind of supervisor and spy. She was a completely asocial person, with shallow affects. Some of the officials were on amazingly familiar terms with her. They regarded her as a part of the jail inventory, used for pumping and denouncing other prisoners, as a scapegoat for their aggression or for intimate talk if it happened to be convenient. A very rude official — herself on a rather low human level — would, for instance, chat with her in whispers about her occasional "adventures" in the city, at one moment, and shout at her without proper cause a little while later.

Apparently, many years of association with convicts had a strong influence on the sexual and personality structure of the officials. Most conspicuous were the paranoid traits which developed in most guards in the course of time.

As a matter of fact, the prison officials were continuously deceived by the convicts who tried in every way to procure some little pleasures for themselves and to break the rigid discipline. But the small crimes of the convicts against regulations — secret talking, smuggling of food or letters — were out of proportion to the amount of suspicion and indignation shown by the officials. They felt persecuted by the convicts, believed unconditionally any information against them and were oblivious to individual differences among prisoners.

The strange emotional relations of the officials to the prisoners as well as their paranoid attitude signified an increase of the homosexual component of their sexual organization. It was further proved by their distrust on this point. Naturally, homosexual relations play a big part with criminal convicts. But the prison officials were on the lookout for hidden homosexual attachments behind any kind word exchanged by the prisoners.

A seriously sick woman was brought into the hospital almost unconscious. There she was received affectionately by a former cell mate, a woman of over fifty years with a severe heart disease. The accompanying guard shouted: "So that's why you wanted to come here! You wanted to make love to her, that would suit you well!" When this scene was brought to the attention of the authorities with reference to the age and the illness of the patient, the captain said: "I daresay the guard is right, the old ones are always worst." This is a typical example.

Ambivalence, sadistic and paranoid manifestations and repressed homosexual traits were common among most officials in spite of the variations in their individual characters. It is not astonishing that more or less striking obsessional mechanisms accompanied them. Their development was greatly favored by the contradictory educational system of cleanliness and order in the institutions.

The cells and big rooms had to be kept according to certain traditional procedures. The blankets had to be laid exactly straight, the towels had to be smoothed out, folded and hung only on certain hooks. The tin covers of pails, the bowls and buckets had to be polished till they shone. But only the upper part of the body was allowed to be washed. Complete undressing was punished. The weekly shower only lasted a few minutes. Soap was scarce, rooms and cells were swarming with bed bugs. And nothing whatever was done about it. The state of sanitation was unbearable. There was no drainage system. One toilet with two seats was provided for one hundred women. The connecting doors to the dormitory were always kept open. The toilet pails had to be emptied and cleaned by the prisoners from time to time. The women had to wait their turn for using the toilet. Consequently most of them were suffering from disturbances of their excretory functions. These unhygienic rules were maintained despite repeated protests.

It must be admitted that this very overcrowded jail cannot be compared with other modern institutions of pre-Hitler Germany or of this country. Yet, in this as in other prisons, the so-called cleanliness consisted mainly of the enforcement of obsessional measures. While the political prisoners energetically fought against the filth in their rooms the criminals used it as an excellent way of gratifying their infantile, anal trends, under the cover of apparent tidiness. The officials were so infected by the dirty as well as obsessional habits of the jail that they "educated" the prisoners with much zeal in this direction. Of course, homosexuality, untidiness, obsessional behavior and aggressiveness of guards and convicts influenced and provoked each other in chain reactions. In the rooms of the criminals wild quarrels and even fist-fights among themselves and with officials occurred frequently.[3]

PENAL SERVITUDE

The external circumstances and rules of the penitentiary in which this group of convicts served their term were rather hard. The greater part of them lived in collective confinement, during the day in the large workshops, at night in overcrowded dormitories. Very young prisoners or those with long terms and, in particular, intellectuals were put in solitary cells, mostly for two to three years. Only those sentenced for high-treason had to stay in cells for their whole term.

Evening conversations were strictly forbidden. During work in the daytime talking was not allowed — only whispering in case of emergency. The possibility of conversation was thus rather restricted, limited to whispers

---

[3] In giving this description of the character traits and attitudes of the average official we must also point out the rare exceptions. In the City Prison more often than in the State Penitentiary there were employees who were humane and helpful, who tried to understand the offenders and to establish a relationship with them without overstepping the permissible limits. One captain, for instance, repeatedly started conversation with the author in order to get information on the psychology of criminals. The librarian of the City Prison was particularly intelligent and refined. Her intellectual and ethical standards were far above those of her colleagues. In many talks she showed remarkable insight into the problems of her profession.

during a recreation time of less than half an hour, and to a few hasty words on the toilet or at bed-time. Recreational evening gatherings and similar mitigations of punishment had been abolished by the new regime. Other favors, such as additional food or longer recreation time were granted to political prisoners only in hospitals.

During the ten hours of work most convicts were kept busy "picking oakum" (the splitting and twining of old rope). Some of them did knitting, sewing, darning and embroidering. In summer, a group of prisoners was allowed to do agricultural work on a farm, which was very desirable, in spite of the hard work.

In his paper, Sievers treats collective confinement and confinement in cells separately. In certain respects, the psychological effects of life in the prison community are different indeed from those of solitary confinement. The latter favors introversion. It invites the prisoner to escape into the world of fantasy but it may also stimulate introspection, self-investigation and contemplation. Collective confinement supports extroversion. It helps to relieve inner tensions by outside actions and reactions toward fellow-prisoners and authorities. On the other hand, continuous life with other convicts in vulgar, dull and brutal surroundings and overcrowded rooms causes permanent tension and irritation. Since delinquents are easily influenced by each other, community life is apt to lower rather than raise the social and cultural level of the group.

With political offenders the emotional and intellectual atmosphere in the community is far more favorable. Bound by a common cause, all the prisoners were eager to improve their ethical and intellectual standards, to preserve and develop their spiritual life and to develop as many interests as possible. Hence they would read good books in turns, exchange opinions in unwatched moments, or discuss various subjects of common interest. In this respect, the inhabitants of cells were rather at a disadvantage though they tried to keep in touch with each other by the well-known methods — smuggling letters, knocking and talking during recreation time. They even managed common discussions. Due to the lack of object-relations, however, regression to an infantile emotional level and neurotic reactions occurred sooner and went deeper in the isolated convicts than with the average prisoner living in the community. As will be described below, they suffered from more frequent and serious depressions or found refuge in daydreams and fantastic illusions. Yet some prisoners stood solitary confinement much better than being constantly with fellow-sufferers who exhausted and irritated them. These latter persons escaped from the troubles and difficulties of captivity by withdrawing their interest from an unpleasant outside world to the extent that the maintaining of object-relations only meant an increased mental effort.

Other more extroverted women stood collective confinement very well
but were overcome by serious depressions if put into solitary confinement.
Excepting these individual variations, the psychological effects of the two
forms of captivity as observed in this group were not essentially different,
though perhaps more definite and traceable in solitary confinement.

Next a picture will be given of the changes in the personality structure
brought about by long-term confinement in this group of convicts. During
the long months of imprisonment pending trial most of the prisoners developed a conspicuous and characteristic psychological attitude which became
more definite during penal servitude.

This abnormal state will be made plainer by giving excerpts of letters
written by political convicts. It is noteworthy that the writers selected had
all passed the age of thirty and were intelligent, observant and articulate
about their inner experiences.

"I could write a book about the emotional changes brought about by
living in jail. Small happenings become events, are exciting, childish habits
reappear, incited by the dependence which we are made to feel with every
step. The mind turns inward during those lonely months. Then again comes
a longing, a compulsion almost to cling to the outer world, to live with others
and for others."

This letter reflects the struggle between the dangerous desire to escape
from the outside unhappiness into the inside world and the craving for contact with the outside world. It describes the change of values: Little incidents become events, big ones become matter of course. The writer also
perceives the danger of giving way to the outside situation which favors
dependent attitudes by reviving infantile reactions.

"When I come out — the most improbable hopes are connected with
these magic words. Here we fall into a mad illusionism . . ."

And in another letter:

"I cannot see beyond the walls anymore."

On one side fabulous fantasies of the future, on the other desperate
resignation!

"Time simply flies. I remind you of Thomas Mann's Magic Mountain
which I read again. What he says on the perception of time in the sanitarium I experience here under similar circumstances."

Actually the prisoners lose any conception of time. The months or years
which they spend in prison seem to them like short weeks or then again like
eternity — as always happens when nothing or too much occurs.

". . . Easter, — it was a quiet festival. Even here these days are different
from others. From the early morning on we listen to songs and to sounds of
the organ — spiritual food — and we get a treat: coffee and cake — for the
stomach."

This letter indicates an increased pleasure in music, a readiness to react
intensely to religious celebrations.

"... Thus many a thought ripens, something is always going on inside. I have been reading many poems. Schiller's moral pathos has impressed me again very much. I have read whole volumes of poetry, just now Droste! Strange, from what resources this person whose life was outwardly completely uneventful must have been drawing."

"... As I have no more knitting to do, and do not care for reading just now, nor want to brood over my case all the time, I am writing poetry incessantly. I have even come across a little pamphlet on the rules of verse and am trying to keep to strictly classical forms."

These excerpts show the deepened relation to poetry, the wish for poetical self-expression and the turning to poets with "ethos", such as Schiller.

In another letter the writer seems astonished and amused at her own craving for writing poetry:

"... It has given me strange satisfaction to write poetry here. It is a substitute for talking to others or keeping a diary which would rather be too sentimental and therefore embarrassing. But shaping poems gives a feeling of distance. — Last year, at this time, life was more tempting, wasn't it? Though to me life does not seem anyhow more than a soap-bubble which may burst at any time — today, tomorrow — what does it matter. ..."

As life affords the writer too little gratification she tries to devaluate it in order to bear it more easily — the origin of many ideologies hostile to life. Letters of other prisoners show similar philosophical, world-weary tendencies. One of them writes, for instance:

"... I do not think I am made for a life in a nunnery. You may open all inner wells, — in the long run they end in the stream of the old philosophical view: All is in vain. The whole of life is a lot of muck and is that worth so much effort?"

Contrary to the previous letters, the following remarks reveal the intense desire for logical thinking and intellectual activities.

"... By training my thoughts I manage to escape imbecility. .... My intellect does not sink into twilight but is always nice and active and that is very important. My craving for work is tremendous! ... I was not capable of doing any reading or writing today. But I have done a good bit of work again this week."

And now some examples of the huge part which observation and enjoyment of nature play with the convicts:

"... Even here there are occasions for secret delight in nature. Through a nearly transparent part of the window we have a lovely view, like a cutting from a picture: the wide hilly country, meadows with flowers, fruit trees, fields, and the mountains in the background. ... Outside the hospital there is a sweet little garden with flowers in all colors and two beautiful acacias which are just now in full blossom. They are sending waves of sweet scent into our poorly aired rooms. Those are the pleasures of our life here. ..."

The following remarks are interesting because they show a phenomenon described by Anna Freud (6).

". . . The capacity of feeling with those who are close to us is very great. The knowledge that they are enjoying life thoroughly out there has a happy influence on our mood. . . ."

The prisoners manage to form altruistic identifications with the happiness of their friends who live in freedom.

In conclusion I quote a few lines which are to give us the key to a deeper understanding of the letters:

". . . Memories and events from my teens come to the fore when you tried to teach me the principles of ancient stoicism. Turn over some time the pages of my autograph book which I kept in those days, and read the sayings by Goethe with which you tried to impress me. . . ."

The teens — the forty-year-old writer expresses what the contents and the emotional quality of all the letters quoted may have revealed already: in the course of their captivity the prisoners seem to return to the phase of adolescence. From a balanced maturity they sink back into the emotional turmoil of that earlier developmental stage.

Sievers described in his paper — without interpretation — the same symptoms which are reflected in these letters: oversensitivity and irritability, intensification and differentiation of emotional and intellectual life, tendency to daydreaming, but also to logical thinking, sharpening of all senses, susceptibility to the beauty of nature, readiness for religious-ecstatic, for esthetic and intellectual experiences and craving for creative work. The latter manifestations are particularly strong with prisoners in solitary confinement. The whole series of phenomena is characteristic of adolescents. As in them, we find in prisoners the intensity and fluctuation of affects from highest elation to the depths of despair, the tendency to uncontrollable fits of laughter or weeping, to outbursts of rage or romantic sentiments. Like adolescent youngsters, the convicts found satisfaction in fantastic daydreams. They suffered from fits of *Weltschmerz* and indulged in overwhelming admiration of nature. Tears were shed about a cloud, a star, a bird's nest. Natural phenomena were watched with sharpened senses. When one group of convicts was taken out for agricultural work for the first time everyone of them wept when they drove through rows of fruit trees in blossom — all of them formerly well-controlled, unsentimental, mature women. The sound of the organ coming from the church would move these usually unreligious persons to tears. Sievers reports on the frequency of religious ecstasy and humble return to God during captivity (Verlaine, Wilde, Pellico) — that this must stem from a sexual source was also apparent to him. Even the political prisoners most of whom had stuck to a materialistic *Weltanschauung* frequently revealed in discussions on religious and philosophical questions a metaphysical longing of which they were often quite unaware.

As in adolescence, nearly all prisoners felt the urge to artistic work, especially to writing poetry. In the cells, where no games were allowed on Sundays, "writing poetry" became quite a hobby with the political prisoners. The contents of the serious or humorous rhymes referred mostly to events of prison life (see Wilde, *Ballad of Reading Gaol* (7)) or to the ideals for which the prisoners were fighting and suffering, though they might also be on general subjects. Naturally part of them were creations of a more mature ego but all had an intense subjectivism and a pathos typical of adolescent productions.

On the other hand, there was a reaction drive toward strenuous physical and exacting intellectual work, a tense effort to train body and mind, much stronger than it had been in freedom. Some of the prisoners went through a systematic study of natural science or geography, history or languages, as far as they could obtain the necessary material for it during their recreation periods. Others read the classics with much attention and learned them by heart though they had never before felt any preference for these poets.

Some women, especially the younger ones, experienced intense inner struggles — such as characterize the adolescent stage, which brought about radical changes in their personalities.

A very intelligent girl of twenty-five had been brought up by her adored stepfather, a radical union man, on strictly communistic ideas, and had spent some years in Russia. In solitary confinement, partly under the influence of propagandistic Nazi literature, her never before questioned political principles broke down. Torn by tormenting inner arguments she passed through an exhausting emotional crisis. During months of high tension she then tried to approach her problem critically and built up her *Weltanschauung* again bit by bit until it stood more firmly and safely than before.

This example shows the truly constructive development which prison confinement may set in motion in strong and intelligent individuals with a capacity for sublimation. The process mostly starts with regression of the mature ego into a state of adolescent dissolution. With the help of richer resources than had been at disposal at that earlier stage a new, more mature structure and integration of the personality may be achieved. Such exceptional cases though must not lead to the assumption that prison confinement is generally of psychological benefit.

A conspicuous and almost grotesque personality change with formation of new ethical codes and sublimations was observed in another prisoner.

A thirty-two-year-old woman had lived as a prostitute before her arrest. She had been married to a procurer on whom she was sexually extremely dependent. For the first time in her life the prisoner met with outward barriers against those impulses which had ruled her so far. Never before had she lived among well-controlled people with intellectual interests and an inherent urge to work. Two years of imprisonment in an unaccustomed environment demanding identification changed her to an astonishing degree. She read and enjoyed hearing good poems which she would learn by heart.

While lying sick in the prison hospital she was eager to arrange for courses in anatomy and first aid and used this opportunity for gaining information in answer to her innumerable questions. She was not only untiring in learning anything she came across but also showed a burning interest for all sorts of spiritual problems as far as her moderate intellect could grasp them. For the first time she questioned her inner self about life in general and her own in particular and developed a painfully contemptuous attitude toward it. In the end she freed herself from her husband, got her divorce while she was still in jail and had lodging and work in another district procured for her.

The sudden development of a morality which rejected promiscuous sexuality went hand in hand with the awakening of sublimations which had never before existed. These changes occurred in the same way as we observe during childhood at the beginning of latency in the phase of the mastering of the oedipus complex: a belated formation of a superego had set in with the imprisonment. This process was to a smaller extent noticeable with the normally developed prisoners. They formed new ego ideals, their superego became severer, forced the ego to a strengthening of the sexual barriers and laws, and influenced their social attitudes, sexual life and personal relationships greatly.

Before discussing this question in detail, I have to point out the differences in the personality and community life of criminal and political convicts. With the first it took place in a most unpleasant, hostile, dirty and generally more infantile, pathological-regressive atmosphere. Toward the officials they would show hypocritical flattery, submission and a readiness to give information about a fellow prisoner at any time for the sake of some little advantages. Now and then the dammed up fury against their tormentors found vent in explosive outbursts of hatred. Among themselves they gave way to continuous fights. Their main ties were common guilt secrets, such as transgressions of the regulations, common daydreams of future criminal actions, dirty jokes and talks and more or less manifest sexual relations. Reading Plaettner (8) we learn that criminals are persons with no firm sexual organization but mainly pregenital habits. Therefore manifest homosexuality and all kinds of sexual perversions are the rule.

The political prisoners maintained an incomparably better level. It was not easy to get exact information about their sexual life. In fact, many of the women showed vivid interests in and understanding of psychological problems but were very reluctant and fearful of discussing their own love life. Only after long and close contact between two or only a few prisoners would personal experiences be exchanged and the theme of love and sex discussed. Even then the discussion was restricted to theoretical topics, such as the question of moral sex codes and similar issues. In spite of all their theoretical interest there existed a kind of unwritten law against discussing personal, in particular sexual, problems. In sharp contrast to the habit of criminal convicts sexual allusions, dirty jokes, vulgar or obscene talk were strictly disapproved of. Careful verbal expression, refined language and pronunciation were overcultivated, as were physical tidiness and manners. Badly groomed newcomers were immediately taught complete bodily cleanliness and daily exercise. Great value was assigned to upkeep and tidiness of clothing; scarfs were nicely pleated, aprons "ironed" by sitting on them, the hair dressed neatly, etc.

Prudery with regard to sex, psychic and physical overcleanliness are easily recognizable as increased reaction formations. They were built up as safeguards against those homosexual and pregenital trends which manifested themselves in the criminals and which were aroused or increased by the disruption of heterosexual relations and by living in an unclean atmosphere and in close contact with other females.

In fact, the majority of the political prisoners did not give up heterosexual desires, nor their genital organization. Many of them produced recurring dreams of intercourse with their husbands or lovers, up to the point of orgasm. Some of the women admitted that they found stubstitute gratification through masturbation. Many convicts however repressed their sexual drives and fantasies as completely as they had done during the latency period in their childhood.

Thus a girl of twenty-six who had lived for years in a happy and normal relationship with a man felt no genital or other sexual desire since her arrest. During the three years of her term she only suffered from an intense affectionate longing for her friend. His image became more and more glorified, the longer she was separated from him.

This is characteristic: most women managed to idealize the lost state of happiness and the beloved person. Altogether the image of their love-relations took more beautiful shapes, the more remote the time of real union and the stronger the sexual repression grew. In the evenings, most girls spoke of their past relations to their husband or lover with a dreamy expression and longing eyes, reviving happy memories but evidently denying any past conflicts or suffering.

As substitute for absent heterosexual love relations affectionate friendships were established. The above mentioned young girl, for instance, had formed a sentimental relationship to a fellow prisoner in which she acted like a very young girl. The two happily married women gave each other little presents, tried to snatch minutes to spend together, called each other by their pet names and so forth. It was found out from the younger girl that until her first intercourse at the age of twenty she had neither masturbated nor felt any conscious sexual desires. Beside some passing flirtations with young men she had maintained similar friendships with women as she did now.

We again are reminded of phenomena in adolescence when beginning flirtations and daydreams about idealized men and love are concomitant with crushes on women or homosexually tinged friendships.

Beyond this, there were groups of friends, cliques, and finally what one
might call a collectively latent homosexual atmosphere. The prisoners tried
to understand and to help each other over their unhappiness. They made
the greatest effort to control irritability with each other which is so frequent
in collective confinement that in the first world war it was called "barbed
wire disease". They understood that it was an involuntary diversion toward
each other of the pent-up aggression against the common enemy. The prisoners did not realize that much of their aggression served the defense against
homosexual temptation. Quarrels were quickly smoothed out and hidden
from the officials. Greatest consideration and respect for the fellow-sufferer
was the fundamental rule of behavior. The prisoners tried to understand
the individual peculiarities of each and to do each other good turns. Birth-
days and anniversaries were celebrated by those who worked at the same
table. Days before, bits of meat, grease and jam, small pieces of soap, etc.,
were saved up as presents. Even in the cells, ways and means were found to
exchange such small gifts. This over-altruistic behavior can be interpreted
as reaction formation to rising pent-up hostilities. Moreover it served as a
harmless, acceptable outlet for increased homosexual trends. During the
whole time manifest homosexuality was never observed with this group of
prisoners, nor could it be traced by questions. I never heard about any other
perverted forms of sexual gratifications.

One interesting report was of a masochistic prisoner. Before her arrest
she had suffered from masturbatory fantasies of being beaten. In prison she
gave them up and replaced them with fantasies of normal intercourse. Her
masochistic wishes seemed to be gratified by captivity to such an extent that
she could allow herself to indulge without anxiety in normal masturbatory
fantasies.

With the younger prisoners it was found that one component of female
sexuality was not at all repressed, but rather increased: the wish for a child
was openly admitted and seemed to be very intense. All young women
planned to have a baby right after their discharge — whatever their material
situation might be. It was easy to see that fantasies about procreation and
childbirth helped to raise the shattered self-esteem of these women and
strengthened their hold on life. I therefore regard them as a reaction of the
injured ego to the traumatic experience of imprisonment, i.e., as a narcissistic effort of restitution.[4]

Additional information gained from discharged male political prisoners
suggested that their sexual life proceeded along the same general lines as
that of the females. A discharged political prisoner who had spent several
years in penal servitude generally confirmed my observations on the prison

---

[4] The fact that the wish for a child is so decidedly in the foreground of interest
in female convicts reminds one of the prominent part which it plays in the mastery of
the castration conflict in adolescent girls and earlier during the oedipus phase.

life of this female group. Men however are used to masturbating more regularly and are less reluctant to discuss their sexual needs with each other. In general one may assume that the psychological phenomena of prison confinement are approximately the same with both sexes.

All the observations reported above confirm the conclusion that in psychologically normal persons prison confinement sets off an emotional and instinctual process similar to that in adolescents. The reasons for this development are apparent.

Adolescence may be defined by two factors: by an uprush of instinctual impulses provoked by the inner secretory development, which then push toward a direct outlet and by a prohibition of sexuality which opposes and frustrates these impulses. The inner struggle even though it may lead to considerable emotional disturbances stimulates the mental growth. The necessity of finding other channels of gratification activates and inspires the adolescent to intense experiences and to creative work which may decrease or cease when with the beginning of his adult sexual life he grows into a mature reality adjustment. The unnatural conditions of captivity artificially create a similar inner situation. I described how the traumatic events of the first phase of captivity upset the stability of the ego, caused a damming up of libido, reactivated infantile conflicts and opened the door to regression. Emotionally healthy persons will overcome the narcissistic disturbance as well as the deep regression at the beginning of confinement. They will recognize their ego and their instinctual life but without returning to the original situation. The narcissistic trauma — in particular the revival of the castration conflict — is too strong to be overcome completely and the damming up of libido and hostility is too severe to allow a completely healthy readjustment, in view of the grave instinct restriction to which convicts are submitted. In addition to the disruption of a healthy sexual life the prisoners are deprived of affectionate object relations by means of the pleasures of a socially active life with material, aesthetic and intellectual gratifications. We know that deprivation and frustration produce anxiety and aggression. But discharge of even normal aggressive reactions to the oppression imposed by captivity is quite out of the question. Consequently, part of the aggression is turned against the ego instead of being discharged on the outside world. This accounts for the development of overstrict ethical standards. Instinctual prohibitions from within are added to the outside restrictions. Hence, the most constructive way out of this impasse is the building up of reaction formations and sublimations. That is how a far-reaching change of personality and of sexual life takes place if a neurotic solution of the conflict should not occur. The normal adolescent passes through similar experiences under the pressure of reawakening sexuality on the one hand, and of outer barriers and inner inhibitions on the other.

The fact that the genital phase was retained and the increased homo-sexuality fairly satisfied in sublimated friendships proves the healthy resist-ance with which the political prisoners actually held their ground against the overwhelming attacks of the external and their own internal world. Pregenital sadistic and anal impulses could partly be fenced off and partly made fertile in the described reaction formations and sublimations (cleanli-ness, aesthetic needs, artistic and intellectual work, social trends, sympathy for fellow sufferers) along socially valuable and gratifying channels. The oral sector was the one which was least well mastered. Poor food, scanty intellectual nourishment, prohibition of talking, restriction and censorship of letters, visits and intramural relations — these are not apt to appease the gnawing physical and mental hunger which the convicts are prone to suffer. In the first phase of imprisonment, because of sudden object losses, primitive oral cravings and wishes for infantile dependency break through unchecked. Even later on they come to the surface periodically in dreams and daydreams of eating orgies, in sudden attacks of hunger and sexual greed or of nausea and eating disturbances.

Beyond these symptoms no prisoner can escape from severer symptom formation of oral origin: temporary depressions which become more and more paralyzing in the course of a long term of imprisonment.

There was no opportunity to observe political prisoners who had been in penal servitude for more than three to four years. Therefore an exact report on their further psychic and mental development cannot be given. On the whole it seems, as previously pointed out, that the convicts keep up better in the long run in the community and prefer it although solitary con-finement may offer advantages in respect to health. Those cell prisoners who had been in jail longest showed increasing signs of a paralyzing lasting depression due to lack of contact with the outside world: a feeling of empti-ness, of plunging into intellectual dullness and a desperate inactivity extend-ing to the smallest things.

A previously lively young woman sentenced to nine years complained after three and one-half years of confinement that she could not pull herself together anymore, not even to sew on a button. "So what, I don't care, what does it matter anyhow!"

As active trends decrease and depressions threaten to cloud the mind, the opposite danger of escaping into illusionistic optimism without critical control grows in the same degree. Sievers also reports that prisoners manage to paint their future in the brightest colors. The same tendency was apparent even with the most sober political prisoners. The longer and more complete the separation from the reality of the extramural world has been, the more fantastic does it appear in the prisoner's imagination. He may still rationally recognize the unreality of his imaginations but this does not protect him from irresistibly sinking into wishful daydreams of a happy future supposed to compensate him for the lost years. These fantasies reached their climax immediately before discharge. It plunges many of the prisoners into a nearly manic state. While the future waiting for them outside is usually uncertain and difficult, their concepts of far removed beloved persons are glorified by imagination, their yardsticks, standards and plans overidealized and exaggerated. Therefore, discharge often means a sudden and violent fall from the heights of winged dreams into the depths of a gray and hard reality.

A young prisoner left jail with the most beautiful hopes of love and with an exacting program of intellectual work. I witnessed the tragic breakdown of her happy plans: her lover had left her while she had no notion of his infidelity. Another man in whose love she had believed had started love relations with her mother. She had to take on very heavy physical work which hardly left her any time for intellectual interest.

It is a fact indeed that most of the prisoners do not succeed in transforming their new life in freedom as they had planned it during captivity. This leads to the question what happens in freedom with the sublimations acquired in prison and thus to the complicated problem of the educational value of correctional methods.

The analyst has reason to doubt that sublimations — formed under the pressure of such an extensive instinct inhibition — are stable and lasting. The political prisoners were normally developed persons who on the whole did not give up their mature organization. Therefore, their increased capacity for sublimation can be regarded as a favorable symptom: as an effective outlet provided by the ego for the pent-up instinctive tensions. In some cases it may even inspire spiritual life after discharge with a certain élan. But with most prisoners the excess of their moral and mental efforts proves their transitory value. They last only as long as they perform their function, to serve as sufficient anti-cathexis in the fight against rising impulses which cannot be gratified in prison. If the women returned to their former environment, their families, and their usual work and pleasure, the return to freedom and normal life also meant relapse into the old habits and ways. The capacity for sublimation artificially cultivated in prison disappeared fairly quickly.

After a short transitory phase of adaptation the prisoners returned to their former pattern of life. The readjustment from prison to freedom is difficult. This is shown by temporary neurotic symptoms about which many prisoners complain in the time immediately after discharge: phobic symptoms (street and accident anxiety), frigidity (or impotence in men), instability of affects, irritability and vasomotor excitability and a certain timidity and inhibition in dealing with other people. These symptoms resemble those of the first phase of captivity and must be understood as the effect of an acute damming up of libido.

Probably they arise from a conflict between the sudden external freedom of instincts and the inner prohibition which is retained from the time of captivity.

The psychological effect of convict prison or penal servitude on criminal characters is quite different and much more harmful. There we are not dealing with healthy persons but with the psychologically deformed; people with insufficient, inhibited or archaic ego and superego formations and pregenital fixations, who relieve their instinctual needs partly in perverted gratifications and antisocial acts, partly in neurotic symptoms and attitudes. What happens when such pathological personalities are exposed to the impact of prison confinement as it has been described? Their masochistic tendencies find gratification, their aggression is suppressed and — newly charged — is ready for future criminal deeds (9). If even healthy persons are pushed into a regressive emotional development by captivity it is evident that the infantility of instinct-driven criminals can only be aggravated by confinement. Their pregenital fixations — greediness, anal, sadistic and other perverse and delinquent tendencies — are tremendously strengthened by the hardships and temptations of their prison environment. Their irresponsible infantile attitude becomes worse through the way they are treated in the institutions. Thus regression is aided in every way and the path is barred to all possibility of progress to mature instinctual aims and normal character development.

Can delinquents, in view of these facts, be "corrected" in prison, or can they acquire a more social attitude toward life? The psychoanalyst has to answer these questions decidedly in the negative. By captivity the convict can only be driven further into antisocial behavior. Habitual criminals will remain what they are. In young ones at the beginning of their criminal career the pathological structure and with it the antisocial attitude will be established more firmly and even intensified.

The fundamental problem is how far social prophylaxis — change of the material and cultural conditions of life — might help to diminish the number of criminals. Apart from that, however, let us suppose that society cannot maintain order without corrective methods. Cannot these measures — used and accepted in all continents — fulfil a more constructive function than that of a — questionable — deterrent or temporary protection against asocial elements?

It has been pointed out before that in solitary confinement a criminal will at least have time for introspection and for moral and spiritual change. There is no doubt that this is impossible in collective confinement where the general standard is even lower than that of a single individual. Hence, Sievers is inclined to look at solitary confinement as a valuable method. In spite of that he knows the psychological dangers which are involved in isolation of prisoners. That is why he suggests common work in small groups with self-government and single cells for sleeping. In this way more responsibility and opportunity for occupation would be given to the convicts while they would be protected from sexual temptations.

But the successful education which he expects in the direction of an increased capacity for sublimation by means of solitary confinement seems illusory. According to psychoanalytic experience, persons who are only ruled by instinctual impulses cannot really sublimate if they are refused all instinct gratification for years.

Criminals will always try to find instinctual primitive pleasure in some way or other. If they cannot do that they will at best accomplish erratic and pathological reaction formations in the moral or intellectual sphere. These will carry the signs of an enforced instinct defense — such as insincerity and exaggeration — and thus will be utilized mainly as partly conscious propaganda action for the benefit of the warden and chaplain of the institution. After discharge they will disappear. The moralist may see signs of improvement in these attacks of morality. The psychologist with his deeper insight will not be deceived by such symptoms. He knows that the whole style of prisons would have to be changed in order to have them serve as corrective institutions. The practical solution of this problem cannot be discussed here in detail. May I be permitted some remarks on the most urgent reforms which, from the perspective of the psychoanalyst, would prepare the ground for corrective work with criminals.

First of all, a minimum of primitive gratification, such as appetizing food, the possibility of normal sexual gratification, decent dayrooms and greater freedom of movement would have to be granted to the prisoners. Only on this basis can the hard work of renouncing primitive instinctual pleasure and of building up social attitudes be expected from them. Above all, however, relations between prison authorities and prisoners and among the prisoners themselves would have to be fundamentally changed. The first prerequisite is proper training of those who are called upon to train the prisoners. Furthermore, it is vital that those concerned with crime and its punishment will come to understand that social and cultural development of criminals cannot be obtained by privations, sadistic measures and senseless hard labor, nor by means of ethical and religious exhortation alone. Consideration of normal instinctual needs, encouragement of positive human relations and constructive occupation is of much greater value. Only in this way could one lay the foundation for an educational method of "correction" — or rather of psychological restitution of convicts.

REFERENCES

1. Sievers, R.: *Die Wirkung der Freitheitsstrafe und Untersuchungshaft auf die Psyche der Gefangenen.*

2. Kretschmer, Ernst: *Physique and Character*. New York, Harcourt, Brace & Co., 1925.

3. Bjerre, Andreas: *The Psychology of Murder*. Trans. from the Swedish by E. Classen. London, Longmans, Green & Co., 1927.

4. Baer, Abraham A.: *Die Hygiene des Gefaengniswesens*. Jena, G. Fischer, 1897.

5. Wilde, Oscar: *Epistula: In carcere et vinculis*. Berlin, S. Fischer, 1925.

6. Freud, Anna: *The Ego and the Mechanisms of Defence*. New York, International Universities Press, 1946.

7. Wilde, Oscar: The Ballad of Reading Gaol, in *Complete Writings*, Vol. 6, New York, Pearson Co., 1909.

8. Plaettner, Karl: *Eros im Zuchthaus*. Berlin, Mopr Verlag, 1929.

9. Alexander, Franz, and Staub, Hugo: *The Criminal, the Judge and the Public*. New York, Macmillan Co., 1931.

NON-VIOLENCE AND SELF-GOVERNMENT IN TRAINING SCHOOLS AND PENITENTIARIES

By Paul Reiwald, Ph.D.*

(*Geneva, Switzerland*)

One of the problems that has been under discussion for a long time, among educators as well as among the public at large, is whether the beating of children, pupils or delinquents, or the flogging of prisoners is permissible. In Great Britain, flogging has been retained as a disciplinary measure in both schools and penitentiaries. Recently, an amendment to the Criminal Justice Bill aiming at the abolishment of this procedure was introduced in the House of Commons. It was defeated.

Mr. Chuter Ede (Home Secretary) said:

"I implore the committee to live in a world of reality. Many prisoners are people who easily resort to violence to get their own way and it is essential that officers should be given as much protection as we can give. . . . Flogging is a brutal necessity which one has to have in present circumstances."

The remarkable successes of British education have been adduced in favor of retaining flogging as a means of punishment in the schools. British education, however, emphasizes the formation and strengthening of character, in contrast to continental aims which instead lay stress upon the transmission of knowledge. Admittedly British education has achieved one important goal, in that the aristocratic ideal of the gentleman with which it began has permeated the nation.

However, the problem of flogging is no more than one particularly conspicuous question within the entire field of education. Generally speaking, one must ask: should force be applied at all in education, and if so, to what extent? It has been objected that the other means of education, such as for example, indoctrination, praise and blame, religious, traditional and environmental influences have proved inadequate for the attainment of an optimal goal. Coercion and force have proved to be indispensable, and perhaps both have been and remain the foremost means of education to date.

Even the most ardent supporters of non-violent education cannot deny

---

* From the University of Geneva, Switzerland.

that force has played a decisive role in the civilizing of man. Those traits which are essential to mankind and which we proudly feel distinguish man from the beast, could never have been developed without the incessant application of the most strenuous methods of force. Conscience, says Freud, is internalized social coercion. Man as a social being who subordinates himself to the community and who follows its essential commands, is very largely the result of force. Therefore if we approve of man as he is today as a result of this development we can hardly question the expediency of force as an educational measure. The experience of many thousand years supports the assertion that no other method has been found to equal the effectiveness of force.

Even those who hold different convictions will not dispute the efficacy of force. Nor will they dispute that Nature itself frequently "educates" by most violent means. Only the experience of burnt fingers can convincingly impart the fact that fire burns. Education by force is also frequently, albeit unintentionally, achieved through one's encounters with other human beings. The opponents of the enforcing methods of education will question whether the effects of force in such cases are not rather like the blind workings of nature, man and destiny, and whether the force involved can be called an educational means at all even though it may have a coincidentally educational effect.

This opinion is supported by studying the effects which using force and punishment have upon the educator himself. Though it seems theoretically conceivable that there can be a reasonable use of violence one hardly, if ever, comes upon an instance of it.[1]

As a rule the use of force is accompanied by an outbreak of affect and this affect is then later justified under the guise of its educational purpose. The culprit, however, who has been punished in this manner understands too well that his mentor responded to his affect with an outbreak of his own. He understands that the educator has descended to his own level and is his superior only by virtue of his physical strength.

In his *Genealogy of Morals*, Nietzsche says: "Through most of human history, punishment rarely has been meted out because the culprit was held responsible for his deed, i.e., solely on the assumption that only he who is to blame must be punished; but rather in the manner in which nowadays parents punish their children, because of their indignation over some inflicted damage. This indignation is vented on the culprit but is checked and modified by the idea that all damage can somehow be balanced and effectively counteracted if only through the pain inflicted on the offender."

---

[1] In the *Psychology of Punishment* (quoted from H. Meng's *Zwang und Freiheit in der Erziehung*, Bern, Hans Huber, 1945, pp. 69ff) Arthur B. Allen and Evan B. Williams report a case in which a combination of violence and non-violence was applied "according to plan".

Whether or not one agrees with Nietzsche's thesis, it suggests by implication that the use of force in education be investigated from a radically different standpoint than has hitherto been done. The main question then is no longer what is the effect of force on the pupil but rather how does it affect the educator? Even at first glance it is obvious that the use of force constitutes an emotional acting-out which is the antithesis of an educational procedure. In this situation there is no difference between parents, teachers, heads of training schools or wardens of penitentiaries. The educational procedures of all of them disclose the gamut of their repressed affects, though it is aggression which is most frequently and intensively revealed. A father slaps his son's face because the boy broke a glass. What is the affect which here finds its expression and outlet?

First of all, the father wants to vent his annoyance on the boy, i.e., he wants to discharge the aggression which he usually represses, in the form of justified aggression. Had he not given in to this impulse, he would probably have calmed down a few minutes later and would again have been able to keep his aggression in check. Furthermore, he wants to assert his physical superiority over the boy. He would not have slapped a guest who broke a glass. As a rule, the relation of the educator to his charge is that of the all-too-powerful to the powerless. There is nothing so easy as to use force in education. It requires neither deliberation, nor inhibition, nor self-control. Small wonder that nearly everyone takes recourse to this means if it is within his reach. The very convenience of its use should have led to questioning its long-range expediency in education. Instead, however, it has only led to the search for probable and improbable reasons whereby to justify and rationalize its use. Instead of admitting that the application of force or violence is an extreme measure, resorted to when the educator is at his wits' end and that it therefore represents a confession of his helplessness, there are ever renewed attempts to emphasize its developmental effects. It is true that force is effective in impressing prohibitions on the memory of a child, an inmate of a reformatory, a delinquent or a criminal. It may be that it also hardens the character of the strong — that is, it creates or strengthens the determination to oppose force with force or cunning. Finally, it may also result in an internalization of coercion. The child may incorporate force, as it were, and may turn it against itself. The adolescent, however, will no longer react in this way.

Perhaps these three effects of force are today still indispensable. But there is no need to justify violence, it takes care of itself and is never at a loss for reasons. The crying need is to investigate the effects of force on those who resort to it. The answer is unequivocal that the effects are detrimental. They can be observed again and again in the administrators of training

PAUL REIWALD
372

schools and of penitentiaries. These officers never hesitate in applying force, they consider it an irreplaceable tool of their trade.

Year after year, Frederick the Great appointed the honorably discharged non-commissioned officers of his army as teachers in the grade schools and thus provided for their old age. These men who had been professionally trained in the use of violence became the educators of the Prussian people with the results known to all the world. It would be important and profitable to establish the qualifications in various countries which determine the appointment of administrators of training schools or penitentiaries. But we can unfortunately anticipate that there is today as much neglect in determining the qualifications of an educator as there was when Frederick the Great appointed his non-commissioned officers.

Force is the only means of education with which all parents are familiar. How should administrators of training schools or penitentiaries know any better? Neither they nor parents have any idea of the high level of educational attainment which is a prerequisite of their function. But what does educational attainment mean in this context? Our first reaction to a child's naughtiness or misbehavior, to a delinquent's attack or a criminal's offense is a purely affective one; our anger, our rage, that is, our own repressed aggression, is aroused. We want to discharge it by venting it on the offender. Up to the present such emotional acting-out constitutes the nucleus of our educational system in respect to normal children as well as criminals, and is the basis of our criminal jurisprudence. Certainly, the director of a training school sits serenely behind his desk and orders solitary confinement for an offender. Lynching of a criminal by an excited mob is no longer practiced, or at least it happens rarely and in only a few countries. Decorously and in their dignified robes, our judges sit in their seats or in the council chamber and mete out justice, apparently remote from all affect. But they are no more and no less devoid of affect than is the audience which throngs the courtroom to witness a sensational trial, or the mystery fan who seeks his supply of tension and discharge in a detective story, or society is in its relation to its criminals.[2]

For the educator, therefore, a high level of educational attainment means to have conquered his tendency to acting-out. Affective reactions manifest themselves in the judge and in the public prosecutor in moral indignation as reflected in the sentences they pronounce. They are revealed in the administrators of training schools and penitentiaries by their unhesitating measures of force against their charges. The affective reactions of the public at large come to the fore in the mass attendance of sensational trials, in the manner in which such trials are reported in the papers and in the

---

[2] I have dealt extensively with affective reactions in criminal justice, in my book, *Die Gesellschaft und ihre Verbrecher*, Zürich, Pan Verlag, 1948.

steadily mounting sales of mystery stories. It is the affective needs of educators and officers of the law which are the important determinants of our educational and penal systems. Yet the only affect which has justification in education or rehabilitation is love and even love should be carefully controlled and guided. Again and again we can observe to what extent educators choose their professional activities as an outlet for their own emotions. They attempt to educate others because they themselves are lacking in education and self-control.

That is the reason why our system of education and punishment constitutes a vicious circle. Every asocial action, be it of the child, of the adolescent delinquent, or of the adult criminal stems from strong affective impulses. Almost without exception one of the unconscious goals of the adolescent offender is to hurt the feelings of those who are in charge of him. As a rule, the offender succeeds only too well. Most "educators" react to the stimulus of an offense or merely of provocative behavior as quickly and as surely as if they had been waiting for it. They drop their controlled, well-balanced attitude, meet affect with affect, and let themselves be dragged down to the level of the one whom they are supposed to educate. The goal has been reached. The educator's emotional acting-out is his charge's triumph.

It is inconceivable that such an educational procedure, such punishment can have a beneficial effect on the pupil. It leaves him exactly where he was before, whereas the educator is thrown back to a level which he may have overcome in other respects. The educator's emotional outbreak is almost inseparable from the use of force. That is why we are such determined supporters of non-forcing methods in education. They presuppose an educated educator, one who has become the master of his affects. They depend on strength of character. If they are the result of weakness — and the child as well as the delinquent has an acute and intuitive understanding of the difference — then they will only encourage the aggression which has proved itself successful.

One of the most impressive examples of the use of non-forcing methods as a means of education is the treatment of a group of aggressive boys as reported by Aichhorn in his book, *Wayward Youth*. Aichhorn realized that even wildest aggression must reach a point of saturation if the goal of hurting the educator emotionally and of inducing him to affective acting-out cannot be reached. Thereafter the delinquent's aggression will slowly be transformed into a pseudo-aggression. Aichhorn's delinquents behaved as do primitive races who give up their strong aggressions by transforming them into play or acting. The rites of initiation stem from castration and killing; and one of the roots of drama reaches back to these same themes.

Mere reform of training schools or penitentiaries cannot by itself effect a change in society's attitudes to its criminals. It is essential that we understand the extent to which the law-abiding citizen is interested in asocial acts because of the opportunities they afford him to discharge reactively his own affects, particularly aggression. Therefore the very measures which are intended to protect him against the asocial members of the community are simultaneously devised to maintain or even to produce crimes and criminals. A classical example is furnished by the penal institutions which not only recently but for more than one hundred years have been called the universities of crime. "It is still in prison that the character of the professional criminal is formed", wrote the London Times on December 3, 1947, when commenting on the discussion of the Criminal Justice Bill. Even more necessary than penal reform is greater insight into the detrimental effects of force upon the educator. We shall disregard here the ethical reasons which may be adduced in favor of its abolishment. We reject force because of our psychological and pedagogical experience that it is unable under prevailing circumstances to transform either the educator or his charge.

It is important to stress that the investigation of non-forcing methods in education is not based upon the experiences of only one outstanding educator like August Aichhorn. Attempts to educate or re-educate without force or with a minimum of force were made far more than one hundred years ago. Though they have been repeated again and again, neither criminologists nor social workers, nor society as a whole has paid any attention to them. This was due to an unwillingness to give up the traditional affective relation both to its asocial members and to its objects of education, and also to society's addiction to the use of force. Again and again reformers found themselves confronted by a unanimous: "Impossible". Yet the possibility of reform has been proved in many countries, it has been successful under the most diverse conditions, with men and with women, with adolescents and with adults. There are examples such as the first training school for delinquents, founded by Jakob Wehrli one hundred and thirty years ago, in Switzerland, the foundation by Thomas Mott Osborne of the Good Conduct League in American prisons, Sing-Sing among others,[3] the foundation of the George Junior Republic in Freeville (U.S.A.), the foundation of the First Junior Commonwealth in Great Britain, shaped after the American model, of the free Work-Colony Bolshewo which existed at least from 1924 to 1934,[4] the Swedish penitentiary in Hall and other institutions in that country, the work-trainings-school in Witikon (Switzerland), which are being conducted

---

[3] Osborne had originally himself gone to prison as a prisoner for a first-hand investigation of prison life.

[4] Because of conditions in Russia, I was unable to ascertain its further development.

according to the principles of modern institutional reforms and modern criminal justice.[5]

A number of these institutions have introduced some degree of self-government. The practice was begun by Wehrli and represented a positive principle, added to that of non-violence. In the long run, no type of education will be fruitful unless it leads to self-education. Prison and training-school as they are conducted nowadays are ineffective because the training-school pupil as well as the prisoner is forced into a passive attitude which is the worst conceivable preparation for his later life. He is relieved of all responsibility. He knows that he will have his food and his bed, a basic security for which he does not have to struggle. Peculiar though it may sound, our penal institutions "spoil" their inmates psychologically in various respects. The prisoner's attitude upon discharge is by no means as unambiguous as one is generally inclined to assume. Consciously, he strives for freedom with all his heart; unconsciously, however, he frequently conceives of the prison as a providing mother. This was revealed particularly clearly in some dreams of a gangster whom Alexander and Healy analyzed in jail and for some time after discharge.[6]

It was a case of a young gangster whose specialty was thefts of cars and armed burglaries and who was particularly prone to develop a passive attitude toward prison life due to his strong mother fixation. I am in a position to confirm from many years of my own experience that the enforced and frequently welcome passivity of the training-school or of the jail constitutes one of the gravest obstacles to later adjustment of their inmates. In spite of all differences, the psychology of the convict with regard to passivity resembles that of the soldier or of the inmate of a T. B. sanitarium. It is true that the soldier also has opportunities for energetic and exciting activity. This does not alter the fact that the basic attitude as compared to that in his civilian life, is one of enforced passivity and the relinquishment of all responsibility. In the same way, the wealthy tubercular patient can also provide himself with all sorts of gratifications. Yet, in his case also, the decisive factor is his passivity: he is nursed and fed, and free of all responsibility.

Both these comparisons point to the necessity not only of keeping the training-school inmate or the prisoner occupied but of jolting him out of his passivity as far as possible. For this purpose, self-government has proved the most effective means. Experience has shown, e.g. that of Thomas Mott

---

[5] Cf. Clara Maria Liepmann: *Die Selbstverwaltung der Gefangenen*, Hamburgische Schriften zur gesamten Strafrechtswissenschaft, Heft 12. (A very important though incomplete contribution.) Paul Reiwald: Verbrechensverhütung als Teil der Psychohygiene, in *Die Prophylaxe des Verbrechens*, Vol. VIII/IX, "Psychohygiene, Wissenschaft und Praxis", Basel, Benno Schwabe, 1948, pp. 203ff. also: idem, *Die Gesellschaft und ihre Verbrecher*.

[6] Franz Alexander and William Healy: *The Roots of Crime*, New York, A. A. Knopf, 1935, pp. 52-55, 58.

Osborne, that it can be introduced everywhere, even among men sentenced to many years in jail.

An additional value in introducing self-government among asocial members of society is the fact that it demonstrates, more than any other measure, the determination on the part of the punishing agents to renounce affective acting-out and the use of force. One may object that such reform in one individual institution, even if successful, does not make much sense in the face of our criminal justice, our sentences and society's general attitude toward its asocial members. With regard to both education and politics, society is convinced that force must be countered by force. It will probably be least ready to relinquish this method in dealing with its asocial members. We believe, on the contrary, that it is particularly important to continue the experiments which have been made for more than one hundred years because in this sphere only practical experience is accepted as proof. Under the prevailing restrictive circumstances only success in individual institutions is convincing. All pioneers in this field were faced with impossible conditions and yet converted into a reality what had been a mere potentiality.

Asocial adolescents in the countries of the vanquished as well as of the victors, have to be counted among the most difficult problems of rehabilitation. It cannot be emphasized strongly enough that the terrible misery and desperate moral situation following the war, particularly in Europe, has more than a merely negative aspect. While this crisis does impede and retard rehabilitation, it also offers new opportunities for such rehabilitation. In Germany, after the first World War, the catastrophic lack of nursing personnel led to the establishment of so-called unsupervised wards in mental hospitals. They proved surprisingly successful. Likewise, the free Working Colony Bolshewo in Russia was created at a time when the country was completely exhausted by civil war and revolution. Frequently, such emergency solutions point the way to the future. It is not true that the mass problem of juvenile delinquency can only be solved by the primitive means of force which has been the main method of our training-schools and our penal institutions. On the contrary, force will keep the educators and their charges in their present state. In many cases, it will not be possible to tackle the problem without taking recourse to camp-life. Delinquents and asocial children and adolescents, without parents, without families or friends, without means, must first of all be removed from the streets. This, however, will be possible only if the camps which house them provisionally will offer them a new kind of life, one with meaningful goals and purposes. Camps and institutions which are run on the principles of non-violence and self-government might create such meaningful goals and purposes.

MENTAL HYGIENE OF CONVICTS IN PRISONS

By Hans Zulliger

(Bern, Switzerland)

I.

The present paper shall demonstrate the desirability of applying all available psychological means to the treatment of prisoners in order not only to protect but rather to improve their mental health.

At first, we must clarify what is meant by "psychological treatment". Its goal is to secure lasting effects in the prisoners by means of re-education which will enable them, upon discharge, to adjust themselves smoothly to life in a community of free citizens. For this purpose, the findings of applied psychology, primarily of psychoanalysis, should be put to use. What we aim at is, above all, prevention; we want to prevent the discharged prisoners from relapsing into their anti-social behavior, which originally had brought them to prison, and which they are bound to repeat if nothing has changed in them during their prison-term. Mere suppression by the criminals of asocial desires is insufficient; the desires themselves rather must be dissolved to the extent that is individually feasible. This necessitates a subtle understanding on the part of the prison personnel of the individual personalities of their wards who should be given the opportunity of undergoing an essential change in their ego structure. Then they would expand the scope of their conscience and achieve mastery of their instinctual drives by transformation and sublimation.

This task requires specially trained prison personnel and the question may arise whether the cost of such training would be justifiable. We believe it is. Experience has shown the value of mental hygiene with normal citizens and in child education. So far it has been possible to correct cases of waywardness, and behavior disorders, adolescent thieves, aggressive delinquents, sexually delinquent children, psychopaths, liars, cheats, and the like, by

377

means of psychoanalytically oriented pedagogy.[1] Therefore there ought to be a good chance of successfully treating similar deviations in adults by the same means.

Obviously, this must not be understood in an absolute, but only in a relative sense. We must not expect to have found in psychological treatment a panacea, effective in every case. Yet, it should be pointed out that deterrence which was the preferred method formerly, was effective in only 10 per cent of juvenile delinquents, whereas nowadays, with the use of depth psychology, 75 per cent of those who were intensively and extensively treated are enabled to resume life in the community without recurrence of their disturbance. If we could achieve a similar increase in educational success with adult prisoners, much would be gained. Even if only a significant reduction in the number of relapses resulted, the attempt would be worthwhile. If we calculate what the state spends for a chronically delinquent child, it is obvious how much less expensive it will be in the long run to invest in appropriate treatment, even if only a small number of delinquents are thus reclaimed for the community. The same is valid in the treatment and re-education of adult delinquents and criminals.

However, we are not only guided by the economic point of view in demanding mental hygiene for prisoners. The state is, for higher, moral reasons, interested in having the smallest possible number of criminals. As enemies of the community, they are at the same time enemies of the state. The one attitude includes the other. Moreover, the state as a social institution has the duty to take care of the welfare of its citizens — which means their mental welfare as well — and, after all, criminals are citizens, too.

II.

We shall now turn to the question of what we can learn from psychology with regard to the re-education of prisoners. First of all, what are the factors that determine the attitudes and character deviations of offenders? These factors can be divided in two groups:

1) The offender has, for inner reasons, developed into a socially unacceptable individual. His heredity is defective. There are drinkers, psychopaths, or psychotics among his next of kin.

2) He has become a criminal in reaction to his environment. As a child,

---

[1] Aichhorn, August: Ueber die Erziehung in Besserungsanstalten, *Imago*, IX, 1923.
——*Wayward Youth*, New York, Viking Press, 1944.
——Zum Verwahrlostenproblem, *Ztschr. f. psa. Paedag.*, 1926.
——*Psychoanalytisches Volksbuch*, Bern, 1927.
Pfister, Oskar: *Die psychoanalytische Methode*, Leipzig, 1913.
Zulliger, Hans: *Schwierige Schüler*, Bern, 1935.
——*Jugendliche Diebe im Rorschach-Formdeutversuch*, Bern, 1938.

he was pushed around and unhappy, and consequently he developed into what he is. He was surrounded by objectionable models in his childhood, unsuitable for introjection as moral conscience. A child in an environment of thieves becomes a thief. A child that is shoved from one foster home to the other every few months (as is frequently the case with abandoned children) cannot root firmly anywhere; he remains innerly isolated and becomes misanthropic; never is he given the time needed to learn to love and esteem a moral model; nor is he given the chance, by loving a real person, to acquire this person's moral standards; least of all is he ever able to achieve the long-drawn-out process of abstracting those standards from the original model and thereafter incorporating them as his own inner law. Therefore his psychic development remains fixated on the infantile level and does not adjust itself gradually to the demands of morality. He withdraws into himself, away from the others; he becomes wayward, delinquent and "matures" into a criminal.

Similarly, his parents' wealth may become fatal to a child; neither in his childhood nor in his adolescence can he learn either gratification or success by personal efforts; he is given everything anyway. Whatever his heart desires — or even more — whatever, in his environment's opinion, he needs or would enjoy, is showered upon him. That is why a child, "blessed" by great wealth, may psychically remain an infant. For much too long a period he is given love without the necessity to reciprocate in kind. He expects this state of affairs to continue indefinitely. When, however, the community limits his gratifications, then he might easily become a defiant criminal. He takes revenge upon his environment for not obeying him like a wet-nurse.

Summarizing it may be said that men become criminals either for their own, inner reasons, or for environmental ones, frequently for both. For the prison administrator, however, it is important to know whether a prisoner has become criminal on the basis of constitution and heredity or because he stems from an unfavorable environment, since the cause of delinquency will indicate to what extent the subject can be re-educated and what treatment will be most suitable.

The former frequently cannot be re-educated at all. There is a good chance, however, that an offender whose deviations are rooted in his under-privileged early environment can be re-educated by proper treatment. On the other hand, the prognosis is less favorable in the case of offenders who turned delinquent in reaction to over-indulgence.

We dispose today of psychological tests by means of which the extent of a person's educability can be established with accuracy within a short time — one or a few hours at most. I here refer to specific tests, such as, for instance, the Rorschach, which can be supplemented by the Wartegg test[2] and by graphology; by applying a battery of tests and by comparing and cross-checking their results, the final conclusions will be fairly reliable.

Whatever the underlying causes of his offense, the man who enters prison finds himself in a completely new environment. The impersonal part of this new environment, the prison proper, assumes for the convict a peculiar role which can best be compared to that of a *mother*. The prison takes care of his physical well-being, it provides a roof over his head, a bed, food, and clothing. He no longer needs to look after these things, just as at the time when his mother took care of him. The deepest unconscious attitude of the prisoner to the prison becomes that of a child toward his mother. In fact, the yearning for the prison which can so frequently be observed in discharged convicts, corresponds in many respects to the yearning for the mother. (Sometimes this yearning may become so overwhelming that the discharged convict resumes his criminal habits only in order to return to "mother".) The prisoners' infantile attitude is re-enforced by the prohibitions and restrictions with regard to sex, smoking, and locomotion. However, re-education is actually facilitated by such infantile attitudes which make adults as accessible to educatory measures as children usually are.

As regards the personal part of the new prison-environment, the supervisory officials, they come to represent father-images, for the prisoners' unconscious. They are conceived of as authority to whom one has to submit like the child to the father.

The fellow-prisoners play the roles of *siblings;* some of them are recognized as equals and are loved, others are rejected with hostility; the sibling rivalry of the nursery is revived in the relations of the prisoners to each other.

Altogether, prison life assumes for the prisoners the meaning of family life, in which they themselves play the parts of the children. Naturally, the prisoners are not conscious of the meaning they are giving their environment, only a detailed, depth-psychological investigation would uncover the parallel to the family circle. Those, however, who are aware of this attitude generally adopted by the prisoners will be able to make pedagogical use of the potentialities of this situation.

III.

Since body and soul are, fundamentally, an inseparable unit, we can influence the "spirit", the soul, through the body. Therefore we take care of the *bodily welfare* of the prisoners without, however, coddling them. Obviously the prisoners must be neither hungry nor cold, nor must their living

---

[2] Wartegg, Dr. E.: Gestaltung und Charakter. Ausdrucksdeutung zeichnerischer Gestaltung und Entwurf einer charakterlichen Typologie. Beiheft Nr. 84 der *Zeitschrift für angewandte Psychologie und Charakterkunde,* Ambrosius Barth, Leipzig, 1939.

quarters or work rooms be furnished poorly or uncomfortably. On the other hand, any kind of "luxury" is liable to have unfavorable rather than favorable effects, both psychologically and educationally.[3]

The most effective means for influencing the prisoners' attitude and re-education is *work*, which, as a rule, means physical work. Regular physical work curbs instinctual drives. Such work, however, must have a purpose which the prisoner can understand and must not be a mere occupation to kill time. We may here point out the favorable effects of soil reclamation which have recently been confirmed by experiences in military prisons.[4]

The prisoner's predilection and fitness must also be considered in the assignment to work. Enjoyment of his work and pride in his achievement — in the sense in which a craftsman takes pride in his productions — will strengthen the prisoner's morale. Therefore it is a mistake to assign any kind of work to anyone. Only a person who has himself no genuine inner relation to work will commit this mistake which corrupts the very concept of work. To put it differently: work is too noble for an indiscriminate distribution of its assignment; if one aims at a maximum educational effect from work, it is essential to put the right man in the right place, even for the hardest labor to be done by prisoners. No doubt that the occupational fitness of prisoners is well worth testing. If convicts are given an opportunity to learn a suitable trade during their term, or to improve their occupational skill, an essential step toward their socialization has been accomplished.

IV.

It has proved favorable for the education of prisoners if *group work* is done by people who belong to the same personality type. They have a stabilizing influence on each other. Just as we would not put sheep and wolf into one fold, just as unwise would it be to bring an anti-social, neurotic querulant or a thoroughly hard-boiled, previously convicted criminal in close contact with a soft-hearted and perhaps penitent and good-natured newcomer; the former would cunningly incite and seduce the latter to reactions which would never have occurred to him in the company of other types of fellow-prisoners. All this goes to show that, in forming groups, the prisoners' personalities should be considered and the composition of the group should be guided by the principle of affinity.

From the point of view of mental hygiene, it is advisable to let the con-

---

[3] As far as I could observe, the provisions and furnishing of most Swiss prisons are sufficient and well-adapted to that purpose.

[4] Kellerhals, H.: *Strafanstalt Witzwil.* Ein Beispiel von Innenkolonisation durch die Arbeit von Straeflingen und Arbeitslosen. Ins (Kt. Bern), 1925.

According to report to the Adjutant General (1943-45) remarkable educational success was achieved with *Military Prisoners of the Swiss Army*, by means of soil reclamation.

victs live together in settlements. This applies particularly to those who have "improved" and are nearing their discharge. It would constitute the task of these special settlements to prepare the transition into freedom, in cooperation with the social agency for ex-convicts. Former prisoners should be permitted to return to this "transaction settlement" if need be. This is how relapses could be prevented; if, for instance, a former prisoner happens to get into an unfavorable environment so that he is tempted to regress and to resume his former behavior patterns, the mere knowledge that he may leave his place of work and return to the transition settlement will give him moral support. The individual groups should be supervised by specially trained personnel. Wardens who may be excellently fit to deal with aggressive prisoners may by no means be fit to deal with impostors, hysteroids or malingerers. Psychopathic offenders must be treated differently than obsessionals. Wardens in charge of the former category need be no more than mentally healthy and free from anxiety; those in charge of the latter must, in addition, be capable of empathy and intuition.

In fact, the supervisory personnel plays a very important role in the mental hygiene and re-education of the prisoners. If a warden is himself unbalanced, his state of mind has a disturbing effect on the group of which he is in charge. The phenomenon of psychic contagion is as active here as anywhere else. Either the prisoners will exploit directly their supervisor's state of mind which they sense rather than understand consciously; or they will react defensively; in either case the situation is educationally unfavorable.

Mental hygiene of the prison personnel is an essential prerequisite for the mental hygiene of the prisoners; this applies, in the first place, to those among the personnel who are in daily contact with the prison inmates. Therefore it is imperative to take the best care of the mental well-being of those wardens whose work subjects them to the most immediate nervous strain. In this context, certain details of the working conditions, which are most liable to have a depressing influence should be pointed out: wardens should be neither underpaid nor overworked, they should have ample vacations and ample opportunity to protect themselves from the psychological hazards involved in their occupation, from becoming mentally rigid through incessant shop-talk, and so forth.

Preferably, a warden should have had some previous experience in a psychiatric hospital. There he would have learned how to deal with people who deviate from the norm. Certain personality traits which recur in attenuated form in the penitentiary, stand out conspicuously in their distortion by mental disease. Criminals are not psychotic (or hardly ever are), but they have many characteristics in common with the mentally ill. The theoretical education of hospital attendants would constitute an additional asset for future prison wardens. They would be familiar with many a trait in the behavior of offenders which would rouse anxiety in and appear enigmatic to others lacking this previous experience.

It has been pointed out before that wardens must be free from anxiety. Anxiety is the worst counselor in education, because it will always lead to inappropriate reactions; either to flight, or to attack in self-defense. A warden's behavior, however, must never be guided by self-preservation as an ultimate principle, not even in an incidental situation, because such episodes have an essential bearing on the way a prisoner feels about his warden. As long as the prisoners remain disciplined, and conceal their short-comings, weakness, and viciousness, no opportunity for specific educational measures will arise. Disciplinary incidents afford the best opportunities to exert educational influence upon individuals and upon the group. Educating, however, is fundamentally different from prohibiting. To do better than to interdict, what is needed is intelligence, clear thinking and freedom from anxiety. Such an educator will remain victorious even in apparently hope-less situations. The inefficient educator will tend, in such situations, to resort to force; he will suppress, instead of offering the chance for channelization or sublimation to a drive that has not yet been mastered.

Regardless of his charge, the *ideal educator* must be a superior, secure, clever and patient person, and consistent in the pursuance of the educational goal; at the same time, however, he must be gentle, kind, and reassuring because he is aware of the distance of the goal and of the impediments on the way to its attainment. He is the mediator between human imperfection and an eternal goal; in the last resort, his mission is of a religious nature.

No one can be an ideal educator because of the innate foibles of human existence. Nevertheless, every educator must undauntedly devote his effort to self-perfection — an educator who has stopped inner development has ceased to live.

V.

Every prison official will, in his contact with the prisoners, occasionally meet with difficulties that he is unable to handle. He does not understand them due to his lack of specialized psychologic-psychiatric training. In such situations he would welcome help from a qualified authority. It should be possible to create an ambulatory institution consisting of no more than, say, one psychiatrist, one neurologist, and two to three psychoanalytically trained pedagogists or psychologists, whose task would be to visit penitentiaries and there to intercede in all those cases in which the less well trained prison per-sonnel failed. Such an institution could go under the name of *Medico-psychological Penitentiary Service*. How many units would be needed for a geographical area could soon be established by experience.

Expenses for such an institution will be low in comparison to those incurred by even one prisoner who cannot be released but must be kept behind bars because he has not been treated properly or not at all. In fact, the benefits of such a Medico-psychological Penitentiary Service must not be evaluated from the point of view of expenses but only from that of the state's services to its citizens. Not only would those prisoners benefit who could be discharged as "cured", but the other citizens who then would no longer be menaced would profit as well.

The sphere of action of such an institution would be manifold and wide in scope. Its tasks could be enlarged to comprise the following:

a) Testing the incoming offenders with regard to their character, the degree of their educability, and their occupational aptitude. Assistance in assigning individuals to groups, respectively to settlements.

b) Specific cases to be diagnosed and treated by the psychiatrist. Neurologic-psychiatric assistance where the routine means of the prison personnel prove insufficient.

c) Advisory functions in the selection of wardens and their assignment to the various groups or settlements.

d) Mental-hygienic social work in the penitentiaries.

e) Training courses for the prison personnel, "reports" and discussion of incidents requiring special measures.

f) The institution to function as a center of scientific research in psycho-pedagogic problems of prison life. Elaboration of test methods, specifically adjusted to the needs of penitentiaries.

g) Advisory assistance to discharged convicts and their social workers.

It is not only imperative to rebuild our prisons in accordance with modern architectural and hygienic principles. Reconstruction and adjustment of their internal organization is at least as important.

Permanent quarantine and isolation of culpable, asocial or antisocial citizens is neither the goal nor the task of prisons. This task much rather consists in the rehabilitation of offenders and in their reclamation for work and independent existence within the framework of the state. Such re-education of offenders, however, can only be undertaken on the basis of psychological knowledge. Only proper mental hygiene will prevent people from deviating and will keep them within the boundaries of normal behavior. With this goal in mind the judiciary will, in the future, have to adjust the sentence, the duration of a prison term, less to the gravity of the crime than to the time necessary for a lasting effect of psychological-pedagogical treatment. Science has provided the knowledge necessary for the re-education of the majority of offenders to the extent of protecting them from relapses. Once the means have been found to reach a goal, an organization must be created unhesitatingly to bring these means to practical use. Otherwise discussions will remain futile; inactivity causes greater damage than a bold attempt to create something new even in view of initial imperfection which will be corrected in due course. The realization of knowledge in utilitarian and constructive action is the task of the day.

SUMMARY

1) Re-education and lasting rehabilitation of prisoners can no longer be thought of without application of modern depth-psychological knowledge and methods. Psychologically well founded treatment of prisoners must be understood in the sense of mental hygiene, with prevention of relapses as its final goal.

2) Only persons who are themselves psychically well balanced are able to apply mental hygiene. Therefore, careful selection of the prison personnel is necessary, particularly of the wardens who are in daily and continual contact with the prisoners. Prison personnel must be provided adequate recreational facilities and opportunities for advancement of their psycho-hygienic knowledge. Otherwise the wardens will be unable to withstand the mental strain originating from their charges and adequately perform the duty of giving maximal care to the mental welfare of the prisoners.

3) The duration of a prison term should be determined less by the "gravity of the crime" than by the subjective requirements of the offender in regard to his re-education.

SURVEYS

SOME SERVICES FOR LONDON'S DIFFICULT BOYS

By Dorothy Archibald

(*London*)

I. INTRODUCTION

This study is mainly concerned with the statutory services provided to deal with difficult and delinquent boys. It is so large a subject that only a superficial survey of the interlocking services can be attempted but it seems possible that out of their multiplicity some new and hopeful patterns of approach may be emerging. Limitations of space and time have made it necessary to omit the great work done by voluntary organizations. For the same reason the picture has been confined to difficult boys, who are a much larger group than difficult girls.

II. THE NATURE AND SIZE OF THE PROBLEM

Some statistics
"Delinquent" Children and their "crimes"
Children "in need of care or protection"
Children "beyond control"
Recidivism

III. THE BACKGROUND OF THE PROBLEM

Blitz
Evacuation
School closure
Shelter life
Absent fathers and mothers
Broken homes
Illegitimacy
Bad housing

IV. THE BACKGROUND OF THE SERVICES

1. Change and development in social attitudes
2. The Children and Young Persons Act
3. The Curtis Report
4. The Education Act 1944
5. The Criminal Justice Bill

V. TREATMENT

Boys before the Courts
The Courts, their procedure and powers
Probation
The Remand Home
Approved Schools
After Care
Approved Schools of the future

I. INTRODUCTION

For a long period, attention has been increasingly focused on the problems which are grouped together under the title of delinquency. From the beginning of the nine-teenth century, many committees have been set up to investigate juvenile crime in London, and report has followed report ever since. Some of the earliest reports have a melancholy familiarity to present-day readers. From one published in 1816, we learn that the principal causes were: "The improper conduct of parents. The want of education. The want of suitable employment. The violation of the Sabbath."[1] Between 1918 and 1939, investigations and reports multiplied; and, although parents continued to behave improperly and education and suitable employment were still wanting and delinquency on the whole increased, much valuable pioneer work was done.

Those dealing with the problem became increasingly aware of the importance of an element in the situation which was new to them, the psychological factor. The old ideas of crime and punishment were dying out and in their place was growing the understanding that delinquent children were those children most in need of help. The educational work of the Child Guidance Council and, in recent years, of the National Association for Mental Health, with which it is incorporated, has been a great factor in this change. And actual experience of the work done by Child Guidance Clinics has convinced thousands of people that their approach to children's problems is the most constructive. The pioneer work of Sir Cyril Burt, whose book, *The Young Delinquent*, was written while he held the position of psychologist to the London County Council (1913-1932); the work and writings of Mr. John Watson, London children's court magistrate and many others; the surveys of delinquency undertaken by provincial cities — all these have contributed to the change. The institution of the Borstal system to prevent the young from being sent to prison and the develop-ment of the probation service were all part of the great advance in the official attitude to difficult children and young persons.

At the same time, the attitude of the whole British nation was changing. An increasing number of ordinary men and women ceased to think in terms of bad boys who need thrashing and began to realize, in whatever words, that delinquency was

---

[1] *Young Offender:* Carr-Saunders, Mannheim and Rhodes. Cambridge University Press, 1942.

a complex psychosociological problem. In short, people were coming to understand that society has a responsibility to its delinquent children which it must fulfill, if only for its own protection. The last war greatly accelerated this new attitude. The drama of the evacuation of London's children and the tragedy of the separation of mothers from children and husbands from wives were burned into the national conscience. No adult who helped in or even saw the operation could remain unchanged. After evacuation came billeting and a great intermingling of the population. For the first time, and in the only way possible, those sections of the nation, rich and poor, who lived comfortable or even decent lives in country districts became aware, by direct experience, of the effects of slum life in our great cities on children.

Parallel with this stimulating experience was the development of the use of modern psychiatric and psychological treatment in the Army. Before the war, the great mass of the people and an influential section of officialdom regarded psychology as a form of quackery, but the needs of uprooted children and of war-shocked soldiers have speeded up acceptance of a new form of treatment; they have, in fact, produced a revolution in the attitude of ordinary men and women.

This change makes it seem worthwhile to attempt a general survey of the present position in the hope of seeing what we have achieved and where we fail. For in spite of all the advances that have been made, the problem remains unsolved. Numerically, it is not a large problem. In the year 1946 to 1947, 4,432 boys and 726 girls came before the London courts, of whom 4,037 boys and 426 girls were regarded as delinquents. The total school age population in September, 1946, was 319,795. Over a period, the proportion of girls to boys is fairly constant, except during the war years when the fact that London was full of soldiers greatly increased the number of older girls brought before the courts. Since the number of delinquent girls is so small and their problems are often of a special type, we have decided to confine ourselves here only to boys. The same services exist for girls as for boys but on a much smaller scale, and everyone working in this field is aware that we have not yet made any real progress in the treatment of sexually delinquent girls. Moreover, we shall only attempt to describe the statutory services provided for London boys and not the great work done by voluntary organizations, although in this, as in all other fields of social work in Britain, the work of voluntary organizations and of statutory bodies is complementary and interlocking.

All provision made for dealing with delinquency is the responsibility of the Secretary of State for Home Affairs (one of His Majesty's Ministers, appointed by the Prime Minister). The local authorities in this country have a statutory obligation to provide remand homes and approved schools for their delinquent children and residential homes for children who come before the courts as being "in need of care or protection". The local authority for London is the London County Council (usually called the L.C.C.), which is composed of 124 councillors[2] elected once every three years by the direct vote of the men and women citizens of London (the total electorate is 2,200,000; in December, 1946, the total population was estimated as being 3,277,100, but it is now much greater). Much of what is regarded as "Greater London" comes under the jurisdiction of adjoining County Councils. Although each of London's twenty-eight boroughs has its own elected Borough Council, the L.C.C. is the overruling authority for the County of London in education, health, housing and town

---

[2] It may be of interest that councillors are unpaid and need to give at least half their time to the work, which is especially heavy for those serving on the Education Committee, which is responsible for 1,600 educational establishments ranging from teachers' training colleges to residential nursery schools.

planning. Its services for difficult and delinquent children are provided for by its Education Committee, which, in 1947 to 1948 is spending £18,500,000 (about $74,000,000) on all forms of education out of the Council's total expenditure of £55,388,640 (about $221,554,560). Approximately half of the cost of the services for delinquency are paid for by a direct grant from the Government, via the Home Secretary, and the rest is paid for by local taxation.

A study such as this, covering so wide a field, can be neither scientific nor exhaustive. At worst, it will be found superficial; at best, it may give an impression of the multitudinous services developed by one great city to help its difficult boys to grow up into good citizens. It is a summary account of one individual's impressions of the present system. Since it is written for overseas readers, every effort has been made to describe the background and to explain peculiarly British procedure and terms. The writer has been greatly impressed by the outstanding work done for difficult children in some parts of the United States, but it should be remembered that the legislation summarized in the following pages applies to *all* British children and that the administrative standards, although they vary from locality to locality, can only vary within certain limits, since the whole country is subject to the same laws enforced by the same central authority.

II. The Nature and Size of the Problem

No satisfactory definition of the word delinquent has yet been formulated nor can be until society has developed techniques of diagnosis and an administrative procedure which enables it to separate difficult children into an infinite number of groups. Then it well may be that we shall discover that each single child is a complete individual problem, different in some respects from all other children. At present, it seems clear that, in the main, delinquency in children is a reaction to delinquency in adults; that it is, in short, one of the many results of a delinquent society which has produced, or inherited, slums, poverty, ignorance and an adult population of which a proportion is both unstable and immature. "Only if we dig deep shall we expose the basic factors and from them alone shall we learn that what matters is not the conduct of the child, but his social and mental background: poverty and slums; disease and drink; immorality; indifference to religion; each of them conducing to that most tragic of all a child's afflictions — a broken home."[3]

It would be simple enough to accept the legal definition of delinquents as those children found guilty of an offence against the law by the children's court, but it is too simple. Apart from those who escape appearing before the courts only by luck, or by the exercise of superior intelligence, it has to be admitted that many children who come before the courts and are not charged with any offence are just as unruly or, in official language, "depraved", as those who are charged. The boys of whom we are writing may therefore appear in the courts either because they were caught committing an indictable offence, or because their parents or guardians are charging them with being "beyond control", or because the local authority, a policeman or any other authorized person, gives evidence that they are "in need of care or protection". The local education authority may also bring a child before the court for persistent absence from school, and if the court is satisfied that the parents are either unwilling or unable to enforce attendance, it may deal with the child as being "in need of care or protection".

---

[3] John Watson: *The Child and the Magistrate*. London, Jonathan Cape, 1943.

One of the problems then arises from our knowledge that there is no hard and fast line dividing these groups of boys. It is often almost a matter of accident whether a child comes before the courts as being "beyond control", "in need of care or protection", or for having been caught committing an illegal action. Further, it is common knowledge, as Sir Cyril Burt pointed out in *The Young Delinquent,* that the same illegal actions are committed by many children who are never suspected of delinquency.

The following tables give a general picture of the cases of boys brought before the London courts:

1. TOTAL NUMBER OF BOYS APPEARING BEFORE THE
COURTS BETWEEN 1934 AND 1947

1934-1935	3,124
1935-1936	3,658
1936-1937	4,299
1937-1938	4,160
1938-1939	3,982
1939-1940	4,107[4]
1940-1941	4,073[4]
1941-1942	4,645[4]
1942-1943	4,524[4]
1943-1944	4,275[4]
1944-1945	4,029[4]
1945-1946	4,483[4]
1946-1947	4,432

The peak year was 1941 to 1942, despite the great number of children evacuated from London. The reasons are not far to seek and are discussed in a later section.

2.

	Delinquency Total		Beyond Control Total		Care or Protection Total		School Attendance Total		Total School Population
	No.	%[5]	No.	%[5]	No.	%[5]	No.	%[5]	
1939-40	3,884	.86	98	.021	98	.021	27	.006	450,000
1946-47	4,037	1.2	170	.053	98	.030	127	.039	319,795

As the total school population in 1946-47 was very considerably lower than in 1939-40, the proportion of boys coming before the courts is of course higher. The school population has risen steeply through 1947, as families have found accommodation and returned to, or moved into, London. There is a striking increase in the number of boys charged by their parents with being "beyond control". In the absence of precise information, we must assume that this increase is due to varied reasons. In some cases, it will be the result of a weakening of parental control, due to broken homes, dead fathers, absence of mothers at work; in others, it will reflect a too sudden tightening of home discipline with the return of long-absent fathers from the Forces and from prisoner-of-war camps.

---

[4] Depleted juvenile population due to evacuation.

[5] Percentages shown are related to the total school population.

3. PROPORTION OF JUVENILE FIRST OFFENDERS (BOYS) TO THOSE CHARGED
   MORE THAN ONCE BEFORE THE LONDON JUVENILE COURTS

	First Offenders	Previously Charged
	%	%
1937-1938......................................	76.3	23.7
1938-1939......................................	68.5	31.5
1939-1940......................................	66.0	34.0
1940-1941......................................	66.9	33.1
1941-1942......................................	64.3	35.7
1942-1943......................................	68.5	31.5
1943-1944......................................	64.6	35.4
1944-1945......................................	62.5	37.5
1945-1946......................................	59.6	40.4
1946-1947......................................	59.8	40.2

These figures are, of all those available, the most disturbing, since they show a rise in recidivism from 23.7 per cent in 1937-1938 to 40.2 per cent in 1946-1947 — a rise which seems to reflect a consistent tendency. If this rise continues over the next few years, when home and school life must be considered to be established on a new post-war "normality", it will indeed be a challenge to all our methods. As it is, it seems to call for a thorough investigation into the causes of failure in 40.2 per cent of the cases.

4. AGES OF BOYS CHARGED WITH OFFENCES BEFORE THE
   LONDON JUVENILE COURTS

1st April — 31st March

Ages in Years	1936-1937	1937-1938	1938-1939	1939-1940	1940-1941	1941-1942	1942-1943	1943-1944	1944-1945	1945-1946	1946-1947
8	69	72	61	51	57	60	97	83	73	97	143
9	164	134	147	144	110	145	177	165	145	177	221
10	271	231	210	210	216	250	287	303	251	251	297
11	399	354	303	331	309	335	312	410	306	365	378
12	442	477	394	440	335	474	498	444	411	449	443
13	596	578	503	595	592	585	534	608	485	603	530
14	485	494	446	507	558	544	504	473	503	519	475
15	640	654	682	773	852	909	686	552	676	772	671
16	815	842	908	883	998	1013	1011	747	810	939	879

Here again, the age distribution of delinquent boys shows some disturbing changes. In 1936 to 1937, only 69 eight-year old and 164 nine-year old boys were charged, that is, 1.7 per cent and 4.2 per cent, respectively, of all those charged with offences; in 1946 to 1947, there were 143, or 3.5 per cent, eight-year olds and 221, or 5.4 per cent, nine-year olds — a very significant increase. Some special factors which may have affected these children are discussed later, but there is immediate need for an intensive study of this age group and its habits. It seems possible, for instance, that in the rapid development of clubs and recreation centers for adolescent boys, the needs of these small boys have been underestimated. There is a lot of time between the close of school and bed time, even for eight-year olds, especially where there is a housing shortage and mothers who go to work have little or no chance to control how these hours are spent.

5. AGES OF BOYS BROUGHT BEFORE THE LONDON JUVENILE COURTS
CHARGED WITH BEING "BEYOND CONTROL"

Year ending 31st March, 1947

Age	Cases
7	21
8	15
9	24
10	14
11	18
12	14
13	12
14	20
15	13

It would not be surprising to find the peak figure of boys charged as being "beyond control" among the fifteen-year olds, but the youngest groups head the list. Born in the immediate pre-war years, these boys probably had less experience of "normal" home life than any other group of children in this country, except their sisters. Their unsettlement began between the ages of two and four and must have made its mark on many of them. Here again, the urgent need is for more information.

6. BOYS BROUGHT BEFORE THE LONDON JUVENILE COURTS
AS BEING IN NEED OF "CARE OR PROTECTION"

	13 years and under	14 years and over
1936-1937	77	70
1937-1938	86	73
1938-1939	66	46
1939-1940	50	48
1940-1941	33	41
1941-1942	36	48
1942-1943	79	48
1943-1944	59	36
1944-1945	66	37
1945-1946	75	42
1946-1947	68	30

The action open to the courts in these cases is discussed later.

7. ANALYSIS OF OFFENCES OF BOYS BROUGHT BEFORE THE LONDON JUVENILE COURTS

Year ending 31st March, 1947

	8	9	10	11	12	13	14	15	16	Total
1. Motor vehicle thefts and Traffic Act breaches	—	—	—	—	3	5	8	44	77	137
2. Thefts of articles from motor vehicles	6	10	14	20	24	32	19	16	24	165
3. Thefts of cycles	5	11	18	22	19	26	26	24	28	181
4. Thefts from multiple stores	3	13	12	20	17	32	23	15	9	146
5. Thefts from other premises	50	67	105	127	137	187	128	172	169	1142
6. Thefts from persons, employers and parents	7	14	18	19	28	33	68	85	101	373
7. Robbery with violence, house and factory breaking, found on enclosed premises, in possession of housebreaking implements, unlawful possession and suspected person	57	91	111	144	165	166	138	220	320	1412
8. Forgery, receiving, false pretences, uttering counterfeit coins and railway frauds	1	3	4	6	7	13	16	11	28	89
9. Attempted murder, man-slaughter and attempted suicide	—	—	—	—	—	—	—	2	1	3
10. Sexual offences	—	—	—	1	2	2	6	5	12	28
11. Malicious wounding, assault, drunk and disorderly, insulting behavior, using obscene language and obstructing police	1	2	1	2	6	4	11	14	31	72
12. Breach of probation	2	2	7	8	18	13	8	24	36	108
13. After supervision	7	3	5	2	5	7	4	9	5	47
14. Other offences	3	4	1	2	4	4	13	22	30	83

The correct legal definitions of the "crimes" listed here seem too clumsy for identifying the actual doings of the boys. Under item 11, for instance, we find one precocious eight-year old charged with one of a variety of very grave offences. Did he maliciously wound or assault someone? There are such cases recorded in the literature of delinquency. Was he drunk and disorderly — that seems unlikely; or was he guilty of insulting behavior, of using obscene language or of obstructing the police? We shall never know what this eight-year old ruffian actually did, but we may hope that at some future date it will be possible to classify the delinquencies of little boys more precisely. The justification of the present method is that the procedure of the courts, from a legal point of view, is as scrupulous as that in any other court of law. The laws of evidence will be fully observed, and the charge must be proved or the case will be dismissed.

The most popular crimes among London boys, even at the age of eight, are those summed up in item 7 as "robbery with violence, housebreaking, found on enclosed premises, in possession of housebreaking implements, unlawful possession and suspected person". This list covers everything from sixteen-year old gangs who, at a time when the London police force was seriously undermanned, successfully carried out a number of burglaries before being caught, to eight- and nine-year olds playing at gangsters on vacant lots and yielding to a sudden temptation to force the window of a factory or warehouse. These two types would be dealt with very differently by the courts.

The general fact which emerges from this table is that the overwhelming majority of charges arise from thefts of one kind or another; 165 from motor vehicles, 181 of bicycles, 146 from multiple stores, 1,142 from "other premises", 373 from persons. No doubt much of this larceny springs naturally from the desire to possess certain things which all boys covet, and it is probably increased by the present shortage of material goods. Some of it may be the result of misdirected adventurousness and bravado — when it is reported to be easy to steal things from the open counters of certain multiple stores, it immediately becomes a sporting challenge, extending even to well brought up and steady boys. We may guess that there is also a group of disturbed children with unhappy home lives who steal compulsively, and this group may account for some of the recidivism. At present, there is no information available on the point.

To sum up, numerically this may not seem to constitute a very serious problem, since the number of London children of school age charged with indictable offences is only 1.2 per cent of the school population; nor are the vast majority of the offences of a serious nature. The gravity of the situation lies in three facts: first, that in spite of all the progress that has been made in the treatment of delinquent children and despite the outstanding improvement in social conditions that has taken place in the last few years, there is no sign of a real decline in total numbers; second, the fact that recidivism appears to be on the increase, and although this may be a temporary phenomenon, our ignorance of its causation leaves it a mystery; third, while all pre-war statistics showed the early adolescent years as the peak for delinquency, the established trend has changed, and for the first time since records existed, the youngest boys equal the adolescents.

III. THE BACKGROUND OF THE PROBLEM

The background of delinquency is, as far as we know, common to all nations, but it is accentuated and perhaps even new elements enter it during wars. We have no precise knowledge because the after-effects of actual experience of war on a population are incalculable by any techniques as yet available to us. We have some rough indices, such as criminal and divorce statistics, the curve of admission to mental hospitals, and of course delinquency figures. It is impossible to establish direct causal connection between these figures but by all these rough tests it may well be thought that the population of London, both civilian and ex-service, has suffered some damage to emotional stability during the war years and can assume that the children have also been affected.

When we consider the possible traumatic effects of bombing on children who come before the courts in the post-war period we enter the realm of speculation. Nevertheless, it is interesting to reflect that the eight- and nine-year olds who formed the biggest single group before the courts in 1946 to 1947 were infants of a year old during the incessant bombardment of London from the Fall of 1940 to the Spring of 1941. We may never know what impressions of violence and terror were imbedded in their unconscious, either by direct experience or through participation in the emotion of their mothers. We can be sure that whatever their particular experiences may have been they were abnormal. The mothers who were evacuated with their babies were often in a state of extreme tension and anxiety about the fate of their husbands, whether left alone in London or on active service. Furthermore, recent statistics gathered by several child guidance clinics indicate that the separation of children under five from their mothers, even when it is followed by periods of apparently normal home life, may be an important factor in the development of one type of delinquent; namely the unresponsive child unable to form affectionate relationships who is so often found among persistent offenders. Research into this association is so far on a small scale but it also shows a correlation between a history of early separation and persistent larceny.

Boys of the older age groups have had very varied experiences. Those now sixteen, for example, may have been evacuated alone or with their school, or with their mothers; many of them returned to London and were re-evacuated several times; some remained in London, sleeping under the stairs, or in communal shelters, or in the tube stations (subway), playing in the rubble of the blitz and running wild in an atmosphere of violent disturbance. A year ago the medical director of a London child guidance clinic expressed his intention to turn the small garden of the clinic into the semblance of a blitzed site by having some tons of rubble dumped on it. "These children," he said, "have spent their lives playing in the rubble of London and they must be able to play it out. At present a garden is meaningless to them."

The experience of evacuation and billeting varied enormously for these boys. Some were fortunate in their billets and in their own adjustment. Others were unfortunate. In both situations the demand made on young children by violent and incomprehensible uprooting from all familiar scenes and from one or both parents, and the effort to adjust to more or less suitable and willing hosts in an entirely strange environment, must have been in many cases a violent trauma. No one who saw the exodus of the children will forget the courage and gallantry of the vast majority who set out cheerfully for a new world with a label round their necks and a bundle in their hands.

One measure of the dimensions of the problems evacuation raised may be found in the fact that by 1941 the Government was alive to the necessity for setting up hostels for "difficult" children in all reception areas.[6] Two hundred and fifty hostels were in fact established. Originally they were intended only as an emergency provision for the children regarded as unbilletable but, by degrees, both hostels and children were sorted out and some of these hostels made a real and lasting contribution to our

[6] *Report by the Shakespeare Committee on Conditions in the Reception Areas.* Published January, 1941.

ideas on the rehabilitation of difficult children. "It came to be realized that it was not enough to provide shelter and care or even a happy and well ordered routine, but they must aim at fitting the children for ordinary life by rebuilding their stability and confidence."[7]

To get any picture of the life of London children between 1939 and 1945 it is necessary to keep the facts of evacuation clearly in mind. In September, 1939, when the first great organized evacuation of children took place there were 450,000 school children in London (i.e. children of five to fourteen). In November, 1939, the estimated number was only 70,000 but as the expected air war had not begun, children were returning in a steady flow from the reception areas. Almost all the teachers had accompanied their children to the country and London's schools were either closed or taken over by the Defence Services. By 1943 eight out of every nine schools were occupied by the National Fire Service, by Air Raid Wardens' Posts, by Rest Centre Service, by the Londoner's Meal Service or by the Light and Heavy Rescue Services. By the end of December, 1939, emergency schools had to be opened as fast as air raid shelters could be provided as about 200,000 children had returned to London. By May, 1940, 163,000 children were enrolled (mostly for half time attendance) in 527 emergency schools — church halls, community centres, missions were pressed into service.

Dunkirk and the air attacks on London which began in the Fall of 1940 produced another great exodus and from then on the waves of evacuation and return ebbed and flowed in and out of the city. Each major change in the child population meant switching teachers about the country and the problems of the education authority became very difficult and were greatly increased by the fact that during air raids 290 schools were totally or partially destroyed and a further 860 damaged.

It is clear that the life of school children who remained in London or returned to it in the early days of the war was undesirable in every way. Apart from the danger to which they were exposed, the black-out and the constant excitement and insecurity must have had its effects. Add to this the ease with which school could be dodged and the temptations to pilfering provided by the blitz damage to houses and property and it is not surprising to find that in the year 1941 to 1942, with an estimated school population of from 150,000 to 200,000 (i.e. less than half the pre-war population) London had its peak figure of children before the courts — 5,460.[8]

It has been truly said that London's education service was a war casualty and the effects on our children would have been far worse but for the devotion of the teachers, whether working in crowded reception area schools or volunteering to return to London to teach in improvised schools under the blitz. As it is, every ordinary school, the remand home and the approved schools all have their little groups of educationally retarded children who require, and receive, special teaching to compensate for what they have missed during the war. The effects of this period can also be seen in the Army, where each group of eighteen year old recruits includes a few illiterates.

It is not easy to form a picture of what shelter life meant to those of London's school children who lived it. Thousands of families slept in communal shelters *every* night, some who had lost their homes lived there. For some wartime adolescents it meant freedom from parental control. Many adolescent girls coming before the courts for sexual offences began their delinquency by going to sleep in a different shelter

---

[7] *Hostels for Difficult Children. A Survey of Experience Under the Evacuation Schemes.* Issued by the Ministry of Health.

[8] This figure and all those referring to evacuation cover both boys and girls.

as a revolt against father or mother. At best the young children were exposed to noise, light, excitement, singing and concert parties organized to keep up morale or to the rush and roar of the trains rushing past in the subway shelters; at worst, they must have witnessed strange and terrible scenes.

The fact that great numbers of the fathers of young families were absent during the war is a factor of incalculable weight. During the war every man between the ages of eighteen and forty-one was drafted and, unless he was working in a reserved occupation (i.e. one essential to the war effort) was put into the Armed Forces. In addition, industrial workers were often "directed" to other parts of the country where their work was needed in war factories rushed up outside target areas. Even those fathers who remained at home had little time to spare for their children. No sooner had they come home from work than they had to turn out for civil defence duties. Absent mothers, also, were sadly usual; all women were urged to go into industry. Some day-nurseries were opened but the supply never met the demand and the school-children probably suffered most as they wandered uncontrolled about war-time London.

This great social problem of absentee parents is still with us. Britain today needs every pair of hands in industry and in the last nine months the Government has again had to call on married women and hundreds of thousands have responded. Perhaps the tragedy of mothers who go to work can be seen most clearly in the children's courts. We remember a desperate faced little girl of twelve brought before the court for the second time on a charge of stealing. The family history was known to the magistrates. The mother was a widow, who went out to work and lived alone with a little son, who was the apple of her eye, and the girl. She looked ill and strained and clearly felt that her daughter's duty was to look after the boy and the home. The probation officer reported that the burden of housework and the hostility between the two children was a big factor in the girl's delinquency. Questioned by the magistrate the child finally broke down and said, "I don't care if you do send me away", and her mother turned on her savagely accusing her of "breaking up the family". She could not afford to lose the service of the child who alone made it possible to leave the beloved son. The girl's resentment of her brother's favored position and of the denial and deprivation of her own childhood had come to a head and the magistrates recognized that her only chance of adjustment was to remove her to a residential school where she would have the same right to a life of her own as other children of her age.

The strain of war and its inevitable separations has greatly increased the number of broken homes in Britain as in other belligerent countries. While the divorce rate tells its own story it only tells part of the story because in the lowest income groups men and women leave their partners or are left by them and seldom have recourse to the law courts for divorce or judicial separation.[9] We know from any cross sample of juvenile court cases that broken homes produce the highest proportion of delinquent children but unfortunately no record is kept of the figures.

Again, we know that out of 48,300 babies born in London in 1939, 3,100 were

---

[9] Divorces registered in London. These figures include many couples who are not resident in London.

1931........3,668	1935........3,942	1939........7,793	1943........ 9,765
1932........3,802	1936........4,199	1940........7,602	1944........11,900
1933........3,934	1937........4,375	1941........6,249	1945........15,221
1934........4,199	1938........6,092	1942........7,456	

illegitimate, while in 1946 out of 65,900 babies born 5,300 were illegitimate.[10] This rise was due to the concentration of allied soldiers on leave in this city. Unfortunately we have no record of the number of illegitimate and adopted children who appear before the children's courts, or the incidence of delinquency among them. The records of the Municipal Court of Philadelphia show that the proportion of adopted children appearing before it is very small which is of great interest for Britain where twice as many couples want to adopt babies as there are babies available.

We have tried to outline the background of the delinquent children of today with its especially unfavorable features; we have not dealt with the permanent factor which perhaps contributes more than any other to the creation of delinquency — bad housing. London's housing problems and their effects on child life are known to the world. Suffice it to say that at the beginning of the 1930's one and a half million Londoners — 313,000 families — had a standard of accommodation of more than three people to one room. In 1934 a Labor majority was elected to the London County Council and in five years 82,999 slum dwellers had been rehoused and 12,652 slum houses had been demolished. This was a notable contribution to London's housing problems but the war put an end to all building and during the war 88,872 houses were destroyed or damaged; of these 78,473 although damaged were habitable and have since been repaired; 7,472 houses were rendered uninhabitable, and of these 7,455 have been rebuilt and are now in use again. Apart from this, since the end of the war 7,411 temporary houses and 1,313 permanent houses, as well as 932 new flats (apartments) have been built. But today there are still tens of thousands of names on the waiting lists for new houses. The need to reduce imports of raw materials which has slowed down the building program will have its effects on the sad procession of children who pass through the children's courts.

When we pause to consider the background of London children over the last eight years, we may well marvel that the proportion who come before the courts is so small and that the majority of their offences are so trivial. Perhaps our attitude should be one of respect for the astonishing adaptability of the majority who seems to adjust themselves to the most unfavorable conditions if they are given reasonable emotional security. This very fact, however, increases society's obligation to understand those who fail, and to provide that missing element in their lives which alone will make their full development into good citizens possible. The obligation is all the greater in a small democracy struggling for economic survival, which has realized that its survival depends to a large extent on the quality of its people. Britain, in the post-war world, can no longer afford to carry a burden of delinquent, maladjusted, criminal or even ineffectual individuals and the new attitude to delinquency shows a deep awareness of this fact.

IV. THE BACKGROUND OF THE SERVICES

The marked increase in social responsibility for difficult children which has come about in the last few decades has found expression in new legislation and a brief survey of the changes made by successive Acts of Parliament may make the development clear.

Last century many thousands of young children were sent to prison every year for trivial offences, but the Children Act of 1908 established juvenile courts and from then on we made slow but steady progress in our treatment. The next step forward

---

[10] These figures have been given to the nearest hundred.

was the Children and Young Persons Act of 1933, a landmark in the treatment of delinquent and neglected children. The interest aroused by its provisions was so lively that conferences to discuss its implementation were held all over the country and were attended by justices of the peace, representatives of local government authorities, probation officers, the police and members of voluntary societies interested in the young. Briefly, the Act extended the powers of juvenile courts to protect children and their jurisdiction to cover all children up to the age of sixteen. Local authorities were charged with the duty of providing remand homes and of providing courts with the necessary information about children appearing before them and were also empowered to act as "fit persons" to whom the courts can commit children in need of care or protection.

The methods of treatment of children appearing before the courts were also made more varied. The two types of residential institutions which had previously been used for young offenders — the "reformatory" and the "industrial school" — disappeared, in name at least, and in their place came the Home Office School, commonly called the "Approved" School, since it is inspected by Home Office inspectors, carried on under regulations laid down by the Home Secretary, and subject to his approval. Local authorities have the obligation to establish schools where there is a need for them but only a few new ones came into being before 1939. Old voluntary, charitable organizations have continued to run their schools under the inspection of the Home Office and with Government grants. It is claimed that the dual system of voluntary and statutory schools has worked well. It is certainly clear that the principles on which the Home Office has developed the approved schools are a great advance on the reformatories and industrial schools. The courts have made full use of their powers to commit children to the local authority for the purpose of being boarded out with foster-parents and to place children not charged with an offence against the law under the supervision of a probation officer or other suitable person if they seem in danger of drifting into trouble.

One result of the Act was the appointment of a much greater number of women Justices of the Peace (lay judges) to fulfil the regulation that children's courts shall have at least one woman justice. It was too soon to judge the full results of the Act before the war but each year has shown an increase in the use of the new methods of treatment.

Approved schools are charged with the duty of educating children and of giving them vocational training. They are therefore organized by the Education Committees and education officers of the local authorities and, despite the handicaps of old and often unsuitable buildings, great progress has been made in the development of the education and training in the approved schools by careful selection of teachers and staff. Above all the official intention has been to get rid of the stigma of the reformatory and to raise the approved schools to such a level that they would be regarded as boarding schools and not as penal institutions.

Up to 1939 the Home Office was still sceptical about the possible contribution which psychiatry and psychology could make to the problems of difficult children, but the idea that the courts might benefit from the expert advice of a "wise" psychiatrist was officially accepted.[11] Further, a proposal to set up residential observation centres for full diagnoses of exceptionally difficult children was gaining ground. The war not only put an end to further progress in this direction but also put the maximum strain on the whole system through shortage of manpower and the increase in delinquency.

---

[11] Home Office. *Fifth Report on the Work of the Children's Branch*. His Majesty's Stationery Office, 1938.

Reference has been made to the shock to the national conscience caused by evacuation and its revelations of the conditions in which many children in our slums lived. This awareness was increased by the fact that the homes of many evacuated children disintegrated entirely; parents disappeared either as a result of the blitz, or, in the case of the least developed and least responsible, because the opportunity offered itself to get rid of unwanted children with a relatively clear conscience. Rural local authorities had the extremely difficult task of providing permanent homes for such children and in one or two cases tragedies occurred. Furthermore the resources of the country districts were entirely inadequate for the provision of remand homes, approved schools, hostels, etc., both in buildings and in trained staff, and children were sometimes placed in unsuitable institutions. As a result of all these and many other problems the nation was roused to the plight of homeless children and to the great increase in their numbers caused by the war. In 1945 the Government set up a distinguished committee, the Care of Children Committee, charged to "inquire into existing methods of providing for children who from loss of parents or from any cause whatever are deprived of a normal home life with their own parents or relatives; and to consider further what measures should be taken to ensure that these children are brought up under conditions best calculated to compensate for the lack of parental care".[12]

It was the first enquiry in England directed to the provisions made for children deprived of normal home life and covering all groups of such children and the *Report of the Curtis Committee* (as it has come to be called) may well prove to be another milestone in the history of deprived children. Based on visits to 451 institutions all over the country, on the evidence of 229 witnesses, on interviews with members and/or officers of 58 local authorities, its findings were of the greatest importance and its scope was comprehensive. The enlightened attitude of the *Report* is shown by its stress on the needs of the individual child. It laid down that a child's welfare demands provision for not only his physical needs but also for those other equally important requirements, an atmosphere of security, personal interest and affection and treatment "as an individual with his own rights and possessions, his own life to live and his own contributions to offer".

The Committee found that the great majority of existing homes were reasonably well run from the standpoint of physical care and that there was little evidence of neglect or harsh usage. Their chief criticisms were of unimaginative methods, of drabness, of unsuitable staffing and of lack of personal interest in, and affection for, the children.

The main recommendations of the *Report* were that responsibility for homeless and deprived children should be unified in one Government Department (The Home Office), and that each local authority should set up a special children's committee and appoint a highly-trained children's officer to be responsible for all such children. Great stress was laid on better selection, training and status of staff at all levels. A Bill has just been presented to Parliament which embodies all the main recommendations made by the *Report*. It covers all homeless children and children whose homes are unfit for them and all provisions made for them, whether by boarding-out, by placement in a children's home provided by a local authority, or in a voluntary home. The importance of this legislation for our subject is clear because, although London has long ago reached a high standard in its provision for homeless and deprived children, the new Act sets a further and more difficult task. The *Curtis Report* proposes that local authorities shall provide substitute homes "which must supply:

---

[12] *Report of the Care of Children Committee.* H.M.S.O., 1946.

(i) Affection and personal interest; understanding of his (a child's) defects; care for his future; respect for his personality and regard for his self esteem.

(ii) Stability; the feeling that he can expect to remain with those who will continue to care for him till he goes out into the world on his own feet.

(iii) Opportunity of making the best of his ability and aptitudes, whatever they may be, as such opportunity is made available to the child in the normal home.

(iv) A share in the common life of a small group of people in a homely environment."

It may be a long time before we learn how to provide such ideal substitute homes, but if we succeeded we might find that delinquency and even adult crime would be greatly reduced since it seems clear that every unhappy child is potentially a delinquent child.

Before the end of the war Parliament passed an Act of supreme importance for all British children, the new Education Act of 1944. This great and visionary piece of legislation makes it possible for education authorities to raise the whole national standard of education without limit, subject only to shortages of materials for building and of trained personnel for staffing. Both directly and indirectly the Act, which came into force in April, 1947, has a bearing on the problem of delinquency.

Its outstanding provisions are for the raising of the school leaving age to fifteen (now in force) and to sixteen as soon as buildings and teachers are available, and the provision of free secondary (or high) school education for all children. In 1938 the indictable offenders per 100,000 of the population were three times as numerous for boys of thirteen as for any age group over twenty-five. It therefore seems probable that one of the best methods of preventing delinquency is to keep children within the framework of a good educational system during the most restless adolescent years. The principle laid down in the Act "so far as possible, all children should receive the type of education best suited to their abilities and aptitudes" opens the door wide for every desirable educational development. The cost of the whole system is shared approximately equally between the government, that is, national taxation, and the local authorities, or local taxation.

The Act made great strides in the recognition that a child is a complex being whose physical, mental and emotional needs must be satisfied if he is to develop fully, and that the duty of an education authority therefore only begins with school room teaching. Whereas under previous legislation progressive local authorities had power to feed and clothe children, when necessary, this Act makes provision of meals and milk part of school life and encourages the provision of clothes for those children in need of them. It also extends and improves the provision for free school medical and dental services.

Most important of all for our purpose, regulations were made for the provision of "special education" for all handicapped children; the blind and partially sighted, the deaf and partially deaf; delicate and diabetic children; the educationally subnormal, epileptics, children with physical handicaps or with speech defects and maladjusted children. While progressive education authorities had, between the wars, made increasing provision for special schools and specially trained teachers for handicapped children, this is the first time that emotional maladjustment has been recognized by the law as a handicap. Moreover the Ministry of Education has published an excellent pamphlet[13] which lays down the necessity for both day and residential schools for such children and makes it clear that the establishment of an

---

[13] *Special Education Treatment*. Ministry of Education Pamphlet No. 5. H.M.S.O.

adequate child guidance service is essential to the fulfilment of the Act. The shortage of child psychiatrists from which Britain is suffering is doubly regrettable at a time when such advances are possible.

Finally, there is before the House of Commons another Bill which will pass onto the Statute Book before long — the Criminal Justice Bill (1947). Formulated by the Home Secretary, its purpose is to bring English law and procedure with regard to criminals and young offenders into line with modern standards and to remove from the Statute Book legal traces of less civilized ages. For instance, the Bill proposes the abolition of the death sentence on anyone under the age of eighteen; it restricts the powers of the courts to imprison anyone under the age of twenty-one; it proposes the abolition of the power of the courts to order whipping as a punishment whether of children or adults. Thus the law is catching up with public opinion which has long ago condemned the legal whipping of children and young people.

The Bill proposes that remand centres be set up for young people between the ages of fourteen and seventeen, and seventeen and twenty-one, where medical and mental tests can be carried out. To avoid sending young persons between fourteen and twenty-one to prison it provides that detention centres shall be established for use when all other methods have failed. It also provides for the establishment of probation hostels in which young people may be required to live as a condition of probation. The Bill gives the Home Secretary power to train probation officers and the staffs of the new probation hostels, approved schools and remand homes and it makes special provision for the supervision of offenders under twenty-one on their discharge.

Taken together, the great legislative changes embodied in the Criminal Justice Bill, the Children Bill and the Education Act (1944), reflect the new standards set by enlightened and informed public opinion and between them they provide a comprehensive children's charter, safeguarding the least fortunate and removing obstacles from the way of the strong and gifted.

V. Treatment

We have written much about the apparatus for dealing with difficult boys, but nothing so far about the boys themselves. They are of many types physically but the impression given by the majority is that they come from the homes of the most depressed section of the community. War time and postwar legislation have already effected a great improvement in the health and physique of England's poorest children. The provision of free milk for every child in school; the great increase in the provision of good school dinners, for which higher rations are provided than for adults' meals in restaurants and canteens; the power of the local education authority to clothe a child where it seems to them that by reason of the inadequacy of his clothing a child is unable to take full advantage of his education; children's allowances; all these and many other reforms are securing a better start in life for the children of this generation, which is reflected in their looks, their health, their size. But still a proportion of the children who pass through the courts appear to have missed these advantages. Too many are undersized and below par in health. When their family background is investigated it is clear that either misfortune or social inadequacy and maladjustment on the part of their parents are robbing them of their rights. Many, too, are the children of the least intelligent section of the population. There are also plenty of happy, ordinary boys with good homes brought before the courts because high spirits have led them into activities which conflict with the law in a congested city.

The deep concern of their parents and their own shame-facedness gives good promise that they will not return.

On the other hand, there are boys who fall into neither of these groups. There was the well dressed, healthy, decent looking man who unhappily charged his eldest boy, aged ten, with being beyond control. The boy was healthy and well turned out and comically like his father. He had a good home and was a good boy but every few months he disappeared and lived no one knew how for a week or two until he was found. The boy himself had no idea why he ran away, neither had anyone else. It seems probable that only a psychiatrist with plenty of time at his disposal could disentangle that knot.

No separate records are kept in London of the proportion of children belonging to minority groups of the population who appear before the courts. The impressions gathered from probation officers, care committee workers and remand home staff suggest that in the case of Jewish boys it is below the average. The explanations offered are that London's Jewish people look after their children too well; that family life and family ties are still strong and divorce very rare and finally that the various Jewish voluntary organizations contribute a notable variety of clubs and recreation centres to the young life of the city. When a Jewish boy does get into trouble, these same organizations give him every possible help.

Like most capital cities which are also ports, London has a varied foreign population and a small colored population, both resident and transitory. The resident colored population is very small and is to be found almost entirely in a square mile round London's docks. A survey[14] carried out during the war showed that about four hundred colored people were living in dockland in some of the worst slums of London. The whole area in which they live is scheduled for demolition and rebuilding by the London County Council. One hundred and thirty-six colored and half-caste children were found attending the schools of the district. It is the opinion of the author of this survey that the colored and white children mix happily and that the school life of these children is good, but in the majority of the cases their home conditions are very bad. In two years alone during the war twenty-three half-caste children from this area were taken into the care of the L.C.C. on its own initiative and fourteen others were placed in its charge by the courts. There is, however, no evidence that any undue proportion of colored children come before the courts charged with indictable offences. For whatever reason they may appear, their treatment will be identical with that described for other boys.

Taken altogether the boys brought before the courts for whatever reason are a cross section of child life in this city. The treatment open to the courts is varied, although still insufficient in the opinion of experts to meet the diverse needs of the children. Probation is the most hopeful and most usual treatment. It will not be discussed here because the principles on which it is based are widely understood.

The courts are guided by the *Children and Young Persons Act* of 1933,[15] which states clearly the principle on which they should be conducted.

"Every court dealing with a child or young person who is brought before it, either as being in need of care or protection or as an offender or otherwise, shall have regard to the welfare of the child or young person and shall in a proper case take steps for removing him from undesirable surroundings, and for securing that proper

---

[14] *Report on Investigation into Conditions of the Colored Population in a Stepney Area,* by Mrs. Phyllis Young, MBE.

[15] Cf. notes in the *Criminal Justice Bill,* pp. 78, 79, 80, 81, 82 and 83 — which relate to proposed new legislation.

provision is made for his education and training."[16] Technically a children's court is still a criminal court, although its central purpose is to promote the welfare of each individual child. Its civil functions are to deal with children charged with being "beyond control" or "in need of care or protection" or with truancy from school, and with child adoption.

The children's courts judges are members of a special panel which in London is appointed by the Secretary of State for Home Affairs from the whole body of justices of the peace. The justices are unpaid and are not lawyers. They are selected because their character and record of public service make them seem specially qualified to deal with children. A court consists of the chairman and two other justices, preferably one of either sex and the chairman may be a woman. There are five children's courts in London and each sits on one day of the week from Monday to Friday.

In London and other big cities children's court justices gain a great deal of experience and the London juvenile courts have been fortunate in securing the services of some outstanding men and women who have contributed much to legislative progress by their work and their books. As in every other field of human affairs the translation of legislative intention into effect depends on the quality of a few individuals in authority. The writer has been privileged to attend children's courts both in New York and London and has been deeply impressed by the swift and sensitive understanding of a child's needs shown equally by a wise chairman of the justices and by an American judge. It is not easy to penetrate behind the silence of a tongue-tied English boy and discover whether fear, bravado or confused misery lies behind persistent bad behavior, but it is done in surprisingly many cases. Good magistrates also make a point of visiting the approved schools and studying their suitability for different children. Some of them manage to establish close touch with children who need it and to maintain a friendly relationship with them throughout their youth.

The courts attempt to be at once dignified and informal. The number of people permitted to attend is strictly limited and a wise chairman will so arrange his court that it is possible for him (or her) to talk intimately and privately with a child. Everyone in the court tries to translate legal terms into simple English, comprehensible to both parents and children. Acquaintance with the vernacular and the way of life of his less fortunate fellow citizens is an important qualification for a children's court magistrate.

The officials of the court include the clerk, who advises the justices on the law, the probation officers, the police and, in London, a representative of the education authority (the L.C.C.) who reports on the child's school record. Many London justices pay high tribute to the sympathetic attitude of the police in children's cases.

Children may be brought to the court as needing care or protection at any age up to seventeen and these cases present great difficulties. They cover children whose parents are unfit to be their guardians, or who fail to exercise proper guardianship; children who are in moral danger or falling into bad company; children who are "beyond control" although their parents have laid no charge; children who have been decoyed or assaulted or are members of a household in which certain sexual offences have taken place. Thus, any child found wandering or destitute or begging or receiving alms can be brought before the court as being "in need of care or protection".

The court may commit the child to an approved school, or to the care of a "fit person", or place him under supervision (probation) for a period of not more than three years, with or without a condition of residence in a fosterhome or hostel.

---

[16] *Children and Young Persons Act* (1933) Section 44 (1).

Finally, the court may order the child's parents or guardian to enter into a bond to exercise proper care or guardianship. Committing the child to a "fit person" normally means removing the child from his home until he is eighteen and the "fit person" must accept full responsibility for the child's upbringing. Nowadays a "fit person" is usually the local authority (for London the L.C.C.), which thus becomes entirely responsible for the child. It may board him out with foster parents, and it should be stated that the L.C.C. has a staff of well qualified and experienced boarding-out officers who, as a result of thorough investigations, have a list of good foster homes, although the supply never meets the demand. It may also send him to an approved school, where he will live and be educated with boys who have offended against the law.

The *Children and Young Persons Act* (1933) also empowers parents or guardians to bring before the court children or young persons on the grounds that they are unable to control them. If the court finds the charge proved and considers such a course to be in the child's interests it may in these cases also commit him to the care of a "fit person" or to an approved school, or place him under supervision (probation) for a period of up to three years — *but in each case only if the parents or guardians consent.*

The underlying causes of these cases vary greatly and they also are difficult to deal with. Sometimes parents, because of their own limitations, are mismanaging a child or are unable to cope with rebellious adolescents, and a good probation officer, backed by supervision order, may be a great help. Occasionally degraded parents or hostile step-parents take this means of getting rid of their children. In such cases it may be desirable to remove the children from their homes for their own protection but not, of course, until full enquiries have been made. It is the duty of the L.C.C. and the probation officer to discover the facts and the court can also ask for a psychiatric report on the child, and can attempt to persuade the parents to visit the remand home psychiatrist. While the enquiries are made the child may be left at home or sent to the remand home which seems to be the better course when the case appears to be one of an unwanted child or of an acute conflict between child and parents. An expanded child guidance service might well reduce the number of cases arising from conflict by helping both parents and children at an early stage.

There is little which needs to be said about truancy cases. Parents are responsible for a child's attendance at school and may have been warned and perhaps fined by an ordinary police court before the child is brought to the children's court. Once it is clear that he will not, for whatever reason, attend regularly, the children's court may commit him to a "fit person" or to an approved school, or put him under the supervision of a probation officer. The court will first do all that it can to get to the bottom of the child's troubles and will often begin by changing his school in consultation with the education authorities. Great care is taken in truancy cases because it is recognized that absence from school may indicate either serious maladjustment in the child or grave disorder in the home.

Turning to the children who are charged with committing an offence against the law, it should be stated that they must be eight years old before they can be charged; that the laws of evidence must be strictly observed and that the child must be helped and encouraged to tell his own story. The chairman of the court threads the difficult path between the absolute necessity for observing legal procedure and the duty of giving a child and his parents the help they so often need. Not only they but also the police must be satisfied that justice is done.

It will be noticed that the court's choice of action is practically the same whether a child is found to be in "need of care or protection", to be "beyond control", or to be guilty of an indictable offence. This may seem illogical and indeed it has drawbacks and produces difficulties for the remand home and the approved schools. Nevertheless it can be argued that, whatever the legal category within which these children fall, their needs are often the same; most of them have a common need for a good home, good parent-figures and a good training for life. In so far as we can supply these good things we may be right to treat all these children alike and to avoid the hypocrisy of stigmatizing and segregating one group of unhappy children as young offenders.

Remands are very usual, except in simple cases, because they give the opportunity for full investigations and reports to be made. Once guilt is established the court has a fairly wide choice. It may dismiss the case if it is not serious or is a first offence; it may, if it seems likely to succeed, bind the child over to be of good behavior, and order the parents to enter into a bond for his good conduct; it may fine the parents in the hope of rousing them to greater responsibility. In the greatest number of cases the courts make a probation order, to which they may attach a variety of conditions, such as boarding out or residence in an "approved" hostel. Unfortunately there are not nearly enough "approved" hostels (i.e. approved by the Home Office). Before the war the existing ones were all run by voluntary organizations but as building becomes possible local authorities will have to provide them. The great advantage of hostels over approved schools is that they do not take boys out of the main current of young life; that there is less "discipline" and that boys can be sent there for as short a stay as six months. Above all, there are hostels where probation cases are mixed with ordinary young people to the great advantage of the probation cases.

A probation order is usually made after the case has been investigated and after consultation with the probation officer. It is unlikely to succeed unless the officer is hopeful and unless the child fully understands what he is undertaking. "It is of the very essence of probation that it rests upon a recognizance, which is a particular kind of promise and acknowledgment. . . . The offender must acknowledge himself bound by all the conditions of recognizance or they are of no effect. . . . Probation really rests upon a promise, not upon compulsion. This is the essential difference between probation and punishment."[18]

It may be of interest to see the number of London boys put on probation during the last nine years and also the number of cases of breach of probation.

Year	Number placed on probation or under supervision	Breach of probation or supervision
1938-39	1,664	170
1939-40	1,631	116
1940-41	1,590	114
1941-42	1,825	133
1942-43	1,687	180
1943-44	1,638	189
1944-45	1,483	173
1945-46	1,514	184
1946-47	1,419	185

Where probation is unsuitable, or has already failed, the court will commit the boy to an approved school, which will involve a period in the remand home. The courts may also send a child or young person to the remand home for a period not

---

[18] L. Le Mesurier: *Handbook of Probation and Social Work*, London, Carswell, 1935, p. 237.

exceeding one month. The theory of this provision is that there are cases where a short, sharp punishment may have permanently good effects. The disadvantage is that the remand home should not be a place of short, sharp punishment as long as it is a place of detention for children who have not yet been tried, and also a temporary shelter for children "in need of care or protection" nor is it such a place in London. We may hope that the provisions of the new Criminal Justice Bill will produce short term residential centres for the group of children who need a sharp lesson. We may also hope that the right children, and only the right children, will be sent to them.

Meantime, the approved school is almost the only resort of the courts when other methods have failed and to send a boy to an approved school is a serious decision because it means taking the child not only out of his home but out of the ordinary life of the community for a period which may be long. The managers of approved schools have the power to release a child or young person at the end of twelve months, but they remain responsible for him and for his care for a further period while he is on license. If he was under fifteen when he was committed he will be on license until he is eighteen; if he was over sixteen he will be on license for three years or up to the age of twenty-one, whichever is the shorter. Moreover any boy may be recalled to his approved school if it seems necessary while he is on license. The maximum period of detention for a child is up to fifteen, and for a young person under sixteen, three years. The average stay at present is about eighteen months, depending entirely on the boy's behavior.

The juvenile courts can only commit to Borstal young offenders who have absconded from, or behaved very badly at, an approved school. Even in these cases the tendency is to try the effect of transference to another approved school before committal to Borstal. It is not proposed to discuss the Borstal system here, partly because it is sufficiently well known already, and partly because it provides for an older age group than that under consideration.

Let us consider the London Boys Remand Home, to which so many of the boys we have been discussing find their way — some 1,200 to 1,300 a year.[19] It is governed by the L.C.C. and, like all other institutions provided by this authority, it is managed by a committee consisting partly of elected councillors and partly of co-opted members, chosen for a special interest in this type of work. The committees meet at regular intervals and, between meetings, the members visit the institutions regularly. Although the powers of managing committees are small their existence is a great safeguard. An actively interested committee, whose members make it their business to be intimately acquainted with the institution for which they are responsible, can do much to ensure that it is run on the lines intended by the Education Committee of the L.C.C. The remand home is also subject to inspection both by the London County Council and the Home Office inspectorate. In the same way the approved schools are governed by managing committees and are subject to dual inspection.

It is a truism among those interested in difficult children that the supreme problem is to find a sufficient number of men and women of fine calibre to deal with them. The L C.C. has met this problem by selecting as heads of its remand homes and

---

[19] *Number of boys admitted to the remand home:*
Year ending 31st March 1942............1415
Year ending 31st March 1943............1447
Year ending 31st March 1944............1325   Average number: 1350
Year ending 31st March 1945............1212

The decline since 1944 will be noticed. It is still maintained and may be attributed to London's recovery from the worst war conditions.

approved schools headteachers drawn from its education service. This system has great advantages; it secures that the heads of these institutions shall be well-educated men, whose training and experience should ensure understanding of boys. Nevertheless the remand home presents staffing problems. Teaching in an institution where boys, ideally, should not stay for more than two weeks is a great sacrifice for good teachers and only a strong sense of devotion to the needs of the boys can secure and keep the right men. The problems confronting these teachers are probably the most difficult in the whole field of education. It is estimated that about 5 per cent of the boys admitted are educationally sub-normal (that is, high grade defectives) and 15 to 20 per cent are educationally retarded, which may be the result of truancy, physical illness or maladjustment. In addition there is a constantly changing population of thirty to one hundred boys, aged from eight to sixteen, and the staff have no means of knowing whether a boy will be with them for two weeks or for many months. When a boy belongs to a religious denomination which supports its own approved schools (Roman Catholic or Jewish for instance) he must be sent to a denominational school and may have to wait many months before there is a vacancy.

The London remand home is extremely fortunate both in its staffing and its site. Although it is in a built-up area it has a large secluded garden, giving ample room for football and other games, for gardening and for keeping animals. The present superintendent is a first class gardener and has a skilled staff, and it is refreshing to see peach trees in bloom and to watch boys from slum streets attending to prize rabbits, hens or dogs, or learning the mysteries of bee-keeping. The building is functionally suitable for its purpose and, unlike most institutions in postwar England, is kept freshly and gaily decorated through the enthusiasm of the supervisory staff working with older boys.

Normal school hours are kept with plenty of opportunity for painting, wood work and varied handicrafts, taught by skilled and inventive craftsmen teachers. The approach to the educational problems of this heterogeneous group of boys is original. The object is to make every lesson a self-contained unit which will interest and appeal to a new boy or an old resident. Lessons are based on known practical familiar objects and situations; thus geography may start from a fish dinner or from the production and distribution of tea. Great stress is laid on speech training, and on helping boys to learn to read for enjoyment. Citizenship is one of the most important subjects. The boys learn of the facilities for recreation and education which are available to them in London and religion, politics, civics, international relations and the United Nations are freely discussed. Teachers try to make real to the boys the development of a democratic people and the necessity for laws and a police force — with special reference to the law as it affects themselves.

A considerable number of the boys are physically and mentally below the average; some are badly co-ordinated, with poor posture and gait, therefore physical training and games play a great part in their curriculum. Whenever weather permits all physical exercise takes place in the open air. They improve rapidly in bodily condition and are helped by music. All marching is done to music and rhythm soon affects their movements. Visual aids are also freely used; they are particularly valuable for educationally retarded boys and the L.C.C.'s libraries of instructional films, film strips and slides keep the home supplied.

The life of the remand home must be conducted behind locked doors, but as soon as boys have proved themselves trustworthy they are allowed out in supervised parties for expeditions to swimming baths, cinemas and so on. The basic principle on which the home is run is to rehabilitate by education and incentive, and punishment is rare. The team spirit is encouraged by dividing the home into two sides, port side and starboard side. Boys receive marks for their school work, their conduct, handicrafts and games. They are classified individually according to their conduct but their marks affect the total of the side they belong to and thus determine the privileges it receives. Good conduct also brings personal responsibility and privilege. Boys appointed as prefects wear honorable badges and enjoy a pleasant sitting room with its own library.

Recreation is varied — games, indoor and outdoor, swimming, boxing (voluntary), reading, radio and entertainment films all fill up out-of-school time. The key note of the atmosphere is struck at morning assembly, where, after a few simple prayers and a well sung hymn, records of great music are played. The superintendent talks about the music and the composers, and from them passes to a simple, brief talk about life and religion, stimulating contributions from the boys. To the observer it seems that the music has released the burden on the spirits of these children. Their faces clear, their anxieties are temporarily lifted and their hearts are open to the wise words of the superintendent.

As soon as the boys arrive they are put into good clothes. They receive a full medical examination and treatment for any minor disorders; hospitalization is arranged for serious treatment. The courts now ask for psychological reports on most of the children on remand and for some years it has been the official intention to establish a full observation centre at the remand home. This has not yet been carried out but progress has been made. For some years the staff have carried out psycho-metric tests and they also initiated an interesting survey of family histories. Out of 100 boys, 48 had home lives which were classified as normal, although the mothers of 9 out of the 48 were engaged in part-time work outside their homes. Normal homes were defined as those in which father and mother lived at home in circumstances which appeared conducive to wholesome family life. The other 52 cases were classified as follows:

Parents legally separated	3
Parents illegally separated	8
(Of.these, five cases came within the category of "co-habiting")	
Father dead	10
Mother dead	6
Step-father in the home	6
Step-mother in the home	2
Father in the Forces	14
Mother out at work	20

In addition the following abnormal conditions were noted:

  (i) Five of the delinquents were illegitimate children; three of the delinquents were adopted children.

  (ii) In one case both parents were blind.

  (iii) In one case the mother was epileptic.

  (iv) In one case the father was completely crippled.

  (v) In one case the father was alleged to suffer from religious "mania".

  (vi) In one case both parents had criminal records.

  (vii) In one case both parents had been convicted of parental neglect.

This very useful study of a sample of the remand home population tells the usual story but it can shed no light on causation in the cases of the 48 boys with outwardly normal home lives.

A visiting psychiatrist interviews those boys for whom the court asks for a psychiatric report, and a teacher has recently been appointed who is a fully qualified psychologist; unfortunately it has not so far been possible to find a psychiatric social worker for the remand home.

To sum up: It is hoped that before long a junior remand home will be opened for eight and nine year old boys and when this is established we may hope that some women will be introduced onto the staff, since it is obvious that maternal failure is the cause of the difficulties of a great many of these boys. Meantime, although we cannot know how the remand home seems to the boys — and perhaps it strikes each one differently — we can be sure that while they are there they are well employed and treated with justice and kindness. It seems probable that boys who come there for "delinquency" caused by sheer high spirits, and those who come because their low mentality and poor background makes them easily misled, benefit greatly. It is not so clear that those who are deeply disturbed emotionally can all be helped by this wise and sane regime. Some will find security in the strength and warmth of the staff but insecurity must be increased by the temporariness of their stay. Some, of course, attend child guidance clinics while on remand.

There has been much discussion of the proposal to classify and segregate remand home boys. While this may be theoretically the ideal procedure it is not clear that, in the present state of our knowledge, it is necessarily the wisest plan. Every good day school carries its proportion of maladjusted or unstable children and it seems possible that in the mixed population of the remand home it is easier to achieve adjustment, *given proper psychological treatment* when necessary, than would be the case in homogeneous groups. Segregation would seem to mean labelling boys as non-delinquents, ordinary delinquents and moral or sexual delinquents (or equivalent terms). Clearly no such rigid lines can be drawn by rough and ready methods. It would require intensive psychiatric study of each boy to approximate to correct classification. This is impossible with the present shortage of skilled child psychiatrists and it seems the better course to allow the boys to learn good and bad from each other in a good atmosphere, remembering that at their ages character is still fluid.

The L.C.C. maintains three approved schools for London boys; a junior school for boys under thirteen on admission; an intermediate one for boys of thirteen and fourteen, and a senior one for boys of fifteen and sixteen. There are at present altogether about five hundred boys in these three schools and about four hundred and fifty of London's delinquent boys are in voluntary approved schools. It is not proposed to discuss the senior school as the boys sent there are passing out of the school age range.

An English visitor to the junior or intermediate school would have the impression that he was approaching a select private boarding school except for the "L.C.C. School" (*not "Approved School"*) on the gate. The schools are housed in well-built red brick buildings; they stand behind sheltering trees, surrounded by green lawns, in open country. Each has its own farm, its football fields, its swimming pool. Inside too is the familiar atmosphere of the typical English boys' boarding school; the long tiled corridors, the old fashioned, unattractive, depressing classrooms, often with high windows, the great hall for meals and assembly, even the shelf of silver sports trophies. There is the same hurly burly of boys, the same lack of anything quiet or homelike, the lack of privacy and of personal possessions. The great reforming wave which produced and followed the *Children Act* of 1933 set out to create good boarding schools for delinquent boys, in place of the old reformatories and industrial schools. To some extent it succeeded. The English boarding school was the ideal educational institution to most of the well-educated men concerned with this problem and they set to work to give antisocial children the best system they knew. It is possible at once to honor their motives and to question their wisdom. English boys of the upper and upper middle class income groups go to their private boarding schools from relatively spacious and, in the main, emotionally secure homes, and they spend four months of the year on holiday with their families. The shock of the large institution must be considerable to boys coming from poor homes with little rooms and its impersonality may well seem menacing to those without secure home ties.

During the thirties a number of smaller experimental approved schools were established up and down the country and but for the war doubtless there would have been great progress in building, or in adapting existing buildings, so that boys could live in smaller units. As it is, 130 to 140 boys live together in each of these schools, sleeping, eating, learning and playing in large groups.

The most striking feature of the schools is their freedom. Here there are no locked doors. The gardens, the farm and the open country invite absconding, yet it is not one of the major problems. It comes in waves, in epidemics and then dies down again. If it is repeated too often by the same boy he may be sent to a different school where he may make a better adjustment. Although one headmaster assured us that the key to the fact that the majority of the boys do settle down was "good food", it is also clear that if a boy finds a real interest among the varied activities available, his problems are solved.

The local authority has the duty of providing education in the schools and the London County Council takes very great pains to select teachers with a vital interest in this work. During the war it was naturally difficult to find sufficient suitable young men but it seems that wartime experiences have produced a number of teachers who wish to devote themselves to boys who have had a bad start in life. It needs devotion to make a good master in an approved school because there is a certain isolation about the life and a fear of being cut off from the usual ladder of promotion.

The age spread in the schools is a great difficulty. In the junior school, boys are admitted from eight to thirteen, but they may stay there up to fifteen and the gap between a boy of eight and a precociously developed boy of fifteen is very great. Similarly, in the intermediate school some of the boys of thirteen are still little boys while the older ones — especially those who are recalled for getting into trouble after leaving — are young men.

The normal school curriculum is worked in the junior school plus a certain amount of domestic activity. Outside school hours there is a great deal of swimming in the indoor baths and all ordinary school games are played. This school competes in national swimming championships and plays cricket, football, chess and table tennis against local schools and boys' clubs. It also visits local factories and public utilities and has visiting lecturers. The boys receive a reasonable amount of pocket money, fixed in accordance with their age.

The intermediate school carries a staff of qualified trade instructors as well as school teachers, and boys of school age attend trade classes one day a week. The choice of trades in this particular school is woodwork, metalwork, farming or gardening. The boys choose their trade while still below school leaving age (fifteen), try it for a period in their weekly trade class and then change if they wish to. When they are fifteen they begin to train seriously, but continue to do one day's schooling a week. Religious teaching in the schools is broad-based, undenominational, and aims at raising the level of thinking and feeling of the boys and at relating the Christian ethic to communal life.

The English "public" (private) school prefect system has been introduced into the schools and in some of them the boys themselves elect their own prefects. This system is intended to develop responsibility and leadership, but it has, we believe, drawbacks. The very fact that most of the boys are below average intelligence and are socially or emotionally undeveloped affects their ability to choose wisely. Critics of the system object that boys tend to elect bullies and then to suffer from them.

What do the boys gain in these schools? They have all the advantages of playing fields, games, good food and medical attention and undoubtedly, they gain rapidly in height, weight and manners. At best — and there are many such cases — they develop self-respect, self-control, responsibility, and good attitudes to life, absorbed unconsciously from one or other of the fine men who are to be found among the teachers and instructors in the schools. Yet unhappiness and insecurity are still there for a major problem in approved schools for boys is enuresis. The education committee of the London County Council has shown great interest in this problem in its residential institutions and has received careful reports on the situation. Apart from the fact that some headmasters are more successful than others in reducing its incidence, no fresh light has yet been thrown on this stubborn symptom. As far as can be observed punitive or reproachful attitudes are disappearing, which is, in part at least the result of the experience gained during wartime evacuation, when the widespread nature of this problem became established and the difficulties of curing it were realized.

The results of the modern approved schools are difficult to assess. What are the tests by which success or failure is to be measured? Certainly if a boy leaves an approved school and then repeatedly changes his job or falls into the hands of the police again and again, something is wrong. On the other hand, the fact that neither happens does not necessarily mean that the boy is a happy citizen, living and working up to his full capacity. Any conclusions therefore can only be rough and ready. In 1938 the Home Office[20] reported that while 25 per cent of the boys from approved schools appeared before the courts again during the first three years after leaving, analysis of their offences showed that only 20 per cent of the charges against them were serious. They therefore concluded that for 80 per cent of the boys the system had, generally speaking, proved a success.

When a boy of school age leaves the junior school to return home he will be helped and watched over, as far as is possible by the special officers of the London County Council who are attached to the education area offices all over London and by the after-care officers. When a boy of fifteen or over leaves he will be found lodgings or put in a hostel if he has no suitable home. Work will be found for him and the after-care officer who is attached to his approved school and will have made friends with him there, will keep in touch with him. Often the headmaster or other teachers visit old boys in their free time, and some boys come back to pay visits to the schools.

The powers of the managers of an approved school over boys under supervision are wide; they may direct them to live in a certain place, to take up a particular job or to return to the school for a period of not longer than three months as they think the interests of the boys direct. All boys receive an outfit of clothes on leaving and are assisted with an allowance of money when they start earning, if their earnings are inadequate to support them and to provide reasonable pocket money. It should be mentioned that parents may be called on by the courts to contribute to the cost of supporting their children in approved schools.

---

[20] Home Office. *Fifth Report on the Work of the Children's Branch,* H.M.S.O. 1938.

Since the war the Home Office has advocated the appointment of "housemasters" to these schools, another institution borrowed from the English private boarding schools. The idea is that the housemaster will be responsible for the happiness and well being of a reasonably small group of boys and, provided that he has the physical facilities to make it possible — a cozy sitting room, books to lend and so on — it might do much to introduce a more personal relationship into the boys' lives. Many experts hold strongly that decentralization is the most urgent step; that boys should live together in houses grouped around the school block, with not more than twenty in a house, in the charge of a husband and wife so that they have some feeling of a "home". If the biggest single cause of delinquency is an arrest or deviation in the development of the emotions and character due to the lack of good family relationships, then this line of advance seems to be essential. Every institution for delinquent children should be staffed so that each child is in the personal care of a good man or a good woman and "institutionalism", however good, must disappear as fast as possible. This will not be easy to achieve because we have not advanced far on the road to scientific selection of the men and women needed for this work, but the techniques are available and sooner or later will be used for this purpose.

Further, we must not forget the proportion of delinquency due to sheer deprivation. It can be simplified by saying that boys like bicycles (and many other things) and that out of many who have virtually no possessions of their own some will steal them. It may even be argued that in our present material civilization the possession of a certain number of things is essential to the full development of the ego. Whether that is true or not, it seems essential that boys who have consistently stolen should, as part of their treatment, be given private possessions and a place in which to keep them securely. By this means they may learn to respect the possessions of others and without it their profound frustration may break out again in stealing at the first opportunity.

Finally, we believe that in any approved school population there is a minority of boys whose experience of life has been so unfortunate that they have no reason to trust or like their fellow human beings. They are called maladjusted and for them psychiatric treatment seems the most economical and promising way of trying to undo the wrong that has been done them. It is not easy to provide, as the schools are all in the country, but it is very necessary that this need should be met. Meantime it is possible to believe that in youth good food, good football and good teaching count for a lot and that the majority of boys adjust themselves to their new life, benefit from the training given to them, and leave with a chance of making a satisfactory life.

VI. PREVENTIVE SERVICES

Since it is not possible to raise the standards of homes and parenthood by any short term policy, the swiftest and surest prevention of delinquency is a fine educational service in the broadest sense of the word. Such a service must of necessity function outside as well as inside school hours and even outside school terms. It must cover as great a span of years as possible, and, in this connection, the British Government's courage in raising the compulsory school age from fourteen to fifteen in 1947 was notable. It increases her already serious shortage of industrial workers but it gives youth another year in which to mature and to learn good citizenship.

A good educational system must provide for all the needs of children — physical, intellectual, spiritual and emotional. It must offer stimulation to the imagination, outlets for the energies and training for the innate talents of childhood and youth. All these things the London education system sets out to do. It will be many years before all its services can be provided for all children, but the patterns of the services had been set in London before the war and now they are steadily extending, limited only by shortage of staff and by the impossibility of building new schools at present. The following summary account of some of the education services may indicate their range and suggest their contribution to the prevention of delinquency.

London is fortunate in possessing 106 parks covering 6,716 acres, and these parks provide football and cricket pitches, open air swimming and Punch and Judy shows, concerts, ballets and theatre for children and adults. In addition to the parks the London County Council has, since 1934, been acquiring land in a vast circle round the periphery of London. This "Green Belt" of parkland, meadow and downland which will be London's playground forever, covers 75,000 acres and before long will reach 125,000 acres, and in it will be playing fields with class rooms attached where eventually all the older children will spend one day a week. Then the younger children will get the sole use of the existing 700 acres of city playing fields.

The Council already uses three holiday camps at which 9,400 children last year spent two weeks, spread between March and November. Teachers accompany their classes and they give eloquent testimony to the physical and emotional enjoyment and the intellectual stimulus arising from the free country life, the varied activities and above all perhaps from the close association between themselves and the children.

Play centres and junior clubs are already organized by the Education Service in over one hundred schools and other centres. They open at the end of afternoon school until seven o'clock from Monday to Friday and many play centres now remain open throughout the school holidays. In addition there is of course a great number of clubs for boys and girls run by voluntary associations. An analysis of the incidence of juvenile delinquency in different months of the year, on different days of the week and at different hours of the day correlated to the periods when schools are closed and to the existing provision of clubs and play centres might establish the great value of these services.

The recreational provision for young people above school age is probably even greater. More than thirty million hours will be worked this year by students in London's technical and evening institutes. Some of the students are teen age and some are adults. In addition a fine new experiment is developing in the provision of evening recreation centres for adolescents. The branch of the Education Service in charge of this work is appropriately named "Youth Service" and is full of promise.

All headteachers are encouraged to organize school expeditions of educational value and in this way parties of London school children are all the time visiting museums, picture galleries, historical buildings, public utilities, hospitals. At last the children are being introduced to their great historical and cultural heritage. Last year good plays were presented by the Children's Theatre and the Young Vic Company to 73,000 children; another 20,000 saw the students of the Royal Academy of Dramatic Art in Shakespeare plays and 132,000 saw special matinees of opera and ballet by our best companies. A series of first class orchestral concerts for school children is given each season in halls all over London and musical appreciation is now taught in the schools.

So much for the cultural and recreational side of the service. It is perhaps on the physical side that the results are most clearly seen.

Early in World War II the British Government, faced with a great reduction in important food and the danger of malnutrition for children, urged all education authorities to provide good hot midday meals and free milk for all school children.

To this measure — and to the special rations for expectant mothers and for infants — we may attribute much of the improvement in the health and size of England's school children over the last eight years. The visitor to a London school today must be struck by the health and vigor of the vast majority of children even in the poorest district.

Last year over 160,000 London children had first class dinners every day in school and the number grows weekly as accommodation is provided, either by the adaptation of old buildings or by the erection of temporary huts. School dinners have come to stay and the Government's policy is to provide free dinners for every child as soon as it becomes possible.

At present the Council provides free milk for all children and charges about five cents for dinners to parents above a certain income level. As the demand greatly exceeds the supply priority is given to delicate children and to those whose mothers go to work.

Last year the Council's school health service carried out 369,635 medical inspections and dental units travel round the schools all the time. Care of the health of the children is, we believe, of great importance in the prevention of delinquency. The steady misery of malnutrition or neglected illness produces psychological ill-health in its train and predisposes to antisocial behavior. In this connection the work of the Special Education Department of the Council cannot be overlooked. It provides special education for 5,043 children in 62 day schools and for 1,152 in 24 residential schools. These children suffer from various handicaps; there are special schools for blind and partially sighted, for deaf, crippled and delicate children, also for educationally sub-normal children. It is noteworthy that physically handicapped children are taught in classes of not more than twenty. A few residential nursery schools are provided in the country for tiny children who are parentless or homeless and, since they are run by highly trained nursery school teachers, these are in many ways wonderful institutions. Physically and mentally the children thrive magnificently although we do not yet know the emotional effect of this life for little children.

The Special Education Sub-Committee is also responsible for a number of residential schools and homes for children of all ages who are homeless, whether temporarily or permanently. These institutions range from old-fashioned barrack-like buildings housing nearly five hundred children (an inheritance from the past) to small groups of homes with twenty to forty children in each. None approaches the ideal standard of homes for eight to twelve children recommended by the *Curtis Report*. All the big ones suffer from the same defects as the approved schools; they are too big and too impersonal; they lack privacy and home-likeness; the children have virtually no private possessions nor any secure place to keep them.

Some provide a complete school on the premises and, as they get older, intelligent children go out from them to grammar and technical schools. From the smaller homes the children attend the ordinary schools of the district. There is much to be said for this system. It keeps the children in the main stream of child life and lessens their sense of "difference". On the other hand, those residential homes large enough to have their own schools have the advantage of being staffed by resident trained and experienced teachers.

Many criticisms are made of the big homes. Those which are for boys or girls only provide a very unnatural life. The children have no experience of the other sex and can form no close emotional ties with adults. It is commonly said by experts that young people who have grown up in them are affectionless, easily led, weak and unable to stand on their own feet when they emerge into the world. It is also said, and we think rightly, that little children should never be put into big institutions and that their deprivation can be measured by their hungry demands for affection from visitors.

The L.C.C. is conscious of these defects and is planning great improvements when they become possible. Nevertheless, some of these institutions do very fine work and all of them help some children. They take in a heterogeneous child population of all ages and types; maladjusted and adjusted, intelligent and otherwise, delinquent (in fact if not in law) and co-operative. They are given healthy surroundings, first class food, good clothes, games, physical training and a diversity of amusements. They do not, and cannot, provide the children with what they need — good homes and parents — but they are infinitely better than the present alternative of leaving them to take their chance in a world which has failed them. The present writer has talked to intelligent, proud, independent children in their teens, still living in the homes but receiving first class education in technical schools or commercial colleges and looking forward confidently to life in the outside world.

The L.C.C. owns a large children's camp by the sea which is used to provide holidays for children in all the Special Education Committee's residential institutions. It holds over four hundred children and last year three thousand spent a fortnight's holiday there. Every boy in the approved schools has his holiday there, in addition to his time at home. The headmasters speak highly of the good effects of this free co-operative camping life where approved school boys mix with every other type of child growing up in the L.C.C.'s homes.

All these institutions for handicapped and deprived children are a further prevention of delinquency, because they give shelter and protection to those children most in need of it. A more direct method was initiated by the L.C.C. many years ago — the Children's Care Section. It is administered by highly trained social workers and there is a trained staff of five or six in each of the nine area education offices in London; for the rest the work is done, under their organization, by voluntary workers. Their function is to promote the well-being of children in their own homes whenever there is need of help and before the war a great work was done by these devoted voluntary workers. Since the war it has been difficult to find a sufficient number of suitable people with enough free time to meet the need, but the work goes on and in addition to women, a substantial number of men — clergymen, club-leaders, professional men, manual workers — give some of their spare time to it.

A staff Care Committee worker attends every medical inspection in every school and sees that, when it is necessary, a worker helps a mother to carry out medical recommendations. Also a staff worker visits each school once a week to confer with the head teacher on any children who are causing anxiety. Increasingly the Care Committee workers are concentrating on children who present psychological problems. For instance, when a "maladjusted" child is taken away from his home, whether by order of the courts or by the L.C.C. for treatment, either the probation officer or the Care Committee worker visits the home to give news of the child's progress; they try to make friends with the parents and do all that they can to improve the home and the parents' understanding of the child's difficulties before he returns. This fine service has proved its value over many years but under modern conditions it needs many more paid full-time workers.

In 1944 another very interesting experiment in preventive work started: the Problem Case Conference. London is divided into nine administrative areas for education, with a Divisional Education officer and staff in each, responsible for about one hundred schools. Any one concerned with children — school doctor or nurse, head teachers, Care Committee workers, parents or others — who believes that a child's behavior is abnormal, reports it to the Divisional Educational officer. He sees the child and, if he considers it necessary, brings the case before the Case Conference, which meets once a fortnight and consists of himself, the District Medical Officer, the District School Inspector and the Care Officer. All the information which has meantime been collected about the child, including both school reports and a report on the home, is considered. The school enquiry officer comes into the picture here. It is his duty, in addition to enforcing attendance at school, to get to know families which are in difficulties and to produce reports when they are needed. Five school enquiry officers work in combination with the Care Committee in each area, three of them specializing on cases of delinquency.

The Case Conference may recommend attendance at a child guidance clinic; if it suspects mental defect it may order a statutory examination so that, if necessary, the child will go to a special school for educationally sub-normal children; it may consider the child to be "maladjusted" under the 1944 *Education Act,* which makes it possible to board him out in a foster-home or to send him to a special residential school for such children. Residential units for maladjusted children are beginning to be formed by the L.C.C. but it is too early to consider their results. Finally the Case Conference may decide that a child is mildly maladjusted and for these cases another approach is being tried. A special day school has been organized where these children spend half their time in groups of not more than eight, with teachers carefully selected for their understanding of difficult children. The rest of their time they spend in their own school.

The object of the Case Conference is, whenever possible, to leave difficult children in their own homes, but to give some help at once so that the problems will not grow worse. It should be pointed out that they have no power to send any child away from home without the consent of the parents.

In the year 1946-47 the Case Conferences dealt with 1,581 children in all, in the ratio of about two boys to one girl. Approximately half the cases are described as behavior problems and most of the rest are either educationally retarded or subnormal. A very high proportion of the children — in some areas the majority — are sent to child guidance clinics.

Here is the beginning of a promising scheme. As it develops — and the number of children dealt with has greatly increased every year — it should be able to give help to a great many children before their problems become too much for them, provided that there is sufficient provision for different methods of treatment. It is interesting to note that many of the workers in this field are pressing for education for parents. The L.C.C. has made a beginning with classes on parent craft at an evening institute; the churches and voluntary organizations like the Marriage Guidance Council are also trying to supply this great need but there is as yet no sign that society as a whole is awake to our failure in this direction. It is estimated that, at the existing rate, one in every five marriages will break down; it is known that in 1947 72,000 children saw their homes broken, but it is still true that our educational system does virtually nothing to make young adults understand their vital responsibility as parents.

The majority of the children referred to the Case Conferences are sent by them to child guidance clinics and nothing has yet been said about London's clinics. It is difficult to generalize, except to say that it is well recognized that the total number is entirely inadequate to the need and that they all have very long waiting lists. Further, the clinics complain that the children are, in the main, sent far too late, when their symptoms have become acute. In the meantime, the parents have become discouraged, their own tension has mounted and, very often, the children have got into trouble. The work of the clinics is therefore handicapped by late referral and by erratic attendance, which is inevitable when children have to be sent to any clinic which has a vacancy even if it entails a long journey across London.

There are about nine voluntary clinics used by the Council, mostly in hospitals, but including such famous units as the Tavistock and East London child guidance clinics. In addition children are sent to the Maudsley Hospital (the Council's most famous mental hospital). Between 1946 and 1947 the Case Conferences referred 981 children to these clinics, or double the number of the previous year.

In the spring of 1947 the Council decided to establish its own child guidance service, but unfortunately shortage of buildings and trained personnel have prevented any substantial progress. Under the *Education Act* it is incumbent on education authorities to provide treatment for maladjusted children and to carry out this provision London needs something like double its present number of clinics. Meantime the Council has appointed a part-time consultant psychiatrist, and a full-time psychiatrist and psychologist to organize the present services and to plan the service of the future which is urgently needed, not only for the prevention and treatment of delinquency, but for the promotion of mental health in children who never come before the courts and, above all, for those children for whom the Council has to provide home life.

It will be clear from the foregoing brief survey of London's preventive services that a great deal of valuable work is being done and that many promising experiments are under way. As they enlarge and develop we feel that, from the very variety of the services and the many angled approach, there will be a great reduction in the number of children who present intractable problems.

VII. The Future

If we believe that delinquency is the failure of the individual to adjust to society, then we should concentrate all our efforts on promoting that adjustment. If, on the other hand, we believe that delinquency is a social disease, then every measure taken to raise the level of society must reduce its incidence. This writer holds the view that children are the product of their environment, that their failure is the result of society's failure, and, therefore, that the great social legislation passed in Britain since the end of the war is of immense importance for the solution of this problem.

Unfortunately, peace did not bring security to this country, but a new struggle for survival in the economic field, and no citizen of Great Britain can write about the future of the social service with any certainty, because, whatever the intentions of the Government and the people may be, the country's economic position is not within our control. Dependent as we are on imported food to support a population which increased fourfold during the hundred and fifty years of the Industrial Revolution; faced by a world whose total food supply falls far short of the minimum needs of its population, the future is not clear. If the people of Britain are to maintain even their present standard of living, it is necessary for them greatly to increase their exports and to find markets for them. Nor can success in this difficult endeavor preserve them unless the world's total supply of food increases, because as long as the present shortage prevails and the price of food continues to rise, British labor must produce more and more goods to pay for the same quantity of imported food. This is the background to the present situation. It has, for instance, necessitated stringent curtailment of Britain's desperately needed building program, because imports of timber must be reduced, and it is more important to increase the labor force in the export industries than in the building trades. It is the background to any picture of the future; we cannot know what proportion of our population can be spared for teaching, for caring for deprived and disturbed children, for psychological and sociological research. It is therefore only possible to outline the Government's policy in all the fields which directly affect the lives of children.

First, and perhaps most important, is the policy of expansion of industry and full employment. Whereas between the wars there were always several million workers unemployed and in want, since the war the fear of unemployment has been lifted from English homes. Next, we should remember the new and comprehensive social insurance system which insures free medical treatment for all and removes the fear of want through illness. The provision of children's allowances, supplemented by free school meals and milk, have also done much to remove the financial burdens of parentage and to raise the living standard of the poorest.

If bad housing is a factor directly contributing to delinquency, then the housing achievements and plans of the Government, of the London County Council and of other local authorities must be taken into account. They are very considerable, especially as reconversion of industry from war to peace has been carried out and the increase of export goods has steadily increased during the same period. Between the end of the war and November, 1947, over half a million families have been rehoused, which means over one and a half million individuals. A total of 315,452 new houses built with Government subsidies to rent to working class families and a further 267,289 under construction is a great contribution towards the national goal of providing a good home for every child in the country.

Today the planning of housing and education go hand in hand. The new *Education Act* (1944) laid it down that every education authority should submit to the Minister its own plan for carrying out the provisions of the *Act*. The London County Council's Education plan is a great work, interlocked with the County of London plan for the rehousing of London. If they can both be carried out together, a new and noble London will rise from the ashes of the old city, which has grown steadily since Roman days, without plan or direction, into a sprawl of such dimensions that it presents the greatest problem in the world to those interested in the creation of good urban life. The Council's plan for schools covers every area and every type of school. At best it will take many years to put it into effect but its achievement would mean a first class school life for every London child. A popular explanation of the plan has been published and the eagerness with which it is bought shows the enthusiasm of the citizens of London for education.

Buildings alone, however good, do not make an educational system. The quality of the teachers and other staff is the most important factor in any institution dealing with children. Everyone responsible for "difficult" or "deprived" or "delinquent" children — or as we might more correctly call them, unfortunate children — is deeply aware that the most urgent need is to find more men and women of fine quality and good education, and to train them intensively for this work. No adults but the best can help children who have already been betrayed and injured by the adult world. This is one of the main objects of the *Children Bill* and of the training schemes for children's officers recently instituted by the Home Office.

In addition to the problems of finding and training the right people to staff residential institutions for children there is the need for trained personnel for research in this field. At every turn the investigator is baffled by the lack of essential information. It would be no exaggeration to say that no scientific survey of delinquency and no real plan for treatment is possible until a thorough statistical survey is carried out. An analysis of the cases which come before the children's courts modelled on that in the Report of the Municipal Court of Philadelphia is a primary necessity. Neither is it possible to plan suitable treatment without an adequate psychiatric service. It may be that many children can be re-educated without psychiatric help but it is certain that some cannot. It is therefore essential to have a first class diagnostic service and to make treatment available for all those boys who are likely to become social problems without it. Congested child guidance clinics, harassed by shortage of funds, cannot fill the need, moreover they only exist in cities; in many parts of rural England, where the residential institutions for children are situated, there is not even a skeleton service. The first essential, it would seem, is the planning of a travelling psychiatric unit, which would survey the field and assess the number of children needing treatment and then plan treatment centres.

Public opinion is ready for this advance and official opinion is gradually accepting the necessity for an experimental use of psychiatry. Great hopes rest on the few psychiatrists working with children in Britain. It is necessary to increase their numbers rapidly and for them to seize the great opportunities offered by the new *Health Service Act,* the *Education Act* and the *Children Bill.* Much depends on their ability to work in cooperation with the officers of local authorities and government departments, and upon their readiness to try out new methods, such as group therapy and the training of psychologists and psychiatric social workers as therapists.

If this paper seems to have stressed the shortcomings of the services London provides for its least fortunate children it is because at this moment the opportunity for a great advance to a positive, creative policy of rehabilitation is present. The London County Council has always been deeply concerned with its responsibility for such children and has, in the past, raised the national standard by its imaginative innovations. It has shown a magnificent concern for handicapped children and has developed many services within its great educational system which are full of promise for the solution of the problems of unhappy childhood. Given peace and economic security we believe that the stubborn figures of boyish delinquency and the unknown numbers of unhappy children destined to become neurotic adults can be materially reduced, if we are prepared to discard old ideas where necessary, to adopt a scientific attitude and to put into practice the knowledge we already possess about children and their needs.

DELINQUENCY IN INDIA

By G. BOSE, M.D.

The term "delinquency" which in ordinary usage means neglect of duty, guilt, sin of omission, misdeed, etc., has come to acquire a special connotation. This term is used in "abnormal psychology" with reference to the misdeeds of juveniles only. An adult offender is not a delinquent in the technical sense of the term. Then again, all offenses committed by juveniles do not come under the category of delinquency. Delinquency comprises only those offenses by minors that would be punishable in the case of adults under the existing legal code. The legal codes of different countries vary to some extent and with it the conception of delinquency in the legal sense also varies. The Penal Code in India does not refer to "delinquency" but uses instead the expression "juvenile offense". The whole problem of delinquency arose from the social and practical necessity of treating juvenile offenders in a way different from that adopted in the case of hardened adult criminals. One cannot draw a sharp line of demarcation to separate juvenile criminals from the adult ones. Mental deficiency is often associated with delinquency but here again no sharp border line really exists between mental deficiency and normal intelligence.

Misdemeanor in early childhood is of special interest to the psychiatrist. Psychoanalysts believe that the seed of much future mischief is laid before the age of five. The antisocial behavior of children before the age of seven is no concern of the law but to the eye of the psychiatrist it belongs to the same category as cognizable juvenile offense. In India the legal tendency is to consider all young offenders from the age of seven up to the age of twenty-one as "juveniles", although the law does not specifically say so. In connection with the Student Welfare Scheme of Calcutta University, I had occasion to conduct a large series of observations on the mental and physical development of the student population of Bengal. The age of maturity was seen to lie within the age groups twenty-one and twenty-two. There is therefore some sort of scientific justification for considering all offenders before the age of twenty-one as belonging to one group, a group that requires special treatment. No juvenile offender can be detained in a Reformatory School after he has reached the age of eighteen which is the legal age of maturity in India but in juvenile jails there are many inmates of ages ranging from fifteen to twenty-one. It is not from any scientific consideration, however, that these offenders are selected to be housed in juvenile jails, nor is there any specific legal direction to that effect. The only justification that the authorities have in view, in selecting cases for admission to juvenile jails, is one of practical convenience from the standpoint of administration and rehabilitation.

THE LEGAL ASPECT OF DELINQUENCY IN INDIA

According to the ancient lawgivers of India, a parent should not administer any
punishment for any offense to a child who is under five years of age. Children of such
tender age should be nursed and educated with love and affection only. After the age
of five punishment may be given in some suitable form such as physical chastisement
or rebuke by the parents. Towards the later half of childhood, however, punishment
should be gradually withdrawn and replaced by advice. From the age of sixteen
upward sons and daughters should be treated as friends by the parents. From the
available records of ancient India it appears that juvenile delinquency was not such
an urgent problem then as it is now.

Coming to modern times it is to be noted that Indian legislators have been active
from a fairly long time past in dealing with the question of youthful offenders. The
present-day *Indian Penal Code* is to a large extent modelled after the British code.
The civil law divides the age of minors, and in some countries of those whose age
is under twenty-five years, into three stages: *infantia,* from birth till seven years of
age, *pueritia,* from seven to fourteen, and *pubertus,* from fourteen upwards. The period
of *pueritia,* or childhood, is again subdivided into two equal parts: from seven to
ten-and-a-half is *aetas infantiale proxima,* from ten-and-a-half to fourteen is *aetas
pubertiati proxima.* During the first stage of infancy and the next half stage of childhood, *infantia proxima,* offenders are not punished for any crime. During the other
half stage of childhood, approaching puberty, from ten-and-a-half to fourteen, they
are indeed, punishable, if found to be *doli capaces,* or capable of mischief, but with
many mitigations, and not with the utmost rigor of the law. During the last stage,
from the age of puberty upwards, minors are liable to capital and other punishments
like adults. Under the English law a child under seven years of age cannot be guilty
of felony; under fourteen though a child shall be *prima facie* adjudged to be *doli
incapax,* yet if it appears to the court and jury, that he was *doli capax,* and could
discern between good and evil, he may be convicted and even suffer death. There are
some offenses, however, for instance, an offense under the *Railways Act* for which an
"infant" below twelve may be convicted and punished by whipping or the guardian
may be bound down to prevent the child from committing further mischief. The
principle of such legislation is that an "infant" below seven is supposed to be absolutely *doli incapax.* "Infants" between the ages of seven and fourteen are criminally
liable if it is shown that they have attained an adequate understanding and can
distinguish between right and wrong. In India the upper limit of age of this qualified
immunity has been reduced from fourteen to twelve on the theory that children born
in the tropics attain the requisite understanding at that age. This fact has also been
considered by the *Indian Majority Act* which fixes the age of eighteen as the ordinary
period of attaining majority; it is thus three years less than the age under English law.
If an adult employs a child below seven years to commit an offense he is liable to
be punished though the child is not. According to the *Indian Penal Code,* nothing
is an offense which is done by a child under seven years of age (Section 82). Again,
nothing is an offense which is done by a child above seven years of age and under
twelve, who has not attained sufficient maturity of understanding to judge of the
nature and consequence of his conduct on that occasion (Section 83). Maturity of
understanding is to be presumed in the case of a child between the ages of seven and
twelve unless the negative be proved by the defense. Naturally also, after twelve the
capacity is to be presumed until the contrary is proved. In the *Indian Criminal
Procedure Code,* it has been laid down that "any offense, other than one punishable

with death or transportation for life, committed by any person who at the date when he appears or is brought before the Court is under the age of fifteen years, may be tried by a District Magistrate or a Chief Presidency Magistrate or by any Magistrate specially empowered by the Provincial Government to exercise the powers conferred by section 8, sub-section (1), of the *Reformatory Schools Act,* 1897, or in any area in which the said Act has been wholly or in part repealed by any other law providing for the custody, trial or punishment of youthful offenders, by any Magistrate empowered by or under such law to exercise all or any of the powers conferred thereby."

The *Reformatory Schools Act* for dealing with juvenile delinquents was first passed in India as early as 1876. This Act was subsequently repealed and an Act to amend the law relating to Reformatory Schools and to make further provision for dealing with youthful offenders was passed on March 11, 1897. According to this Act, a youthful offender was defined as a person who has been convicted of any offense punishable by transportation or imprisonment and who at the time of such conviction was under the age of fifteen years. Rules were laid down for the conduct and management of Reformatory Schools. The act ordains that Reformatory Schools may be maintained by the local government or by any person willing to act in conformity with such rules consistent with the Act as the local government may prescribe in its behalf. Every Reformatory School must provide accommodation for separating the inmates at night, proper sanitary arrangements for offenders detained therein and the means of giving such youthful offenders industrial training. There must also be an infirmary for the reception of such youthful offenders when sick. The Inspector General of Prisons visits such schools at least once a year and reports to the Government on the way it is managed. The procedure adopted in admitting offenders to the Reformatory School is as follows: "Whenever any youthful offender is sentenced to transportation or imprisonment, and is, in the judgment of the Court by which he is sentenced, a proper person to be an inmate of a Reformatory School, the Court may, subject to any rules made by the Local Government, direct that, instead of undergoing his sentence, he shall be sent to such a school, and there detained for a period which shall not be less than three or more than seven years." Special courts known as Juvenile Courts have been established in India for dealing with cases that come under the *Reformatory Schools Act.* In districts where no such courts exist, juvenile offenders are tried in ordinary courts. Again, when any youthful offender has been confined in any ordinary prison in execution of a sentence of imprisonment, the officer-in-charge of the prison may bring him, if he has not then attained the age of fifteen years, before the District Magistrate within whose jurisdiction such prison is situated, and such Magistrate may, if such youthful offender appears to be a proper person to be an inmate of a Reformatory School, direct that instead of undergoing the residue of his sentence, he shall be sent to a Reformatory School and there detained for a period which shall be subject to the limitation previously mentioned. The law further directs that no person shall be detained in a Reformatory School after he has been found by the Local Government to have attained the age of eighteen years. The Local Government may at any time order any youthful offender to be discharged from a Reformatory School or be transferred to another school. The Superintendent of a Reformatory School may with the sanction of the Committee of Management permit any youthful offender who has attained the age of fourteen years to live under the charge of any trustworthy and respectable person or any officer of Government or Municipality, being an employer of labor, on the condition that the employer shall keep such youthful offender employed at some trade, occupation or calling. The license for such transfer shall be in force for three months at a time and is to be renewed after the expiration of the period. The Superintendent at his discretion may cancel the unexpired term of sentence of any youthful offender. For the purpose of the Act, the term youthful offender shall include a girl.

The institutions meant for juvenile offenders in Indian do not admit cases in which there is a marked mental deficiency and in which the offender is considered incapable of taking advantage of the training for rehabilitation. Unfortunately there is not much provision as yet for the housing of mentally deficient subjects. The result is that a mentally deficient delinquent is nobody's charge. The police authorities arrest such cases when any offense is committed and when it is found out in custody that the offender is not of normal intelligence he is discharged. The mental hospitals have no provision for mentally deficient patients and they refuse admission to them as a general rule. Even if they are admitted they are discharged very soon. The whole responsibility of managing such persons therefore falls upon the guardians who are, more often than not, ill-equipped to handle them properly.

In this connection, I remember the unfortunate case of a Jewish girl aged seventeen. She was arrested by the police for theft of an umbrella from a flat and for the offense of solicitation. The police soon found out that the girl was not normal and they sent her to the Police Observation Hospital in Calcutta. From there she was sent to the mental hospital at Ranchi where she received a few electrical shocks as treatment and was discharged. The parents found her unmanageable. She became worse after the treatment and was again arrested for solicitation and again discharged. The parents did not know what to do with her.

Such cases are fairly frequent. Hitherto the British ruling authorities had been entirely unmindful of their responsibility in this direction. The new Indian Government, however, is alive to the problem and plans are at present under consideration for starting homes for mentally deficient subjects.

From early childhood to the age of seven, children showing abnormal and antisocial behavior and also children between the ages of seven and twelve judged to be *doli incapax* (Section 82) are left to be managed at home. These two groups are included in the larger group of what is known as "problem children". There are a few psychological clinics in India that give advice to parents on the management of such children. Cognizable cases between the ages of seven and fifteen are generally dealt with in Juvenile Courts and the punishment consists in removal to reformatories. There are sixteen Reformatory Schools in India with a total accommodation for about thirty-five hundred boys. There are also a few after-care organizations that look to the welfare of the boys after discharge from reformatories. Above the age of fifteen and up to twenty-one the law does not usually take any special consideration and such offenders when convicted are housed in jails with ordinary adult criminals. But the jail authorities whenever they find it necessary or desirable to do so send such young offenders to special institutions called Juvenile Jails of which there are several in India.

THE CLINICAL ASPECT OF DELINQUENCY

Of late the clinical aspect of delinquency has been drawing the attention of many workers. Certain psychiatrists believe that early childhood environment is solely responsible for delinquency. The social, the moral and the economic factors all combine to influence the family life and through it predispose the child to criminality. The psychiatric and the child guidance clinics for problem children mostly work on this supposition, and efforts are made through the activities of social workers and by the education of parents to bring about a healthier atmosphere at home so that the delinquent child may be redeemed. In suitable cases individual mental treatment is also undertaken to remedy the injury already done to the psyche of the child. Just as in other spheres of mental abnormality so also in the field of delinquency, the question whether heredity or environment is the more important causative factor continues to trouble the clinician. The belief that heredity plays a more important role than environment in the creation of delinquents has also a large number of supporters, and since we have no control over the hereditary factor operative in a child, the whole problem of delinquency is looked upon with a feeling of despair in some quarters. It should be remembered, however, that it requires both heredity and environment to produce an abnormality and although we cannot influence heredity we can certainly bring about a better environment by our efforts and thus mitigate the evil to some extent. In my own investigation into delinquency, I have seldom come across a case in which the heredity was normal. If delinquency were due to the environment alone it would have been a comparatively simple matter to deal with the problem. A child with normal heredity, if brought up in the company of thieves and rogues like Father Faggin, will develop criminal traits no doubt, but it would be an easy matter to reclaim such a child when he is removed from the baneful influence. The presence of an abnormal heredity will, however, make the problem immensely more difficult, and in such cases it will require all the skill of the psychiatrist and the social worker to make the child conform to social standards and grow up into a normal person. There is no doubt that proper mental treatment by experienced psychiatrists supplemented by help from social workers will do good in many cases.

I should like to draw attention to a very important aspect of delinquency. There is a type of case in which the abnormal heredity brings about a pathological change which in turn helps to produce delinquency. Sometimes it is possible in these cases to influence the pathogenic factor by proper treatment. There is a close relationship between epileptoid states and certain types of delinquency. I am of the opinion that somnambulism, fugue and some other mental abnormalities showing a periodic variation, really belong to the class of epilepsies. Recent investigations in the field of electro-encephalography tend to point to the same conclusion. Crimes are very often committed by young children during the confusion period following an epileptic attack as also during a fugue. The criminal tendency in such subjects shows periodicity, the behavior remaining absolutely normal during the interval between the attacks. Here are a few illustrative cases:

The patient is a young man who has suffered from somnambulistic attacks from his childhood. After having slept for some time at night, he gets up from his bed in a trance and comes out of the room. If the room happens to be locked he tries to break open the door. Anybody who comes and interferes with his movements is assaulted. The trance attack lasts for a few minutes only, the patient suddenly wakes up and after a few moments of confusion regains his normal mental equilibrium. The heredity shows certain abnormal traits. The mother was insane and one of the paternal uncles used to have bad fits of temper. The patient's next brother is highly unstable. The patient was put under luminal, and made an excellent recovery.

The somnambulistic attack resembles the fugue attack to a great extent. While the somnambulistic trance is generally of short duration, the fugue persists for a fairly long time, viz. from a few hours to several days at a stretch. Some fugue attacks are associated with criminal acts while others are not. Here is a case history.

The patient is a young boy of ten. He was beaten by his maternal uncle for some misdeed and left home suddenly. He came back after a day. The boy does not attend to his studies. Whenever he is rebuked he leaves home. During the period of one year he was on the road eighteen times. The boy tells all sorts of lies to explain his conduct. On one occasion he inflicted a wound on his own leg and locked himself up in a room. The intelligence of the boy is normal. He gives a clear account of his escapades and says that he feels an urge to leave his home and cannot resist it. He also suffers from occasional somnambulistic attacks. The father who talks in his sleep is also a somnambulist. The father's maternal uncle was insane and one of the maternal aunts was eccentric. Treatment along anti-epileptic lines brought about a remarkable improvement in the boy's condition. Apart from the history of self-injury the boy never indulged in any form of violence. This case may be looked upon as a sort of connecting link between the somnambulistic case mentioned before and the following cases of fugue in which delinquency is present.

The subject is a boy aged thirteen. He would periodically steal money belonging to his parents and classmates and would leave the house for some distant place by train without buying any ticket. If detected by the railway staff or if questioned by fellow passengers on the way the boy would concoct plausible stories to explain the fact of his travelling alone and apparently without money. After a few days of adventure the boy would return to the house repentant. These fugue attacks would last for several days at a time. Anti-epileptic treatment cured the boy both of his fugue and of his criminal tendency.

Another boy aged fourteen would leave the house in a fugue state with a confused mind and start for a long walk committing all sorts of mischief on the way. After a few hours he would suddenly wake up as it were and would be surprised to find himself in a strange place. He would return home by questioning passers-by regarding the route. The boy could not give any account as to what happened during the fugue. Reports from outsiders showed that he behaved in an aggressive and mischievous manner while on the road. Here again anti-epileptic treatment achieved a cure.

A police officer reported the case of a house-breaker who periodically committed burglary, and showed extreme cleverness in breaking open safes and in avoiding the police. According to his own confession, his criminal attitude would suddenly disappear when he returned home. He was arrested under peculiar circumstances. He had entered a shop by boring a hole through the roof. After he had collected all his booty he suddenly became dazed and remained sitting in that position till morning when people came and arrested him.

The cases mentioned above show the importance of pathological factors in the genesis of criminality. Mere removal to reformatories, Borstals or jails, and efforts at rehabilitation would be of no avail in such cases but immense good could be done to the offender sometimes by proper physical and mental treatment.

There is another class of delinquents in whom the moral sense seems to be ill developed or absolutely undeveloped. Some workers describe these cases under the category of moral imbecility. It is often assumed that the deficiency in these cases is mainly noticeable with regard to the moral sense; the intelligence of such subjects remains normal. Many observers, however, have expressed doubts as to the existence of moral imbecility. According to them, moral imbecility apart from mental deficiency does not exist. In those cases that came under my care I could always find some sort of retardation of mental development.

The following case is that of a boy of fifteen. He had fits of obstinacy in infancy and in early childhood had periods of depression. He was dirty in his habits and had a voracious appetite. He had no moral sense. He stole books and pens from his school-friends, forged a letter and tried to get some money from a bank by submitting a cheque with a forged signature. He never felt that he was doing anything wrong. He was a good typist and could type eighty words per minute. His intelligence was slightly below normal. The heredity shows a heavy taint. His parents' eldest child was born with imperfect physical developments and died a few hours after birth. The second issue of his parents was a brother who developed into a drunkard. One of the paternal uncles also was an alcoholic. The grandfather and the brother of his grandfather were addicted to drink and women. The grandfather's brother developed insanity.

In contrast to the epileptoid group the pathological hereditary factor in "moral imbecility" does not seem to be amenable to treatment. My case records suggest that psychotic factors superimposed on mental deficiency are at work in creating what is called moral imbecility. The deficient intelligence makes it difficult for the subject to profit by psychoanalysis and the psychotic factor interferes with the development of a proper transference. My own experience of psychoanalytic therapy in "moral imbecility" has not been encouraging. Problem children of other types often show moral lapses but they seem to stand on a somewhat different footing; they respond very well to psychotherapy.

The Social Aspect of Delinquency

Public awareness regarding delinquency has not been fully roused in India. No thorough-going efforts have been made to deal with this important problem. The reformatories and the juvenile jails are the agents that do most of the rehabilitation work. Some of the Juvenile Courts have probation officers attached to them and their services have been found to be very helpful. Unfortunately, as yet, the preventive side of delinquency has not received the attention it deserves. Quite lately, however, the Government and the public have been interesting themselves in this problem. Child guidance, and psychiatric and psychological clinics for dealing with mentally deficient and problem children including juvenile delinquents are now being established in different parts of India. The necessity of looking upon the whole problem from the triple standpoint of prevention, correction and rehabilitation, rather than from that of punishment alone, has been realized. Psychological and out-patient clinics will be regular features of hospitals in India in the near future. The universities also are eager to take up the social side of child management. Calcutta University has a special course in applied psychology with social psychiatry as a complementary subject. At present, however, the number of clinics is very limited.

The reformatories and the juvenile jails all work more or less on the same lines. They try to give affection and considerate treatment to their inmates and to bring about a home atmosphere as far as practicable. In these institutions there are provisions for general education and for certain types of vocational training such as tailoring, carpentry, masonry, agriculture, poultry raising, weaving, printing, sericulture, bee-keeping, toy-making, lacquer work, etc. The Juvenile Jail at Bareilly (U.P.) is one of the best-managed institutions of its kind in India. This institution has developed to its present position as the result of the untiring efforts of Lt. Col. A. H. Shaikh, C.I.E., I.M.S., former Inspector General of Prisons, U.P. Very elaborate records are kept of all particulars affecting the inmates and of their activities. There is accommodation for about two hundred persons. This jail receives convicted juveniles from other jails. There are no direct admissions from the courts. There is a garden and an infirmary attached to the jail and the inmates are encouraged to take up games and hobbies. I have listed below some important statistical findings of social importance relating to the correctional and rehabilitation work done during the years 1939-1943 from the report of the Inspector General. The analysis is based on a record of 201 boys who were given the opportunity of being employed on extramural labor in factories. In 42 per cent of the cases both parents were alive at the time of admission and in about 6 per cent of the cases the father died when the subject was five years old or younger. Seven per cent of the cases lost their mothers before the age of five. In about 65 per cent of the cases the family relationship between the parents was amicable. Parental treatment was good in about 55 per cent of the cases. The father was harsh in about 30 per cent of the cases and the mother in about 6 per cent. Where there is a history of harsh treatment by the father or the brother, the mother generally sided with the child. About 21 per cent were eldest children, 30 per cent were youngest children of their parents and only 6 per cent came under the group "only child". About 53 per cent had sex experience of some kind or other and about 8 per cent of those who had sex experience had homosexual relationships. About 58 per cent came from very poor families and only 7 per cent were comparatively well off. In only 2 per cent of the cases did the family history show a crime record. Fifty per cent of the inmates were illiterate when admitted to the institution. About 70 per cent took to studies on their own initiative and about 3 per cent were found to be uneducable. About 13 per cent were admitted for *dacoity* (gang-robbery), 12 per cent for theft, cheating and counterfeiting, 18 per cent for murder, 22 per cent for attempts to murder and culpable homicide, 14 per cent for assault, 4 per cent for kidnapping, 14 per cent for rape and 3 per cent for miscellaneous offenses. The age distribution was from sixteen to twenty-two. The relative proportion of inmates coming from rural and urban areas was 8:1. This proportion is in accordance with the distribution of the population of the province.

However, it is not justifiable to judge the general crime distribution among delinquents from this table. The Bareilly group from which the statistics are drawn must be considered as a special group. No one who is below fourteen or above nineteen is admitted to this institution, and only those who are sentenced to rigorous imprisonment and whose period of sentence is not less than one year are admissible. Members of criminal tribes, mentally deficient persons and persons with bad physical health are not taken into the institution.

Certain tribes in India have hitherto been regarded as "criminal tribes". Members of the criminal tribe have to live under special police surveillance. No member of the criminal tribe is admitted to juvenile jails. It is believed that social traditions and customs are responsible for fostering criminality in these tribal people. Besides these criminal tribes, there are special communities in certain places which are also subject to regular police supervision. Children belonging to these tribes and communities are taught stealing and other forms of criminal acts by their parents. In some of the big cities of India there are criminal organizations and groups that get hold of orphans and street urchins and teach them the art of pickpocketing and stealing. Juvenile offenders of this class are quite common in big cities. During a recent police drive more than three hundred pickpockets were arrested in Calcutta. The leader of the gang generally appropriates all the booty collected by the members of his organization. In return the juvenile delinquents get food and shelter. Social rehabilitation workers should pay special attention to these organizations as most of the children who belong to such gangs are reclaimable.

There is another aspect of delinquency that demands special attention. Criminals of certain types work only in groups while others are "lone criminals". The *"dacoits"* are gang-robbers. Each *dacoit* gang has a leader called *"sardar"* and has its own rites and religious customs. Before the party sallies forth for an adventure, the members jointly worship their presiding deity, the mother goddess Kali, with some pomp and ceremony. The children of these people very often take part in the criminal acts of their elders. Thieves also mostly work in small groups. The lone criminal on the other hand has no companion. He is an interesting study. The problem of the lone delinquent offers a rich field for the future investigator.

The Hindu social code has some interesting features that are worthy of earnest consideration by the psychologically minded social reformer. The religious manuals of the Hindus repeatedly insist that every member of the society should stick to his *"swadharma"* which may be roughly translated as "one's own code of life". In the *Gita* which is one of the highest authoritative works on Hindu religion, *"swadharma"* has been defined as "that code of life that is in consonance with one's own nature and also with the demands of the society in which one lives". If a person, who is inclined to violence by nature, takes up the life of a highway robber he may satisfy his violent craving but he will be considered to be out of his "*swadharma*" because robbery is not sanctioned by society; again if he adopts the profession of a priest he will be still not following "*swadharma*" as the violent tendencies in his nature are likely to remain unsatisfied as a priest. If, however, such a person enlists himself as a soldier he will be serving his society and at the same time he will have opportunities for satisfying his nature although of course under certain limitations, he will be following his "*swadharma*".

The Hindu social custom takes full cognizance of man's antisocial cravings and it tries to give them an outlet with appropriate safeguards. Intoxicants are not sanctioned by Hindu society and yet it is the religious custom to drink "*siddhi*" which is an intoxicating beverage made from the leaves of the Indian hemp, on a particular day in the year; even those who are totally averse to any form of intoxicant have to put at least a drop in their mouth; others have their fill on that day without any feeling of social guilt. Gambling is allowed by society on the *Kali puja* night and not at any other time. On the day of the Holy festival one may smear his own body or that of any other person with colored powders, liquids and mud and may move about unashamed in the streets. On any other day he would be ridiculed and punished for such conduct. There is a religious prohibition against seeing the moon on certain nights in the year, and if one unwittingly happens to have a glimpse of that luminary one has to do a penance. A curious form of the penance is that the guilty person has to steal something from somebody's house. Young boys very often purposely look at the moon on these nights and then expiate their sin by stealing fruits and vegetables from the gardens of their neighbors or by catching fish from private pools. If they are caught in the act they have to give up their booty and have to put up with the abuse of the offended party. No one thinks of taking any serious action against these juvenile offenders. Thefts of this type on other nights would result in formal complaints and police prosecutions. Occasional licensed digressions from the social standard seem to go a long way toward maintaining normality in many unbalanced persons.

The antisocial and criminal tendencies that lie dormant in human nature break their bounds under certain conditions such as war, political revolutions and social upheavals. The last war has left an aftermath of license and a disregard for law and order resulting in crime waves in many countries. During the recent political disturbances in India boys in their teens coming from respectable families were seen indulging in cruel assaults, loot, abduction, arson and murder often with the tacit approval of their elders. The return of normal conditions has put a stop to these surges but the groundswell will take a long time to subside.

OUTLINE OF THE INVESTIGATION AND TREATMENT OF DELINQUENCY IN GREAT BRITAIN: 1912-1948

WITH SPECIAL REFERENCE TO PSYCHOANALYTICAL AND OTHER PSYCHOLOGICAL METHODS

BY EDWARD GLOVER, M.D.

(London)

To understand the present position of criminological science in Britain, it is necessary to be familiar not only with the various movements which have concerned themselves with delinquency in this country but with the various "theories of conduct" by virtue of which these movements have regulated their policies and efforts. Otherwise it is scarcely possible to estimate the significance of any given criminological policy or to measure the impetus it carries. At the time of writing, for example, the British House of Commons is about to pass into law a *Criminal Justice Bill* which has been eulogistically hailed as an extremely progressive measure, a milestone of social progress. To the casual reader of the provisions of this Bill it might indeed appear that at long last society represented by the State is prepared to recognize the validity of psychological approach to the problem of delinquent behavior. This is very far from being the case. There is no sign that those who framed the *Bill* have been converted to a psychological point of view, or that they are prepared to strike to the roots of the problem. On the contrary the new *Criminal Justice Bill* is largely a measure of prison reform, a tribute to the devoted efforts of Penal Reform Societies but, so far as psychological methods of prevention, treatment and "after-care" are concerned, a timid, unimaginative and cheese-paring measure.

Of the various criminological movements and hypotheses some are sufficiently familiar to the student of delinquency to call for no detailed consideration here. For example the theory of an *unwritten social contract* whereby the community is ready to protect the individual from injury or unwarranted interference at the hands of other individuals and groups (including the State itself), provided always the individual in question is prepared to obey social law, is generally accepted as a rational basis of criminal law. When however we inquire what steps society will take should the individual refuse to obey social law, we find that these rational contracts are but a screen for a more primitive and irrational *moral hypothesis*. In its more sophisticated form this maintains that law breaking is a kind of *sin* calling for appropriate forms of *punishment*. One need hardly add that this moral code is derived from animistic and early religious systems which nowadays seek to conceal their retributive aims on the ground that punishment is an effective deterrent to evil-doers, a theory which still flourishes and will continue to flourish in the face of repeated statistical rebuttal.

At this point a *humanitarian movement,* recruited largely but by no means

433

exclusively from Christian denominations, steps in to mitigate the severity of talion law.[1] Though meliorist in aim this movement does not question the moral hypothesis of wrong-doing; only accidentally, as it were, does it find itself committed to a tentative scientific approach. Seeking for effective arguments against the severities of penal law, advocates of penal reform have found that the theory of deterrence is a rationalization of revenge-impulses that can be easily exploded. But they have not pursued this tactical advantage to press for still more scientific investigations in particular of the causes of crime. Indeed until comparatively recent times penal reformers looked somewhat askance at the efforts of psychologists to revolutionize the approach to criminal behavior. Nevertheless their arguments gained in popular force and, as has been suggested, found their final expression in the present *Criminal Justice Bill.* Indeed it is interesting to speculate on the future of this movement. It can of course continue to press for prison reform or indeed abolition. For the rest it must either divert its energies to more scientific channels of approach or remain aloof from the psychological movement, a rather puzzled and even jealous spectator of more radical procedures.

The history of the *psychological movement,* or rather revolution, in criminological theory and practice will presently engage our attention: For the moment it is sufficient to say that whilst recognizing the practical utility of the social contract, it insists that society should underwrite a charter of individual privileges and liberties; in short it holds that the function of the group is to act as a servant to the individual, not as his master.

Nor does the psychological movement deny that a moral hypothesis of crime however diluted will continue to influence for good or ill individual and social reactions to delinquency. It maintains, however, that the legitimate spheres of moral influence lie in *prevention and after-care,* subject always to the proviso that such influence is appropriate to the case and does not override more important prophylactic and therapeutic considerations. Indeed it goes further to insist that *for its own psychological good,* society must treat the delinquent with more understanding and human kindliness.

On the fallacies of deterrence and on the superstitious elements in criminal law the psychological movement is adamant. Those few psychologists who dally with penal measures on the score of expediency merely take advantage of their professional position to gratify (wittingly or unwittingly) their own moral prejudices. There are always moralists in any psychological field; as witness, the exhortatory group of psychotherapists who are ready on the slightest sign of refractoriness or recidivism on the part of their patients to bully their charges in the same fashion as physiologically trained child-minders. Nor do they stop short of excommunicating their patients, i.e., summarily discharging them as incurable. Even psychoanalysts are not immune from this form of superego disorder.

Surveying "movements" in this rather shorthand fashion, it is possible to "place" various aspects of present day criminology, a process which, however, involves tracing them to their origins. Thus, for example, the long drawn out controversy between the Law and Psychology as to the conditions governing criminal responsibility (known as the McNaghten Rules in this country) is due to the terrified obstinacy with which judges have hitherto defended the unwritten social contract. Fearing that the Law would be hopelessly weakened if any other than psychotic factors were to be adduced

[1] Britain has produced a long and distinguished line of penal reformers. Indeed it would be invidious to pick and choose from amongst their number. The undisputed leader of the movement is Marjorie Fry whose services to the Howard League for Penal Reform, to say nothing of her work on the magisterial bench and on various committees of enquiry, has been a source of inspiration to her colleagues.

in extenuation of crime and convinced, not perhaps unnaturally, that if final authority were delegated to psychiatrists the latter would either be hoodwinked by malingerers or give rein to a sentimental humanitarianism to say nothing of professional and scientific arrogance, judges have ridden roughshod over perfectly valid scientific discoveries such as the nature of psychopathy, have treated psychiatric witnesses for the defense with gross contempt and discourtesy and have stiffened the legalistic backbone of Home Office authorities and Home Secretaries to the point where these naturally timid and conservative creatures have preferred administrative traditions to a courageous recognition of the psychological facts.

To take another example, this time from the chapter of the *disposal* of delinquents: the probationary system in this country is a legacy from the earlier religious and humanitarian movements, one to which the official police system of supervision has contributed not a little. The forerunner of the present Probation Officer was the Court Missionary; and the supervision exercised by such of these as did not choose to apply moral pressure at first smacked of the old ticket-of-leave system. Indeed these disciplinary rigidities, though greatly softened by more adequate selection and training of probation officers, still linger, thereby stultifying to some extent the more understanding techniques now generally employed.

A more complicated trail has been blazed by the Borstal Institution. Sprung originally from the military prison system, it nevertheless fell heir to some of the traditions of the old poor law institution and "reformatory". Gradually, under the influence of Home Office enthusiasts, it took over some pedagogic techniques, in particular the "house master" system of the public (boarding) school and finally graduated to the position of elder and sterner half-brother to the Approved School. Under the new *Criminal Justice Bill* it will continue to play a corrective function for delinquents under twenty-one, a rôle which in the case of those over that age will some day be played by the new Detention Centre. This last is a euphemism for a "reformed" type of prison, as yet merely projected. There are none such in existence. So Borstal is a derivative from the older moralistic penology, modified by Penal Reform influences and by the "segregation" techniques of pedagogy (empirical educational psychology). For psychologists the Borstal system will remain a form of disposal to be sparingly recommended in a small minority of cases and only then if more suitable and humane resources have failed.

On the other hand it has to be admitted that the summary given above does not do justice to the more complicated sources of interest in criminology and penal method. The "movements" described omit, for example, all reference to a special group whose members have played an honorable part in the development of enlightened handling of crime. This group is constituted of persons who either by reason of their sublimated interest in antisocial conduct or because of their sublimated interest in youth and its problems or more rarely because they are interested in psychological puzzles turn a generous and patient mind to the delinquencies of the young. (Relatively few respond with equal understanding to adult criminal conduct.) Many of them had evinced earlier an active interest in Boys or Girls Clubs or Youth Camps, and thereby acquired an empirical knowledge which stood them in good stead when they were caught up in delinquency work. They are a small but enthusiastic band, some of whose members, fortunately for offenders, sit on the magisterial bench, others adorning the Probation Service, others again contributing an influence for good on the staffs of Approved Schools *et hoc genus*. Less active members are content to exert their influence through some of the many societies for penal or social reform whose interests are bent towards juvenile delinquency.

Having surveyed very roughly the field of criminological endeavor, the task remains of outlining the *history of the psychological movement in British criminology.* This involves a two-fold approach; cataloguing the various sections in which some branch or other of psychological thought has obtained expression; and at the same time considering the part played by psychoanalysis, either directly, through the research and therapeutic work of trained analysts, or, indirectly, through the influence it has exerted on persons who, though not themselves analysts, have nevertheless been in a position to develop methods of disposal based on the discoveries of Freud. It is when surveying the second of these approaches that we are able to assess the importance of the work done by Aichhorn.

It would take us too far afield, and without adequate recompense, to enter in detail into the question of historical priority of interest amongst non-analytical psychologists. And it is scarcely worth the trouble because, not to put too fine a point on it, pre-analytical psychology was neither a rich nor a very fruitful clinical field. For yet another reason we need not concern ourselves with earlier approaches which, although of scientific intent, were non-psychological in nature. For although the methods adopted, for example, by followers of Lombroso in this country had scientific intent, their best service lay in indicating the desirability of using other scientific methods.[2] Similarly the publications of early non-psychological psychiatrists impress us nowadays more because of their lack of psychological understanding than because of their contributions to the descriptive aspects of delinquency.

Two exceptions to this apparently sweeping generalization exist. In the first place the attention called by some earlier psychiatrists to the antisocial behavior of psychotic types and of mentally deficient children and adolescents certainly prepared the way for later and more comprehensive groupings of delinquent conduct. And secondly the approach of some exceptional and imaginative medical criminologists was a stimulus to an oncoming generation of workers who were to have at their disposal more powerful instruments of investigation. In this sense the work of Devon, a Glasgow prison officer on the *Criminal and the Community*[3] deserves to be singled out.

For all practical purposes the development of modern methods of dealing with delinquency ran parallel with the development of normal and abnormal psychology, although interestingly enough, in both instances a considerable time-lag developed between the establishment of psychological principles and their specific application to delinquency. Clinical progress in normal and abnormal psychology was stimulated respectively by work done in the field of educational and industrial psychology and in the field of psychoanalysis. But whereas psychoanalysis represented a complete break from existing methods of mental observation and description, educational psychology was based on laboratory studies in mental measurement. For convenience in description it is desirable to outline first the relation of psychoanalysis to delinquency in Britain.

As has so often been the case the application of psychoanalysis to a new field was the result of some stimulating suggestions thrown out by Freud in the course of wider researches. It is no exaggeration to say that his brief article *"Die Verbrecher aus Schuldbewusstsein"* ("Criminality from a Sense of Guilt")[4] laid the foundation not only of a psychoanalytical science of delinquency, but of those freely modified tech-

---

[2] Lombroso's most valuable contribution to criminology was the theory that punishment should fit the criminal not the crime.

[3] Published 1912.

[4] Some Character-Types Met with in Psychoanalytic Work published 1915, *Coll. Papers,* vol. IV, London, Hogarth Press, 1925.

niques practiced by psychotherapists who were not themselves Freudian and who in fact had only the slightest familiarity with work done by psychoanalysts on the subject. But in a very real sense all Freud's early contributions, e.g. on unconscious conflict, guilt, and self-punishment, on the libidinal and aggressive vicissitudes of childhood, on sexual perversions and on unconscious character formation had prepared the ground very thoroughly for research into delinquency. Everything was ready for sweeping advances in the subject save the appearance of psychoanalytical workers ready to specialize in it.

It is all the more interesting to note that this accession of specialized psycho-analytical workers was not forthcoming. Indeed even at the present time when psychoanalytical *principles* and *points of view* are freely applied in delinquency, there is an astonishing dearth of psychoanalytical workers in the field. The number of regular analyses carried out on antisocial types in this country is woefully small. Perhaps this is due to the fact that psychoanalysts are too busy acquiring a satisfactory training and building up a successful analytical practice. Psychoanalysis is a lengthy procedure and it is difficult to persuade young practitioners to devote a substantial proportion of their time to work that is technically difficult, unusually thankless and not particularly remunerative. In fact in the early nineteen-twenties the subject was almost totally neglected. Actually the first public lecture to magistrates on psycho-analysis and crime was given by the present writer in 1923. The clinical material was drawn from some psychoanalytical observations of juvenile delinquents, and the theory was extended to the subject from orthodox Freudian principles. Naturally enough the effort fell distinctly flat and at the time probably did more harm than good. Apart from sporadic efforts of this sort active interest in the subject was promoted mainly by Freudian sympathizers who like Hamblin Smith found that psychoanalytical theories of mental function shed a dazzling light on criminal conduct.[5]

But fresh incentives were soon forthcoming from a number of directions. Rumors of the work of Alexander and Staub in Berlin, of Aichhorn, Reich and Reik in Vienna began to reach this country: from America had already come the linguis-tically more accessible publications of Healy, Bronner and the Gluecks. In Britain itself two additional factors were operative, the expansion of child analysis and the publications of Sir Cyril Burt on backward and delinquent children. It is only proper to add that although Sir Cyril Burt had from the beginning exhibited a friendly interest in psychoanalytical developments, his own original book was derived from a combina-tion of acute clinical observation and steady application of observational methods (both individual and social) developed by "normal psychologists". Indeed it is no exaggeration to say that had he chosen to cast his professional lot with psychoanalysis Sir Cyril Burt might have equalled but scarcely surpassed the contributions he made to the clinical aspects of academic psychology.

It is pleasant to be able to record that the next important step in the direction of specialized work in delinquency in this country was taken by a psychoanalyst, Dr. Grace Pailthorpe. Supported by the Medical Research Council, she carried out inves-tigations on female prisoners and inmates of preventive homes. These observations were based on her psychoanalytical knowledge, and her results were published first in

---

[5] Hamblin Smith's book, *The Psychology of the Criminal* (New York, McBride), which was the result of twenty-seven years' work on criminals was the first purely medico-psychological approach to the problem in this country. It was published in 1922, the year that Pailthorpe commenced her psychoanalytical investigations in Birmingham Prison under Hamblin Smith's direction. (*v. inf.*)

the form of an official report and later in a book entitled *What We Put In Prison*.[6] More important still, she immediately busied herself organizing a private committee whose object it was to see whether the methods she had found so useful in investigation could be applied to the treatment of offenders who had not been in prison. Dr. Pailthorpe, being prevented by ill-health from developing her project, invited the present writer to proceed with the organization of a Clinic. With the assistance of the late Dr. David Eder, a pioneer psychoanalyst who had also done pioneer work in founding School Clinics, of Dr. J. A. Hadfield, a medical psychologist from the staff of the Tavistock Clinic who has taken an active part in the Mental Hygiene movement in Britain and of Dr. E. T. Jensen, a physician who has devoted much interest to the subject of delinquency, a small Clinic was set up in 1932 in a room lent by the West End Hospital for Nervous Diseases, which also provided facilities for physical examination. From these slender beginnings was developed the first *specialized* Institute for the Scientific Treatment of Delinquency now known as the I.S.T.D. London.

But this is to anticipate. In the meantime we can review the general state of research in delinquency from 1930 to the present day, and trace its various tributory sources. We have seen that an occasional *prison medical officer* of exceptional understanding took an objective interest in the subject. This state of affairs has changed very little. The number of psychiatric minded prison officers has increased but only marginally. Training in psychiatry (though not in psychoanalysis) is now an essential qualification; but as a whole the prison service was, and psychologically speaking still is, a backwater. This is not to underestimate the importance of the prison work done by Hubert and backed by Norwood East.[7] Hubert was a psychoanalytically oriented psychiatrist, not a regular prison officer. Even more valuable work may be expected from prison psychiatrists such as Mackwood, Young, Frost and others provided of course, and this is now just barely possible, they are given a free hand by the authorities.[8]

In a review of this kind it is essential to estimate the part played by the *Home Office* and by *Home Secretaries* in either advancing or retarding the progress of psychological research and the expansion of psychological methods of dealing with delinquency. To begin with, the Home Office shows all the characteristics one has come to expect from Government Departments, run by permanent officials with the support of Home Office specialists and a few privately appointed specialist advisors. The Home Office is naturally dominated by an administrative valuation of the social contract. It is also conservative, acutely suspicious of anything new or revolutionary and devoid of social imagination. Its attitude to psychology, in particular psychoanalytical psychology, has been cautious to the point of neglect. Nevertheless it is only fair to say that amongst the junior ranks of its officials some extremely high-grade workers exist whose practical appreciation of psychological factors and policies has been a constant source of support to delinquency workers. The Home Office has

---

[6] Dr. Grace W. Pailthorpe commenced her investigations at Birmingham Prison in 1922 and continued them for a period of five years at Holloway. Her report was published in 1929 and her book in 1932. (*Studies in the Psychology of Delinquency*, London, H.M.S.O.)

[7] Sir Norwood East was originally a Prison Medical Officer, later H.M. Commissioner of Prisons and subsequently Lecturer to London University on Crime and Insanity.

[8] No special mention has been made in this review of *police-surgeons* for the simple reason that the psychological tasks required of them are negligible. An important exception is provided by Baldie, a medical psychologist of Adlerian outlook who combines specialist work with the duties of a police-surgeon.

of course been influenced by the work of various Royal Commissions it has itself appointed; but here again a retarding influence generally makes itself felt. Royal Commissions have never included a psychoanalyst, rarely a medical psychologist of first hand experience in the subject. Bowing to public pressure representatives of penal reform societies came to be admitted and now that, as the result of the war, psychiatry has increased in social influence, a gradual psychiatric leavening of Home Office policy may be expected. But on the whole it will be more influenced by "rational" views of conscious psychology, will rarely if ever be in advance of public opinion and will be more concerned to preserve the traditions of the police service, an organization which though not exactly militaristic is essentially authoritarian, based on the assumption that the social contract must be enforced rather than accepted. Indeed the bias of the Home Office towards the social side of the contract is greatly to be regretted. Whoever controls the Home Office is in a position effectively to thwart or to fulfil the aspirations of the most ardent reformer, or most devoted scientist.[9]

Next in order of strategic importance comes the influence of what might be called normal psychology. This is exerted in the main from university and teaching colleges and training centres and is directed mostly through the channel of educational psychology, e.g., regional directors of education and experts in mental measurement. It impinges on the problem of delinquency directly through the study of behavior patterns, both normal and abnormal, during school age and adolescence and indirectly through the, as yet, only slenderly equipped system of Child Guidance Clinics. Here the educational psychologist and to a considerable extent the psychiatric social worker operates with techniques fostered during training in normal psychology. Normal psychology has also many techniques in common with sociological research, and has naturally contributed a good deal to the statistical investigation of individual factors (backwardness, mental defect and capacity adaptation) and of environmental factors (including many familial and economic conditions that exert a psychological influence on behavior). As we have seen one British representative of this school and method (Burt) gained an international reputation for pioneer work in delinquency and amongst those adopting mainly sociological techniques the name of Herman Mannheim ranks high. Jennings White is also a prominent worker in the combined tradition. Carr-Saunder's approach is largely biometric and sociological. Nowadays students of normal psychology too numerous to mention busy themselves with social and individual aspects of the subject. This increased activity became particularly noticeable during and after the Second World War when evacuation of children from danger areas led to a mass break-up of the family and offered an unique opportunity of studying environmental factors of great psychological consequence for delinquency work.

As to the research value of these methods: whilst it would be premature to say they have outworn their usefulness (for it is always possible for the normal psychologist to apply statistical tests to some of the findings of dynamic unconscious psychology), it can be said that, lacking any training in or understanding of unconscious psychology and debarred by their rules of "controlled" research from applying psychoanalytical methods of interpretation to their data, normal psychologists can contribute little of value to the *individual and etiological aspects of delinquency*. This valuation does not apply so much to the social investigations of normal psychologists although from the

---

[9] From a long line of psychologically unresponsive Home Secretaries, Sir Samuel Hoare (now Lord Templewood) stands out as a distinguished reformer. The present *Criminal Justice Bill* is largely a resuscitation of the measure framed and piloted by him just before the war but abandoned because of the national emergency.

clinical point of view, there is something "distant" (impersonal) even about valid sociological explanations of crime.

Until comparatively recently the contributions of *psychiatry* to research on delinquency have stood in barren contrast to the immense clinical resources of the science. Admittedly formal psychiatry[10] has always had a voice in the matter of criminal responsibility, e.g., testifying in Courts of Law to the presence or absence of insanity in cases of criminal violence. Otherwise the contributions of psychiatrists to the science of delinquency have usually been indirect. Thus they have been able to classify those symptoms of the psychoses, of organic reaction types, and of convulsive states which are responsible for some forms of antisocial or criminal conduct. But these observations do not in themselves constitute research into delinquency, for unless the unconscious etiological factors in e.g., the psychoses, are fully understood (a feat so far compassed only rarely in Britain), it is not possible to make any useful correlations between the conduct of psychotic and non-psychotic types of delinquency respectively. Exceptionally, the work of the psychiatrists Macniven and Dillon has been characterized by understanding of the psychodynamics of delinquency.

On the other hand, psychiatric work on psychopathic states has been a valuable stimulus to research on what is certainly a key problem in delinquency. D. K. Henderson of Edinburgh who combines extensive psychiatric experience with unusual opportunities of studying criminal conduct has produced comprehensive and illuminating observations on this condition. Similarly in the field of mental deficiency, the work of Burt has been amplified by psychiatric studies from Earle E. Lewis and other medical workers. Unfortunately the tendency of workers on mental deficiency is to be content with the demonstration of innate defect and to ignore those psychological factors affecting behavior that are either associated with or a consequence of mental defect. Further progress in this direction will depend on careful psychoanalytical observations. In the meantime the therapeutic amelioration of psychological complications of deficiency goes by default. Institutional and pedagogic procedures have secured too exclusive priority in this field.

Another psychiatric channel of influence is constituted by the *Child Guidance Clinic* which, for good or ill, has fallen under the sway of the psychiatrist. Here the educational psychologist now plays an auxiliary role, sharing with the psychiatric social worker an uneasy equality of status. This has led in some cases to some intriguing professional situations. Under present training conditions, the educational psychologist and psychiatric social worker are trained in the principles of normal psychology and given a smattering of psychiatry; but a number have of their own choice acquired a good working knowledge of clinical psychology, sometimes of psychoanalysis.[11] It is not uncommon therefore to find psychiatric social workers who have a better understanding of the facts of unconscious conflict than their psychiatric directors. Excellent medico-psychological work in this field has been done by, amongst others, E. Miller, Maberley, Pearce (all medical psychologists of repute) and Paterson Brown (a psychoanalytically trained child psychiatrist). The work of so-called "play-therapists" will be considered below.

As has already been indicated the direct application of psychoanalytic techniques to the clinical aspects of delinquency is in absurd disproportion to the overwhelming

---

[10] In this country the term "psychiatrist" has until recently connoted a specialist in the psychoses, not as in the United States a specialist in general medical psychology.

[11] Some of the best psychiatric social work on delinquency in this country has been done by Miss G. M. Wilcox who organized the psychiatric social work of the I.S.T.D. On the educational side of the Clinic Miss D. C. Chaplin has acquired a deserved reputation.

DELINQUENCY IN GREAT BRITAIN 441

indirect influence of *psychoanalysis*. In the course of their regular practice many analysts are faced with delinquent problems but this work has never been organized.[12] Nor with the obvious exceptions of young juveniles and of "neurotic" types of adult delinquency is the classical technique of psychoanalysis altogether adapted to meet the crises that arise with classical cases of delinquency. The most active (medical) psychoanalytical workers in the general field of antisocial behavior are Pailthorpe, Carroll, M. Schmideberg, K. Friedlander and M. Franklin. The work of Schmideberg with advanced cases of the "Dartmoor type" has broken new ground in the psychoanalytic handling of delinquents. But it has involved several modifications of the customary techniques which she has described in various papers on the subject. K. Friedlander has produced a standard work of psychoanalytical reference on juvenile delinquency.[13] Amongst lay psychoanalysts who have also extensive pedagogic experience Barbara Low has played a prominent part in delinquency work and in the education of public opinion.[14]

It has been suggested that in an indirect way all psychoanalytical work has a bearing on antisocial conduct. And it follows that the more direct work done on the mental development of children the more we shall understand the problems of delinquency. It is only proper therefore to record the increasing influence of child psychoanalysis in this country. The founder of child-analysis in Britain was the late Mary Chadwick who produced also several studies of antisocial behavior amongst juveniles. Unfortunately a split on the theory and practice of child-analysis has developed in Britain, a division which threatens to bring about equally acrimonious divergences between those practicing psychoanalysis of adults. On the one hand we have the classical approach of the Viennese school (where child-analysis was first developed), guided in this country by Anna Freud, and on the other a new metapsychological system developed by M. Klein. This split will be briefly considered in an appropriate section. In the meantime it may be noted that these differences are irreconcilable and will reduce the effective thrust of psychoanalytical research in this country by at least one-half. Amongst psychoanalytical workers on delinquency Friedlander follows the classical approach, Bowlby the Kleinian theory.

Inevitably developments in the psychoanalysis of children have given rise to a flattery of imitation amongst non-analytical psychologists. The application of *play-technique* to the needs of child analysis (incidentally, Klein's most useful contribution to the subject) has led to the formation of all sorts of groups of child-therapists. And nowadays there are few psychiatric centres or child guidance clinics which do not include a lay "play-therapist" on their staff. This form of activity has, except in instances where the "play-therapist" is analytically trained, nothing to do with child-analysis. Indeed with the present craze for various forms of "group-therapy" including "play-groups", the mere resemblance between "play-therapy" and child-analysis has been reduced to absurdity.

---

[12] Exceptionally Dr. David Forsyth published a lengthy study, *The Case of a Middle-Aged Embezzler* (1938).

[13] *The Psycho-Analytical Approach to Juvenile Delinquency*. London, Kegan Paul, 1947. New York, Int. Univ. Press, 1947. A book by Schmideberg entitled, *Children in Need*, is about to be published by Allen and Unwin.

[14] Space does not permit an adequate acknowledgment of the work done by various educational journals and child-parent magazines in advancing modern ideas on delinquency in this country. In this connection the work of Leon Radzinowicz and J. W. C. Turner, editors of *English Studies in Criminal Science* (London, Macmillan, 1941, including a volume on *Mental Abnormality and Crime*, 1944), is deserving of recognition.

Equally naturally the differences between Freudian, Adlerian and Jungian *"schools" of clinical psychology* have been accurately reflected in the approach to and treatment of delinquency. In their several ways Adlerians and Jungians are at home in the handling of antisocial conduct which they feel assured can be very convincingly explained in terms of their respective theories. Inevitably the "eclectic" finds an opportunity for applying his compost of theories and methods particularly to the problem child. Indeed at the present rate of diffusion of clinical theories, it would seem that for some time ahead such psychiatric and child guidance centres as are not run by psychiatrists will fall under the direction of eclectics, a state of affairs which bodes ill for any radical progress in research.

Winding up this survey of the more direct approaches to the problem we may note that following the *anthropometric* work of Goring in this country[15] contributions to this method of approach have been made by Burt and later by Norwood East. The *relation of physique to character* has also been followed up but the consensus of opinion is that conclusions based on a study of these constitutional factors should be treated with considerable reserve. And the same may be said of *endocrine investigations* in delinquent types. In any case the psychological influence of these factors on the *development* of mind and character in the child has been very generally neglected.

In an earlier part of this review attention was drawn to the usually retarding influence of the Home Office on the development of modern techniques of investigation and treatment of delinquency. It is pleasant therefore to record that in other official administrative departments psychological methods are acquiring increasing influence and prestige. Seventy per cent of the cases now sent to the I.S.T.D. are recommended by *magistrates* acting in concert with their own probation officers. Amongst magistrates dealing with adult offenders, C. Mullins stands out as a pioneer who has done more than any other to apply scientific procedures of examination and treatment.[16] In the field of juvenile delinquency a similar recognition is due the magistrates Basil Henriques and John Watson. The contribution of Mullins deserves all the more recognition in that he is a firm believer in endopsychic as distinct from environmental psychological factors. Most supporters of a psychological approach are essentially environmentalists and consequently pin their faith for the most part on correction of environmental factors either familial or social. From the therapeutic point of view their faith has of course justified itself, but regarded from the point of view of etiological investigation the approach is a blind alley.

By way of contrast the Higher Courts are notoriously barren of psychological understanding, a fact which any medical psychologist giving evidence for the defense either in mitigation of sentence or on appeal against sentence pronounced can readily attest. It would take us too far afield to discuss the factors responsible for this state of affairs. No doubt the age of the offender and the nature of his offense contribute to this refractoriness on the part of Recorders and Judges by mobilizing their defenses against the "license" of others. The fact is, however, that with the exception of an occasional Recorder ready to listen to a commonsense and plainly expressed statement of the probability of "cure" by scientific treatment, judges at Quarter-Sessions and High Courts of Assize are still critical to the point of open hostility of the evidence of any but Prison Medical Officers or psychiatrists for the Crown.

---

[15] Published 1913.
[16] Mullins drew freely on the medico-psychological services of A. Court, a general practitioner who undertook psychiatric training and carried out his examinations of delinquent cases mostly in private. This raises the interesting possibility that, given the appropriate training, physicians in general practice could function as experts in delinquency. The advantages of such a system particularly in rural districts are obvious.

Returning to the activities of the Lower Courts it can be said without fear of contradiction that the *Probation Service* is by far the most enlightened of all the penal services. Despite their extremely curtailed and inadequate training, many probation officers have followed the example of psychiatric social workers by acquiring, often at great inconvenience, a working knowledge of the psychological and sociological approaches to crime. Next to psychiatric social workers and educational psychologists, probation officers provide some of the staunchest supporters of Institutes such as the I.S.T.D. They are of course handicapped in their individual efforts at re-education and rehabilitation by the excessive case-loads they have to carry and perhaps more decisively, by their divided loyalties. To be a servant of the Court and at the same time to act as counsellor and friend to the offender is a dual rôle calling for unusual qualifications. Certainly no trained psychotherapist would relish being put in this emotionally ambiguous situation.[17] Nevertheless we must be grateful for attenuated mercies. There are few psychological workers in the field who have not had occasion to be thankful for the co-operation of an understanding probation officer. As their training is gradually shorn of irrelevant and tedious studies and extended to include clinical instruction in the psychology of delinquency, the status of probation officers will rise rapidly. Already it is an open question whether they should not be recognized as a special branch of the association of psychiatric social workers.

Much less satisfactory is the psychological status of workers in the various institutions of disposal, e.g., *Remand Homes and Centres, Approved Schools and Borstal Institutions.* Like most institutions these suffer from their divorce not only from ordinary social contact but from the more positive transference influences existing in the family. They are also hampered by their traditional link with poor law institutions, "reformatories" and prison services. It is true that the educational and pedagogic standards particularly of Approved Schools and Borstal Institutions have steadily improved but this does not compensate for the lack of psychological training and distrust of non-disciplinary methods of personal supervision, exhibited in most of these institutions. The position of voluntary institutions run by religious bodies and social welfare organizations is little better, if at all. By way of contrast some individual efforts in this field are of a promising order, witness the contributions of pioneers like Wills (*The Hawkspur Experiment*)[18] and Otto Shaw. It is in this particular department of re-education and rehabilitation that the influence of Aichhorn's work has made itself most felt in this country: although undoubtedly some of the credit should go to the experimental school methods practiced by A. S. Neill. So far however most institutions are psychologically backward and conservative to the point of timidity.

To sum up: modern ideas concerning the handling of delinquents in Britain are derived from the work of normal and educational psychologists, of sociologists, of psychiatrists and of medical psychologists including psychoanalysts, not to mention some workers in more circumscribed fields. These ideas are given practical application in the I.S.T.D., in psychological clinics like the Tavistock Clinic, in the psychiatric centres of teaching hospitals, in child guidance clinics, sometimes at welfare centres and more rarely at special schools and institutions. They have influenced the work of

---

[17] The psychiatrist reporting to the Court from the I.S.T.D. is not a servant of the Court. There is a pretty general feeling amongst clinical workers that he should not hold a Court position. Even if, under a State Medical Service, he should become a civil servant, he still need not be attached to the Court.

[18] Published 1941.

magistrates, Probation Officers, psychiatric social workers, educational psychologists and a number of free lances both medical and lay. It should be noted, however, that the I.S.T.D. is the *only specialized clinic dealing with offenders of all ages*. In all other cases delinquency work is, as it were, a by-product of other clinical activities, not a special department. Nor do these other centres afford facilities for the *specialized training of delinquency workers*.

Translating this into round figures and dividing the specialty into separate sections dealing respectively with diagnosis, treatment and research, the *strength of the psychological movement in delinquency work* can be estimated as follows. There are now a few dozen medical psychologists and psychiatrists throughout the country capable of making an *experienced* diagnosis of antisocial conditions. At a sanguine estimate two-thirds of these are capable of giving the skilled attention necessary for radical treatment. On the other hand, empirical treatment can be given by most medical psychologists and by quite a respectable number of psychiatrists. The number of educational psychologists sufficiently experienced to rate as delinquency workers is about double that of medically qualified specialists in delinquency. Psychiatric social workers suitable for delinquency work are relatively scarce although the number is growing and will continue to do so. The number of first-class probation officers is roughly the same as that of experienced educational workers. Play-therapists are rapidly increasing but their work on the whole is of poor quality and the technique employed of a hit or miss variety. For the rest a few magistrates, a few prison doctors, a few sociologists, a few school-masters and a few institution superintendents are sufficiently experienced in clinical psychology to rate as trained workers in their own particular branch.

When it comes to *research work* the outlook is at first sight much less encouraging. The indirect influence of both conscious and unconscious psychology has already been assessed; but it must be admitted that amongst medical workers directly engaged in treating delinquency the number capable of doing fruitful research can be counted on the fingers of two hands. The number of lay workers in normal psychology capable of contributing to research is much greater. But against this must be set the fact that the theories on which most normal psychologists base their approach are essentially empirical theories of preconscious and conscious mental function. As has been indicated, psychoanalysts are in a specially favorable position to tap the theoretical resources of unconscious psychology, but unfortunately the number of psychoanalysts who can be said to specialize in delinquency work in this country can be counted on the fingers of one hand. Moreover the great majority of all trained workers are centred in London and its environs, an area which, assessed on a population basis, should absorb only a quarter of the total number existing or required. As a matter of interest the further North one goes the more barren are the psychological resources of the land. Scotland, for example, is still in the backwoods and the North of England is little better. Eire is worse.

Fortunately the outlook is not so gloomy as this survey would indicate. So long as a handful of investigators exists and so long as incentive to fresh research comes either from other scientific institutions within the country or from other countries, research will not come to a standstill. It may well be retarded either because those qualified to conduct research are up to their ears in diagnostic or short-term therapeutic work, or because, as seems to be the case at the moment, some psychoanalysts and medical psychologists appear to be flirting with more superficial techniques e.g., group-therapy or "psychosociological" approaches, or, again, because pioneer efforts and organizations may be partly blanketed by the development of a State Mental Service with its paralyzing system of organization by a hierarchy of officials. But it will survive.

Outlines of research into delinquency can be considered under two headings, the *development of techniques* and the *application of existing theories* of mental function having a bearing on the phenomena of delinquency. For a number of reasons it is desirable to commence with techniques.

Delinquency work calls for highly specialized techniques differing in many respects from those applied in the case of psycho-neurotic and psychotic conditions. Also it necessitates a particular form of "team work" which, in the case of classical psychoanalysis, for example, is either undesirable or positively detrimental to progress. Admittedly much of the team work that has been developed in psychiatric centres and child guidance departments is a tacit confession of the weakness of whatever individual methods are employed. A psychoanalyst is his own social worker, although in fact he very rarely makes contact with relatives or friends of the patient and practically never sees home conditions at first hand. His social work is done, as in the case of the psycho-neuroses it certainly should be, through his patients' associations and his own interpretations. But owing to a number of conditions both individual and social this exclusive approach is usually waived in delinquency work. To make this point clear some detailed reference must be made to the experience of the I.S.T.D.[19]

The first concern of the I.S.T.D. is to make a *thorough examination* and the second to arrive at a *provisional diagnosis*. The diagnosis should be sound enough to permit of a satisfactory *recommendation of disposal;* the examination should be comprehensive enough not only to exclude diagnostic error but to permit of subsequent statistical and other forms of *research*. But since the cases investigated are usually on remand from a Magistrate's Court, have frequently been investigated by a Probation Officer, possibly also examined at a Remand Home, and since part of the disposal recommended may take the form of probationary supervision or change of social conditions, it is rarely possible, even if it were desirable, to undertake immediate and exclusively individual forms of contact. Only when persons not officially charged present themselves voluntarily for private treatment can exclusively analytical policies of treatment be followed.

The actual procedure adopted is as follows: the psychiatric social worker who first contacts the case proceeds to compile a *dossier of social information*. This is drawn from the Probation Officer's report, the Remand Centre's report (if any), reports from school authorities, employers or any other social agency that may be concerned in the case. This is amplified from personal interview with the patient, parents or guardians and from the results of a home visit. The educational psychologist then investigates the patient's mental and adaptation capacity, and an organic physician makes a routine physical overhaul, calling for any more specialized examinations or anthropometric survey that may appear desirable to him. Armed with this information the psychiatrist then takes over the case, and having carried out whatever investigations he deems appropriate, makes a provisional psychiatric diagnosis. The whole case is then reviewed by the Director responsible for making reports to the Court. Certain cross-references may still be made but as a rule it is then possible to send in a report indicating the diagnosis and recommending methods of disposal. These latter have

---

[19] See also Edward Glover: *The Diagnosis and Treatment of Delinquency: Being a Clinical Report on the Work of the I.S.T.D. during the Five Years 1937-1941.* London, I.S.T.D. Publications, 1944.

usually been canvassed beforehand with the Probation Officer in charge of the case. Incidentally the clinic's dossier is strictly confidential; under no circumstances whatever are Court or other authorities given more than a "report" which is itself marked "confidential".

The forms of disposal recommended vary in the degree of "supervision" involved. In a great majority of instances the maximum restriction suggested is that of probationary supervision with or without treatment. Should treatment be recommended, it is usually "ambulant", the patient continuing to live at home, and follow his usual occupation, attending the clinic as directed. Changes in home, school and social conditions and/or conditions of employment may be recommended. In rarer cases removal to a foster-home may be suggested or the patient may be boarded out at a progressive school or camp. Still more rarely an Approved School may be indicated or a Borstal Institution. Only in the very rarest instances is a sentence of imprisonment supported. Special educational measures may be carried out particularly in the case of backward children and special courses of training indicated. Contacts are also made with clubs or other social groups. Any recommendations made by the organic physician are followed up and advisory relations are established with the parents. A follow-up lasting five years is aimed at but not often achieved.

From the research point of view the first concrete results of this comprehensive investigation were (a) greater clarity concerning the incidence of different types of disorder, (b) a fuller understanding of the nature of "mixed types". Of course the cases are already "selected" by Court officials but allowing for this fact the percentage distributions are of considerable interest. Thus on the average of five years' work 2.8 per cent were found to be mentally defective, 7.7 per cent "borderline" defective, 1.1 per cent psychotic, 4.3 per cent borderline psychotic and 29.2 per cent psycho-neurotic. During these years psychopathic character types were unfortunately pigeon-holed with sexual perversions, an unsatisfactory overlap which cannot be rectified until a fresh investigation of all such cases is undertaken. The combined group totalled 36.8 per cent of all cases. Behavior problems numbered 5 per cent, alcoholic types 0.9 per cent and organic types 2.1 per cent.

The principle of arriving at a final diagnosis only after "treatment reports" and "follow-up records" are collected has been laid down but so far shortage of staff has prevented a comprehensive reinvestigation of all cases on these lines. The groups calling for most careful screening are the psycho-neurotic and psychopathic groups. Most of the mixed types were distributed between these two groups according to the predominating clinical characteristics present; but when the material is reinvestigated these mixed types will be isolated and subdivided. Final sub-division of psychopathic types has not yet been attempted. It is probable, however, that the psycho-neurotic group is inflated. Certainly if a wider selection of cases were made by the courts the proportion of "behavior problems" and of mild psychopathics would rise considerably.

The immediate research project favored by the Directors of the I.S.T.D. is to establish more exact correlation between, on the one hand, the social and legal diagnosis and on the other the scientific (mainly medico-psychological) diagnosis. This will involve the breakup of various categories of offense, in particular of pilfering (the commonest type recommended to the clinic) and their reclassification in terms either of etiological or of clinical factors. At the moment it is scarcely possible wholly to convert clinical, (mostly) descriptive, classifications into etiological classifications. Nor is the procedure entirely justified. But there is no doubt that it would solve the problem of the mixed type, that bugbear of the statistician.

From the sociological point of view, work is in progress on conditions calling for purely social measures of disposal; e.g., probation, foster-homes, Approved Schools, etc.; and this involves also an assessment of the unconscious factors contributing to the therapeutic success of such disposals. Similarly an assessment of the unconscious factors activated by "bad" upbringing, insecurity in the family, illegitimacy, etc., is overdue. It is already clear, however, that a purely sociological and statistical approach leads to the establishment of descriptive rather than dynamic criteria. As in the case of the legal diagnosis, psychological investigation of sociological (environmental) factors ends in their breakdown in terms of unconscious significance. As has been indicated, it is in this department of research that Aichhorn's work has achieved its most decisive impact.

In this connection it is necessary to remind the reader that the I.S.T.D. is not a purely psychoanalytical Institute. Although its foundation was largely the work of psychoanalysts, and although psychoanalysts have up to the present played a large part in its direction, it is a medico-psychological Institute. Its diagnostic and therapeutic services are representative of all medico-psychological approaches (including for the moment psychiatric methods). Although therefore psychoanalytical concepts and the pioneer work of psychoanalysts like Alexander, Staub, Reik, Reich and Aichhorn have influenced the approach of most medical psychologists, they are by no means accepted in their entirety, even in the diagnostic field. On the contrary the work of Healy, the Gluecks and in this country Burt and Henderson is still in greater favor. This is particularly clear in the case of psychopathy, and is moreover not altogether without justification. Alexander's "neurotic character", based on psychoanalytical reflections on the functions of the ego and superego, does not satisfy the needs of a psychopathic classification and Reich's *"triebhafter Charakter"* (loosely translated equals impulsive character), though clinically closer to a psychopathic standard, is from the psychoanalytical point of view, neither very sound clinically nor very illuminating theoretically. Psychoanalysts on the whole fight shy of "psychopathic" criteria, and although no doubt the issue will be decided when they condescend more to clinical classifications than to unconscious concepts, that time is not yet. Psychoanalytical characterology is still in its infancy.

Yet another factor influences the theoretical views of clinical psychologists, namely, their experience of their own *therapeutic results*. The results of other psychotherapists are naturally never so convincing and in any case cannot always be checked.[20]

Now the individual psychological treatment given at the I.S.T.D. varies widely. Some of it is of necessity advisory and is given during periods of "observation". But even when immediate psychotherapy is recommended, it ranges from hypnosis and suggestion, with or without the use of narcotic adjuvants, through every variety of psychological "influence", with or without some form of "analysis", to pure Freudian, Jungian and Adlerian techniques. Actually, owing to shortage of psychoanalytical volunteers, classical psychoanalyses constitute only a minute proportion of the treatments given. It is consequently reserved only for cases in which it seems clearly indicated or in which the difficulties appear to be too great to admit of the recommendation of other and shorter methods. Short treatment is the rule and although some cases are given as many as three hundred sessions (eighteen months steady analysis),

---

[20] It is one of the virtues of the Clinic system and in particular of the "follow-up" method that it is possible to some extent to check the psychotherapist's assessment of his own work.

the average number of therapeutic sessions for all cases fell during the war to ten, the usual range being five to fifty. Under more settled circumstances the average of all cases, i.e., including a few long analyses and many "incomplete" cases ought to run at about twenty sessions.

Despite this fact the *therapeutic results* obtained at the I.S.T.D. are in many respects striking. The standards laid down are exacting. "Cure" is presumed only when the delinquent has displayed no abnormal conduct for a period of five years after treatment and when in addition the therapist is satisfied that the underlying causes have been resolved. Other apparent cures are for the time being merely rated as "improved". Many cases discontinue treatment and others are prevented from completing it for reasons beyond their control. Two statistical facts have emerged from a survey of these results: (1) that, allowing full correction for spontaneous cure, the number of permanent cures reaches 32 per cent, (2) that except in cases psychoanalyzed the cure does not depend on the length of treatment. As has been said, most treatments are short; but even including cases that have abandoned treatment within a few days or have not attended as long as might have been desired, the percentage of major and lasting improvements reaches an astonishing figure. Indeed it can be said that if suitably selected cases of delinquency are given about 90 per cent become non-delinquent.

As far as psychotherapy is concerned this latter figure must, however, be scaled down for two reasons; first, that an allowance must be made for spontaneous remission or cure, and, second, that in most cases other therapeutic measures, either individual or social, are put into effect. Except in cases undergoing a full analysis, probationary supervision is usually carried out in addition to which changes are effected either in family, school or social environment. These are recommended by the psychiatrist and brought about through the personal influence of the psychiatric social worker and the educational psychologist. So far no exact "ratio of benefit" has been arrived at but taking a conservative view and avoiding over-sanguine and sensational estimates it seems likely that as far as psychotherapy is concerned it can be depended upon to bring about "cure" in at least 30 per cent of cases and major amelioration in about double that figure.

Further research will afford more precise information on these points. In the meantime we are entitled to draw certain conclusions from the existing findings. For instance, although most medical psychologists are agreed that antisocial cases are by no means easy to treat and require various modifications of the customary psychotherapeutic techniques, it cannot be denied that "team-influence", that is to say, the combined efforts, both personal and indirect, of a number of workers on any one case, brings about remarkable improvement in a short space of time. And although no psychoanalyst would dream of suggesting that radical alteration of unconscious mechanisms can be effected by short treatments, he is forced to account for this rapid improvement. If he likes, he can do so simply by saying that the result is a transference manifestation. But in that case he must account for the fact that a "distributed transference" (which psychoanalysts are generally at pains to avoid) so far from hampering progress in short treatment, apparently accelerates it. Indeed he might well speculate whether the form of group therapy most appropriate to regressive types of antisocial behavior is one in which a single patient is the centre of a group of therapists rather than, as in the case of ordinary group therapy, one of a group of patients sharing a single therapeutic leader. Anyhow it is undeniable that the work of the I.S.T.D. has led to a revision of the customary standards of prognosis. The chronic psychopath may be a tough therapeutic nut to crack but when treated with patience, imagination, skill and an unruffled understanding of his compulsive recidivism the outlook is much more favorable than is generally supposed.

Considerations of this sort show how essential it is for successful research not only that clinical data should be constantly screened for their theoretical implications but that existing theories of etiology and therapeutic technique should be repeatedly tested in this, for all practical purposes, fallow field. And since in the writer's view the theory that can be most fruitfully applied to delinquency work is the theory of psychoanalysis it seems appropriate to conclude this review with a brief outline of the theoretical and practical problems arising from the psychoanalysis of delinquency in Britain.

There are two ways by which progress in any branch of psychoanalysis can be achieved, first, by direct psychoanalysis of clinical material and, second, by correlation of existing theories with the results of direct analysis. In the case of delinquency work corroborative evidence can of course be obtained from yet other branches of analysis, e.g., the psychoanalysis of normal or neurotic children and adults, or psychoanalytical interpretations of anthropological material. Unfortunately no anthropological work on crime has been done by any analyst in this country, and the branch of child analysis is riven with dissension on both theoretical principles and technical procedures. For purposes of correlation one is therefore compelled to fall back on the generally accepted theory of psychoanalysis derived mainly from the study of psycho-neurotic adults. It is then possible to enquire how far psychoanalytical observations of delinquent cases corroborate, amplify or correct this general body of knowledge.

Studying the various contributions to research on delinquency in this country from this angle, one is struck by the fact that during the past fifteen years very little has been added to early analytical formulations on the subject. Nor have investigations of delinquency added much to the general theory of psychoanalysis. Indeed it would appear that they have merely corroborated pre-existing analytical theories. This is no doubt a tribute to the validity of the theories but it can also be explained, in part at any rate, by the factor of case selection. Delinquency compromises a number of conditions varying in severity and duration and derived from different levels of developmental structure and function. So far psychoanalysis has been applied mainly to delinquent children in the latency period, to psycho-neurotic types of adolescent and adult delinquency and to some forms of superego disorder giving rise to delinquent character and conduct. Under these circumstances it would be natural for a correspondence to exist between the findings in delinquency and those arrived at in the study of psycho-neuroses.[21]

This factor of selection has given rise to some divergences in therapeutic method between psychoanalytical workers in delinquency in Britain. There are some who, following the tenets of Anna Freud and the orthodox child analysts believe that, owing to retarded or abnormal development of the superego, treatment of delinquency, particularly of the psychopathic type, must follow the lines employed in the psychoanalysis of young children, i.e., it must be divided into two phases, one in which the superego and consequently the ego, is strengthened and a later phase in which psychoanalysis proper is employed.

---

[21] It can be argued of course that these are the types of delinquency most suitable for psychoanalysis and that only the analysis of cases in which a favorable "therapeutic situation" can be developed is likely to lead to new discoveries. This argument not only begs the question of suitability but disregards the fact that legitimate conclusions have been drawn from analytical observations made in refractory cases of every kind.

On the other hand some analytical workers, including the present writer, take the view that, given suitable elasticity of approach, psychoanalytical technique can be successfully applied even in refractory cases of delinquency provided always the patient for one reason or another (the existence of some marginal degree of conflict, or even a desire to escape further penal measures) is prepared to "try" treatment if only as a last resource. According to this view the key to the situation lies in the maintenance by the analyst of a supporting attitude together with an immediate and rapid exploration of spontaneous negative (hostile) transferences and catharsis of the early traumata that so often induce or increase these hostile and aggressive reactions.

The policy of the I.S.T.D. is in effect a compromise between these points of view. Its workers have established that, provided measures of re-education are "dosed" in accordance with psychological principles, they lead to increased stability of mental function. In fact most of the social devices employed by the I. S. T. D. are directed towards this end. *These auxiliary measures are, however, applied simultaneously with analytical (or other) techniques.* This is rendered possible by the "team method" already described. In other words, the team as a whole mobilizes transferences through its *actual behavior* towards the delinquent, whilst the therapist proceeds with his *analytical work.* In practice this constitutes a departure from classical analytical therapy but not from understanding of the dynamics of transference.

From this divergence there arises an issue of considerable moment to research on delinquency. While it is true to say that the importance of disorders of superego development can scarcely be overestimated, it is also true that exclusive preoccupation with this aspect of delinquency deflects attention from research into the reality function of the ego. The psychopathic delinquent, for example, suffers not only from an apparent deficiency in guilt sense but from abnormalities of reality function. As a result partly of predisposition and partly of traumatic infantile experiences, he has lost or has never acquired a normal faculty of anticipation, popularly described as a realization of consequences. This "immediacy" of response to excitation is certainly derived from early instinctual experience. In this respect as well as in the repeated and violent crises of uncontrolled behavior, psychopathic delinquency is closer to a traumatic neurosis than to a psycho-neurosis or psychosis. There is indeed every probability that study of psychopathy will shed more light on ego development than do the more dramatic forms of psychotic abnormality.

If this view be correct it follows that the role of unconscious conflict and of unconscious fantasy formation in delinquency differs from that observed in the analysis of the psycho-neuroses where a fault in repression permits the development of compromise symptom-formations. Not only are the pathogenic fixation points in delinquency earlier in the developmental sense but one faulty fixation is followed by another, with the consequence that the ego itself is in a *constant traumatic state of dysfunction:* this is disguised only so long as his environment provides the potential delinquent with a degree of support and gratification which, judged by normal standards, would be regarded as excessive.

In this connection it is of interest to note that the split amongst child analysts in this country reflects divergences of view on this very matter. The orthodox Freudian school is interested in the phase of early ego development that antedates superego function: the Klein school of child psychology seeks to find superego explanations of function during the first year of life, at a time, that is, when, according to the classical Freudian view, libidinal function is mainly autoerotic and the organization of the mental apparatus mainly narcissistic. It is the writer's view that the Klein school has been carried away by the superficial resemblances between psychotic and infantile function respectively and has thereby been led to a fallacious postulation of psychotic ego-superego-object "positions" in the first years of life.

Another important source of confusion lies in the emphasis laid by different groups on the respective importance of aggressive and of libidinal impulse in infantile development. The orthodox school maintains the overriding importance of libidinal development whereas their opponents, believing in the existence of complicated object relationships in the first year of life, stress the overriding importance of aggressive impulse. Now it cannot be denied that destructive, sadistic and perverse sexual urges play an important part in delinquent disorders. But this does not justify the theory of superego conflict in the first year. On the contrary it suggests that the early increase in aggressive impulse occurring in children who later become delinquent, acts as a traumatic source of overstimulation long before there is any question of superego formation or of the existence of that ambivalence which gives rise to neurotic conflict. Incidentally ambivalence is too frequently regarded as a purely psychopathological factor. Actually its development at an appropriate stage, i.e., when the ego is able to withstand frustration, is to some extent a guarantee against later outbreaks of delinquent conduct.

The foregoing are merely samples of research problems the solution of which will be arrived at by adequate research on delinquent states, in particular on psychopathic types of delinquency. In the meantime we may sum up the position in this country by saying that psychoanalytical research in delinquency is not only held up by the absence of a sufficiency of workers but obstructed by theoretical confusions and fallacious reconstructions of mental development. The outcome will depend largely on whether a sufficiently strong team of psychoanalysts, trained in the accepted theory and practice of psychoanalysis, are able to devote special attention to the study of psychopathy.[22]

But when all is said the paramount need of criminological science in this country is a sufficiency of trained workers in every branch of the subject. No psychological training is demanded of magistrates or of the personnel of foster homes, remand centres, Approved Schools, Borstal institutions. It should be an obligatory condition of appointment that such training is undertaken and proficiency in it secured. The psychological instruction of Probation Officers should be greatly extended and their professional status raised to that of psychiatric social workers. The training of psychiatric social workers should be shorn of many pedantic and old-fashioned courses and should be reinforced by a thorough grounding in clinical psychology and psychoanalysis. Their status should be raised to that of a lay psychiatrist. Psychiatrists including prison medical officers should undergo an obligatory course of orientation in psychoanalytic

---

[22] Even with this scientific equipment, research on delinquency will not get very far unless sufficient funds are made available by scientific foundations. It is an interesting reflection of the general attitude to psychology and to crime in this country that whereas organic research can secure almost unlimited support from university and other scientific foundations, researches in clinical psychology are fobbed off with a miserable pittance. Such funds as are made available go for the most part to students of normal psychology and sociology. Moreover such clinical researches as do secure subsidies are usually promoted by psychiatric centres and medico-psychological groups whose natural bent is towards "generally accepted" technique. Perhaps when a few psychoanalysts succeed in obtaining administrative posts of strategic value, this position may change. But the projected development of state medical services with their inevitable hierarchies of control does not justify too sanguine expectations. Psychoanalysis developed outside the citadels of "generally accepted" medicine, of "formal" psychiatry, and of "normal" psychology, and it seems likely that psychoanalytical research will flourish best under scientific rather than administrative controls.

theory and in any case society will always demand the service of a special group of psychiatrists who can take care of advanced cases without necessarily understanding or exploiting too much the unconscious factors leading to permanent breakdown.

Finally the training of psychoanalysts themselves needs reorganization. The scientific attainments of psychoanalysts in this country and the scientific disciplines practiced by them are not of a high order. Roughly speaking only a half are given a thorough training in classical Freudian analysis. Too often a personal enthusiasm for psychoanalysis is accepted as a preliminary qualification in lieu of scientific ability. Research workers require special training in the techniques of research and in the objective appraisal of evidence. It is unreasonable to expect that therapeutic practitioners should produce good researches. The study of delinquency is a special study calling for special training and experience. If, as seems likely, the standards of mental medicine continue to be regulated by the need to produce "general mental practitioners" few fresh discoveries can be anticipated for some time to come. It should be a binding condition for *all* workers in delinquency that they are specially trained in delinquency work.

SOME REMARKS ON THE INFLUENCE OF AICHHORN'S WORK ON CHILD PROTECTION IN HOLLAND

By Nelly H. C. Tibout, M.D.

(Amsterdam)

The influence of Aichhorn's work on child protection in Holland has been significant indeed nor have its further possibilities been exhausted. In this celebration volume, there is every reason to express our heartfelt thanks on behalf of the Dutch children to the man to whom many of their educators are indebted for better methods. Not from a scientific angle but from the viewpoint of practical work, we regard the following as the most important things Aichhorn has given to us:

1. In him we see a personality with a rare gift of quickly identifying himself with a wide range of human beings and thus able to understand the nature of their emotional life. He is a master in the art of creating a positive transference. His handling of the patient's situation then presents many possibilities for child guidance, both as regards the contact with the parents and the contact with the children.

2. His analytic experience enabled him to invent and formulate the stages of a technique for treating delinquents. He first aimed to provoke a crisis in which resistance was broken down and then understood how to begin the re-education of both individuals and groups. This he did by consciously guiding the balance between indulgence and renunciation. His understanding of the delinquents' need for indulgence during the early part of their therapeutic contact is another of his special contributions to this treatment.

3. Since to the delinquent, identification with others in a group is of paramount importance, Aichhorn pointed out the value of placing such boys in homogeneous groups in the wards of institutions. The homogeneity of such groups is based on the similar positive transference patterns of its members to the group leader.

Apart from these contributions to technique, there is his work as an analyst and theorist, which I need not mention here.

In the child guidance clinics his conceptions have had great influence but I would make special mention of his influence on the institutional educators.

Since the Children's Laws came into force (1905), an increasing number of possibilities has arisen on the one hand in the field of probation work, and on the other in that of foster home and institutional care in Holland.

The education of young delinquents or neglected children mainly consisted of a program of "reconditioning" which in general meant using a positive approach such as arranging for vocational training, recreation and the like. In some agencies, usually those who undertook the permanent care of children, the staff soon came to realize their charges' need of a "positive attachment". On this point, Aichhorn's specific directions and his scientific sanction of a more genial attitude toward such children was particularly helpful. We would mention especially two agencies whose policies were influenced by his work. They are: *Zandbergen* (where Mr. D. Q. R. Mulock Houwer managed this department) and *Tot Steun* (where Mrs. van der Waals-Kirberger is honorary secretary).

Yet great difficulties arose in some other agencies when the educators misunderstood Aichhorn's technique and interpreted it as a blanket permission to "let them have their way", without discriminating support of these young people and without helping them to obtain more insight. In some places, Aichhorn's method stood for "chaos", but this is improving more and more. It is obvious that war and occupation entailed many difficulties. One third of the available space in institutions was destroyed, or occupied, while the number of children that had to be taken care of increased to fifty thousand. The first requisite was to provide for the most elementary material needs. Next came the attempts to relieve the great shortage of educational staff. Though there has been some setback, we may yet hope that, if there is not too great a social upheaval, many new plans will soon be put into practice, even though it must be in the least expensive way possible. We hope to effect a better differentiation of the institutions and a better selection of the children. Such discriminating classification is greatly impeded, however, by confessional differences and there is often no hope of real insight into the psychoanalytic principles involved. Yet since the problems of training pedagogical workers is being vigorously pursued, we can hope for much improvement from that aspect, for most psychiatrists and social workers are today familiar with Aichhorn's fundamental study. More and more work camps and more liberal institutions are being organized. There are, of course, many problems, due to the psychic consequences of war and occupation, but on the other hand there is also a great deal of enthusiasm. The fact that so many of the educational workers and authorities were themselves in the position of "antisocials" during the years of occupation, has undoubtedly had a remarkable influence; we have gained a personal insight into the factors leading to moral construction and destruction (such as poverty, etc.). According to Dutch views, family life should be left intact as much as possible. Interest in child guidance has greatly increased which may help toward this goal. In spite of a great extension of the activities of the Psychoanalytical Association the number of psychoanalysts and analytic psychotherapists is still inadequate; but by means of lectures and courses, our views are propagated more and more. We may only hope that this work will be supported by a personal visit of Aichhorn's before long.

The influence of the American child guidance clinics has been considerable in our country. We think it important to integrate physical, social and psychological care.

Provision for a good school system and working possibilities must be made and social security and psychotherapeutic help to the parents procured insofar as the limited possibilities permit us to do so. It is undoubtedly true, as Kate Friedlander writes, that often the tendency to "retaliation" blocks the good measures that should be taken for delinquents.

But in general the spirit prevailing among the practical workers is good. I am sure that Aichhorn will be glad to learn that during the years of war one matron of a girl's institution hid many people in her home, while another asked the Ration Board for curtain cloth and made dance frocks of it after her direct request for this purpose had been refused and she had realized the importance of this gratification to her charges.

When comparing such attitudes with those which Aichhorn once felt characterized the head of an institution, I would add that to all of us August Aichhorn has been "an inspiring, kind father" from afar. May he maintain this role for many years to come.

BIBLIOGRAPHY OF AUGUST AICHHORN'S WRITINGS

1918 Nochmals zum Fürsorgeerziehungsgesetz. *Zeitschrift für Kinderschutz und Jugendfürsorge,* Vienna.

1922 Lehrlingserholung im Erziehungsamt für Dissoziale. *Blaetter für das Wohlfahrtswesen.* Vienna.

1925 Vom schlimmen Kinde. *Zeitschrift für den Kindergarten.* Vienna.

1925 Zum "Verwahrlosten Problem." *Zeitschrift für psychoanalytische Paedagogik.* Vienna.

1925 *Verwahrloste Jugend.* Wiener Psychoanalytischer Verlag, First edition, Vienna.

1926 Bruchstück aus Verwahrloste Jugend: Die Psychoanalyse in der Fürsorgeerziehung. *Almanach des Wiener Psychoanalytischen Verlages.* Vienna.

1926 Gibt es eine untere Grenze für Schwererziehbare? *Blaetter für das Wohlfahrtsamt,* Vienna.

1928 Psychoanalytische Erziehungsberatung. *Zeitschrift für psychoanalytische Paedagogik,* Nr. 79, Vienna.

1926, 1928, 1938 — Psychoanalytisches Verstaendnis und Erziehung Dissozialer, *Hyppokrates Verlag,* Stuttgart — Berlin.

1930 The Juvenile Court: Is it a Solution? *Revue Internationale de L'enfant,* Geneva.

1930 *Verwahrloste Jugend,* Second Edition. Internationaler Psychoanalytischer Verlag. Vienna.

1931 Lohn oder Strafe als Erziehungsmittel. *Zeitschrift für psychoanalytische Paedagogik.* Vienna.

1931 Besprechung: Der Kindergarten der Frau Dr. Messine. *Freie Stimmen.* Klagenfurt.

1932 Erziehungsberatung. *Zeitschrift für psychoanalytische Paedagogik.* Vienna.

1933 Erziehungsberatungs-Seminar. *Zeitschrift für psychoanalytische Paedagogik.*

1934 Erziehungsberatung. *Almanach der Psychoanalyse.* Internationaler Psychoanalytischer Verlag. Vienna.

1934 Kann der Jugendliche straffaellig werden? Ist das Jugendgericht eine Loesung? *Zeitschrift für psychoanalytische Paedagogik.* Vienna.

1934 English Translation of: *Verwahrloste Jugend.* Internationaler Psychoanalytischer Verlag. Vienna.

1934 Psychoanalyse und Erziehung. *Wiener Mittagszeitung.* October 16. Vienna.

1935 *Wayward Youth.* Viking Press. New York.

1936 Zur Technik der Erziehungsberatung. *Zeitschrift für psychoanalytische Paedagogik.* Vienna.

1936-1938: Erziehungsberatung! *Psychoanalytisches Handwoerterbuch,* ed. Richard Sterba, M.D. Internationaler Psychoanalytischer Verlag. Vienna.

1937 Die Übertragung des Hochstaplers. *Almanach der Psychoanalyse.* Internationaler Psychoanalytischer Verlag. Vienna.

1937 Zur Technik der Erziehungsberatung. Rundbrief: *Die Fürsorgerin.* Vienna.

1937-1938: *Einführung in die Erziehungsberatung. Kurse für Paedagogen.* Internationaler Psychoanalytischer Verlag. Vienna.

1937-1938: *Die Arbeit in der Erziehungsberatung. Seminar für Erziehungsberater,* Internationaler Psychoanalytischer Verlag. Vienna.

1946 Sigmund Freud. *Grosse Oesterreicher.* Gallus Verlag. Vienna.

1946 Die Wiener Psychoanalytische Vereinigung. *Wort und Tat,* Vienna.